Armies of the Great War

MW00646928

This is a major new series of studies of the armies of the major combatants in the First World War for publication during the war's centenary. The books are written by leading military historians and set operations and strategy within the broader context of foreign-policy aims and allied strategic relations, national mobilisation and domestic social, political and economic effects.

Titles in the series include:

The American Army and the First World War by David Woodward
The Austro-Hungarian Army and the First World War by Graydon Tunstall
The British Army and the First World War by Ian Beckett, Timothy Bowman and Mark Connelly
The French Army and the First World War by Elizabeth Greenhalgh
The German Army and the First World War by Robert Foley
The Italian Army and the First World War by John Gooch

The king of Italy on the Carnic Alps

The Italian Army and the First World War

This is a major new account of the role and performance of the Italian army during the First World War. Drawing from original, archival research, it tells the story of the army's bitter three-year struggle in the mountains of Northern Italy, including the eleven bloody battles of the Isonzo, the near-catastrophic defeat at Caporetto in 1917 and the successful, but still controversial defeat of the Austro-Hungarian army at Vittorio Veneto on the eve of the Armistice. Setting military events within a broader context, the book explores pre-war Italian military culture and the interactions between domestic politics, economics and society. In a unique study of an unjustly neglected facet of the war, John Gooch illustrates how General Luigi Cadorna, a brutal disciplinarian, drove the army to the edge of collapse, and how his successor, General Armando Diaz, rebuilt it and led the Italians to their greatest victory in modern times.

JOHN GOOCH is Emeritus Professor of International History at the University of Leeds.

The Italian Army and the First World War

John Gooch

CAMBRIDGE UNIVERSITY PRESS

CAMBRIDGE
UNIVERSITY PRESS

University Printing House, Cambridge CB2 8BS, United Kingdom

Cambridge University Press is part of the University of Cambridge.

It furthers the University's mission by disseminating knowledge in the pursuit of education, learning and research at the highest international levels of excellence.

www.cambridge.org
Information on this title: www.cambridge.org/9780521149372

© John Gooch 2014

First published 2014

Printed and bound in the United Kingdom by Clays, St Ives plc

A catalogue record for this publication is available from the British Library

Library of Congress Cataloguing in Publication data
Gooch, John.
The Italian Army and the First World War / John Gooch.
    pages   cm. – (Armies of the Great War)
Includes bibliographical references and index.
ISBN 978-0-521-19307-8 (Hardback) – ISBN 978-0-521-14937-2 (Paperback)
1. World War, 1914–1918–Italy.   2. Italy. Esercito–History–20th century.
3. Italy–History–1870–1914.   I. Title.
DD569.A2G67 2014
940.4'0945–dc23   2013045307

ISBN 978-0-521-19307-8 Hardback
ISBN 978-0-521-14937-2 Paperback

Contents

List of figures   *page* viii
List of maps   x
List of tables   x
Acknowledgements   xi
List of abbreviations   xiii

Introduction   1

1 Before the war   6

2 From neutrality to action   53

3 1915 – First endeavours   97

4 1916 – Setback and success   146

5 1917 – The year of danger   193

6 1918 – Recovery and victory   247

7 In the wake of war   302

Notes   318
Appendix A   *Chiefs of the Italian general staff and war ministers*   362
Appendix B   *Executions 1915–1918*   363
Bibliography   364
Index   381

Figures

Frontispiece	The king of Italy on the Carnic Alps	*page* iv
	(Source: © IWM, Q 65073)	
Fig. 1	General Cadorna on Monte Cengis, val d'Astico	55
	(Source: © IWM, Q 65129)	
Fig. 2	Italian troops passing through a village	100
	(Source: © IWM, Q 65357)	
Fig. 3	Girl labourers at an Italian munitions factory	125
	(Source: © IWM, Q 19134)	
Fig. 4	Observation post on Monte Nero, Isonzo front	138
	(Source: © IWM, Q 65062)	
Fig. 5	Shelters on Monte Cregnedul	151
	(Source: © IWM, Q 65056)	
Fig. 6	Teleferica	165
	(Source: © IWM, Q 65043)	
Fig. 7	General Joffre, General Cadorna and General Porro	187
	(Source: © Getty Images / DEA / A. Dagli Orti)	
Fig. 8	Hauling a 149-mm gun on the Upper Isonzo front	200
	(Source: © IWM, Q 65141)	
Fig. 9	Italian women constructing trenches	214
	(Source: © IWM, Q 65312)	
Fig. 10	Italian dead after an Austrian gas attack	227
	(Source: © IWM, Q 65049)	
Fig. 11	Abandoned field guns after Caporetto, October 1917	245
	(Source: © IWM, Q 60408)	
Fig. 12	King Victor Emanuel III and General Diaz	250
	(Source: © Getty Images / DEA / A. Dagli Orti)	
Fig. 13	Anti-aircraft gun at Monte Nero	265
	(Source: © IWM, Q 65158)	

Fig. 14   Serving out rations to prisoners   275
             (Source: © IWM, Q 65069)
Fig. 15   Troops in a front-line trench on Monte
             Grappa, 1918   281
             (Source: © IWM, Q 65230)
Fig. 16   Orlando, Lloyd George, Clemenceau and
             Woodrow Wilson at Versailles   309
             (Source: © IWM, Q 48222)

Maps

1. Abyssinia   *page* 16
2. Libya   41
3. The Isonzo front   181
4. The Italian front in 1917   194
5. Caporetto: the attack on XXVII Corps   237
6. Vittorio Veneto   294

Tables

1. Motorisation of the Italian Army 1915–18   *page* 126
2. Financial receipts and payments 1914–19   128
3. Desertions June–December 1916   170
4. Cost of living index, 1913–18   216

Acknowledgements

Once again, my first debt is to the staff of the Ufficio Storico dello Stato Maggiore dell'Esercito in Rome, and in particular to its Head during the years in which I undertook the research on which this book is based, Colonel Antonino Zarcone. His interest in and support of my work was fully matched by the unstinting assistance of all his staff, among whom I would like particularly to thank the archivist, *dottore* Alessandro Gionfrida. A word must also be said about the truly outstanding series of historical publications produced by the Ufficio Storico over the years, many of which figure in this work. My thanks go also to *dottore* Andrea Pelizza and the staff of the Archivio di Stato di Venezia for their courteousness and their help at a late hour. The staff at the Imperial War Museum proved as helpful as always. Materials from the Archivio Centrale di Stato in Rome and from the Royal Archives at Windsor Castle were gathered some years ago in the course of an earlier project on the Italian army; I am very pleased to have the opportunity to thank their staffs once again. Material from the Royal Archives appears by gracious permission of Her Majesty the Queen.

Ever since I began working on the Italian army over thirty years ago, Professor Giorgio Rochat has generously assisted my work with a flow of books and articles. His scholarship is an inspiration to all of us who work in the field of Italian military history and I shall always be very grateful for the interest he has taken in my work and the help that he has given me. No less important to me has been the help and friendship of Professor Lucio Ceva, which I value greatly. Four friends and colleagues have been invaluable in helping me access rare or out-of-the-way published sources and my warmest thanks go to Professor MacGregor Knox in London, Dr Brian Sullivan in Washington, *dottore* Ciro Paoletti in Rome, and Professor Holger Afflerbach in Leeds. Funding research in non-British history presents hurdles all of its own and I am grateful to the Research Fund of the School of History at the University of Leeds for supporting several trips to the archives in Rome.

My wife, Ann, drew the maps and my thanks and appreciation go to her.

Finally I would like to thank my editor at Cambridge University Press, Michael Watson, for his encouragement in this project – and his forbearance when it overran its deadline – and his team for the professionalism with which they have seen this book through the press.

Abbreviations

AA.VV.	Various authors
ACS	Archivio Centrale di Stato
all	allegato [attached]
ASV	Archivio di Stato di Venezia
AUSSME	Archivio dell'Ufficio Storico dello Stato Maggiore dell'Esercito
Avv	Avvocato [a legal qualification]
b	busta
c	cartella
DDI	*I Documenti Diplomatici Italiani*
F	fonogram [order or communication relayed by telephone]
f	fascicolo
Inchiesta	Relazione della Commissione d'Inchiesta (Caporetto)
IWM	Imperial War Museum
N/n/No	Number
RA	Royal Archives
racc.	raccoglitore
ris.mo	reserved
ser.	series
T	telegram
TNA	The National Archives [UK]
vol.	volume

Introduction

In the United Kingdom, the First World War has fastened itself firmly and ineradicably on the public mind. Lutyens's Cenotaph, the innumerable war memorials up and down the country, and the ordered ranks of white gravestones in the official war graves all remind successive generations of the costs of what is still called the Great War. They also act to anchor that war to the Western Front, where Britain and France fought it out with Germany over four long and bloody years. Transfixing though the great battles of the Somme and Passchendaele can be, the mighty clashes in France and Flanders were but part of a much bigger and more complex war. The pre-war alliances, designed to manage and maintain the peace, changed their clothes to become war-fighting partnerships as Great Britain, France and Russia squared up to Germany and Austria–Hungary. Both sides recruited allies, larger and smaller, as the fighting began not just in Belgium and France but also in the Balkans, in Galicia and in East Prussia. In 1915, the Entente powers were glad to woo Italy away from her pre-war partners and recruit her to their ranks.

Italy's decision to abandon Germany and Austria–Hungary and to join in arms with their enemies changed the geopolitical chessboard of the war and readjusted the correlation of forces. Now a new European front drew Austrian forces south, reducing the pressure on Russia and adding, if only indirectly and over the longer term, to the Germans' burden of supporting their weaker partner. To gauge the significance of having Rome in the war alongside London, Paris and St Petersburg we need only consider what would probably have happened if she had not joined the Triple Entente but had instead stayed a member of the Triple Alliance and come into the war in 1914 on the side of Berlin and Vienna. (Non-entry and neutrality – becoming a 'second Switzerland' – was never a realistic option.) France would have been forced to detach more troops from her western front to defend the southern Alps; the flow of French troop transports from North Africa would have been interrupted; Italian units would have joined in the German attack on the Rhône and quite possibly have influenced the battle of the Marne; and Austria–Hungary,

1

with no southern distraction, would have crushed Serbia more swiftly and put greater pressure on Russia, whose two revolutions might then have come sooner – with effects on the other combatants that are simply incalculable. And if Italy had not recovered after Caporetto but had collapsed instead, the political and military reverberations that would have caused would unquestionably have changed the shape of the last year of the war. Afterwards, Winston Churchill thought it might perhaps even have led to a compromise peace.[1] Italy's participation in the Great War on the Allied side was thus a factor of cardinal importance.

In the historiography of the war, by contrast, Italy's involvement has been commonly undervalued and frequently misunderstood. General histories of the war have tended to relegate her to the 'minor' theatres of war along with the Balkans and Turkey – something that Italy's leading military historian, Giorgio Rochat, has put down to the 'cultural imperialism' of the Great Powers 'veined with racialism'.[2] Whatever its causes, overlooking Italy has been a commonplace: in otherwise distinguished comparative studies of the Great War she does not appear at all.[3] All too often Italy has been seen as the fourth wheel on the Allied carriage – with all the subtle denigration that that phrase embodies. Indeed as the Great War ended denigration of her efforts and her contribution by her allies was far from subtle, as we shall see.

Going to war in 1915 – which Senator Pansa at the time called 'an act of madness' and which historians have generally been inclined to regard as at best an egregious error and at worst 'one of the greatest disasters of her history' – was a very particular kind of gamble for Italy.[4] The idea of completing the unfinished business of the Risorgimento enthused the educated volunteers who longed to liberate Trento and Trieste, but it is fairly safe to say that it cut no mustard with the vast majority of the 5,500,000 men of Italy's conscript armies who fought the war that followed. For the average Italian front-line infantryman, unlike his British, French or German counterparts, this was a war without ideals – until October 1917, when history stood on its head and the Italians found the very unity that they had lacked hitherto.

Italy's wartime leaders stood on much shakier political ground than their western allies. In France the *Union sacrée* bound the previously contending political parties together for the first two years of the war before it began to fray a little at the edges in 1917, and in Germany the *Burgfrieden* ('truce of the fortress') did the same thing for much the same length of time. Italy's leaders, by contrast, had to contend with a political society polarised by the Libyan war of 1911–12 in which pro-war elements entirely in favour of fighting and hopeful that 'a fusion of popular and elite culture might create a renewed national community' faced a large – and largely indifferent if not hostile – populace composed of illiterate or semi-literate rural peasants and urban socialist factory workers.[5] During the war successive administrations could count on the active support of the Right but not of the Left – the only socialist in Italy's wartime governments, Leonida Bissolati, had been expelled from the party in 1912 for being too supportive of the government. For the first two and a half years of her war, Italy fought not as a people united but as a nation divided.

With the declaration of war authority shifted from the shoulders of the politicians to those of the soldiers. Although peacetime models of civil–military relations had varied considerably, in wartime the main belligerents in the west trod a more or less common path: for the first two years the *generalissimo* held the politicians at bay and fought the war much as he thought fit. The quintessential example among the Allies was Marshal Joffre, who told the civilians as little as possible about the war and kept parliament at arm's length until the politicians mustered enough determination to remove him in December 1916.[6] In England Douglas Haig, supported by the Conservative party and with the unobtrusive but not unimportant backing of the king, kept full control of his war until the German March offensive in 1918 gave Lloyd George, a radical premier and no great friend of generals, the chance to reconstruct the high command and subordinate Haig to an overall allied commander in the person of Foch and a Supreme War Council.[7] In Italy, thanks partly to the common exigencies of war and partly to the particularities of Italian politics, Cadorna was able to behave in much the same way as Joffre. Indeed, but for Caporetto he might well have stayed in command for a good deal longer as there was no other real contender and no alternative strategy with which to fight the war, unlike in France.[8] In this respect, as in others, Italy's war was a particular version of a general conundrum: how much power to allow to the soldiers and how to get it back when it turned out that too much had been given away.

Like all his fellow commanders, Cadorna had a clear idea of how to win the war. Schooled like them in the Napoleonic tradition of manoeuvre and aggression, he looked to fight a decisive battle or battles within weeks and thereby bring the war to a victorious close. British, French and German commanders learned by experience between August and December 1914 that their nineteenth-century conception of war was now outdated. In May 1915, apparently oblivious to the lessons to be picked up on the battlefields of the western and the eastern fronts, Cadorna launched his armies almost literally bare-headed – as yet they had no steel helmets – against strong Austrian defensive lines. When that strategy proved to be bankrupt, he fell back on a formula that was much the same as the one Douglas Haig would apply on the western front shortly afterwards: '(a) preliminary operations to wear out the Enemy and exhaust his reserves and (b) . . . a decisive attack made with the object of piercing the Enemy's lines of defence'.[9]

The story of Cadorna's eleven battles of the Isonzo is told in the pages that follow. From it readers will be able to make their own judgements about whether, and if so to what degree and in what ways, Cadorna was a poor commander. That story is partly about the exercise of command – something which would be the subject of a remarkable and revealing official inquest at the close of the war – but it is also about means and methods. As far as means are concerned, firepower played a major role in determining events on all fronts. In considering Italy's war we do well to keep in mind the Great War's almost unquenchable appetite for guns and ammunition. At Festubert on 10 March 1915, 340 guns fired 750 tons of ammunition – twenty times the amount fired at the battle of Waterloo – in thirty-five minutes. On the Somme in 1916, 1,750 guns fired one and a half million rounds weighing 52,000 tons in a week-long bombardment. At the crossing of the Canal du Nord in late September 1918, 63,000 tons of ammunition was fired off in three days. The Italian army's heroic efforts on the Isonzo take on a different perspective when its meagre resources are compared with those available – and necessary – on the western front. As far as method goes, the story that follows hinges on the Italian army's capacity – or otherwise – to learn lessons and evolve new tactical and operational methods. The British and German armies did this in the last two years of the war – the Germans evolving flexible defences and infiltration tactics, the British abandoning 'wave' attacks for 'worms' (in the advance) and 'blobs' (for attack and defence) – though the idea that the British army progressed along a seamless 'learning curve' is now starting to be questioned.[10] Italy, it will be seen, had her own difficulties when it came to mastering the changing face of war.

After two or three years of bloody attritional warfare with no demonstrable gains to show for them, the armies of some of the contending parties warped or buckled under the strain. The Austrian army, although it held up almost until the end of the war, showed signs of beginning to shred as early as 1915 with mass desertions of sub-national elements on the eastern front; parts of the French army mutinied in April 1917; and the Russian army collapsed after the failure of the Brussilov offensive in July 1917. The temporary collapse of the Italian armies at Caporetto in October 1917 – the subject of bitter disputes among Italian historians long after the war was over – seems on the face of it to be of a piece with the French mutinies: a case of armies that had been asked to do too much finally reacting in the only way open to them – by withdrawing their labour. Following this kind of thinking, it has been suggested that the French mutinies are best interpreted as a renegotiation by the rank and file of the way the generals were fighting the war whose boundaries were determined by an internalised loyalty to the polity to which they belonged.[11] Caporetto, readers will discover, was in fact a rather different phenomenon with a much more straightforward explanation.

In Italy, as in France, a new commander had the task of putting the army back together and making it into a reliable fighting force that could once again take the offensive. The man who was given the job and who succeeded triumphantly was Armando Diaz. Mostly unremarked and more or less unknown, he stands as an equal with General Philippe Pétain, who put the French armies back together again after the mutinies. Finally, in October 1918 Diaz led his armies to a decisive victory in the field at the battle of Vittorio Veneto. At the time Italy's allies doubted that it was a 'real' victory and many historians have since thought the same. Again, readers will be able on the basis of the evidence to judge for themselves.

Once the war was over Italy like all the other powers faced the problem of demobilising a mass citizen army and absorbing it back into civil society. Unlike them, she also faced volcanic domestic pressures for change stoked up by the war, and almost unanimous dissatisfaction with a peace that denied her some things she had been promised and others – chief among them the city of Fiume – that had never been on the table in the first place. What became known as 'the mutilated victory' did not of itself propel Mussolini to power four years later – but it played a major role in creating an environment in which for many Italians Fascism appeared to be the solution to the country's ills.

1   Before the war

As long as the army is sound there is nothing to fear.
Domenico Farini, 29 January 1894

The First World War began as a clash of contending armies but soon became a conflict that would test to the limit not just the military power but also the state machinery, social cohesion and cultural values of the countries caught up in it. Italy passed that test despite being perhaps the most poorly prepared of the Great Powers to face it. By common agreement the 'least' of them, she along with Germany was also the newest, and she was the weakest. The legacy of five decades of unification was not one that best prepared her for the maelstrom into which she plunged in 1915.

The Italian Risorgimento was a national revolution from above. After 1870 the king of Italy headed a parliamentary monarchy lacking both the popular underpinning provided for the French parliament by the traditions of the Republic and the autocratic authority through which the Kaiser and his ministers governed the German *Reich*. Italian governments stood or fell according to their leaders' success in making and maintaining majorities that were fundamentally unstable and precarious. The country was run by a narrow political and social oligarchy: on the eve of the world war the sociologist Guglielmo Ferrero concluded that thirty people were governing thirty million people for the benefit of three hundred families. The politicians presided over a predominantly rural peasant society: on the eve of the war over half of the active population worked in agriculture, and in turn half of these were rural day-labourers who were employed on average for only 150 days a year.[1] As one century came to an end and another began, reformist and revolutionary socialism and syndicalism rose to challenge the established order in the industrial cities of northern Italy, and took hold among some of the rural labouring poor. Divisive political forces on the Left and the Right were superimposed on deep-seated and fundamental regional, social and economic divisions. The result of all this, it has rightly been remarked, was that pre-war Italy was a country in which social crisis was 'an endemic phenomenon'.[2]

All of this was, of course, reflected in the army. Italy's particular military culture fell awkwardly between France's popular tradition of the nation in arms, dating back to the *levée en masse* of 1792, and Germany's conservative tradition in which an army of short-term conscripts officered by schooled Prussian professionals trained the nation for war. In Italy, the Left saw the army as the tool of oligarchy and the instrument of repression while the Right saw it as the final bulwark against social disorder and collapse. For its part, the army chafed at political interference which frequently caused frustration and on occasion anger. The way it ran itself – its complex organisational structures, stultifying bureaucratic procedures and distant management style – produced further difficulties and dissatisfactions. The result of all this was that on the eve of war the Italian army was not at ease with itself, with the politicians who directed it and with the society from which it emerged. For their part, politicians looked askance at a force that seemed more likely to lose battles than to win them, and a large part of the populace regarded it as at best an intrusive interruption in their lives and at worst as an enemy. The dominant tones of Italy's particular military culture percolated into the wartime existence of the army and formed an important part of the backdrop against which the course of the war was played out.[3]

Military culture in Liberal Italy

Two rival military traditions emerged out of the wars of the Risorgimento. The left-wing tradition of 'people's war' (*guerra del popolo*) was born out of the democrats' attempts to raise partisan war in 1848–9, Mazzini's encouragement of insurrection in the 1850s and the exploits of Garibaldi's 'Thousand' in 1860. Against it was ranged the conservative tradition of the 'royal war' (*guerra regia*) fought by the regular Piedmontese army in 1848–9, in 1859 and again in 1866. Despite having notched up several spectacular defeats, and needing first French and then Prussian help, it was the Piedmontese tradition that triumphed. Garibaldi and his sons remained iconic figures for some republican leftists, and his model of warfare was lauded from time to time: the taking of Tripoli in September 1911, the first act of the Libyan war, was hailed in the military press as the embodiment of 'the Garibaldian spirit – swift and impetuous'.[4] But by the time that the kingdom of Italy took Rome in September 1870 the Piedmontese tradition was firmly in the saddle. It would make its presence strongly felt in the first two and a half years of the world war.

The newly installed king of Italy, Vittorio Emanuele II, needed a politically reliable army that would serve as an instrument with which to create loyal Italian subjects. Given the raw materials it had to work with and the situation in which it found itself, the army could not afford to copy the French Republican model of a mass army of short-term conscripts. Nor could it follow the Prussian–German version, which utilised territorial recruitment by region. There were advantages to such a model as the spiritual father of the post-Risorgimento Italian army, Nicola Marselli, acknowledged: it made for better training, more rapid mobilisation and economies of scale. But, he went on,

> I know also that Italy has been re-united for only ten years, that she is not yet consolidated, that our people are *ignoranti*, and that after administrative decentralisation the army remains like the great crucible in which all provincial elements submerge themselves in Italian unity.[5]

To achieve the goal of 'making Italians', the army mixed recruits from different parts of the country in the same unit. Initially they were recruited from two different regions and stationed in a third, after 1877 they came from five separate regions, and by the first decade of the twentieth century from nine. To ensure that units remained reliable and were not influenced by local interests and affections, they were rotated around the country: in the decade 1875–84 regiments moved on average three times, between 1899 and 1908 only twice. The army certainly sought to generate a sense of *Italianità* in the raw material it was able to reach but it had many difficulties to overcome, not least the illiteracy of the bulk of the population. Judging by results, the system did not do much to break down linguistic and regional barriers.

The disturbing example of the Paris Commune in 1871 reinforced the conviction that Italy needed a system of moral education to spread concepts of patriotism, nationalism and loyalty to the institutions of the new state – foremost among them the Crown. Initially the army was tasked with providing a rural peasantry with a moral education in basic civic virtues, but after 1900 as industrialisation and urbanisation began to make themselves felt it faced cohorts of increasingly better educated recruits, many of whom were either imbued with or vulnerable to the subversive attractions of Marxian socialism and syndicalism.[6] There were frequent complaints in the military press that the officer corps was not trained for what was an increasingly demanding educational role, and that in any case that was not what the army should be doing. Another big problem was that large parts of the male population remained wholly or largely out of reach of the army's efforts to educate it.

National conscription was introduced in 1863, initially for five years. The term of service was shortened to four years in 1874 and then to three years in 1875, where it stayed for the next thirty-five years before being lowered to two years in 1910. This was by no means the whole story, though. From the outset the state made provision for numerous exemptions, some on social grounds such as being the only male child, others on medical grounds. The latter were especially divisive – 'constitutional weakness' and deficient chest development tended not surprisingly to be found more among the leisured class than among labourers – and also encouraged the practice of mimicking illness and the self-infliction of disabling injuries. The resulting contest between unwilling recruits and the authorities became entrenched in the culture and carried on up to and beyond the outbreak of war.[7]

After an initial blip when 11.5 per cent of those legally obliged to present themselves to the examining boards failed to appear, absenteeism (*renitenza*) settled down in the latter part of the nineteenth century to around 4 per cent.[8] In the decade before the Great War it was on the rise, averaging 9.3 per cent between 1904 and 1913 and reaching 10.44 per cent in 1914. Like much else, it demonstrated that there were 'two Italies': Sicily, Calabria and Sardinia sent the fewest conscripts into the army, while Lombardy, Tuscany, Emilia Romagna, Umbria and the northern Marches sent the most. Absenteeism among former conscripts recalled for further spells of service was even more pervasive. In 1912, only 42.2 per cent of those recalled for training turned up at the depots, whereas 70.4 per cent appeared to carry out public-order duties – a discrepancy probably explained by the fact that after 1898 reservists recalled for public-order duties received payment. Emigration, running at almost 700,000 a year between 1909 and 1913, does much to explain the figures for absenteeism. However when the class of 1896 was called up in September 1915, 12.1 per cent were absent even though emigration had fallen from 500,000 in 1914 to only 150,000 in 1915.[9]

The complex and highly bureaucratised organisation of military service, a key component of Italian military culture, was evident in the 1888 law on the composition of the army. Military service was divided into three categories. Recruits who were to be incorporated directly into the ranks for military service went into category I. Those who were judged fit to serve but deemed in excess of the army's needs went into category II, where they received little or no training, and became *truppe di complemento* (i.e. reserves). This category soon languished and was suppressed altogether between 1892 and 1895, and again between 1897 and 1907. In 1913 men in this category were given six months' military training, an improvement on previous years when they had been recalled for only two months. Two years later this virtually untrained manpower pool would be called on to expand the numbers of regulars and trained reserves and go to war. Supporters of families and others deemed exempt from military service went into category III, received no training whatsoever, and in wartime became the *Milizia territoriale*, garrisoning and guarding the coasts and interior of Italy. At the start of the twentieth century there were no fewer than fourteen grounds on which a 20-year-old could be put into category III and absolved from military service.

Once again, there was more to the story than what was codified in the law. Despite her proportionally heavy spending on the army, Italy was a poor country. She simply could not afford to take all the able-bodied men in each annual class into category I, and she could not afford to keep even those that went into it for the prescribed term of three years. Thus the size limit was reset each year: in 1909 it was fixed at 118,469 out of a total available class size of 510,916. Not only was a large slice of the young male population able to keep its civilian clothes on and hold the army at arm's length, but those unfortunate enough to be caught in the net had to be released early for the same financial reasons. In 1902, half of the category I recruits served only two years instead of three, a proportion that dropped to a quarter in 1906–7. In 1896 financial stringency forced the war ministry to introduce a dual *forza massima–forza minima* structure in peacetime which held infantry companies at 100 men for seven months of the year and then reduced them to 60 men for the remaining five months.[10]

The glaring inequalities embodied in the law and in the way it was put into practice did little for the army's reputation and standing in society at large. They certainly did nothing for the army itself. Continual variations in the numbers of men to be inducted each year made planning difficult, and the bellows-like expansion and contraction in the size of infantry companies made effective training extremely difficult if not impossible. Italy's twenty-five-division army, ostensibly manpower-heavy but in practice skeletal for large periods of every year, worried the military authorities as the war clouds began to gather. In 1907 the list of entitlements to category III status was pruned and in 1909 the regulations allowing for exemption on health grounds were stiffened.

Some contemporary opinion interpreted the introduction of two-year service in 1910 as evidence that the authorities were at last prepared to subordinate the time-honoured military function of making Italians to the need to progress a genuine *nazione armata* ('nation in arms'). In fact it was just another attempt to square the circle of an excess of manpower and a shortage of money: even with two-year service, 21,000 category I recruits had to be released in 1910. The news that France had lengthened its term of conscription from two years to three in 1913 was a cause for reflection: for one thing, it was a demonstration of the increasingly widespread view among European armies that conscripts needed more training in order to face a modern battlefield. Italy could not afford to follow suit, either financially or in respect of the founding purpose for which her army existed. Increasing the term to three years and taking in 100,000 men a year would mean finding an extra 90,000,000 lire (one-third of the annual ordinary military budget) and leaving out of the army half the men available to serve in it. A unique argument was invented to justify sticking with the status quo: that such a change would age the first-line army.[11]

If social engineering was the default function for which the army existed, money was the ultimate determinant of its capacity to perform that task. Over the fifty-odd years between unification and the outbreak of the world war the army lived through successive cycles of 'boom and bust'. The newly minted state emerged from the wars of the Risorgimento with a massive public debt, and the 1870s saw pressure to balance the budget which meant reductions in the numbers of men enlisted and shorter periods of effective service. The 1880s, by contrast, were good years – Italy's leading military historian has labelled them 'the happiest years for the army'.[12] Military expenditure rose from 20 to 24 per cent of the national budget, increased numbers of men were taken into the ranks and the officer corps expanded. The end of the decade saw the biggest annual deficit since 1866, after which the state went back to balanced budgets and the army searched desperately for cuts. The good times came back again with the start of an economic boom in 1898, and disappeared once more when the boom collapsed in 1907. Thereafter the national deficit mounted alarmingly from 10,000,000 lire in 1909/10 to 556,000,000 lire in 1912/13.[13]

The army actually managed to do better financially in the deficit years than in the boom years that preceded them: military expenditure averaged 366,000,000 lire a year between 1902 and 1907, and 511,000,000 lire a year (roughly a quarter of total state spending) between 1907 and 1912. The Libyan war somewhat skewed the figures, and the budget, during the last years of peace: when the official and egregiously inaccurate figures were recalculated, the total cost of the war between 1911 and 1914 amounted to 1,015,000,000 lire – a sum equivalent to half the total annual spend of the state. In the last full year of peace, the army got 650,000,000 lire – this in a year when the state spent 150,000,000 lire on public education. Given that it had consumed approximately a quarter of all state spending, the army had not much to complain about – though that did not stop it from doing so! However, the 'concertina' effect of the military budgeting process, and the choices the army made about how to spend its money, meant that it was poorly prepared for a major war in 1914. No less important in view of what was about to happen is the comparative spend. Here the picture was darker yet. On almost every measure one cared to use, military Italy trailed behind both her future enemies and her future allies. In this respect, as in others, she was very much 'the least of the Great Powers'.[14]

If the army did not seem to object too strongly to its task of making Italians, it did object increasingly loudly to the role the state allotted to it in maintaining public order. In 1862 the government had been forced to declare a state of siege in southern Italy and Sicily to combat the brigandage that broke out after unification, and it did so once more in Palermo in 1866. Things did not reach that pass again until the 1890s, when a state of siege was proclaimed six times. The most spectacular eruption of civil disorder and military repression occurred in Milan on 9–10 May 1898. What was originally a *protesta dello stomaco* at the high price of bread became politicised, alarming the government, and when street barricades went up the shooting started. After it was over, the official tally listed 80 dead (one of them a soldier in all probability shot by his own side) and 450 wounded, though the true figures were almost certainly higher.[15] The events in Milan were an expression of many things, not the least among them mounting antipathy to conservative Liberal governance. The army now faced a rising tide of anti-militarism which braided together multiple strands of opposition from the patriotic Left, socialists and anarchists, along with popular anti-conscription feeling. Waves of strikes by industrial workers in the north and agrarian workers in the centre and south hit Italy between 1900 and 1913, organised by revolutionary syndicalists and socialists and exacerbated on the eve of the war by a financial crisis, the slowing down of industrial production and increased unemployment.

The policies pursued by Giovanni Giolitti, prime minister four times between 1892 and 1914 and the dominant political figure in the decade before the outbreak of the world war, made the increasing involvement of the army in the maintenance of law and order inevitable. Prepared to allow strikes within the limit of the law, but not prepared to allocate more money to expanding the police force, he used the army to plug the gaps in the public-order machine. He also obliged officers on public-order duty to put up with a certain amount of abuse, some of it physical, from crowds before they could open fire, though he was prepared to defend officers when they did shoot provided that they were obeying orders.

The army accepted the task of safeguarding the rule of law reluctantly and with mounting resentment; about the only thing in its favour was that it was a ground for asking for more money.[16] Senior authorities were equally unhappy with the role, though for different reasons. In 1910 (during a brief period when Giolitti was not holding office) the war minister, Lieutenant-General Paolo Spingardi, wrote to the premier complaining forcefully about the frequent demands he was getting from prefects for permanent increases in military garrisons on the basis of 'needs that are actually transitory', which could better be met by the temporary transfer of troops, or of 'more or less credible expectations of the possible need of troops in future in the service of public order'. He was not prepared to 'distort' the nature of his office by 'subordinating the distribution of troops in State territory to the uncertain demands of public security'.[17] When, later that year, the civil authorities in Ravenna trod on his toes again by calling out the army, Spingardi read out his letter to the Senate and drove his point home with the argument that the time taken up in public-order duties was even more of a handicap to training now that the army had two years' service and not three.[18]

Although no one in the army much liked it, the maintenance of public order was one of the defining features of Italian military culture. It is therefore not surprising to find evidence that peacetime ideas and practices carried over into war time. Luigi Cadorna, when he became commander of the armies in the field, nursed profound suspicions about the loyalty and reliability of his troops which he quickly expressed in draconian disciplinary regulations, as we shall see. The enthusiasm with which many of his subordinates imposed them is an indication that he was by no means alone in seeing civilians in uniform as an unreliable bunch of would-be strikers ready to down military tools at the first opportunity. Tracing the impact of pre-war experience on the rank and file of the army is a much more difficult task, but it seems a fair guess that for many a wartime conscript donning the uniform of repression in defence of the *patria* must have generated conflicting emotions.

It fell to the officer corps to meet the demands of the state and carry through the tasks it imposed on the army. Coming from socially diverse origins, they were a deeply divided body whose junior members were far from content with the way that their military and civilian masters treated them. The great military families of Piedmont, often noble, set the caste tone of the army and dominated its upper reaches. Close to the king, with whom senior generals often conversed in the Piedmontese dialect or in French, they tended to set much greater store by loyalty than by intellectual brilliance. Being heavily dependent on the Crown for favour and advancement as they climbed towards the top of the military tree made them courtiers as well as soldiers, and helped fuel strong personal rivalries and antipathies which made themselves felt during the war. Middling landowners who saw a commission as an avenue for social advancement sent sons into the army, as did the petite bourgeoisie. The industrial and commercial bourgeoisie, by contrast, seem to have shunned it. Lastly, one-third of all promotions to second lieutenant were reserved for non-commissioned officers until 1896, when the proportion was reduced to a quarter.

Promotion came slowly after 1900 as the bulge created by the expansion of the 1880s worked its way through the middle reaches of the officer corps. Age limits, introduced for the first time in 1896, did do something to speed up movement but still promotions were slow. Social origin magnified the problem: officers from the military schools were promoted faster than ex-non-commissioned officers, who rarely got beyond the rank of captain. Pay was relatively good by Italian standards – only diplomats and naval officers did better – but the official scales concealed a variety of actions by the military authorities such as pay retentions and delaying the publication of promotions decrees which meant that things were worse than they looked. Officers returning from Eritrea in 1895–6 had to take legal action which dragged on for years to get their campaign allowances. Marriage, which required a dowry, was virtually impossible for junior and middle-ranking officers unless they were lucky enough to find a bride from a wealthy family. Finally, officers were always on the move. Emilio De Bono, later to be one of Mussolini's most favoured and least able generals, thought changes of garrison were an excellent thing because they enlarged the horizons and expanded the army's knowledge of the country. Although some officers may have felt the same way, many were doubtless just as aware of the drawbacks of the 'nomadism' to which their vagabond life condemned them.[19]

The frustrations felt by the officer corps at the burdens being laid on it, at its poor economic situation and at what can only be labelled institutionalised maladministration almost boiled over in the first half-dozen years of the twentieth century. Sporadic demonstrations of discontent in which officers paraded in raw winter weather without their capes or all attended the sermons of a particular priest were indirect challenges to the authorities.[20] A more open protest came in the form of a specialist newspaper to which 2,000 subalterns subscribed. The war office tried to prevent officers from writing for it, but was unable to do so because disciplinary regulations allowed soldiers to publish whatever they wished. In May 1907, recognising the pass to which things had come, Giolitti established a parliamentary commission of enquiry into all aspects of military organisation. Under its imprimatur, Alberto Pollio as chief of the general staff and Spingardi as war minister introduced a raft of reforms between 1908 and 1913. Pay, training, food and barrack accommodation were all improved. Officer promotions were made more transparent, but at the same time the criteria were stiffened.[21] Belated reform was better than none at all, but it had little time to bed down before war came. Spingardi did not, in any case, believe that a war was in the offing: in June 1913 he told a subordinate that he did not hold with the possibility of war and believed that diplomacy would find a way of suppressing the 'divergencies' between the Great Powers.[22]

Risorgimento legends and African realities

In November 1888, the British military attaché in Rome summarised Italy's military record over the preceding forty years. 'Recent history does not shine with great military exploits, or brilliant victories on the part of the Italian Army,' he reported, 'in fact rather the reverse ...'[23] The record certainly did not redound to military Italy's credit. After losing both rounds of the First War of the Risorgimento in 1848–9, during which the Piedmontese army suffered a humiliating defeat at Austrian hands at the first battle of Custoza, Piedmont–Sardinia allied with France to fight the Second War in 1859. The preliminaries went well: the diplomatic preparations were adroit, and Colonel Ugo Govone's organisation of the rail movements that brought the French army into northern Italy was a model of what good logistics should be. On the field, however, things did not go so well. To all intents and purposes a French war in which the Italians won a single engagement – at San Martino on 24 June – it was ended by Napoleon III after the battles of Magenta and Solferino. The king and his conservative entourage were ready for peace in order to recuperate, to cleanse revolutionary forces at home and to free themselves from the hated French dominance. Afterwards loyal establishment historians simply glossed over all this, presenting the public with the image of a fighting monarch unswervingly dedicated to the nationalist cause.[24] Piedmont gained Lombardy – from French hands – but lost Nice and Savoy. In June 1866 the newly created Italian army crashed to defeat at the second battle of Custoza but once again Italy received its reward – the province of Venetia – from the hands of an ally after Prussia defeated Austria at Sadowa. The final act of the Risorgimento, the capture of Rome in September 1870 after a four-hour fire-fight with the minute Papal army, was a cross between a walk-over and a charade.

In the years that followed the wars of the Risorgimento were crowned with laurels and the army's reputation gilded as part of the process of securing the House of Savoy on the throne of a newly united Italy. The process of memorialisation began almost immediately and reached its apogee with a grand official ceremony at the ossuary at San Martino (whose tower bore over its door the inscription 'To Vittorio Emanuele II')

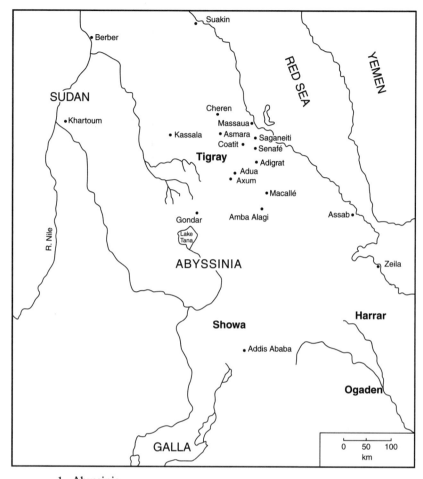

1. Abyssinia

on 24 June 1909, followed two years later by the unveiling of the 'Vittoriano' monument in the centre of Rome marking fifty years of a united kingdom.[25] Underneath the surface, though, bitter memories lingered. Having had to accept Lombardy from the French in 1859, the army's determination not to repeat the experience would play a far from insignificant part in the decision to fight the battle of Vittorio Veneto in 1918. It was also difficult to disguise or forget the fact that the army had suffered humiliating defeats at Austrian hands not once but twice. The second battle of Custoza shook Italians and gave a new impetus to the ongoing and seemingly endless public debate about the nation's deficiencies.

Critics blamed the whole country and not just the military, lamented the disappearance of civic virtues and advised the nation to learn from the Prussians.[26] Thirty-seven years later Alberto Pollio, soon to be appointed chief of the general staff, said that the second battle of Custoza still weighed on the army 'like a leaden cloak'.[27] By that time the Italian army had suffered another and much greater defeat that all but wiped out the legend of the Risorgimento.

Italy's first colonial war was both the product and the expression of two features that characterised her exercises in arms before, during and after her participation in the Great War: political ambitions that outran military capabilities, and military actions that all too readily threw caution to the winds. Her move into east Africa began, like so many of her ventures, as a political calculation in which military factors played virtually no part at all. In 1879, when her only interest in the Red Sea was a coaling station at Assab (see Map 1), no colonial blueprint existed in Rome. Within a short space of time the turns of fortune ignited ambitions and aroused appetites. In 1882–3 Italy was sounded out about joining the British intervention in Egypt but the then foreign minister, P. S. Mancini, did not feel able to take up the invitation. Italy took possession of Assab in 1882, but by the following spring fears were being expressed in the Italian senate that the doors in Africa were being closed to her. The outbreak of the Mahdist revolt in the Sudan in the autumn of 1884 produced a discreet enquiry from London: since the Egyptian garrisons along the Red Sea coast were going to have to retire, why not extend Italy's foothold there? The British were happy to see Massaua in Italian hands and therefore not in the hands either of 'barbarians' or of another, stronger power – France. Nor did they have any objections to Rome taking Beilul and Zeila. Mancini saw more things in the offing than just a larger Italian footfall on the rim of the Red Sea. What now opened up before him, Mancini told the Senate four years later, was 'the probability of our co-operating with England in the Sudan [and] putting a garrison at Khartoum'.[28] 'Why do you not wish to recognise that in the Red Sea, the closest to the Mediterranean, we can find the key to the latter?' he asked of critics who thought Africa a step too far.[29]

On 29 December 1884 the council of ministers decided to occupy Massaua, a decision that launched the Italian army into Ethiopia. As usual, the army was not admitted into the government's thinking. Instead the chief of the general staff, Enrico Cosenz, was asked his opinion on sending out a force to avenge the massacre of an Italian expedition two and a half months earlier somewhere south of Assab. Cosenz thought that it would be useful to have a permanent Italian garrison there to protect the locals but believed that much more in the way of reconnaissance would be needed before thinking of venturing inland. The government kept the military expedition wrapped in a veil of pretence during the preparations, though the navy was told the truth: the target was the occupation of Massaua, not Assab. On 12 January 1885 the designated commander of the expedition, Lieutenant-Colonel Tancredi Saletta, was called to the war ministry and given orders appropriate to the cover story. He was also warned that he might have to change objectives on the way and occupy Massaua.[30] Five days later Saletta's expedition set out from Naples, ostensibly heading for Assab.

When he reached Suakin on the Red Sea Saletta's orders were duly changed. He and his 802 officers and men were now to take possession of the island of Massaua, occupy the foothills around the base as a bridgehead, and reconnoitre three possible lines of advance into the interior: south-west towards Adua and Gondar, west towards Kassala and Khartoum and north towards Suakin on the Red Sea coast. He was advised to pay particular attention to the western route.[31] Arriving on 5 February he at once began to push inland to defend his base, taking two former Egyptian forts at Moncullo and Otumlo, some 10 kilometres outside the city, to protect his water supply. Tactical considerations – raiding by lawless bands in the hills and the threatened departure of the Egyptian garrison – drew him farther out and by August he was at Saati, 50 kilometres from the coast. Small and distant garrisons would later become vulnerable hostages to fortune, in turn generating yet more local pressure for expansion.

On the day Saletta landed at Massaua, news arrived in Rome that Khartoum had fallen. Cosenz had serious reservations about the viability of an expedition there but, not for the first or the last time, the government ignored military advice. In London, Count Nigra conveyed Italian readiness to take part in a British campaign to reconquer the Sudan if invited. The offer was turned down flat, though Gladstone was willing to see the Italians occupy Kassala. Cosenz was unenthusiastic, and the war minister, General Cesare Ricotti-Magnani, advised the government that a solo attempt on Kassala would be 'difficult and imprudent'. Even if it was carried out alongside the English the difficulties would be 'considerable' – not to say expensive at 40,000,000 lire.[32] Shortly afterwards, with tension on the Russian–Afghan border reaching new heights, the British government decided to evacuate the Sudan. London made it clear that there was going to be no joint accord or undertaking over Khartoum, thereby undercutting one of the main planks of Italy's Red Sea policy. Five years later she would remove it completely.

Initially the generals were instructed only to maintain the positions Italy already occupied. Major-General Carlo Genè, who arrived in Eritrea in November 1885, managed at first to obey orders but after a while he succumbed to the ever-present temptation to push farther inland. Faced with demands by the local ruler, Ras Alula of Tigray, to abandon the new Italian outposts, and with instructions from Rome not to let Alula get away with threatening Italy in his pocket, Genè reinforced the 400 local irregulars at Saati with 300 Italian infantry. On 25 January 1887, Alula and between 5,000 and 6,000 Ethiopians attacked the outpost and the local commander telegraphed for reinforcements. What followed was a minor military disaster. The following morning a relief column of 540 white conscripts and 50 irregulars set out from Moncullo under Lieutenant-Colonel Tommaso De Cristoferis. It was within an hour of reaching Saati when it ran into Alula's hordes. After half-an-hour its two old Gatling guns, recovered from an Egyptian depot and put into (briefly) working order, jammed. De Cristoferis ordered his men to retreat to the low hill of Dogali where, unable to hold off the Ethiopians, the column was massacred. At almost exactly the same moment the foreign minister, General Carlo Felice Di Robilant, was confidently reassuring the chamber of deputies that Genè was 'in a position to teach anyone who attacked him a severe lesson'.[33]

In parliament the generals quarrelled, as Italian generals were wont to do. Ricotti blamed De Cristoferis for having accepted combat in what were obviously unequal conditions, at which General Ettore Bertolè-Viale, who would succeed him at the war ministry two years later, pointed out that if he had not done so he could have been subjected to a court of inquiry. The public wanted revenge and so did Genè, who asked for 8,000–10,000 men to march on Bogos and Asmara and raise the local tribes against Adua. Di Robilant dismissed the idea out of hand. If Italy had to fight a campaign in Abyssinia it had to be sufficiently strong, well prepared and well conducted 'as to exclude even the most remote chance of failure'. Either Italy had to commit a large part of her military and financial resources at a moment when there were serious European issues in play, 'or we have to entangle ourselves in the intricate and unreliable maze of African alliances'.[34] Genè was ordered simply to take all steps necessary to secure Massaua and two months later Saletta returned as his replacement.

As long as there were cautious generals in key posts at Rome, politicians could not run wild. All that began to change on 29 July 1887 when the death of prime minister Agostino Depretis brought Francesco Crispi to power. The new premier publicly disavowed any intention of conquering Abyssinia. What Crispi really wanted was action to restore the prestige of Italian arms – as well as that of his government. Asked about recovering the lost forts of Ua-a and Saati, Saletta pointed out that they were respectively 26 and 50 kilometres from Massaua along difficult roads and 60 kilometres apart. He offered the government three choices: a fully fledged invasion of Abyssinia, the occupation of Bogos, or staying inside the fortified camp of Massaua. Personally he favoured retreating to Massaua and waiting on events – 'for example, a revolution in the interior of Abyssinia' – before undertaking decisive action.[35] To get what he wanted, Crispi clearly needed a new general. Saletta was recalled and General Alessandro Di San Marzano arrived at the beginning of November 1887 with 12,500 men and orders to reoccupy Saati and connect it by rail to Massaua – but not to commit Italy to a *guerra a fondo* ('all-out war').

Di San Marzano was a cautious general who knew how to obey orders. Resisting the urgings of his subordinate, Colonel Oreste Baratieri, to rush forward, he advanced slowly building entrenched camps fortified with metal towers every day to protect his men. By mid March 1888 he had reoccupied Saati and completed the railway connection. When at the end of March, Emperor Johannis appeared in front of Saati with 80,000 men Di San Marzano resisted the temptation to sally out from behind his fortifications and give battle in the open field. Johannis was in any case in a fragile position: the dervishes were making inroads into his empire in the north-east and his army was short of provisions. With his forces in disorder and his cattle dying of rinderpest, unknowingly imported by the Italians in cattle bought from India, he retreated.

Di San Marzano's replacement, General Antonio Baldissera, was a forward-minded general who would afterwards admit that his ultimate goal had been the conquest of all Ethiopia. Shrewdly, he realised that the best way to secure the hinterland beyond Massaua was to make use of tribal and religious divisions (the coast was Muslim, the hinterlands Christian) to foment internal discord and only intervene when all parties were exhausted. Internal conditions looked to be going his – and Italy's – way with rivalry between negus Johannis, shortly to be killed by dervishes at the battle of Metemma on 9 March 1889, and Menelik of Showa, and serious disorders elsewhere. Crispi wanted to conquer Asmara. Again Bertolè-Viale rejected a forward policy. The military arguments were overpowering: it would take at least 25,000 men and cost 100,000,000 lire; a road would have to be built from Saati to Asmara and its garrison provided with six months' supplies; preparing and transporting the troops would take at least three months; and since it was now January and large-scale operations in Ethiopia were impossible after April there simply was not time. Replying disingenuously that he was not thinking of a permanent occupation but a 'reconnaissance march', Crispi argued that if Asmara was impossible then they should choose another place. The important thing was for Italy to show herself on the *altopiano*.[36] Baldissera was prepared to try it, but Bertolè-Viale was not. During the course of his discussions with Crispi the war minister, who had been put in charge of African affairs on 17 April 1887, flatly refused to consult the chief of the general staff on the grounds that he alone carried the military responsibility.

Along with the news of Johannis's death came an offer from Menelik, now claiming the throne, of security for Italy in return for guns and ammunition. At the same time Baldissera told Rome that the imperial army was dissolving and that there was complete anarchy everywhere. Nothing, he suggested, was to be lost by waiting. Crispi was eager to move on Asmara, but Baldissera's telegram, Bertolè-Viale's continued caution and resistance from ministers worried about the huge budget deficits that had been built up left him isolated in cabinet. However, this was only a temporary setback for a wily and determined premier. Military considerations alone never carried much weight with Italian prime ministers, and they had more powerful political cards in their hand. Finding backing in parliament, where military senators led by Cosenz argued that now was a convenient moment to go onto the *altopiano*, Crispi won an important vote on 7 May 1889. Caught between the recklessness of the premier and the enthusiasm of parliament, the war minister had no choice but to agree to the occupation of Cheren and Asmara, which Baldissera took on 3 August 1889.

On 1 January 1890, a royal decree created the colony of Eritrea. The new governor and commander, Major-General Baldassare Orero, a fervent admirer of Crispi, wanted to be in Adua on the anniversary of Dogali (26 January) to demonstrate Italy's military power and to punish Ras Alula, the man responsible for the massacre. He also saw political advantage in then handing over the capital to Menelik as a magnanimous gesture. Crispi, manipulative as always, sent off a series of telegrams which, if they were intended to stop Orero, were highly equivocal.[37] Orero went ahead anyway but after only two days at Adua he withdrew. Crispi, greatly annoyed, accused him of 'untimeliness' first in going to Adua and then wanting to leave it and complained that 'You're rash and don't give me a moment to reflect.' For his part, Orero thought Crispi's injunction to stay put at Adua behind fresh fortifications was nonsensical when he already had more forts than men to put in them. Without more troops the only route to security was by recruiting local chiefs to protect the colony's borders.[38] If Orero was a general out of control, then as far as Crispi was concerned it was less because he went forward than because he immediately came back.

Shortly after the abortive parade on Adua, a main plank of Italy's African policy collapsed when London made it clear that she intended to reclaim her title to Sudan and did not propose to allow the Italians in as partners. Crispi struggled hard to maintain Italian rights to Kassala, claiming that its possession was essential to the defence of Eritrea, but fell from office in January 1891. With tensions mounting with France and severe pressure on finances his successor, Antonio Di Rudinì, would have liked to pull out of Eritrea altogether but that was simply impossible. A deal was struck to hand back Kassala, and the new commander, Major-General Antonio Gandolfi, was given his orders: 'Do not extend the boundaries of our colony, eliminate every reason for friction, avoid all causes for hostility with Menelik and our neighbours. I want as the result of this to reduce military expenditure.'[39] Over the next four years the military budget fell by almost 30,000,000 lire (11.5 per cent), and the Eritrean budget was cut from 20,000,000 lire a year to 8,000,000 lire. As part of a policy of seeking security at less cost, Gandolfi was allowed to reach a vague agreement with Ras Mengesha of Tigray. As Mengesha was the natural son of Johannis and therefore a rival for the throne, this hardened Menelik's growing hostility towards the Italians.

In February 1892 Gandolfi's second-in-command, Major-General Oreste Baratieri, succeeded to the post of commander-in-chief and governor of the colony. Three months later, Italy had a new premier. Giovanni Giolitti's priorities were balancing the budget, maintaining cordial relations with all the European Great Powers and democratising Italy. Eritrea, he told the chamber on 23 November 1892, was no longer a subject that preoccupied the government. To keep a lid on financial expenditure and military tendencies to adventurism, the government tried a policy of 'dual accords' with both Menelik and Ras Mengesha. Baratieri was sceptical, but his immediate problem was not the Ethiopians but the dervishes, 12,000 of whom attacked the Italian fort at Adigrat on 21 December 1893. The garrison held against a first daylight assault, but realising that it would probably be overrun that night its commander, Colonel Giuseppe Arimondi, led his men out in a desperate all-or-nothing gamble. His courage paid off handsomely: by early afternoon the bodies of over 1,000 dervishes lay strewn over the field at a cost of 110 Italian dead. Back in Rome a jubilant King Umberto I promoted Arimondi to major-general – making him equal in rank with Baratieri. Sensitive, difficult and authoritarian, Baratieri resented the challenge to his authority and grew jealous of Arimondi's glowing reputation.

Five days before the battle of Adigrat Francesco Crispi returned to power in Rome. The premier had a new aim, making Eritrea an outlet for the emigration that was losing Italy tens of thousands of men a year, and a new policy – encouraging Ras Mengesha of Tigray and Ras Maconnen of Harrar as contenders for the imperial throne. Menelik was in no mood to suffer any more interference from the Italians. He had found out that the Italians had perpetrated a linguistic trick on him in the Treaty of Wichale (1889) and as a result were claiming to represent Ethiopia in the outside world. On 27 February 1893 he notified the Italian government that he intended to terminate the treaty the following year.[40] With an expansionist premier in Rome and an ambitious commander at Massaua, both former followers of Garibaldi and therefore attuned to aggressive risk-taking, Italy began heading down the road to disaster.

Anxious to outdo Arimondi, Baratieri suggested reinforcing Agordat as a step along the road to Kassala, now reoccupied by the dervishes, and the Sudan. At the foreign ministry Alberto Blanc warned against a move which he saw as a provocative act, but Crispi encouraged Baratieri, passing on news indicating that a fresh dervish attack might be at hand. War minister Stanislao Mocenni, who was widely believed to owe his office to his willingness to cut the military budget and nothing more, had no clear idea what to do.[41] Attacking Kassala was to him 'a seductive idea but not one to be undertaken lightly, given that it could have grave conse-quences'.[42] The chief of the general staff, Domenico Primerano, had no doubts. 'The occupation of Kassala would probably not have any other effect than to provoke the forces in the Sudan to turn on us,' he warned the war minister. It might also lead to simultaneous action by the Abyssinians 'which would enlarge our sphere of action.'[43] His advice counted for nothing. Mocenni had already passed on Crispi's approval for Baratieri to do whatever he thought appropriate. Baratieri set off at once for Kassala with a force of local *ascaris*, and on 17 July 1894 he routed a weak garrison at what the dervishes regarded as no more than an outpost.

While Baratieri was concentrating on the dervishes, Menelik was mending fences with the regional lords and tribal chieftains, among them Ras Mengesha. By the autumn of 1894 he had achieved almost complete unity in his empire – an ominous sign. Suspecting Mengesha's loyalty, Baratieri led a reconnaissance in force to Adua at the end of December 1894 but logistical difficulties forced him to retreat after only four days. Mengesha followed him and the two sides fought an indecisive battle at Coatit on 13 January 1895 and another two days later at Senafé, which Baratieri won. Crispi congratulated him for acting like 'a true Garibaldino' and urged him to consider occupying the province of Tigray, which the premier believed now lay open before him.

These were encouraging times for both men, but beneath the surface of recent events there were some disturbing facts. Logistics, always a brake on operations in the highlands but something which earned insufficient strategic consideration until the last moment, had imposed themselves on Baratieri. They would do so again a year later, with dramatic results. His first indecisive battle at Coatit had been fought after a night-time move by Italian troops, a risky business at the best of times in the labyrinthine hills of the *altopiano*. Finally, the Ethiopians were not easy to stop: in two days of battle the Italians had fired 153,725 rounds, taking thirty-four shots to inflict each of the estimated 4,500 casualties. Tactical doctrine put maximum stress on the use of artillery, thought to be the Italians' great advantage. Shortly, more weight was going to be put on the guns than they could bear.[44]

After Senafé Baratieri, now a lieutenant-general, was given four white battalions and authorisation to raise 2,000 more *ascaris* to add to the 4,000 he already had. For once, Crispi had to rein in his own and his general's ambitions: facing elections in May, he could not for the time being increase the colony's budget beyond 9,000,000 lire. Baratieri was therefore instructed to limit himself to 'a pure and simple, but secure defence' at Kassala. As far as Tigray was concerned, what was needed was a defence which, while not passive, was enough to prevent an Abyssinian incursion against Massaua but one which at the same time 'does not weaken the defence from a military point of view by extending it excessively, or from a political point of view by assuming direct controls that could reinforce the hostility of the Abyssinian population'.[45] Adigrat was set as the outer limit of the Italian sphere of occupation, and Baratieri was told that any expansion must be funded locally. When he complained Crispi reminded him tartly that Napoleon had made war 'on the money of those he had defeated', scarcely a helpful remark. Baratieri pressed hard for more resources, telling Rome that he thought it possible there would be a 'great war' with Menelik in the autumn. Recalled to the capital for consultations, he secured an increase of 3,000,000 lire on the 1895/6 budget, which he believed would suffice even if Mengesha opened hostilities, but nothing more. Then news arrived from Arimondi, left temporarily in charge of Eritrea, that things were getting worse.

Baratieri left for Massaua on 15 September 1895 after telling Crispi and Mocenni 'Have no fears; I am lucky, and under me, even in Africa, everything must go well.'[46] Two days later Menelik ordered a general mobilisation. General opinion held that Menelik's empire was weak and overextended and that the first blow would shatter it into fragments. The best-informed expert on the spot, Major Tommaso Salsa, estimated that Menelik could field half his total force of 40,000 men. The Italians could put 600 white troops and 7,000 natives into the field; with another 3,000 men the Ethiopians could be beaten. Like everyone else, he badly underestimated the enemy and equally badly overestimated Italian superiority.[47]

Back once more in Massaua, Baratieri decided that the best and in the long term the most economical way to give Italy a great colony and secure it against any external enemy was to fight a *guerra a fondo*. That would need preparation, white troops and support services. Advancing beyond Adigrat and Adua would, he accepted, be a bigger exercise than Napier's advance on Magdala in 1867–8, but nevertheless he thought he could carry it out more swiftly and more economically. Mocenni was inclined to agree with him. However, that required men, weapons, munitions and most of all money, which Italy did not have. The only option seemed to be to stand on the defensive and wait for better times. Arimondi was established at Adigrat, now the pivot of the colony's defence, and to safeguard his position he set up a forward garrison at Amba Alagi commanded by Major Pietro Toselli. The spiral to disaster was about to begin.

By the evening of 6 December 1895, Toselli's garrison of 2,350 men was surrounded by 30,000 Ethiopians. Baratieri had intended him to withdraw to Macallé if threatened with defeat, but whether by design or accident (Arimondi had recently quarrelled with Baratieri) the order forwarded to Toselli did not include that phrase. Toselli's battle began at dawn next day and after fighting for six hours, with many of his white officers dead and his guns down to their last rounds, he gave the order to retreat to Macallé. He died, along with 1,500 *ascaris*, 20 white soldiers and almost all the officers – most of them shot down during the retreat. Leaving a garrison of 2,000 men at Macallé, Arimondi retired to Adigrat.[48]

The defeat goaded Rome into action. First, Crispi tried to unload responsibility for the defeat onto Baratieri. The chamber voted an extra 20,000,000 lire – but only after 238 deputies had left it. Primerano urged the need to send out more troops and Mocenni duly added another tranche of 3,000 men to the 5,000 he had sent out between 16 and 25 September. A procession of confusing and contradictory telegrams sped down the wires to Massaua. Mocenni urged Baratieri to be prudent and not to risk another disaster by getting fully committed. Crispi first told him the government did not intend to follow an expansionist policy, then advised him to think of victory – 'only that is our duty at this moment'.[49] Baratieri now proposed to fight if the enemy attacked him; to attack one of their columns if they split their forces; or to launch a flank attack if they marched away north-west towards Mareb. He appeared

to believe that with 10,000 men and the reinforcements that were on the
way he could defeat Menelik's 60,000 Ethiopians. Crispi warned him on
Christmas Day that he needed more troops if he was going to take
the offensive.

When Baratieri arrived at Adigrat, where he had built up a force of
14,848 Italian and native troops and twenty-two guns, on 10 January
1896 Major Giuseppe Galliano was already two days into a siege at
Macallé. His position was hopeless from the start. Surrounded by commanding hills from which forty pieces of Ethiopian artillery started to
batter his defences and with the only two wells 400 metres outside the
walls the fort, which had only four guns, was indefensible. After ten days'
fighting, and with his water supply at the point of exhaustion, Galliano
gave his officers a choice: blow up the fort or attempt a break-out. They
opted for the break-out and were about to try their chances when
Menelik offered them a safe conduct back to Italian lines. If he was
willing to try for a diplomatic settlement – and his motives for this act
are contested – Crispi was not. The only terms he was prepared to
consider were recognition of Tigray as Italian territory and the rest of
Ethiopia as a protectorate under Italian sovereignty.

Rome sent Baratieri more troops along with three more generals and a
new chief of staff, none of whom had any African experience, but all of
whom knew (or thought they knew) what to do. Under pressure from
his four brigade commanders, all of whom wanted to fight, Baratieri,
who was by now neither eating nor sleeping and was according to
an eyewitness 'physically finished', cancelled orders to retire on 23
February. Crispi goaded him on. 'This is a military consumption, not a
war,' the premier complained. Not being on the spot he claimed to have
no advice to give, but he certainly had criticisms to make. It appeared
to him that there was 'no fundamental conception underlying the
campaign, and I want that remedied'. Finally the premier twisted
the psychological knife. 'We are ready for any sacrifice to save the honour
of the army and the prestige of the crown.'[50]

At the end of a supply line from Massaua that took the caravans
twenty-four days to journey there and back, Baratieri was by now in
severe supply difficulties. On 27 February he was told that in four days'
time he would get a caravan with enough supplies for five days after
which no more could be guaranteed. Next day he called his brigade
commanders together, explained the situation and asked the crucial
question: advance or retreat? Speaking first as the most junior general,
Albertone was against retreat. So were Dabormida and Arimondi,
the victor of Adigrat confident that against 50,000–60,000 Ethiopians
they could win at least a partial victory. With that the die was cast.

Eyewitnesses saw the chief of staff, Colonel Gioacchino Valenzano, leave Baratieri's tent rubbing his hands and exclaiming 'At last we've got him to attack.'[51]

In one of history's many ironies the battle of Adua, which took place on 1 March 1896, might easily never have happened at all, or have happened differently. Menelik, suffering like Baratieri from considerable supply difficulties, had decided to strike camp and retire next day. Had Baratieri waited one day he would have been following a retreating enemy. The likelihood is that he would have attacked, but the circumstances on the field of battle would have been different and the outcome almost certainly other than what it turned out to be. As it was, Baratieri's intentions, according to his own account, were to move forward to a position from which he could easily repel the enemy if attacked, to retreat to Sauria if not attacked, or to attack the Ethiopian rearguard in the valley of Mariam Sciavitù ahead of Adua if the chance arose.[52] The odds were against him by between six and ten to one: Menelik had between 80,000 and 150,000 men and Baratieri had 14,400 men and fifty-six guns. Circumstances lengthened the odds even before the first shots had been fired. Advancing at night over unreconnoitred ground and using an inaccurate map, the formation got split up when Albertone's native brigade advanced too far west and got well ahead of the other three brigades.

By 0800 on 1 March Albertone's 4,000 men, several kilometres away from the rest of Baratieri's force, were fighting off some 30,000 Ethiopians on their own. An hour and a half later he was struck by another 25,000 of the enemy and completely cut off from the other three brigades. The native troops retreated, covered by the gunners who fired over open sights until their ammunition was exhausted, when they were massacred to a man. In the centre Arimondi's 2,500 men were hit by Showan hordes. General Ellena's reserve brigade was unable to help him as most of it had been detached to fight off attacks on his right. Arimondi fought a semicircular defensive battle until the early afternoon when Baratieri, who had been cut off and lost for an hour, rejoined the command and allowed a general retreat to begin. More men were lost in this phase of the battle than in all the earlier ones, bearing out an established tactical belief that Italians should never retreat in the face of the enemy.

Last to go was General Vittorio Dabormida who, probably misled by the maze of hills and unable to tell where the sound of the firing was coming from, moved away north thinking he was helping Albertone. All morning his 3,800 men fought off Ethiopian attacks. By midday they thought the battle was won, but their Calvary was about to begin. At 1415 the bulk of Menelik's army, having disposed of the other three brigades, descended on them. The brigade fought 50,000 Ethiopians for an hour and three quarters and then, after a desperate last charge, Dabormida ordered the retreat.[53]

Arimondi, Dabormida and Major Galliano died on the field of Adua along with 5,000 Italians (more than in all the wars of the Risorgimento put together) and 1,000 *ascaris*. Another 1,500 men were wounded and 2,700 taken prisoner, including Albertone. Italian casualties included 30 soldiers castrated during the battle and 406 *ascaris* who had their right hands and left feet cut off after it to prevent them from doing any more fighting. Ethiopian losses are difficult to estimate, but probably between 6,000 and 12,000 died and an equivalent number were wounded. Baratieri was quickly tried by a military court at Asmara and found not guilty of the two charges against him: deciding for inexcusable reasons to attack (it was supposed that he knew that the government intended to replace him, something he always denied) in circumstances that were bound to lead to defeat, and abandoning his command during the battle. Although he was exonerated, the court deplored the fact that such an unequal fight in such difficult circumstances had been entrusted to 'a general who showed himself so far below the needs of the situation'.[54] With that, his career was over.

The war came to an abrupt end when Italy signed a peace treaty on 26 October 1896, but the reverberations lingered long afterwards. Italian generals seemed wanting both professionally and personally, and there were bigger question marks than ever over the army's reliability and capability. Adua gave politicians grounds to be sceptical about the military instrument on which they might have to call, and undoubtedly reinforced the well-established practice of leaving the soldiers out of things when it came to international policy-making. The conflict between war ministers and chiefs of the general staff augured badly for military decision-making, and Crispi's harrying of the general on the spot was an example of the power of an Italian premier to take policy by the throat and a demonstration of the complete absence of collective political decision-making. In due course these features of Italy's political–military culture would play their part in her entry into the world war and her conduct of it. The African disaster also gave another general an excuse for a failure of greater proportions. Two decades later Luigi Cadorna would explain Caporetto with the words 'I was the commander of the army of Custoza and Adua.'[55]

The general staff, war planning and operational doctrine

The era of modern war planning in Italy began with the appointment of General Enrico Cosenz as first chief of the Italian general staff in August

1882.[56] Before that little existed by way of an organised and professional staff of the kind that had guided Prussia–Germany to its victories in the wars of 1866 and 1870–1. A War College opened its doors in 1867, and in 1873 an advisory body of general officers was created to contribute on great military questions, but Italy still lagged a long way behind most of her rivals. Two years later an American general, Emory Upton, in a survey of some of the world's major armies, concluded that the Italian army had no planning agency at all.

In one respect the first two chiefs of staff, Enrico Cosenz (1882–93) and Domenico Primerano (1893–6) broke the traditional mould. Both were southerners educated at the military college in Naples and intended initially for the Bourbon army. Cosenz owed his appointment to his distinguished record in the wars of the Risorgimento, in which he had fought with Garibaldi in 1860 and had managed by pure chance to avoid being on the field at Custoza in 1866, and to the fact that he was widely acknowledged to be one of the most intellectual as well as most modest men in the army. His study of the German wars convinced him of the importance of professional preparation, study and direction as contributors to victory.[57] Unlike his opposite number, Helmuth von Moltke, though, he had no real independence. The royal decree that defined his role and determined his functions made him responsible for devising mobilisation and deployment plans under the authority of the war minister, whose agreement he had to secure. Bitter struggles between the two became commonplace during the late nineteenth century as they battled over the army's size, organisation and employment. They would do so up to and beyond August 1914.

Domenico Primerano's short and troubled tenure of office was ended by the débâcle at Adua about which, parliament and the public quickly discovered, he appeared not to have been directly consulted at all. The revelations sparked a short and bitter debate in which the war minister blamed the chief of staff for the fact that no preparatory studies had been made and that as a result 'we entered the campaign unprepared' and the chief of staff pointed out that the war minister, with a general staff section of his own, could and did act quite independently of the general staff. The rumpus came to an end when a new war minister, General Luigi Pelloux, who had been instrumental in persuading Primerano to accept the post in the first place, used a law on seniority that was only days old to retire him. Critics pointed out that the war minister was Piedmontese and his victim was not.[58]

The next chief of the general staff, Tancredi Saletta (1896–1908), was a Piedmontese artilleryman with combat experience in Africa who had served time as Primerano's deputy. Saletta proved to be a safe and competent pair of hands. Trusted both by Umberto I and by his successor, Vittorio Emanuele III, he was able with the new king's backing to negotiate a secret agreement in August 1900 that gave him 'full and exclusive competence' to look beyond the army's mobilisation in his planning and to deal directly with the German and Austro-Hungarian chiefs of staff about 'possible dispositions'.[59] As well as carrying out the now customary duties of the job – mobilisation planning, developing new service regulations and the like – he proved something of an innovator, re-establishing grand manoeuvres in 1903 and introducing modern staff rides on the German model. His position was eased somewhat when changes in the regulations in 1906 and 1908 freed him from some of the oversight that war ministers had been able to impose on him. The chief of staff was now able to develop operational plans that extended beyond the moment when the army was assembled and deployed, as well as being charged with troop training and drawing up regulations for the tactical and operational deployment of divisions and corps. The government was also supposed to keep him informed of the politico-military situation – an obligation honoured more in the breach than in the observance.

The last pre-war chief of the general staff, Alberto Pollio (1908–14) was by common consent the most brilliant of them all. A southerner by birth, he followed a conventional educational path through the Piedmon-tese military academies in the north, culminating in his passing out from the War College at the top of his class. A mixture of staff and active service which included a spell as military attaché in Vienna in the 1890s served as a good preparation for the professional demands of the job, and a period as aide-de-camp to Umberto I doubtless did him no harm in court circles. By the time he came into office he had published studies of Napoleon and Waterloo, as well as an authoritative book on the second battle of Custoza. In addition to taking a major role in directing a war, unlike any of his predecessors, Pollio reorganised the *Alpini*, cavalry and artillery, improved promotion prospects and brought in a system of annual individual assessments for officers. He also fought a continuing battle for more money. A true soldier from his cap to the tips of his gloves (he was always elegantly turned out), Pollio was widely admired in the army.

The general staff over which these four men presided before the world war was relatively small in size – until Pollio's time it numbered only 137 officers. There were several reasons for this. The War College, from whose graduates the junior staff officers were drawn, was not particularly popular. Few officers put themselves forward for the entrance examin-ations and fewer still got through the orals and made it onto the course: in the 1880s some thirty officers graduated each year. Under the influence of many of its senior officers, the officer corps as a whole remained more or less resolutely anti-intellectual and distanced itself from staff work. General Baldissera, on reading in an officer's record that he refused to give lectures, reportedly declared 'But this is a merit! – he commands his battalion splendidly and will command a regiment even better.'[60]

General staff officers were not popular in the army at large. Castigated as *bel, biond, nobil e cirula* ('handsome, fair-haired, aristocratic and blue-eyed'), they were widely held to live a charmed life in Rome where they spent their days smoking, laughing and chatting while the rest of the officer corps slogged away in the territorial commands.[61] An 1882 decree giving officers on the general staff faster promotion caused uproar, and an attempt in 1893 to make the War College more attractive and deepen the pool of prospective general staff officers by giving successful graduates the right to promotion by selection not seniority made staff officers even less popular with the rest of the army. Feelings grew so bad that in 1904 a parliamentary commission recommended abolishing the general staff altogether. It survived, of course, but remained a body in isolation. When war came in 1915 it had neither imbued the army with a school of thought nor shaped command styles and practices to a common last.

Until the outbreak of war in 1914, Italian soldiers looked on France as their most probable enemy and Germany as their most likely ally. Italy had joined the Triple Alliance in 1882. Five years later Francesco Crispi began his first term of office. Acutely sensitive to long-standing threats that the French might take advantage of Italy's strategic vulnerability to sea power and land troops somewhere on the peninsula or the islands, cutting railway and telegraph communications, and to rumours that France was in negotiations with Switzerland, Crispi turned to Berlin for assistance. An Italian military delegation went to Berlin in late December 1887 against the backdrop of an Austro-Russian crisis that, as Rome knew from the reports coming from the Italian military attaché at St Petersburg, was being blown up by Bismarck.[62] Under the terms of a military convention signed on 28 January 1888, Italy undertook to send six army corps to operate on the Rhine in the event of a war with France and an initially hesitant Austria–Hungary undertook in turn to make three railway lines available to get them there – but only if a war involved Russia and herself.[63] Crispi seems to have wanted to use the military link as the platform from which to fight a preventive war with France, but Bismarck swiftly squashed the idea. The scheme did Crispi no good on the international stage as the Russian secret service got hold of his letters to his military emissary and may well have tipped off the French.

The new national military strategy was far from welcome in some quarters. The Italian parliament, in one of its periodic fits of anxiety about a French invasion, was debating the necessity for fixed fortifications to defend the exposed coasts and islands, a preoccupation which began soon after unification and lasted until very shortly before the world war began.[64] The new war minister, General Ettore Bertolè-Viale, was uncomfortable with the convention which might expose a weakened Italian army to a direct attack by France. So was Cosenz, who was unwilling to place much reliance either on the military convention or the Germans, well aware that any system took years to finalise during which time interests and alliances could undergo many changes.[65] His new war deployment plan that year addressed traditional priorities, spreading eleven of the twelve army corps in a defensive net stretching from Alba and Alessandria via Turin and Bologna to Verona intended to protect vulnerable coastal points and serve as a secure defensive deployment from which to launch counter-attacks.

Timing was a critical element of the new commitment and in March 1888 a joint railway convention set out the timetable for a joint Italo-German war. Twenty-eight trains would run every day for twenty-three days, getting the Italian army to the Rhine by the twenty-ninth day of mobilisation. As Italy and Austria together had only half the number of railway engines and two-thirds of the railway carriages needed to carry out the move, it was heavily dependent on a substantial material contribution from Germany. The railway plans were updated four times between October 1891 and May 1898. During the course of the discussions the Italian commitment was reduced from six corps to five and the timetable speeded up by four days.[66]

The railway agreement dealt only with the transport and maintenance of the Italian units, not what they would do once they went into action. In November 1891 the newly appointed chief of the German general staff, Alfred von Schlieffen, sent Cosenz details of the forts of Epinal and Belfort, the likely targets of an Italian force fighting on the Rhine, and in 1893 the staff in Rome was given studies of the invasion routes to Paris and Lyons.[67] The Rhine began to look a more attractive operation after the staff ride of 1891 examined the prospects for an Italian offensive across the Maritime Alps and concluded that the topography and the fortifications put up by the French posed such formidable obstacles that any thoughts of attack were 'brought up short in confusion'.[68] At this point the German general staff did not seem inclined to take the Italians very far into its confidence: General Osio, designated chief of staff for the 3rd (Rhine) Army at the close of the century, complained about the 'scant and nebulous directives' being given to him, though he did recognise that no more could be asked 'from a people who consider us unreliable allies'. One project that was passed to him was for operations against Verdun and plans to transport three Italian army corps there were drawn up during the 1890s.[69] Despite a degree of apparent mistrust on both sides, collaboration in war seemed very much on the cards in the first years of the new century: the German deployment plans of 1905/6 and 1906/7 both mentioned the arrival of the Italians 'dependent on political circumstances'.[70]

With international tensions between Rome and Paris high, and the Italian army looking dangerously weak as a result of budget cuts, France remained the planners' main preoccupation during the 1890s. Their fears of attack or invasion increased when they learned that France had begun to construct a new naval base at Bizerte in Tunisia. With the French clearly in mind, the annual grand manoeuvres in 1892 took as their scenario a major battle in the valley of the Tiber to defend Rome. The following year Cosenz's last staff ride examined the prospects for a French landing in Sicily. The reassuring result was that it would not be a decisive move in a major war and that as long as the Italians kept a foothold on the island all would be well. The same could not be said, however, for Italy's chances of attacking France. The staff rides in 1894, 1895 and 1896 all showed that Italian defences along the French border were weak, that even if Germany were successful on the Rhine Italy might be overwhelmed unless she built more barrier forts and roads and invested in more mountain troops, and that whereas the French could get through the mountains and onto the Paduan plain fairly quickly an Italian attack would find itself tied up in a long drawn-out and costly campaign.[71]

Cosenz's successor, General Saletta, dealt with each of the problems he faced in turn. Determined to secure the French frontier regardless of cost, in 1898 he successfully persuaded a special commission to spend state money to make it secure, even getting some fortifications he had not asked for. In the same year, doubtful about whether the Austrians would necessarily honour their promises over the transport of 3rd Army to the Rhine, he resuscitated the so-called 'second hypothesis' that had been a minor part of staff planning since 1886 and explored getting there via Switzerland. Plans were duly drawn up to move through eastern Switzerland to Lake Constance and thence to Zurich and were communicated to the Germans, who agreed in 1900 to provide the supplies and munitions that 3rd Army would need if it followed this route.[72] In the same year a staff ride concluded that given the difficulties involved in getting across the country it would be best to respect Swiss neutrality. The 'second hypothesis' formally disappeared from planning after 1907, though the staff did explore it one more time in 1910 when they reached the same conclusion. Finally Saletta looked east, where increased Austrian activity along the common frontier was beginning to cause alarm. Defensive deployment plans that spread the army between the Adige and Tagliamento rivers were out of date, and staff rides in 1898, 1899 and 1900 revealed that the frontier was dangerously unprotected and that Italy faced defeat on her eastern front whether she had to attack or defend.[73]

Since the completion of unification the army had traditionally seen France as its number one enemy. With land frontiers bordering on France, Switzerland and Austria–Hungary and a vast coastline to protect its cast of mind during the decades after unification was predominantly defensive. After 1902, the Italian foreign ministry began surreptitiously to shift Italy's diplomatic alignment away from the Triple Alliance and towards accommodation with Italy's Gallic neighbour. At more or less the same time educated public opinion, fanned by the increasingly vociferous rantings of Italian nationalists, grew angry at Austrian behaviour in Trieste and her possession of the so-called *terra irredenta*. Although both of these currents may have had indirect effects on the Italian general staff, its concerns were more narrowly focused on assessing the military capabilities of potential enemies and designing contingency plans to meet the threats they presented. Italy's titular ally, Austria–Hungary, most certainly could not be excluded from such considerations.

From 1900 onwards the Italian high command watched with mounting alarm as Austria built a new series of armoured forts along the frontier with Italy, modernised existing ones, constructed fieldworks, put in new roads, and extended railway lines. Later on the staff calculated that by the time the war began the Austrians had built sixty major permanent works armed with 450 guns, as well as constructing 799 kilometres of trenches and 200 kilometres of new roads. Staff rides compared Italian and Austrian communications, defences and logistical arrangements along the eastern frontier, contributing to the mounting anxiety about the disequilibrium between the two sides. Masses of data poured into headquarters in Rome as the army assembled all the details it could muster about Austrian fortifications, tracked every alteration in Austrian manpower policy and analysed every tactical, operational and technical regulation it could lay its hands on. Simply calculating the numbers of men the Austrian army could put into the field was far from straightforward as there were different ways of counting active soldiers, reservists, the Austrian *Landwehr* and the Hungarian *Honvéd*, but whichever way up the general staff held this piece of paper the outcome was always the same: the 'enemy' was half again as strong as the Italians. In 1905, the Italian standing army numbered on average 207,000 men against the Austrians' 371,000. In 1914, the standing Austrian army comprised sixteen army corps against the Italians' twelve.[74]

In 1900 money was forthcoming to fortify some of the north-eastern valleys and increase the garrisons, but not enough to double-track the railways so as to be able to deploy the whole army on the river Tagliamento. The planners hoped to push two army corps up to the Tagliamento in an advance move, but given the state of the railways they had to settle for deploying the entire force on the Piave. That scheme went into the melting pot when the 1904 staff ride forecast disaster for Italy in a war against Austria, suggesting that Italy could not even hold the line of the Piave. Italian forces were pushed back to the Livenza river in the war game and threatened on their left flank, Italy was shown to be weak everywhere, and unless a great deal of money was spent on railway building it appeared all too probable that the Austrian armies were going to get to the starting line in Friuli first if war came.[75] While Saletta pressed for more money for fortifications – something parliament was becoming increasingly reluctant to provide – the general staff grew concerned about the new chief of the Austrian general staff, Conrad von Hoetzendorff, who made no secret of his anti-Italian views. He was only waiting, they supposed, to be able to collect together forces presently strung out along the Russian frontier before launching an attack into Friuli.

The planned co-operation with the Germans on the Rhine suffered a minor setback when, on 24 February 1901, the newly enthroned Vittorio Emanuele III told the German military attaché that he was against sending 3rd Army to the Rhine as it would dangerously weaken Italy's land frontiers and coastal defences. Saletta reassured Schlieffen in 1902 and again in 1903 that the Rhine plan still stood despite Italy's tightening links with France. He had to do so again in 1906 during the first Moroccan crisis, when Italy's failure to give Germany diplomatic support raised hackles in Berlin. Ironically his successor, Alberto Pollio, a convinced *triplicista*, had to tell the Germans in November 1912 that Italy could not stick to its undertaking.

Pollio had wanted to talk to his opposite number, General Helmuth von Moltke, about the international situation a little earlier but had been reined in by the war minister, General Paolo Spingardi. Then, on 22 November 1912, Moltke suggested to the Italian military attaché that the two general staffs ought to communicate in view of what he felt was a 'most serious' moment in international affairs. The first Balkan war had begun on 4 October, the Turks were going down to defeat contrary to everyone's expectations, and the Russians were backing Serbian claims to a port on the Adriatic. The question in Moltke's mind was what might happen next. If Russia intervened in an Austro-Serbian conflict on Serbia's side this would be the *casus foederis* that would cause Germany to take the field and in all likelihood trigger French mobilisation. Moltke wanted to know how far Germany could count on Italian help.[76]

With not much to go on as far as government policy was concerned other than that the Triple Alliance was likely to be renewed and that aid to Germany was still on the cards, Pollio sent his personal emissary, Colonel Vittorio Zupelli, to Berlin to explain that Italy's strategic options were very limited. She could not count on the Austrians; crossing Switzerland would be 'very difficult'; operating in the mountains on the French frontier would be equally difficult because of French fortifications and the need for siege artillery; and a war with France would expose Italy's coasts and its communications with Libya to attack.[77] In plain language, Italy was not going to be able to honour its 1888 commitment. In reversing that decision, Pollio had two considerations at the forefront of his mind: the war in Libya, which had absorbed the equivalent of three army corps and a great deal of matériel, as well as causing much organisational disruption, and the need to keep 3rd Army as a strategic reserve in case of 'complications' in the Balkans.[78] When Vienna learned that Italy was not going to keep to its military undertakings the general feeling there was that she had acted in bad faith. In less than two years' time, her suspicions about her alliance partner would be confirmed.

In August 1913, Pollio attended the annual German summer manoeuvres and made a good impression on both Moltke and Conrad. Then, on 10 October 1913, all three chiefs of staff met at Salzbrunn in Silesia to discuss strategy. At that meeting Pollio told Moltke and Conrad that he was persuaded that 'in war the Triple Alliance must act as a single state, dealing [as we shall be] with a question of [our very] existence, since the war will be terrible'. To his mind there were no viable alternatives to the Rhine option. An attack on France across the western Alps, as he knew, faced formidable defences and posed considerable logistical problems. It would inevitably be slow and difficult, would occupy no more than two French army corps at most, and was therefore an extremely unproductive use of Italy's military power. A landing in Provence, under consideration by the planners in Rome at the time, was even less viable. There were no convenient landing sites, the few suitable steamships which would take time to assemble could only land a small and therefore vulnerable first echelon, and capturing the only substantial target of such an operation, Marseilles, was likely to make no impact on the fighting along the Rhine. It also depended on Italy first securing a decisive victory at sea. All in all, Pollio told his allies, it was 'risky'.

Personally, he was ready to send two Italian cavalry divisions to the Rhine and to study the employment there of two army corps.[79]

Pollio called his four designated army commanders together in December 1913 and put the idea to them that the Italian cavalry should be sent to the Franco-German theatre – a proposal that had already been approved by the king and the premier – rather than to Silesia, which had been his idea the previous summer. The generals thought the new idea even better than the old one. Pollio, though, wanted to go further. 'How deplorable our conduct would be,' he told the army commanders, 'if we, with extra troops available, were to leave them standing at arms, passive spectators of the great drama unfolding in the Franco-German theatre of war.' If the *Triplice* won Italy stood to make gains, but if it lost then the army would be open to the accusation that it had failed properly to safeguard the nation's interests. Pollio wanted support to resuscitate the plan to send three Italian army corps to the Rhine – and he got it. All four army commanders backed the idea, and Cadorna, who thought a campaign in the French Alps would be indecisive at best, went further: if five army corps and three cavalry divisions were available then they should all be sent 'and even more if possible'.[80]

Whether strategic or political arguments carried the day, and whether the soldiers or the politicians were the prime movers, is unknown but somehow early in the new year the king was persuaded to change his mind and agree to sending three Italian army corps to the Rhine in the event of war. Moltke and Conrad were told in February 1914, and in March Major-General Luigi Zuccari, newly designated commander of 3rd Army, went to Berlin to discuss the arrangements. There he learned that since the German army's mobilisation regulations for 1914 had already been prepared the three Italian corps could not figure in them. In 1915 they would be expected at the end of the third week of mobilisation, and would be tasked either with a diversionary attack on French frontier fortifications or with counter-attacking the French in Lorraine. A transport agreement signed on 10 April made provision for 541 trains to shuttle the three Italian corps to their destinations by the twenty-sixth day of mobilisation.[81] Then, at the eleventh hour, Moltke began to think about using the Italians on the Russian front not the Rhine. A matter of days before Franz Ferdinand's death – and his own – Pollio was prepared to accept that the course of events after a war started might justify such a deployment and ready too to take personal responsibility for it – but for the moment without telling the government.[82]

Although Pollio's sights were set on co-operating with his Triple Alliance partners and his default position was the Rhine plan, neither he nor the planners could afford to neglect the eastern frontier. In 1909, plans were drawn up to put the bulk of the army on either side of the river Piave with a forward deployment on the Tagliamento, from where advanced Italian units could launch cavalry raids to disrupt Austrian deployment. If the right circumstances arose, offensive drives could move on Innsbruck, Bolzano or Villach. The plan assumed that the Austrians would launch their main attack on Italy from the Tyrol salient. After 1910 the Italian general staff changed its mind. The Tyrol salient was difficult for the enemy to move across, occupied an 'eccentric position' in respect of the rest of the Dual Monarchy, and was in any case now covered by new Italian fortifications. By 1913 a new war scenario envisaged the main Austrian attack coming on the Isonzo front, joining hands with a converging attack from Carinthia in the Treviso–Conegliano–Cornuda triangle, and meeting an Italian army that was arriving on the Piave having only just completed its mobilisation and deployment. If things went as the Austrians planned 'the enemy's numerical superiority and the strategic situation, which is so unfavourable to us, would very quickly decide the outcome of the war in Austria's favour'.[83]

A revised plan provided for a more rapid counter-offensive, pushing an army corps forward to support cavalry divisions at Udine, Codroipo and Latisana on the assumption that new fortifications in Friuli would allow the bulk of the armies to get to the Tagliamento before it fell to the enemy.[84] On the eve of the war, revising their assumptions yet again, the Italians expected the Austrians to saturate the mountain zone surrounding Italy 'almost completely' with troops and launch a 'spoiling' attack five divisions strong from the eastern face of the Tyrol. Five lines of probable advance were identified, partly on the basis of where the Austrians had built their fieldworks and partly on where Italy had sited her fortifications. Despite all the difficulties that the previous planning had highlighted, the Italian general staff were confident that they could block the Austrian advance 'and with good luck, blow the enemy's plan to the winds'.[85]

The Libyan war, 1911–12

When Liberal Italy went to war for the second time in 1911, she was satisfying ambitions that went back almost a quarter of a century. In 1887, renewing the Triple Alliance, Austria–Hungary and Italy agreed to the principle of 'reciprocal compensation' if either was obliged to occupy some part of the Ottoman empire, either in the Balkans or on the Aegean coasts and islands. The desire for 'compensation' would be a powerful force propelling Italy to war twenty-four years later. Italian eyes were on north as well as east Africa, and by 1909 Italian diplomats had secured agreements from Austria–Hungary, Germany, France, Great Britain and Russia which seemed to leave them free to develop an Italian sphere of influence in Tripolitania and Cyrenaica when the time came. Awkwardly, though, Italy as a signatory to the Treaty of Berlin in 1878 was a guarantor of the Ottoman empire. Maintaining this façade, Italian ministers regularly stood up to reiterate their commitment to preserving the integrity of the Ottoman empire. As late as June 1911, three and a half months before starting the war, foreign minister Antonio Di San Giuliano confirmed it as an unchangeable and fundamental principal of Italian foreign policy.[86] In the meantime the 'sick man of Europe' was growing demonstrably weaker. From 1909 opportunities began to beckon as the Young Turk regime suffered revolutions in Constantinople and revolts in Albania, the Yemen and the Yasir. In the spring of 1911 the Ottoman high command was forced to send 30,000 troops to the south, stripping their Libyan division of four-fifths of its men and leaving only some 3,400 men there.

Domestic pressure now came into play to advance an avaricious policy, as it would do again four year later. The newly formed Italian National Association stirred up the literate public, Marinetti approvingly labelled the war 'Futurist' and an excited press spread exaggerated claims about Libya's economic potential and wildly misleading descriptions of its abundant natural resources made by people who had never been there. Giuseppe Bevione of *La Stampa*, who did go there in the spring of 1911, described in seductively hyperbolic language the economic possibilities that beckoned in a land where 'olive trees grow bigger than oak trees . . . grapes grow in bunches weighing two or three kilos each, and the melons weigh twenty or thirty kilos apiece'.[87] Politically, economically and ideologically, the idea of a war for Libya was popular on the Right and the Left.

International tension in the shape of the second Moroccan crisis married with mounting domestic pressure when the German ambassador told Di San Giuliano on 1 July 1911 that the German gunboat *Panther* had been sent to Agadir. For the foreign minister, this was the moment when the question of Tripoli 'entered an active phase'.[88] As he saw it, Italy might be forced to carry out military operations in Tripolitania within a few months. There were reasons not to do so, foremost among them the possibility that such an action could hasten a Balkan crisis and 'almost force' Austria–Hungary to act there. However, there were more compelling grounds for quick action. French moves in Morocco could change the Mediterranean equilibrium; Italy would not encounter serious obstacles if she acted now, but that might not be the case if she acted later; and Turkey, facing serious military problems, was evidently in a vulnerable state. Finally, there was domestic politics to think about. Public opinion felt that the government's external policy was 'too docile' and there was a widespread feeling that national energy needed vigorously to assert itself.[89]

During August Di San Giuliano encouraged the European powers to believe that all attempts at conciliation had been exhausted before taking action, though in reality no such moves were ever made. A check around the European embassies confirmed that neither Germany nor Russia would oppose an Italian action and that Austria–Hungary, while uneasy, was not disposed to obstruct it.[90] Then, on Saturday 2 September, Di San Giuliano met Rear-Admiral Corsi, vice-chief of naval staff, in the Grand Hotel Fiuggi and learned that if an Italian expedition to Tripoli was not launched in October or November bad weather would mean waiting until the following April at the earliest. The foreign minister thought delaying until 1912 impossible as by then the international situation would be 'completely changed'.[91] On 14 September, premier and foreign minister decided to launch an expedition in November. Next day Di San Giuliano urged that action be in the first half of October. On 19 September, Giolitti instructed the war and navy ministers to speed up secret preparations for war. At this point, the foremost consideration in both men's minds was the need to act before Vienna and Berlin suspected or got to know about what was happening and exerted mediating action which would prevent Italy from lifting her prize.

Next day came news that the Turks were sending the steamer *Derna* to Tripoli with arms and ammunition, and the day after that further intelligence that the Franco-German talks over Morocco were nearing conclusion. On 23 September France and Germany signed preliminary accords, and the following day the king was asked to consent to the issue of an ultimatum to Turkey. The paper-thin ultimatum was delivered on 27 September. The Porte was prepared to give whatever guarantees Italy wanted regarding the expansion of her economic interests in Tripolitania and Cyrenaica as long as they did not infringe its ultimate sovereignty. This was not enough for Rome, and Italy declared war on 29 September 1911. The conclusion of the Moroccan crisis had been the spur to action, and the nationalist campaign had provided the underpinning. Thirty years later the king told General Alberto Pariani that Giolitti had been against the war until he saw how strongly the senate was in favour of it.

The Tripoli venture did not take the Italian general staff entirely by surprise, as some historians once believed. In fact, war planning had begun as early as November 1884 when the foreign minister, Pasquale Mancini, instructed the war minister to be ready with a force of 30,000 men 'to occupy Tripoli, Benghazi and a few other points, above all at the

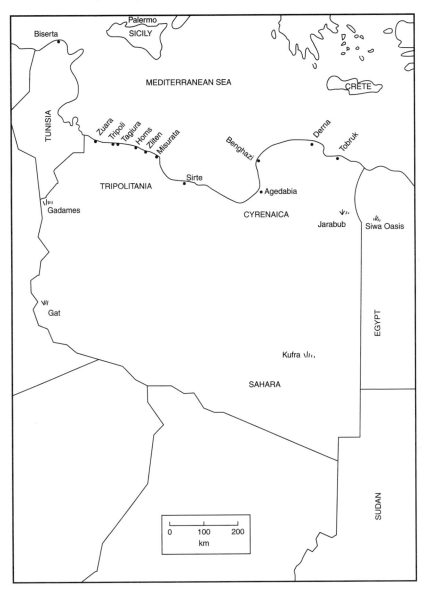

2. Libya

extreme margins of the coast, both towards Egypt and towards Tunisia'.[92] A plan was duly drawn up the following year, revised in 1897 and further updated in 1899. As the twentieth century opened a detailed study of Tripoli was compiled including maps of the defences and tables of ranges and angles for an artillery bombardment, and the general staff began to gather data on Turkish garrisons, defences and port activity. The landing plans were updated during the first Moroccan crisis and six years later, when the moment came for action, they were ready for use, together with detailed mobilisation plans drawn up and issued in 1910.[93]

Along with the war plans went extensive political and military intelligence. From the outset Italian consular staff in Libya, Egypt and Tunisia sent back detailed reports on Turkish troop strength and movements, local political attitudes, economic resources and communications. A secret military reconnaissance in 1903 produced detailed plans and 230 photographs of the Tripoli fortifications. Information was also gathered on the local population. In 1903 the head of Italian military intelligence, Colonel Garrioni, asked the consul general about their likely stance in the event of war. If the Italians landed, the consul believed that the Arabs would neither take up arms against the Turks nor aid any Europeans, but their sympathy could be won by guaranteeing them their ancient rights 'thus hoping to overcome an atavistic mistrust by a population *who at the most could put up a passive resistance*'. Two months before the war broke out Rome was advised that there was nothing much to fear from the local territorial troops and that the only difficulty was 'to secure in advance the support of the Arab chiefs', a task which an undercover officer ought to be able to manage within four to six weeks.[94]

Instructions issued in August 1911 opted for 'a few displays of force at coastal points duly selected as secondary objectives', after which the entire country would be occupied by degrees following 'appropriate political and administrative action on the part of the new government installed at Tripoli'.[95] However, although the local political dimension was acknowledged the general staff assumed that action on that front could be left until after the army had landed. Nothing whatever was actually done by way of political preparation before the guns began firing, perhaps because on the day that Italian sailors landed in Tripoli military intelligence believed that the Arabs would in general be 'if not entirely ready to receive us favourably, then at least neutral and waiting on events'.[96]

Pollio concentrated his entire attention on the local Turkish forces, finding it 'difficult to imagine' that they could retreat and mass in the interior of the country. If they did so this would constitute 'a grave threat'

to the expeditionary force and oblige it to undertake 'a difficult expedition into unknown and difficult country'. He therefore expected that the
Turks would fight on the spot and then retreat towards Constantinople.
The undertaking would not be easy, but the main difficulties he foresaw
were disembarking the troops and then maintaining them 'in a poor and
primitive country'. If Tripoli could be taken quickly by the first echelon
of troops then the expeditionary force would not have to land on open
beaches. Now was the time to dare,'but to dare quickly'.[97] If this conception of a war now looks somewhat blinkered, it was more or less in
line with what the politicians wanted him to do. On 24 September Di San
Giuliano told General Spingardi that the army's task was 'to secure
possession of the coast and to neutralise the resistance of the Turkish
troops ... Any advance into the interior must be avoided as far as
possible.'[98] However, when on 13 October 1911 Di San Giuliano
announced the government's decision to annexe Libya outright the
political face of the war changed completely and with it the strategic task
facing the army.

The special army corps that embarked at Naples numbered 1,105
officers and 33,303 men. Italian intelligence expected it to face 4,000
regular Turkish troops and 10,000 local levies. Their estimate was
remarkably accurate: in 1911 Turkey had 12,000 troops in Libya,
60,000 in Albania, and over 110,000 in the Yemen. Italian mobilisation
proceeded quickly and smoothly, but servicing and equipping the expeditionary force produced a catalogue of deficiencies not unlike those that
would afflict it again three years later. The stores contained boots without
nails and haversacks of such poor-quality leather as to be unusable.
Recruits joined with unsharpened bayonets. There was no proper organisation of reserves for wastage, and specialist units were particularly hard
hit.[99]

The force commander, 66-year-old General Carlo Caneva, had fought
the dervishes in 1897 and had taken part in Libyan war planning in 1905.
When told of his appointment he was less than enthusiastic, though
Spingardi still thought that he would 'do well'.[100] Caneva's instructions
identified four objectives established in the earlier plans – Tripoli, Benghazi, Tobruk and the Djebel Akhdar – but left him to use his own
judgement about moving away from the coast and following withdrawing
Turkish troops. They also emphasised the importance of separating the
Turks, 'considered as the oppressors', from the Arabs, 'considered
the oppressed'. Everything had to be done 'short of weakness' to recruit
the Arabs as allies or at least to ensure their neutrality.[101]

Pollio needed three weeks to ready and move the expeditionary
force, but Giolitti and Di San Giuliano could not wait that long. On

28 September the navy was ordered to blockade Tripoli and call for its surrender as soon as hostilities were declared. If the demand was rejected, Admiral Luigi Faravelli was to bombard the port. Faravelli promptly telegraphed for 3,000 troops and after shelling Tripoli he sent sailors ashore on 5 October. The Turkish garrison fled, and the town was – or seemed to be – securely in Italian hands when the first expeditionary troops began to land on 11 October. Caneva arrived with no plans to penetrate into the interior of Libya, aware of the obstacles to be overcome before any active operations inland – 'which must be prudent and decisive' – could begin. As well as completing the disembarkation and establishing the base, a logistical service had to be organised across a country without resources, the intentions of the Arab population had to be clarified, and they had to be politically prepared 'without prematurely involving them in warlike acts, which must be directed exclusively against the Turks'.[102] 'I don't think this is a real war,' one soldier wrote home, 'just small attacks and we shall soon win ... you'll see that it will all be over before long.'[103]

The *drôle de guerre* was short lived. Italian forces took Derna on 17 October, Benghazi on 20 October and Homs next day. At Benghazi the Turks fought from dune to dune inflicting 130 casualties on the invader, and at Homs, where Caneva had been led to believe that the local Arab tribes would greet the Italians' arrival favourably, the landing force was besieged until the following February. Lines of trenches and barbed wire were constructed to defend the west and south of Tripoli, where the Italians controlled the whole of the oasis; in the east, where they did not control it all, the troops faced a labyrinth of houses, gardens and orchards. There, at Sciara Sciat on 23 October, Turkish officers launched local tribesmen in an assault preceded by diversionary attacks elsewhere along the line. In the course of vicious fighting that cost the Italians 307 killed and wounded and 294 missing, two companies were captured and 250 men massacred in a Muslim cemetery. A second battle three days later cost the Italians a further 251 dead and wounded. Later it was discovered that Italian captives had been mutilated, blinded, eviscerated, crucified, buried alive or torn to pieces.[104] In the fury that followed Arabs found carrying guns or knives were summarily executed and several thousand were deported. The delusion that the war was in any way 'civilising' had ended.

Caneva's men now faced two enemies – the Turks who were fighting a national and imperial war against an enemy state, and the Arabs who were fighting a religious and tribal war against European infidels. The Senussi in Cyrenaica joined in readily as the pan-Islamic notes encouraged by Constantinople grew ever louder. Arab tribes were organised under their own leaders and supplies brought in across the eastern and western borders. The Arab *mehalla*, fast mobile columns whose strength was their fluidity of movement, were difficult targets. Nothing in Italy's military experience had prepared her for a war of this character. Caneva called for – and got – another 55,000 troops and settled down to sit it out, backed by advice from his generals on no account to venture out into the desert.[105]

Having moved from occupation to annexation, the politicians moved the goalposts yet again when, on 5 November 1911, a royal decree proclaimed absolute Italian sovereignty over Libya. This dramatic extension of Italy's original war aim, the establishment of an Italian protectorate under the veil of Turkish sovereignty, changed the politico-military character of the war once again. Not only did the army now have to conquer the entire country instead of merely occupying it as the instrument of a diplomatic demonstration with limited goals, but it had to confront a Turkey determined to fight where previously it had seemed inclined to give way.

Caneva's preternatural caution now came to the fore. The day after the announcement he told Rome that he was not willing to move away from the coast and start operations against the desert caravan routes as he had neither the men nor the resources he needed to do so. He could see no point in pursuing Ottoman forces into the desert, where there were neither significant strategic objectives nor key points whose occupation would subdue the tribes. Nor, he warned, should Rome pin its hopes on winning a decisive encounter. The Turks wanted a long-drawn-out campaign and Caneva could see no alternative to giving them exactly that. His advice was to settle down in the coastal garrisons for a long war.[106] Back in Rome, the question began to be asked: was Caneva the general Italy needed?

Pollio and Giolitti both put pressure on the field commander to act but he was reluctant to move very far. Sticking to the coasts, the Italians fought a nine-hour battle at Ain Zara on 4 December during which the navy bombarded oases east of Tripoli to prevent a flank attack. Casualties were light and the action chased the enemy out of range of Tripoli, but though the Italians gained control of the ground they did not inflict a significant defeat on the Turks who withdrew. Then the army overreached itself. On 19 December General Pecori Giraldi, the victor of Ain Zara, sent out an exploratory column of 1,800 men under Colonel Gustavo Fara to deal with 350 Arabs at the oasis of Bir Tobras. With no maps the column got lost, took seven hours to cover less than 15 kilometres and on arrival attacked the wrong positions. Attacked themselves from the rear, Fara's men dug in and fought until nightfall when both sides retreated. Headquarters sent two brigades out to help him, one of which itself got lost and met him on his way back. Pecori Giraldi was recalled, and Fara was promoted to general for military merit. Caneva and Fara were both Freemasons, unlike Pecori Giraldi. Suspicious minds back in Rome perceived a hidden hand at work in the army.

The army was now fighting a war that required it to conquer, or at least dominate, the vast hinterland of Libya while pinned to the coast and pitted it against mounting resistance from the Arab populations and the Turks, whose presence and backing multiplied the power of the local inhabitants. Arab raids and guerrilla-style attacks caused many casualties and patrols were frequently caught and mauled. The strength of the resistance mounted when, in January 1912, the head of the Senussi in Cyrenaica, Said Ahmed el-Sherif, declared a *jihad* against the invader. Money and support flowed in from across the Ottoman empire. Alongside the resistance Constantinople made a series of diplomatic offers involving ceding parts or all of the Libyan coastline to Italy, maintaining nominal Ottoman sovereignty or granting local autonomy. None were acceptable to Italy, and so the fighting continued.

With 100,000 men and twenty-six generals under his command, Caneva's inactivity was now causing considerable political irritation. Giolitti recalled him to Rome in February 1912 but was not reassured by what he heard and concluded that he was insufficiently aware of the need for rapid action to avoid foreign-policy complications. The problem, as Pollio later complained, was that nothing could be done with Caneva but, for the moment at least, nothing could be done without him. He rarely spoke of the advantages of operations, dwelling instead on their difficulties and disadvantages but doing so in such a way as to make them irrefutable.[107] The other generals were no better. Giolitti thought two-thirds of them ought to be sacked for '*intellectual inadequacy*' or else the military budget would be wasted.[108] In the absence of any obvious successor, and not yet having demonstrably failed even if he had not succeeded, Caneva hung on to his command for another six months while a string of his subordinates were recalled.

Faced with a new kind of war in which the fact that there was neither a substantial enemy force to manoeuvre into battle nor a distinct territorial objective to seize made it pointless to attempt to penetrate into the interior, Pollio revised Libyan strategy. There would be no strategic offensive, but neither would there be a passive defence. The 'third way' was to be one of wearing out the enemy with firepower and counter-attacks.[109] As part of this strategy Caneva agreed to take Cape Macabez west of Tripoli as a jumping-off point from which to intercept enemy caravans moving through the desert to the south. When his troops finally carried out the operation in April they found themselves facing salt lakes and waterless desert which made penetration into the interior impossible. In March work began on a 4.5-metre-high masonry wall around Tripoli, for which the materials had to be brought from Italy. Caneva's strategy was now literally set in stone.

Caneva's foremost concerns were to maintain Italy's military prestige and the image of invincibility which the coastal defences were supposedly instilling in the enemy. Believing that pure force was useless as a weapon against a hostile population, he proposed to move out and occupy territory only when suitable political preparation had created a friendly disposition among the local population. The problem with this strategy, as Di San Giuliano recognised, was that as long as the Ottomans were in the field there was no incentive for the Arab tribes to act as Caneva required. Turkey, for her part, would not pull out until she and the European powers were persuaded that Libya was indeed pacified. If military operations could not create this situation, then they should at a minimum 'produce abroad the impression that it has been created, and give the Turkish government at least a pretext for yielding'.[110] Rome wanted complete conquest of the coast, and Caneva cautiously obliged. In a series of operations between June and mid August he extended his control along it using artillery and naval gunfire, taking Zuara in August and cutting off the inland supply route to Tripoli.

Caution was now as much of a tactical watchword as it was an operational and strategic one. Orders were issued that artillery and machine-gun detachments should not be exposed with insufficient infantry support, cavalry patrols were instructed not to get involved in skirmishes while on reconnaissance, and when advancing infantry encountered the enemy they were ordered to stop and wait for a shrapnel bombardment to clear the ground ahead. Luigi Capello, then a major-general commanding the western district in Libya, fumed at the inactivity that Caneva's defensive tactics were imposing on the army. Waiting for the enemy to break himself against Italian fortifications was 'undoubtedly healthier than the tactical offensive, but does not fit with the concept of a strategic offensive'.[111]

In June 1912 news reached Giolitti that the Turks were willing to treat and diplomatic conversations began in Lausanne on 12 July. Both the premier and the foreign minister had already decided that Caneva had to go, and the need for success at arms to reinforce diplomacy now became paramount. Pollio and Spingardi were reluctant to dismiss him, fearing that the action might be seen as a criticism not of an individual but of the army as a whole, but safeguarding the army's *amour-propre* was not something calculated to appeal to a premier who increasingly despised and despaired of the military. Caneva was recalled to Rome on 31 August and formally relieved two days later. His command was split in two and his successors immediately proved more active and more successful. In Cyrenaica, General Ottavio Briccola lifted a two-month bombardment of Derna on 17 September, and three days later in Tripolitania General Ottavio Ragni took the oasis of Zanzur, which Caneva had dithered over since December, although holding off a counter-attack cost him 553 dead and wounded – the heaviest Italian casualties since Sciara Sciat.

When peace negotiations bogged down in mid September over Turkey's unwillingness to accept Italy's bottom line – full and entire Italian sovereignty over Tripolitania and Cyrenaica – the Italians threatened to break them off and initiate more aggressive action. As September drew to a close things did not look all that promising for Rome. The picture changed dramatically when, on 30 September 1912, Serbia, Bulgaria, Montenegro and Greece began mobilising their forces against Turkey. Though Italy was unable to put direct pressure on the Porte for fear of upsetting either the Austrians or the Triple Entente, the Ottoman empire was now vulnerable to interdiction of its sea communications between Anatolia and Roumelia along which a large proportion of the Turkish army would have to travel. Threats could be made, and they were. On 1 October Italian negotiators announced that if a Balkan war broke out Italy would extend her theatre of operations beyond Libya. Shortly afterwards Montenegro declared war on Turkey.

The Balkan war that followed made it imperative for Turkey to agree terms with Italy, and equally imperative for Italy to avoid an international initiative that might resolve both wars simultaneously to her detriment. After a fortnight of close negotiation the Turks gave way. Under the terms of the secret treaty of Ouchy signed on 15 October 1912, and the Treaty of Lausanne published three days later, Italy got what she wanted – sovereignty over Tripolitania and Cyrenaica.

For Italy, the human costs of the war in Libya were relatively light. Of a force which numbered 100,000 men at its maximum, 3,431 men died – 1,483 of them in combat and 1,948 of illness. Turkish and Arab losses have been estimated at 14,800. Financially, the war proved a heavy burden. In March 1914 Giolitti declared that it had cost just over half a billion lire. When the figures were recalculated, the total cost of the war between 1911 and 1914 came to twice that sum. As well as costing a great deal of money, the needs of the Libyan war seriously disfigured the army. Divisions were broken up as all but three had to send one of their regiments to the war; almost all the machine-gun sections, considerable numbers of guns and enormous quantities of ammunition, rations and clothing intended for war mobilisation went off overseas; and most of the recently trained reservists went too.[112] The Libyan campaign drained the army of weapons, munitions and equipment and weakened it on the eve of what would turn out to be a world war. Reassured by General Spingardi, premier Antonio Salandra told parliament in March 1914 that stocks were back to their proper levels. Over that summer it would become apparent that they were not.

Peace at Lausanne did not bring peace in Libya. While the Turks in Tripolitania surrendered and withdrew, the Berbers retreated to the Djebel to continue the fight. Turkish troops stayed behind in Cyrenaica, where the Senussi continued the war. At the end of 1913 there were reports of Turkish officers and men among the Senussi, and by the following spring when there were still 66,000 Italian troops in Libya it was clear that Enver Bey was supplying the rebels with money, arms and ammunition. In July rebellion broke out in three districts and by November the Italian forces, besieged in Tripoli, Homs and Zuara, were facing a general insurrection. With a European war on his hands, the new chief of the general staff, Luigi Cadorna, categorically refused to send out any more men, and by 1 August 1915 only Tripoli and Homs remained in Italian hands.[113]

The army's record in Libya earned its generals Giolitti's lasting contempt, but though the performance of the Italian armed forces left a lot to be desired this was by no means entirely their fault. Some generals were undeniably cautious, but others were bold almost to the point of foolhardiness. All faced a war which was very different from anything of which they had first-hand experience. Tribal resistance blended with religious hostility in a powerful amalgam, and the operational expertise provided by a Turkish army with unequalled experience of dealing with internal insurrections added depth to the tactical virtuosity of the Arabs and Berbers. Dismissing France's successful model of colonial suppression in Algeria, which Caneva plainly misunderstood, Italian generals had neither the political nor the military tools with which to fulfil the task handed to them by their government. Nor did they have much time to learn how to fight a desert war.

In July 1911 Giovanni Giolitti questioned whether it was in Italy's interest to 'break into fragments' one of the cornerstones of the European balance of power, and wondered whether a subsequent Balkan war might then provoke 'a clash between the two power blocs and a European war'?[114] Almost to a man historians have adopted this 'domino thesis', making its author appear simultaneously both far-sighted and irresponsibly culpable for the coming catastrophe.[115] No one else seems at the time to have thought as Giolitti did, and if indeed Italy did wreak irreparable damage on the international system by initiating the Libyan war then she did herself no military favours in the process.

The army on the eve of world war

In the final year of peacetime (1913–14), the standing army numbered 15,340 officers and 250,000 men. Behind it were a further 27,881 officers and 3,100,000 men in the nineteen annual classes liable for some form of service upon whom the generals could in theory draw. They comprised some 1,700,000 trained category I men, another 200,000 category II men who had had up to six months' training, and approximately 1,000,000 men who had had no training whatsoever. Drawing on the most recent classes of demobilised conscripts, the field army in 1914 was reckoned at 873,000 men; 345,000 men of the older classes in the territorial militia garrisoned the forts and guarded the coasts and railways; and another 44,000 men held on to the Libyan enclaves. The twelve corps of the standing army, composed of twenty-five infantry and three cavalry divisions, after being filled out with recent reservists, would be supplemented with a further ten divisions of older reservists, four of them grouped into two additional corps and the remainder added to existing corps to give them three divisions.[116]

One looming problem for the army was the amount of untrained manpower it was going to have to deal with. Another was the shortage of officers. In August 1914 the army had a total of 45,099 officers of whom 15,858 had permanent commissions, another 15,480 had reserve commissions, and a further 4,380 were officers in the territorial militia. In March 1914, Pollio believed the army was short of 7,500 regular officers. Making up the numbers was difficult not only financially but also because the Libyan war had swallowed up a large number of career non-commissioned officers who had been promoted from the ranks. During the course of the war the army commissioned 13,454 new regular officers, 100,960 reserve officers and 45,777 territorial militia officers. The military academies were only able to produce 1,799 junior lieutenants before they closed in 1916, and thus over 10,000 of the new regular officers had to come from the reserves.[117]

If the army's strength was its manpower, its weakness lay in weaponry, and especially artillery. Shortage of money could easily be blamed, though that was not the basic problem: between 1907 and 1914 the army got 555,300,000 lire in extraordinary budgets and spent 311,300,000 lire on artillery and munitions. What really went wrong was procurement. In 1897 the French introduced the quick-firing 75-mm *Déport* field gun and the following year the Italians began to look for a replacement for their own 75-mm and 87-mm guns, which had been in service for thirty years. What followed was fourteen years of chaos, confusion and mismanagement. First Krupps palmed off on the Italians a gun that was already out of date, not having the recoilless gun carriage that gave the French gun its advantage. Then the artillerymen, who prized mobility and manageability above all other qualities, clashed with the chief of the general staff, who put power above mobility. Finally, in 1909–10 a Krupps 75 was tested against a *Déport* 75. The French gun won – but the rights and the money to build it were not available until 1912. A consortium of twenty-seven Italian establishments was formed to produce the new weapon, but it ran into technical difficulties and the matériel was only just becoming available when Italy entered the war in 1915. The story was much the same for mountain and horse artillery, and worse as far as heavy field artillery was concerned: in 1911 the twenty batteries that were supposed to be in service only existed on paper. Only in June 1912 did the army get round to commissioning a machine-gun from Vickers.[118]

The official tactical and strategic doctrines in force in 1914 were the work of Alberto Pollio. The regulations he had inherited for the tactical deployment of divisions, corps and armies, issued by his predecessor in 1903, took as their fundamental axiom that there were no fixed rules at all for tactical action. They exhorted commanders to think collaboratively – 'all for one and one for all' – and emphasised frontal attack, along with attacking one or both flanks of an enemy position.[119] In his introduction to the revised version of the regulations, published in 1913, Pollio re-emphasised the mutability of conditions in wartime and stressed the non-prescriptive nature of the general norms he would propound. Offensive spirit was the essence of war, but it must be firmly controlled to give the best results and commanders must resist improvised offensives. Infantry were not to wait until the artillery had subdued the enemy before attacking – a proposition that would lead to their being shot to pieces once the world war began. When they got within firing range the enemy's troops should be the artillery's main target, which again turned out to be a fundamental misdirection. Pollio was assuming that battles would most likely be encounter battles and that the Italian armies would attack from the march. As far as 'prepared battles' were concerned, the regulations were simultaneously vague and precise: the best tactical concept was the one that accorded with the strategic situation, and the strategic target should be the enemy's lines of communication.

Pollio's combat regulations, issued in the same year, declared that the unusual conditions of modern combat favoured the attack and not the defence 'because the use of new means, especially modern portable weapons, derives its effects more than in the past from the state of mind of those who use them, that is whoever is better able to make his own moral and material superiority count'.[120] Accordingly the new regulations put particular emphasis on infantry using rifles and bayonets as the principal instrument of attack. Machine-guns were relegated to an auxiliary role as a mobile reserve of fire to be used in support of field guns, themselves an auxiliary to infantry attacks. Heavy divisional and corps artillery were to attack all kinds of targets. One of their main roles, emphasised by Pollio, was counter-battery fire. When the war came, the artillery forgot all about this particular directive.

The stress these pamphlets put on the offensive and on moral impetus was very much in tune with contemporary military thinking across Europe. Their emphasis on flexibility was carried over into the training regulations – also issued in 1913 – which correspondingly aimed at developing the individual's sense of moral responsibility and remarked on the need to leave him free to use his own initiative to respond to situations.[121] However, although considerable stress was being put on the task the infantry had to fulfil, and on the need for flexibility to help them to do so, there was no sign of the devolution necessary to empower them to act in this way. The army was already a rigidly top–down organisation even before Cadorna got his hands on it. In 1914, as far as Italy was concerned, the two sides of war-making – operational doctrine and command practice – did not marry up. Under Cadorna's hand they would be brought into deadly alignment.

2   From neutrality to action

Our sword weighs too little and cannot tilt the balance.
Antonio Di San Giuliano, 12 September 1914

In August 1914 the five European Great Powers went to war and nine months later Italy joined in, fighting against her pre-war ally Austria–Hungary. In coming to this decision, her diplomats had to consider not only Italy's place in a future balance of power but also complex regional issues involving the Balkans, Turkey and even north and east Africa. The final decision was the result of a combination of calculation and guesswork in which domestic policy issues played only a secondary role. Her soldiers had problems of their own to resolve. A half-trained conscript army had to be readied for war; grave shortages of equipment had somehow to be made up; and strategic plans had to be devised in circumstances in which the mobilising army might be surprised by its enemy but could hope for no such advantage itself. Success depended heavily upon favourable strategic circumstances in other theatres – something that was not to be.

A new commander

On 1 July 1914, four days after the Sarajevo assassination, the then chief of the Italian general staff, Alberto Pollio, who was on a visit to Turin, died unexpectedly of a heart attack. In the circumstances the vacant post had to be filled quickly, and it was: on 11 July the press reported that the king had appointed Lieutenant-General Count Luigi Cadorna to the position. However, the selection had not been straightforward. The selection committee of four, of whom Cadorna was one, had been split between him and a younger general. The choice was left to the king. In May 1915, when Italy went to war, Cadorna immediately sacked the general who a year earlier had proposed his younger rival.

Luigi Cadorna had a first-class military pedigree. He was born on 4 September 1850 into one of the most distinguished Piedmontese

53

military families. His father, Count Raffaele Cadorna, had fought in the Crimean war and the war of 1866, and in September 1870 had presided over the symbolic taking of Rome. The son's education followed a conventional path. First stop was the Military College at Milan where he did well academically after a shaky start, passing out second in a class of 167. He was, though, clearly not the easiest of pupils: frequently in the punishment cells, he showed at an early age two of the character traits that would mark his time at the top of the army – irascibility and an absolute inability to accept any criticism. At 15 years of age he entered the *Accademia militare* at Turin, graduating three years later at the top of his class. Most of his early years were spent in staff work and his contact with troops was limited. He kept his social contacts to his own family (he married in 1889) and his professional contacts to his own entourage. In 1892 he made colonel and only then did he finally receive his first direct command of soldiers, the 10th *Bersaglieri* regiment. At this point he began to reveal a predilection for punishing harshly any real or supposed transgression of regulations, earning him an indirect rebuke from his divisional commander which, characteristically, he refused to accept. Later, when in command of the army, a combination of irascibility and paranoia could lead him to what one of his most devoted subordinates termed 'verbal intemperance'.

Over a long career Cadorna climbed slowly into the higher ranks. In 1898 he was disappointed twice over, failing to make major-general and inspector-general of the *Alpini*. In 1900, he was passed over for command of the War College and given a brigade instead. The promotions commission's failure to advance him five places and make him a lieutenant-general in 1904 he took as further evidence that powerful forces were deliberately holding him back. A devout and practising Catholic, he became convinced that he was the victim of a plot by Freemasons in the army to keep him down. Over time, that conviction only grew stronger. Divisional command came his way in 1905, but further disappointment followed when in 1908, despite some active lobbying, he failed to get the post of chief of the general staff. Prime minister Giovanni Giolitti, when asked his opinion of the two candidates, told the king 'Pollio I don't know, but I prefer him to Cadorna, who I do know.'[1] Cadorna again saw the hand of Freemasonry at work. Seniority and an undoubted technical capacity carried him upwards to an army corps in 1910, and in the next year he was made designated commander of 2nd Army in war. He was almost at the top of the military tree – almost, but not quite. Had fate not lent a hand, he would probably never have reached the very top.

Luigi Cadorna officially took up office as the fifth chief of the Italian general staff on 27 July 1914. He was then three months short of 64 years

old – and two years older than his predecessor. In the flesh, he made a
very strong impression. A prominent newspaper proprietor, meeting him
for the first time in December 1914, saw a man who 'with his low
and receding brow, prominent eyes, [and] strong jaw, gives me the
impression of passion and of an obstinate will, rather than of intelligence'. In December 1915, Gabriele D'Annunzio, an admirer, described
him in a celebrated poem as 'cut and shaped from the hardest granite by a
maestro whose vigour was greater than his artistic ability'.[2] As Cadorna
himself said when he read the poem, it was an elegant way of saying
he was ugly. Everyone acknowledged his strengths: he knew the complex-
ities of the military organisation and bureaucracy inside out. He was also
difficult, opinionated, quarrelsome and highly sensitive to any slights,
real or imagined. Later a sympathetic observer confided to his diary
that Cadorna had little 'malleability' (he might as well have said none),
and that dialogue with him was 'simply an impossibility'.[3] A poor com-
municator who deliberately isolated himself from his fellow generals,
many of whom he regarded as disgracefully incompetent, he cared little
for politicians who had interfered too much while disbursing too little.
Most importantly of all, he had never seen action. Many of his generals
had fought in Ethiopia or in Libya, but Cadorna was a metropolitan
general through and through.

    After little more than a fortnight in office the new commander issued
his own 'Summary norms for tactical action'. They put more stress on

Fig. 1 General Cadorna on Monte Cengis, val d'Astico

frontal attacks which, according to their author, were less difficult than they were made to appear. Then, on 25 February 1915, he issued the infamous 'Frontal attack and tactical training'. Based on regulations he had developed from 1905 which had been 'requested by regiments in every part of Italy' before the war, they were, he believed, no more than a remaking of his earlier circular 'more synthetical and taking account of the experience of the recent war'.[4] In fact, the *libretto rosso*, so-called because of its red covers, pushed the doctrine of the offensive and the emphasis on morale to the extreme. According to the new regulations, there were two ways to achieve the demoralisation of the enemy and victory: superiority of firepower and an irresistible movement forward. 'Of these the second is the principal one (to win is to go forward).'[5] The difficulties of advancing over open ground were entirely discounted, the regulations declaring that this could be achieved using portable tools, or at night. Trench warfare – 'this very unusual (*rarissima*) form assumed by war resulting from the lack of predominant force by one of the two parties' – was shrugged off as only apparently contradicting the pre-eminence of the offensive.

Despite today's extended battle fronts which are – in large part – the ineluctable consequence of the perfecting of firearms and the power of improvised fortifications, when one of the parties feels himself stronger than the other he will unleash the offensive, which alone is capable of achieving decisive results: it will always be manoeuvre that decides the outcome of wars.[6]

The chief difficulty revealed by the war so far, Cadorna believed, would be to hold the ground taken by frontal attack. Abandoning his predecessor's concerns with tactical flexibility and initiative, the new army chief stressed the importance of training troops in the mechanism of manoeuvre at all levels. The absolute instrumentalisation of the army as the tool of its commander now became the order of the day.

To achieve his grandiose strategic design, Cadorna would launch his armies across the Isonzo in eleven largely fruitless battles 'with all the sadistic relish of an eighteenth-century drill sergeant'.[7] In doing so he seemingly ignoring the reports he had received from his military attachés in France and Germany about the nature and consequences of trench warfare on the western front. Those reports were, as we shall see, exceptionally informative. They put Cadorna in a better position to envision the shape of combat at the start of his war than was the case with any of the other Allied *generalissimos* when they started their campaigns. But it is not quite true to say that he ignored them. In February 1915 he issued supplementary training regulations requiring that all subordinate commanders employ field fortifications and laying down that there should be four lines of them. Shortly, at least one army commander and numerous corps commanders would ignore this advice. Then, in May, new instructions emphasised the importance of co-ordinating artillery and infantry in the attack. The aim was to make the defender expose himself to the attacker's artillery fire; the method of doing this was by the forward threatening movement of the infantry, protected by field artillery.

Along with them came a pamphlet on French methods of frontal attack in trench warfare. In it Cadorna urged his subordinates to study the western front, though it was 'improbable that our troops will have to have recourse to such procedures, other than exceptionally [and] on very limited portions of the front'. What was unthinkable, and therefore unacceptable, was not trench warfare but the stalemate that might result from it.

Everyone must persuade themselves that trench warfare can and must end, and that that depends upon their energy, their tenacity, and being convinced of their own material and moral superiority.[8]

The solution lay in method: artillery would destroy organised enemy defences, hit personnel, interdict attacks and fire on enemy trenches until the precise instant that the Italian infantry reached them. At bottom, all this was more or less of a piece with pre-war doctrine that was just then piling up French casualties in fruitless attacks at Artois and Champagne and at St Mihiel.[9] Cadorna had not entirely disregarded the war on the western front; rather, Joffre's optimism had trumped Falkenhayn's pessimism.

European war and Italian neutrality

Before his death, Pollio had been growing increasingly worried about the state of the army. It was short of artillery of every kind, of officers and men – he wanted an extra 30,000 conscripts a year – and the rail net needed improving to speed up mobilisation. Without extra money, he had warned, it would not be in a position to support a less 'submissive' foreign policy.[10] There were a good many reasons to be concerned. Tactical exercises were inadequate and target practice was poor. On the north-eastern frontier the Austrians were building new roads in the Trentino, new guns were being emplaced at Trento, restrictions on access to the area were increasing and military intelligence reported a palpable air of concern among the local population 'as if some difficulty were going to arise on our frontier'.[11]

Cadorna warned that the army was going through a crisis which could lead to disaster if some political complication were to arise – something which, if not probable or foreseeable, could well happen unexpectedly. Brigades and regiments were so skeletal that they went to camp as mixed battalions, making realistic training impossible. Because the army was so badly short of junior officers, some units were commanded by newly promoted sergeants or reserve officers, who lacked practical experience and were not being properly guided and encouraged. This in turn contributed to a shortage of sergeants, and the few corporals belonged to the most recent class of conscripts. If this situation continued, he foresaw complete collapse within a very short space of time.[12] Determined to balance the budget, the new premier, Antonio Salandra, was deaf to Pollio's appeals.

The assassination of Archduke Franz Ferdinand was momentarily lost to view by the military attaché in Vienna, Lieutenant-Colonel Albricci, in the face of what he regarded as a less than satisfactory public reaction to Pollio's sudden demise, but on 20 July he was able to report that the diplomatic note containing Austria's demands on Serbia was in Franz Josef's hands. Although he did not know its content, Rome was warned that if the reply was not satisfactory then Austria was prepared to go 'all the way'. Conrad was clearly expecting that if the conflict between Vienna and Belgrade was enlarged and Austria had to go to arms then Italy would honour her obligations under the recently renewed terms of the Triple Alliance. The Austrian chief of the general staff had great faith in Germany's military efficiency, and 'great appreciation for our army especially after the proof it has given in the Libyan war'.[13] Five days later Rome learned that the Serbian reply was unacceptable and next day that secret orders had been issued to mobilise six Austrian army corps.[14]

In the aftermath of the assassination German intentions were of obvious importance. Information reaching Rome on 13 July, and passed to the king and the war minister three days later, indicated that although Moltke, Waldersee and other senior officers had not yet been recalled from leave Germany had evidently decided to support her Austro-Hungarian ally 'in any circumstances'. The decision depended on whether or not there was an armed intervention by Russia. Some of the officers in the German general staff were evidently looking forward to the possibility of war, though General Falkenhayn did not seem enthusiastic.[15] Over the next two weeks it was apparent to both the ambassador and the military attaché, Colonel Calderari, that the decision was deteriorating. On 31 July, Rome learned that Berlin appeared – by her own account – to have miscalculated twice over, first by hoping that in affirming her solidarity with Vienna she would intimidate Russia into giving Serbia 'pacific advice', and second in expecting that Great Britain would stay neutral in a war. Nevertheless, she was ready to fight and confident of success.[16] At 1519 on 31 July, Calderari telegraphed the news that St Petersburg had announced general mobilisation and Wilhelm II had responded by declaring war.

The news of Franz Ferdinand's assassination seemed at first not to cause Russia much concern. Reading between the lines of the newspapers it was evident that they were glad to see the back of someone who was hostile both to Russia and to Slavism.[17] The arrival of the Austrian note on 23 July changed the situation entirely. The military attaché, Major Ropolo, did not see how Russia could stand aside and watch Serbia being crushed without intervening militarily. His guess was confirmed four days later. Russia was clearly not pushing for war – she hoped that Italy might exercise a pacifying influence – and though everyone was ready for it 'at bottom they will not be unhappy if Austria–Hungary's conduct does not lead to war'.[18] Ropolo reported the Russian minister of war's communication to the German military attaché on 27 July that she wished only to act against Austria–Hungary. Three days later he relayed the order mobilising 400,000 men in four Russian military districts, news that was confirmed by Albricci the same day.[19]

The general staff in Rome were being kept well abreast of the developing crisis by their representatives in Vienna, Berlin and St Petersburg. War in Europe was a worrying scenario given the state of the army – which was about to be revealed to the political leadership – but it was by no means the only one. From Rome's standpoint, Turkey seemed as likely to start a war as Austria–Hungary or Germany. The embers of recent conflict in the Balkans still glowed, and three days after the delivery of the Austrian note Cadorna had reason to believe that the oncoming European crisis might breathe life into them again. The Turkish press praised Vienna's sagacity and her readiness to put an end to a situation that had for a long time threatened the empire's security. The Turkish navy minister, Djemal Pasha, declared that Turkey would join in the war at an opportune moment to reconquer the lost territories of Macedonia and Egypt.[20] A Russo-Turkish war was yet another possibility. Although Turkey announced that she would remain neutral in the event of a European war, it seemed highly likely that – 'pushed by Germany and convinced that the *Triplice* is the stronger group' – she would hold herself ready to join in the weakening of Russia 'whose victory [in the war] would signal the end of European Turkey'. In yet another scenario, if Romania backed by Russia joined the war against Austria–Hungary, Turkey could line up alongside Greece against Bulgaria with the aim of regaining western Thrace.[21]

As war began in Europe it appeared to the military authorities in Rome as though it might spread yet more widely. Passing special provisional conscription laws, Turkey began mobilising on 3 August. It looked to the military attaché, Colonel Mombelli, as though the main Turkish deployment would be in Thrace with two or three corps defending the Russian frontier. As the month of August drew to a close Turkey seemed to be in German hands, led by Ambassador Wangenheim and pushed by Enver Bey. Then at the end of the first week in September, just as the battle of the Marne was starting, the danger of further fronts opening in the Balkans momentarily died down. Talaat Bey returned from a visit to Sofia and Bucharest apparently unable to come to agreements with Bulgaria and Romania which would permit Turkey to make war either on Greece or on Russia.[22] By early October the military situation looked to be delicately poised as far as the Turks were concerned. Germany's failure to advance with the speed and success expected made her triumph seem less certain and the result of the war less decisive. The Turks waited on the big battle that was coming in Galicia and southern Poland. The situation was resolved when, on 14 November, a decree from the caliph declared holy war on Great Britain, France and Russia. Turkey was clearly now in the Central Powers' camp, and equally clearly she expected Italy to join her there.[23]

If Turkey's ambitions in Europe presented complications, she also posed a direct military threat to Italy in Libya. Since the end of the Libyan war in 1912 the Turks had been covertly encouraging the Senussi to resist their conquerors. In March 1914 the extent to which the Turks were directly supporting the Arab rebellion against Italian rule in Cyrenaica became public when a Turkish officer, Lieutenant-Colonel Azziz Bey, was arrested and condemned to death for misappropriating 6,000 Turkish lire while commanding Ottoman troops there.[24] Next, intelligence reached Rome suggesting that in the next two or three months the Turks were going to try an *attentat* against King Vittorio Emanuele in the hopes of causing a revolution to break out and forcing the government to pull troops back from Cyrenaica.[25]

There were also reasons to be concerned about the security of the Italian colony of Eritrea: reports in early June from Cairo spoke of arms shipments passing through the Suez Canal on their way to Abyssinia.[26] On the eve of the Sarajevo incident, intelligence reached the general staff in Rome that the Turks had not accepted the result of events in Cyrenaica, Macedonia or Albania and led by Enver Bey they wanted revenge 'starting with Italy, the primary cause of all Turkey's woes'. The apparent friendship they were showing towards Italy was, in the view of the Italian deputy chief of the general staff, 'no more than a diplomatic stratagem'.[27]

As July 1914 moved to a close, and with no reason as yet to think otherwise, Cadorna prepared to go to war alongside Germany and

Austria–Hungary. On the day he took office he told the German military attaché that he fully accepted all the agreements made by his predecessor, repeating his undertaking in writing to his German opposite number, Helmuth von Moltke, the same day. He was kept out of the innermost counsels when, also on 27 July, premier Antonio Salandra called in the two service ministers and asked whether they were ready to mobilise. The navy was, but the army was not. The war minister, General Dino Grandi, hesitated, citing a shortage of uniforms that he claimed not to have known about when he had allowed the premier to assure parliament earlier in the year that the losses suffered in Libya had all been made good.[28] Completely in the dark about both the current foreign policy and its military implications, Cadorna drew up a list of 'urgent military provisions'. They included stripping the Austrian front of fortress artillery and sending it to the French front, filling in the gaps where units were not in their proper places because of public-order duties, and using the press to prepare public opinion for the possibility of war. That same day he asked the king's permission to send all forces not necessary for the defence of metropolitan Italy and Libya to the Franco-German front in the event of war.

On 31 July, as Russia went into full mobilisation, the Italian cabinet convened, listened as foreign minister Antonio Di San Giuliano analysed the crisis, and accepted his view that in the present circumstances 'neither the letter nor the spirit of the Triple Alliance obliges us ... to aid Germany and Austria'.[29] While the foreign minister was guiding Italy towards neutrality, Cadorna presented the king with the outline of the Rhine plan, along with the warning that it would not be immediately possible to carry it out because of the 'abnormal state' of the army.[30] Next day his world turned upside down. Just as the king was approving the Rhine plan, the cabinet decided to adopt a posture of armed neutrality and instructed the war minister, General Dino Grandi, to order a partial mobilisation of the army so that Italy's declaration of neutrality did not appear to be the consequence of weakness.

Because the military were traditionally kept at arm's length by the politicians of Liberal Italy, Cadorna did not know that the line of Italian foreign policy had already been set by Di San Giuliano. In mid July, before it was apparent that Austria was ready to go to war with Serbia if necessary, he had decided that in the event of a conflict between the two Italy must get adequate territorial compensation.[31] Learning the harsh terms of the Austrian ultimatum to Serbia, he told the king on the day after its publication that Italy must get compensation for any Austrian gain in the Balkans and for Italian involvement in the war, which he thought 'possible, but not likely'.[32] On 2 August, settled on a

policy of immediate neutrality, he set out the unpalatable consequences
for Italy in any one of the three possible outcomes of a war. If the Triple
Alliance won, the outcome for Italy would be 'sad'; if it gained a partial
victory it would not be able to give Italy adequate compensation; and
if the Triple Entente won 'there would be neither the interest nor the
desire to give us compensations in proportion to our sacrifices'.[33] In the
circumstances, premier and foreign minister agreed to temporise while
they negotiated an acceptable price for Italian arms. Whatever happened,
Italy was not going to go to war yet.

The news that Italy was going to claim that the July crisis and the
declaration of war did not constitute legitimate grounds for triggering
the military convention of the Triple Alliance went down very badly with
her erstwhile allies. On 2 August Moltke thought that even if Italian
troops were not sent to the Rhine, Italy might still mobilise on the French
frontier. Three days later, shaken and angry that his supposed ally had
not even gone that far despite undertakings from both Pollio and
Cadorna, he wrote to Conrad:

Italy's felony will be revenged in history. May God grant you victory now, so that
you will be able to settle accounts later with these knaves.[34]

In Vienna the German military attaché told Albricci 'with tears in his
eyes' that win or lose Germany would never forgive Italy. Some Austrian
circles, though, still hoped for eventual Italian participation in the war.[35]

A frustrating summer

The war did not begin in the way that the Italian high command had
expected, and therefore planning and preparation had almost to start
from square one. Initial intelligence about Austrian military measures on
the Italian frontier was 'contradictory and uncertain'. Cadorna's staff
read Austria's attitude as based on mistrust of Italy and the expectation
that she might attempt hostile acts. They forecast that she would make
her maximum offensive effort against Russia while defending herself
against Serbia and Montenegro and 'observing' Italy and Romania, and
expected to face two Austrian corps, amounting to perhaps 100,000
men, on the Italian frontier.[36]

By the third week in August, Cadorna had shaped his plans. He knew
that the government wanted the Trentino and Trieste, but felt that it
had no concept of the difficulty of attacking the Trentino without an
adequate siege park of heavy artillery. In the event, the army would have
to borrow heavy guns from the navy. Also, the entire military scenario
had changed in one important respect. Pre-war plans had envisaged that

both sides would mobilise simultaneously. Not only was this no longer
the case but now Austria could move troops rapidly from the Russian and
Serbian fronts as soon as war was declared, putting the Italians at an
initial disadvantage.

Like all his opposite numbers at the head of the combatant armies,
Cadorna was decidedly aggressive. The Italian armies would be deployed
ready for combat by the twenty-second day after the declaration of
war. The campaign would be a swift push along the valleys leading east,
north-east and north-west from the Italian frontier with Italian forces
driving into Austria along the river valleys. The ultimate target was
Vienna. The main thrust from the Tagliamento by 2nd and 3rd Armies
would drive rapidly east to the Isonzo and then press forward along the
Sava river to Krainberg and Ljubljana. A subsidiary strike north-west
would take Flitsch and seize control of Tarvisio as a first step along
the road towards Villach. Meanwhile 4th Army would strike north and
east, seizing Dobbiaco and opening up the options either of driving
west on Bolzano or east along the Drava and Gail rivers towards Villach
and Klagenfurt.[37] There were, it was thought, guns enough and to spare
to subdue the forts of Malborghetto, Hermann and Flitsch which protected Villach.[38]

On the map, it looked simple: Italian forces would penetrate a leaky
mountain barrier like water flowing along the cracks in a pavement.
In fact it was a pipe-dream. The colonial minister, Ferdinando Martini,
thought the plan to seize Vienna in three bounds was 'heroic proof of
fantasy'. He was quite right. In the event, Italian forces did not advance
much beyond the Isonzo, and although they smashed fort Hermann
to pieces they never took the fortress of Kluže (Flitsch), which stands
unharmed at the valley mouth to this day.

August was a month of deep frustration for Cadorna as he tried
unsuccessfully to use military and political logic to overturn the diplomatic decision that had just been reached. He spent the month trying to
persuade the government to move to full mobilisation, to go to war
alongside the Entente, and to do so before the winter came – and failed
on all three counts. Given the state that the army was in at the time, and
the lack of broad popular support for a war that would inevitably
be fought by a mass conscript army, it was perhaps no bad thing in the
long run that he did so – though it certainly did nothing to improve the
already somewhat fragile state of civil–military relations.

Cadorna began by objecting to partial mobilisation as strongly as
protocol would allow. Recalling only the 1889 and 1890 classes of
reservists would not put Italy in a state of armed neutrality, which
depended on properly organised units plus all the necessary support

services they required being stationed in locations ready for action. Far from accelerating general mobilisation when the time came, it would retard it and would complicate deployment. If the army was required to act it would need at least a month before it could start war operations. Facing the unknown, and evidently without anything much by way of guidance on immediate government policy, Cadorna wanted complete mobilisation to begin as soon as possible in case the army was called on to go into action.[39] His case, presented in summary form to the premier, was dismissed by the war minister in very short order. The cabinet had decided against general mobilisation – 'this radical measure' – for reasons of foreign policy and in view of the internal conditions of the country. The idea of mobilising as quickly as possible to gain a time advantage over an enemy, which had been a central feature of pre-war planning, had always been a questionable one, the war minister declared airily. Grandi was quite confident: its strength recently increased, the army could 'tranquilly contemplate a variety of possibilities against which, with only two classes under arms, a few days ago we were almost disarmed'.[40]

Italy's military action – or rather inaction – in August and September 1914 was determined primarily by political considerations. The problem had three dimensions. Should Italy go to war at all? If so, on which side? And what then should be the goals of what Salandra and Sonnino called '*nostra guerra*' ('our war')? Di San Giuliano's determination to stick to his policy was underpinned by calculations about both the war and the army. The war was likely to last a long time. Italy lacked the power to sustain herself in such a war – and the foreign minister did not think she had the social cohesion and fortitude to withstand early defeats. Thus it was impossible to commit Italy to a war 'unless we have the near certitude of victory from the very first operations'. It followed that there could be no break with the Central Powers until Italy could be assured both of victory alongside the Entente and of adequate territorial compensation. It was, he admitted, a policy that was 'not heroic but wise and patriotic'.[41] The political rationale was explained to Cadorna, Grandi and the chief of naval staff, Admiral Paolo Thaon di Revel, on 5 August but Cadorna was not persuaded: delaying general mobilisation he believed would expose Italy to 'irreparable damage' were Germany and Austria–Hungary to be victorious.[42] Certain that, win or lose, the Central Powers would never forgive Italy for deserting them, the new chief of the general staff thought that Di San Giuliano's policy would inevitably make Italy look grossly opportunistic.

Salandra's policy was to stick to neutrality while preparing the army for action in support of a policy whose nature and direction was as yet undecided. Throughout August Cadorna strove to make the government change its mind, backing his urgent pleas with two kinds of military logic. To Grandi, he argued that full mobilisation now would give the government freedom of action, whereas doing what it was presently doing could provoke an Austrian attack which the country would be unable to oppose. His hands bound by the government's apparent desire for a precautionary mobilisation which could last for days or weeks, and might even exclude a declaration of war altogether, Grandi responded with three different and equally impracticable proposals for partial mobilisation.[43] To Salandra, Cadorna argued that since it would be impossible to cross the Julian Alps after the end of October because of the weather, and since call-up would take a month, general mobilisation had to be declared by the beginning of September at the latest in order to have a month in which to crush the Austrians. With a political argument of his own to deploy – 'if Germany and Austria–Hungary win they'll take from Italy whatever they want' – he pressed the war minister for immediate mobilisation on 23, 27 and 28 August.[44] He tried another tack with the foreign minister on 27 August, arguing that since it was impossible to see which side would win, throwing Italy's military weight into the balance could determine the outcome. 'I don't think so,' was Di San Giuliano's dry response.[45]

Cadorna's attempts to alter the government's perspective on war policy got no support from the war minister. Grandi argued, reasonably enough since he was a member of it, that he was bound by the government's deliberations. He was also constrained by the parlous state of the army – something which both men knew but which Grandi kept from the civilians until the end of the month. The deficiencies were considerable. The army was reckoned to be short of 13,500 officers and at least 200,000 uniforms; due to long-running internal problems with the procurement of artillery ten of the 36 regiments of field artillery did not exist; and both the reserves and the militia were badly armed and poorly trained.[46] The deeper one delved, the more parlous things looked. For example, there were only 700,000 of the most modern Wetterlì rifles, introduced in 1891, for a field army of 1,262,000 men, and only 700 rounds of ammunition per rifle. Stocks of ammunition for the most modern heavy field gun (the 149A) amounted to 500 rounds per gun, and 1,200 rounds per gun for the older 75A and 65A models. The artillery had only 595 of the 2,082 trucks and motor vehicles it needed.[47]

Grandi, who had been brought in as war minister by Salandra in March 1914 because he was prepared to run the army more cheaply than a rival candidate, was not the man to admit the extent of the shortages outright and ask for more. As the month went on, the cabinet gradually learned about the state of affairs in the army. In mid August Grandi asserted that Italy had more arms and ammunition than she needed, but did acknowledge a shortage of 250,000 uniforms – itself something of a shock since his predecessor, General Paolo Spingardi, had told the king that the army was only 40,000 short. Not until 31 August, after further pressure from Cadorna, did he ask the cabinet for 12,000,000 lire to make up a shortfall now reckoned at 200,000 uniforms. However, he balked at Cadorna's proposal to add another 7,500 officers to the army, rejecting it in mid August on the grounds that it would cost 32,000,000 lire a year, 'an intolerable burden', and would adversely affect the long-term career structure of the officer corps.[48] On 22 August the cabinet learned that the planned mobilisation of a third division of mobile militia in each army corps was impossible as they were completely lacking in military capacity. That meant that Italy could send into combat only 380,000 men at most. A week later General Ugo Brusati, the king's chief military aide-de-camp and as such a man in the know, estimated that Italy could field only 100,000 men.[49]

As August gave way to September Cadorna fired off another salvo of letters and memoranda urging the recall of reserve officers and demanding winter uniforms and equipment for at least 600,000 men. The Intendance department had by now spent 30,000,000 lire on making good the shortfall in uniforms needed for a summer mobilisation, but they would not be ready until mid October. If the government wanted a winter campaign, Cadorna told Grandi, he needed a further 46,000,000 lire, otherwise it should be 'clearly understood that no military operation of any kind could be undertaken from today until the coming spring'.[50] Grandi referred the matter to the prime minister. Salandra was not prepared to be pushed by the army in a direction he did not wish to go. To his way of thinking, the deficiencies had existed for a long time, and could not be made good in a hurry. In any case, the international situation as he saw it presented Italy with the alternatives of persisting indefinitely in neutrality or exiting from it very shortly, either by entering the field or by an act of mobilisation. In the first case, the expensive measures proposed by Cadorna would not be justified. In the second, they would probably be too late.[51] By way of a footnote, Grandi added that the deficiency in summer uniforms would not now be fully put right until the end of the third week of November.

Cadorna's urgent wish for general mobilisation and his ambitious plans were driven by anxiety that the diplomats might land the army with a winter campaign for which it was entirely unequipped. He had reason to be concerned. As the fighting on both the eastern and western fronts swung back and forth, there was no guarantee that the politicians might not suddenly opt for war to take advantage of the turns of fortune. News of the Austrian setbacks in Galicia and the fall of Lemberg arrived early in September. Ambassador Avarna reported 'much depression' in Vienna, where the hospitals were already crowded with sick and wounded, and reports from St Petersburg told of Austrian armies in full retreat, having come near to disaster. By the end of the month it appeared that the Austrian government was encountering grave difficulties in equipping its armies for a winter campaign, so much so that the Viennese tram service was apparently handing over its stocks of uniforms to make up some of the gaps. Morale among the hospitalised troops was reportedly low, 'especially among troops not of German nationality'.[52] The military attaché, Lieutenant-Colonel Albricci, was a little more circumspect: the Austrians were retreating without excessive losses and the Russian infantry were lazy in pursuit. However, the morale of the Austrian army must have been weakened by the retreat, and although the conduct of the troops 'deserves the greatest admiration' he supposed it surely could not be sustained in the next battle.[53] During November German and Austrian troops were reported to be in full retreat from Poland, the Austrians were falling back along the San river and in the Carpathians, and the German invasion plan appeared to have failed completely.

Grandi's unwillingness to prepare for a winter campaign, and his refusal to agree that this was a time for boldness and daring, infuriated Cadorna. Salandra had his own reasons to be dissatisfied with his war minister. In mid September, urged by Sidney Sonnino to find out exactly what the army's deficiencies were and how quickly they could be remedied, the premier met privately with the recently appointed head of logistical and administrative services, General Adolfo Tettoni, and learned the full extent of the shortages of officers, artillery, winter clothing and horses. While the news can only have confirmed in his mind that the diplomatic line he and his foreign minister had struck at the very beginning of August was the only prudent one, it gave him pause.

On 22 September Salandra called the chief of the general staff to a two-hour private meeting. Cadorna told him bluntly that given the deficiencies in clothing, equipment and weapons, the only way in which Italy could enter the war with any hope of success would be if Austria was heavily engaged elsewhere. At that moment she was: as well as having launched the second of three unsuccessful attacks into Serbia on 8 September, the Austrian armies were busy between 1 and 18 September throwing back a Russian attack in Galicia. According to one member of his cabinet, Salandra apparently came away from the meeting believing that Italy could enter the field under present conditions with some hope of success, possibly by fighting in Istria since a combination of season and climate now ruled out operations in the Trentino or the Cadore.[54] If so he soon changed his mind for two days later he told Sonnino that since 'little or nothing useful' could be done in the immediate future, it would be better to spend the next five months 'in a state of (active) neutrality than in one of (inactive) war'.[55]

Cadorna had no choice but to accept the premier's decision and conform to his policy. On 25 September, after his staff had done a rapid study of how the army could take the field with reduced numbers proportional to the shortage of supplies and equipment and with the knowledge that Tettoni could not say when the winter uniforms would be ready, he told Grandi flatly 'We are not now in a condition to put the army into the field.'[56] At a meeting next day, attended by the premier, the war minister, the chief of general staff and the four generals designated to command Italian armies in wartime, Salandra was told that the lack of suitable clothing ruled out a winter campaign.

Salandra bemoaned the condition of the army in cabinet, and when he got around to writing his memoirs he suggested that its unreadiness for war had tied his hands. Since he did not intend to go to war yet, there was in fact no military 'problem' enveloping Italy's decision for neutrality. The army's material shortcomings did however present him with a diplomatic problem. Until they were remedied, Italy could not negotiate terms of entry with the Entente on a realistic footing. They also presented an immediate political problem. At a moment when neutralist sentiment was strong, and when he had reassured parliament in March that all military deficits had been made up, he was going to have to ask the chamber for extra money. He needed a justification but what Grandi gave him amounted to a clumsy piece of casuistry: the reassurance given to the premier had been that supplies had been restored to 'the state prior to the [Libyan] war', but when reading it out Salandra had changed this to 'every normal [level of] equipment'. The fault, Grandi claimed, was not his. The premier had misled both parliament and the public.[57]

Fate now caught up with Grandi. Enraged at what he dubbed the war minister's 'quibbling', Salandra told the king at the end of September that he did not regard him as up to his job. Within a fortnight he was gone. His successor was the deputy chief of the general staff, Major-General Vittorio Zupelli. He and Cadorna could be expected to work well together, reversing the traditional pattern of separation and rivalry between the holders of the two posts. Zupelli also soon struck up a good relationship with the treasury minister, Paolo Carcano. For the time being at least, Salandra had a team which would work in harmony.

In fact, it was probably a very good thing that Cadorna did not succeed in winning Grandi over to his viewpoint and that the civilian politicians decided in August 1914 to opt for peace and not war, at least for the time being. Much later, giving evidence to the inquiry into the disaster at Caporetto in October 1917, General Tettoni painted a dismal picture of an organisation in serious disarray in August 1914. Wastage of troops and equipment in the Libyan war of 1911–12 had not been made good. There were insufficient stocks of uniforms, with some depots completely lacking boots and others jackets. Four central stores – at Turin, Verona, Florence and Naples – were responsible for supplying all twelve Italian army corps and the units that had to be mobilised to bring them up to wartime establishments. Drastically short of personnel as well as equipment, they could not take in all the reserves and had to reorder the process of induction. The medical arrangements he described as simply 'an enigma'. At the back of all this lay a fundamental failure of direction: the war ministry had never carried out an in-depth study of a general mobilisation.[58]

Choosing sides

As the guns began to fire, Italy found out that she had been manipulated by her erstwhile *Triplice* partners. On 5 August Rome learned that Berlin had backed the Austrian ultimatum in the full knowledge that it would provoke Russian intervention and could therefore involve her in a war. To act otherwise would, she believed, allow Serbia, backed by Russia and France, to undermine the integrity of the Austro-Hungarian empire and the result of that would be 'the submission of all slavism under Russian hegemony'. The action had been co-ordinated in advance, and Italy had been kept in the dark until the last moment. The wool had been pulled over her eyes: German protestations that she knew nothing about the development of Austria–Hungary's policy, and that Russia would limit her protestations to diplomatic notes, were a tissue of fiction. The Italian ambassador, Giuseppe Avarna, had contributed to the deception. Believing that no one and nothing counted in Vienna save the emperor, and that he did not want war, he had discounted Albricci's evidence of a will to war in military and economic circles.[59] When, at the beginning of August, Italy's diplomats read and reported the German *White Book*, they felt her action in declaring neutrality had been entirely justified.

Although Vienna had been ready to start a war, the mood there in mid August was downbeat. There was little evident enthusiasm for the war and none of the anti-Russian demonstrations that were taking place in Berlin. It appeared, on the surface at least, that Austria–Hungary had been sucked into a general war by Germany. The Italian representative, Aldovrandi Marescotti, was assured that Vienna was not going to make any hostile moves in Albania and advised that Italy's position in the Adriatic was not threatened by Vienna but would be when the French were at Cattaro.[60] There was, it seemed, ground on which to manoeuvre.

Between August 1914 and April 1915, Italy undertook a tortuous process of negotiating the price for her military services first from her former partners in the Triple Alliance and then from her future allies in the Triple Entente. The task was made the more complicated by Balkan politics. Italy had long-term interests in the lands on the far side of the Adriatic, foremost among them Albania, and hoped ideally for military support from some of the regional powers, but the diplomatic landscape was cluttered with the débris of the two Balkan wars of 1911–13. The world war gave small powers the opportunity to drive hard bargains for their support, and both parties to the war that had just begun had no choice but to engage in some sharp dealing, which for Italy made matters even more complicated.

As far as Rome was concerned, two issues dominated the landscape of international politics: the *terre irredente* on her northern and eastern frontiers, and the Balkans. The latter was less than straightforward. There, Italy had to deal not with Austria–Hungary alone but with the competing interests and aims of half a dozen smaller powers. The idea of creating a Balkan bloc was dismissed at once as entirely impracticable given the tensions and conflicts between the regional powers.[61] The only option left to Italy was to attempt to stitch one or two of them together to serve her interests as well as their own.

Albania proved the easiest nut to crack. In mid October, Salandra prepared to send in a sanitary mission to prepare the way for 'a more concrete affirmation of our influence'.[62] Fearful that Albania might be given away to Serbia by the Entente, Italy went about registering her interest in Saseno and Valona. Berlin, Vienna, London, Paris and St Petersburg were all ready to fall in line, the Russians being more guarded than the rest. The sanitary mission was thus free to start at once, but Rome needed a local incident to justify a military occupation of Valona. It took only a day for Cesare Lori, the Italian consul at Valona, to cook one up, and on 27 December 1914 Italian forces occupied the city.[63]

Greece was both an actual threat and a potential support. Illegally occupying large areas of southern Albania, she wanted to push her frontier further into Albanian territory up to the river Skumbi. If she was to be brought alongside Serbia against Bulgaria, who had lost Macedonia to Serbia in the Balkan wars, she wanted guarantees from Romania; but Romania wanted good relations with Bulgaria and so

would not give them.[64] Even if it could be engineered, a Greek–
Bulgarian conflict was by no means clearly a good thing for Italy. It
would in all likelihood bring in Turkey, thereby facilitating the crushing
of Serbia and linking Vienna, Sofia and Constantinople in a strategic
chain that would dominate the Balkans.[65] Greece also threatened to
undermine the position Italy was trying to build up for herself in Asia
Minor. Rumours that if Turkey were to be partitioned she wanted
Smyrna and the surrounding region set the telegraph wires buzzing.
Anxiety mounted when Rome learned in February 1915 that the possibility of granting Greece concessions in Asia Minor was indeed being
examined in London.

With the resignation of the Greek premier, Eleftherios Venizelos, on
6 March 1915 Italy lost the only significant proponent of Greek entry
into the war and the country sank back onto its normal line of policy:
neutrality unless and until Bulgaria attacked her. To her sine qua non
for entering the war, a guarantee of her territorial integrity if Bulgaria
did attack, she added the Turkish *vilayet* of Aidin, financial support,
and a free choice of the moment to join in the fighting.[66] Italy had been
willing to go a short distance down that path: having signed a secret accord
with Romania in September 1914, Sonnino learned in January 1915 that
Austrian and German troops were mobilising on the Romanian frontier.
On 6 February he signed a defensive alliance with Romania. It had only
four months' life, suggesting that Sonnino may have been expecting war
by June. Both the Austrians and the French were able to track these
developments almost in real time thanks to their cryptographic services.[67]

As well as immediate concerns about recruiting or losing neutrals,
well-established longer-term strategic issues were also in play as far as
Greece was concerned. The country loomed large in the Italian official
mind as a potential outstation for France in the eastern Mediterranean.
As far as the head of commercial affairs at the *Consulta*, Primo Levi, was
concerned, the wrong side had won the second Balkan war. Had Bulgaria
been victorious Italy would have faced no problems. As it was, Greece
had gained Salonika, Crete and a number of islands. As a result,
she was to be feared on two grounds: the 'rare and undeniable maritime
virtues of her people', and the fact of her geographical position which
made her 'a natural ally for France, if needs be against us'. It would
be to Italy's advantage if the 'new Greece' were reduced during or as
a result of the war.

Levi's fears about Greece and France chimed with those of Admiral
Thaon di Revel, chief of the naval general staff, who forecast that even
if Italy took up arms against Austria and won she would end the war a
weakened power. In such circumstances 'our coasts, our maritime cities,

our islands, our colonies, especially those in the Mediterranean, would inevitably be at the mercy of the French fleet'. Di Revel, who thought the Greek navy a factor that could certainly not be neglected, could only see one way out of the problem: an accord with Great Britain and France 'independent of naval co-operation in the transitory phase of war'.[68]

The leitmotiv of Romanian policy was her preoccupation with Bulgaria. Afraid of being attacked by her, Bucharest also looked with alarm at the possibility that Constantinople might fall into her hands and was not inclined to believe Bulgarian protestations that, for the time being at least, she did not intend to act on her aspirations to Macedonia or Adrianople. Sonnino wanted Romania and Bulgaria to reach an accord so that Romania was no longer paralysed by the threat of a Bulgarian attack – but this was never a realistic option. Italian diplomacy was in fact hamstrung. For one thing, Romania did not trust Italy. For another, given that Italy would not have 'sufficient minimal military preparation' before the end of March 1915, Sonnino felt unable to offer her anything concrete by way of a clear and precise accord. When in February prime minister Ion Bratianu finally appeared to come down off the fence and promise that Romania would take military action simultaneously with Italy if and when she decided to do so, it took only three days for him to come up with a caveat – it all depended on Italy and France fulfilling his orders for war materials.[69] The caveat stayed in place, and by the time that Italy entered the war Romania's price for joining included territorial acquisitions in the Carpathians and Macedonia, as well as Hungarian and Russian territory.[70] She would spend the next fifteen months trying to work out which way the military wind was blowing and how best to profit by it before finally coming in on the Allied side.

Italy faced complications with both sides in wider areas as well as in Europe. In North Africa, German agents were aiding and fomenting the Muslim movement in Egypt and Libya: official assurances were given that they were instructed not to impinge on Tripolitania and Cyrenaica, that no accord had been reached with the Senussi, and that if one was then it would explicitly exclude any action against Italy.[71] More troublesome was the threat posed by the Turks, who had been forced to give up Libya to Italy in October 1912. Already suspecting that Turkey was stirring up Muslim elements in Albania, Rome feared that her entry into the war would extend Islamic agitation to Libya. Turkey repeatedly reassured Italy that both her interests and her possessions in North Africa would be respected, and the German and Austro-Hungarian ambassadors in Rome backed her up. Salandra was not inclined to believe Constantinople's protestations that it was only inciting the Senussi against the British, reading in the general tone of Turkish policy the intention to wage holy war against all Christians and thus free Islam in Africa and Asia from European domination. Sonnino shared his distrust.[72] Both men were right to do so.

The central problem of policy and strategy, though, lay squarely in Europe: on which side should Italy fight? At the end of October Sonnino, very shortly to take over the *Consulta*, posed one part of the two-part dilemma. A decision could not be put off too long, but was Italy able militarily to go into action now? The answer to that was a decided no. The other part of the dilemma was: who to talk to first, and on what basis? As far as reaching any kind of agreement with the Triple Entente was concerned, Salandra was not disposed at the moment to act. It was still far from clear whether the outcome of the war would favour the Entente; the threats to Italy's vital interests in the Adriatic which alone would justify her exiting a thirty-year diplomatic undertaking to the Central Powers had yet to be determined with exactitude; and the army was not prepared for a winter campaign.[73] Feelers put out to the Germans as to whether Austria–Hungary might purchase Italian neutrality were initially met with scarcely veiled scorn. It was impossible to imagine that Austria would engage in 'self-vivisection', Arthur Zimmerman, under-secretary of state at the German Foreign office, told the Italian ambassador in Berlin, Count Bollati – especially for an ally who had abandoned her. Was Italy threatening to go to war unless she was compensated for her neutrality, Jagow wondered politely.[74] For the time being, there would be no help from Germany.

Sonnino – 'Italy's worst ever foreign minister' according to one authority – soon amassed what became an extensive list of desiderata as Italy's price for joining in the war.[75] The British ambassador to Rome at the time, James Rennell Rodd, believed that 'considerations of security and not imperialist ambition' were behind Italy's negotiating position.[76] He was partly right, but partly wrong. The Italian Trentino, the Isonzo frontier and Trieste were irredentist goals; the Brenner Pass, Istria and Dalmatia were strategic issues; Albania spoke both to strategic and imperialist aspirations; and slices of mainland Turkey were undoubtedly expressions of an imperialist appetite. The question in the first four months of Sonnino's time at the *Consulta* was how much of each (apart from the last) was Vienna prepared to give in exchange for Italian neutrality?

Wartime negotiations necessarily took place under intense pressure caused by the ebb and flow of the fighting. After scarcely two weeks in office, Sonnino was very conscious of the fact that the war was moving fast: Serbia, defeated by the Austrians, could be crushed and there was talk of a separate peace between Russia and Germany. Each day that passed was a gain for the army and navy as they prepared for war, and potentially a day lost for foreign policy. By the first week of January 1915, the military situation had indeed changed again, to Italy's disadvantage. Austrian troops had retreated from Serbia, thereby weakening Italy's case for compensation.[77] Tommaso Tittoni, Italian ambassador in France, put the difficulty that the war posed for the conduct of diplomacy rather well:

It seems to be the fate of this war that scarcely has the balance begun to swing towards one of the belligerents than it swings towards the other. The result of these oscillations is an almost perfect equilibrium which makes it impossible to forecast with any confidence either its length or the final outcome.[78]

Italy's decisions were going to be the result of a combination of calculation and guesswork.

Vienna staked out its basic position early in the negotiating process. There could be no question of ceding the Trentino: for one thing, it would encourage irredentism elsewhere in the empire, and for another the emperor (who was count of the Tyrol) would sooner abdicate. If Italy freely joined the war it could be conceded to her at the war's end in compensation for Austria's gains in the Balkans, but it could not be a condition of Italian participation and there could not be any prior undertakings. The *Ballhausplatz* could not see – or would not acknowledge – that a 'momentary occupation' (meaning her invasion of Serbia) triggered by the war, which could from one day to the next be abandoned, justified compensation under clause VII of the Triple Alliance treaty. Austrian diplomats stuck to their guns on this fundamental principle almost to the last – and by then it was too late to change the trajectory of international politics.[79]

Meanwhile analyses of the pros and cons of negotiation and war piled up at the *Consulta*. Alessandro De Bosdari and Andrea Carlotti, ambassadors at Athens and St Petersburg respectively, saw dangers to Italy whatever happened. Either Austria would win, which would strengthen her position in the Balkans, or she would be so weakened that she would have to allow the creation of a 'great Serbian state' which would 'Slavicise' the eastern side of the Adriatic – something that was entirely contrary to Italy's political, cultural and ethnographic interests. Giacomo De Martini, secretary-general at the *Consulta*, saw things in a very similar way. If Austria were victorious, her Balkan aspirations would be directly in conflict with Italy's whether she did indeed proceed according to her manifest intention not to seek territorial gains or, as he believed, would seek to conquer new territories. If the Entente won, Italy's Adriatic interests would be threatened by the Slavs. His suggestion was to start negotiations with Vienna on the basis of the statement she had made on 11 August 1914 that she did not wish to make territorial gains in the Balkans. As a piece of analysis it was logical; as policy guidance, it was utterly unrealistic. Things were never going to be the same again.[80]

From Vienna Giuseppe Avarna, a convinced *tripicista* who followed his government's instructions reluctantly and having no faith in the Italian army thought that Italy ought to avoid war with Austria–Hungary at all costs, put a different slant on the issue. Interventionists were pushing for war because they believed that only thus could they save the dynasty and the established institutions of the state from extremists. If, however, Italy were defeated or if the war lasted a long time, this could well create the conditions in which republicans, socialists and anarchists would provoke a revolution. His argument – that unless Italy stayed loyal to the Triple Alliance a combination of Freemasons and Francophiles would pull down the monarchy, the Russian fleet would be in the Mediterranean, Italy would find herself contesting the Balkans and the Adriatic with Serbia, and his country would get little or nothing out of any division of the Ottoman empire – was self-evidently partial. Sonnino was unconvinced. The force of circumstances was pushing the government in another direction – the need to satisfy national feeling.[81]

While military preparations went ahead at their own pace, the matter of the army's readiness to fight gradually became more closely interlinked with Italy's diplomatic negotiations with both sides about the price that would be paid for her participation in the war. The wish-list was shaped by the politicians and the navy much more than by the army and Cadorna's direct input to the process was limited. In December he sent Salandra maps showing three different positions for the post-war Italian frontier, with a marked preference for one following the Isonzo with a detour east from Tolmino to prevent the Austrians from fortifying the heights. In January, when the diplomatic manoeuvrings were reaching a critical point of decision, the premier was armed with the knowledge that the army set a high value on possessing Bolzano, Cortina d'Ampezzo and Livinallongo.[82] The navy put in a strong claim for the islands of the Cos–Patmos chain and Rhodes: all were essential if Italy were to exercise influence over Anatolia, and Rhodes was important if Italy was to be able to extend her interests in Adalia.[83]

The arrival of Prince von Bülow in December, with the mission of smoothing the road and advancing negotiations between Rome and Vienna, did not help matters much. He was certainly not speaking for Vienna: neither Berchtold nor Burian, the past and present foreign ministers, had any faith in him and Burian thought he was 'gaga'.[84]

His advice to limit Italian demands to the Trentino conflicted with Italy's determination to get both it and Trieste, and Rome was not willing to accept a secret agreement on frontier rectification – despite having previously indicated that secrecy was agreeable. However, his arrival and his half-promises of the Trentino and Fiume generated a widespread feeling that Italy might do quite well out of the war without having to join in at all.

At the end of the third week in January, faced with Austrian intransigence and a scarcely veiled threat that if Italy pressed for compensation before the war ended then Austria–Hungary would make peace with Russia and turn on her, Sonnino decided to dust off the *telegrammone* ('big telegram'), prepared early the previous autumn in case negotiations were opened with London, which laid out all Italy's territorial demands. The time was fast approaching, he told the premier, to make a decision about whether to open serious negotiations with England. Now at a diplomatic impasse with Bülow apparently immovable on the need for Italy to specify what she wanted before negotiations could move forward and he himself unbending on the need for Austria–Hungary explicitly to accept the cession of territory before Italy could specify anything, Sonnino sent the *telegrammone* privately to Ambassador Imperiali in London on 16 February 1915. When nothing concrete came from Vienna he pressed Salandra to make a decision on whether formally to deliver it by 1 March. Still apparently unwilling to let any option slip from his grasp, Salandra accepted the deadline but wanted to know from war minister Zupelli and Cadorna exactly what the military situation was, and wanted also to keep Berlin and Vienna in play.[85]

Another swing in the pendulum of war confirmed the now all but finalised decision to look to the Entente for satisfaction. On 3 March the Italian military attaché in London reported that 15,000 troops were on their way to the Dardanelles – an operation the British expected to complete within two months, Rodd told Sonnino a week later. With the military situation in two war zones of prime interest to Italy apparently about to favour the Allies, and the prospect that the Balkan neutrals might now come off the fence for a price that would not suit Rome, the race for spoils was well and truly on. The instruction went out at once to hand Italy's list of wants to the British foreign secretary. When Sir Edward Grey read it, his first reaction was that Italy's conditions for entering the war on the Allied side were 'somewhat excessive'.[86] Over the next three weeks the discussions came to focus on two major areas of dispute: the eastern Adriatic coast and Turkey.

Over Turkey, where he wanted a zone east of Adalia and the *vilayet* of Konia, Sonnino eventually gave way in the face of Grey's adamant refusal to specify what Italy would get in Asia Minor after the war until she was actually involved in it.[87] The Adriatic, where Russia objected to Italian claims on the Curzolari islands and the Sabbioncello peninsula and backed Serbia's claims on Ragusa and Cattaro, was quite a different matter. The main reason for entering the war on the Allied side, according to Sonnino, was the need to end 'the present intolerable situation of inferiority there vis-à-vis Austria'. There was, though, no point in Italy's going to war to free herself of that incubus if it was simply replaced by a similar threat from 'the league of young, ambitious Yugoslav states'.[88] Salandra felt the same way. Like Sonnino he was prepared, if it came to it, to give up Italian possession of Sabbioncello, but not to jeopardise 'our military supremacy in the Adriatic'. Given that the Allies were not providing Italy with any direct military help or any concrete advantages in the eastern Mediterranean, the only reason to join in with them was to exclude any other power from the Adriatic. Austrian rivalry was less of a threat than Serbian rivalry would be 'because it is an old state in decline'.[89] The navy was right behind them both. With Pola in Italian hands and the Austrian fleet eliminated, Admiral Thaon di Revel was sure that Italy would for some years be absolute master of the Adriatic, but not if 'some eastern power' got its hands on Sebenico, Spalato, Ragusa or especially Cattaro.[90]

On 27 March, in a last-ditch attempt to swing Italy back to her side, Austria offered the south Tyrol and Trento and Germany indicated that she was ready to guarantee a settlement. Not wanting to give the impression that a break was inevitable, Salandra instructed Sonnino to wait a day or two and then tell Vienna that her proposals were insufficient. 'I have not yet decided anything,' he told his foreign minister.[91] There was, though, one insurmountable obstacle to any possible deal with Vienna: she offered Italy no security in the Adriatic. Concerned at the prospect of the Russians in the Mediterranean at the war's end, Sonnino believed that Italy must have dominance over the Adriatic – and that meant possession of Dalmatia and the Curzolari islands.[92]

At the end of the first week in April Italy presented her conditions. They comprised the Trentino, rectifications of the eastern frontier to include Gradisca and Gorizia, Trieste and Capo d'Istria as autonomous states, the Curzolari islands, an Austrian declaration of complete disinterest in Albania and recognition of Italian sovereignty over Valona, Sasseno and the hinterland, and Austria's abandonment of any claims to compensation for Italy's seizure of the Dodecanese islands during the Libyan war. The pill was much too large for either of the Central Powers to swallow. In Berlin, Gottlieb von Jagow, German foreign secretary, told Italian ambassador Riccardo Bollati that he could not 'in conscience' counsel Vienna to accept the Italian terms as they would 'entirely destroy her position as a great power'. In Vienna, Burian told Avarna that large parts of the Italian proposals were unacceptable, including extensions to the eastern frontier (which Avarna had guessed he would accept). He was prepared to extend his offering in the Austrian Tyrol but not as far as Bolzano, which the Italians wanted.[93]

In late March, Imperiali had denied to the Russian foreign minister that Italy was simultaneously negotiating with Austria–Hungary. Now that was indeed the case. The Allies were offering more or less everything Italy wanted in Europe, the Central Powers very little of it. Only one thing remained to be done before the whole business could finally be put to bed. Italy had begun negotiations with London on the basis that she would enter the field alongside the Entente no later than the end of April. She now had to explain to impatient allies why she was committing herself to start fighting within one month of the date of the treaty. The news was evidently both surprising and disagreeable but the explanation – that if Italy pushed her military preparations beyond a certain point before signing she risked being attacked before she was ready – was accepted.[94] On 26 April 1915, the Italian ambassador in London, *marchese* Guglielmo Imperiali, signed the Treaty of London on behalf of Italy.[95] The next day it was in the French press. Cadorna claimed afterwards that as soon as he saw that he knew that 'surprise, which I had worked so hard to ensure, would go up in smoke'.[96] Belatedly, Vienna made further offerings that included the eastern frontier rectifications and Trieste as a free port, but they were too late and too little. For one thing, she was not willing to give up control of the peaks in the Trentino, which Italy believed she had to have.

Sonnino laid out the detail of the secret negotiations and explained the government's rationale to parliament on 20 May 1915 – four days before the war began. A nation did not live by irredentism alone, he declared; it had vital interests that were political, moral, economic 'and expansionist'. Italy had to be concerned with her security in the Adriatic, her position in the Mediterranean 'and the possible development of her colonies'. In his final peroration he called on Italy's sons to fight 'for the freedom and independence of [our] brothers who are today under a foreign yoke' and to safeguard the country's 'vital interests in the Adriatic and the Mediterranean'.[97]

Winter preparations

While Salandra and Sonnino began their progression down the winding path to war, the chief of staff and the new war minister set to work.

Cadorna proposed to enter the field in spring 1915 with fourteen army corps composed of thirty-five infantry divisions and four cavalry divisions. As he was away, Salandra called in Zupelli, still deputy chief of staff, to discuss the programme. Zupelli quickly put some detail into the picture. The training of the categories I and II of the youngest classes of conscripts born between 1893 and 1895 would be improved, and provision made to call up the category III men born during or after 1888, who had previously escaped any military service, for three months. Active-service officers would be swept out of the bureaucracy and returned to the troops; unnecessary instructional courses would end; officers' courses in the military schools would be accelerated and expanded; laws on age limits for officers would be suspended; and suitably qualified volunteers would be accepted as trainee officers. Maximum effort would be made to recruit non-commissioned officers using military schools and graduates of the class of 1892. Finally, the mobile militia would be expanded, with additional artillery, cavalry and engineers, and its equipment improved.[98] The shopping list that went with this programme was substantial but, in the light of what was to come, woefully inadequate: for example, reserves of artillery ammunition were to be increased by a maximum of 600 rounds per gun, and thirty field hospitals would provide a total of 3,000 beds.[99]

Zupelli's energy contrasted strongly with Grandi's torpor. Shortly after being appointed, the new minister told the cabinet that by March 1915 he expected to have 1,250,000 men ready to fight. The public purse was duly opened and Zupelli received 600,000,000 lire in October and November 1914 and a further 340,000,000 lire between January and May 1915. There was plenty to spend it on. Salandra tended to focus on the numbers of men that could be put in the field, and Zupelli had to tell him that the necessary improvements were qualitative and not quantitative. That was true in manpower terms, but not in respect of armaments: for example, where a German army corps had 140 guns its Italian equivalent had only 64, a number Zupelli aimed to raise to 90. As far as manpower was concerned, Zupelli, who had been working to a plan to mobilise a total of 1,515,000 men, learned at the end of December that Cadorna's staff were working to a plan that envisaged mobilising 2,108,000 men. The war minister warned the chief of the general staff 'in the most explicit and formal way' not to go beyond the number he had fixed upon, scarcely veiling the threat that otherwise he would resign.[100] It was a bad omen. Relations between the two men soon worsened and in February 1915 they had a run-in over sending troops to Libya, which Cadorna never wanted to do. Cadorna offered his resignation but the king intervened, as he would at several key moments during

the war, to ensure that he stayed. Over the coming months the relationship between the two men at the summit of the military high command
would sour to the point at which Cadorna would demand Zupelli's head.
Readying the army to carry out Cadorna's grandiose plans was an
enormous task. The tortuous bureaucratic machinery through which
designs for new guns had to pass before 1914 had badly delayed the
introduction of modern recoilless artillery. There was very little heavy
artillery. An order for 140 of the new 149A howitzers, placed in 1911,
had still to be completed. Another, placed with Vickers in 1912 for 940
machine-guns, was also incomplete and to make up the numbers the war
office placed an order with FIAT for a gun they had dismissed in 1911.
The manufacturers undertook to produce fifty a month – but only from
May 1915. Between February and April Cadorna pressed Zupelli and
General Alfredo Dallolio to increase production of rifles and ammunition –
but despite the wealth of information coming both from France and
Germany, he entirely neglected the need to expand production of
ammunition for the artillery.[101]

Although he was enthusiastic about getting into the war, Cadorna had
serious doubts about the reliability of the instrument that he and Zupelli
were forging and about the resilience of the society that stood at its back.
His strategy – to fight a short, fast war when the time came – was based
not so much on the capabilities of the economy as on 'the morale and
disciplinary conditions of our country, on which our success in large part
depends'.[102] Italian plans once 'open' mobilisation (*mobilitazione rossa*)
began, when mobilisation would take place in the depots and not at
the points of deployment, filled him with concern lest the Austrians
attack before Italy could deploy the bulk of its armies, an event which
was unlikely but could have 'consequences of extraordinary gravity,
especially [given] the qualities of our race'. He was reassured that six
army corps would be hurried to the frontier 'in special formation[s]'.[103]

Uneasy about the army that he commanded and the society from
which it was drawn, Cadorna began to formulate disciplinary policies
that would become increasingly ferocious as the war went on. At the
end of September he complained furiously to Grandi about the use of
exemptions from conscription, demanded a new military penal code, and
criticised officers who in their dealing with the troops forgot 'to use
firmness pushed to extreme rigour when necessary'. The military penal
code at his disposal, introduced in November 1869 and based on the
old Sardinian penal code of 1840, was already a fearsome enough instrument: a catch-all clause on desertion prescribed the death penalty for
actions 'in the presence' as well as 'in the face' of the enemy, and another
made abandonment of one's post 'in the presence of the enemy'

punishable by death or imprisonment. During the winter of 1914–15 Cadorna published a new set of regulations allowing him to cast his disciplinary net more widely: wrongly claiming exoneration from military service was made a punishable disciplinary offence and membership of the Freemasons was made illegal in the army.[104] Zupelli was more concerned about maintaining public order in the event of general mobilisation when only a limited number of troops would be available. Although the law would be energetically and severely applied, there could be 'sudden and unexpected disturbances of special seriousness'. Cadorna was more than willing to make 130 battalions of territorial militia available to back the civil power in case of need, at least in the early stages of a conflict.[105]

The date by which the Italian army would be ready to fight slipped back during the winter of 1914–15. Cadorna came away from a meeting with Salandra and Sonnino on 24 November believing that both men were contemplating possibly entering the field in December or January – and submitted written advice opposing such an action.[106] Meeting with Cadorna and Zupelli in Palazzo Braschi on 15 December, the premier and the foreign minister asked the soldiers how the military preparations were going. The answer was that the measures needed to fill the gaps in artillery, machine-guns, men and horses were 'in a state of incubation' and would mature at some point between January and March. That meant that the army could not enter the field until April. To mobilise the army in the meantime simply to stand in front of the Alps would, they were told, be 'folly'.[107]

In purely military terms, Italy's inability to enter the war in the autumn and winter of 1914 when things were going relatively badly for Austria–Hungary and Germany might have been unfortunate for her, but its impact on the diplomatic machinations was actually minimal. Besides the commanding requirement to secure the right territorial deal, foreign minister Sonnino wanted to be as sure as possible that the outcome of the war was turning in the Allies' favour, and he needed to find a justification for abandoning the Triple Alliance. The fact that the army was unprepared for a winter campaign was but one of a number of factors standing in the way of reaching a definitive accord with London – and by no means the most important one.[108] In any case, the same message was arriving in Rome from the embassies in all the major combatant countries: the war was going to be a long one. In Vienna, Franz Josef told the Italian military attaché so in October. In November, Italian ambassadors in Berlin, London, Paris and St Petersburg all reported in identical terms: the nature of their respective hosts' war aims meant that there was no basis for mediation and they were in it to the end.

At his first meeting with the German envoy Prince von Bülow on 18 December, Sonnino offered the opinion that the war could not last beyond autumn 1915. Certainly no less and perhaps longer was the reply.[109]

By December the Italian general staff were in a decidedly pessimistic frame of mind. If Italy intervened in the war now, they expected the German armies to adopt a defensive stance in the West and put a premium on safeguarding territorial inviolability in the East while Austria likewise stood on the defensive against Serbia and Russia. '[F]or political, moral and military reasons' the Germans would want to send troops to fight alongside Austria against Italy.[110] There were historic and cultural as well as strategic reasons why the Austro-German blow was likely to fall heavily on Italy. The mentality of both powers was influenced by 'inexact and partisan' evaluations of the second battle of Custoza in 1866. It was also affected by much broader cultural assumptions: 'Too much has been written about the lack of military preparation, too much observed of discord, indecision, internal pacifism for them not to hope to inflict a fatal defeat on us.'[111] As to where the fighting might take place, winter weather ruled out anything more than minor operations in the Tyrol – 'and their troops are not equal to ours'. The Austrians would most likely try to take advantage of the twenty days' mobilisation time needed by the Italians to move twenty or more divisions up to the Carso and the left bank of the Isonzo. Information that they had abandoned or destroyed their temporary works on the right bank suggested that once there they would adopt a defensive posture.

The fact that Italy would be joining an ongoing war as partner to powers that were already fighting her own probable opponents added an important new dimension to her strategy. Self-evidently, the more intense the pressure that the French and Russians could exert the better things would be for the Italian army. If, on the other hand, the allied armies slowed down then the picture was clouded by grave dangers. From that it followed that Italian entry into the war 'must be preceded by a clear, well defined understanding [intesa] with the other belligerent armies to safeguard our military interests'.[112] The war was not expected to be short. If Italy entered it, the staff warned, she must be ready to sustain heavy sacrifices for a long time to achieve her ends.

Cadorna thought differently. In early December he told Olindo Malagodi, director of the *Tribuna* newspaper, that the Austrian army was in a bad way and that if another army was thrown against it, it must overturn. The balance was swinging against the Central Powers and Italy's entry into the war would be the end of Austria if the Germans were unable to help. As for his strategy, he did not intend simply to take the *terre irredente* for which the nationalists were clamouring but would go all the way. There could be no greater error than limiting oneself to local and limited goals. Wars were won by hitting the enemy in his vital centres. 'Conquering ground means nothing if the enemy is left in a condition to re-attack and take revenge.'[113] A week after receiving the staff analysis, he forecast that a campaign against Austria would involve a big battle within a fortnight of the start of operations two days' march inside the country, and another one six or seven days' march from the frontier within forty-five days of the start of the war. Thereafter the army, having reached the Ljubljana region, would push on towards Vienna. Occupying the Trentino and Trieste was only of secondary importance.[114] The war he had in mind would be quick – and decisive.

Lessons unlearned

At this point, intelligence began to arrive in Rome which might have given the chief of the general staff pause for thought. As Cadorna and Zupelli worked to get the army ready to take the field, a flood of reports from the Italian military attachés in Paris and Berlin opened up a rich vein of information about the new kind of warfare that was appearing on the western front. Some were circulated quite widely: the war ministry and the general staff received them, they were read by the king, and the designated army commanders received copies of the more important ones.

On 25 November 1915 Lieutenant-Colonel Luigi Bongiovanni arrived in Berlin to take up the post of military attaché. Bongiovanni had served with the new chief of the German general staff, Falkenhayn, during the Boxer rebellion. Using this personal connection he was able in mid December to give the Italian authorities a detailed insight into Falkenhayn's thinking about the broad shape of the war and about present and future German strategy. Falkenhayn believed that all the great powers had erred in thinking that the positional warfare that had marked the Russo-Japanese war had been due to particular and local contingencies. The explanation lay in the new weaponry: 'The power of the defensive is incredible,' he told Bongiovanni, and indeed was such as to condemn attacks to certain failure unless they had a great preponderance of force and could take 'unheard-of losses'. Victory could not come until both sides had tired one another out. The moment would eventually arrive when one side felt stronger than the other – 'It's a question of nerves: the Germans have good nerves.' The German infantry had already suffered enormous losses (estimated by Bongiovanni at 600,000 dead, wounded and missing), largely caused by machine-guns. Things could not go on in the way they had begun because that would be 'an absurd waste of human life'. The immediate alternative was a return to some form of positional warfare, though Falkenhayn feared that might fatally affect the offensive spirit of the troops.[115]

Confirmation of much that Falkenhayn had said soon came from the other side of the lines. In November 1914 an early report from the attaché in Paris, Lieutenant-Colonel Breganze, identified the tactical problems that were appearing: the heavy losses suffered by the attacker, the extraordinary effect of heavy artillery and machine-guns, and the spreading of trenches. After visiting the Marne, Breganze sent a massive 165-page report back to Rome at the end of December which described in detail the organisation of a sector of trenches, highlighted the enormous volume of supplies the army was consuming and the large number of trains necessary to provide them, and emphasised the strength of French defensive positions – 'super-human force will be needed to dislodge them'. Breganze too foresaw the war dragging on until one adversary was exhausted. After exalting the perfect organisation and material resources of both sides, he concluded by laying great emphasis on moral force.[116]

A visit to Foch's army group in Flanders early in February 1915 produced another extensive report from Paris. As well as providing Rome with a particularly good account of how the French used interdiction fire in the attack and assessing the effects of artillery generally, Breganze deconstructed trench warfare, dwelling in detail on the creation of fieldworks, the importance of barbed wire, the wearing down effect of this 'work of ants' on the troops, and the 'great, the enormous prevalence of moral factors in the conduct of the war, which enable [men] to keep going in the face of difficulties that seem insurmountable'. Breganze's analysis of the fundamental cause of the situation he described so effectively was less convincing, though it must have been music to Cadorna's ears. It was due, he suggested, to an 'original lack of preparation', the solution for which was to put everything necessary to mobilise all the resources of the country into the hands of the military. As for the future, there were only two ways forward: either the continuation of the war of attrition, or the intervention of third parties.[117]

Breganze returned to Rome in January 1915 and saw the king, Cadorna, and a number of other senior military officials including Dallolio, under-secretary at the war office and the man responsible for the production of weapons and munitions. Dallolio asked him to research the role of private industry in France, especially in regard to munitions production. When it came, early in March, the report earned praise from war minister Zupelli and from the head of the operations section of the general staff, Major-General Armando Diaz. From it they learned that France had had to look beyond the state arsenals and have recourse to private industry, with excellent results. Machinery was ordered from the United States; finance came from the government via contracts that were advantageous to both parties; and specialised labour was selected from among the reservists recalled for military service. The outcome was 80,000 rounds of artillery ammunition a day, which more or less exactly equated with daily consumption.[118] A follow-up report provided the authorities in Rome with more detail about how the French contracting system worked, what prices they were paying, and what they were ordering, which included 12,000 lorries. Because of her late arrival in the international marketplace, Breganze warned, Italy was clearly going to face difficulties. All the big American factories were already contracted, and the French were finding it very difficult to procure munitions from them at reasonable prices.[119] This intelligence seems to have stimulated Zupelli to start mobilising national industry for war production – something for which Cadorna was pressing – though the legal basis of Italy's industrial mobilisation and the conversion of factories to war production was not laid down until 26 June 1915, a month after the war began.[120]

Although Cadorna did not seem to feel the need for more information about the German army, his deputy did. Early in February 1915, Diaz complained that not much information about it had been gathered over the past thirty years because of both powers' membership of the Triple Alliance. This was not entirely true – the archives contained a great deal of information had he or any of his subordinates had the time to go through them – but Bongiovanni more than filled the gap. A visit to East Prussia and Poland in January 1915 left a strong impression. The spirit of the German army was *elevatissima* ('very high') and faith in victory was universal. What struck him particularly was the 'perfectly methodical organisation of all the [ir] enormous national resources with the single aim of greater war-making efficiency'.[121] The chief tactical lesson he drew from his visit was that although modern weaponry had strengthened the power of the defensive, it had not made manoeuvre impossible. 'To win, it will always be necessary to attack and manoeuvre.'[122]

Rome was provided with detailed descriptions of the German, Russian and Austrian trench systems (the latter 'as good as the Germans'). Like his colleague in Paris, Bongiovanni dwelt at length on the enormous consumption of munitions by the artillery, the ineffectiveness of shrapnel and light shells when fired at trenches and the need for heavier guns, especially howitzers. A conversation with Field Marshal Paul von Hindenburg yielded the observation that if the troops were not to get lazy and lose their offensive spirit in the trenches then what was needed was 'a very active defence and the continual improvement of [one's] positions through the progressive conquest of new ground'. This remark at least seems to have found its target: it was one of only two passages marked with triple lines by a reader, possibly Diaz.[123]

The king was impressed by Bongiovanni's reports. Cadorna, on the other hand, was disinclined to believe the reports he received from his attachés in Berlin and Vienna, whom he regarded as 'impregnated' with *germanofilia* and *austrofilia*. Other sources suggested that the situation was not as favourable to Italy's adversaries as Bongiovanni made out, and in any case the observations made by military attachés were affected by 'the very special conditions' in which they were put. Cadorna recommended that Bongiovanni be 'more objective' in the future. Bongiovanni protested. While he admired the German army this had not in any way clouded his judgement: 'sympathy [for the Germans] is difficult to find in anyone who, like me, is forced to live in immediate contact with them'. He was not, though, going to change his views or alter his style of reporting, and if Rome did not like it then they could sack him.[124] For the time being Bongiovanni stayed.

A five-day visit to the German front at Lille in mid February convinced Bongiovanni that the French and British forces, like the Russians, had lost all real offensive strength and that the Germans had the operational initiative – a view queried back at headquarters in Rome.[125] This experience, together with second-hand accounts of the French attack at Soissons on 7 January 1915 and the German counter-attack on 12 January, informed an impressive 54-page report on positional warfare sent to Rome at the end of March. As well as reinforcing and expanding his earlier observations on the practice of trench warfare, the importance of field fortifications and the pre-eminence of artillery – 'artillery dominates positional warfare' – Bongiovanni suggested that attack, although difficult, was not impossible. Unlike in the early stages of the Libyan war, trenches were now no longer simply passive defences but could serve as supports for offensive actions. The lesson of Soissons, in which the Germans advanced to a depth of 4 kilometres along a front of 14, was that a well-prepared attack could get across the *zona battuta* (the zone between the lines beaten by enemy fire) without excessive loss. The real difficulty, and therefore the key to success, was destroying the barbed wire. The best way to cut it was by using medium-calibre artillery. There were also lessons to be learned from the German method of dealing with concentrated French artillery fire, which they did by withdrawing troops laterally or to the rear and then reoccupying their front lines as soon as it ceased.[126] The report alarmed the king, leaving him convinced of the need to be 'on guard against those who spread false impressions (*notizie*) of the condition of the Allied armies so as to draw the country into adventures on which its existence may depend'.[127]

During his last trip to the western front, in early April, Bongiovanni had two long conversations with Falkenhayn. From them Rome learned that the chief of the German general staff was urging his opposite number in Austria, General Conrad von Hoetzendorff, to push his government to accept Italy's terms for a benevolent neutrality, but that if it came to war between the two powers then Germany would be with Austria–Hungary – which can have come as no great surprise. As far as German strategy in the West was concerned, Falkenhayn had abandoned the idea of a major offensive there. 'Better to resist sterile Franco-British attacks which will never succeed in chasing us out of our defensive lines and content ourselves [with our] favourable situation', he told Bongiovanni. With the coming thaw, Falkenhayn expected the Austro-German war to settle down into localised engagements there too. As for Italian intervention in the war, it would not be decisive in ending the campaign:

> Given the strength of the defensive, modern methods of war, [and] the terrain [of] the Italo-Austrian frontier zone … the Italian army will be stuck for a long time in the mountains, and in any case before it reaches Budapest and Vienna it will find itself faced by German forces.[128]

It was an accurate forecast. Falkenhayn also confirmed Cadorna's view by concluding that the result of such a war would be an 'implacable hatred' for Italy.

The last months of peace

If the tactical and operational shape being taken by the war over the winter and spring of 1914–15 presented potential problems, its strategic shape was almost all that the Italians could have asked for. Austrian forces stationed along the Italian frontier were thinned out as units were drawn off to take part in the fighting in the Balkans and Russia. The fall of the Austrian fortress of Przemysl on 23 March 1915, with a loss estimated by the Italians at between 117,000 and 164,000 men, was both a material and a moral setback: on hearing of it, Emperor Franz Josef burst into tears. On the western front the Germans were fully occupied in beating off a non-stop series of French offensives between January and April, and launching strong counter-attacks of their own. In the eastern Mediterranean, the failure of British attempts to force the Dardanelles in February and March led inexorably to the landings of 25 April and the opening of another land front against Germany and her allies. Failure at Gallipoli was a long way off, and Mackensen's sweeping victories against the Russians in the Gorlice–Tarnow offensive, which began on 2 May and saw German and Austrian armies drive as far as Vilna and Pinsk by September, were yet to come.

During the early spring, fear of an Austrian attack forced Cadorna to abandon the principle that the army would first mobilise in its depots and then deploy to its starting positions along the frontier and instead deploy parts of individual army corps to guard the eastern frontier. On 1 March, three days before the government secretly started its final negotiations with the Allies, he gave the order to start *mobilitazione rossa*, thereby secretly beginning to put the army on a war footing. Parts of some army corps had already been sent to the front in case of a sudden Austrian attack, so that the pre-war plans were already in disarray. Sonnino was led to believe that Cadorna expected to have all his forces in the field by 29 May but when the main transports started to roll on 4 May it took forty-three days to move the army to the front instead of the twenty-three days assumed in the pre-war transport plan.[129] The entire army was not in place until the end of June, five weeks after the war began.

At the moment when secret mobilisation began, Cadorna knew nothing about the course of Italian diplomacy. As Salandra and Sonnino were still undecided about which side to join, there was in truth not much to know. In the dark about government thinking, and fearing that he might as a consequence give values to the Tyrol and Isonzo theatres that were different from what the government might require, he asked on 12 April to be included in all ministerial meetings dealing with military–political matters.[130] The blinkers were removed nine days later, when Salandra told him that negotiations with Vienna had come to nothing and that war was therefore coming. At the end of April, Cadorna told the foreign minister that the Friuli army corps would be ready to move on 12 May.[131]

Cadorna was as keen as his political masters to ensure that when Italy sent its armies into the fray their opponent should be as distracted as possible by military action elsewhere. To that end a military convention with Russia was signed on 21 March 1915. Under its terms the high commands of all four allied armies undertook to act in common in deploying all their efforts to vanquish the common enemy and to concert their military operations as much as possible. Italy undertook to enter the war at the latest by 26 May, at which time the other three armies would undertake energetic military measures in order to prevent the Austrians concentrating superior forces on the Italian front. Italy and Russia bound themselves to concentrate the maximum possible force against the Carpathians and the Alps and jointly to select the best directions for their armies when military operations actually began.[132]

At that moment, with the Austrian fortress of Przemysl in the Carpathians about to surrender, the Russian military star seemed to be in the ascendant. When the time came to cash this cheque two months later Russian armies would be reeling back across Poland. Collaboration of the kind envisaged in the convention would remain a pipe-dream. In the meantime, responding to a follow-up by Grand Duke Nicholas, commander-in-chief of the Russian armies, Cadorna revealed that 'secret' mobilisation had been partially carried out and that he expected to have 240,000 men on the frontier by 12 May. General mobilisation would not begin before 15 May, and Italy would be ready for war with all its forces two weeks later.[133] A vigorous offensive by the Russian army was absolutely necessary when Italy began hostilities:

significant enemy forces are already gathered on our frontier, recent work has made the enemy's defensive organization powerful, so that our first offensive leap will be slow, difficult, [and] possible only if there is simultaneous and energetic pressure by the Russian army.[134]

On April Fool's Day 1915, Cadorna issued a revised strategic plan. The institution of *mobilitazione rossa* meant that the army would now deploy on the eastern frontier in successive waves and not simultaneously. That ruled out the offensive bounds that had been the cornerstone of his first plan. Although apparently heedless of the changing physiognomy of war about which his military attachés had given him more than ample warning, Cadorna was aware of new possibilities and alert to at least one potentially significant alteration in the physical circumstances his armies would face. He drew his subordinates' attention to three new elements that had now appeared and would have to be taken into account. First there were the large forces that the Central Powers had been able to put into the field and maintain there. It was thus possible that they could deploy forces adequate enough to meet the Italian offensive. Second, given the defensive works that the Austrians had erected on the Carso and the Friuli front, an Italian offensive in that direction 'may run into tenacious resistance and remain paralysed in the same way as has happened in Flanders and in Poland'. Finally, it was possible that the Tyrol might become a more important theatre than he had previously allowed, both in itself and in relation to the European war.[135]

His operational directives to his field commanders, issued on 1 April, reflected the changed circumstances. They were now to focus on protecting the assembly and deployment of the later arrivals and conquering positions which could be used as starting points for a general offensive once the troops were fully assembled. During deployment, 2nd Army was to keep open the opportunity of taking Caporetto and if possible

Kolovrat and Korada, and 3rd Army was to secure the bridges across the lower Isonzo ready for a subsequent move onto the Sagrado heights. The generals were warned not to take positions which they could easily be forced to abandon and above all to avoid 'partial checks and unduly risky ventures which, by forcing the withdrawal of troops not yet orientated [to the war zone], might disturb the deployment of those units arriving successively at the frontier'. As soon as the army was fully deployed, he intended to launch it against the *altipiani* (upland plateaux) of the Bainsizza and Sagrado.[136]

A study of the military efficiency of the Austrian army carried out at this time estimated that it would be able to put 62 divisions in the field during the war, and that the Italians would face 233 Austrian battalions (approximately 250,000 men). This was a remarkably accurate forecast: on 24 May 1915 there were 155 Austrian battalions on the frontier, but a week later that number had swelled to 234 battalions. Despite the fall of Przemysl and a drastic shortage of junior officers – a problem that the Italian army shared – the general staff could see no signs of disorganisation in the Austrian army, which had hitherto demonstrated 'the most admirable powers of resistance'.[137]

As May began, in Paris the French generals pushed for an immediate Italian entry into the war and war minister Alexandre Millerand observed that it should be no later than 26 May. Cadorna was prepared to commit himself and his armies to a vigorous forward push by the covering forces by 26 May at the latest on the condition that the Russian army launched a vigorous attack around the 20th and that the British and French armies took analogous action to prevent the concentration of Austro-German troops on the Italian frontier at the moment when Italy joined in the war.[138] Assurances of full co-operation quickly came from Marshal Joffre, General French, and General Janushkevich, who promised to 'advance with an energetic offensive where possible'. Cadorna wanted more – fixed undertakings that the Allies would launch an attack some days before Italy entered the war, and that they would also take the offensive if Austria–Hungary launched a surprise attack on Italy before 26 May. Both were steps too far for the western Allies, and he had to content himself with purely verbal undertakings.[139]

Simultaneous conversations with the Russians reached what was, if anything, a more satisfactory outcome. Cadorna needed a Russian offensive because, as he had told the Russian general staff, 'our first offensive jump will be slow, difficult and only possible if there is simultaneous pressure by the Russian army'.[140] At a meeting on 9 May, attended by French and British military representatives, the Russian chief of general staff gave an undertaking to act contemporaneously with Italy and identified the Alps, the Carpathians and Bosnia as the common objective of all parties. It was also agreed that the Serbs would undertake an offensive against northern Bosnia when the time came, synchronising with the drive by the Italian right flank on Ljubljana. Italy's signature to the convention had to be delayed when the Salandra government resigned four days later. Lieutenant-Colonel Ropolo was authorised to sign on 17 May, but not to accept a clause under which Italy was bound to supply Serbia with provisions. The Russians were worried about the effect of this on their ally's morale, and had to be persuaded to sign the agreement.[141] It was not a good omen. Shortly, for different reasons, both parties would fail to provide Italy with the military assistance she needed and expected.

The fact that he was now negotiating directly with his future military allies was a sign of Cadorna's mounting authority and independence. The timing and content of his dealings also raise questions as to whether, as he afterwards claimed, he only found out by accident on 5 May that Italy was committed to war and that his armies were to be in action by the 25th of that month.[142] Wartime collaboration with other armies was both a necessity and something of a novelty – and not entirely a welcome one. Cadorna's staff were not very happy at the thought of being closely tied up with the French. The 'enormous feeling of superiority over everybody else' that was characteristic of the French people was likely to make it difficult to come to understandings with their army. They would probably demand formal undertakings, and since 'every Italian would rebel at such a pretension' the authorities had better be prepared for it.[143] Joffre had already sent unsolicited advice. Given the impossibility of expelling the enemy from well-constructed trenches in present conditions without enormous sacrifices, he suggested that Cadorna would be well advised to dig a line of trenches in the Trentino and along the Isonzo to stop the enemy in case the Italian offensive failed and the army was forced to retreat.[144] Cadorna's reply merely promised a vigorous offensive that would be 'as rapid as possible given the roughness of the ground and the defences which the enemy has been multiplying for some months'.[145]

As war approached, Cadorna became more exercised by what he saw as growing disciplinary problems in the army. The previous autumn he had been appalled that the protests by soldiers of the 1888 and 1889 classes, who had been recalled for service in Libya and who had demanded their release after six months, had gone unpunished. Now officers, some of high rank, were speaking out of turn and 'exaggerating' the deficiencies in manpower and materiel. This was damaging to the spirits of both the troops and the populace, and he demanded that it be stopped.[146] More worrying, no doubt, was the news at the end of April that recalled reservists being marched to trains at Parma, Brescia, Arezzo and Reggio Emilia were behaving in a disorderly and undisciplined fashion. With the newspapers up in arms, Cadorna called for the swift infliction of 'severe and exemplary punishment' on the guilty parties, regardless of the numbers involved.[147]

'The radiant days of May'

The disorders among returning conscripts were symptomatic of a deeper malaise in the nation as a whole. A wave of strikes had broken out in major cities across Italy from Turin to Bari and Naples during 'Red Week' in June 1914, when Salandra had banned anti-militarist demonstrations planned for the festa dello Statuto. Firm government then had put them down at the cost of some twenty dead. During the months that followed Salandra nursed doubts about the pliability of his citizenry if and when it came to war. In December he admitted that arms were being manufactured not just for war against the Austrians but also 'to prevent internal upheavals'.[148] Whether the Italian government would be able to overcome the explicit as well as the innate opposition to war was far from clear as former premier Giovanni Giolitti pursued a campaign to persuade the voters that they could secure 'sufficient' (parecchio) gains without having to fight.

Ready to sign the Treaty of London, Salandra faced a loose grouping of neutralists comprising Giolittians, Catholics and 'maximalist' socialists who confronted an equally disparate but more united grouping of 'interventionists' that combined nationalists, 'reformist' socialists (including Benito Mussolini), republicans, democratic radicals, Freemasons, Futurists and assorted literati.[149] A month earlier, interventionist demonstrations had not made much of an impression on the writer W. Somerset Maugham. In Rome for the birth of his daughter, he had seen 'nothing more than mild promenades of two or three hundred peaceable citizens'.[150] Now both 'neutralists' and 'interventionists' were on the streets in force. A demonstration in Milan on 31 March was broken up with 235 arrests, and the death of a worker during socialist demonstrations led to a general strike in Milan on 14 April. In Genoa 5,000 interventionists led by Peppino Garibaldi marched to the Belgian consulate and applauded.

Salandra needed to test the strength of neutralist feeling across the country – whether in order to assess its impact in the event of war against Austria–Hungary or more prosaically simply in order to ensure the maintenance of public order and the authority of the state remains a matter of some dispute. To find out, he sent out a secret circular on 12 April to all the prefects outside Rome asking for their assessment of public feeling in case Italy joined the war. By 21 April, with about half the replies in, he had enough information to close the enquiry. The overwhelming majority of responses, up and down the country, spoke of a passive neutralism, not organised by socialists but spontaneous and indifferent. In the south the population was preoccupied with economic depression, possible unemployment and the potential of war to damage exports. In Campania, Umbria and the Marches there were signs of indifference, but the prefects reported that although overwhelmingly neutralist the population would accept war if properly prepared for it. The north was much the same, and the majority of industrialists were neutralist. Even the Veneto was neutralist – save only for the province of Treviso.[151]

On 5 May Giolitti arrived in Rome to challenge Salandra. A month earlier, Salandra had believed that the only indispensable conditions for entering the war were the preparation of the army and the conclusion of diplomatic accords. The assent of king and parliament were less important 'because the king never gives a clear opinion and the chamber even less'.[152] However, faced with a split parliament and a predomin- antly neutralist country, as well as Allied military setbacks, the king now took the view that it would be possible to back out of the London Pact either by a change of government or by a vote in parliament. Salandra concurred – as he had perforce to do – and offered his resignation on 13 May, thereby ostensibly putting his administration and the future course of government policy in the hands of the country. In fact he had no intention of putting himself in anybody's hands, calculating that the king preferred him to stay on and that Giolitti would not agree to take office in the circumstances. The extent to which he was also expecting that the piazza and the press would return him to power, as some historians have claimed, is more debatable: on 11 May Sonnino warned him that appealing to the crowds to back a war 'could have an opposite effect'.[153] As 'old Right Liberals', neither the premier nor his foreign minister attached much significance to parties and public opinion as forces in play in reaching decisions about foreign policy, which was above party. This was, indeed, the default position in Giolittian Italy.[154]

Giolitti's neutralism was rooted in his scepticism about the fighting capacity and resilience of the nation in the war that was about to start. The rural peasantry would no longer respond instinctively to war, unlike their more backward counterparts in Russia, he thought; nor did it yet possess the conception of citizenship present in Germany, France and Great Britain. Getting there would take generations. Nor did he think much of Italy's generals. Having joined up in the days when families sent only their most stupid sons whom they did not know what to do with into the army, they were worth little. Only the junior officers, 'educated and technically prepared', were of any quality.[155] Mostly, he was wrong: responding instinctively to war in the social context in which it arrived is more or less exactly what the peasantry did, and Italy's junior officers were wanting in both numbers and preparation. About the generals he may have had a point.

For a week, Italy was without a government. Cadorna was forced to halt mobilisation as Salandra lacked the political authority to allow preparations to continue for a war which, if Giolitti came to power, would not happen. Behind the scenes, though, activity continued: a cabinet meeting sanctioned another tranche of military spending, and the king ordered Zupelli not to slow down or suspend war preparations. The interventionists responded to Giolitti's arrival in Rome by coming out onto the streets. In the south, the traditional *classe dirigente* was joined by social reformists, radicals and republicans, motivated by a mix of anti-Giolittian sentiments (Salandra was from Puglia), anti-Austrianism and monarchism. In central Italy the demonstrations were more evenly balanced. In the north, Milan was massively in support of the war, as was Venice, while Turin witnessed strong anti-war demonstrations.[156]

The crisis was short-lived for, as all the main protagonists recognised, there was now no turning back. On 16 May the king refused Salandra's resignation. Giolitti left Rome next day, and on 20 May the chamber of deputies gave Salandra extraordinary powers amid reports of widespread patriotic feeling. By the king's own account, it had been 'touch and go'. When a count of the likely votes in the chamber showed the two sides were very closely balanced 'he had decided that he must make it known that he was determined to abdicate if the policy he knew to be the right one for Italy were not adopted'. His success had been 'immediate and complete'.[157] On 23 May the chamber approved the declaration of war on Austria–Hungary. Immediately before the declaration, the prefect of Livorno (Leghorn) reported a 'profound transformation' in the public mood.[158] Hostilities began next day.

Much has been made of the political divisions that were evident in Italy as she joined the war, and of the political manipulation that levered her into it: later Salandra admitted that in spring 1915 war was 'understood and desired' only by a small minority of the population.[159] To be sure, Italy had her own special problems: high levels of illiteracy, strong local loyalties (*campanilismo*) and sharp social stratification. But turn the picture around and Italy shared several fundamental features in common with other combatant powers. Everywhere small groups of oligarchic politicians took the decision that war was a justifiable and necessary step. National assemblies all fell into line behind them. Italy went to war in what was perceived by those who made the decisions as the national interest – just like everybody else. And recent research has swept away the idea that the populations of western Europe were drenched in patriotic enthusiasm and militarism in favour of a more nuanced picture of peoples whose dominating emotions combined elements of worry, obligation and resignation. Here too Italy was not that much different from the peoples she would now be ranged alongside and those she would be seeking to defeat.

On 16 May Cadorna issued the commanders of 2nd and 3rd Armies their operational orders. Their troops were to advance on the Isonzo as fast as possible in 'an energetic and improvised irruption' with the aim of securing jumping-off points for further offensives. The Trentino 'wedge' was left aside: while pre-war plans had contemplated cutting it off as a necessary preliminary to any attack to the east, Cadorna lacked the heavy siege artillery he considered essential to reduce the Austrian forts there. Ironically, the objectives he selected for the first 'bound forward' included Monte Nero, Sleme and Mrzli Vrh east of the Isonzo. The Italian army would not reach them until 1916 and would never get beyond them.[160]

Already Cadorna had abandoned any ideas of a quick campaign and a short war.[161] It would be an illusion, he warned Zupelli, to believe that the coming campaign might be brief. The organisation, richness of means and moral solidity of their enemies, especially Germany, gave every reason to think that they would put up a tenacious resistance to the end. It was therefore essential that Italy had new units ready to enter the field in spring 1916. Accordingly he requested that the war minister urgently order the arms, equipment and clothing for another 50 infantry regiments, 14 battalions of *Bersaglieri*, 40 companies of *Alpini* and as many batteries of field, heavy field, mountain and pack artillery as possible. With these reinforcements Italy could assure herself of final victory in 1916 'if it is not given to us to obtain it before then'.[162]

As Cadorna's 400,000 troops began to mass on the frontier for war, almost everything that could go wrong for him did so. The pre-war design was for the Italian attack on Austria–Hungary to coincide with simultaneous attacks by Serbia from the south and Russia from the east. Aware of Italian designs on Istria and Dalmatia and unwilling to help them in any way, the Serbs launched an attack on Albania instead, while the Russians began a five-month retreat into the depths of Russian Poland. The enemy was ready and waiting. The Austrian army had a good background knowledge of Italy's defences and of where she would put her army if it came to war: Austro-Hungarian military intelligence – the *Evidenzbureau* – had been in possession of the plans of the permanent Italian fortifications along the frontier since 1907, and knew in 1910 that Italy's planned deployment had shifted from the Livenza to the Tagliamento. Its deciphering service was well equipped to read its enemy's mind: between 1912 and 1914 it got hold of the *cifrario rosso* used by the general staff in war, the 'Mengarini' code used by Italian troops in Albania (openly for sale in bookshops) and the *Carabinieri*'s 'special cipher'.[163] Thanks to Ambassador Avarna's carelessness, it also had the Italian foreign office cipher: on a visit to the Austrian foreign ministry in 1913, he had left behind a bag containing both the text of a telegram in cipher and its unenciphered version.[164]

Finally, surprise had gone by the board. On 9 May the German military attaché in Rome reported that an Italian offensive was likely very shortly. It was already possible to discern the distribution of Italian forces: 'From this one can deduce that the Italian army will stand on the defensive against the Trentino in order to act *in massa* across the Isonzo.'[165] Conrad had already given orders the previous month to resist on the Isonzo, block the entrances to the valleys around Tolmino and organise the defences along the western edge of the Carso. When the Italian army arrived at the Isonzo, it found the Austrian army ready and waiting, ensconced in trenches protected by three belts of barbed wire and a mined zone 5 metres wide.

With the decision for war taken and the army in action, soldiers and politicians entered an entirely new landscape. Politicians now faced the task of mobilising the material and social resources of the state to support not the short war which Cadorna had initially promised them, but one whose duration was impossible to forecast. Cadorna's powers of command and his generals' operational capabilities would be tried, and his soldiers' mettle tested. In the coming year one issue in particular would come to the fore: who in Italy was in control of the war? The pattern of peacetime civil–military relations would be turned upside down as Cadorna subordinated military and civilians alike to his iron will.

3   1915 – First endeavours

A desperate country to fight in.
Brigadier-General Charles Delmé-Radcliffe, 25 October 1915

Before the war Italy had been 'the least of the Great Powers'. That had been a diplomatic truth but now the opening phase of her war showed that it was also a military truth. Indeed, if Austria–Hungary had not been engaged in driving the Russian army back deep into Poland and had turned her full attentions on her former ally instead, Italy might well not have lived to fight another day. In the first seven months of the war Cadorna fought four battles of the Isonzo (seven more would follow in the years to come) all to no avail. In the face of huge physical obstacles and a well-entrenched enemy strategy failed, commanders failed, and the rank and file of the army began to show the first signs of the very reactions Cadorna feared – disillusion and disobedience. His response was to begin what became an ever more forceful tightening of the disciplinary screw. Behind the firing lines supply, while it did not entirely fail, barely sufficed to keep the armies going. Slowly, and with difficulty, Italy began to build its own version of a war economy.

Like his fellow commanders in the west, Cadorna skirmished with the government over peripheral theatres which either he (in the case of Albania) or they (in the case of Greece) regarded as distractions from the main business of the war. As the New Year dawned he faced the one serious attempt to unseat him as *generalissimo* – and showed himself to be as skilful as a political in-fighter as he was inflexible as a commander.

Going to the war

In May 1915 Giani Stuparich, a 24-year-old volunteer from Trieste, joined the 1st regiment of Sardinan Grenadiers – a crack unit. He left Rome on 2 June, a brand new soldier from his beret to his boots, and had his first encounter with the reality of war next day when his transport passed a hospital train standing in Mestre station which smelled of blood and iodine. Shortly afterwards he was on the Isonzo where the scent of war was a mixture of pine resin and gunpowder.[1] Six weeks later Luigi Gasparotto left Rome to cries of 'Lucky you ... you're [all] going to breath clear air!' In line two weeks later, he experienced for the first time the striking dissonances that made the Italian front a terrifying place. In front of a menacing line of Austrian fortifications, Italian dead from the June offensive lay still waiting to be buried.[2]

Getting to the front in the first weeks of the war could be a wearying and frustrating business. Giovanni Mira, a schoolteacher and a patriot, belonged to the 35th infantry division. Every morning for a month it formed up in columns and marched along dusty roads under the June sun while express trains on the Milan–Venice line ran by half empty. He and his companions suffered from the heat, from thirst, from the dust, from the hours spent in marching columns 'but above all from feeling that we were suffering a useless hardship ... That month could have been put to use to give us rational, intensive, modern training in war service and then we could have been moved up by rail.' Then, climbing up a steep slope above the valle dell'Astico, 'I got a scent of Alpine air and pines and tiredness disappeared.' Around and below him stretched the *altipiani* of Lavarone and Asiago, 'a sylvan rural countryside spread with fields and stands of conifers'.[3]

Soldier T. F. of the 91st infantry regiment had a less agreeable experience with a profoundly unfortunate outcome. He recorded leaving home amidst a general feeling of indifference to the war and universal sadness, and half his unit threw themselves to the ground during their march to the front from a combination of exhaustion and food that was both bad and insufficient. When he and his companions got to the Cadore, the locals attempted to attack one of their encampments. He incautiously went on to record troop movements, the extreme shortage of artillery and the heavy cost of several early attacks before being captured by the Austrians. Extracts of his diary were published in an Innsbruck newspaper and though they were anonymous the authorities worked out who the author was. He was sentenced in absentia to fifteen years in a military prison for having furnished the enemy with information damaging to the state.[4]

The region to which the soldiers were coming – the Veneto – was among the poorest and most backward in the country. Before the war large numbers of the population emigrated to find work in Austria, France and Belgium, or else to go to the United States, Brazil or Argentina, earning it the soubriquet 'the Calabria of the North'. One hundred thousand *veneziani* left between 1909 and 1913, and 162,361 returned in the first months of the war because of the employment crisis everywhere following the outbreak of war. At home, the average daily earnings of workers, agricultural day-labourers and small independent proprietors was between 18 and 80 *centesimi* (one-hundredth part of a lire) a day. They ate no meat or higher-grade cereals. Pellagra, tuberculosis and syphilis were rife, as was alcoholism. In the isolated valleys inbreeding resulted in cretinism. Some of this would have been familiar to many of the conscripts who came from central and southern Italy. What was unfamiliar was the country, which would have its impact on them both as individuals and as fighting men.[5]

For the soldiers arriving at the war everything was new and everywhere was challenging. As they advanced to the front, men asked their officers whether plains or mountains lay between them and Trieste. In the Tyrol they faced well-prepared lines of defences strengthened with steel cupolas and machine-gun turrets. In the distance, the Dolomites sparkled in the clear mountain air. Snow, at first a novelty, would soon become an obstacle and an enemy. It began falling in early October. To Luigi Gasparotto, still capable of seeing beauty amidst the horrors of war, it made the fir trees look like Christmas trees and turned the barbed wire entanglements into silver hedges.[6] Such poetic images were soon displaced by more sombre thoughts. For the poet Giuseppe Ungaretti, writing two years later, snow had become a sign of mourning; 'white gives me the sense of things ending, the iciness of death'.[7]

Arriving at the Isonzo river on 16 September 1915, Benito Mussolini was struck by its extraordinarily blue waters – as one is today. If he is to be believed, he bent and drank a mouthful 'with sacred devotion'. Behind Monfalcone, on the lower Isonzo, the green plains of Friuli stretched away into the distance at the soldiers' backs. To their front, beyond the enemy entrenchments, the Gulf of Trieste sparkled in the middle distance, the Adriatic shimmered beyond it, and the coast of Istria stretched away into the blue.

When the troops reached the Isonzo, they faced an enemy whose powers of resistance were multiplied by the terrain and the weather. The ground across which they had to attack was decidedly not on their side. The front line, stretching some 650 kilometres from the Swiss border to the sea, comprised three separate zones. In the west, the Asiago plateau, centre of the Trentino front, was a heavily wooded undulating area at an average height of 1,000 metres, surrounded by peaks more than twice that high. There were only three routes up to it, and no lateral communications other than mule tracks to either side. In the centre – the *Zona Carnia* – the Dolomites reached up to 3,000 metres. The third main theatre of war, the Isonzo, was dominated by the Bainsizza plateau, averaging some 800 metres above sea level, and further south by the

Fig. 2 Italian troops passing through a village

Carso, described by the British official historian Sir James Edmonds as 'a howling wilderness with stones as sharp as knives', that rose steeply from a thin strip of coastal plain no more than 10 kilometres wide to heights of between 300 and 650 metres.

On the Isonzo, infantry found themselves attacking up slopes at angles of between 20 and 80 degrees, overlooked by elevations varying in height between 100 and 1,000 metres. Italian artillery could not follow them up inclines as steep as these, leaving them entirely without fire support when they reached the enemy's wire. Their possession of the higher ground gave the Austrians distinct tactical advantages: the Italians' visibility meant that they could economise on manpower in defending unthreatened sections of their line, and use their artillery on the eastern bank of the Isonzo to break up attacks launched from the western slopes. One Austrian general said it was like 'firing from a ten-story building'.[8] The narrow river valley itself gave the Italians no space in which to manoeuvre. On the limestone plateau of the Carso, as yet still covered with scattered trees and shrubs, the Austrians turned natural cup-shaped depressions (*dolline*) into strong defensive positions protected by three tiers of barbed wire each between 6 and 9 metres deep.

Ground alone produced unforeseen and crippling tactical consequences. On the second day of the war, the 33rd infantry division found it impossible to keep its cohesion because the rocky ground split the linear formations into fractions with the result that when it reached the enemy's positions it lacked the strength to break through. On only a single day during the first six months of the war was a lone division able to launch an attack across fairly level ground with adequate artillery preparation, advancing 1,500 metres before running out of steam.[9] During the advance to the front, Gasparotto's battalion commander had spent three days reading and commenting on Cadorna's '*Attacco frontale*'. He found it unpersuasive and experience quickly bore him out.

The climate was no friend either. Suffocating heat in the daytime, when temperatures rose to as much as 30 degrees centigrade, was followed by sharp, cold nights. Fog, caused by relatively high humidity and constantly changing temperatures, persisted until early afternoon in the summer and became more severe in the winter, hindering observation and affecting the accuracy of the guns. Sporadic summer storms filled the gullies with run-off water; then, in October, the three-month rainy season began. Downpours often seemed to come on days when heavy bombardments preceded attacks, creating a belief that the artillery was disturbing the atmosphere. There was also the *bora* to contend with – a north-easterly wind which could reach speeds of 200 kilometres an hour. Stuparich quickly felt its full effects:

The wind whistles round corners and furiously chokes the loopholes. The trunks of the pine trees seem to writhe, their branches waving like mad skeletons, and the bushes shake as if they want to leave the earth. The heavy rain, strengthened by the *bora*, passes over like a squadron at the gallop.[10]

Nature exerted the full spectrum of its effects. Men plagued by mosquitoes and lice were enchanted when the guns stopped and the birds at once began to sing.

What the soldiers thought as they trudged up to the front lines and prepared to carry out Cadorna's first attacks is hard to know. Fascist rhetoric afterwards drenched the war and its participants with patriotic and martial verbiage.[11] Enthusiastic nationalists, aching to release Trieste from Austrian tyranny and some no doubt intoxicated by Futurism's hymns to violence, railed against the rank and file's apparently emotionless outlook on the war:

Who knows why, no-one sings. The smell of blood spurts within me like a must in my veins, giving me the cruel taste of joy and violence. Already I seem to possess death as one violently takes a beautiful woman – and they, bent and long- eared like mules, paw grotesquely along the sides of the road without a shout or a song. Why?[12]

Long afterwards, survivors felt baffled as to why they were there – but memory is often an unreliable guide to past emotions.

For the rural peasantry who provided the army with its largest numerical component, there was no commanding moral cause behind the nation's mobilisation for war. Brought into being by the narrow political elite, it was the war of the *signori* – a necessary evil which once begun had to be seen through. Adolfo Omodeo, himself a veteran of the war and later one of Italy's most distinguished historians, thought that what kept the men going was 'a male sense of *bravura*, devotion to their officers, anger and vexation with the enemy, [and] the desire to avenge dead comrades'.[13] Curzio Malaparte, with his own populist line to propound, afterwards saw it differently: the Italian soldier, lacking the collectivist orientation of the Slavs, fought out of a combination of goodness of spirit and 'truly individualistic Mediterranean fatalism'.[14] Marxist socialists, to be found among the industrial workers who made up the other main component of the rank and file, believed at the time and afterwards that the war had been started by the *classe dirigente* to serve their own political and economic interests and to break the workers' movement.[15] No doubt some of the troops brought their pre-war political or ideological perspectives with them as they marched up to the line, but perhaps that is not the whole story. Luigi Gasparotto's unit, the 154th infantry regiment, were socialists to a man: when they left Varese for the front, the only thing to be heard was a shout of 'Down with the war'. By mid August, the first taste of action had turned them into 'magnificent soldiers'.[16]

For the majority of soldiers, the *questione Risorgimentale* – the notion that the war was being fought to expunge the final traces of Austrian rule and complete the unification of Italy by taking the 'unredeemed lands' – was an abstraction. Junior officers could recognise their patriotic duty to the nation and were expected to nurse a sense of honour. To 'revive the aggressive spirit' of the troops, they were issued with notes on how to make every soldier hate the enemy.

Every soldier must see the enemy not in terms of how he personally can be hurt but as the centuries old enemy. Every soldier, confronted by the enemy, must be the avenger and the executioner. Dangerous feelings of compassion arising from shared suffering and danger must be extinguished, and the love of quiet which smothers any provocative acts in the hope of the same treatment must cease. The enemy must be given no rest ...[17]

Discipline – 'the spiritual flame of victory' according to a circular of Cadorna's that awaited Gasparotto when he came out of line on 13 October 1915 – was starting to become an obsession, and there were signs of the decay and dissolution that Cadorna came increasingly to suspect and to fear. During 1915, 845 Italian soldiers deserted to the enemy, the highest annual figure of the war, and there were 8,492 desertions 'not in the presence of the enemy' – a figure that would triple in 1916 and double again in 1917. Discipline was applied – in a rather different way – at the higher as well as the lowest levels of the army as Cadorna began the ongoing practice of sacking generals, an action he thought necessary not least because of the large number of 'pessimists' in Italy at large and in the army in particular.[18]

Opening rounds

In the first fortnight of the war Italy lost what few advantages she might have had. Austrian troops were still relatively thin on the ground at the outset – there were only 35,000 men and 685 guns to guard the Austrian Tyrol – and Conrad, perhaps aware of their uncertain quality, had initially planned to abandon the Carso and let the Italians advance into the heart of the Julian Alps before launching a counter-offensive. The timidity of the Italian advance caused him to change his mind.[19] The piecemeal arrival of units on the frontier, forced on Cadorna by the political and military contours of the weeks preceding 24 May, did not help. Nor, it must be said, did his direction of the armies he commanded. His directives immediately before and after the start of the war were first offensive and then defensive in tone. Army commanders were more or less simultaneously told that the enemy did not intend seriously to contest the Italian advance and that they should therefore profit from this state of affairs 'gaining as much territory as possible', and then required to ensure the inviolability of the frontier and carry the occupation into enemy territory only where it was both possible and convenient in order to procure positions from which to launch subsequent offensives beyond the Isonzo. Barely a fortnight after the war had started Cadorna instructed his generals that it was often useful in mountains to cede ground inch by inch when it was not essential to the defence.[20]

The first Italian moves were mostly hesitant and the effort dispersed. On the left of the front, 1st Army's general Roberto Brusati planned to grab the dominating positions of Monte Pasubio, Monte Altissimo and Monte Maggio. Firing the opening salvo in an exchange which would sink Brusati the following year, Cadorna warned him that they were 'naturally strong positions' whose conquest could well turn out to be both bloody and sterile, and reminded him that the task of 1st Army was 'for the moment defensive'. However, somewhat contradictorily, he then added that the idea of possessing them 'should not be given up completely' and that Brusati should consider conducting an offensive to aid 4th Army to his right.[21] When the fighting started and the Austrians in front of him retreated to their defensive line Brusati's men occupied Pasubio and other important crests. They were the only successes in the first days of the war.

Elsewhere things went awry from the start. General Nava's 4th Army was supposed to break into the Drava valley and swing both east towards Tarvisio, linking with troops advancing from the *Zona Carnia*, and west towards Franzenfeste. The day before the war began Nava issued a 'stupifying' order to his corps commanders: given that the enemy could have brought up large forces, they were to report on what operations were possible without running grave risks. Caution was to be their watchword.[22] Four days later Cadorna ordered 4th Army forward across the frontier, exhorting all his army commanders to take advantage of an enemy 'who does not intend seriously to contest our advance' and to act 'offensively [and] with daring'.[23] One of Nava's corps did indeed occupy Cortina d'Ampezzo, which the Austrians evacuated, on 29 May but then everything stopped for a week while Nava asked his subordinates what they thought they could do without running serious risks. His offensive, when it started, came too late. Over the next three months his troops carried out a series of attacks in parlous circumstances: the siege park could not go into action until 5 July, the guns were short of ammunition, the troops lacked even garden shears to cut the enemy wire, and there was not a single Italian aeroplane in the skies above them. They were bloodily repulsed. On 20 September Cadorna ordered a temporary defensive and five days later Nava was removed.

On Nava's right General Clemente Lequio, commanding the *Zona Carnia*, lacked the heavy siege artillery he needed to knock out the forts of Malborghetto and Predil which blocked the passes leading to Tarvisio and Villach. His artillery bombardments did not begin until 12 June. On the main Isonzo front, General Pietro Frugoni's 2nd Army walked up to the right bank of the river, occupying Mount Kolovrat, Korada and Caporetto and then, instead of pushing on to occupy the heights of Sleme and Mrzli that dominated the left bank, they halted and dug in. When the *brigata Modena* tried twice to take the heights facing them, on 29–30 May and 2 June, the Austrians were ready for them.

Things went no better on the lower Isonzo. Zuccari's 3rd Army lost its commander on the third day of the war when Cadorna sacked him after he refused to occupy Monte Medea immediately on the grounds that his troops were not ready. Zuccari was independent-minded, and perhaps more significantly had been a favourite of Cadorna's predecessor as chief of the general staff, Alberto Pollio. He also had a reputation in the army as a dandy and something of a lightweight. Zuccari's successor,

Emanuele Filiberto duca d'Aosta, was recovering from illness, so for the first few days of the war the army was without an effective commander. Further down the chain of command, General Pirozzi was sacked after his cavalry division dawdled and so failed to capture the bridges across the lower Isonzo at Pieris which would have opened a route onto the Carso, allowing them to be destroyed by the enemy. After the war Cadorna put a positive spin on the first days of his campaign, claiming that as a result of his army's advances the Austro-Hungarians had lost a large part of the offensive value of the Isonzo line, leaving them with only the two bridgeheads of Tolmino and Gorizia, and that the successes in the Trentino made possible the entire two-and-a-half-year campaign in the Julian Alps that was to come and the subsequent defence of the Piave.[24] It was not a convincing defence.

On 30 May, Cadorna moved into the archbishop's palace at Udine. It would be his permanent headquarters for the next two and a half years, a place he left to fight his political battles in Rome and to visit his commanders who were fighting their own battles at the front. Despite its shaky start, he thought the army was in excellent shape, its character quite different from the peacetime manoeuvre army. Discipline was improving daily thanks to the examples he was making. News of the sackings of Zuccari and Pirozzi would, he believed, 'remove all hesitation and give everyone the necessary offensive spirit'. Already the war was confirming his conviction that in the exercise of command what mattered more than intelligence was character and will.[25] Officers who did not measure up to his standards and his demands would be axed ruthlessly and without a moment's hesitation: in little more than two years Cadorna would fire 217 generals, 255 colonels and 337 lieutenant-colonels.

During the first three weeks in June, the Italians made small local advances, crossing the lower Isonzo to get onto the edge of the Carso *altopiano* between Sagrado and Monfalcone and seizing a foothold at Plava on the left bank of the middle Isonzo. An attack on Podgora by two army corps, part of Cadorna's wish to test the defences around Gorizia, was beaten back by Austrian artillery and machine-gun fire. Faced with strong Austrian trenches and barbed wire, Cadorna concluded that there was no longer any place for the kind of imaginative brilliance that relied on rapidity of manoeuvre. Instead, he told premier Salandra, the enemy's positions would have to be tackled using 'method and patience'. Grandiose strategic horizons shrank in the face of the reality of war. The immediate target of operations was now the city of Gorizia, a fortified enemy camp. Taking it would require first capturing some formidable mountain peaks protecting the city: Monte Sabotino to the north, Monte San Michele to the south, and Monte Santo, Monte

San Gabriele and Monte San Daniele to the west. Overcoming the enemy's resistance, he told his army commanders, would necessitate an adequate concentration of men and guns, but above all use of 'the method suggested by the experience of combat in the other allied theatres of operations, avoiding improvised attacks which although they show the valour of our troops do not allow [us] to achieve results proportional to [our] losses'.[26]

His hopes of a fast campaign shattered, Cadorna made the first of many complaints about the discordance of allied strategy and its adverse effects on the Italian front. Intelligence indicated that Austria–Hungary had moved all or almost all its forces in Serbia to the Italian front, as well as some from Galicia. In the front line, untried Italians were facing mountain troops with ten months' war experience. If the enemy attacked and if his troops had to abandon any conquered territory then this would have a bad effect on 'an impressionable country like ours'. The Allies were not helping. The French offensive had not prevented the Germans moving troops, probably to the Tyrol–Trentino front; the Russians had not been able to immobilise the Austrians on the Galician front; and the Serbians were completely passive 'for suspect reasons'. Sonnino's remonstrations with Russian and Serbian diplomats had evidently not worked so Cadorna decided to put the matter to the king. He suggested summoning the Allied military representatives and getting them to fix an exact date for contemporaneous offensives – his preference being late June or early July, when the Hungarian harvest was due. The Austrians would either have to send troops on leave or move entire detachments to do the work or else sacrifice a large part of it.[27]

A weary sounding Salandra told Cadorna that the Russians could not be forced to fight and were probably conducting an enforced retreat in the face of *forza maggiore*, and that pressure was being put on the Serbs. This cut no mustard with the chief of the general staff. Information from St Petersburg suggested that the Russians would be in no shape to resume the offensive for at least two months. The Italian army would soon have in front of it almost all the Austro-Hungarian army as well as some Germans and they might try to invade Italy. Cadorna wanted effective allied support as soon as possible. Among other things Serbia, presently claiming that she was in difficulties as far as fighting the Austrians was concerned because of the flooding of the Sava and Danube rivers, must be reminded of the agreements she had made and the pacts that had been signed.[28]

Scarcely a month after the fighting began, Cadorna acknowledged that things were not going as well as he had expected. The explanation was to be found in material constraints that were afflicting all the Allied armies, and particularly his own. The formidable enemy entrenchments facing him all along the frontier could only be mastered with 'monstrous quantities of ammunition' and more medium- and heavy-calibre guns. Needs must be calculated on the assumption that the war would last through the whole of 1916. With some reason given their woeful peace-time performance in developing and procuring artillery, he believed that the technical departments of the war ministry were not up to the task of large-scale ammunition production. What was now needed, he told Salandra, was a ministry of munitions along British lines, or an autonomous organisation within the ministry as in Russia.[29] The pressing question was: who to put in charge of the new body? Cadorna thought that Salandra should head it himself and suggested General Alfredo Dallolio, currently director-general of artillery and engineers, as his assistant.[30]

Salandra was not willing to contemplate creating a new ministry. Instead the cabinet agreed to set up a special committee under Sonnino to study the question. There were pressing reasons to move more quickly. After a month of combat it was already clear that vast and almost limitless consumption of ammunition was going to be the order of the day. Twenty-two guns had already blown up, for reasons so far unknown. Two more of the older 149A medium field howitzers blew up the following week – between June and December one hundred and thirty-nine 149-mm guns would explode – and by the beginning of July Cadorna was growing increasingly worried that unless there was large-scale manufacture of the new model 145 he would shortly have no medium guns at all and be unable to continue operations.[31]

On 9 July 1915, Dallolio was appointed to the new post of under-secretary for arms and munitions in the war ministry. He at once offered industry a premium for every round of 149-mm howitzer ammunition over contract produced during July and August and promised 30,000 rounds of 149A ammunition for August, equating to ten rounds per gun per day. This was only half what Cadorna believed he needed. Action on the *altopiano* was presently languishing for lack of medium-calibre ammunition, he told the premier.[32] In early September he was still waiting for anti-aircraft ammunition and for thirty-two new 210-mm mortars while premature explosions were destroying guns and howitzers that could not be replaced. His solution – an ideal if ever there was one – was to double the number of state arsenals and private factories and workshops.[33]

Munitions supply was a serious and pressing issue and would remain so for some considerable time to come. It was also one component of the turf war that now developed between the chief of the general staff and the war minister. The back-story was a fast-deteriorating personal relationship which cannot have made it any easier to conduct the war. When he found out in late July 1915 that Zupelli was proposing to establish a special commission to recommend honours for active service, which he thought was the prerogative of the *Comando supremo*, Cadorna was furious.[34] 'With an enemy in front of me, I don't intend to have another one sitting behind me in the *palazzo* at via XX settembre [the war ministry],' he told his daughter.[35] The imbroglio was smoothed over, but it reinforced Cadorna's conviction that he was battling the government and domestic opposition as well as the Austrians. 'I'm getting information from everywhere that Giolittians, freemasons and socialists are working to make me fall,' he told his daughter.[36]

As chief of the general staff and de facto field commander, Cadorna was responsible for the mobilised army, for territory deemed to be 'in a state of war' (the fighting fronts and the regions immediately to their rear), and for the development of military operations. The war ministry in turn was responsible for mobilising, organising, equipping and arming the field army. When Cadorna began to try to make good the desperate shortage of officers by combing as many as possible out of secondary jobs, sending them to the front, and replacing them with officers from the territorial militia and the reserve, and by instituting competitive examinations to nominate suitably educated civilians as reserve officers, Zupelli complained that his authority was being transgressed. Cadorna refused to budge, convinced that he was well within his rights and that Zupelli had been attributing to himself powers he did not have.[37]

On 1 July 1915, Cadorna sent Zupelli detailed proposals for the creation of new units by spring 1916. To forestall possible complaints that he was exceeding his powers, his covering letter stressed that this was not a theoretical study but a concrete programme, and that in ten months it would bring to the field 'forces which could be enough to tip the balance in our favour'.[38] The *Comando supremo* calculated that there were 600,000 men available to keep the mobilised units up to strength over the winter, and another 1,000,000 untrained category III men in the older classes (aged between 28 and 39). Taking in the class of 1896 and re-examining men whose service had been postponed could produce an additional 300,000 young recruits, enough to form eight or ten new army corps. While manpower could be found, officers – especially tested ones – were in very short supply. Accelerated three-month courses for reserve officers at the military schools in Modena and Turin, along with the regimental schools, could produce 9,000 new officers, but that might not be enough even to keep up the numbers in the mobilised army until next spring. New courses of between one and three months would be needed for potential officers in the new units and *aspiranti* in any of the annual classes. The army was also going to have to look to promoting non-commissioned officers and any ordinary soldier whose conduct on the battlefield gave evidence of *merito di guerra*. Artillery was another problem. On the basis that Italy could produce 456 field guns during the year, foreign sources would need to supply unspecified numbers of 75-mm field guns (Italy could provide 240), 105-mm heavy field guns (there were 24 Italian guns) and 149-mm howitzers. At 2,000 rounds per gun for field artillery and 1,600 rounds for heavy artillery, the ammunition demands show that Cadorna and his staff were still seriously underestimating requirements.[39]

The first battle of the Isonzo began on 23 June 1915. Frugoni's 2nd Army put in the main attack, launching divergent assaults on Monte Kuk from Plava and on the heights of Oslavia–Podgora, while Aosta's 3rd Army advanced as far as possible to the rim of the Carso *altopiano* between Monfalcone and Sagrado. Method amounted to no more than launching soldiers almost literally bareheaded – steel helmets did not arrive on the Italian front until 1916 – against Austrian defences. The Italian artillery gave the first evidence of endemic shortcomings, the result of a combination of insufficient numbers of medium and heavy guns, inadequate supplies of ammunition, and poor doctrine. Fire support was weak and not concentrated on the attack points, gaps in the enemy's wire were insufficient, and the troops lacked wire-cutters with which to try to get through the entanglements. The attacks broke down immediately as advancing lines of Italian troops were cut to pieces at close range by Austrian rifle and machine-gun fire. On the Bainsizza, heat and thirst multiplied the troops' agony. The only success came on the Carso, but although Aosta requested reinforcements Cadorna failed to see and take advantage of the opportunity in time. Two hundred and fifty thousand men went into the battle. By the time it ended on 7 July, 2,000 were dead, 11,500 wounded and 1,500 missing. By comparison with what was to come Cadorna's first set-piece offensive was not much more than a particularly bloody skirmish.

Already there were signs of the tactical and operational deficiencies that were to multiply the effects of the enemy's actions and the natural obstructions. Frugoni, a general who did not inspire confidence in the king's aide-de-camp, opened fire all along his line in the afternoon of 8 June in an attempt to get the Austrians to unmask their batteries. A weak response suggested that the enemy, turning the tables, was locating Italian batteries in order to be able to respond when it most suited them.[40] Italian artillery stopped firing a few minutes before assaults started, leaving the troops unsupported. Primitive wire-cutters – in short supply – and tubes of explosives made little or no inroads into uncut barbed wire. The infantry advanced in tight formations, led by officers wearing peacetime uniforms and badges of rank – there were protests when they were ordered to remove the frogging from their jackets – and carrying swords (before the fighting began Cadorna was concerned to know whether officers in the armies that were already fighting carried swords into battle), all of which made them perfect targets for sharpshooters. To Austrian soldiers, they made for better shooting than the targets on the firing ranges. Heavy losses were officially institutionalised when Frugoni issued a circular on 18 June ordering that units must not be thought incapable of carrying on combat until they had lost three-quarters of their strength.[41]

There was little or no help from the air. Thanks to bureaucratic turf wars, Italian air power was in a parlous state when the world war began. An initial budget allocation had been made in 1910, but Pollio was sceptical about the utility of aeroplanes and dirigibles and did all he could before the war to ensure that the air component did not develop into a semi-autonomous *corpo unico* ('separate corps') and remained subject to his authority as chief of the general staff rather than that of the war ministry. In June 1914 war minister Spingardi tabled a parliamentary bill calling for a halt to any large-scale aeronautical developments to allow for 'a period of reflection, of wise and efficacious organization of aircraft presently available [and] careful study of technical, scientific, and employment-utilization issues so that, when circumstances permit an increase of our air fleet, military aviation will be ready'.[42] The imminence of war persuaded the government at least partially to resolve issues of autonomy and authority, and in January 1915 a royal decree established the *Corpo Aeronautica Militare* and the government allocated a budget of 16,500,000 lire. The air arm was, though, as General Zupelli acknowledged in March 1915, in an 'unfortunate and serious condition'. Only four of its fifteen active squadrons were Nieuport fighters in good condition; the remaining forty-four aircraft were more or less obsolescent Farmans and Blériots.

Cadorna's headquarters issued regulations for air reconnaissance on the eve of the first battle of the Isonzo. Experience so far suggested that it only worked when carried out at the same time as ground attacks, a moment at which the enemy was forced to reveal troop positions and movements and the location of his gun batteries. Successful reconnaissance also required close relations between land and air commanders so that the airmen knew what was wanted and could satisfy the needs of the infantry as quickly and as completely as possible. This was to be achieved by daily contact and by establishing rapid and secure telephone communications, which did not presently exist, linking airfields with command headquarters. Where necessary, messages could be dropped on agreed locations near ground headquarters.[43] This counsel of perfection failed to achieve its goals. In the first battle of the Isonzo, Austrian aircraft were able, using air reconnaissance, to identify Italian units on the battlefield and during the course of the battle the station at Cividale was bombed and four Italian observation balloons shot down. The gap between the two sides was even more evident in the second battle of the Isonzo: co-operation between Italian ground and air units was poor, while the Austrians, who had observed the preparations for the offensive from the air, used photographs of the Italian front lines and made the first attempts at aerial spotting of enemy artillery positions.[44]

Making strategy in wartime, Cadorna was learning, was a very different matter than designing it in peacetime. For one thing, Italy was now a member of a military partnership. On 7 July an allied conference at Chantilly confirmed that Italy's military task was to develop the action she had already undertaken towards Ljubljana and Villach as rapidly as possible while Great Britain, France and Serbia prepared large offensives. In practical terms, the more Italy attacked now the more she helped herself by helping her allies. The Austrians, Cadorna calculated, were having to put as many troops on the Italian front as on the French and Russian fronts, which facilitated the work of the British and French on the western front and simultaneously helped the Russians to reconstitute their forces. Italy's actions had therefore to be considered 'not only for the effect they have on our theatre of war, but also and more particularly for their repercussions on the entire European theatre'. If the Allies could co-ordinate their strategies, they would win.[45] A considerable part of the responsibility for achieving this fell to the politicians, of whom he had a uniformly low opinion. He also felt strongly that Italy should declare war against Germany: 'We do much for the Allies, but they do as much and more for us and to keep them in suspense about our intentions is anything but good policy.'[46] As far as enlarging the war as Cadorna wanted was concerned Salandra and Sonnino would keep their alliance partners in suspense until 28 August 1916, much to the Allies' annoyance at the time and afterwards.

Cadorna could not afford to pause and the Allies were anxious that he did not. Grand Duke Nicholas asked for help from the Allied armies and as the second battle of the Isonzo got under way Joffre urged his Italian opposite number in the common interest not to falter: the French were causing the Germans (and themselves) considerable losses and the continuance of the 'energetic' offensive by the Italians was evidence of the convergence of the Allies' strategic efforts. Cadorna, who had just switched the last reserve army corps in the Tyrol to the Isonzo front, thought it unlikely that the Austrians could shift any troops away while the Italian offensives continued.[47] Hard information was difficult to come by: in late July the Italian military attaché in Russia reported intelligence suggesting that Austrian divisions were being withdrawn from the Russian front and sent elsewhere, but a month later he had to admit that though there were lots of enemy troop movements on the southern Russian front he could not say where they were going.[48] On at least one occasion what seemed like confirmatory evidence of Austrian troops movements to the Isonzo front turned out to be regurgitated information originally distributed by Italian military intelligence.[49]

Cadorna's intention was to attempt as much strategic manoeuvre as the situation would allow.[50] Gorizia, which he saw as an outlet from which the enemy could threaten 3rd Army, almost all of which was now across the Isonzo, was the main target. As the first step towards its capture, 3rd Army would tackle the southern pillar of its defences, which hinged on Monte San Michele, while 2nd Army carried out diversionary action at Plava in support. The second battle of the Isonzo began on 18 July and two days later the peaks of San Michele were in Italian hands. Other heights were taken and held, but as was so often to happen in the months to come local success on San Michele was only temporary. A violent Austrian artillery bombardment overnight followed by a two-hour hand-to-hand fight drove the Italians off the mountain next day. Twice more in the following days Italian troops retook the mountain, and twice more they lost it. By the time the battle ended on 3 August 1915 Italian losses amounted to 42,000 dead, wounded and missing, slightly fewer than the 47,000 Austrian losses. While the battle was going on disease too took its toll: 21,000 Italian soldiers caught cholera and typhus and 4,300 of them died.

With two less than successful battles under his belt, Cadorna recognised that the operational methods of the past 'which by now would find us in the heart of Austria' were not going to work and would have to be replaced with new ones. Manoeuvre, which had both allowed and demanded imagination and brilliance, was being wrecked by the labyrinth of trenches and barbed-wire entanglements facing the Italians. Artillery bombardments were less effective than they appeared: the enemy concealed his guns and his men in connecting galleries dug into the hillsides, and hit any troops able to take crests and summits with converging fire from concealed batteries in the rear. Advances were going to be slow and it would be necessary to proceed 'with method' if useless losses were to be avoided. In the prevailing circumstances, a commander needed 'imperturbability' in order not to be unduly impressed by his own side's losses.[51] Over the next two years implacability, as well as imperturbability, would be the hallmarks of Cadorna's leadership of the Italian army.

Cadorna's immediate priorities were to improve air reconnaissance capabilities and air defences. He had no faith whatever in the new director-general of the air corps, Colonel Maurizio Moris: with the war scarcely two weeks old, he had complained that the 'absolute lack of aircraft', shortage of observers and inadequate organisation were making it difficult to locate enemy batteries for counter-battery fire. The consequences were losses in infantry and heavy consumption of munitions and of time, none of which would have occurred had the director-general only done as he had asked.[52] This was the first shot in a campaign which would end with Moris's dismissal in December 1915. Now, with the third battle of the Isonzo about to start, his Farmans were no use because they were unable to gain enough height to dominate the enemy. Manpower was a growing problem too. His squadrons had been in line for three months without pilot reinforcements, and as a result some were having to be broken up. 'How are you going to arrest the crisis?', he asked Zupelli.[53] Above all, he wanted Moris's head.

At the beginning of August Cadorna set out his thoughts on how the military situation on the Italian front would develop in the future in the light of events on the eastern front, which could have consequences of 'exceptional gravity' for Italy. Austrian forces were already being moved to the Italian theatre due to the 'complete inaction' of Serbia. Once Warsaw fell, more might follow. If that happened, Italy would be forced to switch from the offensive to the defensive. The lines currently occupied in the Tyrol and the *Zona Carnia* could be held but he would have to retreat on the Isonzo, abandoning 'a promising but nonetheless precarious foothold' on the Carso. If he had had the ammunition he had asked for, Cadorna declared darkly, he would have been able to form a secure line of resistance there. As it was, the defences were strong enough to resist any enemy pressure until the coming spring when the Russian army would be ready for renewed action. If all this came to pass, Cadorna thought the country should be forewarned 'so that the inevitable repercussions do not hit an unprepared public'.[54] As much a warning as a strategic analysis, this like many of his subsequent communications carried a vaguely menacing undertone. Next day, lacking ammunition for all his guns but especially his 149A heavy field guns – 'the most useful and effective' – and short of officers, replacement troops and aircraft with which to seek out enemy batteries and observe their fire, he suspended his current attack.[55]

At the front the fighting continued in August and September as Cadorna sought 'methodically' to prepare for the next major battles while at the same time keeping ammunition consumption down to a minimum. The French wanted him to start his next offensive on 15 September, simultaneously with theirs, but a lack of munitions, the shortage of aircraft and the slowness with which he was getting replacements meant suspending it for a month. The third and fourth battles of the Isonzo, fought between 18 October–4 November and 10–30 November, were an extended effort right along the line – thus opening Cadorna to post-war charges of failing to concentrate his resources and optimise his army's chances of success. To fight them, the Italian fortresses on the French frontier and the Tagliamento were stripped of their medium and heavy artillery. They were still too few. In May 1915, Cadorna had started the first battle of the Isonzo with 112 heavy field guns; after the third battle he had only 57 guns left.[56]

In the weeks preceding the start of the third battle of the Isonzo, the Milan office of Italian military intelligence passed on evidence from an agent in Switzerland suggesting that General Boroević was planning a 'spoiling attack' with 50,000 troops. There were tell-tale signs: the interdiction of all postal and telegraph communications in Austria and southern Germany, and major troop movements from the eastern front to the west. The motive power behind what could only be a limited military action was held to be anti-Italian propaganda which suggested that the general state of mind in Italy was 'gravely disturbed'. This in turn was interpreted by Cadorna's headquarters staff as being part of a 'Giolittian resurrection'. It was, however, perceived as a trick to make the Italians think very large movements of troops and artillery were happening. More useful perhaps was information deriving from the German military attaché in Berne to the effect that Boroević had a maximum of 280,000 troops at his disposal in the whole of the Gorizia region.[57]

The supply situation on the eve of the coming wave of Italian offensives meant that attacks were once again going to take place without truly adequate fire support. Cadorna had been hoarding reserve supplies of ammunition since the end of July by enforcing economies, which included stopping the firing of heavy field howitzers except for special tasks. Despite his somewhat hand-to-mouth measures the army still lacked adequate supplies of weaponry and munitions for trench warfare, especially hand-grenades and gas shells – the company monopolising the manufacture of liquid chlorine was believed to be using it almost entirely for sanitary and pharmaceutical products. Cadorna laid the blame squarely on the government's shoulders: 'Our directing classes are not sufficiently educated as to the gravity of the struggle in which the Nation is engaged, are over-optimistic about the means we have, and are not preoccupied with the need to co-ordinate all our financial efforts for victory.' What was needed, he told the premier, was 'an apostle' from the political classes to direct and co-ordinate the national economic effort.[58]

Salandra readily agreed that the production of guns and ammunition needed intensifying, but was unwilling – or unable – to do very much about it. Italian private firms often did not meet the obligations they had undertaken, but it was difficult to apply the rigorous treatment they deserved since there were no substitutes and alternative foreign supplies were too far away and too insecure. In such circumstances he did not think 'political exhortation' could produce any concrete results. He did promulgate decrees designed to improve tendering by lessening competition, and militarising munitions workers who were put under military regulation, but that was as far as he was willing to go.[59]

For his third offensive of the year, Cadorna massed 400,000 men and 1,250 guns, only a quarter of them medium and heavy weapons, for a vigorous offensive on the middle and lower Isonzo. First and 4th Armies and the *Zona Carnia* army corps were tasked with local offensives to prevent the enemy from moving reinforcements down to the Isonzo. There, 2nd and 3rd Armies were to take the Plezzo basin in the north, Tolmino and the Bainsizza plateau in the centre, and the mountains of Sabotino, Monte Santo and Monte San Michele protecting Gorizia – which was fast becoming a prestige objective. The third battle of the Isonzo began with a three-day preliminary bombardment by 1,363 guns, roughly half the total stock. This was less impressive than the numbers might suggest: by this time the artillery was firing a total of only 21,000 rounds a day. On 8 October Frugoni issued an order to 2nd Army limiting ammunition expenditure per gun to 60 rounds a day for light artillery, 30 rounds for medium artillery, and 20 rounds for heavy artillery, not to be exceeded in any circumstances including battle. As this would not be enough to open gaps in the enemy's defences, after the opening bombardment it would then be up to the infantry to destroy the wire.[60]

The infantry attack began on 21 October 1915 after a three-day artillery preparation. Four days later Cadorna was forced to pause in order to reorganise his troops, fill in gaps and get up reserves of ammunition. At that stage he had little progress to report. Italian troops had enlarged the bridgehead at Plava and made some progress on the Carso, pushing forward to below the crest of Mon San Michele and towards San Martino, taking 5,000 prisoners. Progress, he was forced to acknowledge, seemed 'not very considerable'. This was due in the main to the enemy's superiority in guns, machine-guns and munitions. If the weather and ammunition supplies allowed, his intention was to continue putting pressure on the enemy front for another three to four weeks with the immediate aim of taking positions around Gorizia and the Carsico *altopiano*. More broadly, this would produce 'the most tangible results as far as the allies and the operations in Serbia are concerned'.[61] New orders were issued: troops were not to be 'concentrated excessively under enemy fire'; the advance was to be methodical, making 'slow but sure progress'; and – somewhat contradictorily – the infantry were to advance in bounds, strengthening themselves at once and not giving up an inch of conquered ground.[62] Nine days later, with the theatre blanketed in heavy clouds and fog, Cadorna suspended operations in order to reorganise his front and give 'new impulse' to the attack.[63] The battle cost the Italians 67,000 dead, wounded and missing – some 23 per cent of the force engaged.

Both sides made more use of aircraft during the third battle of the Isonzo, and for the first time the Austrians were numerically the inferior party. Both used aerial reconnaissance, the Austrians observing train transports. Air power played less of a role in the fourth battle of the Isonzo due to the *bora* and the bad weather, but Austrian aircraft were able to identify forty-five Italian battalions strung out along the Isonzo as far as Plava. The Italians now began to use their long-range Caproni 300 bombers, which proved difficult for Austrian fighters to catch and more difficult to stop after the Italians began to employ them in compact formations rather than singly.[64]

As winter closed in, and with the start of what would be the last battle of the campaigning season only two days away, Cadorna was running out of ideas – but not out of self-assurance. His own offensives, and that conducted by Joffre in Champagne with much greater means than his, had both encountered 'insurmountable difficulties'. The war was imposing its methods on him not vice versa and those methods were 'extraordinarily favourable to the defensive'. As a result, it was proving impossible to achieve 'really tangible results'. Cadorna talked much of 'method' but there was no sign that it consisted of anything more than throwing men against enemy wire. As far as personal responsibility went, he was absolutely confident as the fourth battle of the Isonzo drew to a close that he had done everything possible to succeed.[65]

Salandra was growing increasingly concerned at the frequent enemy incursions into Italian airspace. Air warfare had begun on the opening day of hostilities when the Italian airship *Città di Ferrara* was despatched to bomb Pola but forced to turn back by atmospheric conditions. On the same day two Austrian aircraft dropped fifteen bombs on Venice. Over the succeeding months Italian airships carried out attacks on Austrian ports and cities, though the loss of two airships in June and August led to the realisation that they would not be as useful as pre-war thought had suggested. Austrian aircraft began to bomb Italian cities while Austrian warships bombarded Italian towns on the Adriatic coast. As autumn turned to winter Austrian air attacks intensified. Venice was bombed twice in October, Verona and Brescia in November (thirty-seven people were killed in Verona), and Venice again in November when seven Austrian aircraft dropped twenty-six bombs, most of them hitting the water. When the Italians decided to bombard Gorizia in November, the Austrians launched reprisal air attacks on Venice and Grado. To the politicians, who now faced a new kind of war, it seemed that it would soon be the turn of Milan and Rome to suffer.[66]

The Austrian attacks appeared to be part of a plan for intimidatory reprisals, and Salandra wanted the *Comando supremo* to take all possible steps to defend the most important cities in order above all to reassure their populations.[67] Cadorna was more concerned about the fighting front. The enemy was expecting powerful new planes that would put all the factories on the Paduan plain within range. In the coming winter months he expected the Austrians, aided by the Germans, considerably to increase the numbers, strength and armament of their own planes. He would face them with insufficient numbers of aircraft and pilots and very few anti-aircraft guns. The armaments committee must find a solution – though the army would not have found itself in this situation if the director-general of aviation had been replaced, as he had formally proposed.[68]

The fourth battle of the Isonzo began on 10 November. Cadorna could expect no direct assistance from his Russian ally, whose troops were in no condition to undertake a general offensive and for the time being could only carry out local 'spoiling' attacks.[69] He had some reason to hope for indirect assistance from his enemy, however. Austro-German troops had attacked Serbia on 7 October, and by mid November the Serbian army was in full flight. In the middle of the battle Russian military intelligence reported that Austria–Hungary was shifting 'substantial forces and numerous artillery' towards Cattaro.[70] There was also some encouraging – if highly speculative – arithmetic to back Cadorna's strategy. From St Petersburg, Ambassador Carlotti relayed calculations suggesting that Austria–Hungary and Germany together had 12,000,000 men capable of military service, of whom 7,000,000 were already casualties. With 4,500,000 men now committed on four fighting fronts, that left a reserve of 500,000 plus some 2,000,000 returning wounded, a force 'which must necessarily be exhausted within four or five months'.[71]

The attack went in all along the line from Monte Sabotino to the sea. The intention was to prevent or limit the Austrians' ability to concentrate their fire on any particular zones, and so make incremental progress. The front was blanketed with heavy clouds and thick fog, making Italian artillery even less effective than usual. Support parties were unable to get food up to the forward troops who fought in appalling conditions: Luigi Capello, then commanding VI Army Corps, described his men as walking lumps of mud. With the battle bogging down, Cadorna decided to bombard the town of Gorizia. It was a relatively comfortable zone of recuperation for the enemy's troops, while his own had to live in the open in mud and suffered the consequences of the enormous difficulties of resupplying the front lines. It was also a useful cover for the Austrian gunners, who had sited their weapons near habitations in the certainty that their enemy would not risk damaging the city. However, Cadorna assured the government, there were no Italians there now. All things considered, it was the next logical step: 'As this is a war of attrition,' he told Salandra, 'it is both natural and necessary to do whatever is best to wear down the enemy's strength.'[72]

The fourth battle of the Isonzo ended on 2 December 1915, and with it the campaigning season was over. Together, the third and fourth battles of the Isonzo cost the Italian army 66,908 dead and 48,967 wounded. Total Austrian casualties amounted to 73,797 men, of whom 41,847 were killed. Numerically, Cadorna's armies had paid the higher price. Proportionately the opposite was the case: 23 per cent of the Italian forces taking part in the battles were casualties, compared to 40 per cent of the Austrian forces.[73]

Peripheral distractions

When war came to Europe in August 1914, Italy's political leaders saw the opportunity to satisfy nationalist and irredentist ambitions. Those ambitions stretched beyond her immediate borders, embracing a distant Anatolian Turkey, about which Italy was able to do nothing during the war, and Albania, which was much closer to hand and where she both could and did act, against Cadorna's repeated and strongly worded advice.[74]

Before the war Albania had attracted the attention of leading statesmen and soldiers alike, chiefly because of its strategic value in the control of the Adriatic but also because of its supposed economic potential. Di San Giuliano's interest in it was roused by Sidney Sonnino, who would succeed him on 5 November 1914. In 1907 the general staff drew up plans to occupy the coastal ports of Durazzo and Valona, and in 1911 it had plans for a 38,000-man expeditionary force as a counterweight to Austria–Hungary's occupation of Bosnia–Herzegovina three years earlier. Endemic instability, which was not solved by the creation of an independent principality in 1913, and Greek and Serbian designs on Albania added focus to Italy's gaze and fed ambition and anxiety alike.

The fear that Vienna would steal a march on Rome was the driving force. On the eve of the world war, Di San Giuliano saw among other dangers the possibility that Austria–Hungary might partition Albania with Greece or take Mount Lovcen. While he preferred to threaten military action in order to safeguard Italy's interests in the region, his successor was prepared to take it.[75]

Fearing that the government was threatening to get the army bogged down in what would turn out to be another Libya or Bosnia, where the Austrians had had to mobilise 260,000 men, Cadorna set down his conditions on 27 September 1914: there must be an absolute guarantee of a favourable reception by the local populace and the army could not be drawn into armed conflict with local insurgents, otherwise an entire army corps would be necessary and that would impact on general mobilisation in the event of Italy's joining in the European war. Di San Giuliano was persuaded against military action, but his successor was not. Sonnino raised the issue again in the second week of November and again Cadorna resolutely opposed an expeditionary force. In the face of such obdurate opposition, Sonnino took limited steps: Italian sailors seized the island of Saseno, off Valona (which Cadorna himself had recommended) and occupied the city shortly after Christmas Day. There Balkan matters rested until the following autumn.

On 5 October 1915 French forces landed at Salonika, opening up a new military front in the Balkans. Three days later the Central Powers launched an offensive against Serbia which would defeat her in little more than two months. These developments, which opened a new theatre of war, sparked a serious strategic confrontation between Cadorna and the government. Faced in late September with the likelihood of an Anglo-French intervention in Greece, Sonnino asked the soldiers for their advice. The war minister, General Zupelli, was against the idea. Although Sonnino was only talking of some 20,000 Italian soldiers, he was finding it difficult enough to keep the mobilised army up to desired levels of efficiency in the existing circumstances. An expeditionary force would need powerful artillery and would require resupplying, difficult enough in respect of the army operating in their own country without the additional burden on Italian industry of meeting the needs of an expeditionary force. Cadorna took the opposite view. Supporting Serbia in the imminent conflict was 'opportune'. After the next offensive there would be a pause, winter would allow 'a fairly notable reduction in our front line', and in spring new units would be fully efficient. In the circumstances he could find 20,000 men and another 10,000 could be drawn from Tripolitania.[76] His basic reasoning was simple: Austrian troops drawn down into Greece could not fight Italians on the Isonzo.

Sonnino, who like Salandra shared his war minister's opinion, preferred to pursue one of his own foreign-policy objectives and put Italians into the Balkans via Albania on the grounds that this would assure Serbia's rear and block Greece's advance towards Berat. Cadorna felt it necessary to give the foreign minister a primer in strategic calculation: communications in Albania were poor, an Italian force would find its flanks exposed, and the local population was untrustworthy and warlike. 'Therefore an expedition [there] would run a permanent danger of disaster which, even if partial, would oblige us having lost prestige to send further expeditions of a size which is unpredictable.'[77] Joffre weighed in, sending General Gouraud to Cadorna's headquarters to ask for 100,000 men for Salonika. While making his own views clear, Cadorna allowed that the question was a political one. The matter was decided in the course of a two-day meeting in Rome on 13–14 November 1915 in which Salandra, Sonnino, Zupelli and treasury minister Francesco Tedesco were all firmly against committing Italian troops in Macedonia and all for expanding Italy's foothold in Albania. Cadorna was reduced to insisting that there be no penetration into the interior, which the council of ministers appeared to accept. An Italian contingent would eventually appear at Salonika – but not until August 1916.

A *Corpo speciale* was swiftly created and on 25 November it received its instructions from Sonnino to garrison Valona, Durazzo and the hinterland necessary to secure communications between them, and to provide as far as possible for Serbian resupply without sending troops into the interior. To emphasise the supremacy of politics, overall command of the expedition was denied the chief of the general staff and given instead to the war minister. Much annoyed, Cadorna warned that it would get no more troops. The expeditionary corps landed at Valona on 3 December and next day its commander, General Bertotti, despatched a brigade to Durazzo, a fifteen-day march. Cadorna saw this as exactly the kind of penetration into the interior he had feared. His suspicions that the government's intentions were being masked and that its ambitions would quickly grow were soon confirmed. Twelve days after the troops first landed, he learned from Zupelli that the foreign ministry was enquiring about the viability of occupying Berat on the grounds that peace in the Balkans would probably come on the basis of territory held and that if Valona ended up as an enclave in Greek territory it would lose all worth. Bertotti, like many another general on the spot, favoured a forward move but needed another regiment of infantry, a battalion of *Alpini* and a battery of mountain artillery to do it. Cadorna wrote at once expressly opposing the occupation of Berat or any other operation inside Albania that required additional troops.[78] It was, he reminded Zupelli, exactly what he had warned against: 'As I was easily able to foresee we are now at the start of requests for troops of which no-one can foretell the end.'[79] The government abandoned the Berat gambit next day, and then went into dysfunctional mode. Zupelli decided that Durazzo had lost its value and ordered the column advancing on it to be withdrawn, only to learn that it had already got there. In January the Austrians attacked Montenegro, taking Mount Lovcen, and by the third week of the month the Serbian army had fled to the coasts and was being evacuated by the Italian navy. Salandra decided Durazzo must be abandoned, but Sonnino added the rider that that should only happen when it could no longer be held. The politicians wanted Durazzo held and the defence reinforced by pushing inland. Cadorna pointed out that it was of no value now, that it was too costly to hold, and that Valona needed all the available resources. The only clear outcome of the meeting was that the army had to provide another division for the defence of Valona.

Locally, the Albanian expedition now became a tragi-comedy – and an object lesson in the perils of politically driven strategy. Durazzo was blockaded by the Austrians on 13 February 1916 and a bombardment of the town began. Cadorna recommended immediate withdrawal, but Sonnino insisted that the Italians must not leave too hastily and so give the impression that they were abandoning the position without trying to put up a serious resistance. The local commander asked for a sea evacuation, but decided to stay after Bertotti reminded him of the penal sanctions facing a commander of a fortress who did not put all due measures in place. The garrison was hit first by gastroenteritis and then, on 23 February, by an Austrian assault. Two days later the last Italian defenders embarked, leaving the city in flames, at a cost of 815 dead, wounded and missing. Italian troops settled in at Valona, from where they would conduct what one historian of the Great War has labelled '[a] little mountain war of no significance' until the Armistice came in November 1918.[80]

Cadorna, whose authority and judgement had both been challenged in Albania, had been proved right and told Salandra so. Italian military prestige had suffered 'a serious blow' at Durazzo which would have 'grave repercussions in the ranks of the fighting army'. It was not up to him, he told the premier, to decide where the main blame lay 'for the ineptitude and the obstinate refusal to recognise the dangers', but Zupelli was not up to his job. Durazzo proved it. If Zupelli did not go, he would resign.[81] Getting no immediate satisfaction from Salandra, who brusquely reminded him that constitutionally it was none of his business to tell an administration which ministers it could or could not have, Cadorna tendered his resignation on 1 March. In the meantime, a royal decree on 29 February gave him command of the entire army but confirmed that political directives about the conduct of the war were reserved to the government. The king intervened, hoping that in the light of what had now happened he would withdraw his resignation.[82] Cadorna accepted the revision of his powers – but only so long as the directives he was given were such as could militarily be acted upon and the ends were proportionate to the means. His victory was sealed when, on 6 March, Zupelli resigned. Fifteen months later, in June 1917, Zupelli, now commanding the 20th division at Hermada, was sacked by Cadorna for 'inefficiency'. In March 1918, under a new administration and a new chief of general staff, he returned as war minister and was officially reinstated.

The war economy

Italy went to war in May 1915 *alla Garibaldina*, her decision dictated by idealistic goals not hard-headed calculations, and awoke late and slowly to the industrial dimensions of the conflict she had entered.[83] Not only was she unprepared when the moment came, but she had relatively little with which to prepare: in 1913 industry's share of the Italian gross national product was 25 per cent, fractionally more than one of her coming enemies, Hungary (24 per cent), but less than that of another, the future Czechoslovakia (34 per cent) and well behind Germany (44 per cent).[84] Her economy was vulnerable in almost every respect. Before the war, three-quarters of her imports and exports went by sea, making her increasingly open to the depredations of German and Austro-Hungarian submarines. With the start of the war her land markets in Germany and Austria–Hungary, which provided almost 30 per cent of her imports, were closed to her and access to Russia and Romania, her traditional grain suppliers, was blocked by the closure of the Dardanelles. In the words of one commentator, Italy's industrial frailty 'placed the country in a singularly weak position, always just one step away from collapse'.[85]

By any standards, Italy's mobilisation of the sinews of war was impromptu. In February 1915 Cadorna remarked on the need for a proper industrial mobilisation of the country, and in the same month General Alfredo Dallolio pointed out Italy's lack of raw materials and the need to solve the problem of retaining sufficient specialised labour to keep the factories working. In May 1915 the minister for agriculture, industry and commerce, Giannino Casavola, called together the heads of the main manufacturing associations to identify industry's needs in war. Their recommendations, backed by regional and national industrial bodies, were modest: a consultative presence in the ministry, a place on the local committees deciding who to mobilise and who to put in reserved occupations, and the creation of consortia to control the purchase and distribution of raw materials other than coal, whose provision was a state function. On 26 June a royal decree introduced industrial mobilisation, putting factories producing war matériel and their owners under state direction, and on 9 July the *Comitato supremo per i rifornimenti delle armi e delle munizioni* was established to determine what was needed for the most effective provision of war matériel. The same law created the new office of under-secretary of state for arms and munitions, which was placed in the hands of the current director of artillery and engineers at the war ministry, General Dallolio.[86] Central and regional military commissions with powers to requisition goods and fix prices handled the army's needs for foodstuffs, while mixed commissions did the same thing in respect of industrial products. This did not, however, signal the start of a consolidated mobilisation of the resources of the state, rather the reverse: by the war's end, 297 different government bodies reporting to six different ministries all had the power to allocate resources to the war effort. After the war a parliamentary enquiry into its costs, which the economist Luigi Einaudi estimated to amount for Italy to 40,200,000,000 lire, concluded that they had been inflated by defects in organisation, the absence or inadequacy of effective controls, and the lack of a single regulatory authority which together 'turned the bureaucratic machine into a mastodon'.[87]

Shortly after his appointment, Dallolio introduced a system of regional committees to oversee the manufacture of munitions. Government intervention began to gather pace: a central committee for industrial mobilisation was created and put in Dallolio's hands, and a senior military or naval officer was put on each of the seven regional committees. Workers and industrialists were represented on them, but had only consultative rights and not voting powers. In September 1917 the system was extended to the whole of Italy. The intention behind it was to secure a uniformity of approach and to ensure that government's intentions were faithfully carried through. The regional committees provided central government with manufacturing data, made technical, legislative and economic recommendations to improve output, and were empowered to resolve disputes between owners and the labour force.

Next, the government decreed that factories manufacturing arms and munitions could be declared 'auxiliary establishments', putting their workforce under military discipline: at the end of 1915 there were 221 such establishments, and by November 1918 the number had swollen to 1,976 employing over 530,000 men. With 322,000 men working in the ordnance factories alone, by 1918 one in three of the industrial workforce was working for Dallolio's ministry. Overenthusiastic use of the conscription machinery at the outset quickly produced a labour shortage. To solve it, the army combed through its manpower and created *militari–operai* ('soldier–workers') who wore uniforms and slept in barracks. Eventually the sheer pressure of numbers forced the authorities to relabel them *a disposizione* ('on release') and allow them to live with their families and wear civilian clothes. All told, over 300,000 men were designated *militari–operai* and another 600,000 were exonerated from military service.[88]

Although the committee on arms and munitions was given considerable powers over industry, including the ability to force firms to produce and supply goods and materials, it preferred to leave matters largely in the hands of business. As Dallolio explained after the war, 'the government is inevitably ... slower ... than private individuals, so that in its hands production would have declined ... For this reason, and also because I trusted the patriotism of industrialists and workers, I did not order government requisitions or takeovers.'[89] He was also willing to see the government charged high prices – for artillery rounds especially – in order to keep less efficient small producers in business and encourage new ones in regions where they had not previously existed. His stance on industrial relations was more emollient than that of Cadorna, who bombarded him with complaints about shortcomings in supply, interspersed with the occasional note of congratulation when the under-secretary for arms and munitions had placed a large order. 'Rather than urging on the executive and productive elements we have at our disposal,' he told Cadorna in January 1916, 'we need to steer them, thinking of Italy as one great factory and having a single vision of [our] various needs.'[90] By autumn 1916 his methods were producing 70,000 rounds of artillery ammunition a day and 202 guns each month.

Dallolio's international operations were dextrous. FIAT automobiles and small-calibre guns were exchanged for French steel, and in December 1916, short of convertible currency to pay for overseas orders which the treasury doled out grudgingly, he simply called in the heads of three of the largest banks and got the dollars he needed without any formal orders or guarantees. Even he, though, found it difficult to cope with the shortages of labour and coal which hampered Italian production in the last two years of the war when a chronic lack of shipping meant juggling competing demands for coal, grain and steel. Coal imports, amounting to 10 million tons in 1914, shrank to 5 million tons in 1917, and in April of that year the intendant-general of the army gave Dallolio the choice of cutting down the coal supplies to the factories or reducing the number of trains. A number of steel furnaces had to be shut down to square the economic circle.

Fig. 3 Girl labourers at an Italian munitions factory

Metal manufacturing industry expanded to satisfy the war's gargantuan appetite for weapons and munitions as well as for men. Munitions absorbed the greater part of steel production and by the end of the war the gun foundries had supplied some 16,000 guns of all types and Italian munitions factories had produced 68,265,346 rounds of artillery ammunition, of which the army had fired off roughly two-thirds. Daily output started at 31,800 rounds (20,800 charged rounds) in 1915, rising to 66,189 rounds (52,805 charged rounds) in 1916 and to 73,015 rounds (54,408 charged rounds) in 1917 before falling back in 1918 to 51,649 rounds (77,174 charged rounds). Rifle manufacturing had difficulties in keeping pace with the expansion of the army at first: in February 1916, when new recruits arrived in barracks the army was short of 113,000 rifles, but by the end of the year the situation had improved. In all, small-arms manufacturers produced 2,817,000 rifles and muskets and 37,029 machine-guns. To feed them, ammunition factories produced 3,616,000,000 rounds of small-arms munitions.[91]

Machine-age warfare made its own demands in every sphere except one: the Italian front was entirely unsuitable for tanks and neither side used them. Motor transportation saw a dramatic expansion. More or less unknown in the army logistics service before the war, it employed 20,000 men driving 12,000 motor vehicles by November 1918. In all, the motor industry provided the army with 2,074 motor cars and 40,390 trucks as well as assorted motor cycles, buses, ambulances, towing trucks and the like, while at the same time exporting 15,538 trucks and cars. Some of the army's difficulties during the first two years of the war were due to the gathering pace of vehicle provision and use, as the transportation data in Table 1 illustrate.

Table 1 *Motorisation of the Italian Army 1915–18*

	Officers	Other ranks	Motor cars	Trucks	Tractors
May 1915	500	9,000	400	3,400	150
June 1916	800	20,000	930	8,100	400
June 1917	1,500	60,000	1,460	15,700	830
October 1917	1,700	70,000	1,500	17,000	1,000
June 1918	2,500	100,000	2,000	21,500	900
November 1918	3,000	115,000	2,500	28,000	1,200

Source: Mazzetti, *L'industria italiana nella grande guerra*, p. 45.

The Italian aircraft industry provides an even more striking example of wartime expansion. In 1915 only three firms built planes in Italy; by 1918 there were sixty-two. In 1915 they produced 382 planes; in 1916 1,255; in 1917 3,861; and in 1918 6,523.

The war sucked in imports. Italy used a total of 9,276,000 tons of iron and steel, of which she had to import one-third. Imports of rubber more than doubled, totalling 245.4 thousand quintals. The cotton and wool industries, both heavily dependent on imports, were more or less able to keep pace with demand during the first two years of the war, thanks to overproduction in the pre-war period as far as cotton was concerned, but both were badly affected by the German submarine campaign of 1917. Cotton-thread production fell below pre-war levels in 1917 and fell again in 1918, and wool imports for the whole of the war (236,000 quintals) barely exceed the volume of imports in 1914 alone (216,000 quintals). Italy's pre-war food imports, primarily wheat from Russia, had been of higher calorific value than her exports of fruit, vegetables and wine. Domestic grain production held out until 1917, when a bad harvest saw a 30 per cent drop compared to pre-war levels. Allied sources filled the gap, with the result that in 1918 Italy's food imports were some 40 per cent above pre-war levels.[92]

Factory owners and directors jibbed at being put under closer government control: in October 1916 Vickers–Terni used its lack of freedom of action to justify delays in supplying orders of artillery. In truth, much was in their favour. Contractors were less bound by legal regulation, enabling them to extract high prices for raw materials, delay production without penalty, and extract larger advances. Nor could effective checks be made on them: the lack of technical expertise of the civil servants and the ease with which they could be corrupted made it impossible to verify actual production costs.[93] The index of wholesale prices is a measure of the government's failure to exert pressure on the manufacturers through the early and wide imposition of price controls – or of the industrialists' success. Between 1914 and 1918 wholesale prices in Italy more than quadrupled, where in Great Britain and Germany they more or less doubled and in France the level was a little more than triple the pre-war number.[94]

At bottom, the industrialists had the government over a barrel because when threatened with anything they were not prepared to accept they could slow down the output of the guns that were so badly needed at the front. Thus Ansaldo ignored well-founded technical criticism of some of its products, particularly the 149-mm 1916 model howitzer, first voiced in September 1916, then again in November 1917, and finally in the summer of 1918 (when thorough checks on everything it produced exposed multiple deficiencies) on the grounds that any alterations would mean halting production for six months. Manufacturers failed to adopt better methods to produce better products because they were unwilling to retool their factories. ILVA, which produced iron and steel, resisted putting its entire output at the state's disposal until September 1918; in the meantime, placing some of its production on the open market hiked the prices the government had to pay for its share. External pressure forced the government to extend its powers in some areas: thus British determination to deal only with state authorities led to the state becoming the sole purchaser of coal in February 1917 and of wool in April 1917. In other areas, such as raw cotton consumption, consortia of producers divided up supplies on a monthly basis.

Dallolio's office, which became a ministry in June 1917, favoured extending the new relationship between state and industry into peace-time, and between August 1916 and August 1917 the issue was discussed on a number of occasions. The idea foundered on the twin rocks of the industrialists' dislike of the extent of state interference and their concern at the continued proliferation of stifling bureaucratic structures, and labour's suspicion that the intention was to keep the workforce under tight legal constraints.

The question of who or what controlled the government's contractual relations with industry and foreign suppliers became the subject of a political contest after Caporetto when Francesco Nitti became treasury minister. In December 1917 Nitti pressed his ministry's rights in respect of purchasing in the United States. At the same time he tried unsuccessfully to exclude Dallolio from the *Comitato di guerra* ('War Committee') set up by Vittorio Orlando in December 1917 to improve relations between the government and the *Comando supremo*. The duel continued into the spring of 1918 with Nitti, who had close connections with the Perrone brothers who ran Ansaldo, accusing Dallolio of presiding over 'the most complete administrative disorganization'. Finally the arrest of some of his subordinates on charges of peculation forced Dallolio to resign on 14 May 1918.[95] The transport minister, Riccardo Bianchi, likewise a target of Nitti's manoeuvring to make the treasury the chief economic decision-maker, resigned at the same time.

The final months of the war can only be described as a mess as far as the organisation of arms production went. While the industrialists continued to criticise the excessively militaristic and bureaucratic character of industrial mobilisation, Orlando put the arms and munitions ministry temporarily under the war minister, Zupelli, before in September creating a new combined ministry of transport and arms and then at the end of October resuscitating the ministry of arms and munitions.

Working out what the war cost is an exercise fraught with obstacles: 'ordinary' and 'extra-ordinary' budget allocations, items held off-budget, the underestimation of some costs (notoriously those of the Libyan war 1911–12), and the matter of whether debt servicing and war credits are or are not included all make for complexity. Using the difference between total actual public expenditure and a notional 'peacetime' budget, the 'excess payments' made for civil purposes from 1914–15 to 1918–19 have been calculated at 56,475,000,000 lire; those for military purposes at 77,605,000,000 lire.[96] Four-fifths of the 26,479,000,000 lire net excess payments during the war, another gauge of the 'cost' of the war, went on military expenses and one-fifth on civil expenses. Meeting these costs from her own resources was way beyond Italy's capacity, as Table 2 shows.

Table 2 *Financial receipts and payments 1914–19*

	Receipts	Payments	Excess
1914–15	2.204.000.000	4.481.000.000	2.277.000.000
1915–16	1.727.000.000	6.807.000.000	5.080.000.000
1916–17	1.994.000.000	7.301.000.000	5.307.000.000
1917–18	1.772.000.000	7.534.000.000	5.762.000.000
1918–19	2.018.000.000	7.764.000.000	5.746.000.000

In 1913–14 lire. *Source*: Répaci, *Scritti di economia e finanza*, vol. IV, p. 463.

Paying for the war put heavy pressure on a budget of which, before it began, a third went on furnishing the interest on the national debt and another third on the administrative costs of running the state. Significant sources of revenue disappeared. Before the war, remittances sent home by emigrants covered some 40 per cent of the gap between imports and exports; during the war they fell by three-quarters, and revenue from tourism which had helped make up the difference vanished. Exports, which had paid for three-quarters of Italy's imports in 1914, covered barely 20 per cent of the costs in 1917–18. With a balance-of-payments deficit amounting to a quarter of national income, debt became an important instrument with which to dilute the cost of the war.[97]

During the war years (1914–19), the state raised 34 per cent of its domestic income from direct taxation, 51 per cent from taxes on consumption, and the remainder from indirect imposts – most of that coming from the requirement to put stamps, which were a government monopoly, on almost every document with an official purpose. Regressive taxes on consumption put heavy pressure on a society large parts of which were already grindingly poor. Land and real-estate taxes, which had fallen steadily from the mid 1880s until 1910, were more important to wartime budgets than they had been before, partly because of their relative inelasticity and partly because of the possibilities for evading taxes on wealth and income. Revenue from duties imposed both locally and nationally fell.[98]

One way of financing the war was to print money, and that is what the government did. Even before the war the volume of banknotes in circulation was greater than the amount of gold in the banks' vaults, and when Italy entered it the rules were swiftly relaxed to allow the three issuing banks to print money and extend credit to the government. In July 1914 notes to the value of 2,270,000,000 lire were in circulation. By November 1918 the amount had risen to 11,500,000,000 lire – evidence of the degree to which the printing presses had been used by the government as a weapon in the war.[99] By 1918 the deficit on receipts that had to be covered by borrowing amounted to 70 per cent of total expenditure. Too poor to meet 'excess' cost through taxation, Italy financed approximately 36 per cent of the costs of the war through external debt, 55 per cent through domestic indebtedness, and 9 per cent by inflation. By the end of the war, Italy owed Great Britain, the United States and France a total of 2,961,000,000 dollars.

Intelligence, counter-intelligence and policing

Italian military intelligence – the *Servizio informazioni militari* as it came to be known – was not much more than a decade old when it went to war.

Founded in 1900, and initially staffed by only three officers with a budget of 50,000 lire, its first major contribution to active military campaigning came with the Libyan war of 1911–12. It was not without shortcomings. The surprising force of Arab resistance was an early illumination of the problem of analysing intelligence in addition merely to collecting it.[100] The peace of Lausanne in 1912 brought an end to a war which, its internal history later acknowledged, 'in the field of intelligence lacked adequate preparation, necessary expertise, and appropriate organization'.[101] Over the next two years the *Ufficio informazioni* concentrated its attention westwards. It was therefore not well placed when in 1914 it became increasingly obvious that Austria–Hungary and not France would be Italy's antagonist in war: its sources within the empire, almost entirely 'patriots' or individual confidants, had shrunk almost to nothing, and it put no faith in the refugees who now arrived in increasing numbers.

With Italy's entry into the war, the *Ufficio informazioni* was subordinated to the operations section of the *Comando supremo* under Armando Diaz, who wanted all strategic intelligence passed straight to him. In May 1915, 'detached' sections were established at general headquarters in Udine and at Palmanova, Tolmezzo, Belluno, Verona, Brescia and Milan. The Brescia section under Captain Tullio Marchetti soon became very active, Marchetti establishing a network of informers in the Austrian Trentino and Switzerland. Outside Italy, there was a lone intelligence-gathering station in Switzerland. The service lacked an efficient counter-espionage set-up, an adequate radio interception capability, and appropriate cryptographic capacity. The Milan section under Colonel Achille Brotti soon became a critical component of the intelligence apparatus, acting as the link with expanding intelligence-gathering activities in Switzerland, running agents across the borders, and carrying out counter-intelligence work. Its sources included agents and informers in place in Switzerland and, at a humbler but no less important level, subscriptions to some forty foreign newspapers and journals. In the early months of the war at least, the political intelligence gathered in Switzerland was superior to the military intelligence coming out of the country.[102] The situation at Udine, where the *Ufficio informazioni* was losing the competition with the *Ufficio situazioni* to be the provider of intelligence to Cadorna, meant that neither the strategic direction nor the operational planning of the war made the best use of intelligence resources.

During 1915 the intelligence service began to make progress in cryptography and in the interception of enemy telephone conversations – a capability not discovered by the Austrians until the autumn of 1917. Activities expanded rapidly, running the gamut from the analysis of secret inks to the surveillance and counteracting of the early Jugoslav nationalist groups. Leaflets encouraging would-be deserters were dropped behind enemy lines – to such good effect that General Boroević threatened to hang Italian aviators caught dropping them.

By the end of 1915, the *Ufficio informazioni* at headquarters was beginning to get overwhelmed with the volume of information flowing in from military and diplomatic sources whose source accuracy it had to check and collate. It also complained that the information coming from Marchetti's Brescia office, which cost more than any of the others, often duplicated intelligence received from other sources. Brusati had protected Marchetti from a summons to Udine, and valued his two intelligence sections at Brescia and Verona. Information from the enemy side was far from easy to come by: the Austrians had effectively sealed off the Trentino, which meant that Marchetti relied on agents in the middle or upper Tyrol.

Intelligence security on the Italian side was frequently poor, handing the Austrians an undoubted advantage in the early part of the war. Italian ciphers proved very vulnerable. The Austrian *Evidenzbureau* had already acquired the red cipher, which the Italians began to use on 5 July 1915, and thirteen days into the war it succeeded in cracking the Italian naval cipher. In September 1915 it began work on Italian diplomatic ciphers, and from the end of December it was able to read Carlotti's telegrams from St Petersburg and radio communications between Udine and Albania as well as foreign ministry communications with Serbia and Montenegro. For their part, the Austrians made as little use of radio communications as possible and when they did so they used secure ciphers. As early as June 1915 Austrians picked up Italian telephone conversations on the front line, initially by accident. Two months later a listening station was in action in the *Zona Carnia*, and six more followed, three of them on the Isonzo front. The numbers grew steadily and by June 1917 there were twenty-five Austrian interception stations in operation along the Italian front.[103] In the field, the Austrians used wire-borne telegraph or telephone as much as possible.

In October 1916, the advantage swung Italy's way when the commander of an Austrian telephone intercept post went over to the Italians, taking with him all the details of the Austrian technology. The results were dramatic. In one sector alone, Vipacco–Monte Rombon on the Carso, the Italian decryption service was able to read more than 5,000 messages in the next six months. The quality of the information gained was high: Italian interception stations read the messages sent between 21 and 31 July 1917 giving the number of casualties inflicted by 3rd-Army which enabled them to judge the effectiveness of their artillery. Soon there were thirty Italian intercept stations strung out along the Isonzo front at 2-kilometre intervals.

Unlike the Russians, the Italians very seldom gave out dispositions by radio that indicated their intentions. They did, however, use radio for administrative purposes. This enabled the Austrians to locate and track unit movements and make educated guesses about numbers of effectives and even sometimes intentions: moves by cavalry divisions almost always indicated the beginning or end of major offensives. In this way the enemy were able to follow the arrival of fresh troops at the front before the seventh, eighth and ninth battles of the Isonzo. Heavy early snowfalls on the Isonzo at the end of September 1916 damaged Italian telephone wires, forcing them to make more use of radio communications and increasing their exposure to the enemy.[104]

In 1912 the *Ufficio informazioni* was given responsibility for espionage, or intelligence-gathering from outside Italy, and the *Carabinieri* were made responsible for counter-espionage. When the war began the *Carabinieri* also took on a key role in the maintenance of discipline and in ensuring the success of military operations. Regulations devised at this time emphasised the importance of 'inflexible rigour' in maintaining discipline behind the lines, where the greatest danger arose from panic. The *Carabinieri*'s main task in war was to ensure that the development of military operations was not adversely affected by 'disorders among the troops or in the [civil] population'. To do this required them to carry out a wide range of policing functions: ensuring that the soldiers obeyed laws and regulations for good order at railway stations, on the march and in combat; surveillance of civilians in the army's rear; the prevention and repression of criminal acts; guarding soldiers under arrest, deserters and enemy prisoners of war; watching persons suspected of espionage; and preventing robbery and pillage.[105]

In 1915, there were 80 *Carabinieri* officers and 3,000 men serving with the field army and a further 92 officers and 4,000 men in post behind the lines with the Verona legion and at general headquarters at Udine. Individual sections (1 officer, 7 non-commissioned officers and 40 men) were attached to divisional staffs, army corps and to the Intendance, and 'special sections' to the staff at general headquarters and army staffs. Troop movements on trains and in stations were guarded by 2,906 *Carabinieri* manning sixty-nine railway posts. During the course of the war total numbers would triple, and by the end of the war 488 officers and 19,556 men were serving in Italy, France, Albania, Macedonia, Palestine and Russia. Briefly used in combat in the summer of 1915, they were taken out of line in November when it became apparent that the war would be lengthy and the need for policing was bound to grow.

Policing the war involved undertaking a multitude of tasks. In the early stages, there were 17,000 refugees to be dealt with, forty-two villages in the combat zone to be cleared of their inhabitants, and almost a thousand suspected persons to be processed. Stolen goods belonging to the state had to be recovered, and civilians in military workshops needed policing to prevent espionage and vandalism – or so the authorities felt. Increasing emphasis was put on prophylactic measures to prevent the military 'disorders' that had been envisaged in the 1912 regulations. In September 1915, Cadorna created a special rear inspection service under General Di Giorgio, and in December the *Guardia di finanza* (customs police) were added to the mix to help police the areas behind the lines.

Practices grew ever tighter as the war went on. In September 1916 a control service was introduced on trains to check the identity of all passengers except officers in uniform, and from July 1918, monetary rewards were offered for capturing deserters. In case more direct action was needed, a circular on 28 November 1915 enumerated four measures to be used to snuff out the first signs of cowardice or indiscipline, ranging from sending in reinforcements to using artillery on 'recalcitrants'. On the battlefield, a cordon of *Carabinieri* posts would be established 200 metres behind the main line, advancing when the troops advanced and otherwise ensuring that they did not disband, come to unauthorised halts or fail in any other ways to obey orders. Behind them, small posts of *Carabinieri* manned paths and crossroads to catch any small groups who evaded the first line; and behind them again two large 'reserve posts' would stop larger groups of *sbandati* (disbanded soldiers). In the event of a second refusal to obey their orders, the *Carabinieri* were authorised to shoot.[106]

Crimes and punishments

For many years, the reality of everyday life in the trenches was concealed behind a cloud of patriotic rhetoric. Describing the first winter of the war some fourteen years later, General Pietro Maravigna painted a picture in which, as a result of the country supplying the army's needs, the officers' constant care for their troops and the light-hearted way in which they shared the dangers in their men's lives, discipline was always excellent 'and good will and the most elevated military feeling reigned everywhere'.[107] This was an attempt to paper over truly seismic fissures, among them an intense and lengthy dispute between those who thought the reserve officers drawn from the *borghesia* had been the true artificers of victory, not the regular officers who had safely ensconced themselves behind the front lines, and those who thought that the temporary officers had had no ideals other than material well-being and had been an obstacle to the reconstruction of morale.[108] As far as Maravigna's rosy view is concerned, the truth was quite different. The war had scarcely begun before the first cases of refusal to obey orders, desertion, distributing subversive propaganda and suborning troops to shoot their officers came before the military tribunals. The authorities' reactions to them over the coming months and years would form one of the darkest pages in Italy's military history.

On the first day of the war Cadorna called for 'iron discipline' in the army and reminded subordinate commanders of their responsibility to apply 'extreme measures of coercion and repression' when the situation required them. He also tried to do away with the right of appeal to the Crown, the only legal instrument left in the hands of men condemned by the military tribunals. This failed, but the *Comando supremo* ensured that any such appeals were accompanied by an account of its own and an opinion, both intended to sway the king's judgment. The immediate need, however, was to get as many soldiers as possible to the front and so, within limits, discipline was eased. Half a dozen regulations were issued between May and August 1915 suspending punishment where reasons of military service were paramount, amnestying those who had deserted before the war began, and finally suspending sentences of up to three years' imprisonment for the duration of the war. The 'flight from the trenches' continued nonetheless, and as a result on 17 July 1916 the provisional amnesty was extended to include sentences of up to seven years in prison.

In September 1915 yet another circular advised the army, in somewhat self-contradictory terms, that every soldier would find in his superior when necessary a brother or a father, but also that his superiors had 'the sacred power of immediately shooting recalcitrant and cowards'. Anyone trying to surrender or retreat would be shot by the soldiers behind them or by the *Carabinieri* if they had not already been shot by an officer.[109] In so saying, Cadorna was acting strictly within the law. The civil code had abolished the death penalty in 1889, but Article 40 of the military penal code of 1869, still in force over forty years later, and the 1913 Combat Regulations both referred to the right and duty of officers and non-commissioned officers to shoot soldiers who during an action put at risk the success of the operation or the safety of their detachment. Article 117 carried a penalty of up to three years in prison for any soldier, regardless of his position in the chain of command, who failed to use all means available to prevent a mutiny or a revolt.

With the war barely two months old tensions started to become apparent. At the end of July there were a number of incidents in three battalions of the 12th division in which troops demanded to be relieved and in one case threw themselves on the ground rather than march. The corps commander and his military advocate acted circumspectly: order was restored thanks to the energy and good sense of the officers, General Carlo Ruelle recognising that the men had a case. The authorities were mightily displeased. The head of Cadorna's office for discipline, promotions and justice, General Giuseppe Della Noce, regretted that the first incident had only been a mutiny; had it been a revolt (for which the use of arms was a prerequisite), an extraordinary tribunal could immediately have been convened and the subsequent disorders would never have happened (the ringleaders presumably having been sentenced to death and immediately shot). The military advocate had in any case been far too lax. Cadorna took steps accordingly. The corps commander, General Ruelle, was sacked, the divisional commander punished, and the military advocate removed as 'irresolute and lazy'. Instructions went out to the army and corps commanders reminding them to apply punishments with 'lightning immediacy'.[110] The cardinal criteria of wartime military justice had been established: punishment had to be swift, severe and exemplary regardless of any mitigating circumstances.

Ever since unification in 1861 self-inflicted injuries and infections had been a feature of the battle between the determination of the state to impose conscription and the reluctance of the *contadini* (peasants) to accept it. They now took on a new lease of life. On the Carso in July 1915 the proportion of lightly wounded, normally around 10 per cent, rose to 90 per cent. It needed little medical experience to guess that many of these injuries were self-inflicted: single wounds to the hand or the foot, powder burns, and the fact that the Italian '91' rifle had a 6 ½ mm gauge while the Austrian equivalent was 8 mm all gave the game away. Lists were sent back to army corps headquarters for processing and trial. In the only surviving example, 46 soldiers were put in front of a military tribunal on 16 July 1915. Twenty-seven were found guilty and given twenty years' incarceration. The same phenomenon appeared in the Plava sector in October and November 1915: seventeen soldiers of the 125th regiment were tried and sixteen found guilty and sentenced to twenty years. In the circumstances they were lucky not to be shot: in September a soldier who had shot away three of the fingers of his right hand was sentenced to death and executed by firing squad five days later. The seventeenth soldier got off because he alone had a wound to the foot and since his boot had not been recovered it was not possible to say with certainty that it was self-inflicted.[111]

Soldier D. B. A., who had what were deemed to be self-inflicted wounds to the hand, was executed on 20 September 1915, the first man to be sentenced to be shot in the chest. The niceties of Italian military law allowed for some unfortunates to face the firing squad, thus giving them a last opportunity to cry *Viva Italia!*, while others deemed guilty of

especially heinous crimes were shot in the back. In determining the
appropriate sentence, the law required the military tribunals to distinguish
between crimes committed 'in the face of the enemy' and those committed
'in the presence of the enemy'. Soldier D. B. A. paid the extreme price for
the permeability between these two categories: in fact, his act had been
carried out not 'in the face of the enemy' but 'in the presence of the
enemy', for which the penalty under Article 174 of the military penal code
was five to ten years' imprisonment. In November 1915 the *Comando
supremo* sent out a circular which defined 'in the face of the enemy' as
applying when combat had started or was imminent, but left the military
tribunals a good deal of latitude as far as 'the presence of the enemy'
was concerned.[112]

Cadorna, his judge advocate general, Giuseppe Della Noce, and many
of his senior commanders believed that the citizen army they had in their
hands was a brittle instrument that would break unless tempered by
combat and by discipline. One of the issues foremost in the minds of
the tribunal that sentenced the 27 *autolesionisti* on the Carso in July was
the belief that a propensity to imitation among the troops could easily give
rise to 'a shared criminal determination' unless strongly inhibited. From
the outset, the authorities demanded that the force of the law must make
itself felt. The military tribunals tried 1,900 men in August 1915 and
2,170 in September, whereupon military advocates were advised not to
waste time in laborious legal interpretations but to hold to 'a certain
summariness of judgement not disjoined from strict observance of the
military code'. Cadorna told Della Noce in early October that he wanted
judges to show maximum severity. For the rest of the year, and succeeding
ones, the members of military courts were exhorted to be severe, reproved
when they imposed penalties that were deemed insufficiently heavy, and
threatened with removal if they did not follow directions.[113]

While every transgression caused the military authorities concern,
what worried them most of all was the spectre of collective acts of
disobedience. As the first winter of the war froze the trenches, their fears
took on substance. On 6 November 1915 a riot took place in Aosta when
a group of *Alpini* attacked a barracks, opened two military prisons and
barricaded station platforms to stop trains leaving for the front. Some
six weeks later another and more serious incident occurred at Sacile. On
26 December, 400 *Alpini* left their barracks firing and shouting 'Down
with Salandra, long live Giolitti.' At Cividale they shot out the lights,
plunging the station into darkness, and persuaded 300 infantrymen
about to depart for the front to join them and take it over. Eventually
they were cajoled back into their train by a captain from the Sacile depot –
who was himself subsequently hauled before the judicial authorities for

having made insufficient use of force. Thirty-seven men were tried by military tribunals and thirty-three got sentences of between five and fifteen years in prison.[114] Shortly afterwards soldiers of the 48th regiment mutinied on the eve of their return to the front line; two were shot by the *Carabinieri* during the suppression of the mutiny, and two more afterwards. Then, at Oulx on 7–8 January 1916, some drunken *Alpini* did a modest amount of damage. The local police ascribed the incident to a plotted revolt, of which the military authorities could find no trace.

As the New Year began, questions were raised about what kind of political influence could have caused the Sacile disorders. Cadorna expressed no surprise at the 'indifference' shown by the soldiers when their sentences were read out: unfortunately the conviction was widespread in the army that when the war was over the government would be generous in granting amnesties. The threat of imprisonment was of little or no deterrent value to soldiers who risked their lives every day and who preferred to run the risk of prison rather than that of death. As far as he was concerned the only effective deterrent was the firing squad. Unfortunately in cases such as Sacile evidence was often only circumstantial and as a consequence military tribunals could not impose the death penalty. Cadorna wanted to go beyond even the draconian terms of the regulations. 'It is ... greatly to be deplored,' he told the premier, 'that the current military penal code no longer allows the use, in the case of serious collective crimes, of decimation of the guilty units.' That, he believed, was the only effective way to constrain the riotous and safeguard discipline.[115] Although at least one prominent historian afterwards claimed that decimation never actually occurred, the next two years of the war would see it practised by more than one commander with official approval.[116]

When, in May 1916, Cadorna sent a letter to all headquarters giving his subordinate commanders the power to order summary executions and assuming full responsibility for them, he was for once trailing in the disciplinary stakes. Summary executions without trial were already an established practice.[117] In the afternoon of 30 June 1915, finding themselves exposed to enemy fire in a valley when another battalion retreated instead of counter-attacking to come to their aid, a group of perhaps seventy soldiers of the 93rd regiment (*brigata Messina*) and seven of their officers surrendered. On learning what was happening, the brigade commander rushed forward and ordered the nearest company commander to open fire on the fugitives. 'Unfortunately,' he reported, 'I don't think our fire caused serious losses.' On 30 September a soldier of the Ivrea *Alpini* battalion was shot after raising a white flag. On 28 October, in the course of a desperate attack against strongly held enemy trenches, two soldiers

Fig. 4 Observation post on Monte Nero, Isonzo front

of the 12th regiment (*brigata Casale*) were shot for 'passive disobedience' when ordered to attack. Three days later, a soldier of the 85th regiment (*brigata Verona*) who had left the front line and sought shelter in a field dressing station was shot for abandoning his post in the face of the enemy. The corps commander, General Paolo Morrone, fully approved of making an example of him 'in order to prevent the repetition of shameful acts of cowardice'. On 28 November an unknown number of soldiers of the *brigata Pistoia*'s 36th regiment were shot while surrendering after being hit by a violent Austrian counter-attack while in the enemy's front line.

In all, thirty-one known soldiers and an unknown number of others were summarily executed in 1915. During June 1915 the army also shot twenty-six civilians in the newly occupied former Austrian territory on the west side of the Isonzo. Some were killed in reprisal for shootings at advanced detachments, some were taken with weapons in their hands and presumed to be members of the *Landstürm*, some were accused on flimsy or non-existent evidence of having given away Italian positions or collaborated with deserters, and two were caught in cross-fire between *Carabinieri* and Italian soldiers. Eleven of these shootings happened on a single day – 4 June 1915 – at or near Idersko on the western bank of the Isonzo. Some were apparently shot as a form of revenge by troops who were taking out on the civil population their own failures and lack of success.[118]

In the course of the war, the military tribunals would handle 352,000 cases and find 170,000 officers and men guilty, 23,016 (13.46%) in the first twelve months of the war, 48,296 (28.4%) in the second year, 82,366 (48.16%) in the third year and 2.380 (10.4%) in the final five months of the war. They handed down 4,028 death sentences of which some 750 were carried out (391 for desertion, 154 for indiscipline, 164 for surrender or disbandment, 41 for cowardice or other crimes). In the first twelve months of the war 101 men were shot, in the second year 251, in the third year 342, and in the last months of the war 54.[119]

A winter audit

At the start of December 1915 Cadorna decided that it was time for his troops to have some rest. They had fought for almost fifty days (by his calculation), during which units had been decimated by losses and sickness; they lacked officers; and they desperately needed replacements. Where the fighting front was not covered in ice and snow, the advanced trenches were full of mud and water and enemy fire made it impossible to construct effective cover. There was also the threat of a future enemy offensive to take into account: information suggested that significant enemy forces were being moved towards the Isonzo front from Hungary and Bukovina. There was also talk of concentrations of Austrian and German troops in the Tyrol. Here Cadorna was indulging in some special pleading: the military intelligence office in Milan had put the number of German troops in the Tyrol at no more than 14,000 and did not think they were increasing. The possibility of an enemy offensive made it even more necessary in Cadorna's eyes to increase the strength of the defences so that not a foot of ground captured at such great sacrifice would be lost. While maintaining aggressive contact with the enemy, he planned to fight limited actions in front of Gorizia and Tolmino to complete possession of the right bank of the Isonzo, while on the Carso 4th Army took possession of Monte San Michele and stabilised the front on the line of the Vallone. All this would allow the maximum number of troops possible to be sent on *licenza invernale* ('winter leave').[120]

Organising leave was a matter for the war ministry, not the chief of the general staff. A circular issued early in October announced that provisions for leave were done away with altogether except for those convalescing from wounds sustained on the battlefield. It was subsequently modified slightly to allow army commanders to give permission in really exceptional cases. At the start of December Zupelli suspended restrictive provisions introduced in August and September so as to allow for brief periods of leave to be taken over the next three months. Those who had been under arms longest were to be given preference. The process had to be gradual and numbers were not to swell over the Christmas and New Year periods. The penalties for overstaying leave were draconian: soldiers returning late were to be charged with desertion.[121] Though they were meant to apply after five days, everywhere they were interpreted as meaning only one day.

In some places the difference between coming out of the line and being in it did not amount to more than not being shot at – welcome as that must have been. Giuseppe Garrone, in late November an *Alpini* lieutenant in charge of a position 2,600 metres up in the *Zona Carnia* with temperatures at 25 degrees below zero, received troops coming out of the front line whose conditions were 'truly pitiful' and who lacked even basic items of kit such as mess tins. Because of 'the usual bureaucratic difficulties' he was unable to complete their equipment, feed them properly or issue wine and tobacco. Men reported sick with sprains, sore throats, pneumonia and bronchitis – but no doctor had been sent up to treat them.[122] After leading a truly heroic escape from the Caporetto disaster in October 1917, Giuseppe Garrone would be mortally wounded on Monte Grappa in December 1917 and die in his brother's arms. Eugenio Garrone, fatally wounded in the same engagement, died a prisoner of war some three weeks later.

Leave must have been a welcome respite for those who got it – and bitter for those who did not – for the army was exhausted. It was also showing signs of the dissent that Cadorna had all along suspected lay just below the surface. The first mutinies occurred in the *brigata Ferrara* on 11 December, when two soldiers were shot, and in the *brigata Salerno* on 20 December, when eight soldiers were shot. On 17 January 1916, the 151st regiment of the *brigata Sassari*, which was resting out of line at Caporetto, demonstrated against going back into line and called for leave to be granted. In the coming months incidents of this sort would increase in number.

The causes of the bloody failures that were the first four Isonzo battles, and the sense of gloom and despondency that was beginning to afflict the troops, were probably well summed up in an anonymous letter sent to Cadorna from Genoa in mid December. Almost all generals and many colonels were absolutely ignorant of the terrain. Terrorised by the sackings carried out by their commander, they issued impossible orders. Troops lacked cohesion, the consequence of very young and inexperienced junior officers who did not know one another and were not known by their soldiers being incorporated into regiments on the eve of advances, and of young recruits being sent up to the line without adequate training and preparation. Gunfire was not opening gaps in the line, and reinforcements did not arrive in time with the result that hard-won trenches had to be abandoned.[123] This was well-founded criticism, but things were destined to get worse not better.

The winter pause gave the military bureaucrats time and space to assess the state of the army after seven months of war. Everywhere the story was one of shortages and shortcomings. In July 1914 the army had been short of 7,500 active service officers.[124] The gap had been filled simply by substituting reserve officers who had done short accelerated courses (initially eight to twelve weeks, but later on four to six months) or had been nominated from the military schools and academies. Qualitative deficiencies had been magnified and multiplied by the necessary practice of promoting young lieutenants to captains and company commanders, thereby exacerbating the shortage of trained and experienced subalterns. Non-commissioned officers had been in short supply in the peacetime army, and promotions from the ranks had deepened that particular hole. Officers in some specialist arms were in short supply. The problem was particularly severe in the artillery, where cavalry officers had had to be brought in to fill gaps and field artillery commanders were given impossible assignments to direct fifteen or more batteries (sixty guns). Senior officers were very scarce so that at the start of the war engineer and artillery specialists were given divisional, corps and even army commands. Failings in the promotions procedures, which were producing officers who were not capable of functioning properly in their new grades, were making a bad situation worse.[125]

Command was only one face of the problem. Soldiers were being wounded and falling sick in ever-growing numbers. At the end of the first season's campaigning, the army medical service believed it was doing pretty well. Gaps had been filled on mobilisation using retired personnel, civilian doctors and final-year medical students. Three thousand of its 7,500 personnel had had no experience of military medicine – but time was taking care of that. In certain areas – field incinerators and field laundries – there were shortages but no real lack of matériel. The first months of war had, though, thrown up organisational and managerial problems: the distribution of doctors to units according to their medical specialisms had been deficient; field hospitals had been poorly organised, particularly to deal with epidemics; and there had been a crisis in the direction of the medical services – still unresolved at this time. This had forced the army's Intendance General to intervene, ensuring the supply of prophylactics against venereal disease and separating convalescents from the wounded and ill. The failure of civilian medical authorities to devise plans to counter epidemics and an increase in cholera infections had prompted Salandra to intervene, forcing a fusion of civilian and military health authorities and instituting committees of inspection. Rapid action, the authorities reported, had now contained the threat.[126] Without weapons in its hand and food in its stomach, the army could not fight. For the Italian army, like all armies, supplying and maintaining the men at the front was an enormous task and a novel one. In the first year of the war half a million soldiers were strung out along the line between Gorizia and Monfalcone. Feeding them alone was demanding enough: satisfying the appetites of 200,000 men and 30,000 animals for a single day took 140,000 kilos of bread, 48,000 kilos of meat, 30,000 kilos of pasta or rice, 10,000 kilos of cheese, 30,000 kilos of potatoes, 16,000 kilos of legumes, 3,000 kilos of coffee, 4,000 kilos of sugar, and 50,000 litres of wine.[127] Apart from a manageable problem with grain supplies – stocks had shrunk from thirty to fifteen days' supply – the commissariat believed it was doing well. A real shortage of tobacco at the start of the war due to transport problems had been overcome, but hay was still causing some problems. At the front, though, the picture was not so rosy. The food that reached the soldiers was sometimes rotten or of poor quality thanks to dishonest suppliers, and some comforts such as coffee, chocolate, wine and grappa tended to disappear as they passed forward through many hands. Throughout the war feeding the army always took priority over feeding the civilians but front-line troops, often existing on cold rations that came up all too intermittently, could be pardoned for believing that they were the last in a lengthy queue.[128]

Guns and munitions were, officialdom acknowledged, another matter entirely. At the start of the war munitions supplies were what they should be according to official tables – but not sufficient for foreseeable consumption. Manufacturing output at the start of the war had been wholly inadequate: in May 1915 Italian arsenals turned out 14,000 rounds of artillery ammunition a day (an average of seven rounds per gun); a year later the figure had risen to 50,000 rounds a day. Rifle ammunition began in an equally parlous state: in May 1915 there were 800,000,000 rounds, an average of 800 rounds apiece. By October 1915 three government factories and a private firm were providing 92,000,000 rounds a month, which was just about enough.[129] Medium-calibre artillery, essential for tackling reinforced enemy positions, had been in short supply from the start: Cadorna's only mobile heavy field artillery had been 112 149A howitzers, but he expected to have more taken from fortifications in the New Year, as well as new 200-mm mortars. The army was still short of heavy field artillery, mountain howitzers and heavy-calibre guns. Black powder, used in medium- and heavy-calibre ammunition due to the lack of high explosives, reduced effectiveness; there were no gas

shells; the war ministry had slowly doled out four ineffective wire-cutters
to each infantry company; and the first trench periscopes were only just
arriving.[130]

The air force had made limited progress by the year's end. It now had
135 aircraft, more than twice the number with which it had begun the
war, and 146 pilots. Eighty-five observers were at the front and more
were doing courses. Where only eight aircraft had initially been armed,
all now were. There now were – or were thought to be – enough bombs;
seven months earlier the total stock had amounted to only 900. Twenty-
eight aircraft were equipped with radio-telephones. Resupply was now
much improved thanks to the creation of an advanced supply depot at
Pordenone.[131] However, the Austrians had been the superior side in the
air during 1915, thanks in part to their prior experience. The Italian high
command had yet to learn how to make best use of air intelligence – and
how to gain it. The question of political control tended to shoulder its
way to the forefront of Cadorna's mind, but he had reason to complain
about the government's failure to generate industrial programmes that
would make up for the disparities between the two sides. During
1915 Italian factories manufactured a total of 382 aircraft and at the
end of the year could produce only 50 aircraft and 100 aero-engines a
month. There was no real production of spares, or of propellers, and no
repair service for machines or motors.

Less evident but no less important shortages were hampering the
army, among them a lack of reserve batteries on which to train personnel
and of forward repair shops for firearms in particular. The army had gone
into the war short of all sorts of equipment – flares, lights, radio-telegraph
stations, bridging equipment, sandbags – the list seemed almost endless.
Transport had enough horses but had been short of drivers and of
requisitionable automobiles. Communications, by contrast, were now
thought to be up to the task. The central postal office at Bologna had
initially been overwhelmed, but after a month a regular service had been
established. Almost immediately, postal censorship became an 'invisible
collaborator' in the ever-constricting coils of the military justice system.
Telegraph and telephone networks had initially been unable to cope
with the extra traffic, but after four months the necessary extra lines
had been laid.[132]

If things were not good at the front, they were no better behind the
lines. The railway service had functioned fairly well during mobilisation
and afterwards, thanks in part to the programme of line construction,
double-tracking and station building begun in 1903. The only real problem at that time had been the quality of the personnel, mostly old reserve
and territorial officers who lacked experience. Some lines necessary for

strategic deployment and subsequent development had not been built, though, and others had come into service belatedly: the newly double-tracked Treviso–Udine line was only opened for use on 10 August 1915. The transport service now had to prepare for the coming spring campaign short of some 1,000 waggons, 200 carriages and 150 railway engines, the only external source for which was the United States. It seemed that nothing would be possible until the end of 1916. There were problems transporting wood and coal. Finally railway personnel were tiring. 'Special compensations' might be the answer, but the government had decided against them.[133]

As the year ended and the weary soldiers at the front settled in to face the winter as well as the enemy, storm clouds were gathering over Cadorna. There were signs that the army was losing confidence not in itself but in his leadership. Ministers too were losing faith in him as his strategy was seemingly coming to nought. His brilliant reputation seemed overblown. Cadorna himself was now admitting that the war had become a matter of brute force in which attrition was the only route to success – a fact that Sonnino had recognised the previous July.[134] His relations with the war minister in Rome grew increasingly fraught. In the late autumn the two had a run-in over when to call up the 1896 class of recruits: Cadorna wanting mid November so that they could be in the field by the following spring, Zupelli preferring mid December. Before they managed to settle on a compromise (22 November) Cadorna threatened to resign and Zupelli did hand in his resignation, which he was persuaded to withdraw.[135]

With the New Year not yet a week old, Zupelli challenged Cadorna's military leadership. Writing to Salandra and Sonnino on 6 January 1916, he accused the chief of the general staff of breaking up his forces all along the frontier – clear evidence that there was no commanding strategic concept. There was no reason to believe that renewed attacks would have any better results. Instead, the war minister offered a new strategic formula: an attack in early February instead of waiting until April that would mass at least 500 medium and heavy guns on a 12-kilometre front. The enticing prize that beckoned was Trieste.[136] Zupelli put his idea to a lively cabinet meeting on 26 January. It went down well, particularly with Sonnino who wanted to remove Cadorna and replace him with General Di Robilant, Nava's successor in command of 4th Army. Sonnino went a step further and proposed that a war council be set up that included the top military men. Salandra put the ideas to the king, telling him that generals who had been fired and generals who had been promoted were all saying that continuing to attack in the same place and the same way was banging one's head against a wall. So were junior officers. Could they remain indifferent to what was 'indubitably the spirit of the army and with which the country is every day being infused', he asked the king.[137]

The cabinet sent Zupelli to try out his plan on Cadorna and Vittorio Emanuele sent his chief aide-de-camp, General Ugo Brusati, to sound him out on the idea of sharing strategic and operational power and responsibility. Cadorna was predictably furious, rightly scenting a plot to get rid of him, and refused point-blank to agree to any form of military council. 'Do you think I could ever tolerate this mini-parliament, whose assembly would show lack of faith in me and in which the army commanders would want to express their own views, quite possibly in opposition to mine?' he told Ninetta Cadorna. 'As you see, my greatest enemies aren't the Austrians.'[138] He had history on his side: fifty years before, conflicting military counsels had contributed to Italy's poor performance in the war of 1866.

A shrewd and energetic political in-fighter, Cadorna resorted to a press campaign orchestrated by his friend Ugo Ojetti which praised the high command at Udine and contrasted it with the puny politicians in Rome. More importantly he had the king on his side and at an audience on 21 February Vittorio Emanuele told him not to worry: 'If I had a bad opinion of you, I would not have defended you as I have – more than you can think.'[139] Zupelli's plan disappeared, as one minister put it, like the melting snow and its author soon followed. Cadorna had lived to fight another day – and would survive at least one more attempt to get rid of him before he finally fell from favour.

Italy's first experiences of modern war had exposed a multiplicity of shortcomings – in command at every level from *generalissimo* to platoon commander, in operations and tactics, in weaponry and supply. Some were beyond Italy's capacity to overcome alone: her weak economy entailed an ever-greater dependence on the support coming from her Allies. Others, such as the underpreparation of junior officers for their combat roles, could in theory be remedied although this would require a cultural change in the army. Others again, most notably the shaping and conduct of military operations, could potentially change. Would Cadorna and his generals learn from their own experience and that of their allies, or would they carry on much as before? In 1916, the front-line soldiers would learn the answers to some of those questions – and suffer the consequences.

4   1916 – Setback and success

Who would have imagined a catastrophe like this and lasting so long?
Luigi Cadorna, 17 January 1916

From his post-war vantage point, Cadorna wanted the year 1916 to be judged according to what turned out to be the fundamental characteristic of modern war – lengthy battles of attrition which consumed men and munitions in large amounts without winning much ground.[1] That was not exactly how he conceived of his war at the time, though it was accurate enough as far as the front-line soldier's experience went. On the ground, his armies would come perilously close to defeat in May – chiefly, critics later pointed out, because of the same failings in command that would have such dramatic consequences seventeen months later – before winning a prize in August. Tested under ever more extreme conditions, parts of the army failed, broke and mutinied. Cadorna's unhesitating response was to introduce the most extreme form of exemplary punishment – decimation.

Italy's declaration of war on Germany in August 1916 – rather too belatedly as far as her Allies were concerned – added to the increasing complication of strategy produced by the twists and turns of the war on the western, eastern and Balkan fronts. In dealing with these complications Cadorna always set his course according to what he thought would best serve Italy's military interests and help her win the war. The result was a policy which, while in essentials no different from that adopted by the leaders of all the other major Allied armies, was to all appearances the military version of the rallying call with which Antonio Salandra had justified Italy's entry into the war in the first place – *sacro egoismo*.

The fifth battle of the Isonzo and the threat to the Asiago

Cadorna laid great emphasis on 'method' in his operational and strategical approach to war, urging his commanders over the winter to continue offensive action and using 'mine warfare' methods. The Duca d'Aosta,

146

commanding 3rd Army, took this to mean applying the principles of siege warfare. His first priority was to construct such solid forward lines of defence as to give absolute certainty that they could not at any point be overrun no matter how substantial the attacking forces might be. This was a formula guaranteed to perpetuate the Italian weakness of concentrating as many men as possible in the front line, thereby rendering the army even more vulnerable to the effects of enemy artillery. General Frugoni, commanding 2nd Army, interpreted method in a like manner. Since the artillery must reserve its fire for the final determining phase of the battle, when its job was to hit the enemy batteries and to drop a dense screen of fire to paralyse enemy reinforcements in the manoeuvre zone, the enemy's line must be attacked using the weapons of trench warfare, approach works, and mine warfare. The first phase would entail digging zigzag approach trenches and parallels to within 30 metres of the enemy line and carving out galleries and mines under it. The second 'determining' phase would see 'the opening of the breach and the irruption onto the objective'.[2] The wire was to be cut using explosive tubes placed in position by hand.

At the beginning of February 1916 Cadorna learned that the Allies were going to have to postpone their planned offensive on 1 March as they were not yet fully prepared. The French wanted Italian action at Monastir and Salonika to draw off some of the Central Powers' strength and so make them too weak to act against the Russian 7th Army in Bessarabia and the Romanians. Cadorna brusquely dismissed the idea of operating in theatres that he regarded as sideshows, preferring to fight on the principal fronts where the Austro-German masses could be 'cut to the quick'. He was unwilling 'for elementary reasons of prudence' to send any Italian troops to the Balkans in exchange for Allied artillery, and argued instead that with some Allied guns and ammunition he could draw Austrian and possibly also German forces – 'the only ones we must seek to defeat' – onto his front.[3] The fifth battle of the Isonzo was thus undertaken partly in order to help the French, who were fighting for their lives at Verdun. No specific objectives were set. Instead army commanders were to fix their own according to the results they had already attained and their artillery deployments, bearing in mind that they should result in a step towards the first stage objectives in the advance to the east – Gorizia and Tolmino.[4]

Cadorna unleashed his fifth offensive – 'not really a battle, but a combination of local actions' – on 9 March 1916. First Army's task, together with 4th Army on its right, was to conduct 'energetic partial actions aiming to immobilise enemy forces on the front'. The battle, which lasted eight days, focused on the Carso and the west bank of the Isonzo opposite Gorizia. The ground over which it was to take place was severely affected by flooding and by snow and ice. Forward observation officers were used for the first time but because visibility was down to 100–200 metres they were of little help. Losses were mercifully few: 1,882 Italian and 1,985 Austrian dead and wounded. After it was over Frugoni castigated his subordinate commanders for failing to apply his methods properly. Some had finished their approach trenches too far from the enemy's line (his preferred distance now was a maximum of 20 metres); others had concentrated on digging galleries in caverns, 'an absolutely passive method of access'. The men were also not doing enough digging: there should be as many approach lines as possible to deceive the enemy and multiply the targets he had to hit.[5]

While Cadorna was focusing on the Isonzo, storm clouds were gathering elsewhere. At the start of the war General Roberto Brusati's 1st Army had been allotted a defensive role protecting the flank and rear of the other advancing armies, but when it became apparent that the enemy was not going to contest the Italian advance he was ordered to profit from this and gain as much ground as possible, at the same time instilling an aggressive spirit in his men. He was also instructed to complete the defensive systems on the Asiago. Discovering that one of his corps commanders had not duly done as he had been ordered, Brusati replaced him with Ottavio Zoppi, a relative of Cadorna's. By mid July 1915, Zoppi reported that everything necessary had now been done, and Brusati assured Cadorna in his turn that the front line could now put up 'an effective resistance'.[6]

Brusati nursed offensive ambitions and wanted to invest Trento with an action extending from the Brenta to Lake Garda. Cadorna had thought of a similar action in late 1914 but had then abandoned it. Chafing at the restrictions imposed upon him, and still nursing his grander ideas, Brusati pestered Cadorna at the end of June: 'I am now more strongly convinced that we need to advance.'[7] He was allowed a limited attack in the second half of August – perhaps because it was proposed by Zoppi – but then reminded that his task was to defend not attack. Asked by Cadorna as to how he proposed to protect his 238-kilometre front against an 'energetic enemy offensive', he replied reassuringly that 'If the defences cannot be said to be complete along the entire front, they are at a good point, and in some zones the power of resistance is truly great.'[8]

In September Cadorna agreed that 1st Army should hold the forward positions it had won 'as advanced occupation'. As winter closed down his front, Brusati was encouraged to remain actively vigilant and to undertake limited offensives as long as they did not weaken the general defensive design. However, he was also instructed to give up advanced positions if attacked in force and retreat to the principal defensive line. Cadorna's main concern was not to have to divert parts of the Isonzo armies in order to reinforce Brusati. Confusingly, two weeks later Cadorna underlined the absolute need to maintain conquered positions against Austrian counter-attacks.[9]

At the end of November, the army commanders were told that the *Comando supremo* wanted a defensive wall established from Stelvio at the western end of the front to the sea 'sufficiently solid and deep as to make it absolutely certain that the enemy will not succeed in undermining it at any point, no matter how strong the forces he uses'.[10] Later General Pecori Giraldi, conducting an inquiry into Brusati's failings, acknowledged that he had worked tirelessly over the winter to establish a secure defensive system, repeatedly exhorting, criticising and advising his subordinates. Brusati had good reason to think that his active forward policy was what his commander wanted: when the two men met in early February, Cadorna told him 'You're the only one who has done anything.'[11] Shortly afterwards he gave explicit approval to Brusati's strengthening of his defensive lines, especially the advanced ones, and dismissed his subordinate's worries that if the enemy attacked reinforcements would not arrive in time. Men and guns could be moved from other sectors of the front in time – Cadorna accepted Brusati's estimate of between nine and thirteen days – given 'the capacity for prolonged resistance of well-organised positions'. In line with his general strategic directives, the field commander emphasised that what mattered was the defensive capacity of the *prima linea*, by which he did not mean very advanced positions not linked to the defensive system.[12]

In view of what was to come, it is scarcely surprising that 1st Army's actions during the months preceding the *Strafexpedition* would come to be the subject of bitter post-war dispute. Colonel Roberto Bencivenga, then head of Cadorna's personal secretariat, believed that 1st Army headquarters skilfully presented its actions as obeying orders when in fact it was acting against both the spirit and the letter of those orders. Pecori Giraldi, tasked by Cadorna with inquiring into what turned out to be nearly a disaster, concluded that the essentially defensive conception of 1st Army's task had changed to a 'predominantly aggressive stance' and that although the higher authorities had studied the defensive problem carefully their directives had not been properly complied with and applied. As a result the three successive defensive lines had not been completed when the Austrians attacked and in various sectors flanks were exposed and capable of being turned by the enemy. Brusati bore the final responsibility for his command, but Pecori Giraldi would find eight of his subordinate generals responsible in varying degrees for what went wrong, including the army engineer-in-chief and two successive army artillery commanders. For Zoppi alone there were extenuating circumstances: the

V Corps commander, an aggressive 'thruster' who had been warned by Brusati on at least one occasion not to wear down his corps, admitted often being told that his defences were being neglected but in his defence put forward 'serious and well-founded reasons'.[13] Action was duly taken against the other seven generals but not against Zoppi.

At the start of January 1916, Italian intelligence picked up local signs that an Austrian offensive was coming. Russian and British intelligence offered some confirmation, reporting that Austrian units were being concentrated in Styria and Carinthia, that Austrian troops were being transferred from the Russian to the Italian front, and that there was talk in Vienna of a major offensive against Austria at the beginning of February.[14] Cadorna was personally inclined not to believe in the likelihood of an Austrian attack. The Russians, he knew, were preparing a spring offensive. With Austrian attention apparently focused on Galicia, it appeared unlikely that their forces currently operating there and in the Balkans would be employed on any other front.[15] Reading his enemy's mind – and reading it wrongly – he believed that they must know of the coming Russian offensive, that they would never deploy troops to an 'eccentric' theatre from which it would be difficult to move them to other theatres of war if needed, and that in any case if the Austrians were looking to achieve a great strategic success they would need more forces than they appeared to have on the Trentino front. As he later explained, 'It seemed very strange that the Austrians would choose the Trentino theatre for a major offensive because it was poorly connected to the rest of the monarchy [with] only two single-tracked mountain railways.'[16]

More information trickled through in February that appeared to confirm Austrian intentions. Reaching common ground on interpreting this intelligence proved difficult, partly because there was an ongoing dispute between 1st Army intelligence and the military intelligence office (*Ufficio informazioni*) at general headquarters over the cost of the 1st Army operations and its imperfect organisation.[17] To complicate matters further, competing and sometimes contradictory intelligence assessments were coming from different parts of general headquarters. In late February, Cadorna warned his commanders that the bulletins sent out by the military intelligence office could produce completely different projections on successive days and that only the ones put out by the situation and operations office (*Ufficio situazione e operazioni*) properly represented headquarters' thinking.[18]

Until the autumn of 1915 Cadorna's *Ufficio informazioni* tended to discount information coming from Allied – and especially French – sources about the transport of German and Austrian troops to the Tyrol and the Trentino because they turned out to be on their way to Serbia. As 1916

Fig. 5 Shelters on Monte Cregnedul

began, they inclined to Brusati's view that Austrian preparations in his sector were defensive and were intended to block any further Italian advances. Austrian military intelligence did its best to encourage the misreading of their intentions, swelling radio traffic to and from 10th Army in Carinthia to suggest that troops were being sent there as well as to the Trentino. With fragmentary indications arriving from various sources that an Austrian offensive was indeed forthcoming, Tullio Marchetti, running the Brescia station, began systematically collecting information, using railway watchers, deserters, refugees, field post offices and the Austrian press to identify and track the movements of Austrian units. Putting all his information together and adding the results of aerial reconnaissance, he concluded that it pointed unmistakably to the likelihood that an Austrian offensive would be unleashed in the Trentino, that no German troops would be involved, and that signs of enemy attacks on the Isonzo and in the *Zona Carnia* were deceptions.[19]

The Verona intelligence station confirmed Marchetti's assessment, providing Udine with the numbers of enemy regiments and guns being moved to the Trentino front, but the *Ufficio informazioni* disagreed and so did the *Ufficio situazione e operazioni*, which informed the army that it believed the reports from prisoners of a troop build-up were an exaggeration. Telephone intercepts – a very new source of information as the first equipment was only installed at Plava in 2nd Army's zone at the turn of January/February 1916 – were interpreted as confirming their judgement that the Austrian high command was not in a position to execute a large-scale operation and that its activities were intended at most to correct their most advanced front line. 'What the enemy is preparing [in the Trentino] has a purely local character,' the *Comando supremo* asserted confidently.[20]

Preferring to believe his own intelligence officer, and with all his forces in the front line, Brusati asked to have troops that had been switched to the Isonzo front restored to him. A staff officer was sent to headquarters at Udine to tell Cadorna that an attack was probable within the next three days, and that his army had absolutely no reserves with which to meet it. Brusati was told that it must be met with the resources he already had. After quizzing him about what strategic aerial reconnaissance he was undertaking, and what arrangements he was making to move troops by truck, Cadorna gave Brusati a lesson in command. Only a cool evaluation of events allowed them to be adequately confronted and 'imperious calm' on the part of a commander was a major factor in success.[21] Once again Brusati reassured him. Everything was being done to ensure an energetic defence: artillery was being concentrated at the centre to dominate the two most important rail routes as the wings were not threatened;

sector reserves, more appropriate than central ones on ground broken up by radial valleys and with very poor lateral communications, had been established and two of the reserve divisions had been sent forward. Brusati was fully confident that he could face even the most unfavourable case.[22] Cadorna agreed to the deployment of the artillery and the army reserve. Although unconvinced that the Austrians planned an all-out attack 'and that the enemy's predispositions look above all to mask other movements', he nevertheless sent Brusati seventy-two medium-calibre field guns and two infantry divisions.[23]

In early April Cadorna was still convinced that the Austrians were unlikely to launch an offensive on his front given the difficulties involved. Nevertheless, he used the signs of an Austrian offensive to appeal to Joffre for guns, munitions and a Russian offensive to relieve the pressure on the Italian front, reminding him that Italy had launched the fifth battle of the Isonzo in mid March to prevent the Austrians directly or indirectly reinforcing German action at Verdun.[24] Cadorna got some of what he wanted: the French armaments office promised him 140 guns and 70,000 rounds of ammunition by 15 May. Joffre favoured an attack by the Allies in the second half of May, when Russia and Great Britain would be stronger. As far as the Trentino was concerned, his advice was to limit military action to resisting and inflicting the maximum casualties on the attackers as the French were doing at Verdun, where they had found counter-attacks to have limited effects.[25]

By the end of April the intelligence picture looked very different. On 26 April a Czech deserter, Lieutenant Anton Krecht, fell into Tullio Marchetti's hands. In the course of his interrogation he told his captors that their estimates of Austrian numbers in the Trentino were too low. There were at least six army corps there, guns and munitions had been flooding into the region since the middle of February, and all the hospitals, barracks and private houses in Trento were crammed with soldiers. An action of 'extreme weight' was being prepared and would take place in the Val Giudicarie–Val Lagarina–Val Sugana area.[26] The *Ufficio situazione* at Udine was not minded to believe Marchetti's source, who they believed was mostly repeating hearsay, and preferred their own numbers to his which were too high. The rest, they believed, was hearsay. 1st Army intelligence kept counting and by 14 May they had identified 226 enemy battalions on the Trentino front, 69 more than the *Ufficio situazione* estimate and a 50 per cent increase in three weeks. The presence of a number of generals in the Trentino, including the Austrian army commander General Boroević, was also suggestive.

With action evidently impending Cadorna visted the Val Sugana and the Val Laguna, to which he had not been for seven months, in the last days of April and the beginning of May. During his visit he told officers in the 15th division mess at Val Sugana that he did not believe in the offensive because it was 'a bluff'.[27] What he saw left him very far from satisfied. Brusati had been tasked with ensuring that national territory was not invaded, and had reassured him that the advanced positions taken up did not prejudice maximum resistance on the rearward main defensive line. He had again been enjoined to ensure that the advanced line was in no circumstances reinforced. Cadorna now discovered that Brusati had been ignoring his orders. His advanced line had been so well fortified as to be more suitable for a main defensive line (*linea di massima resistenza*), and needed more troops than it presently had. Both his flanks were vulnerable to turning, and some of his positions were 'tactically absurd'. Cadorna ordered that the advanced works be terminated at once and that only light mobile medium-calibre guns be emplaced in the first line of defence.[28]

Brusati's days were clearly numbered. After a second inspection, Cadorna accused him of pushing his lines dangerously forward everywhere and failing to improve his defensive position despite frequent injunctions to do so. Brusati attempted to counter the accusations, claiming that he had always conformed to Cadorna's winter directives and had had explicit approval for the attack he had launched in Val Sugana that had pushed the line forward. By now, though, Cadorna had had enough and at the end of the first week in May Brusati got his marching orders. His defensive arrangements were deficient, the product of a mistaken conception of the role of fortifications and an imperfect application of the principles of mountain warfare. As a commander, his constant decentralising tendency, evident in his passing command of an additional army corps to Zoppi when he should have kept control of it himself, had revealed 'an excessive fear of responsibility'. Brusati had disobeyed orders and failed to fulfil his mandate, leaving the Val Sugana section of the front in need of far greater forces than would otherwise have been necessary. The king was asked to remove him from command.[29]

Cadorna was now in a delicate position. Brusati had gone beyond his instructions and seized forward positions – and Cadorna had let him do so. The immediate grounds for his dismissal were that he had not prepared 1st Army for a situation which could at any moment turn serious – but Cadorna had repeatedly said he did not believe in the likelihood of an Austrian attack in the Trentino. Cadorna retreated on to ground that was both unverifiable and unchallengeable: the principal cause of Brusati's removal was the 'lack of serenity' he had shown when attack seemed probable. 'As for my disbelief in an all-out attack from the Trentino,' he told the king's chief aide-de-camp, 'it still exists.'[30]

The *Strafexpedition*

Conrad had long nursed the ambition to attack Italy, and in 1916 his chance came. Falkenhayn refused to provide him with nine German divisions, which would have allowed him to release the same number of Austrian divisions on the Russian front, so he went ahead alone. He had 160,000 men and 1,056 guns. Taking personal command of the Italian theatre on 25 March, he planned a straightforward frontal assault 'with all possible force' to break through onto the Paduan plain, seize Padua, and envelope the Italian armies stationed in the Carso and along the Isonzo. After a three-week delay caused mainly by deep snow, and a two-hour bombardment, the Austrian offensive hit 1st Army on 15 May. Half of Brusati's army was up on the advanced line and too far forward and another quarter on the rearward line, leaving only a quarter in reserve, too far behind the fighting front. Cadorna's strategic reserve was in the wrong place: expecting a Russian offensive, and despite the warnings from military intelligence, his eyes were focused on the middle and lower Isonzo and his seven reserve divisions were stationed on the Tagliamento.

On the eve of the battle there was considerable confusion about Russian plans. At Chantilly in March the Russians had promised to start an offensive on 15 May. Then, on 24 April, unbeknown to Cadorna, the Russian chief of staff General Alexiev decided to postpone the offensive until 15 June and then unleash it in the direction of Vilna and not towards the south. French general headquarters claimed to have sent the exact date of the planned offensive to Cadorna, and he claimed to be unaware of it. As it was 'the necessary condition' for the launching of the next Italian offensive, and neither foreign minister Sonnino nor ambassador Tittoni in Paris knew anything useful about it, Salandra was anxious to lever the information out of St Petersburg.[31]

Cadorna was also at least partially misled by Austrian deception. Their intentions were camouflaged in various ways: preparations were kept secret from the Germans as well as their own troops; movements of men and matériel were described as responses to Italian preparations for an attack on the Isonzo (an intention which the Austrians had learned from informers, prisoners of war and censorship of their letters); and false information was placed in Austrian and neutral newspapers. Radio stations on the Carinthian front received much more radio traffic than usual, and at the start of March portable radio stations were brought in to the 10th Army to make it look as if six army corps were being deployed there. Italian aerial reconnaissance in that area suggested to the Austrians that the disinformation had worked, though the head of Italian military intelligence, Colonel Odoardo Marchetti, afterwards denied this.[32] Although the Italians had gradually latched on to the likelihood of an Austrian offensive, Cadorna continued to discount its likelihood or severity.

The first phase of the battle (15–20 May) took place in the Val Lagarina–Val d'Astico sector. The Italian divisional commanders stuck to orders issued by Brusati in mid April and defended forward positions or tried to retake them if they were lost. Pettiti di Roreto's 35th division on the Tonezza *altopiano* (a sector where there were no army reserves) took the principal shock and lost so heavily trying to retake the front line that it was incapable of holding the line of strong points behind it. Its commanding officer, De Chaurand de St Eustache, was sacked two days later. Pecori Giraldi threw in all his reserves in a desperate attempt to hold the Austrian attack and by 19 May had established a line of resistance. The first bulletins from the *Comando supremo* were vague and optimistic, saying nothing about the numbers captured, whereas Austrian bulletins referred to large numbers of prisoners taken. A worried premier quizzed military headquarters: given that the military authorities had said so often that the Trentino and the Asiago were the most vulnerable point of Italy's frontier, how was it that the force there was so small as to be overcome at once?[33] General Carlo Porro's reply on behalf of Cadorna was little more than a rehearsal of an already well-known refrain. Italy's forces in the region were not inferior to the Austrians, whose superiority lay in medium and heavy artillery and inexhaustible munitions. Cadorna blamed his commanders: Brusati had compromised the situation by his 'bad defensive organisation' and the 35th division on the Tonezza *altopiano* had performed badly. Salandra could be reassured that the measures he had already taken would ensure that the enemy would not be able to gain possession of the Asiago plateau and then descend onto the plain below.[34]

Salandra's government was already in a shaky position with Sonnino pressing him to remove Cadorna, something the foreign minister had long wanted, and bring Leonida Bissolati, a moderate socialist, into the cabinet, both demands the premier rejected. Now anxieties mounted rapidly in Rome – as well they might. At the war ministry General Morrone complained at having to rely on what was in the public bulletins to keep ministers informed. Porro stressed the difficulties he and the staff were facing: information was fragmentary, it took time to cipher communications, and the division of the *Comando supremo* into two (an advanced headquarters had been set up at Thiene) was admittedly a problem. Doubtless on Cadorna's orders, or at least in line with his wishes, Porro fended off the idea of direct communications between Rome and Thiene, but did agree that the war minister should have a high-level liaison officer in place at Udine.[35] There was clearly a communications problem, and Porro's subsequent undertaking that all telegrams that he received would go to the premier is not likely to have been much of a reassurance.

Facing the possibility of a collapse of 1st Army on the *altipiani* and an Austrian irruption onto the plains below which would expose Milan and the other major cities of the north to the enemy, Cadorna moved swiftly to shore up the weakened front. On the night of 20/21 May he created a 5th Army under Frugoni, and in a colossal logistical manoeuvre his staff concentrated an army of 179,000 men and 35,600 horses in the Vicenza–Padua–Cittadella zone in only twelve days, thanks largely to the efforts of the intendant-general of 5th Army, General Guido Luzzi. By the time that 5th Army was in place, the third and final stage of the battle was taking place (29 May – 10 June) and the Italians were holding the line of final resistance.

On 20 May Conrad launched a second wave of assaults against Sette Comuni on the Asiago plateau (20–28 May). Cadorna had by this time been able to give his subordinate another forty-two infantry battalions. The Italian reserves were deployed forward to hold the front line – a strategical error according to one commentator.[36] Three days into the second stage of the battle, with Austrian troops at Portule (2308 metres) and the *altopiano* of Asiago at their feet, Salandra was reassured that what was happening was 'not a defeat but an orderly retreat, inflicting considerable losses on the enemy', carried out by the sector commanders to avoid 'useless sacrifice'. Austrian dominance was put down to a crushing superiority in artillery thanks to guns and ammunition supplied by Germany – which was untrue as Conrad had kept the Germans in the dark about his offensive until six days before he launched it. What was needed now, the premier was told, was energetic insistence on Russian intervention. If Austria got reinforcements it could pressure the Italians to abandon the Isonzo line.[37] In the meantime, Cadorna created a new *altopiano* command under General Clemente Lequio, a specialist in mountain warfare.

Facing the prospect of a political as well as a military disaster, Salandra was under pressure from within his cabinet to reform the instrument of war government and in effect to refound the structure of Italian civil–military relations. Sonnino revived his earlier proposal for a council of generals and politicians. Orlando pointed out that this would be the equivalent of dismissing Cadorna. Ever the parliamentary politician, Salandra looked for an acceptable compromise. Cadorna was asked to come with his chief of staff and his four army commanders to a meeting at Padua that would be chaired by the premier and would also be attended by the army and navy ministers and two other members of the cabinet. The military situation would be examined 'in depth and in all its aspects' so that the government had a foundation for its deliberations and on the basis of which it could 'assume its rightful responsibility before parliament and the country'.[38] This was strategy by committee and Cadorna had no intention of putting up with that. He was prepared to meet ministers to give them information – but that was all. Councils of war, with the multiple opinions they inevitably embodied, merely created uncertainties, divided responsibilities and led to temporisation when what was needed was swift decision-making. As long as he enjoyed the trust of the king, he told Salandra, running the fighting was his responsibility; if that responsibility was diminished, then the government should replace him. Salandra backed off at once. Cadorna had misunderstood him: the premier did not intend to convoke a war council. Instead he was sending General Morrone to gather information.[39]

While the council of ministers fretted, the Italian front buckled yet further. On 27 May Austrian troops took Arsiero on the left of the Sette Comuni *altopiano*, and next day they captured Asiago in the centre. They were now on ground that had been Italian since 1866. On 31 May Conrad launched the third and final stage of his offensive along the line from Vallarsa to the Brenta. In the middle of this, Morrone returned to Rome with the news that if Austrian pressure increased Cadorna intended to order a retreat to the Piave to avoid encirclement. Sonnino, Salvatore Barzilai, a minister without portfolio, and Domenico Martini, the colonial minister, all wanted Cadorna replaced: the king should be told it was Cadorna or the cabinet. On 30 May the council of ministers gave Salandra a mandate to propose Cadorna's substitution. This left the issue in the premier's hands, and although the king was prepared to change his chief of the general staff Salandra decided not to sack him after being reassured about the military situation and promised that he would be warned in the unlikely event of a need to retreat to the Piave.

Pouncing on the government's evident weakness, Cadorna put pressure on the premier to release Eritrean and Libyan troops for his war. The government was reassured that 1st Army had been reinforced and 5th Army was being formed on the Paduan plain in case the Austrians irrupted into it, but warned that there were signs that Austrian troops were being switched from Galicia to the Italian front. If that was indeed so then Italian troops would have to be moved from elsewhere and if that in turn left his defences too weak Cadorna would be forced to redeploy behind the Piave 'to avoid a catastrophe'.[40] Morrone flatly refused to give Cadorna any more troops from Africa.

Cadorna now applied pressure of his own on Russia. If she intervened quickly and vigorously, then notwithstanding its current tribulations the Italian army would be in a position to take part in a general Allied offensive within or close to the time limit established at Chantilly for 'contemporary' action. If not, then the Italian army would find itself 'paralysed' on the Trentino front and would for a long time be unable to take the offensive.[41] News arrived the same day that Russia would complete transferring and concentrating her troops by 1 June and begin her offensive at once.[42] General Alexiev, the Russian chief of staff (whom St Petersburg claimed was in direct communication about the offensive, though Cadorna denied this), confirmed to the Italian military attaché, General Romei, that Nicholas II had issued orders for the offensive to begin on 4 June all along the south-west front using three armies. Alexiev added a strategic spin of his own to match Cadorna's, remarking that it would be 'desirable' if Italy launched an energetic offensive by 10 June and raising the possibility that the *Comando supremo* might wish to support the Russian and Serbian idea of launching an offensive at Salonika at the end of June.[43]

Aware that the Russian offensive would begin in three days' time, Cadorna was able to reassure Salandra when the two men met at Vicenza on 1 June that the hypothesis of a retreat to the plain was neither imminent nor probable. Within days the Austrian offensive ground to a halt. Early news from the Russian front spoke of unbroken success there and by mid June there was evidence that Austria–Hungary had moved two army corps from the Italian front to Galicia and Bukovina, that she was combing the rear echelons and the hospitals for officers, and that all her reserves had now been deployed.[44] On 10 June Cadorna launched a counter-offensive around Asiago. Conrad began to withdraw troops and at 1830 hours on 16 June he ordered his armies to go on to the defensive. The Austrians retreated to a prepared line of strongpoints on the night of 25 June. After forty-five days of continuous fighting, the Italian army was too exhausted to follow up the retreat. It was also showing more signs of discontent that was beginning to shade into dissent.

On 4 June, as General Brussilov launched his promised offensive on the Russian front – twenty days later than the date that had been agreed at Chantilly in March – Salandra sought once more to assert his authority. If it became necessary to withdraw behind the Piave, such a decision would have such serious national and international consequences that it could never be regarded as falling within the military's competence and must be communicated to him so that it could be deliberated 'without [feeling] the pressure of immediate and unavoidable necessity'.[45] Cadorna, who now expected to regain the initiative thanks to the provisions he had made to stem the Austrian tide, repeated that retreat behind the Piave was improbable. If the situation got worse, the government would be informed. However, in the 'very remote' likelihood that he did have to withdraw from the Isonzo he had no intention of ceding his authority to take such a decision to civilians as any delay could land the entire army with 'an irreparable setback'.[46] Highly impractical, Salandra's demand to make a crucial military decision also displayed his now weak grip on the war: if he had a military commander whom he did not trust, then why was he still in place?

Only the most robust of governments could have survived such a moment of national peril and Salandra's administration was now far from robust. On 6 June the chamber of deputies reassembled. Neutralists who had never wanted the war anyway joined forces with socialists and with interventionists enraged by what had happened, and four days later Salandra lost a vote of confidence by 197 votes to 158 with 98 abstentions and resigned. His replacement, 78-year-old Paolo Boselli, headed a national government that included right, centre and left Liberals as well as a single republican and an equally lone Catholic. Sonnino and Morrone were kept on. Morrone believed the demise of Salandra's cabinet to be due to a 'very widespread feeling of hostility towards it' combined with 'nervousness' generated by the accounts being given by Venetian deputies and others returning from the front. It would 'perhaps be preferable,' he suggested to Cadorna, to limit politicians' presence in the war zone as far as possible, a suggestion that must have been music to his ears.[47]

The Italian losses at the hands of the *Strafexpedition* amounted to some 148,000 men, Austrian losses to 80,000.[48] The Russian intervention produced the impression that the Italians had been saved once again by the military achievements of others – a picture uncomfortably like that of 1859 and 1866 when first French and then Prussian troops had come to the aid of an ineffective Piedmontese army. In fact, on the basis both of the hard fighting that held the Austrians on the very edge of the Asiago plateau and of the fact that the Austrians did not start withdrawing troops from the front until 20 June, the Italian army could fairly claim to have won the battle thanks to its own efforts.

As soon as it was clear that the Austrian offensive was over, Cadorna began preparing an Italian counter-offensive to assist his Russian ally. On 21 June, with 3rd Army not ready, he decided on an all-out offensive on the *altipiani*. The most that the army could manage would be tactical offensives from Pasubio and Sette Comuni and they would be lacking artillery. On 25 June, thirty-six hours before the offensive was due to start, Conrad retreated. Cadorna first suspended the offensive on 27 June, but then ordered it restarted to help the Russians.

The *Strafexpedition* showed Cadorna's strengths as a commander – and his shortcomings. His reactions once the Austrian attack had begun were quick and well calculated, but he had – as he privately admitted – been taken by surprise. His own explanation was that the attack had been – or had seemed to him to be – strategically illogical. The Italian theatre was not a decisive one, unlike the French or Russian theatres, and therefore a battle won against Italy would not resolve the European war. Nor did it seem reasonable to suppose that Austria would shift its best heavy artillery to the Trentino in the face of an imminent Russian attack.[49] There was, however, rather more to it than that. A confused and inadequate structure for reporting and assessing intelligence, itself a reflection of the way he ran his headquarters, led Cadorna to underestimate the gravity of the threat and thereby contributed to the surprise. So, too, did his practice of running his army commander, Roberto Brusati, on too loose a rein, giving orders that were insufficiently explicit, not following them up closely enough, and not insisting strongly enough that they must be carried out. Looking back a decade later Piero Pieri, doyen of Italian military historians, saw the same errors that Cadorna would repeat eighteen months later in an aggravated form and against a more able opponent.[50]

One thing that did change for the better after the *Strafexpedition* was the intelligence organisation. Before the attack Marchetti had tried to see Cadorna personally to alert him to the true numbers but had been blocked by Colonel Ugo Cavallero and others on the headquarters staff. Afterwards he was called to the *Comando supremo* and there, on 14 September, he poured out his frustrations at Cadorna's failure to heed his warnings to an officer he believed to be General Porro, the sub-chief of staff. It was in fact Cadorna himself. Two days later Marchetti was summoned to headquarters again. 'This time you'll recognise me,' the *generalissimo* remarked drily before inviting him to weekly personal meetings.

To resolve the conflicts that had contributed to the intelligence failure on the Trentino, Colonel Garruccio reorganised the *Ufficio informazioni*, dividing it in two on 5 October 1916. Operational intelligence was subsumed within the *Ufficio situazione e operazioni di Guerra* of the *Comando supremo*, supported by detached intelligence officers (ITOs) in each army, and rear area and foreign intelligence was entrusted to the *Servizio informazioni del comando supremo*. Headquarters in Rome ('R' section) oversaw the new structures, developed a specialisation in economic intelligence, and took responsibility for policing, counter-espionage and censorship, serving as the general link to 'U' section at Udine. As the latter two activities were in the hands of two *Carabinieri* captains and a lone official from the *Pubblica sicurezza* a problem of

overwork soon developed. 'M' section in Milan took on responsibility for
the collection and transmission of all military intelligence from other
centres and free-standing agents, which went to the *Comando supremo*
via 'U' section, and for economic information which went to 'R' section.
Rome also handled telegraph and telephone censorship and the interception and decryption of radio-telephone traffic.[51] The service now had
or planned to have intelligence-gathering centres at Cairo, Athens,
Corfu, Salonika, Valona, Lugano, Berne, Paris, Madrid, The Hague,
Copenhagen, Stockholm, Oslo, Petrograd, Bucharest and Buenos
Aires. General Alessio Chapperon, military attaché at The Hague from
November 1916, appears to have had overall charge of European intelli-
gence operations. Particular care was taken by the Paris section to
develop the fullest exchanges of intelligence with the Americans.

In the firing line

By 1916, the war on the Italian fronts had settled into a pattern. The
generals ordered enemy positions conquered at all costs, apparently
without first-hand knowledge of the ground they were sending their
men across or of the need to capture other positions first, while nature
and circumstance combined to make the infantryman's life difficult and
unpleasant when it was not downright dangerous. The end of winter
brought relief to the troops soldiering in the mountains, but also anxiety.
'If you could see the snow here,' an anonymous infantryman in the high
Cadore wrote to his brother in early April, 'it's almost 8 metres deep but
now the good weather is coming we'll have to advance . . . how many poor
Italians will have to die to satisfy this passion to slaughter us like sheep.'[52]
As summer arrived on the Carso mosquitoes, sunshine and a dusty wind
which got into the shelters increased the discomfort. There were no
latrines and men relieved themselves as soon as they could for fear of
being hit by the enemy, so that immediately soldiers left their shelters
they trod in human waste. The stink was insupportable.[53]

Battle brought with it danger and dread. Austrian 305-mm rounds
arrived like express trains and hit the ground with a shock like an
earthquake. Tackling the enemy wire, all too often left unbroken, led to
calls for volunteers to slide tubes of explosive underneath it. The reward,
for those brave or desperate enough to take what was a big gamble with
their own lives, was extra money or six days' leave. Where they worked,
the enemy immediately filled in the gaps with *chevaux-de-frise*. In the
attack, men bumped into one another as they hurried forward, a strong
smell of sulphur in the air, until they reached an enemy trench 'still warm
like a bed' from the bodies of the men who had left it to attack.[54]

There were on average 1,539,000 men in the field during 1916. Between May and November (the fighting season) 357,400 died or were wounded, a daily rate of 1,670. The patterns of hospitalisation reflected the murderous nature of the infantry's war. In the first six months of 1916, 40 per cent of wounds were caused by machine-guns and rifles and 55 per cent by artillery. Venereal disease accounted for 4.6 per cent, half the rate for the first seven months of the war. Deaths in the field accounted for 8 per cent of the wounded and deaths in hospital for another 10%. At the end of June 1916, the authorities were unable to say how many of the injured were permanently invalided and how many would be able to return to the ranks.[55]

Faced with the horrors of trench warfare, the most notable thing about the Italian army, as Giorgio Rochat has pointed out, is 'not that a minority of soldiers may have sought flight in self-inflicted wounds, in desertion, in neurosis or in other ways, but that the great majority continued to sustain it and to fight'.[56] Exogenous situational factors inherent in the nature of war and the act of fighting played their part. The hierarchical organisation of war and the organisation of large masses of men contributed to the army's cohesion by binding them together in both large and small groups – though this could occasionally lead to disruptive action by groups of disaffected or distressed soldiers. Then there was the enemy – a binding force of not inconsiderable power and one which should not be over-looked. The soldiers also drew strength and stamina from endogenous forces and from the diversions that authority allowed them.

Despite the all too evident social fragmentation, Italian culture provided the fighting soldier with resources that helped him find the will and the strength to keep going. Hard-line members of unions such as the railwaymen may well have carried into the war their hatred of 'the arbitrary and paternalistic systems of individual reward and punishment' to which they had been subject in peacetime.[57] Against this, though, must be set the experience of growing up in a Catholic–peasant society in which deference and the acceptance of destiny were heavily emphasised and widely accepted. Rural peasants and urban workers alike were used to authority figures – the parish priest, the mayor, the local *Carabiniere*. In the army, junior officers were their immediate authorities. By and large they adopted a familiarly paternalistic role, talking of duty while imposing discipline.

Religion operated on many levels. The central government of the Catholic Church explained the war theologically as God's punishment for the apostasy of modern society. This collective sin required expiation, which meant sacrifice in combat. By this logic war became an instrument of collective and personal sanctification. Extending and amplifying the church's core proposition, the bishops saw in the war an opportunity to rebuild society and bring together 'real' and 'legal' Italy, split apart by the Risorgimento. According to the archbishop of Rossano Calabro, Monsignore Orazio Mazzella, war would do much more good than harm since the collective suffering it was causing would produce the same beneficial effects as individual suffering:

It can re-awaken lost energies [and] perfect civil and moral virtues, making felt the need for order, discipline, sacrifice, [and] heroism...[and] reinforce the union between the different classes, sacrificing all on the altar of the *patria*.[58]

Catholicism also allowed the superstitious to get direct personal comfort from their religion by requesting, or being sent, images of saints and other devotional items from their local parish church. The churches played their part in encouraging this religiosity, printing images of the Madonna literally by the million.[59] At the front military chaplains held field masses and gave communion, though according to one authority direct contacts between chaplains and individual solders were rare.[60]

Perhaps the most important contribution made by the Catholic Church to the war as far as the front-line soldier was concerned came in the form of the *Case di soldato*. Modelled on pre-war parochial hostels for workers and emigrants, and extended along the entire front in the autumn of 1916 thanks to the persistence of a priest, Don Giovanni Minozzi, they were a conscious attempt to provide a conservative alternative to official socialism which was held to be sabotaging the war effort. Reading and writing rooms offered tired troops refuges in which to receive and reply to mail (illiterate soldiers were given help to do both), and provided books, newspapers, musical instruments and gramophones. By May 1917 there were ninety-six of them scattered through all the armies. Some idea of their significance can be deduced from the example of the *Casa di soldato* at Vicenza. Between June 1915 and December 1918 it received 1,200,000 visits, sent out 800,000 letters and cards, and put on 300 theatrical and musical shows.[61]

Under Cadorna's iron rule, Piero Melograni has remarked, the mass of his soldiery had only two authorised distractions to mitigate the hardships of war: one was alcohol and the other was *case di tolleranza* (military brothels).[62] Wine was part of the rations, but extra supplies were always welcome and even necessary. It gave peace of mind to the brigade commander about to throw his men against unbroken Austrian wire, courage to the nervous platoon commander about to lead out a patrol, and 'resignation to the poor wretch who doesn't command a cabbage, who has just come out of his seventh battle and already sees the eighth taking shape', according to one of the best of the war's many diarists.[63] A glass of good wine taken from an abandoned cantina could brighten

Fig. 6 Teleferica

the day and help reassure relatives that all was for the best albeit not in the best of all possible worlds.[64]

Casual sex was readily available both unofficially and officially. Paolo Caccia Dominioni, on a train from Rome to the front with a friend, encountered a woman in her thirties who looked as if she came from the 'modest bourgeoisie' until she took off her coat. He turned down her offer of a threesome in Arezzo.[65] Behind the lines, officers and other ranks could arrange for consorts to give them solace. When Cadorna's telegraphist was caught by the *Carabinieri* in Udine with his girlfriend who did not have a pass Colonel Cavallero of the headquarters staff got him off, amused by the fact that she was also a senator's mistress.[66]

Official and unofficial prostitution were both widespread and to different degrees both posed a threat to the army, taking men out of action for no good cause. The war ministry was worried from the start about the incidence of venereal disease among the troops – conscripts were bringing it with them into the army – and on 11 June 1915 Cadorna decreed the establishment of officially controlled military brothels 'in case the war lasts a long time' in order to discourage the troops from visiting clandestine prostitutes.[67] In September an ongoing process of regulation began. As the war went on the army expanded and extended its activities: clinics were set up, prophylactic advice was given, military brothels were visited two or three times a week, soldiers were examined by medical orderlies after using them, and regular changing of sheets (at least twice a week!) and the disinfection of mattresses and blankets were made mandatory.

Conventional socio-medical thought indirectly but influentially supported official policy. Masturbation was thought to be a serious threat to the race (along with tobacco), and there were fears that too prolonged a period of enforced sexual abstinence might lead to homosexuality, rape and sadism.[68] The medical authorities thus took a very practical view of 'official' sex: 1st Army's medical specialist complained that there were not enough *case di tolleranza* for his troops because of 'prejudice and erroneous concepts of morality' by the civil and military authorities.[69] How much was enough it is impossible to say, but in November 1916 the prefect of Udine reported that the military authorities had opened nine brothels and by the following summer 3rd Army had fourteen *case di tolleranza*, mostly either for officers or for other ranks though at Cervignano one was reserved for senior officers only. Demand, to judge by the only statistic we appear to have, was not inconsiderable: in 1916 the Palmanova brothel had 700–900 customers every working day.

Unofficial and amateur prostitution was, or was held to be, common. The bishop of Padua, Monsignore Luigi Pelizzo, complained about 'great floods of prostitution in the occupied areas', and after 3rd Army had retreated from Caporetto to the Piave it reported that it was fighting 'phalanxes of clandestine prostitutes'.[70] In the Bologna military district, women workers in military establishments were believed to be one of the most active sources of venereal infections. Amateurs and *vaganti* ('wandering' prostitutes) posed particular threats to the military because they were harder to control and to the civil authorities because of the collapse in morality they represented. The *Pubblica sicurezza* (security service) had the job of tracking down clandestine prostitutes, ensuring that they had a permit (*libretto*), visiting them regularly, and seeing that they were punished for any infractions of the law or the rules.

While they fought to hold the Austrians, Cadorna's armies were assailed with both lethal and non-lethal bureaucratic missiles as their commander fired generals, their generals had soldiers shot, and the war ministry sent out a stream of irrelevant circulars and entangled everyone in infuriating red tape, as staff officers have always done. At the end of May Morrone sent out a circular warning officers who were sporting sideboards that they were not only breaking disciplinary regulations but were adopting a foreign appearance which, at a moment of patriotic fervour, could be displeasing and give rise to disagreeable comment.

Cadorna had been convinced from the outset that both the regular and the extraordinary military tribunals (convened by regimental commanders) were going to be too soft on the soldiers appearing before them. The events of the winter of 1915–16 appeared to him to bear this out. War tribunals, convened by army or corps commanders and observing all the regulations designed to safeguard the accused, were at the top of the hierarchy of military justice. 'Extraordinary tribunals' could initially only be convoked by divisional commanders or above. To make sure that the extraordinary tribunals did not succumb to the temptation to be merciful, a circular sent out on 22 March 1916 instructed their chairmen to 'make judges understand the serious consequences which can result from excessive leniency'.[71] Then, on 1 June 1916, regimental commanders were given the power to convene extraordinary tribunals. Convoked by middle-ranking officers – during the war regiments were often commanded by lieutenant-colonels – and manned by their juniors who had little or no judicial expertise, they were both directed and enabled to punish severely: for example, according to Article 116 of the military penal code if four or more soldiers refused an order or even made a complaint verbally or in writing, they were guilty of mutiny. In wartime, if this happened in the front line or during a march in which they were exposed to enemy fire, the punishment was death.

In tightening the disciplinary screw Cadorna may have thought that he was putting a lid on his problems, but they were very far from over – in fact, they were only beginning. On the night of 21/22 April 1916 a battalion of the 3rd *Bersaglieri* was due to go back into line to renew an attack. From the barracks there were shouts for peace and rest and shots were fired at regimental headquarters. Officers quickly restored order but four soldiers took arms and refused to leave the barracks. Three were shot at once, the fourth escaped. As so often, the circumstances surrounding the event were complex. A month before 450 men, including the three who were shot, had been transferred from another brigade which they had left with regret, and several days before the battalion commander had fired on two of his own companies when they had been trapped in no-man's-land by Austrian machine-guns. The day after the incident an extraordinary military tribunal sentenced five soldiers to death (by shooting in the chest), one to hard labour for life, one (a corporal) to fifteen years' military jail, and the remaining 337 to three years' incarceration for complicity. The condemned men were shot next day – Easter Sunday – in thick snow. Cadorna praised the regimental commander for the energy he had shown in repressing the trouble.[72]

Having hitherto been attacking, or fighting off enemy counter-attacks, the Italian army was now fighting an entirely novel kind of battle in which the enemy had the initiative. Confronted with this new and unforeseen circumstance, the leading historian of such matters has adjudged, the high command 'was easily induced to believe in the inefficiency of the troops and to over-value episodes of fear and disbandment'.[73] The number of such episodes was about to increase. When the Austrian *Strafexpedition* was barely ten days old Cadorna discovered that while the troops on the Val Sugana and Val d'Adige were fighting well there had been 'deplorable incidents' on the Asiago.[74] On 26 May, with Monte Cimone in enemy hands and Arsiero about to fall to the Austrians, elements of 141st infantry regiment panicked when hit by violent enemy artillery fire and a sudden attack. Several hundred soldiers fled the front line and took refuge in woods to the rear. Cadorna upbraided General Lequio for the 'shameful events' that were occurring on the *altipiani* where 'easily defensible positions of capital importance have fallen into the hands of [only a] few of the enemy without any resistance [being put up]'. Lequio was told to take 'energetic and extreme measures' and to use summary executions to shoot the guilty immediately regardless of their rank.[75] The next morning the regimental commander, following orders, selected by lot a lieutenant, three sergeants and eight men from among the men who had dispersed and shot them – the first unequivocal case of decimation.[76] Commanders were now ordered to shoot the guilty without trial and on 4 June Cadorna met with Lequio personally and ordered the most severe punishment for anyone 'giving in'. More 'deplorable incidents' occurred in the days that followed. On 19 June elements of the 138th regiment (*brigata Barletta*) broke up after the death of their battalion commander. The commanding officer of its sister regiment, 137th infantry, machine-gunned them and three days later became the first individual officer to be named by Cadorna in an Order of the Day, praised for taking energetic measures against troops who had 'disbanded'. Multiple summary executions now became more common and commanders more ready to carry them out. After heavy fighting on Monte Nero and then on the Asiago, where they suffered many casualties, the exhausted men of the 89th infantry regiment were launched in repeated attacks on Monte Interotto. On 1–2 July 1916 groups of soldiers tried to go over to the enemy. Some were reported to have succeeded. The divisional commander ordered his artillery and machine-guns to fire on them. The corps commander, General Ottavio Zoppi, then withdrew the battalion from the front, and next day two men from each of the four companies involved were summarily shot. They included soldiers decorated for valour and wounded soldiers who begged for the opportunity to die in battle.

Official reports skated over the fact that the battalions had been sent into indefensible positions with no trenches and ignored the desperate circumstances of the units concerned, many of whose members after being wounded had been pinned down for two days between the lines under enemy fire, making any attempt to rescue them impossible. Instead three officers, one of whom had himself already been wounded and was no longer in command when the supposed desertions took place, were put on trial for having put the operation at risk through negligence. The case against all three was subsequently dropped. Nevertheless, General Porta, the divisional commander, General Zoppi and Cadorna were all pleased with actions which were both unjust and illegitimate.[77] When the affair was made public by a parliamentary deputy in November 1916, Cadorna admitted that only one of the eight men executed had been declared guilty and that four had been chosen by lot from the two companies involved, something which he believed proved that selection by lot had not 'struck blindly' but had ensured that punitive justice was 'exemplary and sure'.[78]

Cadorna's ire extended up the hierarchy as well as down it, though the consequences for senior officers who felt it were considerably milder. Lequio, his performance in the mountains disappointing, was fired two weeks after he was appointed and replaced by General Ettore Mambretti. De Chaurand had already gone, and he was joined by Major-General Gustavo Rostagno, commanding 32nd division, who paid the price for

Table 3 *Desertions June–December 1916*

June	July	August	September	October	November	December
[1,925]	[1,925]	1,627	1,612	1,364	1,328	1,817

Source: Tables of deserters, AUSSME L13 b.143/f.7. Figures in brackets are averages

the earlier loss of Cengio. Frugoni, put in command of the new 5th Army by Cadorna, was removed from command immediately after the *Strafexpedition* after making a bad impression on Salandra. An enquiry resulted in 'justified accusations of negligence, frivolity (*leggerezza*) and ignorance'. Frugoni was found to have 'passed entire days in cafes ogling every little seamstress who passed by'.[79]

The official statistics reflected the increasing disciplinary problems within the army. In the second full year of the war the incidence of acts deemed to be crimes under military law began to climb. In the war zone, 11,598 men were charged with desertion between June and December 1916.

Desertion was not confined only to the war zone. Between May 1915 and the end of November 1916, 10,222 men deserted from the territorial military districts, and 6,830 of them remained at large. Palermo, Rome and Milan were at the top of the list. In all, 28,000 men were condemned for desertion in the second year of war, 2,300 for surrendering to the enemy, and 3,118 for self-inflicted wounds. As far as the latter category was concerned, sitting the war out in the relative comfort of prison ceased in October 1916, after which sentences were suspended and the men were sent to the front line. From December, military tribunals interpreted self-wounding 'in the face of the enemy' as an act of cowardice punishable by death. As a result of both measures, cases of self-wounding diminished in the third year of the war and fell sharply in the final year.

On 1 November 1916 Cadorna did as he had threatened to do and issued a circular instructing his commanders to draw lots for summary executions. The response was instantaneous. On 30 October there was a revolt by men of the 125th infantry regiment (*brigata Spezia*). The *Carabinieri* were used to persuade them to attack, and when they did so they took 8,000 prisoners. After this ultimately successful action five men were shot by decimation. On the same day, men of the 1st battalion 75th infantry regiment, protesting at not being taken out of line, refused their rations, fired a couple of shots and threw stones at two of their officers. Two men were chosen by lot and shot next day, earning a word of praise for their commander. The following day something very similar happened in the 6th *Bersaglieri* regiment when soldiers who had just been taken out of the front line on the Carso were put in positions where they were hit by their own trench mortars. In the protest that followed hand grenades were thrown and an officer injured. Five soldiers selected more or less at random were immediately shot by order of the corps commander. Drawing these events to the attention of his army commanders, Cadorna reminded them that where it was not possible to identify individuals responsible for acts of indiscipline it was their right and their duty to select soldiers by lot from the unit in question and execute them. It was, he emphasised, an 'absolute and indeclinable obligation'. As an extra punishment for a unit that had obviously got off too lightly, all winter leave was suspended.[80]

As the year drew to its close, the increasingly severe application of military justice began to cause political ripples. In November there was talk in parliament of the decimations that had supposedly taken place the previous July, in which forty-eight soldiers had been shot. To arm himself against potential difficulty Boselli asked Cadorna for the facts. After setting him straight on the numbers, Cadorna told the premier that the current code of military discipline was simply too lax. More extreme measures were necessary. Modern mass armies 'with improvised officers and soldiers' were less solid than in the past; modern wars, which were longer and harder than in the past, 'inevitably provoke[d] acts of indiscipline'; and finally soldiers came from backgrounds which for many years had educated them to indiscipline. After complaining that the military tribunals were afflicted with the same 'morbid sentimentalism' that affected the rest of the country, Cadorna gave the premier a clear warning not to allow public debate on the matter.[81]

The executions continued remorselessly. In 1916 there were at least 83 summary executions and 242 'regular' executions after trial, 76 accused were found not guilty, and a further 761 soldiers were sentenced to death *in absentia*. While senior officers were commonly enthusiastic punishers, their juniors occasionally found ways of saving their men from the condign punishments dished out by the tribunals. Emilio Lussu's divisional general was sacked for unjustifiably losing a position on the Asiago during the *Strafexpedition* and replaced by an unsympathetic bullying know-all. When he ordered a man shot for no good reason as an example, he was deceived with the use of a corpse.[82]

Balkan attractions and distractions

Cadorna's attention was focused chiefly on the Italian theatre of war, and he was always ready to urge the diplomats to pressurise Italy's allies for supporting offensives elsewhere. Pressure also came from the reverse direction as his own foreign minister and the statesmen and diplomats in Paris, London and St Petersburg pursued their own strategic and diplomatic goals. The Serbians proved difficult partners from the start, and were far too interested in Albania for Sonnino's comfort. To Cadorna's way of thinking the Serbs were unco-operative, failing to hold down Austrian troops and prevent them from shifting across to the Italian front.[83] As far as the British campaign at the Dardanelles, which began in April 1915 and expired with a successful if ignominious withdrawal in January 1916, was concerned Cadorna refused absolutely to have anything to do with it.[84] The Balkan theatre became more tangled after the French broached the idea of an Allied expedition to Salonika. Sonnino supported an Anglo-French landing but made it plain at the outset that there could be no Italian participation on land, though the navy might be able to contribute something. Supposing that Italy's refusal to join the expedition would be put down to military considerations, Cadorna announced that he could find a 30,000-man force for an overseas expedition without diminishing the strength of the offensive he was about to unleash against the Austrians.[85] The Salonika venture made the politics of Italian strategy easier for Cadorna as he was able to set it against Albania: if there was going to be an Italian military contribution in the Balkans, then he was adamant that it should be in the former theatre and not the latter.[86]

Separately and together, Albania and Salonika set Sonnino and Cadorna against one another, and probably had more than a little to do with Sonnino's attempt in January 1916 to persuade the cabinet to dump the chief of the general staff. Much exercised by what he saw as Greece's intention to invade Albanian territory around Valona and by the possibility that the French might move into the region to open up a second supply route to Serbia, Sonnino believed that if the French went in then Italy would have no option but to do the same. Cadorna was unmoved by either scenario: if the French were disposed to try such a risky undertaking then they should be dissuaded, and if the Greek threat became a reality then he was prepared at most to find a small corps to occupy the hinterland of Valona.[87] Sonnino used the chief of the general staff as an unwitting shield in January 1916, claiming to his allies that the *Comando supremo* 'absolutely exclude[d]' any possibility of sending Italian contingent to Salonika.[88] This was untrue and had Cadorna found out it would undoubtedly have worsened an already difficult relationship.

Tensions over the Balkans rose yet further when, at the end of the second week in January 1916, Rome learned that the French had occupied the islands of Castellorizzo, Mytilene and Corfu. The Italian ambassador to Athens and the soldiers on the spot, Generals Marro, Mombelli and Piacentini, who were deeply suspicious of Greek intentions in the region, itched to slip Rome's leash and take action. Sonnino was forced to instruct Cadorna to rein in Piacentini lest he start a war with Greece, and order him to await instructions from the government and the *Comando supremo*.[89]

Throughout this time, Italy and the other allies were engaged in the stop–go game of persuading Romania that her best interests would be met by joining in the war. Within a week of Italy's entry into the war, Italian and British diplomats advised that the state of Russian military operations would be crucial in dealing with the Romanians.[90] As the Russians were in full retreat the immediate prospects were not good, and Salandra for one doubted that a Romanian commitment to the war would be serious. Reports of the deplorable position of the Romanian army, too weak to defend the length of its northern frontier and much inferior to the Austro-German and even the Bulgarian armies, gave military substance to political doubts. The only remedy for her strategic vulnerability was a Russian army in Bessarabia or at some other point near her territory strong enough to allow her to resist a possible invasion by Austrian, German and Bulgarian troops.[91]

Well aware of the ins and outs of Italy's membership of a military–diplomatic alliance, Cadorna was as ready to ask what his allies could do for him as he was to suggest what he could do for them. The shifting sands of Balkan politics did not impinge directly on Italian strategy, but enemy activity on the Italian front most certainly did. Planning what would become the sixth battle of the Isonzo, he wanted to know when the Russians were going to start the offensive they had undertaken to launch at the Chantilly conference. Joffre was evasive, Kitchener did not know, and Cadorna knew nothing of the telegram that the French *Grand quartier générale* claimed to have sent him giving the date. As the Austrians irrupted into the Trentino, Russia's immediate military intentions were a mystery. The best that Ambassador Carlotti could get out of his sources in St Petersburg was that a Russian offensive was not likely until the second half of June and that the Russian military proposed to wait for a big German attack they expected shortly on their northern front.[92]

Sonnino pressed the Russian ambassador to act quickly, Cadorna pressed Joffre, and Ambassador Carlotti pressed General Alexiev and Count Sazanov, the Russian foreign minister. He was told that no offensive was possible immediately and at the same time reminded that Italy's failure to declare war on Germany created an unfavourable impression in Russia.[93] Finally Italy brought her king into play. On 24 May Vittorio Emanuele III sent a personal message to Nicholas II.

At last, Rome got a definite answer: the transfer of troops and artillery to the southern front would be complete by 25 May [7 June new style] and the offensive would then begin.

As the Austrian *Strafexpedition* wound down, Cadorna launched a limited counter-offensive, partly to improve his positions and partly to tie down Austrian troops and so assist the Russian offensive in a theatre where easier terrain allowed for more decisive blows. It would, he warned Rome, face 'serious obstacles' and would likely produce 'less than brilliant results' because of the superior Austrian artillery.[94] At the same time he supported Alexiev's suggestion that an Allied offensive at Salonika in the last third of June would be effective. His headquarters also suggested that a demonstration at Valona, which must be of limited range given the limited number of troops there, would presumably help.[95] Cadorna's willingness to support Alexiev's proposal for a common Allied offensive at Salonika was a cheque with a very limited value. When Sir William Robertson, chief of the imperial general staff, made it clear early in June that he favoured neither an Italian demonstration in Albania nor an operation at Salonika, which could have no significant effect on the Italian front, he was swiftly reassured that the Italians did not think much of Salonika either. Cadorna had wanted to support Alexiev only out of the Allies' common interests.[96]

Italian strategy now came under pressure from both France and Russia. Joffre tried to persuade Cadorna that the combination of Russian victories in Galicia with a check to the Bulgarians on their southern front would create a situation 'eminently favourable' to Romanian intervention. The Franco-Serbian army was 'entirely organised for mountain warfare', and the British general staff had greatly exaggerated the maritime transport difficulties.[97] As the Austrians moved forces from the Italian front to Galicia, pressure from St Petersburg for energetic Italian action also increased. When Sonnino asked how he should respond, Cadorna explained that he intended to widen the offensive action presently under way on the Asiago *altopiano* as soon as possible, but he could only do so as far as was 'compatible with our lack of heavy weaponry'. The Russians could be assured that the Italians had exactly the same view as they did about the value of a simultaneous attack on the Austrians.[98] He was also prepared to support French proposals for action at Salonika, despite British reservations. The Allied forces already there could not make their weight felt elsewhere, even if there were the means to transport them. In the Balkans, however, Allied action could have more decisive results than hitherto both in persuading Romania to enter the war and against Bulgaria, now deprived of useful support by the Central Powers who were heavily engaged elsewhere.[99]

On 25 June Joffre informed Cadorna that the preparatory artillery bombardment for the forthcoming Anglo-French offensive on the Somme would begin next day. The Russian offensive would be enlarged and intensified. It was, he told his Italian opposite number, 'indispensable' that the Italian army attack the enemy with all its resources to fix and defeat it in accordance with the Chantilly directive. Cadorna's emollient reply gave nothing away. He was ready to develop offensive action on the Trentino and Isonzo fronts to the full, but wished to know what had been decided about Salonika so as to be ready to take demonstrative action at Valona.[100] As Cadorna was and remained absolutely opposed to widening the Albanian campaign, which he regarded as a dangerous distraction, his reply may have been purely diplomatic.

Joffre used the combined Allied offensive to put pressure on the Romanians to join the war, arguing that the present circumstances were ideal ones in which Bucharest could invade and occupy Transylvania without risk, and invited Cadorna to do the same. Cadorna at once fell in line with the French and Russian policy of putting maximum pressure on the Romanians.[101] At the end of June he learned that an Allied offensive at Salonika had been postponed because of the objections raised by the British, but that as far as Joffre was concerned it was far from dead and buried. 'I think,' the French *generalissimo* told him, 'that important events such as Romanian intervention [in the war] could lead us at any time to undertake [it].' Italian forces at Valona must therefore be ever ready to carry out local actions.[102] The French offensive was timed to start on 17 July and the Russian offensive two weeks earlier. Reports from the Russian front soon spoke of substantial numbers of prisoners of war taken, of Slav units of the Austrian army surrendering 'easily' and of considerable quantities of heavy artillery being transferred from the Italian front.[103]

While grappling with the complications of Balkan strategy, Cadorna also had another potential front much closer to home to consider. The possibility that German and Austrian troops might transit Switzerland, and that Swiss forces might be brought into action against Italy, had been much on the mind of the Italian general staff at the start of the world war.[104] In March 1916 Rome learned that the Swiss general staff had secretly provided the German and Austro-Hungarian military attachés with 170 military bulletins dealing with the whereabouts of troops on the frontier, the movement of military trains and the location of artillery. Cadorna was worried that German agents might be at work in Switzerland preparing for a moment when the German general staff wanted to turn the enemy's lines. With seven good roads leading from the frontier Lombardy and Milan were wide open to invasion. Orders were issued at once to fortify a 120-kilometre stretch of the frontier in the Val d'Ossola and along the right bank of Lake Maggiore.[105]

In the aftermath of the *Strafexpedition* Cadorna's anxieties resurfaced. A serious situation would arise if significant German and Austrian forces were free to cross Switzerland. Large forces would be needed to hold them off, compromising the situation on other fronts. If the Swiss army joined in things would be 'very serious'. Such a scenario was, to be sure, improbable or at worst far off, but if it were to arise he intended to take the initiative and cross the frontier to occupy stronger defensive positions.[106] Joffre sought to put Cadorna's mind at rest. It was only because the Italian general staff had taken precautionary measures that the Swiss government was keeping 'relatively important' forces on the Italo-Swiss frontier. The eventuality envisaged by the Italian chief of the general staff was 'more than ever unlikely'.[107] Cadorna's suspicions were not allayed. All the Italians had done was to dig trenches, an entirely defensive action. The presence of Swiss troops was of an entirely different character, and he was not willing to rule out the possibility that the Swiss were concealing offensive intentions.[108]

To further their Balkan strategy the French now tried to pressure Italy into taking the theatre more seriously. As part of the campaign to get Romania into the war, the French premier Aristide Briand claimed that he had British consent to take the offensive at Salonika – which was untrue.[109] Once again the French knocked at Rome's door: in the event of an offensive at Salonika, could the Italians launch some kind of military demonstration in support? Now they wanted an Italian division, and not a single brigade, to support an offensive.[110] Cadorna, who had his mind on the sixth battle of the Isonzo and the capture of Gorizia, was far from eager to fall in with the French request. At most he was prepared to initiate a local demonstration at Valona to stop enemy forces moving from Albania into Macedonia, and then only if the allies launched a simultaneous offensive from Salonika. If such an offensive were to take place, Italy would send a single brigade to Salonika 'essentially to ensure the presence of our flag there'.[111]

At this point Cadorna changed his mind about Salonika. The almost interminable negotiations with Bratianu, which tried the patience and tested the skills of Allied diplomats, were approaching their finale. At the end of July Sonnino told Cadorna that it was almost certain that Romania would enter the war on 10 August, ten days after an Allied attack had been launched from Salonika (she in fact did so on 27 August). Sonnino asked for an Italian brigade, and Cadorna offered a division. He now accepted that defeating Bulgaria by an Allied offensive from Salonika reinforced by Russian and Romanian offensives on the Danube would result in 'a most compromising situation for the Central Powers'.[112] The 'suction pump' effect of Balkan politics was also drawing him in: he wanted diplomatic action to get Greek troops out of Epirus, which would remove a threat to Valona and end a situation in which, he believed, the connivance of the Greek authorities with the Central Powers enabled Austria 'seriously to embarrass' Italy in Albania and forced her to disperse forces there which would be better used elsewhere.[113]

Having sought to influence Italian strategy in the Balkans, the French now sought to prod the Italians into renewed efforts on their own front. For the Russian offensive to develop under the best possible circumstances it was of the greatest importance that the Austrians were not reinforced from other fronts. All or parts of nine Austrian divisions had arrived on the Russian front. The situation, Joffre insisted, was favourable for an all-out Italian attack which would prevent new reliefs transferring from the Italian front and considerably increase the Austrian army's difficulties. The Isonzo offensives must be unleashed with the least possible delay.[114] In case Cadorna was minded to pay too much attention to French exhortations, Porro told his chief that the date for his own offensive was already fixed and could not be brought forward without compromising the success of the operation. A check by headquarters staff showed that ninety-four Austrian battalions had indeed been withdrawn from the Italian front since the *Strafexpedition.* Unwilling to give any hostages to fortune, Cadorna told the French that grandiose results could not be promised from the coming offensive, about the date of which he said nothing, because of the persistent shortage of artillery, but promised that every effort would be made.[115]

For Cadorna, who looked at the business of war largely from a strategic point of view, domestic and international politics were unavoidable intrusions. Italy's relationship with her allies was for him strictly a functional question: what could they do for Italy and what was it in Italy's interests to do for them? His support for an Italian declaration of war on Germany, which took place on 28 August 1916, was just such a combination of military and diplomatic calculation: it would not significantly alter the balance against Italy, and if it did this would be compensated for by 'an improvement in [our] diplomatic position in respect of our allies'.[116] Events now gave some support to his scepticism about Balkan entanglements. The Romanians did not attack Bulgaria but launched an ill-judged offensive against Austria instead. Greek interest in northern Epirus, which had been ceded to Albania in 1913, threatened to get Italy drawn further into military sideshows when the Allied commander at Salonika, General Maurice Sarrail, wanted Italian troops to seal it off. Cadorna was reluctant to get involved in

Greece and had no wish to do Sarrail's job for him.[117] Sonnino was unable to say exactly what Italian policy was with regard to northern Epirus, and therefore envisaged a 'provisional occupation'. The Italian commander in Valona, General Bandini, confirmed that he would be able to occupy Santa Quaranta and Agirocastro with the troops he had to hand, and the move duly went ahead with local forces on 2 October 1916.

The twists and turns of international diplomacy were now playing into Cadorna's hands. Italian diplomats had been kept ignorant of the agreements made by Britain, France and Russia over the dismemberment of Turkey until Italy's declaration of war on Germany. Sonnino was greatly displeased when he learned what had been decided. As part of the process of carving out a share of the spoils for Rome, he cooled on the idea of sending a division to Salonika.[118] During October repeated British and French requests for more troops for Salonika were turned down. The idea of a triple offensive against Bulgaria was not dead, however, and Joffre proposed to put it on the agenda of the Allied military conference that was scheduled to convene on 15 November.

Cadorna was now very doubtful about the idea of sending more troops to Salonika, foreseeing the danger of an enemy offensive the size of the *Strafexpedition* against multiple points of the Italian line. Nor did he think a reinforced Salonika army could develop an action which would decisively influence the course of the war. If the Allies were to agree to a simultaneous joint offensive there and Russia undertook to stand on the defensive everywhere else it would become what it presently was not – a principal theatre of war. Only then would it be in Italy's interests to send more troops to Salonika – militarily because then the Central Powers would have to abandon attempts at large-scale offensives on the Italian front, and politically because it would reinforce Italian claims to Turkish territory in Asia Minor.[119] On 7 November he learned from the Italian military mission in St Petersburg that a powerful Russian offensive against Bulgaria was unlikely. With that, the principal incentive for Italy to increase its military stake in Salonika disappeared.

There had been a good deal of politics in the debating and decision-making about Balkan issues, and therefore over questions of military strategy, during 1916. As the year drew to a close they threatened to grow yet more intrusive. Premier Boselli sent Cadorna some of the documents dealing with the Allied negotiations over Asia Minor, and let him know that the government saw a satisfactory solution to them as being closely linked to the military sacrifices Italy was prepared to make. This was too much for Cadorna. Strategic decisions such as those relating to Allied operations in the Balkans could not be influenced by political criteria 'even when of the highest importance such as those involving territorial concessions in Asia Minor', he told Boselli. In making judgements about whether or not to join in a Balkan offensive 'the only norm and guide must remain military advantage, which dominates over all other [considerations]'.[120]

Joffre's military conference convened at Chantilly on 15 November 1916. Cadorna did not attend but was represented by his deputy, General Carlo Porro. The move, which was undoubtedly deliberate, ensured that no decisions binding on Italy could be reached since everything would have to be referred back to the chief of the general staff at Udine for his yea or nay. It may not, however, have been wise – not least because of the impression Porro tended to make. Later in the war the head of the British military mission, Brigadier-General Charles Delmé-Radcliffe, noted that he was full of 'complicated and unsatisfactory theories which are pleasing to the timid members of the Government who would like an easier way out of their difficulties than by fighting'.[121] Some of Porro's strategic ideas were certainly imaginative: the following spring he was proposing changing the course of the Isonzo river or creating a permanent gas cloud over part of the Carso.[122]

In Paris, Aristide Briand, who was about to sack an over-mighty Marshal Joffre, told his fellow politicians that governments must take decisions about operations, leaving their execution to the soldiers, and that the war must be looked at from a collective viewpoint. The first objective must be to crush Bulgaria and put Turkey out of the war. Prime minister Asquith, who was himself shortly to lose office, and Count Isvolsky, the Russian ambassador to France, fully agreed. The Italian representative, treasury minister Paolo Carcano, reserved his opinion but personally agreed with the first point. At the military meeting General Alexiev reiterated the military priorities identified by Briand. Everyone agreed that their armies must be active in winter and that concerted offensives should be delivered the following spring. May appeared to be the month on which all could agree. In the afternoon Joffre raised the necessity of trying to knock out Bulgaria at once. Cadorna could only accept such a strategy, Porro told the meeting, if there was little or no likelihood of an offensive on the Italian front. There were, though, indications that such an offensive was possible. Now that Italy had declared war on Germany, it was necessary to envisage a German attack across Switzerland: Italy had another 200 kilometres of frontier to defend, and at the moment Milan was threatened.

Cadorna's strategic logic did not go down very well with his military partners. General Palatsin, the Russian chief of staff, pointed out that all the allies were under more or less the same threat and that there was no point in Italy waiting until they were approaching Sofia before consenting to join in. After Palatsin confirmed that the Russians proposed to defeat the Bulgarians, he and Joffre joined forces to argue that Cadorna's conditions for sending troops to Salonika were now being met. Porro said they were not as Russia had yet to execute an offensive plan against Bulgaria. The meeting then dissolved as each side politely but pointedly stuck to its respective guns. Joffre wound it up by asking Porro to inform Cadorna of the situation resulting from their discussions and insist on the immediate despatch of three Italian brigades to Salonika.[123]

Gorizia and the Carso

In June 1915 Cadorna had envisaged crossing the Isonzo and taking up a defensive line based on two major bridgeheads at Gorizia and Tolmino, fortifying the heights of the Carso west of the Cormen depression.[124] The first battles on the Isonzo had shown the strength of the Austrian defences and the obstacles presented by the enemy and by nature. In March 1916, before the Austrians temporarily took the initiative away from him, Cadorna began to lay plans to take Gorizia when the good weather came by removing the two pillars of its defences: first moving against the heights of Monte Sabotino–Oslavia on the right bank of the Isonzo above the town to push the enemy beyond the river, then attacking Monte San Michele and Monte San Martino on the left bank below it.[125] Now for the first time attacks were to be preceded by massive artillery fire which would totally dismantle the enemy's defences. The *Strafexpedition* disrupted his plans but, more importantly, he was now being watched. Leonida Bissolati, Boselli's link with the *Comando supremo* and a war hero who had won a *medaglia d'argento* on Monte Nero, was interrogating everyone about the Trentino. What was worse, Bissolati was a Freemason. Cadorna badly needed a victory.

As the dangers of the *Strafexpedition* passed Cadorna revised his plan, limiting Aosta's offensive to the Gorizia bridgehead for the time being and excluding San Michele. The change was needed partly because of the losses that had just been suffered, but also so that Aosta could focus a large mass of artillery on a small area. 'Only by raising to a very high level the tonnage of projectiles thrown at the enemy is it possible to overcome defences prepared at length and carefully and open up easy gaps for the infantry', Cadorna told him.[126] On 27 June Aosta extended the northern end of his attack front as far as Plava. Cadorna reined him in, repeating his order and taking 2nd Army, over which he had had interim command, away from him. There was as yet no intention of taking the heights

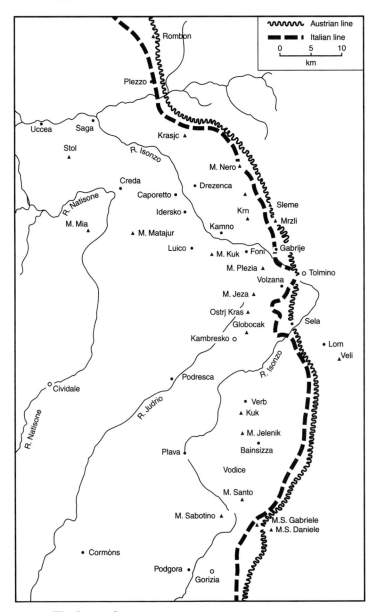

3. The Isonzo front

east of Gorizia. Cadorna, Aosta and Luigi Capello, commander of VI Army Corps, all agreed that at this stage only small bridgeheads on the left bank of the Isonzo were in view. What Cadorna had in mind, he told his son, was 'a manoeuvre on interior lines in the modern manner'.[127] The VI Corps commander was raring to go: when Cadorna visited his headquarters at Brazzano near Cormòns two days before the battle began, Capello told him 'In four hours we'll be on the Isonzo, in four days [we'll be] beyond Gorizia.'[128]

Monte Sabotino was the starting point for the attack. The ground had been well prepared. During the previous winter the Italians had defended it with a single line of trenches stretches of which had fallen down, lacking loopholes and shelters, and reached by two mule tracks completely open to the enemy. Since then a great deal of work had been done on it so that it could now be considered 'a classic example of field fortifications and of the offensive preparation of terrain'.[129] The transformation, which was the basis for the success that followed and which opened the door to Gorizia, was chiefly the work of Colonel Pietro Badoglio.

The idea of advancing gradually on Monte Sabotino using parallels, a classical method taught in the advanced officers' schools, was first put forward in November 1915 by General Luca Montuori, commanding 4th division. Badoglio inspected Monte Sabotino and put the same idea to Cadorna, who gave him the 74th regiment to carry it out. The result was the first significant improvement in the design, construction and use of Italian trenches since the war began. Where previously they had been too wide, too shallow, not masked by close entanglements of barbed wire and very visible because covered by sheets of metal and wood, Badoglio had covered walkways constructed, underground caverns and shelters created to lessen losses, and *teleferiche* (cable ways) installed. Stone was quarried and brought forward to build walls that would form the besiegers' parallels, and he encouraged a more active surveillance of no-man's-land. Greatly impressed, Capello called him away to become chief of staff to VI Army Corps, where he supervised the excavation of huge caverns capable of holding two battalions and linked to one another while still returning twice a week to monitor progress on Monte Sabotino. After the attack on Monte Sabotino, Badoglio was made a major-general at the age of 45 with a salary of 10,000 lire a year.[130]

On 25 July Cadorna told Joffre that 'grandiose results' were not to be expected from the coming offensive.[131] In some respects, though, the auguries were good. From St Petersburg came Russian general staff reports that considerable quantities of Austrian heavy artillery were being moved from the Italian front to Russia, and that according to prisoners of war Austrian troops were 'really demoralized'.[132] On the eve of the attack, Russian general staff calculations suggested that there were now twenty-six Austrian divisions on the Italian front, four fewer than two weeks earlier, and that since May the Austrians had lost over 500,000 men on the Italian and Russian fronts. Manpower reserves were now believed to be getting scarce for both Austria–Hungary and Germany, which had called up the class of 1917 and in some districts the 1918 class too.[133]

To Cadorna, artillery was the key that would unlock the door and open up the enemy's lines. All experience went to show that it was only by 'raising to a very high co-efficient the tonnage of rounds fired in a limited period of time' that defences which had been patiently constructed over a lengthy period of time could be overturned and destroyed, thereby opening up 'broad and easy gaps for the infantry'.[134] However, Cadorna's conception of how artillery was to be used had serious limitations. The most important thing, to his mind, was that the guns should be brought into action simultaneously and by surprise. Since it was difficult to neutralise enemy fire with artillery, the main need was to remove 'passive obstacles' so that the infantry would be exposed to enemy fire for as short a time as possible. Enemy batteries should be targeted only at the decisive moment of attack. Counter-battery fire, far from being a central task for the gunners, took its place towards the end of a list that included demolition of the obstacles directly blocking the advance, interdicting reinforcements and jamming the enemy's main centres and arteries.

Aosta's design for the battle comprised two attacks. Capello's VI Army Corps with six divisions, 471 guns and 40 batteries of heavy trench mortars (*bombarde*) would launch the principal assault on Monte Sabotino–Podgora, while XI Army Corps with three divisions, 270 guns and 20 batteries of *bombarde* carried out a secondary action against Monte San Michele. The attack, which began on 6 August, covered a front 35 kilometres in length. In thirteen days (4–16 August), a total of 1,260 guns and 768 bombards fired 535,000 rounds, an average of 41,153 rounds per day. Awe-inspiring as this must have been to the participants, it was insufficient. Over time artillery fire increased in volume and intensity, as it did on the western front, so that by the time of the eleventh and final battle of the Isonzo (18 August – 15 September 1917), 2,160 guns and bombards fired 1,202,919 rounds along a front half the length of the Gorizia battle at a rate of 168,988 rounds a day or 73 rounds per linear metre.[135]

At 0615 hours on Sunday 6 August 1916, under clear and serene skies, the Italian artillery opened up. At 1600 hours the infantry attacked, wearing white discs on their backs so that the artillery could spot them. Sent forward in waves, their battle orders instructed them not to bunch as this made them too good a target and not to stop in captured positions when the enemy withdrew and there was no further resistance to overcome. The Austrians did not expect the Italians to be in a condition to launch a surprise attack after two months of continuous combat, and Italian troops were in their front lines before they recovered from the bombardment. Monte Sabotino, Oslavia, Podgora and San Michele fell quickly, but Austrian counter-attacks and the obstacles formed by the re-entrants of the river Isonzo stopped the Italians opening wide breaches in the enemy lines.

Next day, encouraged by his early success, Cadorna extended his design: Monte Santo, Monte San Gabriele and the heights east of Gorizia looked to be there for the taking as soon as the troops were reorganised. However, the Austrian defence was managed shrewdly. They had not fallen for a diversionary attack on Sei Busi two days before the main attack, and now abandoned Gorizia and fell back, using their reserves to stiffen their second line of defence stretching from Monte Santo via San Daniele and San Gabriele to Monte San Marco.

Although at least one of his divisional commanders was keen to irrupt onto the left bank of the Isonzo, Capello was at first reluctant to reach beyond his original orders to take the right bank. Then, seeing what looked like the beginnings of a rout, he ordered his troops to go for the heights east of Gorizia. As they assaulted the Austrian positions east of the river, Cadorna ordered 2nd Army to take advantage of the situation and attack Monte Kuk and Monte Vodice from Plava in order to turn the Austrian positions from the north.

Gorizia was occupied on 9 August, and the next night Austrian forces withdrew to the eastern side of the Carso to avoid being turned on their flank. Austrian reinforcements were already coming up to the front. Capello's attack on Monte Santo and San Gabriele and VIII Corps' attack ran into trenches protected by wire and machine-guns and manned by fresh troops. Cadorna complained to Capello about the slowness with which operations to secure the heights surrounding Gorizia were proceeding. At a summit meeting of commanders at Brazzano on 11 August, when Aosta tried to get him to redirect his offensive onto the Carso towards Hermada and then Trieste, Cadorna stuck to his earlier orders to attack San Gabriele and Monte Santo in order to open the path to the Ternova *altipiano* and thence to Ljubljana.

At the outset Aosta had split his efforts; afterwards some commentators thought that if he had concentrated on a single attack there was at least the possibility that he might have broken through. Now Cadorna pushed his army well beyond his original planning envelope in an attempt to capitalise on what seemed to be a propitious turn of events. What looked to be a possible rout was in fact a well-organised retirement so that within a matter of a very few days Italian troops ran up against exactly the kind of strength in defence that had arrested almost all progress hitherto. The Italian heavy artillery was left far behind, one reason why the second act of the battle did not end as its protagonists hoped, and why it would now be necessary to start all over again. Cadorna acknowledged as much to General Piacentini as the sixth battle of the Isonzo ended: the enemy had retreated to what were not simply rearguard positions but 'real and genuine fortified lines'. To attack them would require 'complete and methodical preparation'.[136]

After ten days the sixth battle of the Isonzo ended with Gorizia in Italian hands at last. The cost was considerable: 51,221 Italians dead, wounded or missing as against 37, 458 Austrians. The Austrians had lost an important and threatening bridgehead and a dominating position on the Carso from which they had overlooked the rear of the Italian line for a year. Afterwards Cadorna called it 'a model break-through battle', which was a gross exaggeration.[137] To one historian it was 'a beautiful victory' whose echo 'resounded throughout the country', not least because after fifteen centuries 'a wholly Italian army had defeated a great foreign army'. Whether it left the Italians strategically much better off when the Austrians still held their main defensive line on the heights east of the river was, though, a matter of debate.[138] It certainly made Badoglio's reputation as a rising star and confirmed Capello as the most aggressive and offensive-minded of Cadorna's generals – something which for the time being did him no good at all. Seeing the VI Corps commander as a potential successor being lauded by the press and groomed by Bissolati, Cadorna packed him off to the Asiago for four months. Finally, it encouraged Cadorna to believe in his strategy. A lack of medium-calibre ammunition, shortages of officers and troop replacements, and what he described as a 'serious lack' of aircraft suitable for artillery spotting had forced him to suspend the Carso offensive, the second stage of his strategic original plan.[139] With adequate means, the right preparation and sufficient drive, it seemed that bigger victories lay within his reach.

After Gorizia, Cadorna turned his attention to the Carso. His plan was to push 3rd Army across the Vallone, putting it in a position to turn the Austrian positions on the heights east of Gorizia from the south while 2nd Army attacked them from the west. Much hope was placed in the new bombards and 600 were concentrated to support three brief battles, but bad weather reduced their effectiveness. The seventh battle of the Isonzo, fought around Cormen, began in torrential rain and lasted only three days (14–16 September) before it had to be stopped. The eighth battle, fought at Vipacco (10–12 October) was brought to a halt by a combination of heavy enemy gunfire and thick fog. Storms ended the ninth battle (1–4 November), previously delayed by heavy rain and fog. Together the three battles, which saw 3rd Army advance onto the western Carso but did not act as the prelude to a new offensive against the Austrian positions on the Bainsizza, cost the Italians 125,000 dead and wounded.

After the first battle ended, Boselli wanted to know what strategic purposes his field commander was now pursuing. Cadorna listed them for him: breaking the enemy's defensive line; inflicting losses; improving Italy's position by winning territory to the east and so lifting the threat of enemy fire on Gorizia; capturing prisoners; and easing the pressure on Romania by detaining enemy forces on the Italian front. Continued military activity also had the broader purpose of confusing the enemy as to Italian intentions, disorientating him, and keeping him in a state of alarm.[140] The explanations he advanced afterwards for what he called 'modest' results – that enemy wire was not properly cut, the artillery stopped firing before the infantry reached Austrian positions, and the guns switched to second-line defences too soon – were in fact an acknowledgement that Italian tactical and operational practice was failing in vital respects.[141] That was not how Cadorna saw it, though. It is not difficult to read his mind as he faced the second winter of the war: nothing was wrong with his strategy that more guns, more ammunition and more men could not solve.

Strategy and politics at the *Comando supremo*

As he went into the Gorizia offensive, Cadorna knew that he was under closer political scrutiny than ever before. From conversations reported to him by subordinates he believed that his enemies in the government could well move against him once it was clear who was responsible for the Austrian invasion of the Tyrol. Boselli was already accusing the *Comando supremo* of not taking the necessary precautions. Leonida Bissolati, now a minister without portfolio with responsibility for liaison between the government and the army, was pressing Cadorna to start an inquiry into the Austrian offensive. He was also becoming a second voice in the cabinet on military matters; while it was unlikely that he would wish to take over the war ministry directly, having two ministers speaking on military matters would be an even more dangerous situation for the *Comando supremo* than one, as at present.[142]

Cadorna told both Bissolati and Boselli bluntly that the war minister was the only legitimate representative of the chief of the general staff in government, and that while visits by ministers and members of the government to the troops were 'welcome signs of affectionate interest'

Fig. 7 General Joffre, General Cadorna and General Porro

he would not put up with any external interference in any branch of the military's activity. Since even the best intentioned critic could wander off the right path, disturb the peace of the army and thus cause serious damage, in future any military missions to the war zone must be restricted to those with 'extremely well defined tasks [and] limited functions'. It was, he reminded both men, the war ministry's responsibility to administer the provision of the means of war and the *Comando supremo*'s responsibility to decide how they were to be employed. Boselli imediately assured Cadorna of his complete agreement.[143]

Cadorna waged an increasingly intense war against politicians of every kind and degree as the year went on. A circular went out to army commanders notifying them that all visits to units under their command must be signalled in advance before they were agreed, and that the *Comando supremo* would decide whether or not they were to be allowed. In September orders were given that any parliamentary deputies serving under arms were to be extracted from command headquarters and sent to active units. (Morrone subsequently got this modified.) Cadorna's personal conflict with Bissolati, who he was convinced wanted to torpedo him, simmered on. At the end of August 1916 an anti-Cadornian diatribe by Colonel Giulio Douhet, a bitter critic of the general's, that was intended for Bissolati, fell into official hands. Douhet was arrested, tried in October and sentenced to a year in prison. Cadorna was convinced that Bissolati had instigated the whole thing. The two men were finally reconciled in March 1917 when Bissolati in effect accepted that Cadorna had the unquestionable authority to run the war.[144]

Cadorna also took the offensive against the government on the long-established issue of manpower needs. The *Strafexpedition* and the sixth battle of the Isonzo had shown the need for a larger number of divisions if he was to be able to develop his plan of operations, 'which is to concentrate a sufficient mass [of troops] in the direction of the attack without diminishing our capacity at least to defend the other parts of the front'. According to the *Comando supremo*'s calculations, the British, French and Belgians had 174 divisions strung out along an 800-kilometre front, while it had 49½ Italian divisions to cover 600 kilometres. The mountainous nature of the theatre did not attenuate this disproportion very much. The Trentino front had been stripped of troops 'to the extreme limit of its defensive capacity' and was in any case a perpetual Sword of Damocles hanging over Italy. Now that Italian troops were across the Isonzo, it was more difficult to switch men and weapons between sectors because of the greater distances involved and the lack of railway lines. Between Gorizia and Ljubljana – 75 kilometres as the crow flew – was harsh mountainous country with little water. Extra men would be needed as the army advanced, both to replace wastage and to guard the lines of communication. Carefully calibrated alarmism was always a prominent ingredient in Cadorna's strategic appreciations for the government; this time he stressed the 'seriously worrying inconveniences' that would arise if the enemy tried an irruption across Switzerland. To meet all his needs he needed as an absolute minimum four new divisions.[145]

Manpower, for Cadorna as for every other military supremo during the First World War, was the bedrock on which combat was founded. The numbers on which he and the war ministry worked were more than a little frayed around the edges. On 1 March 1916 the bureaucrats estimated that Italy had a total of 2,362,000 men under arms, some three-quarters of whom were in the active army while the rest (349,499 men) were in the territorial militia – a number which did not include losses through deaths, going missing in action, not meeting call-up standards or desertions, for all of which there were no precise data. Three-quarters of them were presumed to be in the infantry – but there were no exact figures. By 1 July 1916 the total number under arms was believed to be 2,762,080, again an estimate and this time one which incorporated educated guesses at the number of men reviewed by the conscription boards and called up at a second hearing. Another 200,000 men might be found from men aged 35 to 40 who should have gone into the territorial militia, and a further 250,000 by further extending that age limit to include men aged 41 to 43. The next major tranche of manpower for the active army were the 260,000 men of the class of 1897, but they could not be enrolled before the middle of the coming autumn.[146] A more detailed inquiry revealed that there were 2,495,273 men in the active army on 1 August, of whom 1,380,000 were in the infantry. A further 382,591 were in the territorial army, and then all that was left in the manpower pot were 259,857 untrained category III men aged between 38 and 40.[147] By the close of the year, the war ministry estimated the total number of dead since the start of the war at 166,275 men.

As well as manpower shortages, Cadorna's army was also starting to feel the lack of experienced officers. In the sixteen months since the start of the war, the army had lost 14,841 officers, all but 836 of them in various branches of the infantry.[148] As the Gorizia offensive came to an end there were 107,755 officers on the books – 20,328 were on permanent active service and the remainder were almost all reservists or territorial militia officers.[149] By December 1916 the loss rate of officers dead, wounded and missing, was running at 3.2 per cent of total casualties.[150] In all, 16,867 officers would die during the war, 8.2 per cent of the total number.[151] Among the higher ranks, 36 lieutenant-generals left the mobilised army between May 1915 and June 1916 (eleven of them, including Frugoni and Lieutenant-General Vittorio Elia in the last month), along with 52 major-generals. Some indication of the reasons for their departures may be gleaned from the 14 major-generals who left the army in June 1916: one was wounded, seven left through illness, and six went because of inadequacy (*insufficienza*).[152]

As the autumn approached Cadorna's operations staff conjectured as to future German strategy. Aware of the broad outlines of the dispute between Hindenburg and Falkenhayn at the opening of the year about whether to prioritise the eastern or the western front, and of Falkenhayn's failure at Verdun, they now expected Germany to retreat to a fortified line along the Meuse–Scheldt rivers and switch her attentions to the east. There Russia, not yet supplied with the weapons to arm its millions and with no time to construct defences, could easily be beaten. If and when this happened, neither France which was almost out of men, nor Great Britain who could not fight a land war alone, nor Italy who would be simultaneously threatened with German action on the Trentino and Austrian action on the Isonzo and in Albania, could resist peace overtures.[153] Another analysis, which imagined greater co-ordination between the German and Austrian high commands than was actually the case, forecast a sequential cycle of offensives against what the Central

Powers perceived as the weakest points of the Entente, the most recent being Romania. If everything possible was not done to snuff out renewed German activity in the Balkans soon, the cycle would recommence and it could quickly be Italy's turn to face it. That could mean a winter campaign. The conclusion drawn from this analysis was that whatever was done in the Balkans to prevent German success would distance the danger to Italy's front and therefore favour her success.[154]

By the end of October, Cadorna's natural tendency to concentrate on his own front was becoming yet more deeply entrenched. With the Austro-German forces piling up successes in the Balkans the only Allied option left was Salonika and that offered little prospect of a decisive victory: Sarrail's army was too small, the ground over which it would have to advance was too difficult, and the direction chosen was to Cadorna's way of thinking the wrong one. No longer could two Italian divisions be spared for it. They were needed now to supplement the big Italian offensive on Trieste he intended to unleash and to face an enemy offensive in the coming spring which, given the failure of the *Strafexpedition*, would certainly be launched 'with the largest possible force, probably from the Trentino and the Isonzo simultaneously'. As far as Alliance strategy was concerned, Cadorna had his own recipe. Russia must do everything possible to save Romania now and launch offensives in Galicia and Transylvania next spring; the Salonika army 'reinforced with all that Great Britain and France can give it' must keep as many Bulgarians occupied as possible; and Britain and France should continue their offensives on the western front. Italy's share of the action would be to advance on Trieste and towards the Sava valley next spring.[155]

In preparation for the mid November conference of the heads of the Entente armies, the Italian general staff did some forward thinking. Simple and somewhat speculative arithmetic on manpower resources produced the conclusion that the Germans and Austro-Hungarians could, while maintaining resilient defences, make twenty-five divisions available for an offensive – thirty if the Germans moved from four- to three-regiment divisions. Winter operations against France or Russia were unlikely, the former because of the Verdun experience and the latter because of the climate. Austro-German objectives were presumed to be Romania, Macedonia, Valona and then Italy. Since it was not logical to suppose that they could launch a big operation in the Trentino during winter, the most probable target was the Isonzo.[156] A month later, Cadorna's staff thought their world a somewhat safer place. A combination of calculation and forecasting involving adding up numbers of enemy divisions, projecting their possibilities for movement between fronts and excluding 'eccentric operations' produced the conclusion that the forces the Central Powers would be able to deploy in the coming spring would not be 'overpowering' unless 'new unexpected deficiencies' appeared in Russia.[157]

As the year came to its end, the war ministry too was alert to the difficulties in Italy's war. Some were geo-strategic: unlike either Britain or France, Italy had a massive salient in the shape of the Trentino jutting into her lines as well as an unknown threat in the shape of Switzerland. More important, though, was the manpower question. France, with 40 million inhabitants, had an army of 140 divisions whereas Italy, with 36 millions, had only 55 divisions. One hundred of France's divisions had been improvised since the start of the war, where Italy had only improvised thirty divisions. If she were to put in the same effort as her ally, Italy should have 126 divisions, sixty-two of them created after hostilities broke out. As it was, the Italian army was stretched out at an average of one division for every 10 kilometres of front, whereas on the western front a division had to cover a frontage of only 3.9 kilometres. To General Di Giorgio, intent on advising General Morrone, this more than the harshness of the theatre of operations or the shortage of artillery and munitions explained the difficulties Italy was having. As a consequence of this ratio, troops had to be held in the front lines for prolonged periods and the army lacked a strategic reserve.[158]

Di Giorgio's solutions were simple – not to say simplistic. As far as finances went, Italy should borrow whatever money it took to secure victory, or raise it through forced loans. As for her lack of artillery, since they were engaged in a war of position not of movement a shortage of field guns could be accepted without undue worry: 'not being able to give artillery [to the fray], we do better at least to give infantry alone'. This alarming recipe for battle reflected the traditional Piedmontese worship of manpower as the crucial factor in battle – a view that the world war would entrench in the Italian military mind for more than a decade afterwards. Behind it lay a calculation that others undoubtedly shared. A strong army was the only way to win a decisive victory and thereby 'get complete satisfaction of our national aspirations'. But if it came to a compromise peace, a strong army was the only guarantee in a tempestuous period of negotiation when 'the weak will be sacrificed to the interests of the strong'. At the end, what would matter would be the sacrifices made and the results gained.[159] Apart from the artillery question, Cadorna would likely have found little or nothing here to disagree with. In the third year of the war he would continue his manpower-intensive strategy, either oblivious to or prepared to disregard the basic truth about trench warfare – that a strategy of attrition cuts both ways.

The first full year of the war ended with Cadorna more firmly in the saddle than ever, having fought off the *Strafexpedition* and taken Gorizia.

As long as his allies were all actively in the field, and as long as the war minister and his civilian cronies in Rome could send him fresh men and more guns, he was confident of winning in the end. The only things that gave him pause for thought were the worrying signs of lack of solidity in the army – but he believed he had the remedies for that – and the apparent inability of the politicians to bear down on left-wing subversion in the country at large. In 1917, social tremors and international upheaval would be the precursors of a military disaster that would put the army and the country to the greatest test either had faced since Unification in 1861.

5   1917 – The year of danger

The state of morale of the troops is not very high.

Rino Alessi, 29 June 1917

In 1917 the elements that sustained and supported Italy's war began to come apart. The two Russian revolutions in February and October removed an important strategic distraction and tilted the balance of forces in her theatre of war against her. The western Allies were unable or unwilling to take up the strategic slack: the French army was more or less immobile after the mutinies in April and May, and the British army remained obdurately focused on the western front. On the home front political fissures began to widen – partly as a result of the events in Russia – and social discontent deepened as inequalities and shortages grew more evident and more painful. At the same time, apparently oblivious to the possibility of a mismatch between appetites and capabilities, an ambitious colonial ministry added to the list of aims for which the war was being fought.

At the front, what would turn out to be the last two battles of the Isonzo in May and August gave the generals grounds to believe that their tactical and operational methods – which with one exception remained more or less unchanged – might yet produce victory. Two months later a catalogue of errors, misjudgements and mistakes would put Italy in jeopardy. For the army, 1917 was the worst year of the war. Deaths in action rose from 66,000 in 1915 to 118,880 in 1916 and then to 152,790 in 1917 before falling in 1918 to 40,250. The numbers of wounded too reached a plateau, climbing from 190,400 in 1915 to 285,620 in 1916 and then to 367,200 in 1917 before falling to 103,420 the following year.[1] Although they had not by any means lost their capacity to fight, the soldiers were tired and starting to feel dispirited. 'Today we've been at war for two years and we're at the same place we started, except for having taken Gorizia and lost a slice of the Trentino – and several hundred thousand dead,' Paolo Caccia Dominioni noted at the start of third campaigning season.[2] Cadorna had no doubts as to the source of the disobedience he perceived to be germinating within the army. It was

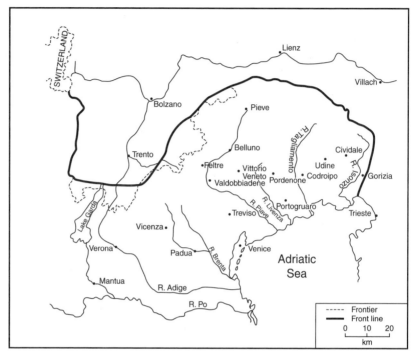

4. The Italian front in 1917

being stimulated by 'poisonous propaganda' against the war in Sicily, Tuscany, Emilia Romagna and Lombardy. The culprits were being aided and abetted by a weak government, which was practising excessive tolerance in the face of 'the most perverse theories of our domestic enemies'.[3] When disaster overtook him, he found the explanation not in his own failings or in his enemies' operational virtuosity but within the ranks of his own army.

War aims and domestic politics

After a brief initial flurry, public and political debate over why Italian soldiers were fighting and what the country's war aims were – or should be – went quiet for almost two years before coming to life in the latter part of 1916 and 1917. In the autumn of 1915 local Piedmontese deputies agitated to redraw the 1861 frontier with France and do away with French territory that projected onto their side of the Alpine crest. Sonnino intervened swiftly to block them, and in France President

Poincaré squashed his own prime minister after Briand had said that he would look at the idea 'with the greatest benevolence'.[4] At the *Consulta*, Sonnino was concerned chiefly with European and Balkan matters, his guiding star the need to ensure Italian security. Part of the rationale behind his wish to control Dalmatia – always a high priority – was the idea that it would protect Ancona in the same way that La Maddalena, the naval base at the north end of Sardinia, protected Genoa, Livorno and Palermo. At the Colonial Ministry, officials with an appetite to assuage Italy's pre-1896 ambitions saw an opportunity to expand her empire at the war's end when the victorious Allies would surely expand their own colonies at their enemy's expense, 'thereby giving them the means of satisfying, if not all, at least a good part of our demands'.[5] In November 1914 his staff handed the colonial minister, Ferdinando Martini, a list of wants comprising Jibuti, Kisimaio, Lake Tsana, the Yemen, Kassala, Jarabub, the Portuguese colonies, and Ethiopia. Not yet a formal programme, it was put on ice until circumstances changed.

Several factors combined to open up the war aims debate in mid 1916. After the conquest of German Cameroon in February 1916 the only enemy colony still holding out was German East Africa, raising the possibility of a share-out of the spoils. The Italian declaration of war on Germany on 28 August 1916 opened the door, and three months later Martini's successor, Gaspare Colosimo, handed Sonnino the first definitive statement of Italy's colonial war aims. It came in two parts: the 'maximum' programme amounting to 2,947,000 square kilometres staked a claim to a vast East African empire including Ethiopia and a large swathe of sub-Saharan Africa embodying the hinterland of Libya as far south as Lake Chad, while the 'minimum' programme, amounting to 722,000 square kilometres, reduced Italy's claim over the Libyan hinterland. Preoccupied with securing an Italian foothold in the Near East and Asia Minor, Sonnino did not respond until early February 1917. When he did, he refused to take a definite stand on the colonial programme and would go no farther than allowing that part of the 'minimum' programme might be fulfilled within the terms of the general peace settlement.[6]

The colonial ministry's programmes, leaked to journalists, played into what became an intense campaign by the nationalist press, stimulated partly by the announcement on 9 May 1916 that Great Britain and Russia were in 'full agreement' over Eastern questions, and partly by Italian participation in the Salonika campaign. The tone was set by Senator Leopoldo Franchetti, writing in the *Corriere della Sera* on 8 October 1916: 'It is certain that the Italian nation, just as it wants its unredeemed lands and military predominance in the Adriatic, also wants its share of the Mediterranean coasts.'[7] With that, the newspaper men began carving up the Ottoman territories between the Great Powers, claiming most or all of Anatolia from Smyrna to Alexandretta for Italy. Along with this went calls for 'greater guarantees' for Italy with respect to Tunisia, Morocco and Egypt, the reintegration of the Libyan *retroterra*, exclusive influence in Abyssinia, and Jibuti. The occupation of Baghdad by British troops in March 1917 intensified the press campaign. Nationalists and journalists wrapped all the goals up together in a *memoriale* presented to Premier Boselli and backed by some 3,000 signatories who included D'Annunzio and Mussolini.

The colonial ministry's policy was based on the supposition that Great Britain and France would take Germany's colonies at the war's end and be forced to give Italy compensation. The change in the complexion of international politics that developed during 1917 and 1918 did nothing to help Italy secure either the declaratory goals for which she had entered the war or the aims which she nurtured during the following months and years. President Woodrow Wilson's demand in January 1917 for 'a peace without victory' rang alarm bells in Rome. The publication of the secret Treaty of London by Bolshevik Russia in November 1917 caused growing concern, and anxiety increased at the start of 1918 when Lloyd George announced his support of national self-determination and Woodrow Wilson published his Fourteen Points, the fifth of which spoke of 'A free, open-minded and absolutely impartial adjustment of all colonial claims.' Sonnino's ambitions were likewise threatened by the twelfth Point which demanded 'an absolutely unmolested opportunity' for 'autonomous development' for all the non-Turkish nationalities in the Ottoman empire.

The Boselli government was being propped up by an uneasy amalgam of the same political forces that had jettisoned Salandra. Their respective war aims agendas overlapped in some places but diverged in others. On the far Right, Trento and Trieste were not enough for D'Annunzio: a 'colossal hecatomb' was needed to cleanse Italy of 'the filth, the pusillanimity, the cowardice of centuries' and reinvigorate her.[8] Nationalists and interventionists saw every reason to keep on with the war in order to complete the Risorgimento and carry through the colonial programme that had been brought to a standstill at Adua in 1896 and then hesitantly restarted with the Libyan war in 1911–12. The Catholic hierarchy tended to sit on the fence: Cardinal Ferrari told Salandra at Milan in November 1915 that Italy required 'a lasting, stable and tranquil peace', to which the then premier replied 'Yes, Eminence, peace – but only after victory.' Catholic youth, on the other hand, saw the opportunity for the first time since 1870 to immerse itself in the mainstream of national unity and to participate in the final formation of the state.[9]

No political grouping was more divided over the war than Italian socialism. Its declaration of neutralism at the start of the world war provided a flimsy shelter for a wide spectrum of attitudes and positions that included Francophilia, sympathy for the Entente, internationalism (now abandoned by virtually every other European socialist party except the Swiss) and revolutionary activism: when Milanese socialists revived the idea of an insurrectional strike in the event of war in February 1915, the French socialist Gustave Hervé accused them of 'revolutionary cretinism', and was told in return that he had 'a lot of balls to treat us as eunuchs'.[10] In May 1915, meeting at Bologna, the Italian Socialist Party reaffirmed its neutralist stance but carefully avoided appealing to the working classes to oppose the war openly. Instead, seeking to achieve internal equilibrium between contending forces, it adopted the formula *né aderire né sabotare* ('neither adhere nor sabotage').

By 1916 the party had split into two distinct factions. With Boselli now at the head of the government and Vittorio Orlando at the interior ministry, the 'reformists' or 'minimalists' were ready to participate in a tacit partnership with Rightists. This included support for at least some of the multiplicity of war aims now being identified: on 17 December 1916 Filippo Turati publicly endorsed two of the baseline war aims, 'rectification of the frontier' and 'strategic guarantees' for Italy. At the same time the 'intransigents' or 'maximalists', led by Giacinto Menotti Serrati, lined up with Lenin and Trotsky. During 1917 the gap widened. 'Reformists' backed Woodrow Wilson's January 1917 formula and welcomed the disappearance of Tsarist Russia from the ranks of the Allies, while 'intransigents' castigated Wilson's pronouncement as a 'capitalistic act' and greeted the arrival of a mission from Petrograd and Moscow in August 1917 with spontaneous cries of 'Viva Lenin'.

On 30 June 1917, Turati inadvertently gave the 'maximalists' ammunition. Speaking in parliament, he suggested that the government open peace negotiations, declaring 'In the coming winter there must be no [more] war', a measured pronouncement that was converted by his fellow socialist, Claudio Treves, into something that sounded more like a firm statement of intent – 'Next winter no longer in the trenches.'[11] In August 1917 Pope Benedict XV added his voice to the chorus, condemning the 'useless slaughter'. However, neither Catholic condemnation of the war nor socialist defeatism appears to have played much of a role, if any at all, in undermining the army in the run-up to Caporetto.[12]

Strict censorship and the banning of socialist newspapers in the fifteen provinces that had been declared war zones made it very difficult for any political grouping not overtly supporting the government directly to influence the soldiers at the front. By 1917, though, they had preoccupations of their own. Staring into the abyss of war in a world bounded by barbed wire and perpetually galvanised by bombardments, attacking and defending heights that seemed on the face of things to be of no account, and watching the gaps in their ranks mount remorselessly induced 'a sense of profound discouragement ... against which the ideals for which Italy had undertaken the war, which required a capacity to distance oneself from the daily facts of existence, were not an apt remedy'.[13] Visiting the front in January 1917, Olindo Malagodi, director of the *Tribuna* newspaper, found 'an air of dejection and weariness, and in some place of irritation and discontent'.[14] Later one of the earliest and shrewdest commentators on the war said that if, when they were defending the line of the Piave after Caporetto, Italian soldiers had been told by their officers that they had to fight for Spalato and Jibuti 'they would first have shot at them and then retired back to the Po and beyond'.[15] Even before the army's morale was shaken by that battle, its dogged commitment to the war was by now instinctual and no longer, if it ever had been, the product of abstruse intellectual calculations about what Italy needed in order to be a Great Power.

War fighting methods

The Italian army as learning as the war went on – but it was a slow and uneven education, not all of which carried a positive message: in March 1916 orders went out that when in range of enemy fire officers should advance following and not leading their men, which cannot have done anything positive for troop morale. In the early autumn of 1916, the *Comando supremo* circulated some lessons from recent experience. Attacks should be on as wide a front as possible to make it difficult for enemy artillery to concentrate fire, and commanders should not worry about the alignment of their assault waves. It was now evident that the maximum success came on the first day of an attack, after which gains diminished and losses increased until on the third day the point was reached when it was not worth attacking, a formula that was applied between September and November 1916 in the seventh, eighth and ninth battles of the Isonzo. Once the critical point had been reached, commanders must be ready to inflict maximum losses on enemy counter-attacks. Lengthy bombardments were to be avoided because they meant losing the advantage of fast action and did not fit with the state of munitions supplies. At the same time, and somewhat contradictorily, the *Comando supremo* stressed the importance of gaining maximum advantage from artillery action: 'The infantry grow more precious every day, above all because of the growing difficulty of recruiting officers for them; they represent an energy that must be expended judiciously.'[16] These were, of course, counsels of perfection, some of which collided with reality. Thus, for example, achieving surprise was well-nigh impossible given the propensity for long preparatory artillery bombardments.

One of the contributors to the success of the *Strafexpedition* was believed to have been Brusati's inclination to pack the forward line with troops, a practice shared by other commanders. In December 1916, Cadorna's staff had a stab at reversing it. The 'persistent tendency' to hold too many troops in the trenches, which increased losses through enemy bombardments and made it difficult for divisional and corps commanders to use their forces either in attack or in defence, was to be kept to a minimum. Instead, defences should exploit improved positions and make use of the increasing numbers of machine-guns that were now becoming available. In the most advanced trenches, the staff recommended that men be stationed 30 or 40 metres apart – a move from one extreme to the other. Enemy attacks were to be thrown back by artillery, machine-guns, and counter-attacks by fresh troops 'who have been protected from enemy artillery'.[17] Like much else, this last was easier said than done. Densely packed front lines remained a feature of the Italian front throughout 1917 and after, as they did on parts of the French front as late as March 1918.

Although more guns, especially siege batteries, heavy field artillery and anti-aircraft artillery, arrived during 1917, this did not open the way to substantial reforms in established practice. In March, the artillery was instructed to concentrate all available fire on enemy infantry who were about to launch an attack and suffocate it before it happened 'since the quality of the artillery and aerial means at our disposal do not permit us to effect counter-battery fire that is sufficiently resourced and effective as to silence our adversary's artillery'.[18] In May, Italian artillerymen were enjoined to reduce the length of firing time by limiting their preparatory fire to the enemy's wire and the vital elements of his defence, and not to try to demolish all the obstacles in the infantry's path. Counter-battery fire was to aim at the temporary neutralisation of the enemy's guns by making ample use of gas rather than attempt systematic destruction, which was difficult and consumed lots of ammunition. A raft of directives on defensive action came from Udine during the spring, emphasising the maintenance of strong reserves for counter-attacks and the need to defend principal defensive positions to the last man. Once again, inherent contradictions in declaratory doctrine were not resolved. The regulations told the generals not to give up a foot of ground, but Cadorna also told them in March and again in April that positions were being held that were tactically very unhelpful and that excessive numbers of troops were still being held in them despite his repeated advice.[19]

Fig. 8 Hauling a 149-mm gun on the Upper Isonzo front

If advances in infantry and artillery operational doctrine and practice were slow and at times lacked internal consistency, this was not entirely the case where infantry tactics were concerned. Austria–Hungary provided both a model and a stimulus. During the campaign in the summer of 1916 the *Kaiserlicher-und-Königlicher Armee* began using specialist bombing sections in its attacks. Then, in December 1916, following its experience fighting alongside the German army against Brussilov's offensive that summer, the Austro-Hungarian army issued regulations for the development of *Stürmtruppen* on the German model. By the end of January 1917, the *Comando supremo* had picked up the enemy's use of assault platoons in small-scale actions along the Isonzo front. Storm troop units armed with grenade-throwers, flame-throwers, machine-guns and machine pistols were used in action on the Asiago plateau on 15 March, on Monte Maio and Monte Pasubio on the Trentino front in mid May, and during the tenth battle of the Isonzo (12–16 May 1917).[20]

The first Italian assault detachments – which would become the *Arditi* – developed as an expansion of small units of *esploratori* who probed enemy defences in the mountain zones during the first year of the war. In March 1916, General Ottavio Zoppi institutionalised them in every regiment of his V Army Corps, though not without expressions of anxiety from his divisional commanders about the loss of their best men to specialist units. Two months later, on the Gorizia front, General Luigi Capello invited the divisional commanders of VI Army Corps to do likewise. Spearheading the waves of attacking infantry, the *Arditi* were to destroy any obstacles that had survived the preparatory artillery bombardment, speeding up the attack and magnifying its impact. The successful use of terrain and automatic weapons by the Austrians during the course of the *Strafexpedition* contributed to the next stage of development. During the summer of 1916, Colonel-Brigadier Francesco Saverio Grazioli, whose mind had been on the creation of specialised attacking units for several months, set up special platoons in his brigade to develop infiltration tactics and used them to break into the flanks and rear of enemy positions ahead of the main assault, taking maximum advantage of surprise and the portable fire-power of machine-pistols. Capello picked up the idea on the eve of the Gorizia offensive in August 1916, remarking that the enemy was beginning to use similar techniques and that they could produce excellent results for his army 'given the incontestable physical and moral superiority of our soldiers'.[21]

Arditi units seem not to have been used during the Gorizia battle, but the idea of specialist assault troops was very much in the air over the winter of 1916–17: in January, 3rd Army circulated lessons from the German conduct of the battle of the Somme which stressed the need for special training for assault troops, and in March the *Comando supremo* drew attention to the Austro-Hungarian assault detachments and encouraged the adoption of similar units. On 8 November 1916, Major Giuseppe Bassi sent General Giardino, commanding 48th division, a memorandum on the employment of machine-pistols in the attack. At some point over the following winter Bassi's memorandum was passed along to Grazioli, and in March 1917 he began experimenting with assault companies. Other corps and divisional commanders followed suit. Grazioli's brigade tried the new method on the opening day of the tenth battle of the Isonzo (12 May 1917), when small groups broke into the enemy line but were soon isolated and then destroyed by enemy artillery fire.

After watching successful exercises by Bassi, and aware of the spread of *Stürmtruppen* through both the Austro-Hungarian and German armies, Capello set up an experimental *Arditi* company in 2nd Army on 12 June 1917, and two weeks later a circular from General Porro, Cadorna's deputy chief of staff, invited all army commanders to form units at least a company strong to be made up of volunteers, preferably from *Bersaglieri* regiments. The line infantry were also slowly evolving in response to the demands of trench warfare and in 1917 each rifle company now had one squad equipped with rifle-grenades and another with hand-grenades to accompany two rifle squads. *Arditi* companies, armed with revolvers, machine-pistols, knives, bombs, and incorporating a flame-thrower section, were built around four 'attack platoons', each comprising a ten-man 'assault squad' whose task was to cut the enemy wire, deal with his sentries, cut telephone wires and open gaps in the second line, and three ten-man 'attack squads' which dealt with the enemy's strongpoints, fanned out in a covering arc, and fought off any counter-attacks. The whole edifice was built up from two-man 'pairs', giving it a particularly strong psychological foundation.[22] A training camp was established at Sdricca where select detachments were put through a comprehensive course of individual, squad and platoon exercises involving gymnastics, hand-to-hand combat, grenade-throwing and shooting and culminating in a simulated company-level attack on an enemy trench line. Five hundred and sixteen 'live fire exercises' were held between 15 June and 24 October 1917, each using 12,000–15,000 explosive charges, 30,000–40,000 rounds of ammunition and 5,000–6,000 grenades, resulting in only a single death and no severe woundings.

The immediate goal was to professionalise the men by teaching them routines where run-of-the-mill infantry doctrine still aimed to turn out automata. Beyond that, they were to serve as a model for the army at large as well as an instrument with which to overcome the tactical stalemate. Now the *Arditi* were seen not as specialist units within separate regiments but as autonomous detachments controlled and directed at army level. As yet in the experimental phase, in 1918 they would evolve into a two-division corps with a strategic role. Morale was high, thanks in part to better food and living quarters, extra pay, less formal discipline, more leave and special uniforms. Although the high command had set itself against too many distinguishing badges, the *Arditi* were allowed two – the double black *fiamme nere* flash on their collars, and a roman sword encircled in oak leaves on their sleeve. The men revelled in their role: later, former members recalled regarding war as 'a festival . . . the place at which our desires converged', and going into action with 'explosions of barbaric joy'.[23] Out of the front line they could be no less rumbustious. On 2 October 1917 an open fight broke out after the *Carabinieri* tried to escort a group of *Arditi* who had gone to Udine without leave back to camp at Sdricca. The *Arditi* first threw stones and then bombs at them and the *Carabinieri*, taking shelter in a farmhouse, fired back, wounding two of their attackers before officers intervened to calm things down.

Second Army's *Arditi* companies received their baptism of fire in the eleventh battle of the Isonzo. Their fortunes were mixed. During the night of 18/19 August 1917, three companies successfully forced a crossing of the Isonzo at the foot of the Bainsizza plateau, but after taking

Monte San Gabriele on 4 September they were driven off with heavy losses, partly caused by Austrian artillery fire which prevented reinforcements reaching them and partly by the retreat of some of their men who, without officers, thought they had done their job. In the weeks that followed Capello added *Arditi* companies to the eight corps of 2nd Army, and other army commanders set about incorporating the new elements into their own forces. The lesson that Capello drew from the experiences of the summer was that the 'small' Austrian successes were due to 'minute and exact preparation, in which the enemy has unfortunately hitherto been our master'. The assault units were 'a very precious element which at all costs must not be subjected to exhaustion or depression'. Therefore they must only be employed in actions which, if risky, 'contain all the elements for certain success'.[24] Shortly afterwards the *Arditi* found themselves struggling to stave off defeat as 2nd Army streamed back from Caporetto.

Strategy and international politics

Cadorna's end-of-year report in December 1916 was brief and upbeat. '[T]he very strong fortress of Gorizia' had fallen and with it the 'formidable system of defences on the Carso to the west of the Vallone'. The 'constant and full success' on the Julian front was borne out by the 42,000 prisoners, 60 guns and 200 machine-guns taken between August and December. The army was waiting 'in perfect readiness' to renew its efforts.[25] What those actions would be was decided when the fourth Allied conference met at Chantilly on 15–16 November 1916. The French general staff, for whom Germany was the main enemy, wanted to concentrate the Entente's efforts in the coming year on the western front. Believing no decisive result could be achieved in the Italian theatre, Joffre wanted the Italian army to launch a general offensive in spring 1917 to draw in Austrian reserves and thus ease the pressure on the eastern front. A general offensive on all fronts was slated for the spring, and immediate Allied aid was promised to any power attacked by the Central Powers in the meantime. Cadorna responded positively, telling Boselli on 4 December that an offensive using French and British units in conjunction with Russian forces could have decisive consequences and would put into practice the unity of effort the Allies had so far failed to achieve.[26]

The Italian army, represented at Chantilly by General Porro, did not trust the Allies to give them effective aid if they needed it, and David Lloyd George did not entirely trust his own generals, putting a higher strategic value on the Italian front than they did. Accordingly, the newly installed British prime minister called a conference in Rome on 5–7 January 1917 at which he proposed temporarily loaning Italy 300 guns with which to back an offensive aimed at inflicting a decisive defeat on Austria–Hungary and taking Trieste. Neither the French general staff, preparing the Nivelle offensive that would begin on 16 April, nor their British opposite numbers were prepared to see the focus of the Allies' military gaze switch from France and Flanders to Italy. Sonnino, too, opposed the idea for diplomatic and not strategic reasons, fearing that it would reduce Italy's leverage at the eventual peace conference. With that, Cadorna's only recourse was direct negotiations with the British and French high commands over possible aid.[27] Even General Dallolio was not keen on having British guns, which he regarded as antiquated.

Intelligence suggesting that an enemy offensive was in the making came drifting in to army headquarters. In mid January an Austrian deserter reported that his officers were talking about a coming offensive in the Trentino. At the start of February, King Vittorio Emanuele III told General Porro that he had received information that the Austrians were going to attack 'from the Carso to the sea' on 18 February. Indications that something unpleasant was in the offing began to multiply. New Austrian units were arriving on the Gorizia front, as were medium and heavy guns (information confirmed by telephone interceptions); the enemy had been taking prisoners 'here and there' with the evident intention of gathering information about the exact location of Italian forces; new transport lines were being laid down on the Carso; and special training exercises were being held for the Austrian assault detachments. Everything pointed to a 'spoiling' attack, perhaps in co-ordination with a similar attack by the Germans on the western front, some time after the end of February. Reports that Hindenburg and Ludendorff had travelled to Innsbruck and Vienna in mid January to hold discussions with Emperor Karl I and his senior military commanders, and that Ludendorff had then visited the Val Sugana, suggested that an enemy offensive from the Trentino was possibly in the offing once the snows melted. However some of the agent reports of troop movements were demonstrably untrue, and headquarters suspected that at least part of the incoming intelligence was disinformation.[28]

Cadorna wanted at least eight more divisions to be able to reach the Julian Alps and Trieste. A meeting with Nivelle, whom he found 'very gentlemanly and *simpatico*', on 1–2 February produced nothing much for Italy as the Frenchman was convinced that his offensive would produce decisive results before the Austrians attacked on the Italian front, but it did leave Cadorna believing that 'within a few months the war will be over'.[29] On 17 March Nivelle told Cadorna that his offensive was fixed to begin on 8 April, and asked for an Italian offensive no later than the middle of that month. By the time that Cadorna met the British chief of staff, General Sir William Robertson, for the second in his round of individual talks on 23 March, Italian military intelligence was more inclined on the basis of informers' reports and troop counting to believe in a forthcoming Austrian offensive in the Trentino, preceded by diversionary attacks against Gorizia or on the Carso. The *Zona Carnia* was thought to be safe from attack until the end of April, when the snows would begin to melt, but military intelligence warned that if and when the time came Italian forces in the mountains would only get short notice of an enemy attack.[30]

As always, artillery was much on Cadorna's mind. At the end of January Dallolio had promised him at least 520 heavy- and medium-calibre guns by the end of April, and at the halfway point he complained that he had not received a third of that number. Field and mountain guns, too, were a matter of concern: at thirty-two guns per division numbers were insufficient if the army were to be attacked on a wide front, the more so because the nature of the ground made it difficult to switch guns around rapidly. Struggling with the lack of raw materials on the international market and the tonnage to ship them, as well as the action of enemy submarines which had just cost him 4,100 rounds of 305-mm ammunition, Dallolio promised thirty-one batteries of 75-mm anti-aircraft guns and fifty-seven batteries of 65-mm and 75-mm guns by June – some 452 guns in all. It was impossible, he told Cadorna, to buy in field and mountain artillery from abroad.[31]

There were also much larger strategic concerns to add to the mix. Strikes and demonstrations in Russia began on 22 January 1917 and by 16 March the Romanov dynasty was gone, replaced by a provisional government. There was now an ongoing concern that the Italian proletariat might follow the Russian example: when reports came in that workers' organisations in Turin were beginning to show signs of shifting from violent talk against the war to real demonstrations, the war ministry complained that the prefects and the police were being 'too weak'.[32] As international events began to unfold, Ambassador Carlotti was inclined to think that the Russians would stick to their agreement to contribute to the co-ordinated Allied offensives to be launched during April, confirmed at the Petrograd conference (1–17 February 1917), but thought that the Russians' contribution would be delayed because of the upheavals inside the country and transport difficulties. Therefore Italy could not count on 'a vigorous, effective and prolonged Russian offensive this coming spring'.[33] A long analysis by the Italian military attaché, General Romei, early in April was even less sanguine. The 'miasma of indiscipline' had reached the soldiers at the front and the revolutionary socialists 'who see in a disciplined and compact army a potent weapon [that could be used] against their designs' had already won a considerable victory with the institutionalisation of soldiers' committees in every army unit. If the indiscipline in the army were not halted it could lead to disaster.[34]

When Cadorna and Robertson met at Udine on 23 March, the Italian chief of general staff understood that his British opposite number was under considerable domestic political pressure to reach an accord of some kind with him.[35] For his part, Cadorna was not prepared to launch a major offensive on the Carso until he was sure about the position on the Trentino. The host put pressure on his guest. Notwithstanding the healthy defensive position that had been achieved, Italy was still vulnerable. A simple tactical setback could present her with 'events of extreme gravity' and a reverse could have 'fateful political repercussions', which meant that particular consideration must be given to the possibility that the enemy would turn his offensive forces on her in order to win a decisive success. In such circumstances diversionary offensives elsewhere were of no value whatsoever; only direct aid could help. Robertson was obdurate: the forthcoming Allied offensive would fix the enemy on the western front, denying him any other initiative, and any decision on direct support must be conditional on its outcome. Reviewing the overall strategic situation, which to his mind was clearly in the Entente's favour, he noted that Italian forces were twice the size of the Austrians facing them. Cadorna deployed the Trentino threat, which for the moment paralysed any hopes of an Italian offensive on the Julian front, and an offer to take the offensive on the *altopiano* of Sette Comuni in tandem with an Allied offensive on the western front 'compatible with the difficulties of terrain and season', but to no effect. Robertson was willing to authorise preliminary logistical studies but any decision about direct support for Italy would be taken 'at the right moment' by the respective Allied war committees. That, Cadorna told him, could be too late.[36]

'What blockheads!' Cadorna complained after Robertson and Colonel Maxime Weygand had left. 'I talked myself hoarse for two hours [trying] to make them understand that if the Austrians and Germans mass against us and we don't do the same we'll be beaten one at a time. They are infatuated with their offensive in France, which will achieve nothing very much.' However, he was confident that the army already had the means to hand to face any eventuality.[37] Frustrated with the Allied process for making big strategic decisions, he persuaded Sonnino to press the case for the Allied military commanders to be given the authority to decide the timing and size of reinforcements for any threatened front, but although Lloyd George privately agreed with the proposal he was a prisoner of his

war cabinet, which did not.[38] Robertson, who was not at all persuaded by
Italian perceptions of the threat of an Austrian attack, noted both the
great superiority in infantry and 'the considerable superiority in artillery
which the Italian army possesses' and hoped both would be used 'in a
vigorous offensive action as soon as possible' to support the coming
Allied offensive on the western front. To that end he offered Cadorna
forty 6-inch howitzers plus ammunition, to arrive by the last week
of April.[39]

Next to arrive at Udine, at Cadorna's request, was General Ferdinand
Foch, charged by war minister Paul Painlevé with preparing the necessary measures 'for the direct support' that France intended to provide in
the event of an Austrian offensive via the Trentino.[40] Cadorna first
explained the shape of Italy's military strategy. Trieste was the target of
attack partly because it was the 'most sensitive point' of the Central
Powers and therefore one to defend which they must mass considerable
force, to the profit of the Entente, and partly because the lack of sufficient
heavy artillery made it impossible to attack the fortified camp of Trent
(Trento). His worst-case scenario included the possibility of simultaneous Austrian attacks on the Isonzo and the Trentino, as well as subsidiary attacks in the *Zona Carnia* and the Cadore. If checked, the country
'which already presents symptoms of lassitude' could demand peace and
provoke a change of government, which would take Italy out of the war.
Moving into detail, the two generals agreed a possible schedule for the
arrival of up to ten Allied divisions plus heavy-calibre artillery twenty-five
days after the start of an enemy concentration. The spadework done on
this occasion would prove its worth at the year's end. Cadorna got on
well with Foch, whom he found 'very frank, decisive, *simpatico*', and was
pleased with the outcome of the talks, which he saw (or claimed to see) as
evidence of the 'intimate fraternity' between the two nations and
their armies.[41]

Almost at once the French shifted their ground. Cadorna had promised on several occasions to act on his front at the same time as an Allied
offensive. Now Nivelle wanted to know exactly what his intentions were
and what conditions he was counting on to carry out his operations.
Cadorna was ready to help – on his own terms. Preparations for a major
attack on the Isonzo front were advancing, and when he deemed the time
to be ripe it would be unleashed 'with lightning rapidity'. But that would
not be until August. In the meantime, he was preparing to start an
offensive on the Sette Comuni *altopiano*, where although Austrian preparations for an offensive seemed recently to have paused there were no
grounds for thinking that the enemy had given up an idea 'so long
cherished and prepared for'.[42] French pressure mounted. Painlevé

evoked memories of Magenta and Solferino, and Nivelle, whose offensive was in trouble after only four days, urged Cadorna to unleash his planned Isonzo offensive within the next few days. On the basis of evidence that the enemy's plans for a Trentino offensive were now less immediate, Cadorna ordered preparations for thirty Italian divisions, backed by 1,300 medium- and heavy-calibre guns, to launch an offensive on the Julian front in the first week of May.[43]

Cadorna's assertion that an Austrian threat was building on the Trentino front was not backed by incontrovertible evidence – as he knew. At the start of April military intelligence reported that information about enemy movements on all the Italian fronts was 'somewhat contradictory' but that there was evidence of the suspension of movements of troops and war matériel to the Trentino, which suggested a pause for the time being at least. Austrian units that had been believed to be at or on their way to the Italian front were now turning up on the Russian and Romanian fronts. On the basis of a ragbag of bits and pieces which included evidence from a radio intercept that Conrad was at Bolzano, the transfer of three generals to the Italian front, and the departure of four and a half Austrian divisions from the Russian and Romanian fronts, the *Ufficio situazione* concluded towards the end of April that 'the enemy has not given up the idea of an offensive [on the Trentino front] and is working actively to complete preparations [there]'. Three days later the same office concluded from credible information and aerial reconnaissance that no important Austrian troop concentrations had been taking place in the Merino–Bolzano–Bressanone region up to 23 April. It was also forced to admit that the number of Austrian divisions on the Russian front had been under-counted by a factor of four (40 instead of 10), and that it was far from clear whether the forces that had been supposed to be intended to attack Italy (36 infantry divisions, 8 cavalry divisions and 5 German army corps) were indeed intended for an offensive or were the entire enemy force concentrated on the Italian front.[44] The presence of any German troops on the Italian front was in any case a dubious matter: prisoner-of-war interrogations during April revealed that Austrian soldiers were ordered to give false information if captured and particularly to invent the presence of German troops and exaggerate the strength of Austrian defences.[45]

On 11 April 1917, under pressure from Bissolati who was worried that the international situation might deteriorate and wanted a decisive action that would give Italy Trieste before it did, as well as from the western Allies, Cadorna ordered 3rd Army and the *Zona Gorizia* to complete preparations for an offensive by 10 May. The tenth battle of the Isonzo was planned as a three-phase engagement. After three or four days of preparatory artillery bombardment, Luigi Capello, now in command of the newly created *Zona Gorizia*, would cross the Isonzo with three corps and take Monte Kuk, Monte Santo and Monte San Gabriele. Then 200 guns would be shifted to 3rd Army which would attack on the Carso striking at Hermada. Cadorna was employing a new operational method: advancing in limited bounds with intervals of several weeks between them to move supporting artillery forward for the next one. But if he had faith in his method, he had little in his subordinates. Visits to the Trentino and Asiago fronts during April left him extremely unimpressed by the quality of many of his generals. A number of the artillery commanders were 'not worth a button', and the Asiago commanders needed continued goading or they all went to sleep. 'Nullities' and 'poltroons' were everywhere. The only answer was to incite fear – otherwise 'nothing gets done'.[46] Luigi Capello was different – able, energetic and capable of inspiring confidence in everyone, the new commander was 'entrepreneurial' and a 'doer' – but one whom Cadorna sensed needed holding on a short rein.[47] Five months later Capello would slip his tether and thereby make his contribution to disaster.

Capello acted to prepare 3rd Army for the coming battle psychologically as well as materially. Assuming command of the *Zona Gorizia* in March 1917, he selected dozens of *candidati oratori* from among the officers who were to educate the men to war. What was needed, he told them, was that 'we ourselves transform our spirit'. Italian soldiers were brave but gentle and averse to violence, 'reacting only to direct attack'. Their task was to dispel any sense of pity for the enemy that came from sharing common dangers and hardships and quell the soldiers' love of a quiet life. Only when the enemy was convinced that the Italian soldier was his superior in aggressiveness and determination would there be peace. The themes that Capello wanted instilled into his men included 'the necessity of our war', 'the inconveniences of a hasty peace', the importance of discipline, comradeship and the reciprocal trust between officers and men, and the importance of the '*spirito aggressivo*'. When the attack came, he wanted his soldiers to 'follow the fleeing enemy and put a bayonet in his kidneys'.[48]

Cadorna massed 220,000 men and 4,000 machine-guns for the tenth battle of the Isonzo (12–16 May), facing 147,000 Austrians with 1,660 machine-guns. The infantry would attack in simultaneous waves, not firing but using the bayonet. As always, guns and ammunition were a serious problem. Some 2,000 heavy- and medium-calibre guns supported the offensive. Third Army, including Capello's *Zona Gorizia*, calculated that it needed 1,414,000 rounds of ammunition but three weeks before the operation it was 700,500 rounds short. Central magazine assigned 247,700 rounds but was completely out of some calibres. Cadorna and his intendant general scratched around to find Capello more ammunition: the day before operations began Cadorna sent him 31,600 rounds with the injunction that they were to be considered 'untouchable' and only to be used in case of direst need and with the explicit prior authorisation of the *Comando supremo*.[49] The attack by 3rd Army had an average of 40 guns per kilometre on the Gorizia front and 90 guns per kilometre on the Carso front; if it lasted twelve days then with the supplies available the guns could fire an average of between 35 and 46 rounds per day each, depending on type. On the eve of the attack there was disagreement about whether the attacking army corps should each have their own allocation of counter-battery fire, and about the value of 'dismounting' counter-battery fire. Because of limited supplies gas shells, which could give the attack notable advantages, had only been used on 'neutralising' counter-battery fire and had not been tried out against enemy troops.[50]

The high command was still working out artillery methods as the battle went on, Cadorna sending out injunctions about which kinds of guns to use for which kinds of fire. By the time it was half over it was evident that 'dismounting' counter-battery fire was not working and also, more importantly, that the number of Austrian gun batteries revealed when the Italian infantry attacked was much greater than had been thought and that 3rd Army therefore lacked sufficient counter-battery capability.[51] Cadorna had allocated Capello 521,000 rounds of ammunition for his operation. On 22 May he calculated that Capello, who had fired 291,000 rounds on 19 May, had 130,000 rounds left and sent his final offering – a last 34,000 rounds.[52] Firing on average between 40,000 and 50,000 rounds a day, that left Capello with four days' fighting time. On 26 May the battle did indeed end. Total consumption, reportedly more or less what the commanders had requested, had amounted to some 3,000,000 rounds, excluding bombards.[53]

The Isonzo offensive took the Austrian commander, who was expecting to be attacked on the Carso, by surprise. However, once again the defence proved stronger than the attack. The guns cut some of the wire, but cratered the ground and left the deep caverns behind the front line in which the enemy troops sheltered untouched. The waves of assaulting infantry faced murderous enemy fire. Heroic advances were made but went unsupported: on the first day a battalion of the *brigata Campobasso* climbed 600 metres to get to the top of Monte Santo but, left to hold out alone, only seven officers and 100 men remained alive to surrender next day. Badoglio, jumped over the heads of three other generals by Capello on the eve of the battle to command II Corps, did well, taking Monte Kuk and Monte Vodice both of which were deemed untakeable, and was promoted to lieutenant-general for merit after the battle.

Once his attack began, Capello was reluctant to hand over the artillery to 3rd Army as planned and abandon the attempt to take Monte Santo. He was allowed to hold on to the heavy guns for another two days and this, together with bad weather, delayed the start of the Carso offensive by five days. By the time it began on 23 May, Boroević was able to bring up reinforcements. Aosta's 3rd Army advanced to a depth of 4 kilometres, taking three lines of defences, before it ran out of steam in the face of Austrian counter-attacks. Cadorna halted the Carso phase on 28 May. Capello's attacks on the Bainsizza continued for another three days and then the battle died down, leaving his troops holding the slopes of Monte Kuk and Monte Vodice but unable to keep hold of Monte Santo. Austrian counter-attacks on the Carso on 4 June retook almost all the lost ground. The Italian losses amounted to 36,000 dead (a figure that subsequently rose to 43,000), 96,000 wounded and 25,000 missing. Austrian losses totalled 54,904 killed and wounded and 5,278 missing or prisoners of war. The most important strategic result of the battle was to create a foothold on the eastern side of the Isonzo from which further attacks could be developed.[54]

Reviewing after-action reports and information from prisoners of war, confirmed by his own observations, Cadorna's artillery commander concluded that artillery regulations were still not working. There was a balance to be struck between giving responsible commanders the power to choose the guns and methods they thought locally appropriate and general norms for the use of artillery, and it had not yet been found. Instead of diminishing, the tendency to try completely to destroy the enemy's first-line defences was actually increasing, as was the weight of fire being delivered behind the enemy lines in attempts completely to dismount his artillery. Instead, 'seeking speed and surprise, [the artillery] needs simultaneously to uproot [all] the successive defensive lines which the infantry columns are scheduled to attack'.[55] Commanders needed to employ different calibres of gun with more discrimination, using bombards, small-calibre howitzers and mortars on the first defensive line and field artillery and medium-calibre guns on rear lines, while keeping heavy-calibre guns for distant targets and counter-battery fire with gas shells. As far as the latter went, dismounting fire (*tiri di smonto*) used enormous amounts of ammunition for little return. The gunners should stick to neutralising fire. Third Army practice had been to classify enemy batteries into three categories but then to distribute fire across a whole category of batteries; what was needed was to split the categories into zones and concentrate on those that were most trouble.[56]

Cadorna was generally pleased with the Gorizia offensive, a successful manoeuvre 'which in another age would have decided the campaign'.[57] Predictably incensed when wrongly informed that during the defence of

212   1917 – The year of danger

Hermada against Austrian counter-attacks on 4–6 June three Sicilian regiments had surrendered, he was outraged to learn that 10,000 Italian prisoners of war were in Austrian hands. If he could, he fumed, he would write to Boroević and ask him to shoot them all. Lieutenant-General Felice D'Alessandro's advice was incorporated into a circular at the end of May which emphasised that dismounting fire was to be 'completely renounced'. Characteristically, Cadorna added a few thoughts of his own which threatened to undercut the views of his gunnery expert. Protracted counter-battery fire 'on the basis of an aprioristic and inopportune division of objectives' was absolutely to be avoided; and commanders were where possible to use guns for which additional ammunition was most easily available, even if they were not the most efficient for the particular task in hand. As far as the artillery was concerned, the watchword was still: economise.[58]

The war and Italian society

Socially, economically and geographically fractured, Italy carried the burden of her immediate past into a war that opened the gaps yet wider and imposed new pressures on a people already under strain. By 1917, a combination of unresolved pre-war structural inequalities, latent and at times not so latent political conflict, and wartime stresses and strains was beginning seriously to test the social fabric. Increasingly weary of the war, its costs and its effects, Italian workers and their families began to make their restiveness ever more obvious, to the alarm of the civil and military authorities. One noted Italian historian has seen this as nothing less than a maturing crisis, exacerbated by socialist propaganda and the stirrings of revolution in Russia, that 'reached its zenith in the events at Turin in August' – and, according to some, at Caporetto.[59]

Italy had entered the war suffering from economic deflation after a decade-long 'economic spurt' came to an end around 1908. The war greatly stimulated the concentration and expansion of the older-established industries of cotton and silk textiles and the new steel, chemicals, motor vehicles and machinery industries in the industrial triangle of Turin–Milan–Genoa. The most important and most obvious consequence of the war was the shift from artisanal to industrialised patterns of production: before it began, only 3,207 out of an industrial workforce of 2,304,438 worked in factories employing over 100 people.[60] To feed the war's appetite, the industrial cities of the north sucked in labour from the countryside, absorbing semi-skilled workers from the rural craft workshops and unskilled labour from the fields. Big business and war advanced hand in hand. FIAT, the Turin-based automobile company, grew to become the third largest public company in Italy after Ansaldo and ILVA, expanding its workforce from 4,000 to 40,510, tripling the value of its fixed capital and increasing its financial reserves from 1.5 million to almost 92 million lire.[61]

Rising industrial pay rates increased social divisions and tensions. In 1917, the average unskilled worker in industry earned 9 lire a day, a sum which, when set against the infantryman's daily pay of 0.5 lire, made the factory workers' lives look luxurious while the value set by the state on the lives of its soldiers' appeared nugatory. Pay averages, lower in Rome than in northern Italy and lower again in the south, concealed sharp differentials – something which, writ large, was one of the features of wartime Italy. In Brescia, a city known for arms manufacture since the early nineteenth century, where by the middle of the war all seventeen steel and machine factories were working exclusively for the government, the daily wage in 1918 averaged 9 lire but most metal workers made 12–15 lire and some earned as much as 40 lire. A textile worker in the same city earned 1.80 lire a day, and railway workers' real salaries plunged to below 1914 levels.[62]

More pay did not produce better standards of living for the industrial north. In Piedmont, one of the better-off regions of Italy whose inhabitants were on average the second richest after the province of Lazio, overall meat consumption per person fell by 20 per cent between 1916 and 1917 (from 63.8 kg per person to 50.4 kg), and horsemeat increasingly replaced beef and pork. Sugar consumption fell by half. In Milan, where the pre-war diet had been insufficient to sustain ten hours' labour a day, average calorific intake excluding wine (which averaged 215 calories a day) fell from 2,613 calories in 1913 to 2,528 in 1916 before rising to 2,732 calories in 1917. Once more, gross averages conceal sharp differences: calorific intakes in 1916 ranged from 1,852 at the bottom to 3,684 at the top, and in 1917 from 1,936 to 3,612 calories. The fact that more Milanese families were enjoying higher calorific intakes in 1917 than in 1916 was indicative both of a spreading of income and also of a widening gap between more 'haves' and fewer 'have nots'. By way of comparison, soldiers consumed on average 3,846 calories in 1915, 2,947 in 1916, 3,240 in 1917 and 3,578 in 1918.[63]

In 1911, some 28 per cent of the working population were engaged in industry of some form and 55 per cent, or 9,085,597 people, worked in agriculture. According to official figures, approximately one-third of that labour force was made up of women, but the census under-counted their number and therefore their contribution; where the official figure was 2,973,000, economists subsequently calculated the true figure at 4,197,000. With large numbers of men taken out of the fields and into

Fig. 9 Italian women constructing trenches

the army, women bore an increasingly heavy burden as the war went on. Of those engaged in agriculture and related activities, 2,612,000 men and 1,604,000 women were day-labourers (*braccianti*).[64] They and the regularly paid rural labour force (*salariati*) were hit in different ways by the war, the *braccianti*, who predominated in the south, being hit worst. The remainder of the *agricultori* owned, rented or shared ownership of the land they worked. Behind these figures lay yet one more example of the divisions within the country: in 1913 the five northern provinces – Piedmont, Lombardy, Veneto, Emilia Romagna and Liguria – produced half the country's gross annual agricultural product by value.

Before the war, the agricultural sectors had lived in extreme misery. A social enquiry in the province of Bologna in 1881 noted that 'the concentration of families of day labourers is sometimes dreadful; in a few hovels perhaps a hundred families live heaped together'.[65] Almost thirty years later and hundreds of kilometres further south things were as bad or worse. An analysis of family budgets in the Basilicata in 1909 reported:

The day labourers live in great poverty: food is scarce and of little nutritional value ... one or at most two rooms on the ground floor for a family of seven ... there is nothing in the house which can stir a feeling of love for life, the hope of improvement! The only hope for these poor people is a change in the social order.[66]

To escape from these conditions men – they were mostly men – left the country in droves. In the pre-war decade, emigration drained Italy of the equivalent of one-sixth of its actual population. Between 1905 and 1914, 6,579,809 Italians left the country; of that number, 3,904,418 went overseas, the majority to the United States of America. Apart from the Veneto, the largest numbers came from the southern provinces: in 1913, 146,000 Sicilians left the island (the largest figure for a single province since statistical records started in 1876) and in 1914 another 46,610 of their compatriots followed them.[67] Some returned once the war began, but one consequence of the flight from the countryside was that by September 1917 the army was short of 329,545 conscripts who had gone abroad to friendly or neutral countries.

In 1915 the army took 2,500,000 men out of the labour market and put them in uniform, and over the entire period of the war 5,758,277 men were conscripted, more than half the active male labour force. To keep the economy going, it was necessary to relieve some workers from the obligation to do military service. The exonerations, as they were called, fell unevenly across social classes and occupational groups. In September 1918 a total of 603,985 workers fell into this category. They comprised 163,090 agricultural labourers, the largest numbers in Lombardy, Tuscany and Emilia Romagna, and 440,895 industrial workers, half of whom worked in the metal industries, most of them in Lombardy, Liguria and Piedmont.[68] Umbria had the highest proportion of exonerated rural labour, Basilicata the lowest. This distribution of human resources was both necessary and justifiable, but with some 46 per cent of the rural peasantry (*contadini*) in uniform, it bred discontent that was exacerbated by sharp differences between industrial wage rates on the one hand and soldiers' pay and rural wages on the other.

On the face of it, the countryside was quieter during the war than before: the number of rural strikes fell from 68 in 1915 to 61 in 1916, 27 in 1917 and 10 in 1918 and number of strike days lost from 19,941 in 1915 to 18,217 in 1917 and 3,270 in 1918. Strikes, which were in the main about preventive agreements and salaries, were concentrated overwhelmingly in Lombardy and the Veneto. In Bologna, the need for social cohesion resulted in government putting pressure on landowners to make concessions to labour in order that, in the words of the prefect of Bologna, 'there will be no dissent or anything that disturbs the harmonious union of all the national forces during the period in which Italy

Table 4 *Cost of living index, 1913–18*

	Italy	UK	France	Germany
1913	100	100	100	100
1914	95.1	97.6	102	106
1915	132.7	127.1	139.8	142
1916	199.7	159.5	158.2	153
1917	306.3	206.1	261.6	179
1918	409.1	226.5	339.2	217

Source: Prato, *Il Piemonte e gli effetti della guerra sulla sua vita economica e sociale*, p. 185

confronts its historical destiny'. Employers' and labourers' organisations, now subject to arbitration, accepted a truce that held throughout the war.[69] However, unmistakable signs of mounting discontent became apparent as the war went on. The numbers of land workers organised in leagues fell initially but then began to rise. Likewise, numbers in the *Confederazione generale del lavoro* (the main left-wing union) fell from 125,000 in 1914 to 91,000 1915 and 82,000 in 1916 before rising again to 87,332 in 1917. Catholic leagues too began to organise and expand during 1917, tripling in size by the end of the war.[70]

Town and country alike were increasingly affected by rising prices, which eroded the value of the wage rises in the industrial north and increased the impoverishment of those in rural Italy who did not farm for themselves and could not retain a part of their output to feed their families. Once again national statistics conceal substantial regional and local differences: between 1913 and 1916 prices rose 40 per cent in Modena, and 87 per cent in Potenza. However, the overall cost of living index tells its own story.

The government's failure to take control of food supplies until late in the day made most peoples' lives worse. Disorientated by the novel circumstances it faced in 1915 and unprepared for them, the government took no significant steps until December when, faced with a poor harvest, the state entered the grain market. In January 1916 General Tettoni was put in charge of a new central committee set up in the war ministry to co-ordinate the purchase and distribution of cereals by state-backed consortia. A central provisioning commission was established in the ministry of agriculture to regulate prices and control the market, and state intervention was gradually extended to meat, sugar, eggs and milk. The inter-provincial importing of foodstuffs was forbidden to ensure that the big cities got enough, distorting the pre-war market but not solving the problem. Finally, in mid 1917, rationing was introduced and price controls extended to foodstuffs not distributed by the state. The food queues were thought to have contributed to defeatism and the introduction of ration cards (*tessere*) would, the authorities believed, improve morale since things were demonstrably the same for everyone. The government's ban on dividends over 10 per cent and its harsh crackdown on excess profits in 1916 did little to redress the grievances of the poorer parts of society.

The complex interplay of supply and demand, labour and wages, prices and costs during the war had drastic effects on rural Italy. The *braccianti*, whose existence had been precarious at the best of times, saw their living virtually disappear, while the *salariati* enjoyed greater security of employment but were not insulated against rising prices. Sharecroppers and small peasant proprietors were particularly hard hit by conscription, but where they had large families and could produce for the market they were able to benefit from rising prices: wheat prices increased by 30 per cent in 1915 alone. Government intervention in autumn 1915 extended all agricultural contracts for the duration of war. Leaseholders, paying rents that were frozen at pre-war levels with inflated currency, made huge profits while, in Bologna at least, enjoying a virtual monopoly on exemptions from military service. As the war went on, the increasingly hard-pressed *contadini* watched the proprietors do well out of rising prices; average farm incomes in Cremona rose 330 per cent during the war.[71] The divisive consequences of all this cannot be underestimated. In the words of one commentator, 'The war changed the terms of social conflict in Italy.'[72]

State action to help those in need was limited until the government was jolted out of its non-interventionist mindset after Caporetto. Subsidies for the families of soldiers in need were fixed on 13 May 1915, and remained unaltered until they were increased by 20–30 per cent in April and July 1917. Additional funds were provided by provinces and communes, but in Tuscany they were either denied to the rural peasantry or suspended during harvest times on the grounds that the families had access to the means of subsistence.[73] Local and regional voluntarism stepped in to fill the gap. Patriotic mobilisation and welfare committees – *Comitati civili* – undertook work that mixed together propaganda, welfare and charity, sending comforts to the troops at the front, assisting the wounded and sick, providing *posti di restauro* for soldiers on leave and in transit, helping refugees, organising lotteries and benefit evenings, and setting up local clothing manufacturing schemes to provide the poor with an income from work at home. Mostly the Catholic clergy played an enthusiastic part in local and regional works but there were regional exceptions, notably in the Veneto. In Pavia, one of the most expensive cities in Italy, a clerico-moderate administration did not intervene much. In the socialist-led communes, communal ovens, food kitchens and price controls spoke to a very different agenda. Good works were surely of some aid and comfort, but they were understandably regarded ambivalently by the working class who saw them as both traditionally paternalistic and the personification of the very interventionism that had taken Italy to war in the first place.[74]

The general health of the population suffered the consequences of difficult economic and social circumstances. Pre-war Italy had been more or less in the middle of the European table for mortality, with an average life expectancy of 47.4 years, compared to 49.0 in Germany and 53.4 in England and Wales. Subsequently statisticians calculated that Italy suffered approximately 600,000 'excess' civilian deaths during the war years. The young and the old were especially at risk, though in the last two years of the war there was a marked excess of non-infant deaths. Epidemics of cholera in 1915–16 and cerebral–spinal meningitis in 1915–17 played their part; deaths from malaria, heart and lung diseases, typhoid fever, diphtheria and malaria (in Tuscany there were five times as many deaths in 1917 as in 1915) increased; and childbirth became ever more risky. Deaths from syphilis remained more or less at the pre-war average (1,774 per annum).[75] Again, national figures masked marked regional differences. Death rates were high in the Veneto because of the war, and high too in Basilicata, Puglia and Sardinia because of wartime infective illnesses, but in Piedmont they were almost stationary until late 1918 when Spanish flu arrived. Birth rates fell steadily from 31.84 per 1,000 in 1911–13 to 18.9 per 1,000 in 1918, with a brief spike in January 1916, ten months after Italy went to war. The greatest falls were in Lombardy, Piedmont and Tuscany, and the steepest in 1917 and 1918. At the time and afterwards, the causes were variously identified as declining matrimony, the scarcity of foodstuffs, and decreasing hope for tomorrow.[76]

By 1917 it was becoming widely believed that it was the agricultural peasantry in the south who were doing most of the fighting – 'I contadini lo fanno la guerra' – while the industrial workers in the north were shirking their military duty and raking in hefty wages on the factory floors. In fact, the south was proportionally underrepresented in the army. The national average of 745 men in uniform per 1,000 liable for service concealed a marked regional differential: the average in the north was 781/1,000, in north–central Italy 832/1,000 and in the south and the islands (Sicily and Sardinia) 627/1,000. However, the contadini had a point: proportional death rates among southerners at the front were higher than the national average of 10.5 per cent. While the northern and north–central provinces were mostly on or near the average, Campania, Calabria and Sardinia were all higher and in Basilicata, which suffered worst, the death rate was over 21 per cent.[77]

The countryside's problems surfaced in parliament in March 1916, when socialist deputies contrasted the contribution that the *contadini* were making to the war in blood with the harshness of conditions in the countryside. The independent socialist deputy Arturo Labriola warned that the concentration of war production in the north was shifting wealth yet further away from the *Mezzogiorno*. A campaign against absentee owners and the non-cultivation of land began to gather pace with occupations in Lazio, and on 6 August 1916 a national congress at the Teatro Argentina in Rome demanded the requisition of all uncultivated land and its distribution among the working population, a demand echoed in similar gatherings at Piacenza and Milan in September and December. During that year the slogan '*la terra ai contadini*' ('land to the peasants') began to make itself heard. Landowners, particularly those with holdings in the south, predictably resisted. At the second congress of the reformist socialist party, held in Rome in April 1917, a motion calling for 'the general expropriation of the land and the sub-soil' was accepted with acclamation. Hostility to the war in the countryside gathered pace as the sense mounted that the peasants were being called on to make a disproportionately large sacrifice and getting little or nothing in return. News of the first Russian Revolution gave the growing movement more wind, and sharpened antagonisms that were no longer latent. 'We shall see,' the socialist party newspaper *Avanti!* mused, ' if our bourgeoisie continues to applaud a revolution that wants what they don't want: land to the peasants.'[78]

The first signs that serious trouble might be about to break out behind the front lines, threatening the entire war effort, came at Christmas 1916. Encouraged by the German peace note of 12 December, long processions of women wound through the lower Arno valley carrying white banners bearing the word *Pace* ('peace'). The Prefect of Florence thought things might be on the point of an explosion, fearing that there were 'many soldiers (and some officers)' who might be 'ready to support an insurrectional movement in some way'. This was a characteristic misapprehension by the authorities of what was actually going on. In the succeeding months thousands of women took to the streets, tired of the war, burdened with supporting families that included the old and infirm, lacking money and short of food. Nine thousand women working in the arms, cotton, tobacco and shoe industries went on strike in March and April 1917. There were frequent strikes by male metal workers in Liguria. In April, May and June, roads were blocked, telephone and telegraph wires cut, and stones thrown when the authorities sent in the cavalry. At bottom an updated version of the traditional *protesta dello stomacco*, the agitation was also being fuelled by attempts to fuse together opposition to the war and the struggle for radical social change, and by a socialist presence at the women's demonstrations. Popular anxieties also played their part, among them the fear that compulsory vaccination was a measure being introduced by the government to reduce a population that it could no longer afford to feed.[79]

By the end of April the authorities believed that almost all of Emilia Romagna was 'in the hands of the extremist parties' and that demonstrations which had a political character were being 'masked by an economic appearance'. Everywhere in northern Italy the prefects saw the not-so-hidden hand of socialism at work. Even moderate political activity alarmed the Prefect of Bologna: at the end of December 1916 he warned Rome that the activity of the subversive parties was 'persistent but cautious and therefore much more dangerous'. South of Rome, demonstrations were relatively few and were generally recognised by the prefects as being economic – a fact explained by the weakness of the socialist party's organisation and its few supporters. Maximalist socialists, led by Giacinto Menotti Serrati, had indeed been actively propagandising over the winter, castigating the *signori* ('masters' or 'bosses') as *imboscati* ('shirkers') and telling the workers that it was better to start a revolution against the bourgeoisie than to fight a war on their behalf.[80]

Between 30 April and 10 May 1917 4,000 women demonstrated in the city of Milan itself and almost double that number in the surrounding localities, protesting at the shortage of all foodstuffs but especially rice. The backdrop was a widespread exasperation with the *signori* who had wanted the war and who were held responsible for their difficult economic circumstances. The local police chief rightly put the disturbances down to a shortage of foodstuffs and blamed the prefect for failing to take appropriate action. The civil authorities, on the other hand, were on the lookout for political manipulation. General Dallolio, sent to the city early in May, wanted the interventionist party reinforced to form 'a bulwark against the open and concealed moves of neutralists, socialists and catholics'. The prefect, forced to recognise that the reformist socialists were carefully not taking political advantage of the agitation and were working to keep local extremists in check, saw in their wanting to distance themselves from the movement in Milan but not to disavow it completely 'a sign of weakness that does not leave me with peace of mind about the future'.[81]

In early August 1917 a bread shortage in Turin provided the spur for serious trouble. Intransigent socialists – *i rigidi* – were the preponderant political force in the city, strike action had been in the air for several months beforehand, and agitators had been encouraging the workers to down tools and thereby stop the war. On 13 August a demonstration in support of the Russian provisional government turned into an anti-war protest, and on the same day Giovanni Giolitti emerged from his self-imposed silence and speaking at Cuneo called the war 'the greatest catastrophe since the Great Flood'.[82] The papal peace note two days later added fuel to the flames. Spontaneous demonstrations on 22 August became a general strike next day which was almost total in all the main factories. The prefect called in the army and over the next four days rebels and soldiers battled for control of the city. At the end, 41 people were dead and 193 wounded and 1,000 had been arrested. The socialist party leadership kept well clear of the disturbances, and all but one of the Piedmontese deputies said during parliamentary debates in mid October that shortage of bread was the only cause of the riots. Though Communists and others of a Left persuasion would afterwards try to portray the 'Turin days' as an armed insurrection by the workers, what happened there and happened also in Bologna, Modena, Parma, Florence and elsewhere during the spring and summer of 1917 was a new form of protest by a newly emerging working class hatched by the war in which economic distress, social dissatisfaction and political aspirations found expression in a shared desire for an end to the fighting and for peace.[83]

Dallolio's productivist attitude to labour relations during the first two years of the war led to limited but significant concessions in such matters as labour representation on the regional mobilisation committees, a maximum working week (60 hours) and equal rates of pay for equal performance, but only when change was necessary to keep the war running and workers' demands did not threaten output or social order. After the disorders in Turin in August 1917 he first took a hard line, ordering the chairman of the Piedmontese committee of industrial mobilisation to concede nothing and demanding that justice be 'severe and implacable'. His attitude softened thereafter, and in mid October he instructed local officials not to apply sanctions to the innocent. Some workers had been taken off the restricted service roster and sent into the army simply for signing memoranda, an act he deprecated, saying that it had not been intended 'to remove the right to free assembly for economic motives'.[84] In all, some 300 Turin workers had their exonerated status removed and were sent to the war zone, where they were put in labour units not combatant corps and so were not able to 'infect' the front line with revolutionary and defeatist sentiment, notwithstanding Cadorna's belief to the contrary. Their presence, and agitation in Lazio and the Po valley, contributed to the concern felt by the authorities on the eve of Caporetto about the state of mind of the rural population and of the *soldati–contadini* at the front.

Ortigara and the eleventh battle of the Isonzo

In the early summer of 1917, the Italian lines above the Asiago *altopiano* ran more or less north–south from the Brenta valley to the Assa valley, facing Austrian positions entrenched along a line of mountains some 2,000 metres high. Naturally strong Austrian defences had been improved over the winter, which in the mountains lasted until June and during which snow 7 metres deep blanketed the region. A complete absence of local water supplies was not the least of the many difficulties the troops faced. The offensive, designed to put the Italians in a favourable position to attack the Val Sugana, was brought forward after an Austrian counter-attack on Monte Hermada between 4 and 6 June. On 10 June, eager to recover territory lost to the enemy the previous autumn, General Ettore Mambretti launched the four corps of 6th Army against the Austrians in mass frontal attacks. The offensive was initially intended to focus on the zone around Ortigara covered by Lieutenant-General Luca Montuori's XX Corps, but by extending it right along the line Mambretti ensured that Montuori had only 648 of the 1,504 guns available. Inadequate artillery preparation and support would be one of the causes of a bloody failure. Only on Monte Ortigara itself would the attack succeed – and then only briefly.

The job of taking Ortigara was given to the *Alpini* of 52nd division. The divisional commander, General Sabina Como Dagna, and one of his brigade commanders, General Antonino Di Giorgio, tried unsuccessfully to persuade Montuori that using small groups to penetrate the mountain chain would be more effective but the corps commander dismissed their advice, afraid that the troops might not leave the trenches. The attack, launched at 0515 on 10 June 1917 in appalling weather, was immediately repulsed everywhere except on the northern flank of XX Corps, where Como Dagna's men took a 2,000-metre mountain flanking Ortigara. It was suspended next day because of bad weather and after resisting an Austrian counter-attack it was renewed on 18 June. Making a super-human effort, Di Giorgio's brigade got to the summit of Monte Ortigara. At 2045 Mambretti ordered a halt all along the line except Ortigara, where there was to be 'local action to assure our occupation of [the] region on a tactically favourable line'.[85] The Austrians were now able to devote their undivided attention to the *Alpini* crammed on the summit of the mountain, an easy target for Austrian batteries overlooking them from nearby slopes. Battered incessantly by the enemy's guns with little effective response from their own artillery, desperately short of food and especially of water, fighting in snow littered with corpses and covered in excrement, Di Giorgio's men were attacked in the small hours of 25 June by Austrian *Stürmtruppen*. Six hours later the crest had fallen. Attempts to retake the summit were cut to pieces with rifle and machine-gun fire. Orders finally to retire were issued that night.

Misguided, mishandled, but fought with incomparable bravery, Ortigara cost the Italian army a total of 23,736 men and achieved nothing. What followed showed the senior reaches of the Italian officer corps at their worst. Mambretti tried to offload responsibility onto his corps commanders on the grounds that 'moral preparation' had been lacking, something that was the commander's responsibility, seemingly oblivious of the fact that ultimately that meant him. Corps commanders criticised junior officers for being inexpert and unable to infuse their troops with the necessary courage. Mambretti and Montuori both tried to blame Como Dagna, and Montuori withdrew a proposal to promote him *per merito di guerra*. Although he had a soft spot for Mambretti, who had taken an unattractive command during the *Strafexpedition*, Cadorna rejected his shuffling off of responsibility for the débâcle. After considering a number of reports, he concluded that the causes for the failure were 'bad weather, deficient preparation of the ground on which the attack was to be launched, and insufficient moral preparation of a portion of the troops'. All were basically Mambretti's responsibility. Four years later he changed his mind, holding that the principal cause of the failure was 'diminished combative spirit in part of the troops due to subversive propaganda' – a charge from which he exempted the *Alpini* of 52nd division.[86] Regretfully Cadorna replaced Mambretti, now a general with a reputation for presiding over failure thanks to his 'accursed bad luck', but instead of sacking him as he had many generals who had presided over lesser setbacks Cadorna sent him to command the Swiss frontier.[87] The only good thing to come out of the fiasco was Cadorna's decision to give up the idea of an offensive on the Pasubio on the grounds that it would almost certainly fail.

On 28 May Cadorna suspended the tenth battle of the Isonzo, meanwhile encouraging his subordinates to continue 'particular operations . . . useful for the purposes of the future offensive'.[88] His intention was to attack the Austrian lines on either side of the Vipacco river, aiming first for the *altopiano* of Ternova and then for the Bainsizza. Five days later, Capello outlined the objectives of his next offensive. From the foothold 2nd Army had established on the left bank of the Isonzo he intended to take Vrh (600 metres) and Jelenik (788 metres) while developing his principal attack from Vodice in two directions – a north-eastern thrust would move on Kobilek (627 metres) and Jelenik before heading for the eastern edge of the Bainsizza, while a second thrust south-east would drive for the Dol Gap below Monte Santo and then aim to take Monte

San Gabriele (646 metres), opening up the Ternova *altopiano*. Once again, heavy reliance was to be put on artillery. Eight or nine hours' firing by bombards would destroy the wire and parapets of the first line, while medium and heavy guns dealt with the second line.[89] Unaware that Capello's real objective was Tolmino, Cadorna raised no objections. At the same time the duke of Aosta expanded 3rd Army's role from a supporting action to an attack all along its lines aiming at Trieste.

As the date for the attack grew nearer, intelligence interpretations produced moderately encouraging news. The Ortigara offensive was held to have 'disorientated' the enemy, who were unable to explain its brief duration, while on the middle Isonzo he was still feeling 'the surprise and violence of our offensive'. The collapsing Russian front would in all likelihood draw at least three Austrian divisions away from the front south of Tolmino. An Austrian offensive on the northern Italian front was extremely unlikely: the time needed to transport troops from the eastern front and the narrow fighting gap before winter closed in meant that if they did not start to move by mid August there could be no Austrian offensive in the Trentino in 1917. The same calculation did not apply to the Isonzo, though, where seasonal limits on campaigning were much smaller if indeed they existed at all.[90]

Briefed by Bongiovanni at the beginning of June on the failure of Nivelle's offensive, Cadorna appeared to agree with the new French doctrine of waiting and wearing down the enemy by limited attacks where possible until a breakthrough battle became possible.[91] His plans suggest otherwise. Cadorna designed his eleventh – and last – battle on the Isonzo to fulfil both 'extrinsic' and 'intrinsic' strategic functions. As well as preserving the initiative in operations, something to which he attached great importance, it was intended to synchronise with British and French operations on the western front, where the Passchendaele offensive was to begin on 31 July, and to ease the pressure on the Russians, whose last offensive launched on 1 July had quickly collapsed. Locally, it was intended to create a stronger defensive front resting on the Bainsizza and Comens as the northern and southern bulwarks linked by the Gorizia amphitheatre. Tolmino, which could not be taken frontally, could then be squeezed out and Comens would smooth 3rd Army's way to Trieste. The attack by 1,200,000 men supported by 3,747 guns and 1,882 bombards, was launched along the entire length of the front from Tolmino to the sea in order to deny the enemy free play with his reserves.[92]

With 3rd Army attacking the Comen *altopiano* and Monte Hermada, and 2nd Army attacking the Bainsizza and Ternova, the eleventh battle of the Isonzo was already assuming gigantic proportions. Capello added yet more complexity to the design. Three days before the battle was scheduled to start, Cadorna learned that 2nd Army's commander had extended the front as far north as Mrzli, that the weight of the Bainsizza offensive was now on the left and not the right, and that the main objective was now the conquest of the Tolmino bridgehead.[93]

On 17 August 2nd Army's artillery opened up, next day 3rd Army's artillery followed suit, and on 19 August the attacks went in. The enemy was well placed to resist. Austrian artillery had doubled since the May battle and there were good stocks of ammunition. The caverns, deep and winding walkways and armoured observation points at Monte Santo gave the defenders huge advantages. The Tolmino attack failed first. Short Italian artillery fire ignited a wood concealing bridging materials for the northernmost crossing, bridges were not thrown across, and the troops faced well-prepared defences. Capello sacked XXVII Corps' commander, General Vanzo, replacing him with Pietro Badoglio, and blamed the troops' inability to manoeuvre and mediocre dash. In the centre, Lieutenant-General Enrico Caviglia's XXIV Corps took Monte Kuk, aided by II Corps' attack on Kobilek further south which, though it did not take the heights, did draw in enemy reserves. At this point Cadorna and Capello both made strategic errors. Cadorna halted 3rd Army's offensive in order to transfer artillery to the Bainsizza, thereby allowing Boroević to concentrate on a single front. Reinforcing failure instead of backing success, Capello threw in XIV Corps on the northern flank to strengthen Badoglio's attacks at a moment when his Austrian opponent, Boroević, had ordered a withdrawal. Badoglio's attack failed, and Boroević cancelled his order. The Austrians abandoned counter-attacks and put their newly arriving reserves into a rearward defensive line out of reach of Italian guns. On 25 August the Italians hit it. Instead of pausing to bring forward medium and heavy artillery, Capello with Cadorna's backing ordered his troops to press on. The attacks next day failed, and at the same time violent Austrian counter-attacks hit XXIV Corps. On 29 August, Cadorna ordered 2nd Army to stop. Third Army's attack had stalled equally quickly, thanks largely to the killing done by hidden machine-gun nests. When the fighting ended on 10 September, Italian losses amounted to 143,334 dead, wounded and missing, Austrian losses to 110,000. In the words of Cadorna's biographer, 'Italy had experienced the worst blood-letting since the start of the war.'[94]

Seemingly blind to the technical shortcomings of his commanders, Cadorna blamed the failure on the troops who had shown 'too little dash'. Their 'lack of enthusiasm' was ultimately the fault of 'the fatal internal policy of a determinedly laissez-faire government'.[95] Capello's explanation was more measured. The battle, which had begun superbly, had gradually lost forward momentum until it had stopped. This was partly the result of a series of 'natural reasons': logistic difficulties, lessening support by the heavy artillery, ignorance of the ground, increasing resistance by the enemy, 'and, let us admit it, the tiredness of the troops'. It was also the result of failures that should have been avoided. Infantry–artillery co-ordination had been poor, particularly in the second phase of the battle when the effects of concentrated fire had been wasted because it had not been followed by any infantry action. The troops had been poor at manoeuvring, largely because they had been poorly prepared and trained by their officers. Corps commanders sat too far away from the battle lines – some had been 8 kilometres behind the front – and relied too heavily on the telephone.[96] They were also at fault for using entire brigades where a company or a squad of *Arditi* would do much better.

Against a handful of machine-guns a large attacking column is an inert and incapable mass, uselessly suffering casualties through artillery and machine-gun fire when supple and agile nuclei could master the difficulties and act.[97]

Third Army had apparently done better as far as infantry–artillery co-ordination was concerned, but its commander too identified 'a number of grave deficiencies and lacunae in the command and management of the infantry'. In particular, despite clear and repeated orders there had been 'a deplorable crowding in the galleries and the front lines which gave the enemy easy successes and allowed the capture of numbers of our soldiers'.[98] After more than two years of war and eleven battles along the same front, Italian generals still had a lot to learn. Until they were properly trained, orders properly given and he could be sure that they would be carried out, Capello ordered his brigade and divisional commanders to put themselves at the head of their men to ensure that they advanced at the right time and in the proper manner.

Caporetto

On 14 September 1917, Cadorna issued orders to abandon the second stage of the Isonzo offensive, which he had planned for October, and prepare a *difensiva ad oltranza*. Three days earlier, armed with a half promise of British heavy and medium guns and French 75s for the following spring, and planning in the meantime to reduce the size of Italian divisions from four regiments to three, he had intended to resume the offensive shortly and then launch a much larger operation the following May.[99] Two things changed his mind. One was the worsening situation on the Russian front and evidence that fifty Austrian battalions

Fig. 10 Italian dead after an Austrian gas attack

had arrived from the eastern front. Another forty were expected, and more would certainly be on their way. The *Ufficio situazione* calculated that a separate peace would release 105 German and Austrian divisions, as well as freeing 1,250,000 prisoners of war, and would provide the Central Powers with abundant supplies of labour, raw materials, petrol and grain. There was only one place where they could be used before winter arrived, and that was on the Julian front.[100] The other was that no more replacements were available to make up the losses already suffered, and medium- and heavy-calibre ammunition was running low. Launching another offensive would require plundering strategic reserves, which he was not willing to do. With its numerical superiority decreasing day by day, the Italian army was no longer in a position to inflict a blow on its enemy hard enough to deprive him of any hopes of launching an offensive of his own. If the Austrians launched a successful attack, Cadorna foresaw having to withdraw from exposed forward positions which were of little defensive value. He could not presently afford a failure, he told the war minister. That would have 'very grave repercussions' on the army, which would lose at least 100,000 men, 'and above all on the country'. Preparations for the offensive were accordingly suspended, and instead a 'clear and precise' operational order – one of the few operational orders issued by the *Comando supremo* – went out to prepare a solid defence on all fronts.[101] British objections that his decision would annul 'the entire Allied offensive plan' were brushed aside: Italy's 'energetic potential' constituted a very grave threat to Austria and was immobilising the major part of her strength.[102]

Cadorna had pressed Dallolio in early September for 650,000 rounds of medium- and heavy-calibre ammunition by the end of the month on the basis of figures that Dallolio believed were often incorrect and ignored the fact that thousands more rounds of artillery ammunition than he had asked for were sitting in magazines in the rear. On 8 October, having received 'a very precious increase' in supplies and acknowledging that output had reached unprecedented levels, Cadorna allowed that this would permit him to set aside 6,000,000 rounds of medium and heavy and 20,000,000 of light ammunition for spring 1918 'to undertake two successive offensives at a short interval'.[103] Meantime he set in train further defensive measures. Artillery was shifted from 2nd and 3rd Armies to 1st and 4th Armies and the *Zona Carnia* covering the northern arc of the frontier, leaving them with 1,292 and 580 guns respectively, though this still left the recipients short of half their estimated needs for a *difensiva ad oltranza*.[104] The commanders of 2nd and 3rd Armies were also told that they would each lose five divisions as part of a plan to create a central reserve whose fifteen divisions would be rotated one at a time through special training camps.[105]

The orders given to Luigi Capello, 2nd Army commander, appeared unequivocal. If the enemy launched an offensive 'big style', he was to adopt the *difensiva ad oltranza*. The front line should be held with limited forces which should resist as long as possible but not be reinforced as this risked premature attrition. Behind it there should be two lines of main resistance. The many caverns on the front were to be used to set up flanking positions to make maximum use of artillery and machine-guns. Capello was told that he had more than enough guns for an effective defensive, and might have to lose some to other parts of the front if rapid reinforcements were needed elsewhere.[106] The *Comando supremo* was already concerned that Capello had too many of his heavy and medium guns on or close to the left bank of the Isonzo.[107] Capello reassured headquarters: he had arranged to move one-third of his artillery ammunition back near his railway stations and to remove 270 medium and heavy guns and fifteen batteries of light guns from their forward positions.[108] However he had a plan of his own to meet an enemy offensive, which he expected would try to turn and then retake the positions on the Bainsizza *altopiano* south of Tolmino recently won by the Italians but not yet solidly reinforced.[109] In the worst hypothesis, the enemy would attack all along the line and target Monte Jeza before driving west along the crests and valleys towards the plains beyond. The front lines were to be defended where and as long as the troops could be protected from enemy artillery fire by suitable defences and counter-attacks launched to retake lost positions. The key to success was swift and effective artillery fire to smash the attacking enemy, paralysing him and providing a favourable opportunity for a large-scale counter-offensive. Only IV Army Corps, holding the northern portion of the line from Tolmino to Plezzo, was to remain on the defensive, its task to hold its ground.

As well as departing from Cadorna's intentions, Capello's strategic design hinged on an unrealistic degree of preplanning and intrinsic co-ordination.[110] The 'mechanism of defence and counter-offensive' was to be so pre-arranged 'in full agreement between artillery and infantry' that it could unfold automatically 'even if enemy fire were to completely destroy all communications'.[111] If the concept was clear, the details were not. Corps commanders were told that 'only what is indispensable' must remain beyond the Isonzo, leaving them to figure out what that was. Capello warned them that artillery deployment was 'excessively offensive', but then went on to advise them that rather than face 'a crisis of artillery' it was better to have some batteries placed in positions 'that theoretically could be said to be too far forward for the defensive'.[112]

Apparently blind to the contradiction between his own concept of a defensive battle and Capello's counter-offensive design, Cadorna approved his subordinate's directive. Apart from drawing Capello's attention to the need to pull back the bulk of Badoglio's XXVII Corps from the left to the right bank of the Isonzo, the only significant addition he made was to stress the need to hit the enemy's jump-off trenches with 'murderous' fire as soon as his preparatory bombardment, which might be very brief, began so that the attack would be disorganised and destroyed before it got going.[113] At this point Capello envisaged launching a counter-offensive on the northern side of the Bainsizza – and told Porro so on 11 October. Confined to bed with kidney trouble and so unable to go in person to Vicenza, Capello reprised his counter-offensive plan to Colonel Ugo Cavallero and asked for another army corps of three divisions which he wanted to put behind Monte Jeza, so allowing him at the opportune moment to unleash a 'lightning counter-offensive'. Cadorna gave him Bongiovanni's VII Corps without a moment's demur.[114]

As the hour of destiny grew close, command arrangements and strategy were both in a state of some confusion. Capello, suffering from nephritis, was in bed for ten days in mid October and away on leave between 20 and 22 October, though he said afterwards that he kept a close eye on things. His gaze fixed on the Bainsizza, he was aware that the enemy might advance up the Isonzo from the Tolmino basin and then swing left – but did nothing about it.[115] The interim commander of 2nd Army, General Montuori, was unsure whether the enemy intended to attack IV Corps and the left of XXVII Corps with the aim of turning the defensive line and getting to the heads of the Judrio and Natisone valleys or chase the Italians off San Gabriele and reoccupy Monte Santo. He seemed confident of his defensive arrangements but less so of the proposed counter-offensive, for which he had only seven brigades and not the thirteen he needed.[116] In an order that was to have dramatic tactical consequences, Montuori defined the front of Badoglio's XXVII Corps as reaching up to the Isonzo while Lieutenant-General Alberto Cavaciocchi's IV Corps was responsible for the defence of the river. Asked to define exactly what 'defence' meant, Montuori replied that it meant preventing the enemy from crossing from the left bank to the right.[117] Meantime Capello was gingering up his army commanders for 'offensive action in great depth', but was unable to say whether the counter-offensive he envisaged developing from the Vrh basin would go north-east, east or south-east.[118] For a month, Capello could believe that he was authorised to undertake a plan which, according to one critic, 'had no chance of succeeding'. Belatedly, Cadorna stepped in. On 20 October he told Capello that his idea of a counter-offensive was impractical given the strength of his units and the shortage of replacements and that he must restrict himself to 'a tenacious active defence' and local counter-attacks.[119]

In the meantime, indications were mounting that the enemy might be planning an offensive of his own. Intelligence arriving from the Berne station and from the Milan section of the *Ufficio informazione* throughout September and October all pointed in that direction. In mid September Sonnino forwarded intelligence from Copenhagen and Stockholm suggesting that German divisions were on their way to Italy as part of preparations for an offensive, possibly erupting from the Trentino.[120] At the end of the month, French intelligence passed on reports that German and Austrian units were on their way from the Russian and Romanian fronts to Italy and that the main enemy offensive would likely be in the Trentino with a secondary offensive on the Carso.[121] On 30 September it appeared to the *Ufficio situazione* that the enemy had for the moment abandoned the idea of a major offensive on the Julian front and six days later a telephone conversation intercepted on the Bainsizza *altopiano* indicated that an order suspending leave for Austrian soldiers on the middle Isonzo had been revoked. But by 9 October enough information had been obtained from deserters and prisoners of war, confirmed by observation, for Capello to be certain that German troops were present on his front and that preparations for an offensive were under way. The enemy did his best to make life difficult for the newly arrived head of the *Ufficio informazione*, Lieutenant-Colonel Odoardo Marchetti: twenty-one radio stations created false traffic suggesting a strong enemy presence in the Tyrol, the Austro-Swiss frontier was closed, and German troops were ostentatiously moved to the Trentino.

Confronted with differing 'and certainly exaggerated' reports of a German presence Colonel Ricardo Calcagno's *Ufficio situazione* discarded the scenario of an attack in the Trentino and acknowledged that an offensive on the middle Isonzo, where 'our positions [are] in conditions of tactical inferiority' was possible. Given the size and worth of the forces available, the enemy could not be aiming at 'grandiose objectives' and was likely only to seek to restore the position as it had been before the May battles.[122] Next day, modifying its interpretation on the basis of 'very credible informers' and prisoner-of-war depositions, it concluded that the enemy's intentions were defensive or counter-offensive and not offensive and that his aim was probably to block the possibility of a twelfth battle of the Isonzo, although once again an offensive could not be ruled out.[123] The very next day it reversed itself yet again, concluding on the basis of a continuing exodus of Austrian troops from the Trentino to the Julian front and other evidence that there was now a significant German presence there and that an enemy action on the sector from Tolmino to Monte Santo 'must be considered as very probable and possible'.[124]

If Cadorna believed in the coming attack – a matter over which there is disagreement – he certainly took insufficient account of the intelligence that pointed to an imminent enemy offensive in making preparations to meet it.[125] The way in which the *Ufficio situazione* presented its digests allowed – if it did not encourage – the commander-in-chief to underestimate the danger he was in. Inclined to hedge its bets when faced with what was often contradictory and fragmentary information, it faithfully reported the many and various starting dates given by deserters as they came and went. Absent evidence was given as much weight as actual evidence. Thus barely a week before the storm was due to burst it reported that the conventional indications of the immediate proximity of an operation, such as increased transport activity in the enemy's rear, ranging fire by newly emplaced batteries, extra aerial reconnaissance and *nervosismo* in the front line, were all lacking. In fact movements were being carried out at night and German artillery techniques imported from the western front did away with preliminary ranging fire. However, there was evidence of notable activity in the preparation of gun positions and the construction of approaches. The conclusion, on the basis of information from the latest deserter, was that an offensive was being prepared but could not start before the last ten days in October.[126]

In the last days indications that an attack was imminent piled up. A document taken from a German officer killed in a road accident on 5 October, but only translated and circulated two weeks later, gave details of the method of the coming attack including the use of gas, short bombardments, and attacks north and south of the Isonzo. On 21 October 2nd Army's Intelligence Section circulated a translation of the operational order for 1st Infantry Regiment's coming attack on the slopes of Mrzli and Hill 1186, and orders for 12th German Division's advance up the Isonzo to Caporetto.[127] That same morning two Romanian officers deserted on IV Corps' front and gave detailed information backed by documentary evidence on the Austro-German attack, which was now expected to begin on 25 or 26 October. This included the timings of the four-hour preliminary gas bombardment and the ninety-minute rolling bombardment, the first day's target (Caporetto), and the overall objective – 'an invasion in depth as happened in Romania'. Second Army intelligence thought their information reliable, not least because it confirmed the interrogation of another officer who had provided intelligence about the very effective German use of gas at Riga on 3 September 1917, and matched intelligence handed over by two Bohemian deserters the previous day.[128] At 1900 on 22 October General Montuori, now temporarily in command of 2nd Army, reported a telephone interception on IV Corps' front suggesting that the enemy attack would begin that night. Bad weather postponed it for twenty-four hours.

On the eve of the battle Cadorna had a clear and accurate picture of the enemy's plan. The main effort would be made on the sector Plezzo–Tolmino, its immediate objectives being the slopes of Kolovrat and the line Monte Matajur–Monte Mia, after which it would invade the plain. The entire Julian defensive line was to be turned from the north. He expected subsidiary attacks in the *Zona Carnia*, the Cadore and the Trentino, whose defence necessarily reduced the forces he could concentrate in the threatened sector. He was confident that the enemy attack would find his army prepared, with an adequate 'though not very abundant' amount of artillery and sufficient munitions. The only thing he was short of was replacements. Nevertheless, the arrangements he had made, he told the war minister and the king, were 'such as to allow me to await the enemy's blow with serene confidence of being able to repel it victoriously'.[129]

Cadorna's last-minute direction of his defences was too little and much too late. A poor understanding of the threat he was facing, in part due to his failure to absorb in time the intelligence warnings he was given, and a blinkered strategic vision worked in tandem with an over-reliance on his subordinates understanding his intentions and carrying out his orders. In the absence of a clear central defensive plan, the commander of IV Corps, General Alberto Cavaciocchi, was told not to withdraw his left-hand division covering the Plezzo sector from the advanced line of defence and at the eleventh hour given a single additional division to reinforce his front. Bongiovanni, commanding VII Corps, was given three separate tasks – to reinforce the wings of IV and XXVII Corps, to garrison the important defensive line Kolovrat–Matajur, and to man-oeuvre counter-offensively at the opportune moment. On the day, his corps could carry out none of them: it was too far away from IV and XXVII Corps, wrongly aligned to support their internal wings, and too spread out for the counter-offensive.[130]

Capello was asked to confirm that the deficiencies in his defences to which his attention had been drawn in March 1916, particularly in the Luico–Globocak sector (which would become one of the key fighting zones in the battle to come), had been put right and was told to make his defence 'very much more economical than that proposed'.[131] Afterwards he claimed that while sickness had kept him away from the troops between 4 and 23 October his subordinates had failed to carry out his orders to improve the efficiency of their units. The imminence of the offensive had not been apparent until three days before it happened, and when it did reports from observers led to the judgement that the enemy's artillery bombardment was having little effect.[132] When Cadorna met Capello on the afternoon of 23 October and discovered that his orders had not been obeyed, a shouting match reportedly ensued.

A last-minute shift of one division from VII Corps to IV Corps and its replacement with a division from 1st Army did nothing to remedy what was perhaps the single most important strategic fact: Capello's army reserve and Cadorna's strategic reserve were too far away to be of any immediate use in the battle to come. Cadorna's nine-division reserve was spread between Palmanova and Cormons–Cividale, behind Capello's reserves. Capello's nearest reserve was 30 kilometres from Caporetto and 50 kilometres from the Saga Pass, leaving the left wing of his army 'completely abandoned to itself'.[133]

The heavy rain that had forced a postponement of the enemy attack ended soon after midnight on 24 October 1917. Two hours later 2,400 guns opened up all along the line from Monte Rombon to Gorizia. German veterans of the Somme and Verdun said afterwards that they had never heard such a din. At 0430 it died down. Then at 0630 it started up again, and for the next two hours the Italian lines experienced the heaviest bombardment they ever suffered. A thirty-second gas bombardment at

Plezzo killed 600 men of the 87th infantry regiment instantly. Unlike all previous bombardments, this one concentrated not on the Italian front lines but on the gun positions, magazines and communication centres behind them.

In essence, the enemy's plan was simple. Two Austrian and German attacks would cut off the 22-kilometre salient held by IV Corps, the *Gruppo* Krauss driving south-west down the upper Isonzo valley on an axis Plezzo–Saga–Caporetto and aiming for the spine of Monte Stol while the *Gruppo* Stein knifed north up the middle Isonzo valley from Tolmino to Caporetto, severing IV Corps from the rest of 2nd Army. Simultaneous attacks due west by the *Gruppo* Berrer and the *Gruppo* Scotti would hit Badoglio's XXVII Corps on the hills overlooking the middle Isonzo, shielding Stein's drive up the valley. Rapid exploitation of early success would give the enemy possession of the mountain chain protecting the valleys of the Judrio and the Natisone, beyond which lay the open plains of northern Italy. The weather was on their side. High on the mountains of Cavaciocchi's IV Corps front a covering of thick snow hid the paths along which some of his troops would shortly try to retire and freezing winds blinded them. Elsewhere torrential rain, strong winds and fog blinded defenders and masked the advancing German and Austrian columns.

Fourth Corps had pulled its heavy artillery back as ordered so that the Austrian front lines were at maximum range. Interpreting Capello's order to open fire 'shortly after the enemy bombardment has begun' in their own way, the guns of its three divisions opened up as soon as the first enemy fire hit their positions – but for four and a half hours they were on their own. Artillery doctrine, laid down afresh in March, dictated that Italian guns should not start firing until the enemy began the brief phase of 'destructive fire' that forecast an attack, when it should smother his front-line trenches to suffocate the action as it began. Capello and his interim replacement Montuori had both confirmed this in orders distributed in the days before the battle, and Badoglio passed them down to XXVII Corps.[134] When the preliminary enemy bombardment began 2nd Army's artillery commander, General Giuliano Ricci, wanted to open fire and objected to Montuori's interpretation of the March doctrine but was overruled by the chief of staff, Colonel Silvio Egidi.[135] Badoglio's artillery commander, the aptly named Colonel Alfredo Cannoniere, also asked permission to open fire at 0200 but was likewise refused. 'Absolutely nothing may be changed', Badoglio reportedly told him, 'we only have munitions for three days and I don't know if I can let you have any of it. At any rate, we'll see.'[136] Doing more or less exactly as the high command intended, XXVII Corps' heavy and medium artillery opened up at 0630, and its divisional light artillery at 0730 when the enemy attack began.

Artillery played a major role in the Italian battle plan, such as it was, but when it came into action – hindered by fog that obstructed observation, waterlogged ground in which rounds failed to explode, and with little or no communication with the infantry who depended heavily upon it – it was already too late. Poring over the causes of the defeat in 1918, the Caporetto Inquiry was inclined to blame the artillerymen for failing to grasp the principles and prescriptions laid down by the higher military authorities and for acting in ways that did not conform to theory.[137] In fact, as a clearly incensed General Dallolio pointed out, artillery doctrine was complex, confusing and open to misinterpretation, and included no provision for true counter-preparatory fire.[138] Later Marshal Caviglia, who had commanded a corps on the Bainsizza during the battle, was highly critical of a 'complicated method' that made it difficult to know when to open the different kinds of fire prescribed by the regulations, made worse by an unwise tendency to economise on ammunition before and during attacks.[139]

Hit by Krauss's attack, Cavaciocchi's left held until mid afternoon. On Monte Rombon successive Austrian attacks broke against the Italian position, and in the Plezzo basin, where they enjoyed a slight numerical advantage, soldiers of Major-General Giovanni Arrighi's 50th division fighting from earthen trenches held the enemy at bay. In his centre the 43rd division lost Monte Rosso when an enemy mine exploded beneath them but held the line Krasjc–Monte Nero, fighting off nine Austrian attacks. On Monte Nero troops fought to the bitter end. At 0800 the *Gruppo* Stein launched its attack on Cavaciocchi's right wing, and the 46th division, clinging to the steep treeless slopes of their advance line between Sleme and Mrzli, where the rain had turned the trenches into muddy bogs, was soon in trouble. Taking the explosion of an Austrian mine on the summit of Mrzli in their stride Italian troops held the mountain until mid afternoon, but by 1100 the enemy was penetrating gaps in the line and had taken Krn behind them. Rapidly losing contact with the division, regimental commanders were fighting their own individual battles.

The southern end of Cavaciocchi's line, anchored to the Isonzo, was thinly held and at Gabrije two Italian companies (300 men) gave way when hit by twelve companies of Silesians. Masked by the mist and rain, the 12th Silesian division began its advance up the left bank of the Isonzo, reaching Kamno at noon just as Austro-German units advancing up the right bank reached Osteria opposite them. Attacked from the front and the flank, a lone battalion of 147th infantry regiment fought to the bitter end, its commanding officer, Lieutenant-Colonel Maurizio Piscicelli winning a posthumous *medaglia d'argento*. Idersko, where a defending *Carabinieri* unit was destroyed, fell next at about 1330. Cavaciocchi chose not to tell Capello, believing the reports might be exaggerated, but ordered Arrighi to hold Saga. He still had troops to commit, having kept at Caporetto two of the three regiments given him by Cadorna as a general reserve, but both had previously suffered heavy losses on the Bainsizza in the eleventh battle of the Isonzo. With his headquarters at Creda far behind the lines and communications non-existent, Cavaciocchi was unable to comprehend his battle, let alone direct it.[140]

Badoglio's deployment of XXVII Corps and his conception of how he would direct the counter-attack demanded by Capello at the last minute greatly advantaged his enemy. Instructed – in an order that appears not to have reached him – to shift the bulk of his corps from the left to the right bank of the Isonzo, he left three of his four divisions on the far side of the river holding the 8-kilometre southern portion of his line, while Major-General Giovanni Villani's 19th division guarded the 13-kilometre northern section alone. Montuori's ambiguous order two days before the battle delimiting XXVII's front at the Isonzo while allocating the defence of the river to Cavaciocchi and the 46th division on the other side of it created a potential weak spot. Badoglio's dispositions made matters a good deal worse. While one brigade fronted the river and a second stood on the hills behind Volzana, a single battalion amounting in all to some 450 men held the wooded steeply-sloping 2 ½ kilometres from Plezia to Foni and the Isonzo. Five battalions of the *brigata Napoli* were stationed some way behind the forward and intermediate positions. Doubting the wisdom of this arrangement, Villani's chief of staff, Colonel Giulio De Medici, telephoned Badoglio's chief of staff, Lieutenant-Colonel Pellegrini, who confirmed that one battalion looking over the river was enough.

Badoglio seems to have been very confident about the coming battle. 'We don't need to fear anything big on [M] Jeza from German troops used to the undulations of Flanders,' he reportedly told his divisional commanders.[141] Exactly what he planned to do when the expected attack came remains far from clear. His detractors afterwards claimed that he intended to entice the enemy forward into the 'Volzana trap' and smash them there, which seems unlikely. His positioning of five of the six battalions of the *brigata Napoli* on the higher ground at Kolovrat and the Passo Zagradan, above Monte Plezia, suggests that he intended to launch them in a counter-attack if the lower position fell. His orders to his subordinates two weeks before the battle were to hold their front lines thinly and have reinforcements ready for counter-attacks.[142] Colonel De

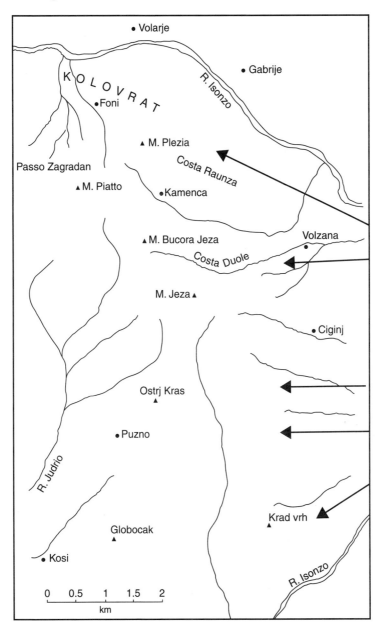

5. Caporetto: the attack on XXVII Corps

Medici told the Caporetto Inquiry that if the Plezia–Foni–Isonzo line was lost his corps commander intended to use repressive fire on Plezia. Under political pressure to whitewash a general who was by then deputy chief of the general staff, the Caporetto Inquiry discovered yet another explanation for his failure properly to guard the right bank of the river. Badoglio had been correct in taking his main task to be the defence not of the Isonzo but of the head of the Judrio valley, which informed his distribution of his troops and his own line of conduct.[143]

What Badoglio did on the day was to disappear – which is the more striking in that he told his subordinate commanders in the briefing he gave them two weeks before the battle to 'remember that in this type of war command action essentially consists in control'.[144] Abandoning his headquarters at Ostri Kras, which gave him a good view of the battlefield, the previous night after it was hit by Austrian ranging fire but leaving his corps artillery command in the caverns of nearby Puzno, he withdrew to Kosi in the Judrio valley. With telephone lines soon cut, he left Kosi at 1100 to make his way forward, came back again at 1400 and then moved to Kambresko. Effectively out of touch with everyone, he remained throughout the day 'strangely passive'.[145] Meanwhile both his and Cavaciocchi's fronts began to collapse.

On Badoglio's front, the fifteen rifle companies (3,560 men) of Villani's *brigata Taro*, with 56 machine-guns and 20 machine-pistols, strung out along the heights from Costa Raunza to Val Duole, were hit by the 75 rifle companies of Berrer's *Alpenkorps*, armed with 450 light machine-guns and 246 heavy machine-guns.[146] With only a couple of hundred defenders and half a dozen machine-guns, the wooded slopes between Monte Plezia and Foni on Villani's left were hanging in mid-air. Württemberger mountain troops led by a young Erwin Rommel reached Monte Plezia soon after noon and had taken it by 1500. Foni, defended by a single platoon, was taken before dark.[147] Monte Kamenka fell in the late morning, and with that Villani's centre began to collapse. On the right Ostri Kras, Puzno and Krad Vrh were all under heavy attack. With the *Gruppo* Scotti making progress there, Villani pulled his units back to Bucova Jeza in mid afternoon. Monte Jeza was defended tenaciously until nightfall and then relinquished. Under heavy artillery fire, reinforcements ordered forward to Bucova Jeza never made it and a second force trying to reach it met two brigades that were already retreating.

While five Silesian battalions marched up the right bank of the Isonzo, brushing aside a lone Italian platoon and a couple of field guns, the main force, mistaken initially for Italians and then for prisoners of war, pushed on up the left bank. At about 1500 they reached Caporetto, cutting off 46th division and opening up the Staroselo Pass and the head of the

Natisone valley. Meanwhile Cavaciocchi's front caved in. Ordered to attack, General Farisoglio left 43rd division headquarters at Drezenca for corps headquarters to clarify instructions which left him unsure whether he was supposed to hold the crests or stop the enemy advancing from Kamno, meanwhile ordering his troops to withdraw – a decision that has been labelled 'incomprehensible'.[148] His orders did not reach some of the front-line troops, who fought on, but did reach the support services and the artillery who began a disorderly retreat. Farisoglio got as far as Caporetto where he became the first Italian general to be made a prisoner of war. At 1800, aware that Caporetto had fallen, General Arrighi ordered the troops of the 50th division holding the pass at Saga to withdraw – 'a fatal error' according to one of Cadorna's sternest critics because it opened up the Uccea valley.[149]

While IV and XXVII Corps fought their battles, VII Corps stood by and watched. Although its commander, General Bongiovanni, knew the attack was coming he spent the night of 23 October at Carraria near Cividale, 30 kilometres behind the front, thinking that the rain would once again force the enemy to call it off. The attack caught VII Corps with one of its two divisions deployed along the Jeza–Kolovrat crests while the other (which had been rotated through all six armies over the previous seven days) was in the process of taking up positions on Monte Matajur and at Luico. Told by Badoglio's headquarters at about 1100 that the front seemed calm after the cannonade, Bongiovanni was ordered by Capello at 1140 to defend the line Matajur–Jeza–Globocak. By noon the roads were so crowded that he could not reach his command post at Luico, and his reserves were unable to get forward either. Following the revised orders, the *brigata Salerno* deployed on Matajur and then did nothing as the enemy marched up the Isonzo valley 1,400 metres below. Shortly after 1800 Capello told Bongiovanni to attack the flanks of the enemy column that was nearing Caporetto – which had fallen two hours earlier. Bongiovanni gave the order at 1900, which was by then far too late.[150] An energetic commander could have done much more with his corps, but Bongiovanni was not such a man. The Caporetto Inquiry, genially taking full account of the speed of events, found him culpable only for 'lack of intuition and activity equal to the supreme tragedy of the moment'.[151]

Cadorna rose early on 24 October and wrote to his daughter, brimming with confidence. 'We are,' he told her, 'on the eve of great events.' The enemy expected that at the first shots his army would show their backs, but they were in for a surprise. The appalling weather was 'a great advantage for us'.[152] His immediate concern was to husband his artillery ammunition in order to fend off an enemy offensive that he expected to last at least a month, during which consumption would be heavy and prolonged.[153] Orders were telephoned to Capello telling him to exercise the strictest parsimony and only to fire when absolutely necessary in view of the fact that the operation could be 'very prolonged'. He was also told to keep in mind the need to ensure a strong build-up of munitions 'for operations next spring'.[154] Capello's misplaced confidence was if anything greater than that of his commander. 'It seems they want to attack me and I couldn't ask for anything more,' he had remarked happily a week earlier. 'I shall be able to add some Germans to my prisoner-of-war collection.'[155] The first news – of the loss of Plezzo – reached general headquarters in mid morning but caused no evident anxiety. At noon Capello reminded Cavaciocchi that counter-offensive attacks which caught the enemy between pincers were the best way to deal with the situation – evidence of how far out of touch with reality he was. It was not until early afternoon that a telephone call from Capello reporting that an enemy column was marching on Caporetto began to sound warning bells. Only at 1600, when Badoglio was finally able to get to a telephone, did 2nd Army's commander begin to get some idea of what was happening on XXVII Corps' front. By then the battle was well and truly out of his grasp – and Cadorna's too.

Next day the collapse gathered pace as the commanding heights behind the Isonzo, whose possession was crucial if the attack was to be held, fell to the enemy one by one. Units of 50th division held out on Monte Stol till nightfall, but Monte Mia was abandoned. Monte Matajur held by a company of Lequio's 63rd division fell, earning Rommel the coveted *Pour le mérite*. Stein's men took the sides of Kolovrat, and Luico. Attempts to retake Kolovrat, Monte Piatto and Bucova Jeza were easily brushed off. Units of XXVII Corps held Globocak until the evening (Badoglio had wrongly reported it lost the day before) when they were finally forced off it. Already the roads were jammed with retreating troops, as yet mostly from the rear services, making movement impossible. Reserves could not get forward, and staff officers had to abandon their motor cars and wade through masses of weary and disheartened soldiery. On the Bainsizza Italian forces were pushed back to the Kuk–Jelenik line and some troops began to cross the Isonzo.

With the backbone of his mountain fortress broken, Cadorna was momentarily at a loss. 'Even a Napoleon couldn't do anything in these conditions,' he complained to his staff. Capello, about to surrender his command and go to hospital, advised retreating to the river Torre or better still the Tagliamento.[156] At 1947 on 25 October Cadorna telegraphed the war minister to tell him that he was ordering a retreat to the Tagliamento and gave Porro the authorisation to begin the move at once.[157] Then he changed his mind, by his own account reluctant to abandon ground that it had taken two and a half years of bloody fighting to conquer, his mind and heart rebelling at the prospect of having to leave 'the magnificent provinces and patriotic population of the Veneto in the enemy's power'.[158] In reality he seems to have been swayed by the argument put to him by one of his staff, Colonel Ugo Cavallero, that retreating would leave 3rd Army at the mercy of the enemy and that it needed thirty-six hours to extricate itself from its position on the lower Isonzo.[159] Cavallero hurried off to Montuori's headquarters and after three hours of discussion Montuori, once again in command of 2nd Army, agreed to hold a line running from Monte Maggiore via Monte Korada, Kuk and Vodice to Monte Santo.[160] Cavallero's intervention may well have saved 3rd Army from a fate like that of its neighbour.

On 26 October the order went out to 2nd Army to defend the line Monte Maggiore–Kuk–Monte Santo 'to the last man': 'ON IT WE MUST WIN OR DIE,' Cadorna declared. Third Army would withdraw to a line running from Gorizia via the bridgeheads on the lower Isonzo to the Vallone. Ground was to be defended foot by foot and the road to invasion barred at all costs.[161] It was immediately followed by another, reserved for army commanders only, preparing them for the possibility of a retreat to the Tagliamento 'which I should think very unlikely (*poco probabile*)'. Third Army was to move after 2nd Army but not uncover its northern flank. Detailed lines of retreat were assigned to 3rd Army, less detailed ones to 2nd Army.[162] Preparing for his worst-case scenario, Cadorna put General Maglietta in charge of all defensive works west of the Tagliamento and instructed him to complete the works on the right bank protecting the bridges and prepare small bridgeheads on the left bank. Forewarned at the eleventh hour, the intendants-general of the two armies were told to make their own individual arrangements for the rapid movement of services such as field hospitals and bakeries, materials and the movable sick and wounded.[163] Here lack of foresight would make its contribution to the disaster that was beginning to unfold.

Over the next fifteen days the Italian armies fell back into the heart of the northern plains. Increasingly concerned about the left of his line, Cadorna switched General Francesco Rocca's 63rd division from 3rd Army to the *Zona Carnia* on 26 October, while the remainder of Montuori's command began preparations to withdraw. While two battalions of *Alpini* defending Monte Maggiore were being attacked from three sides, forcing their commander, Colonel-Brigadier Sapienza, to order a withdrawal, Cadorna created the *Special Army Corps* under General Di Giorgio to act as a covering force on the Torre bridges in case a retreat became necessary. The Natisone valley was now flooding with Württembergers and

Silesians, and the enemy was beginning to pour down the Luico–Cividale road and the Judrio valley, where by the day's end they were closing on Monte Korada. At 0200 hours on 27 October, Cadorna gave 2nd and 3rd Armies twenty-four hours' notice to pull back to the Tagliamento. He and his staff left Udine that day for Treviso while the rearguard, intended to defend the river Torre for two days and allow 2nd Army to retire, was being more or less destroyed at Cividale.[164] The enemy entered Udine next day, fighting a stiff battle with *Arditi* and *Bersaglieri* who were trying to buy time to destroy the stores and magazines.

Third Army's withdrawal, planned by Aosta and his chief of staff, Colonel Giuseppe Vaccari, was well organised. On 26 October, while Cadorna still hoped to hold his line, the corps commanders were ordered to put up a 'vigorous obstinate resistance' to allow the Isonzo army time to reorganise itself. With commendable foresight, they were also given sketch maps of each corps' line of movement in case they had to withdraw to the Tagliamento.[165] Next day, divisional generals were personally given the tasks of blowing the bridges on the Isonzo to ensure that this happened after the troops had crossed but before the enemy could infiltrate the lines. Second Army, holding more or less intact in the neighbourhood of Cormons, was supposed to march diagonally northwest across the Friuli plain – and the enemy's front – to bridges at and near Pinzano, leaving the nearby bridge at Codroipo for 3rd Army. With only half a dozen crossing points on the Tagliamento between the foothills and the sea, there was not much alternative – but as a plan it asked a lot of armies falling back in disorder and soldiers anxious to get away from the advancing enemy. It went wrong from the start as elements of 2nd Army converged on the Codroipo bridges along with fleeing refugees: on one single day it was estimated that over 300,000 people crossed there, along with tens of thousands of horses and carriages. With another of his bridges unusable because of high water levels, Aosta gave his corps commanders clear and exact details about which units were to use which bridges and ordered that all military and civilian elements belonging to 2nd Army be 'inexorably re-directed' to their allocated crossings further north.[166] Then, about midday on 30 October, Aosta's men heard three loud explosions. After responsibility had been passed down the chain of command, a Major Luraschi had blown up the Codroipo bridge, leaving 3rd Army with only two crossing points.

One million troops and 400,000 refugees now jammed the roads. The chaotic scenes as troops without officers and officers without troops hurried to get away from the battlefield left a lasting impression. Soldiers ransacked houses, shops and stores, consuming all the drink they could find and staggering off with whatever they could carry: Luigi Gasparotto saw one man carrying an oven and another an enormous mirror.[167] Houses were set on fire, sometimes for pleasure, sometimes because the inhabitants had refused requests for food or had overcharged for it in the past, and sometimes because of the pressures of the moment: Paolo Caccia Dominioni's flame-throwers lightened their load by setting fire to a house – 'One less for the Austrians.'[168] Curzio Malaparte, an author searching among the survivors of Caporetto for a revolutionary proletariat, described Bacchanalian scenes and claimed that troops were seen carrying naked prostitutes out of the military brothels in triumph.[169]

Although some officers kept their heads and maintained discipline, in general leadership seems to have collapsed. A year later General Viganò summarised the overall impression succinctly: 'Everyone, from the top to the bottom, lost their heads.'[170] Divisional commanders gave way under the strain and had to be relieved. Marshal Caviglia saw higher commands rush to save themselves, leaving it to their troops to decide whether to fight or not.[171] Officers abandoned themselves to flight, some commandeering lorries to carry off armchairs and pianos. Although many deserted their troops some did not, and others became separated from their men, but enough behaved badly to leave an indelible stain on the officer corps. Towards the end of the retreat, Arnaldo Soffici was shocked to come across senior headquarters staff gorging themselves on food and drink while one of their number launched into a diatribe against soldiers who had thrown away their rifles and ought to be shot.[172] In fact many of the retreating troops belonged to support services and had never had rifles in the first place, and others had been ordered to surrender them.

A scratch defence of the bridges on the Tagliamento was cobbled together in the face of the rapid approach of the enemy's advance guard. To the retreating troops, everything seemed to be chaos and disorder. Soffici, trying to find his post as part of the defence, found one bridge totally blocked by overturned lorries and when he got to another after hours fighting his way through huge tailbacks he found it blocked by a furious major with a revolver in his hand who was turning back anyone he did not care for.[173] No one seemed to have the faintest idea about directing traffic. Torrential rain which caused the Tagliamento to flood carrying away some of the bridges added to the difficulties.

The crossing began two days later, but with the enemy hard on their heels and realising that resistance there was impossible Cadorna was already contemplating halting organised troops at the Livenza and collecting disarmed and disbanded troops beyond the Piave. He warned the government that he intended to retreat to the Piave but that if enemy pressure continued he could not long resist there and would have to retire to the Mincio and the lower Adige, the only line where he could contest the invasion of the country.[174] His staff had a different impression. On 31 October, with the army now arrayed on the right bank of the Tagliamento, Colonel Melchiore Gabba, head of Cadorna's secretariat, thought they could stand there for a fortnight. Two days later, noting that the enemy army seemed to have come to a halt which might turn out to be prolonged, Cadorna ordered that the pause of the Tagliamento 'be prolonged as long as possible' and turned into 'a final standstill' if circumstances permitted.[175]

On the night of 2/3 November, as the river passed its high point and the waters began to go down, the enemy crossed the Tagliamento. A day later the order was given to retreat to the Piave. At the northern end of the line almost all of Lieutenant-General Giulio Tassoni's XII Corps, which had been holding the *Zona Carnia*, was cut off by the Austrians; an earlier and better planned retreat might have saved many or most of them. While 2nd Army retreated on Pordenone and 3rd Army on Portogruaro, Di Giorgio's *Corpo speciale* contested every foot of ground in the upper part of the plain separating the Tagliamento from the Piave. Austrian troops followed the retreating Italians, securing the Livenza crossing on 8 November, but their pursuit was slowing down as Italian units began to put up more resistance and their own men were waylaid by the abandoned stores. Strategic misdirection also came to the Italians' rescue: instead of using the *Gruppo* Krauss, the strongest formation on the southern side of the Tagliamento, to hit the flank of the retreating 2nd and 3rd Armies in a battle of annihilation, the Austrians swung it north towards Longarone in the foothills of the Alps in pursuit of retreating Italians. Slowed down by Di Giorgio's *Corpo speciale*, General Vittorio Litta Modigliani's 2nd cavalry division and groups of *Bersaglieri* cyclists, the Austrians took five days to reach the Piave. With their last units across it, the Italians blew the bridges on the afternoon of Tuesday 9 November.

At the same time as directing the retreat – which some have seen as his finest hour, though others have not – Cadorna started to hunt out those he held responsible for it. He had no doubts about who they were. His official bulletin, composed on 28 October and unwisely passed to the press as well as the government, laid the blame on the non-resistance of parts of 2nd Army that had 'retreated like cowards without fighting or ignominiously surrendered to the enemy'. Reading it, one of his staff remarked 'That will be the ruin of Cadorna.' Vittorio Orlando, sworn in that day as premier in place of Boselli, issued a revised version toning down Cadorna's language but the damage had been done. Six days later, as his armies abandoned the Tagliamento, an unrepentant Cadorna told the new premier that the army was in the grip of 'an incurable moral crisis'

Fig. 11 Abandoned field guns after Caporetto, October 1917

and that what had happened was 'a military strike'.[176] The now established 'combat deficiency' of his army required that he withdraw to the Piave. If he succeeded, he now intended to play his final card – a decisive battle – there since further retreat to the lower Adige and Mincio would expose him to the loss of almost all his artillery and would 'completely annihilate what remains of the efficiency of the army'.[177] On 6 November, as the army reached the Piave, his army commanders were instructed to conduct a 'thorough, minute, exhaustive' enquiry to ensure that 'the traitors, the cowards, the slackers' who were responsible by acts of commission or omission for what had happened were punished.[178] General Andrea Graziani's special detachment roamed behind the lines, looking for men who appeared to have deserted the front without reason and summarily executing anyone he deemed guilty: one unfortunate was shot simply for smoking a pipe and looking challenging as Graziani's car passed. Fourteen years later Graziani was found lying dead beside a railway track in circumstances which suggested that someone had taken their revenge.

When the Italian army came to rest on the Piave it had retreated for 150 kilometres, losing 10,000 dead, 30,000 wounded and 265,000 prisoners of war on the way. A further 350,000 were adrift from their units or had deserted. In all, an army which had been 1,800,000 strong on the eve of Caporetto now had 800,000 fewer effectives. The losses in weaponry – 3,152 guns, 1,732 trench mortars and 3,000 machine-guns – were no less significant and harder to replace. The losses in military stores were enormous: they included 321,000 pairs of boots, 430,000 pairs of trousers and 672,000 shirts. The political consequences were less dramatic but no less important. Boselli's government fell and so did Cadorna, kicked upstairs on 9 November to sit on the newly created Supreme War Council at Versailles. As the army regrouped on the Piave, the country faced the greatest question in its history: could it survive and win the war, or would it go down in ignominious defeat to the power that had dominated it until the Risorgimento and the ally it had deserted in 1914?

6   1918 – Recovery and victory

This is a holy war – but what a horrible thing war is.
Luigi Gasparotto, 28 October 1918

In the aftermath of Caporetto things did not look good for Italy. The army had lost hundreds of thousands of men and vast amounts of weaponry and equipment, all of which would have to be replaced if the country was to keep its war going. Wild stories of moral collapse abounded, encouraging dark speculations about social disintegration and even revolution. Recovery was the first priority. Many things contributed to the revival of Italian arms during the first six months of 1918, among them Allied military and economic assistance, the effects of a long war of attrition which was now wearing down Austria–Hungary faster than Italy, and Germany's preoccupation with winning the war on the western front. All this gave Italy time, which she used to good effect. For twenty-nine months the war had been run by a Piedmontese general in the Piedmontese way. What now happened was revolution in military affairs, invisible to outsiders. For decades southern generals had had the reputation of being political soldiers first and foremost. Now the war was handed over to one of them. Diaz proved to be just the man the country needed. Under his guiding hand the Italian army was rebuilt on new foundations, strategy was forged to fit it, and policy shaped and timed by military practicalities.

Diaz's unwillingness to dance to the tune of his French and British allies and launch what he regarded as an unnecessarily risky and premature offensive did not go down well in London and Paris. He had good reasons for caution, being more aware than they were of his army's limitations. Ready at last, the Italian army began the climactic battle of Vittorio Veneto on 24 October 1918 – a battle which the Allies thought at the time and historians have since believed was a last-minute attempt to cash in on a war that was already over. In fact, planning for the battle began several months before it happened and when it did the Italian army inflicted a decisive defeat in the field on its opponent, something its British and French partners were unable to do in the West.

247

A new commander

After Caporetto, there was little or no chance that Cadorna could survive (though there is some evidence that the new premier, Vittorio Orlando, may have wanted to exonerate him). On 28 October, the day that he took the oath of office, Orlando by his own account secured the king's agreement that a replacement be secretly prepared. Shortly afterwards the cabinet decided to send the new war minister, General Vittorio Alfieri, to the war zone to discuss the reorganisation of the high command with the king. At Peschiera on 4 November the king was presented with the proposal that the duke of Aosta, whose conduct of 3rd Army during its retreat had been the one bright spot on an otherwise dark canvas, become the new chief of the general staff and that Generals Armando Diaz and Gaetano Giardino be joint sub-chiefs. Vittorio Emanuele had no desire to see a potential heir to the throne take up a post which might eclipse his own, and preferred Diaz. At this Bissolati, wanting a counter balance to Giardino for whom he did not much care, proposed his fellow Freemason General Pietro Badoglio. The suggestion went down well with the king who, though usually cool and reserved, showed unusual warmth towards Badoglio when they met by chance.[1] The substitution was done behind Alfieri's back – somewhat to Diaz's surprise.[2] Thus when at Rapallo on 5 and 6 November Lloyd George and Foch made Allied reinforcements conditional on a new *Comando supremo*, the die was already cast. The problem of what to do with Cadorna was solved by one of the British officials, Lieutenant-Colonel Maurice Hankey, who suggested making him the Italian representative on the newly created Supreme War Council.

The new field commander of the Italian armies was different in every way from his predecessor. A Neapolitan, and therefore not a member of the conservative Piedmontese military caste that had dominated the Italian army throughout most of its existence, a gunner by training, and only 55 years old, Diaz had amassed both an impressive amount and a wide variety of experience. Before the world war he had seen action in the Libyan war of 1911–12 (like Capello but unlike Cadorna) and had done several stints at general staff headquarters, serving as the head of Pollio's secretariat in the year before the war, as well as acting as *relatore* (presenter/reporter) of the military budget in parliament. Recalled from a brigade command in October 1914 to serve as head of the operations section, he had then commanded first a division and subsequently a corps on the Carso between June 1916 and November 1917. The one blot on an otherwise glittering record occurred in 1900 when, while on manoeuvre, he had moved his troops through a valley and not along

the crests as current doctrine prescribed, earning him a telling-off from
General Caviglia – whose superior he now was! Personally calm, modest,
firm in judgement but relaxed in manner, Diaz was an instinctive com-
municator. He was also a man who made an immediate impression.
Before his appointment he had met the king only three times, first in
1913 when he was decorated for his actions in the Libyan war, and then
on the Carso in June 1917 (when, in the middle of fighting off an
Austrian counter-attack, he had kept the king waiting twenty minutes)
and again in July. After the latter meeting, the king reportedly remarked
to his aide-de-camp 'One day this general will be useful.'[3]

When Diaz took up command, his tasks were self-evident: to arrest the
invasion and resist on the Piave, to reconstruct the army, and to improve
the strategic co-ordination of the war by the soldiers and the politicians.
However, for a moment all the cards were up in the air. On 3 November
the cabinet heard from Bissolati that the army might possibly not be able
to hold on the Piave and might have to retreat yet further to the Mincio.
Some observers doubted whether the army that was arriving on the Piave
had the physical or moral strength to stand there: the colonial minister,
Gaspare Colosimo, heard from one source that unless fresh British and
French divisions arrived to reinforce the Piave front 'only a miracle can
save what remains of the Italian army'.[4] On 9 November – the day after
Diaz took up his new post – Orlando brought back the news that the
Allies had agreed to help Italy provided that she resisted to the death on
the Piave to give them time to do so. General Dallolio, back from
inspecting the new front, was deeply pessimistic. Conditions there were
'very grave, almost catastrophic – No matériel, morale lacking, officers
without confidence, the army in pieces.' The Piave could not be held,
and with the army in dissolution a catastrophe could occur. Aroused by
Dallolio's defeatism, Sonnino lectured his fellow ministers: 'The Allies
will help us if we stand on the Piave. We must be calm, confident,
courageous – anything else is a betrayal.'[5] Afterwards Orlando claimed –
falsely – that he had closed this session with a declaration that every inch
of Italian soil would be defended to the last. As yet, the government had
no such declaratory policy.[6]

On 11 November, with a number of his generals still in favour of
retreating to the Mincio–Adige line, Diaz confirmed the halt on the Piave
but prudently ordered the preparation of a provisional line from Vicenza
to Fusine and a last-ditch defensive line on the Mincio–Adige. An
Austrian telegram enquiring whether Venice was to be declared an 'open
city' pushed everyone to a decision. As Alfieri pointed out, the defence
of Venice was inseparably bound up with the issue of whether or not to
stand on the Piave. Four days later the brand new War Council met for

Fig. 12 King Victor Emanuel III and General Diaz

the first time to decide the matter. The king, the premier, Generals Alfieri and Giardino and Admiral Thaon di Revel, the chief of naval staff, heard what Orlando described afterwards as a 'luminous' exposition from Diaz explaining why retreating to the Mincio was not an option. The new government had handed the responsibility for the decision to the new field commander, and he now made it. As Venice was an important naval base, di Revel was much relieved.

When the news of the unfolding disaster at Caporetto reached the Allies on 26 October aid was soon on its way thanks to the transport arrangements made earlier in the year, but it was not without strings. A French offer of four divisions and forty-four batteries of artillery on 27 October was followed next day by the offer of two British divisions. However, Cadorna's proposal to put the French troops straight into line on the Piave met with a blunt refusal from Foch and his British opposite number, General Sir William Robertson, when they arrived in Italy on 30 and 31 October. The Italian armies, on whom the responsibility for defending Italy rested, must stand firm on the Piave; their forces were only 'a contribution' to that defence.[7] This decision reflected both generals' lack of confidence in Cadorna: when Foch arrived in Rome for talks with the soon-to-be-discarded field commander, he made it plain that he had no confidence in the way the army was being run by the current high command.[8] When the first French divisions arrived at the beginning of November they were deployed between Verona and Brescia, safe from immediate harm in the event of another collapse. The decisions to make a stand on the Piave and to replace Cadorna were necessary not just in themselves but also to bolster Allied confidence. At a meeting between the three heads of government and the king at Peschiera on 8 November, the Allies agreed to increase their contribution to six French and six British divisions (though one of the latter was kept in France as a consequence of the battle of Cambrai). The transport arrangements worked without a hitch, and between 30 October and 8 December 1,413 trains carried 266,000 men, 63,000 horses, more than 1,000 guns and 24,000 vehicles into Italy.[9]

The presence of Allied troops on Italian soil was a mixed blessing and after initial enthusiasm their absence from the front line, their apparent ambitions to control and command Italian divisions, the better treatment their officers and men enjoyed, and their scarcely concealed lack of esteem for the Italian army soon began to arouse resentment.[10] French soldiers were initially shocked by the power of the Catholic Church, and its priests in turn described the French soldiers as 'degenerates' who were not to be fraternised with. The number of shirkers ensconced behind the lines, the circumstances in which Italian soldiers had to live, and the vast gulf between the officers and their men all made a negative impact. Official French regulations were designed to prevent fraternisation with Italian soldiers, who set a bad example with their habit of passing time in cafes at all hours of the day and night and going on leave without permission, and with civilians for fear of pacifist contagion. Individually, though, soldiers found their way around these obstacles – as soldiers will.[11] Foreign observers too were inclined to see the ways of the Italian army as sloppy, or worse. 'The officers here are a nasty illbred arrogant set,' the novelist John Dos Passos, working in an ambulance unit, noted in his diary after watching a Sardinian officer kicking a sergeant waiter.[12]

Diaz styled himself 'Military Representative of the Government', a sign that the politicians were no longer going to be held at a respectful distance from both military action and military decision-making. Where Cadorna's headquarters had had a distinctly Catholic tone, his was masonic – which meant, in practical terms, collaborative but also sceptically anti-clerical.[13] One of his first priorities was to do away with what one of his biographers termed 'certain injurious ganglia' that had been formed in the nerve centre of the army, where the ambitious, the passed-over and the self-proclaimed unrecognised geniuses had colonised competing offices and jousted with one another.[14] The most pernicious element of what was unflatteringly termed the *Comandissimo* was Cadorna's secretariat, which had acted as a cut-out between him and everyone else. The new chief eliminated the *Comandissimo*, simplifying and reducing the number of offices, decentralising responsibility and establishing clear vertical lines of authority. The co-ordinating role, which Porro had conspicuously failed to fulfil, was shared between the new sub-chiefs: Badoglio took responsibility for reorganising the army, Giardino for strategic planning.[15]

Where Cadorna had held some reins only loosely, Diaz held them more tightly; where Cadorna had held them tightly, Diaz loosened them. Only headquarters could now suspend leave, and local military actions were no longer permitted unless and until the *Comando supremo* had inspected the situation and was satisfied of their usefulness. Cadorna's practice of using bullying telephone calls – known as 'torpedoes' – to threaten his subordinates to the point of tears was disdained, and instead army commanders found themselves engaged in dialogue with his successor.[16] Liaison officers were sent out to take the pulse of the army. Cadorna's most feared weapon of command was publicly and uncompromisingly discarded. In a circular sent out on 20 November 1917, Diaz announced that he did not intend to take severe measures against 'anyone who makes a mistake as a result of inexperience or of a praiseworthy initiative that does not meet with success'. Sacking officers, especially those with a good record, would be an absolutely last resort and would only happen 'after having put into practice all the means that a superior [officer] has to correct a junior'.[17]

The issues that were of the most fundamental concern to Diaz were the strength and the underlying consistency of his army. The statistics that were gathered – never wholly consistent with one another – indicated that of the 1,001,400 men of the 1st and 2nd Armies and the *Zona Carnia* who had taken part in the fighting on 24 October, 25,000 had died, 250,000 had been taken prisoner and 300,000 taken to flight when their units dissolved. In one way, the situation was not as bad as it looked. Overall, between 20 and 24 October the Italian army had lost 1,200,000 (including deserters, sick and wounded) but could expect to count on 1,800,000 men, a figure that included 50,000 sick and wounded and 170,000 fresh reserves. The latter were mostly made up of men of the class of 1899, sent into line in November 1917 and now being formed into separate regiments instead of being inserted into existing units to avoid their coming into contact with 'tired' troops.[18]

Cadorna had scandalously accused his army of cowardice, believing its moral fibre had been rotted by pacifist propaganda (though three months later he changed his tune), and more than one of the army's senior generals still felt the same: asked by the Caporetto Inquiry whether defeatist propaganda had played a part in the debacle, General Morrone thought that 'you could not deny that it had exercised an influence where dense masses of men were concerned'.[19] The underlying morale of the army had undoubtedly taken a knock – but it was bruised, not irredeemably broken. None of the army commanders had reported any evident reasons for alarm on the eve of Caporetto, and neither had the commanders of IV, XXVII, XXIV and II Corps when they were visited by liaison officers five days before the battle.[20] An enquiry conducted in the two months immediately afterwards confirmed their judgements. After rising between May and August 1917, the number of crimes reported had fallen markedly in September. In the case of some crimes – desertion to the enemy and the abandonment of a post – there had been no recrudescence of the levels reached in 1916, and in the case of crimes of indiscipline, insubordination and the refusal to obey orders the number had gone down proportionately to the increase in the size of the army. *Carabinieri* reports bore this out. Although giving a nod to the role of increased socialist pacifist propaganda, the report laid considerable stress on the effects of tiredness, discouragement at the lack of evident military success, and complaints about suspensions of leave, particularly the *licenze agricole* that allowed peasants home to help bring in the harvest. The lack of appropriate propaganda and the inability of inexperienced junior officers to inculcate a spirit of duty into their men were important indirect causes of the collapse.[21]

Despite the upbeat talk there were signs that the army was still very fragile. On 16 November an entire brigade surrendered almost without fighting; on the *altopiano* 25,000 men, mostly from units previously tested under fire, surrendered on 4–5 December; and in mid December three companies of infantry on Monte Grappa went over to the enemy. Sporadic protests by groups of *Alpini* and *Bersaglieri* against being sent back into line were an ongoing phenomenon. Faced at the start of the New Year with signs of war weariness and a desire for peace, Orlando feared that the army might take to heart talk of Caporetto as a military strike or a politico-military revolt and do what it had not thought of doing on 24 October. That meant not only that its military value was doubtful but also that its usefulness as an instrument for maintaining civil order was questionable – this at a moment when Naples was apparently 'on the eve of an uprising' and when the *Carabinieri* were reporting that only two of the twelve provinces of central Italy (Rome and Pisa) were in a normal condition.[22] Tasked at the end of January with assessing the state of army morale via soldiers on winter leave, the prefects reported that it was generally good, though Turin and Florence were notable exceptions. The reorganisation of trench tours and improvements in leave were having a positive effect, but everywhere there was evidence of weariness with the war and discontent, some of it directed at the tolerance of shirkers and some at officers who appeared to have little interest in their men. Ubaldo Commandini, general commissioner for civil aid and domestic propaganda, reported much the same thing in early May.[23]

As the army settled down in its new lines along the Piave it seemed both to officials and to at least one well-placed outside observer that there was no need for great concern about its morale. An analysis of soldiers' correspondence carried out by a special section of the intelligence service in early December found an almost unanimous determination to resist the invasion and throw the enemy off Italian soil. The troops were animated by a new sense of purpose and only 10 per cent showed signs of tiredness, due more to physical discomforts than to moral fragility.[24] As the New Year opened Brigadier-General Delmé-Radcliffe, head of the British military mission and a friend of the king, saw some encouraging signs: 'there is very little talk about retiring now & not much thinking about it either. The Italian army is hardening & improving by the day.' Some of this he put down to 'hints from us' about front-line strengths, the proper use of artillery and machine-guns, and the establishment of training schools for all arms. Morale in the country at large was improving too, and there was now 'more sign of the offensive spirit'.[25] General Plumer, commander-in-chief of British forces, was a little more cautious. After three months' work the Italian army, though capable of making 'a brilliant attack or a stubborn defence' was still incapable of any but the simplest manoeuvres and 'uncertain if called upon for any sustained or prolonged effort either in attack or defence ...'.[26] His opposite number, General Fayolle, in an otherwise critical and sometimes caustic survey of Italian military capabilities, remarked that the 'raw material' – the human element – was 'not bad and will be able to give good results if properly used'.[27]

The existence of defeatist propaganda behind the front line was a matter of concern as work began to put the disbanded armies back together. Towards the end of November the task of forming 5th Army out of the remnants of his former 2nd Army was given to Luigi Capello, still on active service but shortly to be suspended when the Caporetto Inquiry began in January. The prefect of Mantua pointed out that almost all the population in the provinces west of the Po that had been selected for the reorganisation of the 5th Army subscribed to the official socialist party. A worried Orlando thought that it might be wise to re-examine the proposal. Diaz calmed him down: strategic necessity dictated the choice, but the premier could count on the 'appropriate necessary disciplinary measures' that were in place and which 'for other obvious reasons too' must be severe.[28] Soon, though, Diaz found his difficulties multiplying. There was not enough clothing and equipment for the 5th Army or the troops in 'concentration' camps, which began to affect morale and discipline as well as military readiness. The local population was another worrying factor. Leaflets deploring the government's failure to take up the Pope's peace proposal were circulating in Bassano, and the agricultural populations of Verona, Mantua and Padua were demonstrating against the Allied troops that were arriving there. If these provinces were not put in a state of war, and therefore subject to full military control, the *Comando supremo* would be 'disarmed against any subversive action and especially the possible renewal of anti-war propaganda'.[29] The necessary decree, signed by the king, was already on Alfieri's desk, to be signed by Orlando when he returned from Versailles.

Orlando's concerns were not quietened for long. Alarmed by news from some of his prefects that discipline among the 'disbanded' troops of 2nd Army left a lot to be desired, he suggested that the camps be broken up into smaller units and spread more widely around the country to places outside the war zone where subversive elements were not preponderant, making surveillance easier. Badoglio, who was overseeing the reconstruction process, reported that propaganda was not active and that the troops, as well as being closely supervised, were extremely heavily occupied. There had been no 'disbanded' elements of 2nd Army for the last twenty days; the camp commandants were reporting that everything was in order; and in the camps there was 'a notable combative spirit' and a sense of the effort necessary to hasten the resolution of the war. Diaz reassured the premier that thanks to good management, support by the *Carabinieri* and regular inspection, discipline in the four 'concentration camps', which had initially left something to be desired, was now substantially improved and numbers falling: of the 200,000 men initially housed at the infantry camp at Castelfranco only 65,000 now remained. As for desertions, about which the premier had also complained, 'the number would certainly diminish if there were an active propaganda effort in the interior of the country to set against the pacifist and anti-militarist ideas with which the deserters are for the most part imbued, ideas which they try to spread among their companions when they reach the camps'.[30] Anti-war demonstrations and propaganda in the war zone continued to cause the high command concern, and on Christmas Eve Diaz ordered his army commanders to set up a special intelligence service to give him accurate and up-to-the-minute information about the influence that 'elements of disorder and propaganda hostile to the war' were having on the population in the theatre of operations and the troops located there.[31]

Servizio P and the regeneration of morale

Diaz's anxiety about the state of his army's morale was triggered in part by an Austrian propaganda campaign targeting the Italians which began in late October 1917 when the retreating troops were showered with manifestos encouraging them to give up the war. Over the winter the campaign intensified as leaflets, newspapers and letters from prisoners of war were reinforced with megaphone exhortations and 'bottle-post' messages sent down the rivers. It increased yet further in the spring, as the Austrians prepared for their forthcoming June offensive. On the Piave, 110,000 leaflets were launched into Italian lines in March 1918 and 150,000 in April. Fraternisation was encouraged: Austrian cigarettes were a popular barter for Italian bread and oranges, and on at least one sector of the front there were regular Austrian visits and hour-long 'coffee breaks'.[32] As the campaign gathered momentum, its themes changed. At first Austrian leaflets spoke in general and rather impersonal terms of British imperialism and Austro-German military superiority, but as time went on they became more 'bolshevik' in tone. Italian soldiers were encouraged to disobey their officers and join their erstwhile enemies as brothers in a common rebellion against the people who had brought them to the slaughterhouse. There were worrying signs that the enemy's exhortations were making an impact on the troops.[33] Evidently alarmed, on 9 March 1918 the Comando supremo announced that anyone trafficking with the enemy would be shot – a warning it felt it necessary to repeat eleven days later.

The idea that the discipline of persuasion could be a complement, and not an alternative, to the discipline of coercion had been developed by Capello during the six months before Caporetto. Taking a leaf from his book, Diaz proposed early in January to distribute 'the good press' among the better instructed elements in order to combat defeatist propaganda within the army. The war minister enthusiastically backed the idea and suggested in addition publishing a bulletin that would explain in easily understood terms the meaning and significance of current international events.[34] At more or less the same time, General Giardino proposed establishing a propaganda service to gather information on troop morale in each of the individual armies. Shortly this would become Servizio P, one of the most important instruments in Diaz's armoury of command and control. The next step was to introduce designated specialist officers into every army to take charge of propaganda. Trusted soldiers (*fiduciari*) would mix with the troops to monitor their feelings and put in a positive word where necessary. 'Simple and persuasive' gatherings for officers, non-commissioned officers and especially the ordinary soldiers would put across the purposes of the fighting and the message that only the defeat of the enemy would hasten peace. The needs of the troops were to be identified via censorship and the questioning of individuals and reported up the chain of command. A soldiers' newspaper would speak to the troops' personal interests, and when they went out of line cinemas and sports competitions would be laid on to entertain and distract them.[35]

The innovation was a response to both positive and negative stimuli: while on the one hand it was an important component of the reformist agenda of the Diaz regime, on the other it was also a tool with which to stem desertion rates that were a concern to the high command and a worry to Orlando. It was also a recognition of the changing face of war as exemplified in the growing volume of American and Allied propaganda and the reverberations of the Russian Revolution. The job specification was simple: *vigilanza, propaganda ed assistenza* ('vigilance, propaganda and help'). Translated into practicalities, this meant evaluating morale and countering subversive influences, propagating 'defensive' propaganda which explained why Italy was fighting using lectures, films and newspapers, and providing places behind the lines where soldiers could rest, write letters and generally recover their mental strength in civilised surroundings. The strategy was a shrewd one, if perhaps somewhat belated in its genesis and application, and also a successful one thanks in no small measure to the enemy. Until July 1918, Austria–Hungary concentrated on 'offensive' propaganda, apparently to no great effect. As Brigadier-General Delmé-Radcliffe remarked, simply distributing leaflets as the Austrians were doing did not appear to be very effective. What did work, to a limited degree, was fraternisation but rigorous methods were used to counter it.[36]

The new service was run by the intelligence section of each individual army and both content and means were left largely to them, though general guidance was given out from time to time. Thus the *Comando supremo* suggested various means to get the government's message across including using former prisoners of war who could recount 'the sufferings experienced in prison' and soldiers' masses 'in which patriotic sentiment can, with appropriate moderation, be grafted onto religious sentiments'.[37] Ordinary newspapers now circulated much more freely, carrying propaganda materials thanks to government encouragement and inducement (the government bought thousands of copies in return). A circular sent out by 2nd Army to its propaganda officers listed fifty topics for conversations with the troops; they included 'Engineers and factory workers aren't shirkers', and 'A premature peace means factories closed, an invasion of German capital and workers, unemployment and hunger for us.'[38] These and other themes were repeated and expanded in the trench newspapers in terms that ranged from the sophisticated – German-owned factories and banks had taken the fruit of the workers' labours and their own money was now paying for the guns that were killing them – to the simplistic. Thus *Savoia!* urged its readers on 27 June 1918 to 'Kill the damned race ... that wants to have your women, steal your crops and livestock ... throw the thieves into the street, kill the filthy violator of Italian women.'[39]

Trench newspapers, previously local in origin and with a simple thematic content, became important vehicles to propagandise an army half of which was semi-literate, and by June some fifty were circulating among the troops. Intellectuals signed on with enthusiasm, eager to take part in a process which, according to the leading historian of the genre, allowed them to 'restore [their] privileges, collaborate in the construction of a new bourgeois party and [take part in] its struggle for internal hegemony'.[40] A variety of themes were developed to appeal to different instincts and predilections. Much was made of the idea that in defending the *patria* a soldier was defending his home (*casa*), his women and his property, and that betraying it by surrendering was betraying the *Mamma*. A more elevated appeal explained that Rome, as the wellspring of European civilisation, was fighting not for conquest or dominion but to complete her work and to defend the idea of right. Appeals were made to religious feeling, too, with the explanation that fighting (and dying) for justice was doing the work of God, although this sometimes took a decidedly secular turn. The 138th Fusilier Regiment had its own Ten Commandments: the second instructed soldiers in the trenches to be 'as cunning as a wolf', and the eighth only to fire at a sitting target. The papers varied in popularity according to the degree to which they were official in tone and central in origin. Some, according to one contemporary, were used as toilet paper.[41]

By the time that the war ended, some 1,500 officers were actively engaged in the multiple roles of assistance, vigilance and propaganda. They were usually men with wartime commissions, carefully selected for their intelligence, practical capacities and records of valour and standing with the troops. Their presence represented something of a revolution for an army that had traditionally taken for granted the natural capacity of all officers to act as educators of their men, and to some eyes the *Servizio P* personnel looked uncomfortably like Russian commissars. In August 1918 Zupelli fired off a missive to Orlando complaining about the uncontrolled activities of the mutilated officers who were participating in the propaganda offensive, and made it clear that he wanted no civilians involved in it but only officers, who would avoid 'any danger of discussion'.[42]

A new regime

If the army's morale was to improve, then it also had to be better led. It was not enough, Diaz told his army commanders, simply to harp on about the *grandezza* of the ideals for which the soldiers were fighting: they had to be 'personally convinced that we are caring for them, that their well-being, their needs, their sacrifices are recognised'. There were still too many abuses and too much favouritism. Soldiers were getting only half their due or less: drinks were being adulterated, tobacco rations were often minimal or non-existent, and attempts to improve things were being hampered by 'the egoism of a few privileged [people]'. All of this was going on right under the noses of the troops, creating resentment or worse, and it all had to change. Army, corps and divisional commanders were now to carry out frequent inspections, and so were their subordinates, and anyone committing or tolerating the slightest injustice was to be punished 'inexorably'.[43] Middle-ranking and junior officers also had to play their part. That meant reversing past practice. Cadorna had warned officers about the 'tendency to familiarity with the troops' which was often 'a sign of weakness and an unhealthy desire for popularity'.[44] Faced with ongoing evidence of war-weariness and a widespread desire for peace, Diaz complained that there was insufficient 'moral contact' between officers and men. It was 'absolutely necessary' that all officers, and not just junior ones, live the same life as the soldiers and share their hardships 'with serenity and in good spirits'.[45]

Problems of low morale persisted during the spring, exacerbated by talk on the home front of the need for peace at all costs which particularly affected soldiers returning from leave in Piedmont. Censors' reports suggested that behind the lines discouragement and tiredness were growing thanks to failures in local administration, commercial speculation and requisitioning.[46] Plain-clothes *Carabinieri* watched in restaurants and cafes for any signs of anti-war propaganda, and the courts cracked down hard on this as on other transgressions: in May, writing down a defeatist song in a letter earned an artilleryman two months in prison, and singing one landed a corporal with six years in prison and a 200-lire fine.[47] Symptoms of tiredness and low morale lingered in some units into April, due to poor rations, heavy labouring work when out of line, and in the case of the Brescia zone because troops who had not been out of line for two and a half years were being reinforced by elements of the 2nd Army whom they did not trust after Caporetto. There was, the head of military intelligence pointed out, 'a certain analogy between the situation in this zone and that which existed in the Caporetto sector last year.'[48]

For some months the military authorities and the *Comando supremo* were, as Diaz acknowledged, 'in the dark' as to what the true state of morale among the troops actually was: troops on leave were apparently saying that the army was very tired of the war and ready to surrender or flee, but when interrogated they claimed to have said exactly the opposite because they were afraid of being judged impressionable, or cowardly, or defeatist.[49] The generals put out a much more positive message. After conferring with army commanders and the general staff, Nitti told a journalist friend that the troops' morale was 'really good, better than it has been for a year and perhaps since the start of the war.'[50] Diaz was more circumspect. At a meeting of the top civil and military leadership on 9 March 1918, he told Orlando that the morale of the troops was 'fair but not very offensive [-minded]'.[51] The German offensive in the west that began twelve days later sent a shiver down the collective spine lest the Allied troops leave Italy, but those anxieties proved unfounded. Diaz's doubts about the army were finally overcome when the head of military intelligence, Colonel Marchetti, reassured him on 12 April that morale was good, though a month later Orlando was still worried about desertion rates which he thought were as bad as in Cadorna's day and possibly worse.

Diaz handled the delicate situation he had inherited with a combination of carrots and sticks. Rations were improved, so that the average calorific intake rose from 3,067 in November 1917 to 3,508 in June 1918, and military co-operatives sold food, drinks and other necessities cheaply. Troops now got an extra ten days' leave on top of the fifteen days already their due, and there were more exonerations for agricultural workers. Pay stayed the same, but a state-funded scheme provided free life insurance policies worth 500 lire for the rank and file and 1,000 lire for officers. On 1 November 1917 the government set up a new Ministry for Military Assistance and War Pensions, a sign of its intention to take greater care of fighting men and their families.[52] Remarking on the 'notable disproportion' between the awards for valour given to officers and to the other ranks, who made up 97 per cent of the army, the high command ordered that they be made more equal.

At the same time, stiff discipline was maintained. In the aftermath of the Monte Grappa incident in December, Diaz ordered commanders to use 'extreme rigour' where necessary. In January, military courts were instructed to use Article 92 of the military penal code which mandated execution by shooting in the chest, deemed slightly less demeaning than being shot in the back, where soldiers voluntarily abandoned their rifles or ammunition. The distinction between defeatism and betrayal was clearly defined in order to ensure that the harshest sanctions were applied, and the interrogation reports of returned prisoners of war were closely scrutinised to identify those who could not completely justify their capture. On 12 May the *Comando supremo* made known its displeasure at the weakness of the sentences being handed down and ordered that 'weak judges' be replaced; and eight days later, faced with the enemy's mounting propaganda offensive, it made any act of familiarity with the enemy punishable by death.[53] All this is very redolent of Cadorna's methods, but there were several important differences. Decimation disappeared, summary executions all but vanished, and the authorities were now more concerned to find out the causes of military crimes. However, the firing squads still did their miserable work. Under Cadorna's regime soldiers were shot at a rate of seventeen a month – under his successor that rate rose to more than nineteen a month.[54]

Fending off the Austrians and the Allies

As what would turn out to be the last year of Italy's war began, Diaz's thirty-three infantry and four cavalry divisions faced fifty-three Austrian and German divisions along a line running from Stelvio via Lake Garda, the Brenta river, Monte Grappa, Montello and Ponte di Priula to the sea. Counterbalancing this numerical inferiority, the Italian line had been reduced in length from 650 to 300 kilometres, and with the plains behind them the Italian troops had good road communications along which to bring up support. The Austro-German forces were at the very end of their long supply lines and in the mountains could only use mule tracks and footpaths to bring forward weapons, ammunition and food. For two months they lived off captured Italian stocks. After that their rations grew increasingly meagre.

A crucial two-phase battle took place between 10–26 November and 4–25 December as Conrad launched attacks on the Asiago plateau, against Monte Grappa and on the Piave. The attacks on the *altipiani* were finally stopped on Christmas Eve at the very edge of the uplands. Monte Grappa was a naturally good defensive position, but conditions were appalling as Italians fought to hold improvised positions in freezing winds and dry snow with temperatures falling to 15 degrees below zero. Resistance was tough and determined, some units fighting to the last man. Austrian detachments got across the Piave on a 3-kilometre front on the first day but could get no further, partly due to the fact that the river was under the guns of Italian artillery on Monte Grappa. Between 20 and 24 November the Austrians had a second try at breaking the Italian front, launching sixty battalions on a 24-kilometre front, this time without the support of artillery. Swift Italian counter-attacks and the abandonment of uselessly exposed positions brought it to a halt. Taking German advice, the Austrian high command ordered the suspension of the offensive. Conrad continued smaller-scale actions for the next three weeks, achieving a local success against Melette on 4 December where the Italians committed their old errors – too many troops held in the front line and insufficient depth in their defences – and lost 22,000 men, more than half of whom were taken prisoner. Four British and French divisions came into line that day, reinforcing a defence that was already holding firm. After further unsuccessful attacks on the lower Piave between 9 and 18 December, the Austrians abandoned their bridgehead at Zenson on 27 December and withdrew to the left bank. Surprised and impressed by the Italians' fighting power, Conrad confessed to his wife on 3 January 1918 'We can no longer count on victory in Italy.'[55]

The first major action by the Italian army in the New Year took place at Tre Monti on 28–31 January 1918. Italian artillery began the battle with counter-battery fire, followed by a brief passage of destructive fire to open gaps in the wire and then interdiction fire to protect the infantry once they had breached the enemy lines. The field guns used French munitions with contact fuses that were more effective than the Italian version. Sardinian infantry, *Bersaglieri*, *Alpini* and *Arditi* assault sections attacked in flexible formations and attack columns were ordered to adapt their movement to the lie of the land and not to be excessively preoccupied with keeping laterally in line. Miraculously, the first attackers were not hit by enemy fire even though the attack was launched at 0930 on a clear January day with perfect visibility. The idea was to employ infiltration tactics, leaving specially designated sections to mop up strong points, though in fact what took place was more a conventional direct assault on the strongpoints. The *Arditi* abandoned the line as soon as they had taken their positions, and after three of the four designated strongpoints had been captured the action was halted with losses totalling 5,000. Although by no means an unvarnished success, the battle marked notable progress in the use of artillery.[56]

The question of Italy's military strategy for the coming year was high on Diaz's agenda. The Allied Supreme War Council, to which Cadorna had been shunted after Caporetto, produced a first Note on 13 December 1917 proposing a defensive strategy along the entire front from the North

Sea to the Adriatic in 1918. A further Note on 24 December concluded that for the time being it was neither possible nor desirable to take the offensive in Italy. Italy's role in the strategic discussions at Versailles was affected by the fact that Orlando and Diaz held Cadorna at arm's length, while the French viewed the Italians as lightweight one-time allies of Germany who were quick to ask for aid but slow to pull their weight.[57] Nevertheless, Diaz needed to know what the British and French intended for the year ahead. His divisions would be ready to take the offensive come the spring, but men and matériel would have to be moved to the appropriate locations. If the Allies were waiting for the Americans to arrive, then Italy should continue concentrating on defensive works and wait too, undertaking only such limited offensive actions as would improve her position. If he could not rely on the continued presence of the eleven British and French divisions currently in Italy, this would limit or even exclude any offensive action. In those circumstances, action would have to be taken as quickly as possible to readjust and realign Italian forces.[58]

The Allied military representatives at Versailles were indeed minded, as Pétain had put it, to *attendre les chars et les américains* ('wait for the tanks and the Americans'), and proposed waiting until 1919 before undertaking a decisive offensive – a conclusion from which Marshal Foch forcefully dissented. At the Supreme War Council meeting held between 30 January and 2 February 1918 and attended by Orlando, Sonnino and General Alfieri (who found Cadorna's presence at the table among the Italian delegation very disagreeable), it was agreed broadly to wait for a year before launching a major Allied offensive and the respective general staffs were tasked with preparing appropriate plans in detail and forwarding them to Versailles. The proposal to create a general Allied reserve carried alarming implications, as it raised the possibility that some or all of the British and French troops that Diaz wanted to keep might be withdrawn from his front.[59]

In circumstances of some uncertainty, the *Comando supremo* began working up its strategic plans for the year. If the general reserve, which would entail the withdrawal of four French, three British and seven Italian divisions, were not insisted on then it would be possible to carry out a large-scale operation from Lake Garda to the river Brenta, along with minor operations at Monte Grappa, Stelvio and elsewhere to distract the enemy's attention. The main offensive, using four French, four British and four Italian divisions in the first line, six Italian divisions in the second line and other British, French and Italian divisions in the third line, would take place on the Asiago plateau. The objective would be to recover as much ground as possible up to the Val Sugana and towards Rovereto and thereby secure the Italian front against the threat of invasion –'which must always exist so long as the enemy were close to the exits into the plain,' Badoglio told Delmé-Radcliffe. If the general reserve had to be kept back, then a limited offensive on the Asiago plateau using two British, two French and five Italian divisions would seek to recover the eastern half of the plateau. New roads were being constructed, troops moved and stores and munitions brought up. Everything, including a stock of 928 new medium and heavy guns, would be ready by 1 May.[60]

Working up the army

Spring 1918 was a time of intense activity for Badoglio and the army commanders as they worked to reorganise the army, reform its tactics and revise its operational practices. Infantry regiments, now smaller than at the start of the war (2,672 men as against 3,586 previously) and therefore more flexible, were equipped with a flame-thrower section and now had thirty-six instead of thirty machine-guns. Badoglio reorganised the artillery, creating homogeneous groups of batteries of the most modern and powerful types, and army commanders were ordered to give more attention to positioning their guns so that if or when it came to a defensive battle they had nothing more to do than fit them into pre-assigned places.[61] Successive defensive lines were organised on the plain between Astico and the Piave to allow a prolonged defence in depth in case the enemy broke through the front again, troops familiarised with the positions they would occupy, and reserves were stationed in strongpoints on the second line.[62] To keep the offensive spirit alive, and to take prisoners as sources of valuable intelligence, Diaz ordered commanders to carry out small local attacks. Rewards of 100 lire per prisoner and ten days' leave per soldier were offered to every patrol capturing enemy personnel to incentivise the troops. Mistakes were still being made – too many commanders relied only on surprise and neglected preparation – but the army was beginning to learn.[63]

The Italian armies were now being handled in new, more flexible ways. Divisions would no longer be broken up and brigades treated as separate entities, a process which had fragmented the army and weakened morale, and corps were given the authority to cede divisions temporarily to one another in case of need. Addressing practices which had contributed to the poor performance of Cadorna's army, Diaz ordered all commanders to organise defensive positions on their own initiative immediately after an engagement had come to a halt, and simultaneously to link up with flanking units 'whatever [the shape of] the front that results'.

Fig. 13 Anti-aircraft gun at Monte Nero

Retreat for fear of being turned or outflanked was 'formally and absolutely forbidden'. If the enemy broke through, commanders must create
a defensive flank, seal the breakthrough and use reserves to form defensive compartments.[64] To ensure that his subordinates conformed with
the new doctrines he was introducing, Diaz ordered his engineers when
constructing trenches not to join up separate elements in order to
counter 'the pernicious tendency' to put most of the available force into
line, 'thereby subjecting it to rapid attrition and useless losses and, what
is most important, thereby removing any possibility of manoeuvre in the
event of an enemy attack'.[65]

   High on the list of priorities was the replacement and renewal of
artillery. In the retreat from Caporetto the army had lost 2,116 guns,
almost a third of its total park, and 1,732 trench mortars. Legend
afterward had it that the armaments firm of Ansaldo had stepped up to
the plate, offering the state six hundred 105-mm guns it had manufactured off its own bat. In reality, the plaudits belonged to Dallollio.
The munitions programme for July 1916–June 1917 had fixed on a figure

of 7,031 guns for the year, but by the time it ended in June 1917 the armaments industry had only managed to deliver 1,845 guns. This kind of slippage gave the army a bad name: Riccardo Bianchi, the minister for transport in 1917–18, believed the military to be bad organisers with 'a very curious idea of organization: to do anything they want an enormous excess of means and don't think of ordering things in relation to the country's means and needs'.[66] In fact there were good – as well probably as not so good – reasons why the armaments industry was falling so badly behind: the ongoing shortage of labour in the arms factories had still to be resolved, and Italy's coal imports in 1917, amounting to 5,038,000 tons, were only 52 per cent of her needs. On 2 July 1917, Dallollio published the 1917–18 armaments programme, reducing the target to the more realistic total of 4,292 guns. By 30 November 1917 industry had already delivered 1,994 guns, 46.5 per cent of the annual total.

In fact, output of guns was on a rising curve from July 1917 until the end of the war. Although it only passed the pre-Caporetto total of 6,918 guns in October 1918, much of what had been lost was obsolescent or antiquated. In that respect Caporetto was not entirely the disaster it seemed at first sight. The steady increase in industrial output – matched in the automotive industry – was the result of a complex of industrial factors. Coal imports increased in 1918 to 5,840,300 tons, four-fifths of which now came overland from France not by sea from England as had been the case the year before. Domestic production of iron ore doubled, reaching 1,803,000 tons in 1917. Imports of semi-finished steel from France saved valuable coal. In May 1917, following the example set by the Allies, labour laws were relaxed to allow women to be employed in munitions factories and elsewhere, and by the end of the war 200,000 were working in the war industries. Finally, expert labour was released from the army, the number of exonerations rising from 256,351 at the end of October 1917 to 437,389 eleven months later.[67]

Although Diaz was beginning to make strides in his efforts to increase the army's fighting power, the commanders of the newly arrived British and French forces could see a great many faults that still needed remedying. Plumer was particularly critical of Italian staff work, which was theoretical and impractical.

Paper is the ruling factor, and they issue orders which cannot be carried out . . . All staffs are inclined to think that once an order is issued it is as good as done, which is far from being the case, and staff officers do not go out to see that the orders are being carried out.[68]

Fayolle picked up the lack of method and organisation and added a litany of tactical defects, almost all of which Diaz was very well aware of.

Front lines were packed with troops and defences lacked depth, guns were pushed too far forward, and although the technical training of the artillery was good it lacked the spirit of co-operation with the infantry, did not know how to carry out destructive fire, and showed a marked reluctance to carry out counter-battery fire. Training was notably poor, chiefly because no measures appeared to have been taken to develop it: nothing was being done to train the reserve army other than a few exercises or marches at company level, and so far not a single divisional training ground had been established in the war zone. Only Capello, in charge of 5th Army, appeared to be occupying himself with problems connected to training. Fayolle estimated that there were forty-five usable Italian divisions, twenty-seven of which were fresh and the remainder tired. Morale was 'not bad' and could be improved with more food, an adequate system of turns in line, and regular leave.[69] When a copy of the report came into Diaz's hands in May 1918, he recognised that though in some respects out of date it contained some fair and accurate observations, and ordered that its contents be summarised and passed on to the army commanders.

Diaz was not left alone to get on with his job. In early January, worried by news that the Swiss–German frontier had been closed, Orlando warned him that another enemy offensive on the Piave or the *altipiani* might be in the offing. Diaz calmly reassured the premier that there was no other intelligence to that effect and no signs of an imminent enemy attack but all the necessary steps were in hand to employ the troops 'in the best possible way'. A few days afterwards, news of strikes in Austria prompted the premier to question whether the policy of non-fraternisation might not in fact mean the loss of possible opportunities to capitalise on the enemy's weakness. Two and a half hours later, another telegram to the field commander relayed reported dissatisfaction with troop rotations into and out of line.[70] Prime ministerial interference had to be borne, but parliamentary interference did not and Diaz complained about it. Senators and deputies were deluging him with letters about supposed shortcomings, most of which were unjustified or exaggerated and all of which created extra work. The unceasing enquiries were overwhelming his resources and thus threatening discipline. Shrewdly appealing to the premier's political instincts, he pointed out that changes and improvements were being attributed not to the government but to 'this or that protector, something which seems to me of great importance for the war and for what comes afterwards'.[71]

An important component of Diaz's reforms was the reorganisation of the intelligence services. Regulations issued on 10 January 1918 divided intelligence into two distinct activities: broader strategic intelligence on both sides of the front was now the province of the *Servizio informazioni*, while local tactical intelligence gathered at and immediately behind either side of the fighting front by officers attached to army commands was the province of the *Servizio informazioni sul nemico presso le truppe operante* or ITO, responsible to the head of the *Ufficio situazione*, one of the branches of the *Comando supremo*. The heads of the intelligence centres attached to each army now met with their chief at least once a week to relay new information upwards and receive fresh instructions. The intelligence collection centres, eventually attached to every corps and to some divisions, gathered information from interrogations of prisoners of war and deserters, captured documents and correspondence, intercepts, and aerial reconnaissance. They also made use of 284 Czech, Yugoslav, Serbian, Polish and Romanian prisoner-of-war volunteers, whose role in propagandising their former comrades-in-arms would grow in importance. The results of the local centres' activities were checked against intelligence from the *Servizio informazioni*, from foreign military missions and from the domestic and foreign press before finally being shaped into a daily war bulletin and an authoritative fortnightly appreciation of the enemy's situation on the Italian front.[72] With clear channels and an integrated structure, Diaz now had an efficient and increasingly effective instrument in his hands.

Over the spring and early summer intelligence work advanced. In February Giardino took advantage of the growing movement for independence within the Austro-Hungarian empire and assigned 24 officers and 260 men chosen from volunteer Czecho-Slovak, Yugoslav, Serbian, Polish and Romanian prisoners of war to 1st, 3rd and 4th Armies, considerably improving translation capabilities. They were given the same pay as Italians and special indemnities. From the end of May, Italian military intelligence began landing agents behind enemy lines and air-dropping carrier-pigeons to carry messages back. With naval co-operation, agents were inserted into enemy territory across Lake Garda and the Adriatic. Specially trained *Arditi* units recovered important documents from recently occupied enemy positions. In June a phototelemetary section was established, greatly improving the army's ability to locate enemy artillery.[73]

A better understanding of the enemy's methods was a means both to strengthen the army's defensive capability and to improve its own fighting power. The international exchanges now taking place could involve some important indirect routes: in May 1917 the Allied intelligence and counter-espionage service in Paris passed on information from Russian sources about Austria–Hungary's use of *Stürmtruppen*. Though the Russian source dried up, an ever-increasing volume of intelligence of all types became available during the last ten months of the war. German lessons drawn from the Flanders campaign in 1917 were used to illustrate more effective tactics: defensive artillery fire should be as close as possible to one's own front line, individual detachments should not try to halt enemy advances with counter-attacks that were easily beaten off but seek to slow them down, divisional counter-attacks should be under the command of the sector commander regardless of his seniority, and defences should not be so thick and high as to be easily recognisable.[74] Up-to-date information was circulated shortly after the March offensive began about the latest German methods of defence and attack, illustrating and emphasising the importance of depth and flexibility in the former and the advantages that could result from holding troops as far back as possible until the last moment in the latter.[75] In May 1918, the *Ufficio operazioni* began publishing a regular series of bulletins reporting on British and French operations on the western front and including translations of captured German and Austro-Hungarian documents dealing particularly with tactics, training, organisation and armaments. The learning process now taking place was helped by the fact that British and French units were located in Italy and Italian units in France.[76]

At the beginning of February, Italian military intelligence reported information pointing to an enemy build-up along the mountain front with operations aimed at Brescia and Verona in the spring seemingly in view. Prisoners were being used for road works, notable quantities of ammunition and artillery were arriving, reinforcements were being sent up and shelters built. While none of this could be confirmed, it could reflect the enemy's intention to launch simultaneous offensives on the Franco-British and Italian fronts to prevent the Allies shifting troops from one theatre to the other. Counting the Central Powers' divisions suggested that they could pull sixty-one out of Russia, giving them a twenty-three-division superiority in France and a seven-division margin in Italy.[77] In early March information believed credible by the head of the Berne centre suggested that the Germans planned to attack Italy with twelve divisions in mid April – an action that would, military intelligence pointed out, be in tune with their guiding concept of concentrating on the weakest enemy. Although there was only fragmentary evidence to support it, Colonel Cavallero, head of the operations office, was inclined to believe it because, among other things, Italy's policy of reaching accords with the Slav populations of the Austro-Hungarian empire might be a sufficient inducement. Also, Austria's internal conditions might well impose on her the need for a major effort to put out of action 'the only enemy she has left to fear' – Italy.[78]

By the beginning of March Diaz believed that the enemy was readying himself for a great effort in which the Italian front would be an important component, if not the principal one. The attack was most likely to come on the northern front, between the Val Giudicarie and Monte Grappa, though neither the western nor the eastern fronts could be excluded. Thanks to the reorganisation and re-equipment already carried out, he was confident that the army was ready to face any eventuality. Army commanders were instructed to prepare counter-offensives to meet any attack, and pre-emptive offensives to stifle it. Clearly learning from Cadorna's mistakes, Diaz spread out his nine reserve divisions between Lake Garda, Vicenza and Mestre in positions from which they could support the northern front or if necessary swing to reinforce the western front. If attacked, the army must resist to the last, looking to contain the enemy in the smallest possible space by means of swift counter-offensives and local counter-attacks.[79]

The Germans' 'March Offensive' bore out Diaz's analysis, but not in the way he had imagined. It also threw a spanner into the Italian works. The immediate consequence was that he lost half his Allied contingent. Over the next three weeks four French divisions and one English division returned to France, accompanied by two Italian divisions whose transfer had been agreed just before the German attacks, leaving Diaz with three British and two French divisions. By the time that the last two French divisions left, evidence was building up that the Austrians were planning an offensive against Monte Grappa. There were also the political consequences of the German offensive to be considered. On 31 March General Giardino (who had replaced Cadorna at Versailles) reported the decision taken at Doullens five days earlier to give Foch strategic direction of Allied operations in France and warned that premier Georges Clemenceau intended to extend the arrangement to the Italian front. His advice to Diaz was to find some way of acknowledging Foch as *generalissimo*. At issue was not the different situation on the two fronts but whether or not Italy remained isolated 'without a voice at Versailles and without [any] direct connection to the general war – that is a risk'.[80] Two days later Clemenceau asked Orlando to adhere to the Doullens accords, just as Giardino had warned he would.

The decision effectively creating a unified Allied command threatened Diaz's authority and his plans. He objected forcefully to giving up *Comando nazionale* for *Comando unico*, claimed that the French did not understand Italy's situation and her natural environment, and deplored the French tendency to consider the Italian front as subsidiary to the western front.[81] Behind these complaints lay a fundamental divergence of views. Diaz's strategy was designed to knock out Austria–Hungary, the weaker prop of the Central Powers. Foch wanted to defeat Germany. Orlando was in two minds about what to do, fearing French interference in Italy's war but recognising at the same time that it might be the way to get more Allied troops in action on the Italian front. The decision taken by the Supreme War Council at Abbeville on 2 May extending Foch's co-ordinating powers to the Italian front and giving him overall command if Allied armies fought together there was a mixed blessing. Italy remained military master in its own house, but only so long as the Allied aid that Diaz wanted did not arrive in force. On the other hand, Italy was now part of a single strategic front extending from the North Sea to the Adriatic, and the possibility that Allied armies might indeed be put into play to defeat the Austrians was now rather more likely.[82]

From this time onwards, Italian generals and statesmen came under ever-increasing Allied pressure to take the offensive. Although it was not apparent to outsiders, the army was as yet by no means strong enough to be confident of the outcome. Diaz had therefore to resist pressure to commit his troops to what he rightly regarded as a premature action and fortunately he had a strong and well-placed political ally to support him – the recently appointed Treasury minister, Francesco Nitti. Widely believed to be after the premiership himself in due course, Nitti's immediate goal was to win the war in such a way as not to compromise Italy's future, which meant adopting a military policy of not wearing down Italian manpower until a decisive battle or battles could be fought. Nitti was well placed to exert influence: he knew Capello, the duke of Aosta and a number of other generals and admirals personally, his wife and Diaz's wife were friends, and Orlando seemed content mostly to leave day-to-day cabinet oversight of military policy in his hands. When he learned of the decision to create a unified Allied command under Foch, taken at a meeting at which the Italian representative, General Giardino, had not been present, he joined Orlando and Diaz in strongly opposing *Comando unico*. Then, at Abbeville on 2 May, Orlando sold that pass by accepting the principle of 'co-ordination'.

Although the German attacks on the Lys had been stopped, the French feared new ones and were more than a little unhappy that Italy was as militarily immobile as Austria–Hungary. As pressure for action from Foch and the French ambassador in Rome, Camille Barrère, mounted Nitti grew increasingly alarmed lest Italy lose at least partial control of the war. Militarily, Italy was fighting her own war and should look after her own interests by counting only on herself. She faced a nation of 53 million people with a long military tradition and the possibility of drawing on Bulgarian, Turkish and perhaps also German reserves. If Italy tried an offensive and did not get the desired results, he reasoned, who would come to her aid? 'We are Italians, and we must save Italy,' he told Diaz in mid May. 'I urge you therefore to listen only to your [own] conscience and choose the offensive or the defensive (as a general programme, be it understood) only according to its military suitability.'[83] With the third anniversary of the war about to occur, and Bissolati too pressing for an offensive, Nitti urged Diaz to stand firm. The army had been reconstituted with enough guns and ammunition for defence 'and perhaps to attack', there was now enough grain to last till the harvest, enough coal, and the socialists were divided and mostly benevolent if not favourable towards the war. Six months earlier such a position would have been inconceivable. But this was not the time to dare, or to show weakness in the face of Allied pressure: if Italy gave way she would finish up like Serbia, Romania or Russia. Diaz must have 'a firm will and nerves of steel'.[84]

Hearing that Orlando was on his way to the front to agree a coming battle, Nitti told Diaz not to pay any attention to the minister or to parliament but to think only of the military situation. As he saw it, the French were trying to weaken Italy and decide the great duel on the western front. An Italian offensive would have the advantage for the French of distracting German forces. 'But would it not be the death of us?' he asked. 'We now have 20 or 30 fewer divisions than Austria. Do they want to send us to the slaughter-house?' Nitti was prepared to be faithful to the alliance – but not to be sacrificed to it. Italy was playing its last card and must play it wisely.[85]

Prisoners of war

If life at the front for Cadorna's troops was unremittingly hard, it was worse for the 600,000 Italians who were unlucky enough to be made prisoners of war. Under the terms of the 1907 Hague Convention, to which Italy had adhered, prisoners were to be maintained at the expense of the 'host' government and receive treatment equal to that accorded to its own troops. Parcels could be sent to individuals as long as they were the result of private initiative. Britain and France modified these terms as the war went along. Arrangements were made to send wagon-loads of food for general distribution at state expense, to transfer wounded and sick prisoners to Switzerland and to exchange certain categories of prisoners. Flint-hearted generals and politicians ensured that Italy did almost nothing to succour its prisoners of war – if anything, quite the reverse. As a result 100,000 of them – a figure equal to one-sixth of the deaths in combat – never returned. Mostly they died of malaria, tuberculosis and dropsy brought on by hunger.

The first reports about conditions in the camps which began to circulate early in 1916 were reassuring, though they were not in fact accurate. The *Comando supremo* grew alarmed: desertion would only be encouraged by the supposed attractions of prison. The government was told in no uncertain terms that it must publicise everything that put the treatment of Italian prisoners in a bad light. Stories that the Austrians were seizing prisoners' parcels for their own population, which began to circulate as the first realistic (and bad) news about conditions started to emerge, were denied by the Italian Red Cross but encouraged by the government. Thousands of individual parcels began piling up at the frontier due to maladministration, a dysfunction officially attributed to the enemy. Censorship ensured that reassuring news from the camps was stifled, but nothing was done to prevent the press publishing information about poor treatment. As Porro explained to the premier, 'such news is a corrective to the fancy to desert'. If the enemy were to threaten reprisals over the exaggerated stories of what was happening to Italian prisoners, then the prisoners' families would 'certainly find in their patriotism the strength to put up with the fate of their loved ones'.[86]

Politicians were every bit as adamantine as generals in their determination to do nothing to help captured Italian soldiers. None was more determined than Sonnino who opposed giving prisoners of war any state aid whatsoever. It would be a cost to Italy; the Hague Convention made it clear that Austria–Hungary was responsible for looking after its prisoners; and if it were to be provided there was no guarantee that it would get through. Boselli agreed with him. However, the policy only applied to the rank and file and not to the 19,500 officers who were prisoners of war. While the Italian Red Cross was only allowed to organise private parcels for individual soldiers, it was permitted to provide collective aid for officers in the shape of wagon-loads of food, clothing and other necessities. The costs were initially met by the Red Cross, which was then reimbursed from the officers' bank accounts or by their families. As officers were given pay by the Austrian and German governments, as well as getting money from their families and personal parcels, they enjoyed better conditions than the men they had commanded. This was reflected in the statistics of mortality. In all, 550 officers died in prison camps, their annual death rate of 2 per cent being one-sixth that of the men.[87]

The first seriously wounded prisoners of war got back to Italy in October 1916 and began to speak about their experiences. By the start of 1917 their reports were in the newspapers. The army was more than happy for returned prisoners of war to report on their maltreatment and thereby propagandise the troops: as the war minister General Morrone explained to Sonnino, 'the soldiers must be inspired by the horror of prison'. Morrone wanted to go tighten the screw yet more, stopping all food parcels and public subscriptions 'because such aid, known to our soldiers, would confirm them in the belief that prisoners one way or another manage to do alright'.[88] Things did indeed get worse for Italian prisoners of war during 1917, due as much to the actions of their own government as to the growing economic stresses bearing down on their captors. Any prisoner of war helping another who was accused of desertion or of some lesser crime lost the right to family aid. In early October an official ordinance forbade the inclusion in individual aid parcels of bread, wine, grapes, fruit, cheese, meat, fish, any goods such as sugar, shoes and leather that the enemy might be short of, civilian clothes and articles of uniform.

Official policy did not change greatly after Caporetto, and where it did it was for the worse. Thanks to Cadorna's publicising of the idea of 'voluntary surrenders', the walking skeletons who now inhabited what they called 'camps for the dying' were castigated by D'Annunzio as 'shirkers beyond the Alps'. Aid wagons for officers were temporarily suspended, and thanks to Sonnino no packages of any kind were allowed for prisoners of war in Germany until February 1918. In the same month the government passed a decree giving the Italian Red Cross sole right to send bread to prisoners of war – the only formal government act for the support of prisoners of war passed during the entire war. Prisoners' families now had the ability to send other foodstuffs. To do so, they had to obtain a special permit from the *Carabinieri*. Prisoners guilty or suspected of desertion, or of a comparable crime, got no parcels at all because their families were denied the necessary permit. The effect of all this, and of the increase in the population of the camps after Caporetto, was to swamp the offices handling parcels and letters. The frontiers had to be closed in March and April 1918, the sending of parcels was temporarily forbidden, hundreds of packages were destroyed or had to be repacked to remove parts of their contents, and 17 tons of post that had built up at the censors' offices was destroyed.[89] To make matters worse, aid arrived sporadically (during offensives no wagons got to the frontier at all), and when it did it was often in a ruinous state because railway carriages that would not or were not shut let in the rain, or had been packed too full so that heat ruined the contents.

Until the summer of 1918 there was no widespread sense of how bad things were in the Austrian and German camps and tales of 'atrocities' were regarded as lying enemy propaganda. When, in June, Diaz learned enough of the truth, he demanded reprisals against the prisoners of war held in Italy. Sonnino coolly pointed out that the Austrians had three times as many Italians as Italy had Austrians, and that in any case half of the Austro-Hungarian prisoners belonged to the sub-nationalities and would have to be excluded. In August Italy at last experimented briefly with a system of state-funded aid, sending single wagon-loads of biscuit. All along, the government's overriding concern was to ensure that the rank and file in the army were thoroughly disabused of any notion that being captured might be a good thing and that prisoner-of-war camps were an agreeable or at least a tolerable way of sitting out the war. Returning prisoners of war were suspect to the last. In mid September 1918, on the basis of evidence supplied by the prefect of Rome, the interior ministry believed that the Austrians were repatriating the worst elements, particularly those who had contributed to the disaster at Caporetto, and that they had given undertakings to engage in 'propaganda or worse against our war effort'.[90] The authorities remained implacable to the end: on 3 October Alfieri told Orlando that because of the army's needs it was 'absolutely impossible to give our prisoners of war even the minimum amount of clothing'.[91]

To begin with Italy had few Austro-Hungarian prisoners of war to handle. The first significant influx came in October 1915 when the

Fig. 14 Serving out rations to prisoners

retreating Serbs brought 24,000 officers and men with them. They were interned on the island of Asinara where, in the blackest episode in this story, some 7,000 died from cholera (which they brought with them), typhus and tuberculosis before the remainder were shipped to France in the summer of 1916.[92] By January 1917 the total number of prisoners of war in Italy had climbed to 79,978, lodged in 111 camps. On the day that the battle of Vittorio Veneto began the figure had reached 180,000, and in the last ten days of the war the army took another 300,000 prisoners.

Conditions in the Italian camps were, or were perceived to be, fairly relaxed and comfortable to begin with: the regulations allowed prisoners of war the same rations as Italian soldiers in peacetime (as were Italian prisoners in Austrian camps until the blockade began to bite in 1917), and table wine and beer too if they could afford it. In January 1916 the *Comando supremo* circulated extracts from prisoners' letters describing 'the excellent Italian treatment' they were receiving and rejoicing in being 'among men of culture'. This was of course by no means the whole picture, and Austrian prisoners of war complained about reductions in rations, narrow cells infested with mice, the impossibility of getting proper exercise, being forced to work in malaria-infested regions, and especially about the harsh punishments handed out for minor acts of indiscipline.[93] Complaints of extreme punishments were summarily rejected at the time, though afterwards the foreign ministry's representative on the joint Italian–Austrian prisoner-of-war commission acknowledged that they had some force and that the Italian authorities had sometimes acted 'with intemperate zeal'.[94] As far as the general population was concerned, the treatment being given to the enemy was far too relaxed. In August 1915 the mayor of Pavia complained to Salandra that Italian cities had been 'invaded' by 'lazy' prisoners who cost the state a great deal and gave it nothing in return, and a year later in the chamber of deputies General Morrone was grilled about the civilian clothes, cultural visits, dinners, suppers and games of football supposedly being enjoyed by the occupants of the camps.[95]

For both sides prisoners of war were an obvious source of labour, and also a legitimate one: Article 6 of the 1907 Hague Convention allowed for the employment of other ranks, but not officers, on work that was not directly connected with the war. General Spingardi, who was in charge of prisoner-of-war affairs at the war ministry, enquired in July 1915 whether agricultural workers could be used. The answer he got – in December – was that work could only be done in the camps. Pressures on manpower were too great for such a policy to last, and in May 1916 the authorities decided to allow the 'exceptional' use of prisoner-of-war labour to meet needs 'that cannot otherwise be provided for'.[96] At first only a few thousand were used to help bring in the harvest, but in 1917 demand intensified and that year roughly 80,000 prisoners of war worked in the countryside, down the mines or building roads. At the year's end Spingardi was able to report to Orlando that 'other than those unable to work and the sick, no-one has been allowed to loaf'.[97] By the following April 130,000 prisoners of war were making a contribution to the Italian war economy: 60,000 were working in agriculture, 30,000 were cutting wood or peat and mining lignite, 2,153 were working on the railways and another 1,098 were employed by Ansaldo.

As well as providing much-needed labour, prisoners of war were also a potential resource in the undermining of Austria–Hungary. As such they became increasingly important contributors to Italian strategy in the last year of the conflict as both sides waged energetic propaganda wars against one another. In June 1916 prisoners had been split into two national groups, Slavs (Bohemians, Poles, Slovaks and Croats) and Germans and Hungarians, in order to prevent 'friction' and to avoid 'discussions of a political character'. After the meeting of the Congress of the Oppressed Nationalities in Rome on 8–10 April 1918, Italy took on a leading role in propagating their cause, though there was considerable ambiguity in the government's position. At this stage Orlando still backed Sonnino's policy of not breaking up the Austro-Hungarian empire, and the Italian government only issued a statement acknowledging the Yugoslav movement for independence as 'corresponding to the principles for which the Entente is fighting' as late as 25 September 1918.[98]

Militarily, though, there was something to be gained from backing some if not all of the parties in the developing sub-nationalities mêlée. Czechs, Poles and Romanians were the preferred nations – and the ones Italy would privilege when it came to the order in which prisoners were released after the war ended. An agreement reached at Palazzo Braschi in April 1918 resulted in the formation of a Czech Legion which by October numbered more than 3,000 men (only eighteen of whom were Slovaks). Another 12,000 former Czech prisoners of war were integrated into Montuori's 4th Army. In February 1918 General Alfieri supported the creation of a Polish Legion, but although men were trained it never reached the front line. The collapse of Russia forced Romania to come to terms with the Central Powers on 7 May 1918, but Romanian volunteers fought on the Piave in the last days of the war. Among the leftovers after Russia exited from the war were 30,000 Austro-Italian prisoners from the Trentino and Trieste. Offered their freedom if they fought with Italy, 2,500 of them accepted.

The battle of the Solstice

After holding off two Hindenburg offensives, Foch pressed Diaz at the beginning of May to attack 'without delay'. On the premise that the Austrians were numerically inferior on the Italian front and were showing 'no offensive will', he asked for the general outlines of his plan of attack, the role to be played by Allied forces, and the date. Diaz assured Foch that he was fully signed up to the principal of action as soon as the moment was favourable, 'one of the immutable laws of war', and then laid out the reasons why he did not propose to act on the request. Austrian strength was at least equal to that of Italy, and he was not disposed to put too much weight on the supposedly vulnerable state of Austrian morale. The enemy's inaction was likely due to a combination of the uncertain situation in Russia and the weather, which was improving. If he went beyond the limited operation on the Asiago *altopiano* that was in the planning stage, he would have to use the ten divisions currently being kept as a general reserve. This would allow the enemy either to achieve a local superiority on other sectors of the front or 'to start a vast counter-offensive when ours stopped, either of which would find us without adequate reserves to deploy'. If he was going to accede to Foch's request, Diaz first wanted assurances about the reinforcements that the Allies would give him. Evidence that the Austrians were planning an attack, and the inability of the Allies to launch counter-offensives on the western front, strengthened his determination not to be pushed into premature action and underpinned a request for yet more Allied assistance with foodstuffs, raw materials and coal.[99] Nevertheless, he was prepared to undertake a limited offensive on the Asiago *altopiano* starting on 18 June to help the allies, now under pressure from Hindenburg's third offensive on the Aisne that began on 27 May.

The Austrians were indeed planning an offensive. On 23 March 1918, Emperor Karl approved the outline of a plan for a 'clamorous victory' against Italy. His chief of staff, General Arz von Straussenberg, promised that it would take Austrian armies to the Adige and bring about Italy's military collapse. The Austrians intended to launch major attacks on the Tonale pass and on the Asiago *altopiano* and Monte Grappa, with a secondary push on Treviso, to force the Italians to abandon the Piave. Aware of increased Italian activity intercepting and deciphering their communications, they ordered the complete cessation of radio communications in April, removed just before the battle, and cut back on telephone communications, forbidding any telephone activity while preparations were made for the attack.

By spring 1918 Italian military intelligence was in some difficulties. A regular trickle of deserters and prisoners began to dry up after the enemy had been thrown back behind the Piave, and air reconnaissance was proving inadequate in identifying enemy units and pinpointing their locations. In one section of the line, north of Ponte di Piave, there was no contact whatever with the enemy for several months, which worried the head of 3rd Army intelligence, Colonel Ercole Smaniotto. His solution was to insert agents into the main enemy centre at Vittorio Veneto and at Pordenone, where the main railway artery could be observed. An agent was put in by air at Vittorio (Veneto) on 30/31 May, but communication by carrier-pigeon proved difficult and he was reduced to using sheets to signal. The first written message did not get back until 29 June. Three attempts to land agents for Pordenone failed. The battle of the Solstice would eliminate the three small areas of direct contact with the enemy, and dry up the trickle of prisoners of war. To fill the intelligence gap, seven agents were subsequently inserted directly by aircraft, seaplane and MAS torpedo boat to watch and report on troop movements.[100] After initial hesitations the first parachute drop of an agent, Second-Lieutenant Alessandro Tandurra, took place on 9 August 1918.

There were, though, enough sources of intelligence to indicate that the Austrians intended to launch an offensive on the Piave with subsidiary actions on the Asiago *altopiano* and at Monte Grappa. Deserters brought information about the movement of troops from the Trentino to the Piave and practice assaults using pontoons on the river Livenza. Six days before the battle Italian intelligence knew that the main front would extend from the Asiago to the lower Piave with a secondary action in the Val Lagarina. They also knew that no German troops would be taking part.[101] On 14 June an Italian radio interception station picked up the exact time when the Austrian offensive would start. Colonel Finzi, head of 6th Army intelligence, confirmed the time and date of the attack, 0300 hours on 15 June, and Colonel Marchetti, head of 1st Army intelligence, was able to confirm the limit of the attack front east of Astico. This enabled Badoglio to get the artillery ready to crush the attackers and Diaz to make better use of his reserves. Some commanders, though, preferred their own intelligence: 8th Army planned a changeover of troops on the night of 14/15 June, and 3rd Army took no immediate measures for counter-preparation.

On 12 June Foch renewed his pressure on Diaz, pointing out that the expected Austrian attack had not come and encouraging Diaz to go back to the original plan. The double Austrian offensive began next day with an attack on Tonale. The Italian positions there had been improved thanks to a brilliant action by *Alpini* in the previous month, and as a result the Austrians took only two summits before they were brought to a halt. The main offensive began two days later. On the Asiago *altopiano* the guns of General Montuori's 6th Army opened up half an hour before the Austrian attack began. British and French divisions lost their positions but took them back with immediate counter-attacks. The Austrians were able to take three mountains and held them against counter-attacks until the end of June.

Monte Grappa was a different story. The centre had been well fortified but the position had no depth and the flanks were only lightly held. Thanks to a thick fog the Austrians were able to stave in the position held by General Emilio De Bono's IX Corps, defending the left slopes. In less than five hours they had broken through three lines of defences and were only 5 kilometres as the crow flew from the plains below. The attack was held thanks to effective artillery fire by 6th Army, which sealed the battlefield and prevented the Austrians from bringing up reinforcements. The situation was retrieved by assault troops led by Major Giovanni Messe (who would command Italian troops in Russia and North Africa in the next world war). De Bono was adjudged to have done well: promoted to lieutenant-general two days after the battle ended and awarded a third *medaglia d'argento*, he ensured his celebrity by composing a popular song about the battle.[102]

Where Conrad's attacks in the mountains had failed, Boroević's on the plain initially succeeded. The Austrian attack began at 0330 hours and three Austrian divisions got across the Piave under cover of fog in the first two hours. The Austrians threw six bridges and fourteen footbridges across the Piave in the first three days, pushing back a thin line of Italian defenders and taking the heights of Montello and a strip a few kilometres wide running from Grave di Papadopoli to the sea. Then, at 0800 hours on 18 June, the summer floods began. Over the next twelve hours the river rose dramatically, taking a further twenty-four hours to go down. With this the battle split into dozens of small engagements in a stretch 22 kilometres long and up to 5 kilometres deep. Italian defences, initially overwhelmed, were saved by artillery and aircraft attacks on the pontoon bridges thrown over the river by the Austrians. The Austrians rebuilt them at night, and Italian guns and aircraft knocked them down again during the hours of daylight. When the river fell, the battle entered its second and final stage. As the Austrian supply situation grew critical, 600 Italian aircraft joined the guns and attacked the remaining bridges and the enemy troops on the west bank. At 1916 hours on 20 June, in the face of violent Italian counter-attacks, Emperor Karl ordered Boroević to retire, which he did over the next three days.

Fig. 15 Troops in a front-line trench on Monte Grappa, 1918

Both sides made full use of intelligence during the battle, the Italians doing better than their enemy. Before it began the Austrians knew the location of the Italian army commands, twenty corps commands and forty-one divisional commands, and during it they picked up lots of information about the enemy's situation and losses. For their part, the Italians took telephones away from front-line company commanders and used searchlights, flares, optical means or runners to communicate between commands. On the fifth day of the battle the capture of part of the Austrian cipher enabled the Italian cryptographic service to learn that the enemy had committed all his reserves and that therefore there would be no more surprises. Intercept stations, particularly one on Monte Grappa, provided useful near real-time information. Away from the front, Italian intelligence was busy corrupting telegraph officials to get duplicate copies of telegrams, and pilfering copies from neutral post and telegraph offices.[103]

The battle blooded Diaz's army, but it also showed up ongoing weaknesses. Some units proved fragile, mainly due to inadequate numbers of junior officers and non-commissioned officers and deficiencies in their training; some counter-attacks were poorly directed or too precipitous; and artillery–infantry co-operation still left something to be desired. The training of junior officers, long one of the army's gravest weaknesses, was now taken firmly in hand. The grade of *aspirante* (officer candidate) was abolished and training courses, which increased in length from two months to five with a final sixth month in the march battalions (replacement units), were removed from individual armies and centralised in five schools overseen by an inspector general. Platoon, company and battalion commanders attended special courses, and monthly divisional exercises were mandated under the direction of army commands.[104] Expanding the army's knowledge base was every bit as important as improving its intellectual capacities. Thus after the battle, 3rd Army issued a collection of studies of enemy operations during it based on a large trove of captured enemy documents. A detailed statistical analysis of the thousands of prisoners revealed that the enemy were making much less use of Czech soldiers – now a dubious quantity – on the Italian front and were relying more heavily on Poles, Croats and Hungarians 'three of the races on whom the monarchy has up to now been able to count unreservedly'.[105]

The 'battle of the bridges' cost the Italians 85,000 in dead, wounded, missing and prisoners of war. Austrian losses amounted to 143,000 men. The river had played an important part, and the Italians knew it: when the general commanding the *brigata Mantova* reached it on 24 June, he knelt down and kissed the water. The guns, too, had played a crucial role, firing 3,500,000 rounds in the course of the engagement. In cities across Italy a jubilant population celebrated: 40,000 turned out in Naples, and in Turin 100,000 crowded into Piazza Castello and swore a collective oath 'to resist, bearing any sacrifice, until victory'.[106]

The Italians had achieved more than either they or their allies realised at the time. The Austrians dated the beginning of their collapse from their failure on the Piave, and Hindenburg too saw it as the end of any Austrian threat to Italy. One thing alone clouded the victory. On 19 June Major Francesco Baracca, Italy's leading fighter ace with thirty victories to his credit, was shot down over Montello while strafing enemy lines. The king wrote in sympathy to his mother, the royal family was represented at his funeral, and in the inter-war years he was adopted by the Fascist regime as a model hero. Roads, squares and schools were named after him, as was the aeroplane in which Italo Balbo flew the Atlantic in the winter of 1930–1 and a submarine which, like its namesake, also went down, sunk in the Atlantic by the British on 8 September 1941.[107]

Vittorio Veneto

On the day that the battle of the Solstice ended Orlando congratulated Diaz and asked whether the Austrian collapse did not open the way for an energetic pursuit of a broken enemy. Diaz, who had only six complete divisions left after the battle, was determined not to put the ultimate goal of winning the war at risk by undertaking what he regarded as adventurous operations. 'Did it not seem enough to throw the enemy back so decisively?' he complained to his wife. 'People have been dreaming of returning onto the Carso and going to Vienna. And who is going to give me the troops to carry out these flights [of fancy]?'[108] He did, though, see the victory on the Piave as the stepping-stone to greater things. Over the next two months he waged a paper offensive to try to persuade Foch that the Italian front was Germany's weak point and therefore the place with a decisive potential for the Allies. An Italian offensive in the mountains wore out the troops to no purpose. The solution to the war was a resolute offensive to defeat Austria, which would isolate Germany and lead to her fall. Struggling to halt the German offensive on the Chemin des Dames, Foch ruled out an inter-Allied offensive in Italy but pressed Diaz to attack in the mountains in order to open up the road to Trento and Feltre as a preliminary to a general offensive in September. Unless the Italians first extended their occupation of the mountain front between Pasubio and Monte Grappa, there could be no question of an offensive beyond Fiume.[109]

With no prospect of any immediate help from the British and French, Diaz's mind turned to the possibility of getting American troops in his theatre. Orlando quickly ruled that out of court because of the enormous political ructions it would surely cause. Like Foch, the premier thought that Austria had suffered a serious defeat on the Piave, and that its internal condition ruled out any rapid reconstitution of the army. It was doubtful whether an injection of German strength would be enough to change that. Italy should agree to an offensive that coincided with the general Allied offensive that Foch was planning for September, but insist on Allied help if the Germans came to Austria's aid.[110] Sticking to his last, Diaz advised Foch that Austria–Hungary might renew the offensive on his front, that he was keeping up the pressure on the Austrians with a series of local attacks, but that he was short of replacements and needed matériel, including 1,000 trucks and 25 tanks. Foch pressed for details of the operations Diaz was planning to undertake, withholding the tanks until both parties agreed on when and how they would be used.[111] In reply he was told that Diaz's plans were for 'a strong push on the Asiago *altopiano* with the aim of gaining space and allowing a similar advance on [Monte] Grappa'. For the time being though there was no question of an offensive on the Piave which would be 'neither opportune nor convenient in terms of direction, objectives and results'. The operations had to be carried out before the weather closed in in October, but nothing could be done without 30 tons of yprite and 60,000 gas shells for the artillery, a small number of tanks, and replacements.[112]

Having broken the final German attack in the Ludendorff offensive launched on 15 July, Foch wanted to exploit the situation as quickly as possible and heighten the shock effect on enemy morale. He now offered Diaz the gas, the gas shells and seventy-five tanks. He was not, however, prepared to part with any of the 70,000 Italian soldiers sent in January as a labour force. Diaz was far from happy with the offer. He now wanted at least 1,500 lorries but, most importantly he needed at a minimum 45,000 of the Italian workers as the 50,000 replacements he currently had were not enough to undertake a major action.[113] Foch thought Diaz was dragging his feet. 'You have everything you need to act in the way of men and matériel when you decide to do so,' he told the Italian. 'The circumstances are most favourable, which it would seem ought to hasten your decision.' Diaz assured him that planning was already under way, and would be completed by September. He proposed to attack using twenty-one Italian and five Allied divisions, almost his entire force. However, once the battle was over he would not be able to replace the losses. Calculations by his staff suggested that Austria–Hungary had 40,000 replacements available, to which would be added the 350,000 men of the class of 1900 and prisoners of war returning from Russia, while the Italian class of 1900 would probably only produce 200,000 recruits. Finally, he had to have the lorries, which were 'indispensable'.[114]

During that summer many people did not see the full consequences of Austria–Hungary's failure on the Piave. Nitti was one of them. French pressure was growing more intense with every day that passed, and now Sonnino, concerned that Italy's apparent unwillingness to collaborate with her ally at a decisive moment might mean her losing out at the peace table, added his voice to those of Foch and Camille Barrère. In late June, considerably overrating the enemy's potential, the Treasury minister suggested to Diaz that more potent enemy attacks might be in the offing, perhaps backed up with German resources, and warned that the illusion that she had escaped from danger might actually be a serious threat to Italy. By now, though, Diaz had no need of Cassandra-like utterances to buttress his earlier caution. Nitti was told that the dangers were no longer as great as they had been and that he was being too pessimistic.[115] After Foch began his offensive on 8 August, Nitti again urged Diaz to resist pressure to attack, and in the first week of September he was still counselling against any offensive action without direct Allied aid to back it up.

While the great men were wrangling with one another, combat knowledge was steadily improving. General Giardino returned from Versailles in May with a 'treasury' of practical knowledge and new theories of war he had learned from the defenders of the Somme.[116] To it Diaz and Badoglio added an analysis of the technical and tactical lessons of the battle of the Solstice. A number of important lessons were drawn from it. The location of the main elements of defence must be concealed from the enemy by camouflage; the movement of troops and supplies must take place at night; and deceptive plans based on false objectives and simulated targets must conceal true intentions. There was a vitally important distinction between immediate counter-attacks, to be carried out locally by commanders on the spot without waiting for artillery preparation, and counter-offensives carried out by fresh and well-prepared reserves. Badoglio lectured army corps chiefs of staff on the importance of keeping divisions intact and not breaking them up, as they were the best instrument with which to carry out the counter-attacks which were 'the most effective means of defence'.[117] The commandant general of engineers, General Marieni, echoing Diaz, emphasised the importance of deploying machine-guns in front of the trenches to foil infiltrations and counter attacks. Drawing lessons was one thing, though, and learning them was another. Almost none of the lower commands were studying the way the enemy fought, Diaz complained; it was from that knowledge that 'opportune employment of our forces derives'.[118] In July he organised a special section of the *Comando supremo* to monitor the disposition of his own armies and report any changes or reinforcements that were necessary.

In September 1918 new regulations for attack by divisions (*grandi unità*) were issued. Described as 'the principal doctrinal innovation of the war', they marked a transition from positional warfare to a war of movement. The application of maximum force on a narrow front, the importance of surprise, and the role of camouflage and deception in masking intentions were the core of the new doctrine. The master concept was the 'breakthrough battle' to open a breach through which reserves could irrupt. The method to be used, which resembled that embodied in French regulations issued in December 1917, prescribed a series of articulated attacks co-ordinated rapidly to succeed one another. Preparatory fire was now to aim at neutralisation rather than destruction. The object was to achieve as much penetration as possible so that reserves could be used not against zones of resistance but where there was most progress. Artillery was once again advised, as it had been for some months, that it must move forward quickly to support and protect the attacking infantry.[119]

The new doctrine represented an advance on what had gone before, but although the army as a whole began to receive flame-throwers, Stokes mortars and light 37-mm trench guns during the course of 1918 it still lacked the volume of firepower, manoeuvre capacity and penetration strength needed to develop widespread infiltration tactics of the kind being used on the western front. Tanks were virtually unknown and armoured cars only arrived on the eve of Vittorio Veneto, along with yprite from France which proved a more effective agent in neutralising enemy artillery in mountainous areas. The war ended before experiments in mobile warfare could get beyond the developmental stage. Only the specialist assault corps, formed in the summer and composed of *Arditi*, *Bersaglieri*, cavalry and cyclists, which was lightly armed (all its equipment and weapons were designed so that they could be broken into pieces and carried on the backs of men and mules) had anything like the capability that the British, French, German and Austrian armies were developing, and it was not a suitable model for dissemination across the army at large.

On 21 August, orders went out from the *Comando supremo* to prepare actions designed to deepen the positions on the Asiago *altopiano* in order to secure a more economical defensive line and a favourable starting point for future operations against Trento or the Feltre basin. Five days later a top secret directive from Badoglio asked the commanders of 3rd and 8th Armies for plans to force the line of the Piave. Eighth Army's objective was the heights of Valdobbiadene, 3rd Army's the line of the river Livenza.[120] Orlando, aware that Foch's second offensive had begun, pressed the *Comando supremo* to move more quickly and more convincingly. Neither Diaz nor his subordinates were going to be hurried. 'Give me a written order to attack,' Badoglio apparently told the premier, 'and I'll tell you how many minutes later I'll resign.'[121] Diaz took himself off to Paris between 30 August and 6 September, and in talks with Foch, Pershing and others again pushed the line that a major inter-Allied offensive against Austria could have enormous results but to do it required another twenty to twenty-five divisions. In default of such an offensive he wanted the Allied general reserve located in Italy so as to protect her against another attack and be on the spot when the time came for a major assault. He came back empty-handed.

Four days after Diaz left Versailles, the Supreme War Council's Note 37 declared that decisive victory required the complete defeat of the German army, only achievable on the western front. Other theatres would be subordinate contributors to the overarching goal. Italy's role over the coming winter and spring would be to continue to wear down the enemy in preparation for a general Allied offensive in spring 1919, to which she would then contribute with an offensive *in grande stile*. Foch exhorted the Italians to fulfil their share of the joint strategy by attacking in the Trentino. The *Comando supremo* was less than happy with the French *generalissimo*'s design, seeing a Trentino offensive as strategic-ally unproductive, risking a Carso-type undertaking, and opening up the possibility for a dangerous Austrian move on Piave.

Aosta's and Caviglia's staffs sent in their plans and on 14 September – the day on which Austria–Hungary approached Italy for non-binding discussions about ending the war – Diaz adopted what was now an outline for a dual offensive. At the same time he provided Orlando – whom he thought likely to push Italy into unwise adventures – with strategic guidance for the premier's discussions in Paris. Once more Diaz refused to be hurried into what he believed would be premature action. As well as lacking adequate reinforcements, he had lost nine English battalions. Until they were replaced the only Allied support available amounted to two French divisions. Any major action by Italy must be 'subordinated to the most favourable situation'. Diaz sketched three scenarios in which he would be prepared to act: either repercus-sions from decisive victories in France, or serious internal risings in enemy countries, or armed support in the shape of more troops. If the government explicitly ordered him to act he would of course do so, he told Orlando, but he would have then to use the class of 1900. That would in turn have serious repercussions on operations in 1919. Orlando assured him that he would never order an action that was not fully and freely supported by the military authorities and left for Paris, deter-mined that Italy must at all costs avoid finding herself in a situation in which the Allies did not assume the responsibility to act but left her with 'the responsibility for not acting'.[122] Always dubious about Orlando's reliability – he was after all a politician – Diaz advised the now absent premier that he would launch an all-out offensive only if the situation on the French front was in its favour. Otherwise he would continue with minor operations in order to fix Austrian forces and start his offensive when the French resumed theirs. If, however, they met with a decisive check, 'I think we must seriously consider the likelihood ... of an Austro-German attack in Italy, whom they would think their weakest adversary.'[123]

Diaz stood his ground again at a war committee meeting on 21–22 September, citing evidence of Austrian troop concentrations north of Montello and on the river Livenza to support his refusal to have anything to do with Foch's favoured offensive. He said nothing about the plans his staff were developing. Then suddenly part of the enemy front buckled. Marshal Franchet d'Espérey's troops defeated the Bulgarians at the battle of Dobro Pole (15–21 September), and the Bulgarian front began rapidly to collapse. This was a favourable strategic turn for Italy, albeit not the one Diaz had envisaged. Austria would now have to shift forces away from the Italian front to shore up her position in the Balkans, giving Italy her chance. Then, on 25 September, a memorandum landed on Diaz's desk laying out the strategic rationale for what would become the battle of Vittorio Veneto.

Arguing that the enemy must have noticed Italian preparations for a limited offensive on the Asiago plateau and that the ground was so difficult that an attack there could easily degenerate into a Carso-type offensive with no appreciable results, Colonel Cavallero suggested that what was needed instead was an operation combining 'brevity of preparation with the possibility of surprise'. An appropriate target did indeed exist: the single supply line for the Austrian 6th Army, which ran from Sacile via Vittorio and Val Mareno. Cut it and the entire 6th Army would fall into Italy's hands.[124] Cavallero's plan arrived at the moment when the complexion of the war suddenly changed. Franchet d'Espérey's victory in Macedonia split the German and Bulgarian armies apart and put the whole front in motion. Simultaneously, Allenby's success at the battle of Megiddo (19–21 September) signalled the end of Turkey as an active ally of the Central Powers. To watch Austria being attacked by Allied armies in the Balkans while the Italian army stood motionless on the Piave was to run a considerable political and military risk. Diaz approved the new idea at once, suspending the Asiago plan and keeping the decision for the time being to a very small circle of immediate subordinates. Foch was told and disapproved, thinking the new plan which was self-evidently not the mountain offensive he favoured risky and bound to fail. Orlando was kept in the dark.

The modified plan was accepted on 29 September and the proposed start date put back from 12 to 20 October to give 8th Army's artillery commander, General Ricci, time to get his guns in place.[125] That same day came news that Bulgaria had signed an armistice. As the planning cycle got under way, international politics added another complicating factor to the military equations. On 4 October Germany and Austria–Hungary asked Woodrow Wilson for an armistice based on the President's Fourteen Points. The cabinet meanwhile was at sixes and sevens over an offensive. At a ministerial meeting on 26 September, just as the big Allied attack on the western front was starting, Orlando argued against an Italian attack on the grounds that the enemy's position on the Grappa–Piave front was too strong and too well defended. Nitti, who did not expect the war to end quickly, stuck to what was by now his customary line: if the Allies sent troops then Italy should move, and if not not. On 20 October, with the battle four days away, Nitti, who was getting police reports from Turin about worker agitation and preparations for a strike, advised Orlando not to pressurize Diaz. 'A failure would be a disaster,' he warned the premier.

'The country would not survive it and we would face a revolt, if not a fully justified revolution.'[126] His pessimism continued to the last. On the eve of Vittorio Veneto he told Diaz that victory would change little but defeat would mean ruin, and four days after it began he wrote to Orlando (with whom he had by now entirely fallen out) deprecating the offensive, forecasting disaster and threatening to resign.[127]

The battle plan that was meanwhile emerging covered a front from the Brenta river to the sea. The guiding intention was to separate the Austrians in the Trentino from the Austrians on the Piave and then envelope the mountain front and bring about its fall. The main thrust by Caviglia's 8th Army, hitting the junction between the Austrian 6th and 5th Armies, would drive on Conegliano, Vittorio (not yet Vittorio Veneto) and Sacile, cutting the main enemy supply route. The advance would then swing north-west around the rear of Monte Grappa to take Feltre before driving up the Belluna valley to Cadore, the Val Cismon and Val Sugana.[128] When he saw it, Colonel Alberto Pariani, who was acting head of Caviglia's secretariat, was not impressed by what he felt was far too casual a study: the artillery was too far back and logistic preparations were insufficient. On 11 October, after he had consulted with Caviglia, 8th Army dropped Feltre as its second target (it went to 12th Army), and substituted Belluno.[129]

The first operational directive, issued on 12 October, laid out the plan which now included supporting attacks by 4th and 3rd Armies at the north-western and southern ends of the front. The general intention was to hit the junction of the enemy's 6th and 5th Armies with maximum force in order to cut 6th Army's communications and pin it against the Piave, making retreat impossible, after which the army would exploit the possible consequences of the manoeuvre.[130] As the Italians hauled 4,750 guns into position along the front of the coming battle, international politics again speeded up the strategic clock. Evidently perturbed at the possible outcomes of President Woodrow Wilson's response on 8 October to a German note about possible armistice conditions, Orlando mused confusingly to his *generalissimo*. If an armistice were accepted an attack would not be worthwhile, but if it were not accepted then one would be. There were powerful reasons why the liberation of Italian territories should not follow a diplomatic act. The only way to reconcile these 'opposing and very delicate needs' was to make future Italian operations 'appear like the natural development of normal actions rather than a large scale offensive'. Diaz, who had just briefed his army commanders, was not disposed to postpone or abandon his planned attack, as Orlando seemed to be suggesting. 'I do not think that waiting on a possible future armistice which would be due to the Allied armies and which may give us the possibility of securing the advantages we want without wearing ourselves out would be a desirable solution, and it would not at all correspond with our position and the size of our aspirations,' he told the premier.[131] This war would end differently than the wars of 1859 and 1866.

As the staffs worked on the plan the details changed and its scope widened, necessitating the creation of two new armies. The orchestration of the battle split the front in two. On the left a new 12th Army, given to the French general Jean-César Graziani, would take the heights of Valdobbiadene and then drive on Feltre via the rear of Monte Grappa, while 4th Army waited on the outcome before it pushed a corps along the Val Brenta to Val Cismon. On the right, Caviglia's 8th Army would drive on Vittorio and beyond, supported on its right by Cavan's newly created Anglo-Italian 10th Army which would cross the Piave at Grave di Papadopoli and advance on the Livenza river, covering Caviglia's right flank. Behind the battle line Diaz formed a reserve – 9th Army – which included the Assault Corps and forty-eight batteries of motor-towed artillery.

Preparations for the attack were pressed ahead in appalling weather, and with the Piave rising fast Diaz issued a second operational directive on 18 October accepting that the planned action to cross it would have to be somewhat delayed. He now proposed an offensive on Monte Grappa 'as quickly as possible'. Giardino's 4th Army, initially tasked to await the outcome of the Piave battle, would launch an offensive there to fix the enemy's reserves in the Belluna basin behind it so that they could not be moved to the Piave.[132] Three days later, he changed his mind again. The final directive, sent out on 21 October, altered the timing once more. Both attacks would now take place on the same day, the Monte Grappa attack in the morning and the attack on Vittorio in the afternoon. The exact date for both would be set by the *Comando supremo* according to the state of the river Piave and the weather.[133]

As the *Comando supremo* finalised its plans, military intelligence provided growing reassurance that the odds were moving in Italy's favour. Diaz frequently attended the regular weekly meetings of the ITOs, as did Orlando, and he and his two sub-chiefs maintained close contact with them. Throughout the summer the intelligence service fed the army commander with information about the capabilities of the Austro-Hungarian army from a variety of sources that included agents landed behind the lines by the navy, former prisoners of war (especially Czechs) infiltrated by a special aviation group set up on 1 September, deserters, informers and press sources monitored by the Berne centre and others. In early June, evidence of mutinies in the Austro-Hungarian army came via the Swiss press with a cautionary note attached: it was still possible that an enemy offensive might happen as the government had the means to suppress or limit any disturbances within the army and an ever-watchful Germany stood behind it.[134] In July there were signs that the enemy's army was growing more fragile. According to a Ruthenian deserter, whose evidence was confirmed by others, 'only soldiers of German nationality, [who are] still fanatics, still have any faith in the outcome of the war ... all the other soldiers, including many Hungarians, see unavoidable catastrophe getting ever nearer'. The only nationalities still fighting with any conviction were the Germans and the Croats. Hungarians fighting on the Italian front were increasingly preoccupied with the spectacle of a Russian invasion of Hungary, something the Slavs devoutly hoped would happen.[135]

In September the Austro-Hungarian pacifist offensive, which included leafleting and financing the fringe of the Italian socialist party in the hopes of stimulating a revolution, intensified but Italian counter-espionage and the close monitoring of troop morale by *Servizio P* gave the *Comando supremo* a reassurance that it had not had before Caporetto. For its part, Italy mounted a skilful and sophisticated propaganda offensive targeting the separate sub-nationalities, dropping tens of thousands of leaflets in which Germany was declared responsible for 'the spread of alcoholism [and] pornographic literature, corruption, [and] the destruction of family life', and Hungarian Magyars were told that they were tied to a corpse and that their only hope for salvation was total separation from Austria and the suppression of the Hungarian landowning elite. Whether all this effort had much effect remains somewhat doubtful.[136]

As before Caporetto, there was contradictory intelligence about the possibility of an Austrian offensive in the Trentino – always an alarming prospect after 1916 – and the influx of German troops. Military intelligence concluded cautiously in September that offensive attempts by Austria 'to try to improve their own general situation' with or without German aid could not be ruled out. The Austrian army appeared still to be in good order though provisions were in very short supply. As more evidence about the enemy's internal political and economic situation became available the picture brightened. On 2 October, Diaz, Badoglio and Orlando were told at an ITO meeting that morale in the enemy army was starting to collapse. Although the line army was still strong, in colonel Marchetti's opinion it was 'like a pudding which has a crust of roasted almonds and is filled with cream'. The crust would be hard to break but if a hole was pierced in it and the cream – the reserves – was reached then it would melt away.[137] The collapse of Bulgaria and Turkey, and the arrival of Spanish flu, were likely to undermine the enemy's cohesion yet further.

Evidence that Italy faced an ever-weaker enemy now began to pile up. On 10 October military intelligence learnt that Austro-Hungarian officers did not think they could halt an Italian offensive. Two days later the next meeting of the ITO officers received an analysis by Colonel Marchetti showing that the march battalions of 18-year-olds were arriving at the enemy front with little or no combative spirit. On 17 October they learned that the Austrians knew that an Italian offensive was about to be launched in a few days and had reinforced their old line on the Isonzo in case of retreat. The enemy was indeed well aware that something was brewing. Austrian intercepts picked up urgent messages to the *Comando supremo* about the state of the water in the river Piave, and Austrian military intelligence was following the movement of Italian troops and the preparations being made for action.[138] However the Italians knew that the Austrian army, weakened by troop transfers to Bulgaria and Serbia, was in the grip of dysentery and cholera as well as Spanish flu. On 20 October news arrived of the first revolt of Hungarian troops in Val Sugana, and on the same day the Austrian press announced that the Skoda armaments works had stopped production two days earlier for want of coal.[139]

Logistical preparations for the battle were not helped by a complex and over-bureaucratised chain of command and poor co-ordination: the *Intendenza generale* only established a liaison office at the *Comando supremo* on 14 May 1918. The logistic service also lost 5 per cent of its manpower in July 1918 as a consequence of Diaz's comb-out of the rear areas. On 17 September 1918 the *Comando supremo* instructed army commands to 'prepare minds and organisations for a war of movement' and eleven days later the *Intendenza generale*, still thinking about an offensive in 1919, issued generalised instructions to the support services to study ways of improving communications, methods of transport and the movement of the wounded, given that railways would probably be unusable. Intendance officers in each army were left to identify and solve their own problems with whatever means they had available.[140] One improvement at least was now to hand – mechanised Weiss field ovens, which would mean that fresh bread would be available immediately to front-line troops.

The main task was to amass and distribute munitions, which the logistic services were able to do. However, on 20 October, four days before the battle started, the *Comando supremo* warned that the railways were experiencing 'a serious crisis which is hindering and slowing down military transport', exacerbated by the faster cycle of reusing rolling stock. Everyone was asked to reduce unloading times to a minimum. Measures were taken 'on the hoof' to support the offensive: when, during the battle, first 8th Army and then 4th Army signalled that they were running out of flour and foodstuffs the *Comando supremo* gave priority to trains carrying rations. For the first week (24–30 October) the fact that the battle was taking place in a fairly restricted space helped resupply of the front line, but even so continuous interruption of the bridges over the Piave as a result of the combined effects of flooding and enemy gunfire produced a logistical crisis. Limited but effective use of air supply helped overcome it. Thereafter the intendance services had to supply not only fast-moving columns but also large numbers of prisoners of war and the civil inhabitants of the formerly occupied territories. The last days have been seen by the leading historian of logistics not as a true war of movement but as a steady follow-up by an army that did not want to be burdened with lots of Austrian prisoners.[141]

Despite calling up the 1900 class in March 1918, Diaz was barely able to make up the losses suffered at Caporetto and afterwards (between June and November the army lost 2,000 men a day, mainly to Spanish flu and malaria), so that for the battle of Vittorio Veneto he had at his disposal a field army that was slightly smaller than it had been a year before. Abandoning Cadorna's offensives had reduced casualties: during the eleven months of combat in 1918 168,903 men were killed and wounded (and another 111,613 died from illness), whereas between May and November 1917 killed and wounded amounted to 461,000. To maximise front-line manpower, headquarters staffs at corps level and above were reduced by a quarter, support services above brigade level lost 5 per cent of their numbers and rear echelons were swept of anyone fit for front-line service, yielding another 150,000 men.[142] At the start of October 1918, Diaz's army numbered 79,000 officers (5,000 more than before Caporetto), 2,092,000 other ranks (about the same number) and 312,000 horses (62,000 fewer), together with 2,500 motor cars and 28,000 trucks, motor ambulances and buses. Far from enjoying the three-to-one superiority held to be necessary for a successful attack, he was one division weaker than his opponent.

The weather determined the final decision. The Piave was too high to get across and so on 24 October Giardino's army began the attack on Monte Grappa. Over the next five days vicious fighting cost the Italians 5,000 dead, 20,000 wounded and 3,000 prisoners of war with little ground gained – confirming the Italians' belief that whatever might be happening back in the Empire, Austria–Hungary's front-line troops were still in fighting shape. After two days the flooded river began to go down and during the night of 26/27 October Caviglia's men began to cross. The task of breaking into the Austrian defences fell to the two *Arditi* divisions of Grazioli's *Corpo d'Armata d'Assalto*. Zoppi's orders to his 1st Assault Division were to get on with the job in hand and fight in the way

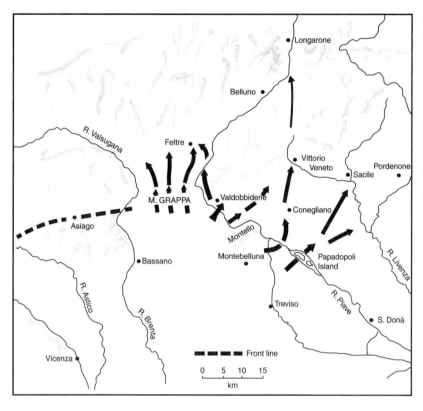

6. Vittorio Veneto

they were accustomed to fight: 'No elaborate manoeuvres ... simplicity and irresistibility ... Of one hundred who set out ten will arrive, but these ten will resolve the situation.'[143] Success for the lightly armed *Arditi* turned on accurate preparation and surprise, neither of which was possible: Zoppi's men only received their orders on 22 October, two days before the battle was due to start. Instead they were going to have to rely on brute force, speed and sheer determination.

Some of Zoppi's men got across the Piave late in the evening of 26 October, but the rest were held up by a combination of high water and Austrian machine-guns. The intention was to link up with Major-General Ernesto De Marchi's 2nd Assault Division crossing a little lower down at Ponte di Priula and drive north and east, but a combination of Austrian artillery and Italian river water delayed De Marchi's crossing for three days. The plan was starting to go awry. A strenuous Austrian counter-attack pushed Zoppi's *Arditi* back and Austrian guns smashed the bridges behind them. For two days they clung on, resupplied by boats and by aircraft dropping boxes of ammunition while new bridges were built at night, enabling Caviglia's VIII Corps for whom they were supposed to be breaking and entering the Austrian lines to cross behind them. By that time XXVIII Corps had two regiments across on the left, XXII Corps was across in the centre but all the bridges behind it had been destroyed, and on the right a combination of machine-gun and artillery fire and a rising river meant VIII Corps could not get across at all. To unlock the door, Caviglia ordered XVIII Corps to get across at Grave di Papadopoli and open the way for his right hand corps.

The British XIV corps had been assigned the task of seizing the island of Grave di Papadopoli and then leapfrogging to the left bank of the Piave. The river at this point was some 2.5 kilometres wide and after heavy rain that began on 14 October the current was running at 16 kilometres an hour. Cavan asked for artillery to support seizing the island twenty-four or twenty-eight hours ahead of the main attack but Caviglia refused on the grounds that this would simply focus Austrian attention and firepower on the attempt. During the night of 23/24 October elements of the British 7th division established a foothold on the top end of the island, while Italian units simultaneously occupied the island of Caserta next to the bottom end. Next day neither could get any further thanks chiefly to heavy rain which made resupply and reinforcement well-nigh impossible. Everything came to a halt that evening when the *Comando supremo* ordered a temporary delay in the main offensive. Over the next two days the troops fought off enemy counter-attacks and took possession of the island while the engineers built bridges and coped with currents twice as fast as they had expected.[144]

The Piave was bridged on 26 October, and with that leverage in his hands, Diaz ordered 10th, 8th and 12th Armies to attack next morning. Over three days 4th and 10th Armies fought bitter battles for Monte Grappa and the *altipiani*, costing them a total during the entire battle of 5,000 dead and 19,000 wounded. In the meantime General Lord Cavan's troops completed their crossing of the Piave and began to push forward, even though neither 3rd Army flanking it on the right nor 8th Army on the left were yet in evidence. By the end of the day Caviglia's 8th Army had put a division across the Piave at Sernaglia, but the two bridgeheads were 10 kilometres apart. French troops of Graziani's 12th Army forced their way across the Piave at Pederobba on 27 October against Austrian artillery fire that repeatedly hit the bridges. Over the next three days, against gradually weakening opposition, French and Italian troops forced their way onto the heights of Valdobbiadene and pushed on to Feltre in support of 4th Army, which was meeting strong resistance on Monte Grappa. Given another corps by Caviglia, Cavan pushed up the east bank of the Piave, forcing the Austrians to fall back and thereby allowing 8th Army to build the bridges it needed to cross the Piave at Ponte di Priula. Caviglia's troops crossed the river early on 29 October to link up with the Sernaglia bridgehead.

On the morning of 28 October Italian military intelligence intercepted a message from Count Julius Andrássy to Robert Lansing, American secretary of state, announcing that Austria–Hungary was ready to agree a negotiated peace and accepted American conditions for negotiating an armistice.[145] Seeing a potential threat to Italy's bargaining position at the upcoming peace negotiations – already somewhat weakened by her earlier inaction – Orlando asked Diaz to antedate the offensive to 24 October. Diaz tartly reminded the premier that he knew the dates of the preparations, that the taking of Grave di Papadopoli was the first act of the battle, that it had been reported in the official communiqué that day (24 October) as a *colpo di mano* solely in order not to call the enemy's attention to it, and that subsequent action had been delayed by bad weather. There was more than enough evidence to back up the facts. Foch had been told of the plans on 10 October, the French liaison officer Colonel Parisot had been briefed during his visit between 26 September and 17 October, and the French General Graziani had been briefed on 10 October.[146] Orlando's telegram, suggesting that the battle of Vittorio Veneto was an extemporisation spatchcocked together to look better than it was, did Italy no favours and started an historical hare that has been running ever since.

On 29 October – the decisive day of the campaign in Austrian eyes – the emperor met with his ministers and concluded that the struggle could not be continued any longer. That night Boroević, whose armies were already in retreat, was ordered to evacuate the area under his command. The combined advance that began that day, exploiting the Austrian retreat, had been made possible by 10th Army's achievements lower down the river. Altogether, the fighting on and across the Piave between 24 and 30 October had cost the Italians 9,500 dead and 20,000 wounded. Rapid movement now became the order of the day as 8th Army drove on Monticano, which it took after hard fighting next day. The Italian armies pursued the retreating Austrians as fast as possible in order to deny them any time in which to organise defences in the narrow Piave valley. On 30 October 1st Assault Division was withdrawn from the battle, embittered at not being allowed a triumphal entry into Vittorio Veneto. The varied experiences of the two *Arditi* divisions were reflected in their battle statistics: 1st Assault Division, some 8,700 strong, suffered

1,172 casualties and took 3,500 prisoners, while 2nd Assault Division took 4,500 prisoners at a cost of only 166 casualties.[147] Vittorio Veneto fell on 30 October to a light force of cavalry and *Bersaglieri* cyclists. 'What's happening is a Caporetto in reverse,' a jubilant Diaz told his wife, 'because now it's a matter of putting the whole enemy army out of action.'[148]

Pursuing the retreating enemy, the British took Sacile on 31 October and closed up to the Livenza river, crossing it next day. In the meantime, with the Austrian centre collapsing, troops of the 8th, 12th and 4th Armies raced towards Feltre and Belluno. On 4 November, the last day of the war, British troops splashed across the Tagliamento. Their role in victory had been of great importance, as the duke of Aosta afterwards acknowledged. 'Without the presence of you and your troops,' he told Cavan, bidding him farewell in January 1919, 'there would have been no Vittorio Veneto.'[149]

Air superiority played an important role in the victory at Vittorio Veneto. Between 25 and 31 October some 650–700 Italian, British and French aircraft faced at least 478 enemy aircraft. They flew a total of 2,533 missions at an average rate of 700 flights a day, shooting down 32 enemy fighters and 11 balloons, dropping 200 tons of bombs, and firing over 300,000 rounds of machine-gun ammunition at enemy troops. Copying a formation they had observed in France in 1916, and had first used at the battle of the Solstice in June, the Italians united 120 aircraft in a mass fighter formation to create a barrier against incursions by enemy planes. Aerial and photographic reconnaissance and artillery spotting were force multipliers for Italian arms. Aircraft dropped food and munitions to troops cut off on the islands at Grave di Papadopoli, as well as deluging the enemy with hundreds of thousands of leaflets.[150]

The two sides had been fairly evenly matched at the start of the battle, 57½ Italian and Allied divisions with 7,700 guns and 1,750 bombards facing 58½ Austrian divisions with 6,000 guns and 1,000 bombards. The guns had played an important part in what was, for the first six days, a battle of attrition: between 24 and 31 October the Italian artillery fired 2,446,000 rounds, half the total available stock and the equivalent of one month's war production. The logistical effort required to fight the battle was commensurate. Moving the troops consumed 9,240 tons of petrol, the equivalent of 637 tons a day, requiring 3,500 wagons. Simply moving the bridging materials took another 3,500 railway wagons. The battle cost the Italians some 37,000 casualties of which perhaps as many as two-thirds were suffered by 4th Army on and around Monte Grappa. Vittorio Veneto was certainly not, as some foreign historians have hinted, a *passeggiata* (promenade). However, once its front line had cracked open the Austrian army rapidly dissolved as starving troops clung to the roofs and doors of trains in a desperate effort to get home. On the morrow of the armistice the Brenner railway line was so thick with the corpses of those who had fallen off that the local authorities had to close it.[151]

Armistice

The first steps towards a cessation of hostilities were taken by both sides in the weeks immediately preceding the start of the battle of Vittorio Veneto. On 4 October the Austrians established a commission at Trento to look into possible armistice conditions. At that moment they were contemplating nothing more punishing than a ceasefire in place. On 13 October, Orlando asked Diaz for ideas about a future armistice. An armistice line was approved next day and Colonel Pariani, who had been seconded to headquarters staff as one of the group working on the armistice, was sent off with it to Versailles. On his return to Rome ten days later he discussed the terms of an armistice with the war minister. Zupelli was inclined not to insist on the Tyrol but believed that for political reasons Trieste and Istria were 'indispensable'. Next day Pariani explained to Orlando, Sonnino and senior naval representatives the *Comando supremo*'s rationale for believing that the only properly defensible border ran along the mountain watershed and down to the Gulf of Quarnero east of Valona. On 27 October Diaz's staff settled the line of occupation to be held once Austria capitulated: it ran from Innsbruck via Villach and Ljubljana to Fiume – the latter added by Pariani.[152]

Once the battle had begun events moved quickly. On 28 October, General Viktor Weber was ordered to reassemble the armistice commission and make contact with the Italian supreme command, and on the same day Boroević signalled that he could no longer rely on even his most disciplined units to stand fast. Later that night the Austrian armies were given orders to withdraw. Next day Vienna indicated that it wanted to move to an armistice and the first Austrian plenipotentiaries turned up at the Italian lines. General Weber arrived to lead the delegation on 30 October, but was not allowed across the line until the *Comando supremo* had given its express agreement at 2030 that evening.

When discussions began in Paris on the armistice terms for Germany and Austria–Hungary on 29 October, Austria–Hungary had already agreed to complete independence for the Czechs and Yugoslavs, and President Wilson had made it clear that she must clear out of all occupied Italian territory. Next day Orlando advised his fellow statesmen that Weber had arrived with authorisation to treat for an armistice on the basis of Wilson's Fourteen Points, though Diaz did not consider him yet fully accredited to do so. He also relayed the content of an intercepted radio message from Emperor Karl requesting an immediate suspension of hostilities on the grounds that a fighting evacuation of the plains would damage the region. Lloyd George leaped at the chance to conclude an armistice with Austria–Hungary before negotiating with Germany, and the assembled diplomats put together a list of terms. It included the demobilisation of a number of enemy divisions, occupation of the line embodied in the Treaty of London, the free movement of Allied troops by road, rail or water, the occupation of key strategic points, and the release of all prisoners of war and allied internees. 'Aren't you going to ask for the Emperor's britches?', Clemenceau reportedly exclaimed when the list finally came to an end.[153]

The Austrian delegation arrived at Villa Giusti, near Padua, early in the evening of 31 October. Motoring there, they thought they had landed in another world: 'The men we see are rosy-cheeked with happy faces; they eat the whitest of bread and sing joyfully. Their equipment is best quality, the horses are fat and well-nourished. Automobiles, motorcycles and guns drawn by motors go to and fro in great numbers, meeting one another every ten yards.'[154] A German delegate sent by Hindenburg attempted to join in but was sent away. Diaz was happy with the terms set that day at Versailles. 'If they accept our conditions, which amount to a true surrender,' he told his wife, 'we can move against Germany through Austria, if the Germans don't give up. If they don't accept then we'll carry on and it will be a disaster for the Austrian army, after which we'll move against Germany wherever it resists.'[155]

Diaz's staff had in fact begun planning for follow-on operations against southern Bavaria, and it was at his express request that the armistice conditions included the right of free Allied movement across Austria. The planners estimated that using four railway lines twenty divisions could be moved by rail to Lindau and Kufstein and another twenty to twenty-five divisions to Salzburg within three weeks. The major problem was the decayed state of the railways on the Venetian plain, which would take two months to repair. Foch simultaneously unveiled his plan for a dual attack on southern Bavaria, using twenty to twenty-five Italian and Allied divisions, and on Saxony using Czech troops. Although concerned about the mounting pressure from Yugoslavia which the army had to face, Diaz telegraphed Orlando on the day that the armistice came into force telling him that the army was readying itself to cross Austria and act against Germany. The German armistice meant that the plan never had to be put into effect. This was probably fortunate because to carry out the troop movements Italy would have needed from her allies 650 railway engines, 15,000 railway wagons, 85,000 trucks and various other vehicles besides, as well as 2,500 tons of coal and 700 tons of petrol a day. The plan was finally discarded in mid December 1918 and the units scheduled to carry it out were demobilised.[156]

At 1000 on 1 November General Badoglio arrived to head the Italian armistice commission with Colonel Pietro Gazzera and Colonel Pariani in tow. In discussion with Badoglio that afternoon Weber, anxious to hasten the moment when the fighting stopped, wanted an immediate cessation of hostilities. Badoglio was immovable – there could be no ceasefire until the armistice was concluded. Pariani, who was unhappy with what had come back from Paris about the surrender of arms and matériel, and who thought the armistice line too vaguely defined, suggested an 'additional protocol'.[157] The Austro-Hungarian high command was momentarily overwhelmed by the severity of the conditions and for a while seemed undecided whether to agree to them or not. Next day, Diaz was instructed to give them forty-eight hours to decide. The original French text arrived at Villa Giusti early that afternoon, along with further instructions that the last moment for their acceptance was midnight on 3/4 November.

Weber wanted to go on with the war, but the Hungarian war minister had sent out orders to all Magyar units on 31 October to lay down their arms. Talks went on long into the night as the Austrian delegation tried to alter the condition that twenty-four hours must elapse after the signing of the armistice before it came into effect – a requirement that was not part of the terms devised at Versailles but something Badoglio held was indispensable if the necessary orders were to get through to Italian troops who were advancing everywhere at full speed.[158] More likely, Badoglio had at the front of his mind the stipulation that the front line in Italy had been defined as that reached by the most advanced Italian and Allied units at the moment that the armistice went into effect. The document, with the protocol appended to it, was finally signed at 1520 that afternoon.

According to the agreement, hostilities were to cease at 1500 hours on 4 November. A brief interlude of complete confusion followed, for which responsibility seems chiefly to lie with the Austrian high command and in particular the chief of staff, General Arz von Straussenburg, who announced at 0200 that same day that armistice terms had been accepted and that all hostilities were to cease immediately. Fifteen minutes later another message annulled the ceasefire order, whereupon the Austrian army commanders protested that the first order had already been distributed and they could not now go back on it. A subsequent message went out to all units that hostilities would cease at 1600 the same day. Different Austrian units were given different times when fighting was to stop. Italian units went on with the war for another twenty-four hours, while their enemies believed that it was over at last. In some places commanders behaved prudently, not risking lives unnecessarily, but in others men died obeying the order to keep the war going for one more day. Austrian units that had maintained their cohesion and kept their weapons passed through the Italians and made it home. Most of them did not: an estimated 300,000 prisoners were taken in the last twenty-four hours.[159] Finally, on 4 November, the guns fell silent. In Padua thousands of jubilant inhabitants mobbed the king's car and many tried to kiss his hands in what was doubtless as much an expression of exhausted relief as it was of patriotic enthusiasm.

Having won her war, Italy now plunged into the complex waters of peacemaking at Versailles. Expectations were high on all sides: diplomats looked for gains that had been unattainable in the continuum of peace that had preceded the conflict; the military, habituated for the first time to being an equal and independent partner in the business of state, cast its net wide as it sought for security in a post-war world; and the toiling masses now sought their reward for years of hardship and loss. Forces that had been roiling just below the surface of Italian politics and society for three and a half years were about to spill out into the open.

7   In the wake of war

Just when we've learned how to make war, the war has ended.
Italian soldiers after the battle of Vittorio Veneto

For all the participants in the war, the transition to peace was a lengthy and difficult process. Every country experienced its own variants of the same general pressures: soldiers keen to get home, politicians concerned about post-war majorities, diplomats under pressure to forge a lasting peace that would solve the ills in the international system and in their own circumstances that had got their countries into the war in the first place. For Italy, the transition from war to peace was particularly difficult. Her perspective on peacemaking was fundamentally out of joint with the 'nationalities principal' that President Woodrow Wilson intended to foster and with the new international order that he proposed to shape, and to make matters more awkward it went along with an increasingly unstable domestic situation The war had sharpened appetites in the foreign and colonial ministries, among the interventionists and nationalists, and amongst the rural and urban working classes. Far from dying down when the fighting formally ended on 4 November 1918, the emotions and desires that it had engendered took on new vigour.

The government in Rome had serious problems to resolve. Something had publicly to be said about the disaster at Caporetto, but if criticisms bit too deeply a conservative officer corps might retreat back to the nineteenth century and focus its loyalty on the throne. At Versailles, Italian diplomats and statesmen were expected to gain the promised territorial rewards and more, enhancing Italy's 'security' in circumstances in which eastern and south-eastern Europe in particular were in a state of apparently uncontrollable flux. At home the country wanted demobilisation, but for technical, political, and military reasons that was no easy matter. The war might be over but its aftermath would shape Italian national life for the next four years and beyond.

Caporetto – the inquest

Caporetto was a disaster whose reverberations resounded throughout the country. The immediate effects were visited on the political Left: the secretary of the socialist party and the director if its newspaper *Avanti!* were swiftly imprisoned. An official enquiry was inevitable, and its outcome was potentially seismic. When Orlando formally presented the idea in December 1917 a parliamentary enquiry was rapidly ruled out in the interest of getting to the bottom of the causes of the defeat – or as near to them as possible – because it was reckoned that the presence of the Judge Advocate General would inhibit witnesses. Instead, a commission of inquiry was established under royal decree and headed by Italy's most senior general, Carlo Caneva.

The commission began its work in January 1918. Over the next eighteen months it interviewed 200 generals, 450 other officers and 350 non-commissioned officers and privates, along with 21 senators, 35 deputies and a number of newspapermen, received 127 private letters (and interviewed nine of the authors), and waded through 200,000 pages of documents. The process of inquiry was neither as comprehensive nor as straightforward as the bare statistics might suggest. The war ministry put pressure on the commission to pronounce on officers it wanted to promote or decorate, and some officers simply refused to turn up to be questioned. The final report was handed to premier Nitti on 24 July 1919 in difficult circumstances. The country was in a state of mounting upheaval and the government had no wish to undermine the *vittoria nazionale*, nor did it want to undervalue the sacrifices of those who had returned alive or those who had died achieving it. Once the report was published a debate began which has continued, with brief interruptions, from that day to this. The basic question, then as now, was whether Caporetto was the outcome of military mistakes or moral collapse.

Caneva and his team concluded that Caporetto had been a military defeat – not a collapse or a military strike, as many people at the time and afterwards were disposed to think – and that its causes were predominantly technical and moral. The technical causes included errors in the conduct of operations, a failure properly to set up defensive lines, and the mishandling of reserves. Moral causes, which had played 'a really effective role in the disaster', derived from command practices and included excessive sackings, bad relations between superior officers and their subordinates, errors in governance, inadequate consideration of the moral well-being of the troops, and a failure to redress inequalities and injustices.[1] Cadorna was held chiefly to blame. His 'coercive tendencies' were damned and so was his inability to distinguish between the multiple causes of defeatism on the one hand and the consequences of 'the mis-government of [his] men' on the other. The command system over which he had presided was roundly castigated, his favouritism in promoting junior officers from his own secretariat criticised, and his 'egocentrism' uncompromisingly condemned. Completely 'lacking in self-criticism', the wider repercussions of his policies and methods which included fostering insincerity, paralysing initiative, discrediting the military hierarchy, spreading a sense of injustice, and generating a fatalistic expectation of the inevitable had entirely escaped him.[2]

A handful of generals were held partially to blame. Capello's personal system of coercion – said in a portion of the draft report later excised to 'match his character' and to be 'almost Carthaginian' – had aggravated the defects of Cadorna's system of governance.[3] He had spent blood prodigally and had not achieved proportionate results. Carlo Porro was culpable for failing to moderate the excessive sackings of officers, for not inquiring into the factors that had depressed the army's morale, and for failing adequately to interpret the politico-military situation. Somewhat bizarrely, his only other failing was in not properly directing the employment of aircraft. Montuori was let off lightly, his shortcomings as substitute commander of 2nd Army going unremarked, and was held partly responsible only for excessive delays in the retreat to the Piave and the loss of some units. Bongiovanni's shortcomings went more or less unremarked, and instead a substantial share of the blame for his ineptitude was heaped on the shoulders of General Cavaciocchi, at fault for not maintaining closer links with the commander of VII Corps and 'making clear [to him] the need for opportune dispositions', thereby making the arrival of reinforcements and the blocking of the enemy's manoeuvre more difficult.[4]

One person was missing from the line-up of guilty men – Pietro Badoglio. Capello had only criticised him to the commission for not having enough reserves available and for losing contact with his units, and in his own submission Badoglio had emphasised the collapse on the left bank of the Isonzo and played down what had happened on his side of the river. There was enough evidence, though, to raise serious questions about his share of the blame. They were never asked – or if they were, the answers were deliberately suppressed.[5] One explanation, popular at the time and afterwards, saw the hand of Freemasonry at work: Caneva, himself a Mason, had saved Badoglio, Montuori and Bongiovanni who were fellow Masons. There were in fact pressing military and political reasons not to put the sub-chief of the general staff in the dock. Diaz needed him – another story had it that when Caneva demanded Badoglio's head, Diaz replied 'If he goes, I go too' – and so, given his undoubted organisational talents, did the army.[6] The committee's conclusions about him smacked of a whitewash, a belief that was given added credibility years later when Senator Paratore revealed that he had been sent by Orlando to see the parliamentary representative on the inquiry, Orazio Raimondo, and had persuaded him to suppress thirteen pages of the report critical of Badoglio.[7] The search for those missing pages – which may never have existed – still goes on.

The socialists and the Giolittian neutralists greeted the report with enthusiasm. *Avanti!* saw it as an enquiry into the Italian *borghesia*: 'All, all responsible, albeit in different ways and to different degrees ... [because they] wanted or accepted the war.' The socialist press trod the fine line between its declaratory anti-militarism and its desire not to alienate the demobilising masses. Catholic papers were inclined to give the military hierarchy the benefit of the doubt and entrust the future reorganisation of the army to it. The nationalist press stuck to its guns, the *Corriere della Sera* affirming that 'socialist and Giolittian defeatism (even if not by means of direct propaganda) was at the root of the moral subsidence of October 1917' and reminding its readers that Italy had after all won an outright victory. An adolescent Fascism was happy to blame Cadorna as the figurehead of the old militarism – 'lots of shootings and not enough to eat' – and laud the *nazione armata*. It too reminded its readers that Italy had in the end won 'a military victory [that is] Roman in kind and scope'.[8] Nitti simply wanted to draw a line under the inquests, and suggested that the nation did too. 'That men made errors, that there was blame, I would dare to say is a matter of indifference to the nation,' he told parliament on 13 September 1919. 'We shall accept responsibility, but we maintain that the enterprise was successful.'[9] A battle of memoirs now began, and aggrieved generals appealed to the Senate to reverse the verdicts passed on them – to no avail. In 1924 Mussolini put the genie of Caporetto back in the bottle as far as contemporary politics were concerned by appointing Cadorna, towards whom he was personally hostile, one of the first two Marshals of Italy together with Armando Diaz.

Problems of peacemaking

Italian diplomats were acutely aware in the last weeks of the war that they needed to sit down at the peace table with a victory in their pockets. Orlando went off to Paris at the beginning of October advised that among other things he had to pressure the *Comando supremo* to expedite the offensive on the Italian front and resist any attempt to change the agreed war aims.[10] Nine days before the battle of Vittorio Veneto began, the

Italian ambassador in Paris warned that it would not displease France 'if Italy were to end the war with a victory like that of the Piave, purely defensive and now somewhat old' as that would make it easier to liquidate the territorial exchanges agreed in April 1915.[11] When a victory duly came, it and Italy's entire war effort were pushed hard and far in support of her peace aims. An extensive list of African territorial wants was founded partly on Italian claims to have brought the war to a victorious end 'against the entire Austro-Hungarian army', and on the somewhat flimsy grounds that Italy had 'contributed' to the Allies' victories in Africa by her possession of Libya.[12] Dalmatia, which had been Venetian until 1797, had been taken by force and now won back – a claim to possession by right of arms in Italian minds.[13] Italy's war was used – and believed – to support a peace programme that was the expression both of ambition and of anxiety. As far as the latter is concerned, Italy's military and political leaders had shared a sense of strategic vulnerability for almost half a century.[14] Now was the moment to assuage appetites and to carve out some security by, as Orlando put it, closing the doors of the house.

Four days after the armistice Sonnino told Colonel House, Wilson's aide and confidant, that the concepts driving Italy in the war that had just ended were 'nationality and independence, but also security', and at least one historian has seen security as his 'supreme objective'.[15] If so, it was an all-embracing and elastic concept that encompassed a good deal, for Sonnino went to Paris determined to press claims that rested on three separate 'rights': those pre-dating the war, those 'born' during it, and those that were a 'necessary consequence' of the post-war situation.[16] The first and third of these 'rights' fed Italy's colonial war aims, which the colonial minister, Gaspare Colosimo, saw primarily as 'valorizing Italy's old [i.e. long-standing] colonial possessions'.[17] His wants stretched from the Arabian peninsula, to which Italy should have economic access, via Kassala in the Sudan to the Jarabub oasis on the Egyptian–Libyan border. They focused on Ethiopia, where Italy needed to recover the position of predominant influence she had lost in 1906 by turning the clock back to the time before the defeat at Adua. Securing the colonial ministry's goal of 'organic unity' of her colonies in the Horn of Africa required getting possession of the British port of Kisimaio (on the basis of a claim going back to 1888) and the French port of Jibuti, which Colosimo regarded as a 'must have'.[18] Sonnino was not much interested in the colonial programme: his chief concern was that it must not compromise Italy's demands in the eastern Mediterranean.

Italy's immediate and long-term security was at stake, and everything was seemingly in play at the peace table in Paris. For the first time the army, long held at arm's length in the formulation of Italy's external policy, had both a place and a voice in the highest counsels of state.[19] It went into the business of geopolitics with a will. Where Sonnino saw past, present and future 'rights', it saw strategic and economic imperatives. Diaz signed up to the African programme and the idea behind it of making Italy the economic master of Ethiopia.[20] So did Badoglio. The war had made the military consequences of Italy's economic weakness all too apparent, and with the army down to ten days' supply of meat at the beginning of January 1919 and the country reduced to coal stocks for only two weeks in March, Badoglio was acutely conscious of the need to secure access to foodstuffs and raw materials. Coal concessions could be secured in China, and grain in the provinces of Konia and Aidin in Asiatic Turkey. 'It would be useless militarily to reinforce our borders if we were not at the same time to make provision to resist independently of the good will of other [powers],' he told Orlando and Sonnino.[21] The army's Turkish ambitions, which it shared with the navy and the foreign office and which were backed by the king, rested on a half-share of Anatolia granted to Italy in the treaty of St Jeanne de Maurienne on 19 April 1917, now declared void, and on the expected partition of Turkey. Weakened by the fact that the Italian army had played no part in the defeat of the Ottoman empire, they were effectively extinguished by the mandates system created for former Turkish possessions and by the outcome of the Greco-Turkish war in 1922, though plans were still being laid for a military invasion several years later.[22]

The army had strong views on Italy's land frontiers. Diaz regarded possession of the Brenner Pass, which everyone agreed was ethnically German, and the southern Tyrol as essential for future security against Germany (which meant primarily Austria). The country could defend itself with a weak eastern frontier 'but with the Brenner passes in enemy hands it was indefensible,' he told the cabinet.[23] The army was less interested in Dalmatia than the civilians and the navy. A study prepared for Cadorna in February 1915 had excluded occupying it on the grounds that extending Italy's defensive lines that far would require major resources, and on Boxing Day 1918 Diaz, who saw little strategic value in the region, proposed ceding it in exchange for Fiume.[24] Admiral Thaon di Revel, naval chief of staff, refused to consider doing so. Yugoslavia, newborn and showing every sign of a healthy and even insatiable appetite, posed fresh strategic threats to add to traditional ones. Her push up to Klagenfurt would mean that a stretch of the Vienna–Udine railway line would run through her territory, a prospect that alarmed Badoglio. The creation of a corridor connecting a Yugoslavia north of the Drava with a Czecho-Slovakia south of the Danube was even more threatening. The Czechs sympathised with Yugoslavian aspirations to Fiume – which, along with Trieste and Istria, Badoglio believed 'are our territories' – and if allowed this frontier they could intervene on Belgrade's behalf. Beyond this lay the spectre of economic and military union of the two states, and then complete fusion. If Czecho-Slovakia and Yugoslavia united they would, the deputy chief of staff warned, be 'a force more dangerous to us than the union of German Austria and Hungary, two weak states, would be'.[25]

Woodrow Wilson was prepared to allow Italy the Brenner and the southern Tyrol, but neither he nor the other allies were willing to agree to Italy's broader demands, embodied in the formula 'the London Pact plus Fiume' with which she entered into negotiations. The British thought Italy's policy towards her eastern neighbours 'perfectly insane' and saw in her demand for Dalmatia an outright rejection of the idea of national self-determination, and Clemenceau thought her claim to Fiume, which according to the Pact of London was destined to go to the kingdom of Croatia, 'an absurdity'.[26] Orlando and (to a lesser extent) Sonnino were ready to try some backstairs bargaining to get Fiume, but coalescing forces ruled out anything smacking of the 'old diplomacy'. The Yugoslavs demanded Istria, Fiume, Dalmatia and the islands along the eastern Adriatic coast, and were backed by France. Woodrow Wilson favoured Yugoslavia, partly on the 'nationalities' principal and partly out of fear that if the Slavs felt they had been unjustly dealt with 'that would make the abyss unbridgeable and open the road to Russian [i.e. Bolshevik] influence'.[27] On the Italian side, an intransigent Admiral Thaon di Revel, with the king behind him, presided over the navy's seizure of ports and islands along the length of the Adriatic from Trieste in the north to Durazzo in the south. Vittorio Emanuele III fired off letters to Orlando supporting Thaon's programme and the demand for Fiume, and warned the premier that the country would take it very badly if its 'just aspirations' were not met.[28]

In the end the peace process gave Italy some of the things she wanted, denied her some things she could fairly claim, and left her with several things she did not want. The *terra irredenta* on the northern frontier was recovered. Austria–Hungary, Italy's traditional enemy, was destroyed as a military power, but as a consequence her empire was broken up and replaced with a power vacuum in the Danube basin and a unified Slav state which threatened to dominate the Balkans and spread its tentacles yet wider. Istria was partitioned and Fiume was made a free city. Zara and four islands off the Adriatic coast went to Italy, and the rest of Dalmatia to Yugoslavia. The western Allies gave themselves the mandates to former German colonies in Africa, disregarding Article XIII of the Pact of London which promised Italy fair compensation if Great Britain or France assumed title to any of them. Italian troops landed at

Fig. 16 Orlando, Lloyd George, Clemenceau and Woodrow Wilson at Versailles

Smyrna in May 1919, backing aspirations in Asia Minor which the king also supported. It was an action which did country more harm than good, reinforcing the impression left by Fiume that she was a greedy imperialist power. The Italian occupation of Anatolia lasted, with successive reductions in size, until May 1922 when the garrison was withdrawn to Rhodes as a result of the Greco-Turkish war. The peace of Lausanne in 1923 ended all foreign claims to Anatolia.

Initial Italian demands for a mandate in Albania were reduced to Valona and its immediate hinterland in June 1920, but proved to be militarily unsustainable in the face of mounting nationalist agitation. As the army withdrew towards the coast small garrisons were overwhelmed and soldiers shot. The local commander, General Piacentini, supported by Badoglio, wanted to bomb Albanian bands forming up at Tirana and Elbasan to support the insurrection in the south, but the civilian war minister, Ivanoe Bonomi, squashed the idea. With malaria taking its toll of the defenders, and strikes and demonstrations in Italy against sending more troops there, a pact was agreed with the Tirana government on 2 August 1920 and the Italians left.[29]

Nitti claimed that Italy's frontiers were now more secure than those of any other European nation including France.[30] If that was true, it was also true that what lay beyond them, geographically and temporally, was insecure and uncertain. Italy's diplomats had not got Italy what they had gone on record as determined to get her, largely as a consequence of their having played a weak hand badly. Her soldiers, who had put her in a position to hope for something better, were slandered by Allied leaders: Clemenceau suggested that the figure of 500,000 Italian war dead should not be taken 'too literally', and Lloyd George claimed that when compared to the experiences of the British, the French and the Americans, 'the Italians have no idea what the fighting meant'.[31] In October 1918, D'Annunzio had told the public that Italy's victory must not be 'mutilated', in December, Thaon di Revel had warned of the possibility that it would be, and now Orlando and Sonnino told Italians that it had been. In doing so, they were storing up a good deal of trouble for the future.

Demobilisation

Returning Italy to a peacetime state was a technically complex process made the more difficult because of the external and internal political issues that unavoidably impacted upon it. The bureaucratic difficulties arose because there existed not one army to send back to its homes, but two: the field army under the control of the *Comando supremo* and the territorial militia that came under the jurisdiction of the war minister. The fact that the colonial ministry had a share of responsibility for the army in Libya was a further complication.

International politics acted as a brake on a process that could not happen fast enough for the soldiers and their families. Although armistices were signed with Austria–Hungary and Germany in November 1918, the danger that the war might be reignited could not be ignored. American troops continued to arrive in France until April 1919, and at the inter-Allied council Italy was warned of the need to slow demobilisation in order to be able to act as a counterweight in the event of a renewed German war. Additionally, Italy now faced an unstable situation on and beyond her borders which necessitated the maintenance of a substantial military capability. As well as confronting intransigent Serbs, Croats and Slovenes who were out to forge a new multi-ethnic state out of the wreckage of the pre-1914 world, and needing possibly to defend with force her newly voiced claim to Fiume, she had overhanging military commitments in Albania and Macedonia. Shortly her military footprint would spread yet wider. As 1918 ended Italian troops were occupying Bulgaria, and in February 1919 an Italian brigade entered Constantinople following pressure from the Italian foreign ministry, which also wanted Italy to occupy Thrace. For Italy, it has been suggested, 'the First World War had not in fact ended but had spread along the east margins of Europe in a vast arc running from the Balkans to Anatolia'.[32]

At close of hostilities, the army in the field numbered 81,867 officers and 2,150,919 men. By the year's end that had fallen to 70,812 officers and 1,646,096 men. The officers and men of the oldest classes (1874–84) were released in four blocs between 5 November and 28 December 1918, along with those physically unable to withstand the stresses of war, soldiers from the invaded provinces and those with pressing family or economic needs. In all 25,000 officers and 1,176,300 non-commissioned officers and men were discharged. One-third of the total force had been released, but only 44 per cent belonged to the field army; the remainder were militarised workers and territorial militia.[33] With no clear plan there was bureaucratic chaos from the start: soldiers returning to their homes received neither material nor psychological assistance (though the latter would have been somewhat in advance of the times), and discharge certificates and pension papers took months to come through.

In framing policy the war minister, General Zupelli, had to take into account the fact that the path to the future was far from clear. At one extreme national armies might be abolished and a League of Nations force created, and at the other Italy might need a stronger national army because of the insecurity of Europe's new frontiers. He had also to consider the needs of domestic reconstruction: not only had the army to remain strong enough to enforce the armistice conditions and be able to face 'the very unlikely but not impossible' resumption of hostilities, but it also had to take account of the needs of civil society which required a faster release of officers who, because of their backgrounds and education, must play a prominent part in the nation's economic and social regeneration.[34] At home, demands for action gathered pace. The socialists called for immediate demobilisation and pardons for all those condemned for political and military crimes, and the interventionist press too wanted fast demobilisation but also and potentially contradictorily a policy of force, especially where Yugoslavia was concerned. Acting on behalf of an evidently concerned general staff, Badoglio told the press that demobilisation was necessarily slow because of problems in the Adriatic and on the eastern frontier, the growing acuteness of the Fiume question, and a mounting feeling that the Allies were not going to support Italy's peace aims. The pace of releases could be speeded up after the signing of the peace treaty and agreement on frontiers as long as peace policy did not follow the 'irresponsibles' who wanted all of Dalmatia down to the Bocche di Cattaro.[35]

On 18 January 1919, four days after Badoglio's interview was published, Zupelli was sacked. His departure seems to have been triggered by what was for the Italian army a perennial issue – the maintenance of public order. Zupelli wanted the field army demobilised ahead of the territorial army, which the minister controlled and which was the last resort in the event of public disorder. Diaz wanted the territorials demobilised first because of the need to keep a fighting force in being.[36] Zupelli was replaced as war minister by General Caviglia. Much revered throughout the army for his concern for the rank and file, Caviglia was probably appointed as much to reassure a public opinion which thought that the army was dragging its heels as for his intrinsic talents. In fact he quickly showed himself to be an improvement on his predecessor, setting up a special demobilisation office inside the war ministry and releasing officers belonging to the classes up to 1885 – up to now only officers belonging to classes before 1877 (i.e. over 62 years of age) had been allowed to go.

Foch was worried about the continued existence of a 700,000-strong German army, and told the Supreme War Council as much on 24 January 1919. Itself reluctant to release any more men until the international situation was clearer, the *Comando supremo* undertook to keep thirty-one divisions in being until 1 April and to suspend the release of the 1885–8 classes. It kept to the spirit but not the letter of the agreement. In February 1919 the class of 1900 was demobilised, creating discontent in older classes still in uniform some of whom had been under arms for nine years. In that and the following month the 1885, 1886 and 1887 classes were released. By the end of March 1919 2,000,000 men had been sent home, but roughly the same number were still under arms. At that point Caviglia, always aware of public feeling and pushing demobilisation as hard as he could, had to give way to Diaz and Badoglio, whose concerns were with the politico-military exigencies facing the army.

Tensions were now rising over Fiume and possibility of conflict there began to loom ever larger. On 24 April the Italian delegation came back from Paris with the news that the Allies were not prepared to endorse Italy's claim to the city. The army now faced a mounting irredentist clamour and the possibility of a test of force with Yugoslavia. On 6 May the delegation returned to Paris and tension temporarily declined. The possibility that the army might have to use force did not, however, and the likelihood that it would have to intervene in Carinthia to prevent a clash between Austria and Yugoslavia became a reality when, on 6 June, Yugoslav forces occupied Klagenfurt. The Italians sent in two brigades and the Yugoslavs withdrew. At the same time a general strike broke out in Rome, accompanied by absenteeism from work in Milan and elsewhere. An anxious government pulled seven brigades out of the war zone and relocated them to Rome, Milan, Turin, Piacenza and Emilia. Orlando asked Foch for fifty light tanks to back them up, but did not get them.

International and domestic exigencies put demobilisation on hold for three months. Abroad, Italian troops were spread across Europe and Asia. There were still 54,000 men in Albania, 24,000 in Dalmatia, 4,000 in the Dodecanese, 40,000 in Macedonia, 10,000 in Asia Minor, 500 in Palestine, 71,000 in Libya, 1,000 in Eritrea, 10,000 in the Rhineland and small contingents on the Barents Sea, in Siberia, and at Murmansk. Yet another task appeared in 1919 when Italian troops deployed to Czecho-Slovakia. At home, Italy was in the grip of what became known as the *biennio rosso*. Demands for social and economic reforms, some stimulated by wartime changes and others dammed up by the authorities during the conflict, were sharpened by inflation and a steep rise in food prices. Agrarian agitation fused with industrial strife. In the south, ex-servicemen's associations took leading roles in the occupation of vast managed estates, and in central and northern Italy the socialist *Federterra* organisation led agricultural strikes which peaked in the summer of 1920. In the cities the new industrial proletariat, again led by socialists, tried unsuccessfully to carry over and extend the wartime factory grievance committees. In September 1920 the *biennio rosso* reached its climax with the occupation of the factories. Thereafter, undermined both by failure to achieve its demands and by recession, labour militancy deflated. The army, tradition-ally the force of last resort, was in an unsettled state: in June 1920 military units in Ancona mutinied when told they were transferring to Albania. In this time of troubles the *Carabinieri* were expanded, reaching a strength of 60,000.

On 11 June 1919, the Orlando government decided to withdraw all Italian troops from the Balkans in July save for one regiment which would remain at Constantinople. Caviglia was able to revive demobilisation, and eight days later he ordered the release of the class of 1888. The Orlando government fell the same day. Orlando had wanted an army over 300,000 strong – more than Italy had ever had in peacetime – primarily for policing duties it has been suggested.[37] His successor, Francesco Nitti, headed a government committed to hastening demobilisation in order to reduce costs. There were to be no more expeditions overseas and many of the units stationed abroad would return home. Only in Anatolia, where Italy hoped to find 'compensation for the disappointments we have experienced in the solution of other questions', did the occupation forces expand.[38]

314 In the wake of war

Although Nitti had faith in Diaz and believed he recognised the need for rapid demobilisation, he did not share the soldiers' ongoing preoccupation with the Yugoslav threat. 'Demobilization cannot seriously proceed as long as the soldiers claim they need a large number of divisions ready for Yugoslav aggression,' he told his foreign minister. 'They appear respectful but are rather obstructionist.'[39] Caviglia was anything but obstructionist. Under his direction, government support was at last provided for men returning to civilian life. The rank and file were given grants of 100 lire for first year of war, and 50 lire for each successive year plus an additional 50 lire for non-commissioned officers; aid to families was extended for ninety days; parcels of clothing were handed out (though stocks ran out and had to be replaced with money); and travel home was free. Officers naturally did rather better: two months' salary for the first year of war and one month's for each successive year, plus a 250-lire clothing allowance. The release of university students was accelerated, but officers were released more slowly and from the older classes, at least to begin with.

A moment of high tension occurred on 20–21 July 1919 when Italy joined in an international general strike. Thirteen brigades were recalled in case of trouble but the occasion passed without incident. The pause in demobilisations ended that same month when the class of 1889 was released, and over the next four months the classes of 1890, 1891, 1892, 1893, 1894, 1895 and 1896 followed. The logic of releasing classes consecutively was obvious, but it led to unequal treatment and dissatisfaction: because of the Libyan war some members of the 1889–93 classes had served nine years by the time they were able to take off their uniforms. By the end of the year, there were 490,000 men left in the army.[40] Category I men of the class of 1897, called up in September 1916, were only released in June 1920, having served for almost four years. Not until 1921 was the army fully demobilised.

Only at the end of November 1919 was the danger from the east deemed by Diaz and Badoglio to have subsided. That was by no means the only problem the army had to be ready for. With frustrations mounting among the nationalist Right, there was always the likelihood that overenthusiastic junior officers might do something foolish – as indeed they did. On 24 September, four officers with a few armoured cars seized the Dalmatian port of Trau and held it for a few hours until an Italian naval force arrived and shepherded them back to the Italian lines. Twelve days earlier, as Italian units garrisoning Fiume were being withdrawn in advance of the creation of an inter-Allied military commission which was to run the city, a group of a thousand or so 'volunteers' led by Gabriele D'Annunzio and including soldiers and *Arditi* occupied the city.

The army, Fiume and the advent of Fascism

The post-war Italian crisis, in the words of one of its historians, 'aroused new forces against which the traditional liberal equilibrium was powerless'.[41] Men newly out of uniform and men still in it were one of the components of those forces and contributed to the crisis. Ex-soldiers returned home to find themselves without employment: in Ferrara in early 1919, a third of 7,000 returning soldiers found they had no jobs. Bad feelings smouldered as they and many others contrasted their position with that of the *imboscati* who had avoided serving at the front and stayed comfortably ensconced in factories and offices that now had no need of pre-war employees. The Nitti government, swamped by thousands of ongoing criminal proceedings left over from the war and burdened with the costs of tens of thousands of military prisoners, passed a general amnesty for crimes committed during the war, including evading call-up, which understandably angered many ex-soldiers and their families. It was a gift to the nationalist–Fascist Right, who hung the label 'the deserters' president' around Nitti's neck.

Ex-soldiers were involved in strikes, demonstrations and land seizures up and down the country, but none matched the *Arditi* for causing trouble. Their wartime divisional commander, Grazioli, recommended their disbandment in November 1918 on the grounds that otherwise it would be 'extremely difficult for anyone to contain their unruly and exuberant nature and avoid deplorable infractions of discipline and perhaps crimes ...'.[42] Even when demobilised, they would prove a powerful force for disorder. Orlando and Nitti wanted them dissolved, but Caviglia kept one division in being (saying afterwards that it was as a check on demobilised and politicised *Arditi*) and his successor followed suit. The *Arditi* set up a National Association and its Milan section engaged enthusiastically in the Fascist *squadrismo* of 1920–1 as the Right's counteroffensive followed the collapse of the Left's *biennio rosso*. Although the National Association publicly distanced itself from Mussolini in July 1921, requiring anyone who was a member of the *fasci di combattimento* to resign, ex-*Arditi* were and remained among the most active and savage members of the gangs that helped Mussolini to power.[43]

Nationalist extremism was actively or tacitly encouraged by generals who were 'disposed for any adventure, from anti-Yugoslav provocations to civil war'. The *oltranzisti* ('ultra') generals, who included the duke of Aosta, Giardino, Grazioli and Pecori Giraldi, and who had the support of many of their subordinates, were a threat to the internal cohesion of the army and to the relationship between it and the country.[44] A line was crossed when, on 15 April 1919, a nationalist mob that included officers in uniform destroyed the offices of the socialist *Avanti!* newspaper. As Nicola Tranfaglia has put it, 'the army, unlike what had always happened in the past, had openly taken part in a political dispute in which "patriots" confronted "bolsheviks"'.[45] Tacit encouragement at the top of the army and activism lower down were both very evident when D'Annunzio and his followers seized Fiume on 12 September 1919.

President Nitti, who was well aware of the rising tension in the city but underrated the complicity and tolerance of many of the generals, did no more than dissolve 3rd Army, stationed in the region, and place its commander Aosta under the authority of the reliable General Di Robilant. Badoglio, who was approached by the man financing the venture in late July, refused to join in but did not tell Nitti. When D'Annunzio acted, total confusion ensued. Men from Zoppi's 1st *Arditi* division, ordered to stop him, joined forces with him instead. Demobilised officers and sailors joined in and when senior officers tried to stop them the impression got about that they were actually supporting the action. Supposedly secure units went over to the secessionists and bewildered local and regional commanders tried to work out whether the government secretly supported D'Annunzio or not. By the end of the month he was estimated to have 285 officers and 4,700 men at his disposal.

In the circumstances the best the military could do was to throw a blockading cordon around the city. Badoglio, still sub-chief of the general staff, was made extraordinary military commissioner for Venezia Giulia and given authority over all military commands in the region. Nitti expected him to act 'with all your usual energy', but in fact Badoglio had some sympathy for the rebels – on the day after the seizure of the city he told Nitti that D'Annunzio was 'the new Garibaldi' – and counselled patience not military action, using the widespread support for D'Annunzio and the possibility of local clashes and a rising in Trieste to justify his policy.[46] More units went over to the secessionists and Badoglio's attempts to negotiate their departure failed, though they did take some of the heat out of the situation. It was not resolved until late the following year. On 12 November 1920 the Treaty of Rapallo settled the eastern frontier. With the security of Trieste and Istria assured Italy renounced claims to Dalmatia except for city of Zara, and Fiume became a free city. Defections of soldiers and sailors still continued and eventually, after the navy refused to bombard the city, the army launched a mass frontal attack on 24 December. Initially it made little progress, but after a pause for Christmas Day and then several days of fighting D'Annunzio announced his resignation, triggering negotiations that concluded on 31 December 1920.[47] Together the solution to the Fiume problem and the fixing of the eastern frontiers allowed the army to make further manpower savings of 120,000 men.

Fiume was an event of huge importance in Italian civil–military relations – and Nitti knew it. 'For the first time,' he told the chamber of deputies the day after D'Annunzio and his followers seized the city, 'albeit for idealistic aims, sedition has penetrated the army.'[48] A conspiracy leading to a planned coup with the intention of overturning government and installing a nationalist dictatorship with tacit military backing, it was in many ways the forerunner of the March on Rome in October 1922. The army had not crossed the Rubicon to carry out a political *pronunciamiento*, nor would it do so in the twenty-two months before Mussolini came to power. But on the night of 23/24 October 1922, Diaz told the king that while the army would do its duty if ordered to stop the Fascists it would be better not to ask it to do so. In that moment, the military signalled its complete loss of faith in the political structures of Liberal Italy and in the politicians who had first got them into the war and then lost the peace.

Notes

NOTES TO INTRODUCTION

1 Winston S. Churchill, *The World Crisis 1911–1918* (London: New English Library, 1968 [abridged edn. first published 1931]), vol. II, p. 825.

2 Mario Isnenghi and Giorgio Rochat, *La Grande Guerra 1914–1918* (Milan: La Nuova Italia, 2000), p. 534. 'Perhaps contempt remains deep rooted,' Professor William Philpott has recently suggested in noting the failure of two recent studies of France's strategy and policy in the Great War to pay any attention to her Italian ally: William Philpott, 'France's forgotten victory', *Journal of Strategic Studies* vol. 34 no. 6, December 2011, 909.

3 For examples see (or rather don't see): Richard Wall and Jay Winter, eds., *The Upheaval of War: Family, Work and Welfare in Europe 1914–1918* (Cambridge: Cambridge University Press, 1988); Jay Winter and Jean-Louis Robert, *Capital Cities at War: Paris, London, Berlin 1914–1919* (Cambridge: Cambridge University Press, 1997); Roger Chickering and Stig Forster, eds., *Great War, Total War: Combat and Mobilization on the Western Front 1914–1918* (Cambridge: Cambridge University Press, 2000).

4 Gian Enrico Rusconi, 'L'azzardo del 1915: Come l'Italia decide l'intervento nella Grande Guerra', in Johannes Hürter and Gian Enrico Rusconi, eds., *L'entrata in guerra dell'Italia nel 1915* (Bologna: Il Mulino, 2005), p. 61; Holger Afflerbach, 'Da alleato a nemico. Cause e consequenze dell'entrata in Guerra dell'Italia nel Maggio 1915', in *ibid.*, pp. 75, 89, 90–4, 99; Denis Mack Smith, *Italy and its Monarchy* (New Haven CT: Yale University Press, 1989), p. 313.

5 Walter L. Adamson, 'The impact of World War I on Italian political culture', in Aviel Roshwald and Richard Stites, eds., *European Culture in the Great War: The Arts, Entertainment and Propaganda, 1914–1918* (Cambridge: Cambridge University Press, 1999), p. 308.

6 Jere Clemens King, *Generals and Politicians: Conflict between France's High Command, Parliament and Government, 1914–1918* (Westport CT: Greenwood, 1971); Arthur Conte, *Joffre* (Paris: Editions Olivier Orban, 1991).

7 David R. Woodward, *Lloyd George and the Generals* (London: Associated University Presses, 1983), pp. 221–81; David French, *The Strategy of the Lloyd George Coalition 1916–1918* (Oxford: Clarendon Press, 1995), pp. 148–70.

8 Guy Pedroncini, 'Trois maréchaux, trois stratégies?', *Guerres mondiales et conflits contemporains*, année 37 no. 145, January 1987, 45–62.

9 Gary Sheffield and John Bourne, eds., *Douglas Haig: War Diaries and Letters 1914–1918* (London: Weidenfeld & Nicolson, 2005), p. 178 (8 January 1916).

10 On lesson learning, see Paddy Griffith, *Battle Tactics of the Western Front: The British Army's Art of Attack, 1916–18* (New Haven CT: Yale University Press, 1994). For recent correctives to the literature it presaged, see Jonathan Boff, 'Combined arms during the Hundred Days campaign, August–November 1918', *War in History* vol. 17 no. 4, November 2010, 459–78; Jim Beach, 'Issued by the General Staff: Doctrine writing at British GHQ', *War in History* vol. 19 no. 4, November 2012, 464–91.

11 Leonard V. Smith, *Between Mutiny and Obedience: The Case of the French Fifth Infantry Division during World War I* (Princeton NJ: Princeton University Press, 1994), *passim*.

NOTES TO CHAPTER 1

1 Giorgio Candeloro, *Storia dell'Italia moderna*, vol. VII, *La crisi di fine secolo e l'età giolittiana* (Milan: Feltrinelli,1974), p. 132.

2 Antonino Répaci, *Da Sarajevo al "maggio radioso": L'Italia verso la prima guerra mondiale* (Milan: Mursia,1985), p. 41.

3 For a helpful list of components of 'military culture' in general, see Isabel V. Hull, *Absolute Destruction: Military Culture and the Practices of War in Imperial Germany* (Ithaca NY: Cornell University Press, 2005), p. 98.

4 'Arte Garibaldina', *L'esercito italiano*, 1 November 1911.

5 Nicola Marselli, *Gli avvenimenti del 1870–71* (Turin, 1873), vol. I, pp. 139–40. On Marselli, see also Piero Pieri, *Guerra e politica negli scrittori italiani* (Milan: Ricciardi, 1955), pp. 275–97.

6 Nicola Labanca, 'I programmi dell'educazione morale del soldato: Per uno studio sulla pedagogia militare nell'Italia liberale', *Esercito e Città dall'Unità agli anni trenta: Convegno nazionale di studio*, (Perugia: Deputazione di Storia Patria per l'Umbria, 1989), pp. 521–36; Angelo Visentin, 'Esercito e società nella pubblicistica militare dell'ultimo secolo', *Rivista di storia contemporanea* vol. 16 no. 1, 1987, 31–58.

7 Bernardino Farolfi, 'Dall'antropometria militare alla storia del corpo', *Quaderni Storici* vol. 42, 1979, 1056–91.

8 John Gooch, *Army, State and Society in Italy, 1870–1915* (London: Macmillan, 1989), pp. 13–14, 19–23.

9 Piero Del Negro, *Esercito, stato, società* (Bologna: Capelli, 1979), pp. 230–1, 239; Virgilio Ilari, *Storia del servizio militare in Italia*, vol. II, *La "Nazione Armata" 1870–1918* (Rome: Rivista Militare, 1990), p. 360. Del Negro and Ilari differ over Sardinia, the former putting it in the 'lowest attendances' category while the latter puts it in the group of 'minimal absences', possibly due to their covering different time periods.

10 Del Negro, *Esercito, stato, società*, pp. 218, 222; Amedeo Tosti, *Storia dell'esercito italiano (1861–1936)* (Milan: Istituto per gli Studi di Politica Internazionale, 1942), p. 124.

11 'La politica militare italiana', *L'esercito italiano*, 26 February 1913; 'La ferma triennale in Italia', *L'esercito italiano*, 6 June 1913. For more substantial

arguments against three-year service from both the conservative Right and the liberal Left, see Gooch, *Army, State and Society*, pp. 128–9.

12 Giorgio Rochat and Guilio Massobrio, *Breve storia dell' esercito italiano dal 1861 al 1943* (Turin: Einaudi, 1978), p. 115.

13 Candeloro, *Storia dell'Italia moderna*, vol. VII, p.234

14 See the figures and tables in David Stevenson, *Armaments and the Coming of War: Europe 1904–1914* (Oxford: Oxford University Press, 1996), pp. 2, 4, 5, 6, 8.

15 Umberto Levra, *Il colpo di Stato della borghesia: La crisi politica del fine secolo in Italia 1898/1900* (Milan: Feltrinelli, 1975), *passim*.

16 Gooch, *Army, State and Society*, pp. 118–19, 128, 136.

17 Fiorenza Fiorentino, *Ordine pubblico nell'Italia giolittiana* (Rome: Carecas, 1978), pp. 67–8 fn.4.

18 'La questione delle truppe in servizio di p.s.', *L'esercito italiano*, 17 August 1910.

19 Emilio De Bono, *Nell'esercito nostro prima della guerra* (Milan: Mondadori, 1931), p. 372; Vincenzo Caciulli, 'Gli ufficiali italiani e i trasferimenti di guarnigione: Nota per una ricerca', in *Esercito e Città dall'Unità agli anni trenta*, pp. 169–83.

20 Eugenio De Rossi, *La vita di un ufficiale italano sino alla guerra* (Milan: Mondadori, 1927), p. 182.

21 Gooch, *Army, State and Society*, pp. 125, 129, 135–6.

22 F. De Chaurand de Ste Eustache, *Come l'esercito italiano entrò in guerra* (Milan: Mondadori, 1929), pp. 330–1.

23 T.N.A. Slade to War Office, 14 November 1888. F.O. 45/603.

24 Piero Del Negro, 'Villafranca: La leggenda di un "Re nazionale"' in *Esercito, stato, società*, pp. 71–124.

25 Jonathan Marwil, *Visiting Modern War in Risorgimento Italy* (New York: Palgrave Macmillan, 2010), pp. 192–210, 213–14, 217–20.

26 Silvana Patriarca, *Italian Vices: Nation and Character from the Risorgimento to the Republic* (Cambridge: Cambridge University Press, 2010), pp. 57–8.

27 John Whittam, *The Politics of the Italian Army* (London: Croom Helm, 1977), p. 99.

28 Intervento alla Camera, 30 June 1887: Mario Montanari, *Politica e strategia in cento anni di guerre italiane*, vol. II, Part I, *Le guerre d'Africa* (Rome: Ufficio Storico dello Stato Maggiore dell'Esercito, 1999), p. 93.

29 Giorgio Candeloro, *Storia dell'Italia moderna*, vol. VI, *Lo sviluppo del capitalismo e del movimento operaio* (Milan: Feltrinelli, 1970), p. 305.

30 AUSSME, Memorie sulla prima spedizione d'Africa del generale Tancredi Saletta, pp. 3–4. L7 racc. 9.

31 Gooch, *Army, State and Society*, pp. 74–5.

32 Ricotti to Mancini, 7 April 1885: Montanari, *Le guerre d'Africa*, p. 129.

33 Angelo Del Boca, *Gli italiani in Africa orientale dall'unità alla marcia su Roma* (Bari: Laterza, 1976), pp. 221, 240–2.

34 Robilant to Genè, 18 February 1887: Montanari, *Le guerre d'Africa*, pp. 172–3.

35 Ministero della Guerra, *Storia militare della Colonia Eritrea* (Rome: Comando del Corpo di Stato Maggiore Ufficio Storico, 1935–6), vol. I, pp. 307–15.

36 Bertolè-Viale to Crispi, 3 January 1889: Del Boca, *Gli Italiani in Africa orientale*, p. 320; Crispi to Bertolè-Viale, 6 January 1889: *Storia militare della Colonia Eritrea* vol. I, p. 190.
37 Del Boca, *Gli italiani in Africa orientale*, pp. 366–7.
38 Crispi to Orero, 30 January 1890; Crispi to Orero, 2 February 1890; Orero to Bertolè-Viale, 4 February 1890: Montanari, *Le guerre d'Africa*, p. 204.
39 Rudinì to Gandolfi, 18 February 1892: *ibid.*, p. 207.
40 On the Treaty of Wichale (Uccialli), see Harold G. Marcus, *The Life and Times of Menelik II: Ethiopia 1844–1913* (Oxford: Oxford University Press, 1975), pp. 127–34; Sven Rubenson, *The Survival of Ethiopian Independence* (London: Heinemann, 1976), pp. 389–92.
41 Domenico Farini, *Diario di fine secolo* (Rome: Bardi, 1962), vol. I, p. 366 (15 December 1893).
42 Note by Mocenni, 2 July 1894: Gooch, *Army, State and Society*, p. 82.
43 AUSSME, N.1816, Primerano to Mocenni, 14 July 1894. L13/b.119.
44 Gooch, *Army, State and Society*, pp. 76, 83.
45 Blanc to Baratieri, 1 February 1895: Montanari, *Le guerre d'Africa*, p. 224.
46 Oreste Baratieri, *Memorie d'Africa (1892–1896)* (Turin: Bocca, 1898), p. 183.
47 Salsa to his brother, 2 May 1895, 16 July 1895; Salsa to his mother, 6 February 1896: Emilio Canevari and Giorgio Commisso, *Il generale Tommaso Salsa e le sue campagne coloniali* (Milan: Mondadori, 1935), pp. 259–60, 261–4, 282.
48 Gooch, *Army, State and Society*, p. 85. On the question of the order to Toselli, see Montanari, *Le guerre d'Africa*, p. 241 fn.3.
49 Del Boca, *Gli italiani in Africa orientale*, pp. 607–8; Gooch, *Army, State and Society*, pp. 87–8.
50 Crispi to Baratieri, 25 February 1896: Gooch, *Army, State and Society*, p. 89.
51 Del Boca, *Gli italiani in Africa orientale*, p. 646; Gooch, *Army, State and Society*. pp. 88–90; Montanari, *Le guerre d'Africa*, pp. 264–5.
52 Baratieri, *Memorie d'Africa*, p. 370
53 Raymond Jonas, *The Battle of Adwa: African Victory in the Age of Empire* (Cambridge MA: Harvard University Press, 2011), pp. 176–217; Gooch, *Army, State and Society*, pp. 91–4; Montanari, *le guerre d'Africa*, pp. 270–3.
54 Montanari, *Le guerre d'Africa*, p. 277.
55 Whittam, *The Politics of the Italian Army*, p. 193.
56 The following section draws from John Gooch, 'Italy', in Richard F. Hamilton and Holger H. Herwig, eds., *War Planning 1914* (Cambridge: Cambridge University Press, 2010), pp. 202–11.
57 Massimo Mazzetti, 'Enrico Cosenz, scrittore militare', in AA.VV., *Il pensiero di studiosi di cose militari meridionali: Atti del congresso* (Caserta: Società Storia Patria di Terra di Lavoro, 1978), pp. 103–4.
58 On the events leading to Primerano's departure, see Gooch, *Army, State and Society*, pp. 98–100.
59 Lucio Ceva, 'Comando Militare e Monarchia Costituzionale italiana (*1848–1918*)' in *Teatri di guerra: Comandi, soldati e scrittori nei conflitti europei*, (Milan: Franco Angeli, 2005), p. 56.
60 De Bono, *Nell'esercito nostro prima della guerra*, p. 197.

61 De Rossi, *La vita di un ufficiale italiano sino alla guerra*, pp. 80–1; De Bono, *Nell'esercito nostro prima della guerra*, pp. 24–96.

62 AUSSME, Dogliotti, nos. 68, 75, 79, 7/19 November, 30 November/12 December, 14/26 December 1888. G29 racc. 80.

63 Massimo Mazzetti, *L'esercito italiano nella Triplice Alleanza: Aspetti della politica estera 1870–1914* (Naples: Edizioni Scientifiche Italiane, 1974), pp. 59–63, 77–89.

64 On the fortification debates prior to the 1888 agreement, see Fortunato Minniti, *Esercito e politica da Porta Pia alla Triplice alleanza* (Rome: Bonacci, 1984), pp. 58–68, 89–113.

65 Francesco Guardione, *Il generale Enrico Cosenz* (Palermo: Alberto Reber, 1900), p. 87.

66 Mazzetti, *L'esercito italiano*, pp. 149–50, 163, 167, 175–7.

67 AUSSME, Zuccari to Cosenz, n.132, 20 November 1891; Zuccari to Cosenz, 14 February 1893. G29 racc. 50.

68 AUSSME, Viaggio d'istruzione, 1891, p. 117. G28 racc. 22.

69 De Rossi, *La vita di un ufficiale italiano sino alla guerra*, p. 138; Maria Gabriella Pasqualini, *Carte segrete dell'Intelligence Italiana (1861–1918)* (Rome: Ministero di Difesa [edizione fuori commercio], 2007), p. 164.

70 Terence Zuber, ' "There never was a Schlieffen Plan": A reply to Gerhard Gross', *War in History* vol. 17, 2010, 247.

71 AUSSME, Relazione del Viaggio di Stato Maggiore 1894, pp. 71–7; Relazione del viaggio di Stato Maggiore dell'anno 1895, pp. 71–2; Stralcio delle relazioni sui viaggi di Stato Maggiore degli anni 1895–1896, pp. 87–90: G28 racc. 23, 24, 25.

72 Gooch, *Army, State and Society*, pp. 104–5, 110–12; Gooch, 'Italy', in Hamilton and Herwig, *War Planning 1914*, p. 213.

73 AUSSME, Relazione del viaggio di Stato Maggiore, 1898, 1899, 1900. G28 racc. 27, 28, 29.

74 Filippo Cappellano, *L'imperial regio Esercito austro-ungarico sul fronte italiano 1915–1918* (Rovereto: Museo Storico Italiano della Guerra, 2002), pp. 28–33, 48–9, 87–8; Maurizio Ruffo, *L'Italia nella Triplice Alleanza: I piani operativi dello Stato Maggiore verso l'Austria–Ungheria dal 1885 al 1915* (Rome: Ufficio Storico dello Stato Maggiore dell'Esercito, 1998), pp. 197–214, 236–54.

75 AUSSME, Relazione del viaggio di Stato Maggiore nell'anno 1904. G28 racc. 33.

76 AUSSME, Calderari to Pollio, 25 November 1912. H5 racc. 45/1912.

77 AUSSME, Istruzioni per colonello Zupelli, 27 November 1911. H5 racc. 45/1912.

78 AUSSME, T.275, Pollio to Albricci, 28 December 1912. H5 racc. 49/4.

79 AUSSME, N.103, Pollio to Spingardi, 12 October 1913; H5 racc. 45/1913. See also Paul Halpern, *The Mediterranean Naval Situation 1912–1914* (Cambridge MA: Harvard University Press, 1971), pp. 270–2; Mazzetti, *L'esercito italiano*, pp. 365–6.

80 AUSSME, Verbale riservatissimo della seduta tenuta in Roma dai comandanti designate di armate in guerra e dal capo di stato maggiore dell'esercito, il 18 dicembre 1913. H5 b.12/f.11.

81 Mazzetti, *L'esercito italiano*, pp. 381, 385, 393–4.
82 AUSSME, T.149, Pollio to Zuccari, 16 June 1914. H5 racc. 45/1914.
83 AUSSME, Studio sulla radunata delle truppe austro-ungariche alla nostra frontiera e sui concetti informatori in presunto piano d'operazione. Deduzioni circa le modalità di attuazione in piano stesso, 16 September 1913, pp. 1–6, 41–3 (quo. p. 42). F3 b.388.
84 Ruffo, *L'Italia nella Triplice Alleanza*, pp. 134–59.
85 AUSSME, Studio circa occupazione avanzata austro-ungarico alla nostra frontiera, 1914, pp. 1, 22, 24, 25 (quo.). F3 b.388.
86 Timothy W. Childs, *Italo-Turkish Diplomacy and the War over Libya 1911–1912* (Leiden: Brill, 1990), pp. 7, 25, 39.
87 Francesco Malgeri, *La guerra libica (1911–1912)* (Rome: Edizioni di Storia e Letteratura, 1970), p. 51.
88 James Rennell Rodd, *Social and Diplomatic Memories 1902–1919* (London: Edward Arnold, 1925), p. 141.
89 Promemoria 28 July 1911 (original emphasis): Claudio Pavone, ed., *Dalle carte di Giovanni Giolitti: Quarant'anni di politica italiana* (Milan: Feltrinelli, 1962), vol. III, pp. 49–56.
90 Childs, *Italo-Turkish Diplomacy*, pp. 51, 56.
91 Di San Giuliano to Giolitti, 2 September 1911: *Dalle carte di Giovanni Giolitti* vol. III, p. 59.
92 Angelo Del Boca, *Gli italiani in Libia: Tripoli, bel suol d'amore, 1860–1922* (Bari: Laterza, 1986), p. 15.
93 AUSSME, Studio dal Capo Ufficio di S.M., 15 March 1897; Studio dal colonello Pittaluga; Studio per il bombardamento di Tripoli, November 1901; Sbarco in Tripolitania/Libia: Appunti, 1905; Disposizioni esecutive per la eventuale mobilitazione di un corpo speciale destinato ad operare in zone pianeggiante d'oltre mare, March 1910; L8 racc. 6/119, 7/1, 7/10, 191/2.
94 Pasqualini, *Carte segrete dell'Intelligence Italiana 1861–1918*, p, 182 (original italics); Andrea Vento, *In silenzio gioite e soffrite: Storia dei servizi segreti italiani dal Risorgimento alla Guerra Fredda* (Milan: Il Saggiatore, 2010), pp. 110–11.
95 Studio per l'occupazione della Tripolitania, August 1911: David G. Herrmann, 'The paralysis of Italian strategy in the Italian–Turkish war, 1911–1912', *English Historical Review* vol. 104 no. 411, 1989, 335.
96 Montanari, *Le guerre d'Africa*, p. 400.
97 Memoria sulla occupazione della Tripolitania e della Cirenaica dal Capo di stato maggiore dell'Esercito, 19 September 1911, Ministero della Guerra, *Campagna di Libia* (Rome: Comando del Corpo di Stato Maggiore Ufficio Storico, 1922/38), vol. I, pp. 267, 271, 274.
98 Di San Giuliano to Spingardi, 24 September 1911: Herrmann, 'The paralysis of Italian strategy', 334.
99 Malgeri, *La guerra libica (1911–1912)*, pp. 157–9.
100 ACS, Spingardi to Brusati: Carte Brusati 10/vi-4–36.
101 AUSSME, Pollio to Caneva, 6 October 1911: L8 racc. 1/28.
102 AUSSME, Caneva to Spingardi, 18 October 1911: L8 racc. 2/10.
103 Innocenzo Bianchi to his father, 20 October 1911: Salvatore Bono, 'Lettere dal fronte libico', *Nuova Antologia* no.2052, 1971, 530.

104 *Campagna di Libia*, vol. I, pp. 127–33, 159 fn.2.
105 Carlo De Biase, *L'Aquila d'Oro: Storia dello Stato Maggiore Italiano (1861–1945)* (Milan: Edizioni del Borghese, 1970), p. 248.
106 Sergio Romano, *La quarta sponda: La guerra di Libia 1911/1912* (Milan: Bompiani, 1977), pp. 166–8; Montanari, *Le guerre d'Africa*, pp. 423–5.
107 ACS, Pollio to Brusati, 16 May 1912: Carte Brusati 10/vi-5–37.
108 Giolitti to Spingardi, 7 March 1912: Montanari, *Le guerre d'Africa*, p. 439 (original italics).
109 AUSSME, Memorandum by Pollio, 14 February 1912: L8 racc. 2/10.
110 AUSSME, Di San Giuliano to Spingardi, 9 June 1912: L8 racc. 3/56.
111 Capello to Ragni, 30 April 1912: Malgeri, *La guerra libica*, p. 175.
112 Gooch, *Army, State and Society*, pp. 141–8.
113 Aldo Cabiati and Ettore Grasselli, *Le guerre coloniali dell'Italia* (Milan: Corbaccio, 1935), pp. 249–59.
114 Montanari, *Le guerre d'Africa*, pp. 370–2.
115 Sidney B. Fay, *The Origins of the World War* (New York: Free Press, 1966) vol. I, p. 427; James Joll, *The Origins of the First World War* (Harlow: Longman, 1984), p. 162; William Mulligan, *The Origins of the First World War* (Cambridge: Cambridge University Press, 2010), pp. 74, 79.
116 De Chaurand de St Eustache, *Come l'esercito italiano entrò in guerra*, pp. 268–70.
117 Massimo Mazzetti, 'Note all'interpretazione interventista della grande guerra', *Memorie Storiche Militari* 1979, pp. 97, 103.
118 De Chaurand de St Eustache, *Come l'esercito italiano entrò in guerra*, pp. 106–113.
119 'Norme generali per l'impiego tattico delle grandi unità di guerra': Filippo Stefani, *La storia della dottrina e degli ordinamenti dell'esercito italiano* (Rome: Ufficio Storico dello Stato Maggiore dell'Esercito, 1984), vol. I, pp. 404–5, 408, 411, 418.
120 'Norme per il combattimento', *ibid.*, pp. 458–9.
121 'Regolamento di istruzione', *ibid.*, p. 496.

NOTES TO CHAPTER 2

1 Olindo Malagodi, *Conversazioni della guerra* (Milan: Ricciardi, 1960), vol. I, p. 199 (17 November 1917).
2 Gianni Rocca, *Cadorna* (Milan: Mondadori, 2004), pp. 13, 45 (the newspaperman was Olindo Malagodi).
3 Angelo Gatti, *Un italiano a Versailles (Dicembre 1917–Febbraio 1918)* (Milan: Ceschina, 1958), pp. 238–9, 299.
4 Appunto, 25 February 1915: *cit.* Giorgio Rochat, 'La preparazione dell'esercito italiano nell'inverno 1914–15 in relazione alle informazioni disponibili sulla guerra di posizione', *Risorgimento* vol. 13, 1961, 28 fn.20; Luigi Cadorna, *La guerra alla fronte italiana* (Milan: Treves, 1934), p. 61.
5 'Attacco frontale e ammaestramento tattico': quo. Rocca, *Cadorna*, p. 83. (Emphasis in original.)
6 *Ibid.*, p. 84. See also Stefani, *La storia della dottrina*, vol. 1, pp. 506–10.

7 MacGregor Knox, *To the Threshold of Power, 1922/33: Origins and Dynamics of the Fascist and National Socialist Dictatorships* (Cambridge: Cambridge University Press, 2007), vol. 1, p.165. For a similar criticism, see Rocca, *Cadorna*, p. 85.

8 'Procedimenti per l'attacco frontale nella guerra di trincea in uso nell'esercito francese'; quo. Stefani, *La storia della dottrina*, vol. I, p. 516.

9 See Robert A. Doughty, *Pyrrhic Victory: French Strategy and Operations in the Great War* (Cambridge MA: Harvard University Press, 2005), pp. 141–52. French operational and tactical regulations issued in 1913 said of the attack, 'The artillery does not prepare attacks; it supports them', much like Cadorna's regulations: *ibid.*, pp.26–7.

10 AUSSME, N.53, Programme vari per migliorari le attuali condizioni dell'-Esercito e l'organizzazione difensiva dello Stato, 21 March 1914, p. 3. F3 b.85/f.6. See also Gooch, *Army, State and Society*, pp. 153–4.

11 AUSSME, Ufficio Informazione promemoria n.284, 19 April 1914. G29 racc. 17.

12 AUSSME, Cadorna to Pollio, 4 March 1914. H5 b.17/f.5.

13 AUSSME, Ufficio Informazione promemoria n.504, 25 July 1914. G29 racc. 17.

14 AUSSME, Calderari T.186, 20 July 1914; T.192, 25 July 1914; T.193, 26 July 1914. G29 racc. 17.

15 AUSSME, Calderari n.119, 13 July 1914; T.124, 25 July 1914; n.124, 25 July 1914. G29 racc. 13/3.

16 AUSSME, Calderari n.128, 28 July 1914. [This despatch reached Rome on 31 July.] G29 racc. 13/3.

17 AUSSME, Ropolo n.177, 11 July 1914. G29 racc. 88.

18 AUSSME, Ropolo T.188, 27 July 1914; T.189, 27 July 1914 [quo.]. G29 racc. 88.

19 AUSSME, Ropolo T.195, 30 July 1914. G29 racc. 88.

20 AUSSME, Mombelli n.184/123, 26 July 1914. G29 racc. 111.

21 AUSSME, Mombelli n.185/125, 1 August 1914. G29 racc. 111.

22 AUSSME, Mombelli n.193/139, 23 August 1914; n.197/143, 30 August 1914; n.199/145, 6 September 1914. G29 racc. 111.

23 AUSSME, Mombelli n.218/170, 5 October 1914; n.261/22, 6 December 1914. G29 racc. 111.

24 AUSSME, Mombelli n.117/35, 18 March 1914; n.127/50, 14 April 1914. G29 racc. 111.

25 AUSSME, Caccia n.17/31, 28 April 1914; n.22, 29 April 1914. G29 racc. 123.

26 AUSSME, Caccia n.30, 9 June 1914. G29 racc. 123.

27 AUSSME, Camerana to Mombelli n.2241 ris.mo, 23 June 1914. G29 racc. 111.

28 Antonio Salandra, *La neutralità italiana [1914]: Ricordi e pensieri* (Milan: Mondadori, 1928), pp. 260–1.

29 Quo. William A. Renzi, *In the Shadow of the Sword: Italy's Neutrality and Entrance into the Great War, 1914–1915* (New York: Peter Lang, 1987), p. 79.

30 AUSSME, Memoria sintetica sulla nostra radunata nord-ovest e sul trasporto in Germania della maggiore forza possibile, 31 July 1914. H5 b.12/f.10

31 Di Sangiuliano to Bollati, 14 July 1914. *DDI* 4th ser. vol. XII no. 225, pp. 159–60. (Note spelling Di Sangiuliano in *DDI*.)
32 Di Sangiuliano to Vittorio Emanuele III, 24 July 1914. Quo. Salandra, *La neutralità italiana*, pp. 78–80.
33 Quo. William A. Renzi, 'Italy's neutrality and entrance into the Great War: A re-examination', *American Historical Review* vol. 73 no. 5, June 1968, 1419.
34 Moltke to Conrad, 5 August 1914. Quo. Mazzetti, *L'esercito italiano*, p. 447.
35 AUSSME, Albricci to Cadorna, T.217, 3 August 1914; T.218, 3 August 1914. G29 racc. 17.
36 AUSSME, Ipotesi circa le forze che l'Austria–Ungheria potrebbe destinare verso la frontiera italiana nella situazione attuale contro la nostra offensive nel settore del Friuli, 9 August 1914. E2 b.131.
37 Ruffo, *L'Italia nella Triplice Alleanza*, pp. 161–7.
38 AUSSME, Circa l'attacco degli sbarrimenti austro-ungarico in caso di offensive nel settore orientale, n.d. [1914]. E2 b.131
39 AUSSME, Cadorna to Grandi, 2 August 1914. G9 b.9/f.1.
40 AUSSME, Grandi to Salandra, 4 August 1914. G9 b.9/f.1.
41 Di Sangiuliano to Salandra, 9, 12, 4(2), 16 August 1914; Di Sangiuliano to Imperiali, 26 August 1914; Di Sangiuliano to Tittoni, 30 August 1914. *DDI* 5th ser. vol. I nos. 151, 219, 244, 246, 281, 453, 503, pp. 83, 127, 142 (2), 160, 245, 278.
42 AUSSME, N.754, Cadorna to Grandi, 8 August 1914. F3 b.85/f.6.
43 AUSSME, N.221, Grandi to Cadorna, 19 August 1914; N.241, Grandi to Cadorna, 22 August 1914; N.303, Grandi to Cadorna, 26 August 1914. F3 b.85/f.6.
44 Cadorna–Salandra audience, 13 August 1914; Cadorna–Grandi meeting 23 August 1914: Giorgio Rochat, 'L'esercito italiano nell'estate 1914', *Nuova Rivista Storica* vol. 45 no. 9, 1961, 330, 332 fn.3. On Grandi's proposals for partial mobilisation, see Salandra, *La neutralità italiana*, pp. 265–6.
45 Cadorna to Di Sangiuliano, 27 August 1914 and encl.; *DDI* 5th ser. Vol. I no. 468, p. 255.
46 Ministero della Guerra, *L'Esercito italiano nella grande guerra, 1915/1918* Ufficio Storico dello Stato Maggiore dell'Esercito (Rome: 1927/74), vol. I, pp. 67–9. The document is undated but is more or less the same as that referred to in Rochat, 'L'esercito italiano nell'estate 1914', 338, where it is dated 9 August 1914.
47 De Chaurand de St Eustache, *Come l'esercito italiano entrò in guerra*, p. 271, 274–5.
48 Rochat, 'L'esercito italiano nell'estate 1914', 336, fn.3.
49 Ferdinando Martini, *Diario 1914–1918* (Milan: Mondadori, 1966), 9, 15, 22, 29 August, pp. 27, 38, 50, 66.
50 Cadorna to Grandi, 10 September 1914: Rochat, 'L'esercito italiano nell'-estate 1914', 342. (Emphasis in original.)
51 AUSSME, Salandra to Grandi, 16 September 1914, encl. with N.438, Grandi to Cadorna, 19 September 1914. F3 b.85/f.6.
52 AUSSME, Avarna to Esteri [unnumbered], 7 September 1914; T.1293, 28 September 1914. G29 racc. 17. Avarna T.9502, 26 September 1914. G29 racc. 88.

53 AUSSME, N.97, Situazione generale, 25 September 1914. F3 b.85/f.6.

54 Martini, *Diario*, 22 September 1914, pp. 115–16.

55 Salandra to Sonnino, 24 September 1914: Brunello Vigezzi, 'I problemi della neutralità e della guerra nel carteggio Salandra–Sonnino (1914–1917)', *Nuova Rivista Storica* vol. 45 no. 3, September–December 1961, 412.

56 AUSSME, N.1257, Cadorna to Grandi, 25 September 1914. F3 b.85/f.6.

57 Sidney Sonnino, *Diario 1914–1916*, ed. Pietro Pastorelli (Bari: Laterza, 1972), p. 15 (16 September 1914); Salandra, *La neutralità italiana*, pp. 270–1, 291; 'Circa le deficienze nelle dotazioni di mobilitazione', 23 September 1914 [Grandi], *ibid.*, pp. 272–7.

58 AUSSME, Caporetto: Seduta Inchiesta 25 aprile 1918, pp. 1–4. H5 b.13/c.10.

59 Luigi Aldovrandi Marescotti, *Guerra diplomatica: Ricordi e frammenti di diario (1914–1919)* (Milan: Mondadori, 1936), pp. 23–5.

60 Despatch, 11 August 1914: *ibid.*, pp. 40–2.

61 Salandra to Tittoni, 4 November 1914; Tittoni to Salandra, 5 November 1914; Squitti to Sonnino, 6 November 1914; Fasciotti to Sonnino, 6 November 1914; Tittoni to Sonnino, 13 November 1914: *DDI* 5th ser. vol. II nos. 123, 137, 141, 142, 194, pp. 91–3, 104–5, 107–8, 108–9, 163.

62 Salandra to Lori, 20 October 1914: *DDI* 5th ser. vol. II no. 9, pp. 5–6.

63 Bollati to Salandra, 21 October 1914; Avarna to Salandra, 21 October 1914; Imperiali to Salandra, 21 October 1914; Carlotti to Salandra, 22 October 1914; Tittoni to Salandra, 24 October 1914; Aliotti to Salandra, 27 October 1914; Sonnino to Lori, 22 December 1914; Lori to Sonnino, 22 December 1914; Lori to Sonnino, 23 December 1914: *DDI* 5th ser. vol. II nos. 16, 17, 19, 20, 35, 51, 456, 460, 469, pp. 10, 10–11, 12, 12–13, 24, 38, 377, 379, 388.

64 Fasciotti to Sonnino, 7 December 1914; De Bosdari to Sonnino, 2 January 1915; De Bosdari to Sonnino, 9 January 1915: *DDI* 5th ser. vol. II nos. 351, 533, 589, pp. 288–9, 438–9, 482–3.

65 Tittoni to Sonnino, 9 November 1914: *DDI* 5th ser. vol. II no. 174, pp. 145–6.

66 Tittoni to Sonnino, 5 January 1915; Bollati to Sonnino, 5 January 1915; Avarna to Sonnino, 8 January 1915; Imperiali to Sonnino, 2 February 1915: *DDI* 5th ser. vol. II nos. 558, 561, 586, 754, pp. 460, 461–2, 481, 625–7; De Bosdari to Sonnino, 7 March 1915; De Bosdari to Sonnino, 18 March 1915; Carlotti to Sonnino, 24 April 1915: *DDI* 5th ser. vol. III nos. 49, 131, 447, pp. 31, 106–8, 353–4.

67 C.J. Lowe and F. Marzari, *Italian Foreign Policy 1870–1940* (London: Routledge & Kegan Paul, 1975), pp. 132–5.

68 Levi to Sonnino, 23 November 1914; Thaon di Revel to Sonnino, 28 December 1914: *DDI* 5th ser. vol. II nos. 272, 508, pp. 226–9, 416–20 [quos. pp. 417, 418].

69 Fasciotti to Salandra, 24 October 1914; Fasciotti to Salandra, 30 October 1914; Fasciotti to Salandra, 3 November 1914; Sonnino to Fasciotti, 13 November 1914; Sonnino to Fasciotti, 26 January 1915; Fasciotti to Sonnino, 23 February 1915; Fasciotti to Sonnino, 26 February 1915: *DDI* 5th ser. vol. II nos. 37, 82, 119, 198, 715, 855, 872, pp. 25, 62, 88, 165–6, 588–9, 731–2, 745–6. Imperiali to Sonnino, 30 March 1915: *DDI* 5th ser. vol. III no. 223, pp. 184–5.

70 Renzi, *In the Shadow of the Sword*, p. 224.

71 Bollati to Salandra, 17 October 1914; Borsarelli to Bollati, 20 October 1914: *DDI* 5th ser. vol. II nos. 5, 8, pp. 2–3, 5.

72 Salandra to Bollati, 20 October 1914; Piacentini to Salandra, 22 October 1914; Piacentini to Salandra, 23 October 1914; Salandra to Bollati, 28 October 1914; Bollati to Salandra, 30 October 1914; Salandra to Bollati, 1 November 1914; Garroni to Salandra, 2 November 1914; Garroni to Salandra, 4 November 1914; Aliotti to Sonnino, 20 December 1914: *DDI* 5th ser. vol. II nos. 10, 24, 30, 58, 80, 103, 106, 109, 130, 436, pp. 6–7, 14, 21, 44–5, 60–1, 77, 80–1, 99, 361.

73 Salandra to Tittoni, Imperiali, Carlotti, 26 October 1914: *DDI* 5th ser. vol. II no. 43, pp. 29–31.

74 Bollati to Avarna, 26 October 1914; Bollati to Avarna, 10–11 November 1914; Bollati to Sonnino, 11 December 1914: *DDI* 5th ser. vol. II nos. 45, 185, 367, pp. 32–4, 153–6, 302–4.

75 Richard Bosworth, *Italy and the Approach of the First World War* (London: Macmillan, 1983), p. 134.

76 Rodd, *Social and Diplomatic Memories*, pp. 243–4.

77 Sonnino, *Diario 1914–1916*, pp. 36, 62 (24 November 1914; 6 January 1915).

78 Tittoni to Sonnino, 20 March 1915: *DDI* 5th ser. vol. III no. 149, p. 120.

79 Avarna to Sonnnino, 18 November 1914; Avarna to Sonnino, 12 December 1914; Bollati to Sonnino, 11 January 1915; Avarna to Sonnino, 14 February 1915: *DDI* 5th ser. vol. II nos. 239, 371, 607, 808, pp. 196–9, 308–10, 496–7, 686–8.

80 De Bosdari to Sonnino, 6 November 1914; Carlotti to Sonnino, 6 November 1914; De Martino to Sonnino, 30 November 1914: *DDI* 5th ser. vol. II nos. 145, 146, 311, pp. 110–11, 111–12, 254–62.

81 Avarna to Bollati, 15 December 1914: *DDI* 5th ser. vol. II no. 407, pp. 333–8.

82 Cadorna to Salandra, 11 December 1914; Salandra to Sonnino, 25 January 1915: *DDI* 5th ser. vol. II nos. 368, 697, pp. 304–6, 573–4.

83 Viale to Sonnino, 19 November 1914; *DDI* 5th ser. no. 247, pp. 203–5.

84 Avarna to Bollati, 19 February 1915: C. Avarna Di Gualtieri, 'Il carteggio Avarna–Bollati luglio 1914–maggio 1915', *Rivista storica italiana* vol. 62, 1950, 71.

85 Sonnino to Salandra, 30 December 1914; De Martino to Sonnino, 9 January 1915; Sonnino to Bollati, Avarna, 16 January 1915; Sonnino to Salandra, 22 January 1915; Sonnino to Salandra, 23 January 1915; Avarna to Sonnino, 23 January 1915; Sonnino to Salandra, 26 January 1915; Sonnino to Imperiali, 16 February 1915; Bollati to Sonnino, 21 February 1915; Sonnino to Salandra, 26 February 1915; Salandra to Sonnino, 27 February 1915: *DDI* 5th ser. vol. II nos. 518, 596, 640, 672, 681, 689, 712, 816, 844, 868, 874, pp. 426, 488–91, 525, 553–4, 561–2, 568–9, 586–7, 692–6, 718–20, 741–2, 748.

86 Imperiali to Sonnino, 9 March 1915: *DDI* 5th ser. vol. III no. 67, pp. 47–9.

87 Sonnino to Imperiali, 18 March 1915; Imperiali to Sonnino, 21 March 1915; Sonnino to Imperiali etc., 24 March 1915; Imperiali to Sonnino, 25 March 1915; Imperiali to Sonnino, 26 March 1915: *DDI* 5th ser. vol. III nos. 138, 162, 183, 195, 199, pp. 111–12, 132–3, 152, 164, 166–7.

88 Sonnino to Imperiali etc., 21 March 1915: *DDI* 5th ser. vol. III no. 164, pp. 134–5.
89 Salandra to Sonnino, 2 April 1915: *DDI* 5th ser. vol. III no. 257, p. 211.
90 Di Revel to Sonnino, 15 April 1915: *DDI* 5th ser. vol. III no. 334, pp. 266–7.
91 Avarna to Sonnino, 27 March 1915; Salandra to Sonnino, 29 March 1915: *DDI* 5th ser. vol. III nos. 208, 211, pp. 172–4, 175–6.
92 Sonnino, *Diario 1914–1916*, pp. 120–3 (2 April 1915).
93 Sonnino to Avarna and Bollati, 8 April 1915; Bollatri to Sonnino, 12 April 1915; Avarna to Sonnino, 16 April 1915: *DDI* 5th ser. vol. III nos. 293, 312, 357, pp. 236–8, 249–50, 285–90.
94 Imperiali to Sonnino, 16 April 1915: Sidney Sonnino, *Carteggio 1914–1916* ed. Pietro Pastorelli (Bari: Laterza, 1974), pp. 399–400.
95 For the detailed terms, see Accordo di Londra, 26 April 1915: *DDI* 5th ser. vol. III no. 470, pp. 369–74.
96 Cadorna, *La guerra alla fronte italiana*, p. 104. The other thing that destroyed his planned surprise, he thought, was Italy's denunciation of the Triple Alliance treaty on 4 May 1915.
97 (Notes for a parliamentary speech, 20 April 1915): *DDI* 5th ser. vol. III no. 735, pp. 577–81.
98 'Memoria circa proveddimenti per l'esercito', 11 October 1914: Salandra, *La neutralità italiana*, pp. 317–28.
99 AUSSME, Promemoria per S E il Capo di Stato Maggiore, 11 October 1914. F3 b.85/f.6.
100 AUSSME, N.119, Zupelli to Cadorna, 29 December 1914. F3 b.85/f.6.
101 Rochat, 'La preparazione dell'esercito italiano', 27 fns. 9, 10.
102 AUSSME, N.8, Cadorna to Zupelli, 26 November 1914. F3 b.85/f.6.
103 AUSSME, Attuali condizioni dell'esercito in relazione alle eventualità di una mobilitazione, January 1915 [quo.]; N.52, Crisi nell'ipotesi di mobilitazione rossa, 31 January 1915; Ufficio Mobilitazione: promemoria, 9 February 1915. F3 b.85/f.7.
104 Rocca, *Cadorna*, pp. 59, 64; John Gooch, 'Morale and discipline in the Italian army, 1915–1918', in Hugh Cecil and Peter Liddle, eds., *Facing Armageddon: The First World War Experienced* (Barnsley: Pen & Sword, 1996), pp. 438–9.
105 AUSSME, N.1224, Zupelli to Cadorna, 23 January 1915; N.95, Cadorna to Zupelli, 18 February 1915. F3 b.85/f.2.
106 AUSSME, N.8, Cadorna to Zupelli, 26 November 1914. F3 b.95/6.6.
107 Rocca, *Cadorna*, pp. 60–1.
108 Salandra to Tittoni, Imperiali, Carlotti, 26 October 1914: *DDI* 5th ser. vol. II no. 43, pp. 29–31.
109 Avarna to Esteri, 23 October 1914; Imperiali to Salandra, 4 November 1914; Bollati to Salandra, 4 November 1914; Carlotti to Sonnino, 7 November 1914; Sonnino to Bollati and Avarna, 20 December 1914; *DDI* 5th ser. vol. II nos. 31, 125, 129, 151, 433, pp. 21–2, 94–5, 97–9, 118, 356–8.
110 AUSSME, Data la presente situazione politico-militare, nell'ipotesi di una dichiarazione di Guerra da parte della monarchia austro-ungarica e della

Germania, quale e quante forze è presumabile potremmo avere di fronte, dove, e in quanto tempo di raccolta? [draft], 15 December 1914, p. 1. E2 b.121.

111 *Ibid.*, p. 9.

112 *Ibid.*, p.10. (Emphasis in original.)

113 Malagodi, *Conversazioni della guerra*, pp. 33–5 (2 December 1914).

114 Promemoria al Capo Ufficio mobilitazione, 21 December 1914: Rochat, 'L'esercito italiano nell'estate 1914', 332, fn.2.

115 AUSSME, Bongiovanni N.16, 15 December 1914. G29 racc. 13/f.3 Another, and more discursive, version of this interview can be found in Angelo Gatti, *Uomini e folle di guerra* (Milan: Treves, 1921), pp. 145–6.

116 Rochat, 'La preparazione dell'esercito italiano', 17–18 (quo), 29 fn.34, 30 fn.38. Breganze's 'Diario dal 9 al 29 novembre [1914]: Visita al fronte dell'Esercito Francese' in AUSSME, F1 b.65/f.5.

117 Rochat, 'La preparazione dell'esercito italiano', 19–22, 31 fn.45.

118 *Ibid.*, 32 fn.66.

119 AUSSME, Breganze N.63, 16 March 1915. G29 racc. 40/f.1.

120 Emilio Faldella, *La grande guerra*, vol. I:*Le battaglie dell'Isonzo (1915–1917)* (Milan: Longanesi, 1978), pp. 30–1.

121 AUSSME, Bongiovanni N.36, 31 January 1915. G29 racc. 13/f.4.

122 AUSSME, Bongiovanni N.39 all. 2: 'Note tattiche', 6 February 1915, p. 1. G29 racc. 13/f.4.

123 *Ibid.*, p. 10.

124 AUSSME, Diaz to Bongiovanni N.410, 28 February 1915; Bongiovanni to 'Egregio generale e caro amico' [Diaz], 4 April 1915. G29 racc 13/f.5.

125 AUSSME, Bongiovanni N.61, 25 February 1915. G29 racc 13/f.4.

126 AUSSME, Bongiovanni N.68 'Guerra di posizione', 30 March 1915, pp. 3, 8 (quo.), 17, 38–9, 45, 46. G29 racc. 13/f.5.

127 Undated annotation by Vittorio Emanuele III: Rochat, 'La preparazione dell'esercito italiano', 31 fn.43.

128 Bongiovanni, 13 April 1915: cit. Adriano Alberti, *Il generale Falkenhayn: Le relazione tra i capi di S.M. della Triplice* (Rome: Libreria dello Stato, 1934), p. 99. A rather more discursive version, which does not follow the original in the archives, can be found in Gatti, *Uomini e folle di guerra*, pp. 151–3. Ambassador Bollati gave Sonnino an accurate account of the content of the conversations: Bollati to Sonnino, 13 April 1915: *DDI* 5th ser. vol. III no. 317, pp. 253–4.

129 Sonnino to Carlotti, Imperiali, Ruspoli, 30 April 1915: *DDI* 5th ser. vol. III no. 521, pp. 411–12.

130 AUSSME, N.146a, Cadorna to Zupelli, 12 April 1915. H5 b.17/f.1.

131 Cadorna to Sonnino, 30 April 1915: Sonnino, *Carteggio 1914–1916*, p. 464.

132 AUSSME, Convention militaire entre les hauts commandements des armées russe et italien, 8–21 March 1915. H5 b.12/f.4. This would appear to be the original document referred to in subsequent negotiations, when Italy refused to undertake an obligation to provide Serbia with foodstuffs, which the editors of the Italian diplomatic documents were unable to find: *DDI* 5th ser. vol. III no. 727, pp. 572–3 fn.

133 Sonnino to Carlotti, Imperiali, Ruspoli, 30 April 1915: *DDI* 5th ser. vol. III no. 521, pp. 411–12.

134 Sonnino to Carlotti, encl. Cadorno to Ropolo, 2 May 1915: *DDI* 5th ser. vol. III no. 540, p. 427.
135 Cappellano, *L'Imperial regio Esercito*, pp. 75–6.
136 Cadorna, *La guerra alla fronte italiana*, pp. 97–103; Faldella, *La grande guerra* vol. I, pp. 39–46. Afterwards, Cadorna shaped his memoirs to suggest that this is what he had been intending all along: *La guerra alla fronte italiana*, p. 53.
137 Capellano, *L'Imperial regio Esercito*, pp. 73–83, 85.
138 Sonnino to Ruspoli, encl. Cadorna to Montanari, 2 May 1915: *DDI* 5th ser. vol. III no. 542, p. 428. An analogous letter was sent to Lt.-Col. Ropolo in St Petersburg via Ambassador Carlotti.
139 Aldovrandi to Cadorna, 3 May 1915; Montanari to Cadorna, 5 May 1915; Carlotti to Sonnino, encl. Ropolo to Cadorna, 4 May 1915; Tittoni to Sonnino, 6 May 1915; Sonnino to Tittoni, 7 May 1915: *DDI* 5th ser. vol. III nos. 547, un-numbered, 568, 585, 612, pp. 432–3, 448 fn.1, 448–9, 463–4, 483.
140 Sonnino to Carlotti 2 May 1915, encl. Cadorna to Ropolo: *DDI* 5th ser. vol. III no. 540, p. 427.
141 Carlotti to Sonnino, 9 May 1915; Sonnino to Cadorna, 14 May 1915; Sonnino to Carlotti, 17 May 1915; Carlotti to Sonnino, 19 May 1915: *DDI* 5th ser. vol. III nos. 639, 684, 700, 727, pp. 503–5, 541–2, 552, 572–3.
142 Rocca, *Cadorna*, p. 66. This purportedly occurred when he attended the unveiling of a monument to Garibaldi's *Mille* and, after listening to an uncompromisingly anti-Austrian speech by Gabriele D'Annunzio, tackled Salandra directly.
143 AUSSME, Promemoria N.54, Scacchiere Occidentale, 3 April 1915. G29 racc. 40/f.1.
144 Tittoni to Sonnino, 25 April 1915: *DDI* 5th ser. vol. III no. 456, pp. 358–9.
145 AUSSME, Cadorna to Joffre, 19 May 1915. H5 b.17/f.3.
146 AUSSME, Cadorna to Zupelli, 15 March 1915. H5 b.17/f.2.
147 AUSSME, N.145, Zupelli to Cadorna, 26 April 1915; N.124, Cadorna to Zupelli, 26 April1915; N.128, Cadorna to Zupelli, 28 April 1915 [quo.]. H5 b.17/f.3.
148 Avarna to Bollati, 15 December 1914: *DDI* 5th ser. vol. II no. 407, p.334.
149 Giorgio Candeloro, *Storia dell'Italia moderna*, vol. VIII, *La prima guerra mondiale, il dopoguerra, l'avvento del fascismo* (Milan: Feltrinelli, 1978), pp. 38–46; Knox, *To the Threshold of Power*, pp. 174–82.
150 W. Somerset Maugham to William Heinemann, 7 March 1915: Selina Hastings, *The Secret Lives of Somerset Maugham* (London: John Murray, 2009), p. 195.
151 Alberto Monticone, 'Sonnino e Salandra verso la decisione dell'intervento', in, *Gli italiani in uniforme 1915/1918: Intellettuali, borghesi e disertori* (Bari: Laterza, 1972), pp. 67, 70–86. See also Brunello Vigezzi, *Da Giolitti a Salandra* (Florence: Vallecchi, 1969), pp. 321–401.
152 Salandra to Sonnino, 16 March 1915: quo. Brunello Vigezzi, 'Le "Radiose giornate" del maggio 1915 nei rapporti dei Prefetti (Parte Ia)', *Nuova Rivista Storica* vol. 43 no. 3, 1959, 334 fn.2.

153 Sonnino to Salandra, 11 May 1915: Vigezzi, 'I problemi della neutralità', 435.
154 *Ibid.*, 436; Brunello Vigezzi, 'Politica estera e opinion pubblica in Italia dal 1870 al 1945', *Nuova Rivista Storica* vol. 42 nos. 5–6, 1979, 551–4.
155 Malagodi, *Conversazioni della guerra*, vol. I, p. 59 (9 May 1915).
156 Brunello Vigezzi, 'Le "Radiose Giornate" del maggio 1915 nei rapporti dei Prefetti (Parte IIa)', *Nuova Rivista Storica* vol. XLIV fasc. I, 1960, pp. 54–11.
157 R.A. Delmé-Radcliffe to Stamfordham, 12 June 1915. RA PS/GV/Q.688/21.
158 Vigezzi, 'Le "Radiose Giornate" del Maggio 1915 (Parte IIa)', 109.
159 Antonio Salandra, *Memorie politiche 1916–1925* (Reggio Calabria: Edizioni Parallelo, 1975), p. 9.
160 AUSSME, N.203G, Cadorna to Comandanti 2a, 3a Armati, Zona Carnia, 16 May 1915. H5 b.17/f.1.
161 Cadorna, *La guerra sul fronte italiana*, pp. 77–8.
162 AUSSME, N.2492, Cadorna to Zupelli, 21 May 1915. H5 b.17/f.3.
163 Albert Pethő, *I servizi segreti dell'Austria–Ungheria* (Gorizia: LEG, 2001), pp. 46, 173.
164 AUSSME, N.951/A, Attività dei reparti crittografici dell'esercito austro-ungarico durante la guerra, 14 March 1919, p.3. The Austrians could also read eight French diplomatic ciphers, and had broken enough Russian ciphers to know the precise date and strength of Russia's entry into the war and to possess all the data on the Brussilov offensive in June 1916: *ibid.*, pp. 1, 3.
165 Quo. Rocca, *Cadorna*, pp. 77–8.

NOTES TO CHAPTER 3

1 Giani Stuperich, *Guerra del '15* (Turin: Einaudi, 1978), pp. 5, 20, 30 (3, 7, 10 June 1915).
2 Luigi Gasparotto, *Diario di un fante* (Milan: Treves, 1919), vol. I, p. 19 (26 August 1915).
3 Giovanni Mira, *Memorie* (Vicenza, 1968), pp. 94, 96: quo. Lucio Ceva, 'Veneto e Italia di fronte alla grande guerra: Memorialisti e letteratura di guerra', *Storia della cultura veneta dall'età napoleonica alla prima guerra mondiale* (Vicenza: Neri Pozzi, 1986), p. 775.
4 Enzo Forcella and Alberto Monticone, *Plotone di esecuzione: I processi della prima guerra mondiale* (Bari: Laterza, 1968), pp. 24–6.
5 Lucio Ceva, 'La grande guerra nel Veneto: Scrittori e memorialisti', *La Cultura* vol. 26 no. 1, 1988, 83–9.
6 Gasparotto, *Diario di un fante*, vol. I, p. 42 (5 October 1915).
7 Quo. Mark Thompson, *The White War: Life and Death on the Italian Front 1915–1919* (New York: Basic Books, 2009), p. 193.
8 Lucio Fabi, *Gente di trincea: La grande guerra sul Carso e sull'Isonzo* (Milan: Mursia, 1994), p. 34.
9 J. F. Gentsch, *Italy, Geography, and the First World War*, PhD thesis, University of London, 1999, pp. 110–11, 120. The division was the 20th, the date 30 July 1915. I have followed this excellent source in describing the strategic geography of the war.

10 Stuparich, *Guerra del '15*, p. 97 (11 July 1915).
11 For example, Pietro Maravigna, *Le undici offensive sull'Isonzo* (Rome: Libreria del Littorio, 1929), p. 7: 'On the Carso, on the Alpine crests, on the sacred Isonzo, Italian youth rediscovered in itself the civic and warrior virtues it had thought lost for ever, and spent them with noble generosity.'
12 Arturo Rossato, *L'elmo di Scipio* (Milan, 1934), p. 93; quo. Mario Isenghi, *I vinti di Caporetto nella letteratura di guerra* (Vicenza: Marsiglio, 1967), p. 21.
13 Adolf Omodeo, *Momenti della vita di guerra: Dai diari e dalle lettere dei caduti 1915–1918* (Turin: Einaudi, 1968), p. 10.
14 Curzio Malaparte, *Viva Caporetto! La rivolta dei santi maledetti* (Milan: Mondadori, 1981), pp. 73–4.
15 Giorgio Rochat, *L'Italia nella prima guerra mondiale: Problemi di interpretazione e prospettiva di ricerca* (Milan: Feltrinelli, 1976), p. 78.
16 Gasparotto, *Diario di un fante*, vol. I pp. 6, 9, 11, 12, 19 (12 July, 30 July, 2 August, 26 August 1915).
17 Quo. Fabi, *Gente di trincea*, p. 147.
18 Cadorna to his wife, 30 May 1915; Cadorna to Ninetta [Cadorna], 26 September 1915: Luigi Cadorna, *Lettere famigliari* (Milan: Mondadori, 1967), pp. 105, 126.
19 Faldella, *La grande guerra*, vol. I, p. 109; Tim Hadley, 'Military diplomacy in the Dual Alliance: German military attaché reporting from Vienna, 1906–1914', *War in History* vol. 17 no. 3, July 2010, 305, 307–8.
20 Rocca, *Cadorna*, p. 79; Piero Pieri, *La prima guerra mondiale* (Udine: Gaspari, 1998), p. 90; Faldella, *La grande guerra*, vol. I, pp. 52–3.
21 Cadorna to Brusati, 27 April 1915; quo. Rocca, *Cadorna*, p. 125.
22 Faldella, *La grande guerra*, vol. I, p. 92.
23 Cadorna to Army Commanders, 27 May 1915: *ibid.*, p. 79.
24 Cadorna, *La guerra alla fronte italiana*, pp. 130–1.
25 Cadorna to his wife, 30 May 1915: Cadorna, *Lettere famigliari*, p. 105.
26 Operation Order N.7, 11 June 1915: Rocca, *Cadorna*, p. 82.
27 AUSSME, Cadorna to Salandra, 17 June 1915. H5 b.17/f.1.
28 AUSSME, Salandra to Cadorna, 21 June 1915; Cadorna to Salandra, 25 June 1915: H5 b.17/f.1. Cadorna to Sonnino, 11 June 1915: *DDI* 5th ser. vol. IV no. 147, p. 86.
29 AUSSME, Cadorna to Salandra, 13 June 1915. H5 b.17/f.3.
30 AUSSME. Cadorna to Salandra, 18 June 1915. H5 b.17/f.3. Cadorna first thought of Gulgielmo Marconi, but then crossed his name out.
31 AUSSME, T.1177, Cadorna to Salandra/War Ministry, 2 July 1915. H5 b.17/f.3.
32 AUSSME, T.514, Cadorna to Salandra, 29 July 1915. H5 b.17/f.3.
33 AUSSME, N.3535, Cadorna to Salandra, 6 September 1915. H5 b.17/f.3.
34 AUSSME, N.509G, Cadorna to Zupelli, 28 July 1915. H5 b.10/f.7.
35 Cadorna to Carla [Cadorna], 6 August 1915: Cadorna, *Lettere famigliari*, pp.117–18.
36 Cadorna to Carla [Cadorna], 17 September 1915: Cadorna, *Lettere famigliari*, p. 123.
37 AUSSME, N.711, Cadorna to Zupelli, 26 June 1915. H5 b.17/f.3.

38 AUSSME, N.880, Cadorna to Zupelli, 1 July 1915. H5 b.17/f.3.
39 AUSSME, Costituzione di nuove unità pronte ad entrare in campagna nella primavera del 1916, 30 June 1915, p. 7. H5 b.17/f.3.
40 Francesco degli Azzoni Avogadro, *L'amico del re: Il diario di guerra inedito dell'aiutante di campo di Vittorio Emanuele III* (Udine: Gaspari, 2009), p. 52.
41 Rocca, *Cadorna*, p. 92.
42 Andrea Ungari, 'The Italian air force from the eve of the Libyan conflict to the First World War', *War in History* vol. 17 no. 4, November 2010, 409, 413–16.
43 AUSSME, Ricognizione coll'aeroplano, 17 June 1915. E2 b.20.
44 Alessandro Massignani, 'La guerra aerea sul fronte italiano', in Paolo Ferrari, ed., *La Grande Guerra aerea 1915–1918: Battaglia–industrie–bombardamenti–assi–aeroporti* (Valdagno: Gino Rossato Editore, 1994), p. 27.
45 Cadorna to Carla [Cadorna], 11 July 1915: Cadorna, *Lettere famigliari*, p. 113.
46 Cadorna to Ninetta [Cadorna], 30 September 1915; *ibid.*, p. 125.
47 AUSSME, French military mission to *Comando supremo*, 20 July 1915; T.488G *Comando supremo*, 20 July 1915. E2 b.14.
48 AUSSME, T.59T/2555, 23 July 1915; T.5963, 25 August 1915. G29 b.89/f.1.
49 AUSSME, T119, 23 September 1915; undated note, Diaz to Ropolo. G29 b.89/f.1.
50 Faldella, *La grande guerra*, vol. I, p. 140.
51 Cadorna to Carla, 10 June 1915; Cadorna to [Raffaele Cadorna], 9 July 1915; Cadorna to Ninetta [Cadorna], 4 August 1915 [quo.]; Cadorna to Ninetta Cadorna, 23 October 1915: Cadorna, *Lettere famigliari*, pp. 107, 112, 115–16, 127.
52 AUSSME, T.329G *Comando supremo* to Ministero della Guerra, 10 June 1915. E2 b.20.
53 AUSSME, N.566, Cadorna to Zupelli, 19 August 1915. H5 b.17/f.3.
54 AUSSME, Cadorna to Salandra, 2 August 1915. H5 b.17/f.3.
55 AUSSME, Cadorna to Zupelli, 3 August 1915; H5 b.17/f.3. N.530G, Cadorna to Salandra, n.d. [3 August 1915]; H5 b.17/f.1.
56 Ministero della Guerra, *L'esercito italiano nella Grande Guerra*, vol. III, Part 1, pp. 28–9.
57 AUSSME, N.1018, *Ufficio speciale* Milano to *Ufficio informazione*, 22 September 1915; N.1053, *Ufficio speciale* Milano to *Ufficio informazione*, 28 September 1915. F17 b.36/f.10.
58 AUSSME, N.4169, Cadorna to Salandra, 24 September 1915. H5 b.17/f.3.
59 AUSSME, Salandra to Cadorna, 27 September 1915. H5 b.17/f.1.
60 AUSSME, II Army Operational Order N.8, 8 October 1915. E2 b.5. See also Avogadro, *L'amico del re*, p. 106 (19 October 1915).
61 AUSSME, T.8819, Cadorna to Salandra, 26 October 1915. E2 b.26.
62 Rocca, *Cadorna*, p. 100.
63 AUSSME, T.937G, Cadorna to Salandra and Zupelli, 4 November 1915. E2 b.26.
64 Massignani, 'La guerra aerea sul fronte italiano', 27.
65 Cadorna to Maria [Cadorna], 6 November 1915; Cadorna to Carla [Cadorna], 28 November 1915: Cadorna, *Lettere famigliari*, pp. 128, 130.

66 Achille Rastelli, 'I bombardamenti sulle città', in Paolo Ferrari, ed., *La Grande Guerra aerea*, pp. 189–95.
67 AUSSME, T. Salandra to Cadorna, 20 November 1915. E2 b.20.
68 AUSSME, N.1028, Cadorna to Salandra, 20 November 1915. H5 b.17/f.3.
69 AUSSME, T.156, Ropolo, 10 November 1915. G29 b.89/f.1.
70 AUSSME, T.163, Ropolo, 19 November 1915. G29 b.89/f.1.
71 AUSSME, Carlotti to Sonnino, 31 October 1915. G29 b.89/f.1.
72 AUSSME, T.1010G, Cadorna to Salandra and Zupelli, 18 November 1915. E2 b.26.
73 Faldella, *La grande guerra*, vol. I, p. 148.
74 On Italy's Turkish ambitions, see Marta Petricioli, *L'Italia in Asia Minore: Equilibrio mediterraneo e ambizioni imperialiste alla vigilia della prima guerra mondiale* (Florence: Sansoni, 1983), *passim*.
75 R. J. B. Bosworth, *Italy, the Least of the Great Powers: Italian Foreign Policy before the First World War* (Cambridge: Cambridge University Press, 1979), pp. 384, 404–5.
76 AUSSME, Zupelli to Cadorna, 25 September 1915; Cadorna to Zupelli, 26 September 1915. H5 b.12/f.4–1.
77 Cadorna to Sonnino, 20 October 1915: [Mario Montanari], *Le truppe italiane in Albania (Anni 1914–1920 e 1939)* (Rome: Ufficio Storico dello Stato Maggiore dell'Esercito, 1978), pp. 39–40.
78 AUSSME, T.1359, Porro to Cadorna, 16 December 1915; T.1217, Cadorna to Porro, 17 December 1915; T.795, Porro to Cadorna, 18 December 1915. E2 b.26.
79 Cadorna to Zupelli, 17 December 1915: [Montanari], *Le truppe italiane in Albania*, p. 47.
80 C. R. M. F. Cruttwell, *A History of the Great War 1914–1918* (Oxford: Clarendon Press, 1964), p. 236.
81 Cadorna to Salandra, 27 February 1916 [Montanari], *Le truppe italiane in Albania*, pp. 297–8.
82 AUSSME, Undated note [*c.*2 March 1916] by Vittorio Emanuele III, H5 b.10/f.1.
83 Roberto Tremilloni, 'Aspetti economici della guerra' in AA.VV., *1915–1918: L'Italia nella grande guerra* (Rome: Presidenza del Consiglio dei Ministri, 1970), p. 267.
84 Daniele Marchesini, 'Città e campagna nel specchio dell'alfabetismo (1921–1951)', in Simonetta Soldani and Gabriele Turi, eds., *Fare gli Italiani: Scuola e cultura nell'Italia contemporanea*, vol. II, *Una società di massa* (Bologna: Il Mulino, 1993), p. 26.
85 Francesco L. Galassi, *Hanging off the Windowsill: Italy at War 1915–1918*, ms. n.d., p. 7.
86 Luciano Segreto, 'Statalismo e antistatalismo nell'economia bellica: Gli industriali e la Mobilitazione Industriale (1915–1918)', in Peter Hertner and Giorgio Mori, eds., *La transizione dall'economia di guerra all'economia di pace in Italia e in Germania dopo la prima guerra mondiale* (Bologna: Il Mulino, 1983), pp. 301–334.
87 Tremilloni, 'Aspetti economici della guerra', 294.

88 Massimo Mazzetti, *L'industria italiana nella Grande Guerra* (Rome: Ufficio Storico dello Stato Maggiore dell'Esercito, 1979), pp. 12 fn.38, 18–25; Luigi Tomassini, 'Gli effetti sociali della mobilitazione industriale', in Daniele Menozza, Giovanna Procacci and Simonetta Soldani, eds., *Un paese in guerra: La mobilitazione civile in Italia (1914–1918)* (Milan: Unicopli, 2010), p. 34. As always, figures differ slightly.

89 D. J. Forsyth, *The Crisis of Liberal Italy* (Cambridge: Cambridge University Press, 1993), p. 81.

90 Dallolio to Comando Supremo, 8 January 1916: Vincenzo Gallinari, 'Il general Alfredo Dallolio nella prima guerra mondiale', *Memorie Storiche Militari* 1977, 127 [original emphasis].

91 Mazzetti, *L'industria italiana nella Grande Guerra*, pp. 36, 38, 40–1.

92 Gerd Hardach, *The First World War 1914–1918* (London: Allen Lane, 1977), pp. 111, 132–3. 1 quintal = 100 kilos.

93 Segreto 'Statalismo e antistatalismo', 314–15.

94 Hardach, *The First World War*, p. 172.

95 Gallinari, 'Alfredo Dallolio', 139–41.

96 Francesco A. Répaci, *Scritti di economia e finanza*, vol. IV, *La Finanza dello stato: Scritti vari* (Milan: Giuffrè, 1974), p. 460.

97 Tremilloni, 'Aspetti economici della guerra', pp. 276–7.

98 Antonio Pedone, 'Il bilancio dello stato', in Giorgio Fuà, ed., *Lo sviluppo economico in Italia: Storia dell'Economia Italiana negli ultimi cento anni* (Milan: Franco Angeli, 1974), vol. II, pp. 207, 221–3.

99 Carl-Ludwig Holtferich, 'Moneta e credito in Italia e Germania dal 1914 al 1924', in Peter Hertner and Giorgio Mori, *La transizione dall'economia di guerra all'economia di pace in Italia e in Germania dopo la prima guerra mondiale*, (Bologna: Il Mulino, 1983) pp, 668–71.

100 See John Gooch ' "The moment to act has arrived": Italy's Libyan War 1911–1912', in Peter Dennis and Jeffrey Grey, eds., *1911 Preliminary Moves* (Canberra ACT: Army History Unit, 2011), pp. 184–209.

101 SIFAR, *Il servizio informazioni militare italiano dalla sua costituzione alla fine della seconda guerra mondiale* (Rome: Stato Maggiore della Difesa, 1957 [declassified 1977]), p. 10.

102 Pasqualini, *Carte segrete dell'Intelligence italiana 1861–1918*, p. 289.

103 Pethö, *I servizi segreti dell'Austria–Ungheria*, pp. 167–70, 173–4.

104 *Ibid.*, p. 176.

105 Filippo Cappellano and Flavio Carbone, 'I carabinieri reali al fronte nella grande guerra', in Nicola Labanca and Giorgio Rochat, eds., *Il soldato, la guerra e il rischio di morire* (Milan: Unicopli, 2006), pp. 171–2.

106 *Ibid.*, pp. 198–9.

107 Maravigna, *Le undici offensive sull'Isonzo*, p. 120.

108 Piero Melograni, *Storia politica della Grande Guerra 1915/18* (Bari: Laterza, 1977), vol. I, pp. 229–231; Ilari, *Storia del servizio militare in Italia*, vol. II, pp. 454–5, 508.

109 C.3525, Disciplina in guerra, 28 September 1915: *cit.* Marco Pluviano and Irene Guerrini, *Le fucilazioni sommarie nella prima guerra mondiale* (Udine: Gaspari, 2004), pp. 9–10.

110 *Ibid.*, pp. 20–1.
111 Forcella and Monticone, *Plotone di esecuzione*, pp. xix–xxi, 3–6, 10–14, 27–30.
112 'Presence' was defined as 'all crimes committed in the presence of the
    enemy, on the occasion of marches against the enemy, in scouting and
    security duties, etc.': *ibid.*, p. 420 fn.16. In a circular of 24 November
    1915, Della Noce made known his view that desertion 'in the presence of
    the enemy' should apply to detachments in rear positions. As time went on,
    tribunals were allowed to punish soldiers behind the front line as if 'in the
    face of the enemy' if two-thirds of the unit was serving in the front line, even
    if at the time of the act those held guilty of it were not.
113 *Ibid.*, pp. 483, 488.
114 *Ibid.*, pp. 45–6.
115 AUSSME, Cadorna to Salandra, 14 January 1916; H5 b.17/f.1. Ilari con-
    cludes that 'The logic of war could not be other than in complete opposition
    to the logic of law' – a moral judgement with which I strongly disagree:
    Storia del servizio militare in Italia, vol. II, p. 463.
116 Faldella claims that it did not occur: Faldella, *La Grande Guerra*, vol. II,
    pp. 303–5. Monticone demonstrates that something very close to it occurred
    on at least three occasions in 1916 and 1917: Forcella and Monticone,
    Plotone di esecuzione, pp. 452–3.
117 Ilari, in an attempt to defend the indefensible, calls Cadorna's decision
    'courageous'and suggests that it was 'probably' as much an offence to his
    conscience as it was to the Caporetto Inquiry: *Storia del servizio militare in
    Italia.*, vol. II, p. 464. The former judgement seems to me wrong and the
    latter demonstrably untrue.
118 Pluviano and Guerrini, *Le fucilazioni sommarie*, pp. 203–13.
119 Ilari, *Storia del servizio militare in Italia*, vol. II, pp. 466–7.
120 AUSSME, Cadorna to Salandra, 7 December 1915. E2 b.26.
121 AUSSME, C.24700, Concessione di breve licenze durante il period inver-
    nale, 7 December 1915. F1 racc. 23/1.
122 Pinotto [Giuseppe Garrone] to Mariella Garrone, 26 November 1915;
    Pinotto to Vittorio Pansini, 26 November 1915: Virginia and Alessandro
    Galante Garrone, eds., *lettere e diari di guerra 1914–1918 di Giuseppe ed
    Eugenio Garrone* (Milan: Garzanti, 1974), pp. 171, 172.
123 AUSSME, Anon. to Cadorna, 12 December 1915. H5 b.17/f.1.
124 This figure derived from Pollio's March 1914 memorandum. The post-war
    head of the general staff historical branch, Colonel Adriano Alberti, the
    author of a number of important works, disbelieved the figure: Ilari, *Storia
    del servizio militare in Italia*, vol. II, p. 455.
125 AUSSME, Promemoria per la Segreteria del Capo di S.M. dell'Esercito:
    Risposta a promemoria 1145 del 5 dicembre, 13 December 1915. H5 b.17/f.3.
126 AUSSME, *Ufficio sanitario*: Unheaded memorandum, 8 December 1915.
    H5 b.17/f3.
127 Fabi, *Gente di trincea*, pp. 283–4.
128 Melograni, *Storia politica della Grande Guerra*, vol. I, p. 121.
129 Ministero della Guerra, *L'esercito italiano nella grande guerra*, vol. III, Part 1,
    pp. 50, 102.

130 AUSSME, Deficienze di materiali d'artiglieria e del genio all'inizio della campagna, 15 December 1915. H5 b.17/f.3.

131 AUSSME, N.1045, *Ufficio servizio aeronautica*: Riassunto delle deficienze, 14 December 1915. H5 b.17/f.3.

132 AUSSME, N.725, Intendente Generale to *Comando supremo* (Ufficio del Capo): Sintesi delle principali deficienze riscontrate nei servizi dipendenti all'inizio della campagna, 14 December 1915. H5 b.17/f.3.

133 AUSSME, Intendenza Generale to *Servizio dei trasporti*: Communicazioni circa le deficienze per il servizio dei trasporti, 13 December 1915. H5 b.17/f.3.

134 Malagodi, *Conversazioni della guerra*, vol. 1, pp. 108, 67 (2 January 1916, 26 July 1915)

135 Cadorna, *La guerra alla fronte italiana*, pp. 148–50.

136 Melograni, *Storia politica della Grande Guerra*, vol. I, pp. 173–5.

137 Salandra to Vittorio Emanuele III, 30 January 1915: *ibid.*, pp. 175–7.

138 Cadorna to Ninetta [Cadorna], 2 February 1916: Cadorna, *Lettere famigliari*, p. 138.

139 Rocca, *Cadorna*, p. 110.

NOTES TO CHAPTER 4

1 Cadorna, *La guerra alla fronte italiana*, pp. 318, 337, 339–40.

2 Procedimento metodico (3a Armata), 6 December 1915; Operazioni offensive metodiche (2ª Armata), 17 January 1916: Ministero della guerra, *L'esercito italiano nella grande guerra (1915–1918)*, vol. III Part 1 *bis*, pp. 136–8, 139.

3 AUSSME, Appunto sulla conversazione tenuta nel pomeriggio del 12 febbraio nello studio di S.E. il Capo di Stato Maggiore dell'esercito italiano [quos. pp. 4, 6]. H5 b.17/f.2

4 Ripresa offensive sulla fronte dell'Isonzo [Cadorna], 6 March 1916: Ministero della Guerra, *L'esercito italiano nella grande guerra*, vol. III, Part 1 *bis*, p. 172.

5 Attacco metodico (3ª Armata), 30 March 1916: *ibid.*, pp. 252–3; Faldella, *La grande guerra*, vol. I, p. 172.

6 AUSSME, Relazione sulla sistemazione difensiva nella fronte tridentina all'inizio dell'offensiva austriaca del maggio 1916, April 1917, Parte 1a, p. 16. E2 b.56.

7 Brusati to Cadorna, 29 June 1915: quo. Pieri, *La prima guerra mondiale*, p. 90.

8 AUSSME, N.5430, Brusati to Cadorna, 7 September 1915: Relazione sulla sistemazione difensiva, Parte 1a, p. 24.

9 AUSSME, Cadorna to Brusati, 11 September 1915 and 26 September 1915: *ibid.*, pp. 27–8, 29.

10 AUSSME, N.1065, Comando supremo to Army Commanders, 24 November 1915: *ibid.*, p. 40.

11 Rocca, *Cadorna*, p. 128.

12 AUSSME, N.1574G, Cadorna to Brusati, 24 February 1916. H5 b.17/f.1.

13 AUSSME, Relazione sulla sistemazione difensiva nella fronte tridentina all'inizio dell'offensiva austriaca del maggio 1916, April 1917, Parte IVa, pp. 10–11, 15–16, 30, 31.

14 AUSSME, T.4 Romei, 6 January 1916. G29 b.89/f.1.

15 AUSSME, T.16, Romei, 21 January 1916. G29 b.89/f.3.

16 Cadorna, *La guerra alla fronte italiana*, pp. 204–6.

17 Pasqualini, *Carte segrete dell'Intelligence Italiana 1861–1918*, pp. 305–7.

18 Capellano, *L'Imperial regio Esercito*, p. 160.

19 SIFAR, *Il servizio informazioni militare italiano*, pp. 24–5; Paolo Ferrari and Alessandro Massignani, *Dietro le Quinte: Economia e intelligence nelle guerre del novecento* (Milan: CEDAM, 2011), pp. 36–7; Vittorino Tarolli, *Spionaggio e propaganda: Il ruolo del servizio informazioni dell'esercito nella Guerra 1915/1918* (Chiari Nordpress, 2001), pp. 85–8.

20 Circa le voci di offensive di grande stile da parte dell'Austria–Ungheria, 3 April 1916: Ministero della Guerra, *L'esercito italiano nella grande guerra*, vol. III, Part 2 *bis*, p. 37. By January 1917 there were 37 telephone interception stations on the Isonzo: Cappellano, *L'Imperial regio Esercito*, p. 108.

21 AUSSME, N.1831, Cadorna to Brusati, 6 April 1916. H5 b.17/f.1.

22 AUSSME, N.8752, Brusati to Cadorna, 6 April 1916. H5 b.17/f.1.

23 AUSSME, N.1840, Cadorna to Brusati, 8 April 1916. H5 b.17/f.1.

24 AUSSME, T.1980, Cadorna to Joffre, 26 April 1916. E2 b.14.

25 AUSSME, T.505 M.13, Breganze to Comando Supremo, 27 April 1916. E2 b.14.

26 Verbale dell'interrogatorio del tenente Anton Krecht, 28 April 1916: Ferrari and Massignano, *Dietro le Quinte*, pp. 53–5.

27 C. Petorelli Lalatta, *I.T.O.* (Milan: Agnelli, 1931), p. 97, quo. Tarolli, *Spionaggio e propaganda*, p. 89.

28 AUSSME, N.2004, Cadorna to Brusati, 30 April 1916. H5 b.17/f.1.

29 AUSSME, N.2106G, Cadorna to Brusati, 8 May 1916. H5 b.17/f.1.

30 Cadorna to Ugo Brusati, 14 May 1916: quo. Rocca, *Cadorna*, p. 135.

31 AUSSME, T.60113, Sonnino to Cadorna, 14 May 1916; T.2165, Cadorna to Sonnino, 15 May 1916; T.1936, Salandra to Cadorna, 15 May 1916. H5 b.17/f.6.

32 Pethö, *I servizi segreti dell'Austria–Ungheria*, p. 177.

33 AUSSME, T.1957, Salandra to Porro, 18 May 1916. E2 b.26.

34 AUSSME, T.2199, Porro to Salandra, 18 May 1916; T.2201, Cadorna to Salandra, 18 May 1916. E2 b.26. Cadorna, *La guerra alla fronte italiana*, pp. 200–2.

35 AUSSME, Morrone to Porro, 18 May 1916; T.2230, Porro to Morrone, 19 May 1916. E2 b.26.

36 Faldella, *La grande guerra*, vol. I, p. 205.

37 AUSSME, T.2283, Porro to Salandra, 23 May 1916. E2 b.26.

38 AUSSME, Salandra to Cadorna, 24 May 1916. E2 b.26.

39 AUSSME, T.5, Cadorna to Salandra, 25 May 1916; T.2048, Salandra to Cadorna, 25 May 1916. E2 b.26.

40 AUSSME, N.2346, Cadorna to Morrone, 28 May 1916. H5 b.17/f.1.

41 AUSSME, Porro to Colonel Enkell, 30 May 1916. E2 b.14.

42 AUSSME, T. gab 722 24, Sonnino to Salandra, 30 May 1916; T. gab 728 26, Sonnino to Cadorna, 31 May 1916. H5 b.17/f.6.

43 AUSSME, T.25006, Romei to Cadorna, 1 June 1916. E2 b.14.

44 AUSSME, T.37, Romei to Comando Supremo, 6 June 1916; T.38, Romei to Comando Supremo, 6 June 1916; T.39, Romei to Comando Supremo, 7 June 1916; T.56, Romei to Comando Supremo, 18 June 1916. G29 b.89/f.3.
45 AUSSME, Salandra to Cadorna, 4 June 1916. H5 b.17/f.6.
46 AUSSME, N.100, Cadorna to Salandra, 7 June 1916. H5 b.17/f.6.
47 AUSSME, Morrone to Cadorna, 11 June 1916. H5 b.17/f.6.
48 Rocca gives an Italian total of 147,710 (15,433 dead, 76,642 wounded and 55,635 'dispersed') and an Austrian total of 80,000: Rocca, *Cadorna*, p.148.
49 Cadorna to Carla [Cadorna], 16 June 1916 Cadorna, *Lettere famigliari*, p. 155.
50 Pieri, *La prima guerra mondiale*, pp.113–14.
51 Pasqualini, *Carte segrete dell'Intelligence Italiana*, pp. 310–13.
52 Anon. to his brother, 2 April 1916: Giovanna Procacci, *Soldati e prigionieri italiani nella Grande guerra* (Turin: Bollati Boringhieri, 2000), p. 424.
53 Stuparach, *Guerra del '15*, p. 45 (21 June 1916).
54 Emilio Lussu, *Un anno sull'Altopiano* (Turin: Einaudi, 1998), p. 116.
55 AUSSME, Alcuni dati statistici sulla campagna Italo-Austriaca, n.d. [30 June 1916]. L13 b.143/f.7.
56 Giorgio Rochat, 'L'efficienza dell'esercito italiano nella grande guerra', in Rochat, *Ufficiali e soldati: L'esercito italiano dalla prima alla seconda guerra mondiale* (Udine: Gaspari, 2000), p. 29. See also, Lucio Fabi, '"Se domani si va all'assalto/soldati non farti ammazzare": Appunti e riflessioni sulla vita e la morte del soldato in trincea', in Nicola Labanca and Giorgio Rochat, *Il soldato, la guerra e il rischio di morire* (Milan: Unicopli, 2006), pp. 153–65.
57 Richard A. Webster, 'From insurrection to intervention: The Italian crisis of 1914', *Italian Quarterly* vol. 5/6 no. 21, Winter–Spring 1961–2, 34.
58 Marcello Malpensa, 'I vescovi davanti alla guerra', in Daniele Menozzi, Giovanna Procacci and Simonetta Soldani, eds., *Un paese in guerra: La mobilitazione civile in Italia (1914–1918)* (Milan: Unicopli, 2010), pp. 295–315 [quo. p. 307]. See also Daniele Menozzi, *'Chiesa e città'*, in *ibid.*, pp. 269–74.
59 Antonio Gibelli and Carlo Stiaccini, 'Il miracolo della guerra: Appunti su religione e superstizione nei soldati della Grande Guerra', in Labanca and Rochat, *Il soldato*, pp.125–36. On the eve of the war, the Santuario di Pompei printed almost 2,000,000 images of the Madonna, as well as 3,000 small portraits and 1,500,000 medallions.
60 Roberto Morozzo della Rocca, 'I capellani militari cattolici nel 1915–1918', in Giorgio Rochat, ed., *La spada e la croce: I capellani italiani nelle due guerre mondiali* (Bolletino della Società di Studi Valdesi no. 176, 1995), p. 67.
61 Mario Isnenghi, *Giornali di trincea (1915–1918)* (Turin: Einaudi, 1977), pp. 12–25; Angelo Ventrone, *Piccola storia della Grande guerra* (Rome: Donzelli, 2005), pp. 116–17.
62 Melograni, *Storia politica della Grande Guerra*, vol. I, pp. 245–6.
63 Paolo Caccia Dominioni, *1915–1919 diario di guerra* (Milan: Mursia, 1996), p. 79 (2 November 1916).
64 Filippo Guerrieri, *Lettere dalla trincea (Libia–Carso–Trentino–Macedonia)* (Vallagarina: Arte Grafiche R. Manfrini, 1968), p. 136 (17 June 1916).
65 Caccia Dominioni, *1915–1919*, p. 35.

66 Tito A. Spagnol, *Memoriette marziali e veneree* (Vicenza: Mario Spagnol Editore, 1970), p. 86.

67 Emilio Franzina, *Casini di guerra: Il tempo libero dalla trincea e i postriboli militari nel primo conflitto mondiale* (Udine: Gaspari, 1999), p. 94.

68 *Ibid.*, pp. 97, 198 fn.7.

69 Antonio Sema, *Soldati e prostitute: Il caso della terza armata* (Valdagno: Gino Rossati, 2003), p. 43.

70 *Ibid.*, pp. 42, 51.

71 Massimo Magli, *Fucilazioni di guerra: Testimonianzi ed episodi di giustizia militare dal fronte italo-austriaco 1915–1918* (Chiari: Nordpress, 2007), p. 22.

72 Pluviano and Guerrini, *Le fucilazioni sommarie*, pp. 50–5. Forcella and Monticone, *Plotone di esecuzione*, p. 70.

73 Forcella and Monticone, *Plotone di esecuzione*. p. 497.

74 Cadorna to Ninetta [Cadorna], 26 May 1916: Cadorna, *Lettere famigliari*, p. 151.

75 Cadorna to Lequio, 26 May 1916: Pluviano and Guerrini, *Le fucilazioni sommarie*, p. 115.

76 Forcella and Monticone, *Plotone di esecuzione*, pp. 449, 452.

77 Pluviano and Guerrini, *Le fucilazioni sommarie*, pp. 98–105

78 Cadorna to Boselli, 20 November 1916: Melograni, *Storia politica della Grande Guerra*, vol. I, pp. 215–17.

79 Rocca, *Cadorna*, p. 156.

80 Cadorna to army commanders and XI Army Corps, 10 November 1916: Magli, *Fucilazioni di guerra*, pp. 34–5.

81 AUSSME, Boselli to Cadorna, 15 November 1916; Cadorna to Boselli, 20 November 1916. L13 b.143/f.6.

82 Lussu, *Un anno sull'Altopiano*, pp. 58–60.

83 Sonnino to Imperiali, 15 June 1915; Sonnino to Imperiali, Tittoni, Carlotti, 28 June 1915; Cadorna to Sonnino, 30 July 1915; Sonnino to Imperiali, etc., 3 August 1915; Sonnino to Salandra, 16 October 1915; Sonnino to Cadorna, 19 October 1915: *DDI* 5th ser. vol. IV nos. 188, 292, 499, 517, 922, 934, pp. 109, 176–7, 301–2, 317–18, 580–1, 586–7.

84 Sonnino to Imperiali etc., 14 September 1915: *DDI* 5th ser. vol. IV no. 742, p. 467.

85 Sonnino to Imperiali etc., 27 September 1915; Sonnino to Salandra, 7 October 1915; Sonnino to Imperiali, etc., 13 October 1915; Cadorna to Sonnino, 16 October 1915: *DDI* 5th ser. vol. IV nos. 813, 880, 903, 916, pp. 511–12, 550, 568, 575–6

86 Cadorna to Salandra, 20 October 1915; Cadorna to Salandra, 1 November 1915: *DDI* 5th ser. vol. IV no. 941, pp. 591–2; 5th ser. vol. V no. 48, pp. 36–7.

87 Sonnino to Cadorna, 21 October 1915; Cadorna to Sonnino, 23 October 1915: *DDI* 5th ser. vol. IV nos. 950, 958, pp. 597–8, 602–3.

88 Sonnino to Imperiali, etc., 23 January 1916: *DDI* 5th ser. vol. V no. 362, p. 257.

89 De Bosdari to Sonnino, 13 January 1916; Galanti to Sonnino, 30 April 1916; Piacentini to Sonnino, 19 May 1916; Sonnino to Cadorna, etc., 19 May 1916: *DDI* 5th ser. vol. V nos. 309, 755, 833, 835, pp. 215–17, 557, 618–19, 619–20.

90 Imperiali to Sonnino, 1 June 1915: *DDI* 5th ser. vol. IV no. 70, pp. 34–5.
91 Fasciotti to Sonnino, 25 January 1916: *DDI* 5th ser. vol. V no. 366, pp. 259–60.
92 Carlotti to Sonnino, 17 May 1916: *DDI* 5th ser. vol. V no. 826, p. 614.
93 Carlotti to Sonnino, 26 May 1916: *DDI* 5th ser. vol. V no. 861, pp. 642–3.
94 AUSSME, Cadorna to Morrone, 20 June 1916. H5 b.17/f.1.
95 AUSSME, Porro to Delmé-Radcliffe, 5 June 1916. E2 b.14.
96 AUSSME, Delmé-Radcliffe to Cadorna, 10 June 1916. E2 b.14.
97 AUSSME, De Gondrecourt to Comando supremo,19 June 1916. E2 b.14.
98 AUSSME, T.2489, Cadorna to Sonnino, 22 June 1916. H5 b.17/f.6.
99 AUSSME, Cadorna to Porro, 21 June 1916. E2 b.14.
100 AUSSME, De Gondrecourt to Cadorna, 25 June 1916; Porro to De Gondrecourt, 26 June 1916. E2 b.14.
101 AUSSME, Joffre to Cadorna, 27 June 1916; T.2257/2509, De Gondrecourt to Cadorna, 2 July 1916; T.2529, Cadorna to Ferigo, 2 July 1916; N.2525, Porro to De Gondrecourt, 3 July 1916. H5 b.17/f.6.
102 AUSSME, Joffre to Cadorna, 30 June 1916. H5 b.17/f.6.
103 AUSSME, T.126, Romei, 18 July 1916. G29 b.89/f.3.
104 R. A. Delmé-Radcliffe to Grey, 10 August 1914. PS/GV/Q.688/2.
105 Paulucci de' Calboli to Sonnino, 1 March 1916; Sonnino to de' Calboli, 8 March 1916 encl. Cadorna to Salandra, n.d.: *DDI* 5th ser. vol. V nos. 531, 562, pp. 389–90, 412–14.
106 AUSSME, N.308, Cadorna to Sonnino, 6 July 1916. H5 b.17/f.1.
107 AUSSME, De Gondrecourt to Comando supremo, 1 August 1916. E2 b.14.
108 AUSSME, Tagliaferri to De Gondrecourt, 3 August 1916. E2 b.14.
109 AUSSME, T.930 37, Sonnino to Cadorna, 12 July 1916. H5 b.17/f.6. In fact, the British general staff was only willing to support an extension of operations in Greece if the Romanians had already agreed to join the Entente, which they did not do until 17 August 1916, and were prepared to attack Bulgaria, something they obdurately refused to do.
110 Sonnino to Cadorna, etc., 17 July 1916; Sonnino to Cadorna, etc., 21 July 1916: *DDI* 5th ser. vol. VI nos. 136, 154, pp. 92, 102.
111 AUSSME, T2559, Cadorna to Sonnino, 15 July 1916; T.2590 Zama [Porro] to Sagunto [Breganze], 22 July 1916. H5 b.17/f.6. Cadorna to Sonnino, 19 July 1916: *DDI* 5th ser. vol. VI no. 138, p. 93.
112 Cadorna to Sonnino, 24 July 1916: *DDI* 5th ser. vol. VI no. 177, p. 188.
113 AUSSME, N.10806, Cadorna to Sonnino, 29 July 1916; N.10916, Cadorna to Sonnino, 30 July 1916. H5 b.17/f.5.
114 AUSSME, De Gondrecourt to Comando supremo, 26 July 1916. H5 b.17/f.6.
115 AUSSME, N.2623, Cadorna to De Gondrecourt, 28 July 1916. H5 b.17/f.6.
116 Cadorna to Sonnino, 11 July 1916: *DDI* 5th ser. vol. VI no. 103, p. 69.
117 Cadorna to Sonnino, 14 August 1916; Cadorna to Sonnino, 18 August 1916: *DDI* 5th ser. vol. VI nos. 268, 287, pp. 182–3, 194–5.
118 Sonnino to Cadorna, 24 September 1916: *DDI* 5th ser. vol. VI no. 477, pp. 319–20.
119 Cadorna to Boselli and Sonnino, 30 October 1916; Cadorna to Boselli, 7 November 1916: *DDI* 5th ser. vol. VI nos. 636, 676, pp. 433–4, 463.

120 Cadorna to Boselli, 10 November 1916: *DDI* 5th ser. vol. VI no. 691, p.473.
121 IWM. Delmé-Radcliffe to Derby, 8 October 1917: IWM 06/1/1–4/26.
122 Rino Alessi, *Dall'Isonzo al Piave: Lettere clandestine di un corrispondente di guerra* (Milan: Mondadori, 1966), p. 51 (6 April 1917).
123 Conferenza militare interalleate, 15–16 November 1916: *DDI* 5th ser. vol. VI no. 712, pp. 488–502.
124 Cadorna to Salandra, 9 June 1915: *DDI* 5th ser. vol. IV no. 137, p. 80.
125 Cadorna, *La guerra alla fronte italiana*, pp. 264–8.
126 Cadorna to Aosta, 15 June 1916: Rocca, *Cadorna*, pp. 159–60.
127 Cadorna to [Raffaele Cadorna], 30 June 1916: Cadorna, *Lettere famigliari*, p. 157. (Original emphasis.)
128 Rocca, *Cadorna*, p.162.
129 Pieri, *La prima guerra mondiale*, p. 122, quoting Francesco Zingales, *La conquista di Gorizia* (Rome: Ufficio Storico della Stato Maggiore, 1925).
130 Piero Pieri and Giorgio Rochat, *Badoglio* (Turin: UTET, 1974), pp. 91–106; Silvio Bertoldi, *Badoglio: Il generale che prese il posto di Mussolini* (Milan: Rizzoli, 1993), pp. 44–8. Others who claimed to have had a large hand in the new measures included General Garioni, II Army Corps commander, Major Nastasi (who arrived months after Badoglio had started work on them), and Major Carotenuto, an engineer.
131 Faldella, *La grande guerra* vol. I, p. 221.
132 AUSSME, T.133, Romei to Comando supremo, 21 July 1916; T.158, Romei to Comando supremo, 3 August 1916. G29 b.89/f.3.
133 AUSSME, T.166, Romei to Comando supremo, 7 August 1916. G29 b.89/f.3.
134 Cadorna to Aosta, 16 June 1916: Pieri and Rochat, *Badoglio*, p. 107. (Original emphasis.)
135 Fabi, *Gente di trincea*, pp. 51–2. During the seventh, eighth and nineth battles of the Isonzo (14–16 September 1916, 10–12 October 1916, 1–4 November 1916) average daily rates of fire along fronts of approximately 10 kilometres were 58,000 rounds, 83,600 rounds and 72,400 rounds.
136 Cadorna to Piacentini, 17 August 1916: Rocca, *Cadorna*, p. 168.
137 Cadorna, *La guerra alla fronte italiana*, p. 294.
138 Pieri, *La prima guerra mondiale*, pp. 119–20.
139 AUSSME, N.530, Cadorna to Salandra, 3 August 1916; T.529, Cadorna to Zupelli, 3 August 1916. E2 b.26.
140 AUSSME, T.2764, Cadorna to Boselli, 19 September 1916. E2 b.26.
141 Cadorna, *La guerra alla fronte italiana*, pp. 318–19.
142 AUSSME, Bertotti to Porro, 4 August 1916. H5 b.17/f.1.
143 AUSSME, N.2663, Cadorna to Bissolati, 7 August 1916; N.2664, Cadorna to Boselli, 7 August 1916; N.19.4.1.7, Boselli to Cadorna, 9 August 1916. E2 b.26.
144 Melograni, *Storia politica della Grande Guerra*, vol. II, pp. 200–6.
145 AUSSME, N.543, Cadorna to Boselli, 18 August 1916. E2 b.44.
146 AUSSME, Situazione dell'esercito italiano alle successive date del 1o marzo 1916, 1o Maggio 1916 e 1o luglio 1916, per quanto si referisce a forza sotto le armi e disponibilità forza in congedo. L13 b.144/f.2.

147 AUSSME, Forze alle armi e forza a ruolo in congedo alla data del 1o agosto 1916. L13 b.143/f.7.
148 AUSSME, Perdite in ufficiali dall'inizio della campagna sino al 10 settembre 1916. L13 b.143/f.6.
149 AUSSME, Situazione numerica delle forze ufficiali al 30 sett. 1916. L13 b.143/f.6.
150 AUSSME, Riassunto dei dati statistici alle perdite dall'inizio della campagna al 31 dicembre 1916 comunicati al Ministero dai Comandi di deposito e centri di mobilitazione, Tabella III. L13 b.143/f.7.
151 Mazzetti, 'Note all'interpretazione interventista', *Memorie Storiche Militari* 1979, 97.
152 AUSSME, Elenco di ufficiali generali che hanno cessato dal commando militare, 1 July 1916. L13 b.143/f.6.
153 AUSSME, Il problema attuale della Germania, 9 September 1916. E2 b.67.
154 AUSSME, La situazione militare attuale, 4 October 1916. E2 b.67.
155 AUSSME, Autograph note by Cadorna, 31 October [1916]. H5 b.17/f.7.
156 AUSSME, Possibilità degli austro-tedeschi durante l'inverno sulle diverse fronte – Risorse – Riserve – Possibili operazioni, 4 November 1916. E2 b.129.
157 AUSSME, N.19972, Le possibilità prossime per gli imperi centrali, 14 December 1916, pp. 4,5. E2 b.129.
158 AUSSME, La situazione militare e politica, Di Giorgio to Morrone, n.d. [?November 1916], pp. 1, 2, 8, 9. L13 b.143/f.9.
159 *Ibid.*, pp. 9–11, 20, 21.

NOTES TO CHAPTER 5

1 Répaci, *Scritti di economia e finanza*, vol. IV, p.6. Ilari gives slightly different figures: deaths in action (recalculated removing deaths through sickness and rounded to 0.1%) with wounded in brackets – 1915, 81,606 (190,400); 1916, 107,660 (285,620); 1917, 111,780 (302,446); 1918, 45,289 (120,607). In 1918, 113,620 troops died of sickness, which could be wound-related. Ilari, *Storia del servizio militare in Italia*, vol. II, *La "Nazione Armata"*, p. 444.
2 Dominioni, *1915–1919*, p. 131 (27 May 1917).
3 Cadorna to Boselli, 6 June 1917: Magli, ed., *Fucilazioni di guerra*, p. 110.
4 Mario Toscano, 'Il problema del confine occidentale durante la prima guerra mondiale', *Rassegna italiana politica, letteraria e artistica* vol. 58 no. 301, June 1943, 243–51.
5 René Albrecht-Carrié, 'Italian colonial policy, 1914–1918', *Journal of Modern History* vol. 18 no. 2, June 1946, 127.
6 Robert L. Hess, 'Italy and Africa: Colonial ambitions in the First World War', *Journal of African History* vol. 4 no. 1, 1963, 108–11; Albrecht-Carrié, 'Italian colonial policy', 132–8.
7 Saverio Cilibrizzi, *Storia parlamentari politica e diplomatica d'Italia: Da Novara a Vittorio Veneto Volume sesto (1916–1917)* (Naples: Tosi, 1950), p. 337.
8 Tommaso Gallarati Scotti, 'Idee e orientamenti politici e religiosi al Comando supremo: appunti e ricordi', in Giuseppe Rossini, ed., *Benedetto XV, I Cattolici e la prima guerra mondiale* (Rome: Edizioni 5 lune, 1963), p. 513.

9   *Ibid.*, p. 511.
10 Carlo Pinzani, 'I socialisti italiani e francesi nel periodo della neutralità italiana (1914–1915)', *Studi Storici* vol. 15 no. 2, 1974, 385, 388.
11 Luigi Cortesi, 'Il PSI dalla "settimana rossa" al Congresso nazionale del 1918', *Rivista Storica del Socialismo* vol. 10 no. 32, 19–30.
12 Isnenghi and Rochat, *La Grande Guerra*, pp. 108, 279–80.
13 Vittorio De Caprariis, 'Partiti politici ed opinione pubblica durante la grande guerra', *Atti del XLI Congresso di Storia del Risorgimento Italiano (Trento 9–13 ottobre 1963)* (Rome: Istituto per la Storia del Risorgimento Italiano, 1965), pp. 130–1.
14 Malagodi, *Conversazioni della guerra*, vol. I, p. 106 (23 January 1917).
15 Novello Papafava, *Appunti militari 1919–1921* (Ferrara: STET/Tadei, 1921), p. 29.
16 'Alcuni importanti ammaestramenti di esperienza', 20 September 1916; 'Altri ammaestramenti di esperienza', 17 October 1916: Ministero della Guerra, *L'esercito italiano nella grande guerra (1915–1918)*, vol. VI, pp. 338–43, 344–6 [quo. p. 345].
17 'Quantità di truppa tenute in trincea', 4 December 1916; *ibid.*, p. 349.
18 'Impiego dell'artiglieria', 1 March 1917: Stefani, *La storia della dottrina*, vol. I, p. 642.
19 Enrico Pino, 'La regolamentazione tattica del Regio Esercito Italiano e la sua evoluzione nell'ultimo anno del conflitto', in Giampietro Berti and Piero Del Negro, eds., *Al di qua e al di là del Piave: L'ultimo anno della Grande Guerra* (Milan: Franco Angeli, 2001), pp. 287–90.
20 Alessandro Massignani, *Le truppe d'assalto austro-ungariche nella Grande Guerra* (Novale: Gino Rossato Editore, 1999), pp. 33–9, 47–51, 64–73.
21 Basilio Di Martino and Filippo Capellano, *I Reparti d'Assalto Italiani nella Grande Guerra (1915–1918)* (Rome: Ufficio Storico dello Stato Maggiore dell'Esercito, 2007), pp. 7–20, 25–32 [quo. p. 32].
22 Giorgio Rochat, *Gli Arditi della Grande Guerra: Origini, battaglie, miti* (Milan: Feltrinelli, 1981), pp. 23–8; Salvatore Farina, *Le truppe d'assalto italiane* (Milan: La Libreria Militare, 2005), pp. 56–7, 65–8, 95–8, 104–9. Unlike line infantry practice, if one man was wounded his partner accompanied him back to the nearest dressing station.
23 Rochat, *Gli Arditi della Grande Guerra*, pp. 35–6.
24 'Costituzione di nuovi reparti d'assalto' 21 September 1917: Di Martino and Capellano, *I Reparti d'Assalto Italiani*, p. 78.
25 'Official Report by Commander-in-Chief Luigi Cadorna', 26 December 1916, available at www.firstworldwar.com/source/gorizia_cadorna.htm.
26 Faldella, *La grande guerra*, vol. I, p. 260.
27 Alessandro Gionfrida, *L'Italia e il coordinamento militare "interalleato" nella prima guerra mondiale* (Rome: Ufficio Storico dello Stato Maggiore dell'Esercito, 2008), pp. 58–63.
28 AUSSME, N.917, Accenni ad una offensiva contro l'Italia, 15 January 1917; N.2360, Offensiva austriaca sul Carso, 5 February 1917; N.2767, Offensiva austro-tedesca nel trentino, 11 February 1917; N.2, Notizie segnalate circa l'offensiva austro-tedesca alla nostra fronte, 28 February 1917. E2 b.67.

29 Cadorna to Ninetta [Cadorna], 4 and 6 February 1917: Cadorna, *Lettere famigliari*, pp. 185–6, 187.

30 AUSSME, N.4478, Situazione generale alla fronte italiana e probabili future operazioni del nemico, 7 March 1917; Promemoria No. 6158, 31 March 1917. E2 b.67.

31 AUSSME, N.1898, Cadorna to Morrone, 9 March 1917; N.1931, Cadorna to Morrone, 12 March 1917; Morrone to Cadorna [14 March 1917]; N.1526, Dallolio to Cadorna, 16 March 1917. L13 b.143/f.8.

32 AUSSME, N.8006, Morrone to Boselli, 30 March 1917. L13 b.145/f.11.

33 AUSSME, T.118, 9 March 1917; T.136, 30 March 1917. G29 b.89/f.5.

34 AUSSME, N.73 all., 'La Rivoluzione Russa (Dal 14 febbraio al 31 marzo 1917)', 10 April 1917, pp. 66–7. L3 b.76/f.1.

35 AUSSME, T.540, Boselli to Cadorna, 22 March 1917. H5 b.17/f.2.

36 AUSSME, N.2042, Note riassuntive sulle questioni trattate nel convegno tenutosi a Udine presso la sede del Comando supremo il mattino del giorno 23 marzo 1917, pp. 1–2, 5. H5 b.17/f.3.

37 Cadorna to Raffaele [Cadorna], 24 March 1917: Cadorna, *Lettere famigliari*, pp. 195–6.

38 AUSSME, T.443, Sonnino to Imperiali, 27 March 1917; T.129, Imperiali to Sonnino, 27 March 1917. H5 b.17/f.2.

39 AUSSME, Robertson to Cadorna, 5 April 1917. H5 b.17/f.2.

40 AUSSME, Painlevé to Cadorna, 7 April 1917. H5 b.17/f.2.

41 AUSSME, Conférence entre S.E. le général Cadorna et le général Foch à la date du 8 avril [1917]; Cadorna to Painlevé, 13 April 1917. H5 b.17/f.2. Cadorna to Maria [Cadorna], 12 March 1917: Cadorna, *Lettere famigliari*, p. 193.

42 AUSSME, De Béarne to Comando supremo, 15 April 1917; Cadorna to De Gondrecourt/Nivelle, 17 April 1917. H5 b.17/f.2.

43 AUSSME, N.2263, Cadorna to Nivelle, 20 April 1917; N.2264, Cadorna to Nivelle, 20 April 1917; Cadorna to Robertson, 20 April 1917. H5 b.17/f.2.

44 AUSSME, Promemoria N.6724, 7 April 1917; N.6789, 8 April 1917; N.8071, Offensiva austriaca alla fronte italiana, 26 April 1917; N.8300, 29 April 1917. E2. b.67.

45 AUSSME, N.5743, Situazione generale, 25 March 1917; N.8146, Promemoria, 27 April 1917. E2 b.67.

46 Cadorna to Carla [Cadorna], 6 March 1917; Cadorna to Ninetta [Cadorna], 20 March 1917; Cadorna to Raffaele [Cadorna], 24 March 1917; Cadorna to Carla [Cadorna], 12 April 1917: Cadorna, *Lettere famigliari*, pp. 192–3, 194, 196, 197.

47 Cadorna to Raffaele [Cadorna], 2 March 1917; Cadorna to Carla [Cadorna], 28 April 1917: Cadorna, *Lettere famigliari*, pp. 190–1, 198.

48 Isnenghi, *Giornali di trincea*, pp. 26–33; Rocca, *Cadorna*, p.198.

49 AUSSME, Compito globale approssimative del munizionamento occorrente (Vanzo), 23 April 1917; N.43414–1, Lombardi to Cadorna, 25 April 1917; N.2487, Cadorna to Capello, 9 May 1917 [original emphasis]. E.2 b.44.

50 AUSSME, N.2046, D'Alessandro to Cadorna, 7 May 1917. E2 b.44.

51 AUSSME, N.2184, D'Alessandro to Cadorna, 18 May 1917. E2 b.44.

52 AUSSME, N.2629, Cadorna to Capello, 22 May 1917. E2 b.44.
53 AUSSME, N.2382, D'Alessandro to Cadorna, 29 May 1917. E2 b.44. Subsequently Cadorna claimed to have fired 1,300,000 rounds. The difference in the figures may be due to different forms of counting – or it may reflect a wish by D'Alessandro to present the artillery in the best possible light.
54 Faldella, *La grande guerra*, vol. I, pp. 276–87.
55 AUSSME, N.2381, Azioni d'artiglieria, 29 May 1917, p. 3 [underlined in blue in original – ? by Cadorna, who read the document]. E2 b.44.
56 AUSSME, N.2420, Azione di controbatteria, 30 May 1917. E2 b.44.
57 Cadorna to Carla [Cadorna], 26 May 1917: Cardona, *Lettere famigliari*, p. 201. Marshal Caviglia afterwards believed that with eight more divisions, denied her by the Allies, Italy could have collapsed the Austrian front completely: Pieri, *La prima guerra mondiale*, p. 126.
58 AUSSME, N.2750, Altri ammaestramenti di esperienza, 30 May 1917, p.2. E2 b.44.
59 Renzo De Felice, 'Ordine pubblico e orientamento delle masse popolari italiane nella prime metà del 1917', *Rivista Storica del Socialismo* vol. 6 no. 20, 1963, 467–8.
60 Gisueppe Prato, *Il Piemonte e gli effetti della guerra sulla sua vita economica e sociale* (Bari: Laterza, 1925), p. 69 fn.3.
61 Valerio Castronovo, *Giovanni Agnelli: Il fondatore* (Turin: UTET, 2003), pp. 112–13.
62 Melograni, *Storia politica della Grande Guerra*, vol. II, p. 327; Alice A. Kelikian, 'From liberalism to corporatism: The province of Brescia during the First World War', in John A. Davis, ed., *Gramsci and Italy's Passive Revolution* (New York: Barnes & Noble, 1979), pp. 221 *et seq.*
63 Prato, *Il Piemonte*, pp. 178–9, 220; Stefano Somgyi, 'Cento anni di bilanci familiari in Italia (1857–1956) Part1', *Annali dell'Istituto G. G. Feltrinelli* vol. 2, 1959, 173, 174; Répaci, *Scritti di economia e finanza*, vol. IV, p. 20.
64 Ornello Vitale, *La popolazione attiva in agricoltura attraverso i censimenti italiani (1881–1961)* (Rome: Istituto di Demografia Università di Roma, n.d.), pp. 16, 171, 188–9. Serpieri gives slightly different proportions: in the 1911 census 26,580,048 people aged 10 or over: 40% worked in agriculture, 18.8% in industry, 3.5% in commerce, 5.3% in liberal arts and professions, the remaining 32% mostly women being non-specified. Arrigo Serpieri, *La guerra e le classi rurali italiani* (Bari: Laterza, 1930), p. 3.
65 Anthony L. Cardoza, *Agrarian Elites and Italian Fascism: The Province of Bologna, 1901–1926* (Princeton NJ: Princeton University Press, 1982), p. 25.
66 Somgyi, 'Cento anni di bilanci famigliari', p. 165.
67 Anonymous, *L'emigrazione italiana dal 1910 al 1923* (Rome: Edizioni del Commissariato Generale dell'Emigrazione, 1926), vol. I, pp. 819, 824–5.
68 Prato, *Il Piemonte*, p.31.
69 Cardoza, *Agrarian Elites and Italian Fascism*, p. 223.
70 Serpieri, *La guerra e le classi rurali*, pp. 254–5, 263, 267, 285.
71 Cardoza, *Agrarian Elites and Italian Fascism*, pp. 229–34; Alberto Cova, 'Problemi dell'agricultura cremonese negli anni della prima guerra mondiale (1914–1920)', in Peter Hurtner and Giorgio Mori, eds., *La transizione*

dall'economia di guerra all'economia di pace in Italia e in Germania dopo la prima guerra mondiale (Bologna: Il Mulino, 1983), pp. 166, 174–5.

72 Kelikian, 'From liberalism to corporatism', 233.

73 Simonetta Soldani, 'La Grande guerra lontano dal fronte', in G. Mori, ed., *Storia d'Italia: Le Regioni dall'Unità a oggi – La Toscana* (Turin: Einaudi, 1986), p. 423.

74 Andrea Fava, 'Assistenza e propaganda nel regime di guerra (1915–1918', in Mario Isnenghi, ed., *Operai e contadini nella Grande Guerra* (Bologna: Capelli, 1982), pp. 174–212; Luigi Tomassini, 'The home front in Italy', in Hugh Cecil and Peter Liddle, eds., *Facing Armageddon: The First World War Experienced* (Barnsley: Pen & Sword, 1996), pp. 583–5.

75 Giorgio Mortara, *La salute pubblica in Italia durante e dopo la guerra* (Bari: Laterza, 1925), p. 227.

76 Répaci, *Scritti di economia e finanza*, vol. IV, pp. 8, 11; Mortara, *La salute pubblica*, p. 107; Prato, *Il Piemonte*, pp. 170–3.

77 Soldani, 'La Grande guerra lontana dal fronte', pp. 351, 358.

78 Antonio Papa, 'Guerra e terra 1915–1918', *Studi Storici* vol. 10 no. 1, 1969, 6–23 [quo. pp. 20–1].

79 Soldani, 'La Grande guerra lontana dal fronte', pp. 442–6.

80 De Felice, 'Ordine pubblico e orientamento delle masse popolari', 481, 483, 484, 494.

81 Morrone to Orlando, 15 May 1917; Prefect of Milan to Interior Ministry, 5 May 1917: *ibid.*, 473, 502.

82 Mazzetti, *L'industria italiana nella Grande Guerra*, p. 110.

83 Alberto Monticone, 'Il socialismo torinese ed i fatti dell'agosto 1917', in *Gli italiani in uniforme 1915/1918: Intellettuali, borghesi e disertori* (Bari: Laterza, 1972), pp. 89–144; Giovanna Procacci, 'Popular protest and labour conflict in Italy, 1915–1918', *Social History* vol. 14 no. 1, January 1989, 42–3, 46–7; Natalia De Stefano, 'Moti popolari in Emilia-Romagna e Toscana 1915–1917', *Rivista Storica del Socialismo* vol. 10 no. 32, 1967, 201, 204–5, 212–13.

84 Gallinari, 'Alfredo Dallolio', 134.

85 Alessandro Tortato, *Ortigara: La verità negata* (Valdagno: Gino Rossato, 2003), p. 155.

86 Cadorna, *La guerra alla fronte italiano*, p. 382; Tortato, *Ortigara*, pp. 166, 167, 168, 169, 206.

87 Cadorna to Carla [Cadorna], 13 and 15 July 1917: Cadorna, *Lettere famigliari*, pp. 209, 210.

88 Pieri, *La prima guerra mondiale*, p. 140 fn.5.

89 AUSSME, Promemoria Comando 2ª Armata, 2 June 1917. E4 b.2A/3 (3 GM).

90 AUSSME, N.12180, Situazione generale del nemico alla nostra fronte, 17 June 1917; E2 b.67. Influenza dell'offensiva russa sulla dislocazione nemica della nostra fronte, 12 July 1917; N.15425, Influenza della situazione generale sulla possibilità di una offensive a.u. alla nostra frontiera, 29 July 1917; E2 b.129.

91 Angelo Gatti, *Caporetto: Dal diario di guerra inedito (maggio–dicembre 1917)* (Bologna: Il Mulino, 1964), p. 92 (8 June 1917).

92 AUSSME, L'offensiva sulla fronte giulia Agosto 1917 – Note sul concetto operative e sulla condotta della 1a fase, [?16] September 1917; E2 b.2A (3GM). Nota 8a sull'offensiva della Bainsizza, n.d. H3 b.14/c.3.

93 AUSSME, N.3684, Promemoria riflettente le prossime operazioni, 15 August 1917. E4 b.2A/3 (3 GM).

94 Rocca, *Cadorna*, p. 245.

95 Cadorna to Carla [Cadorna], 29 August 1917: Cadorna, *Lettere famigliari*, p. 217.

96 AUSSME, N.4458, Capello to Corps Commanders, 30 August 1917; N.4480, Capello to Corps Commanders, 31 August 1917; N.4688, Capello to Corps Commanders, 5 September 1917. E4 b.2A (3 GM).

97 AUSSME, N.379, Impiego delle forze, 1 September 1917. E4 b.2A (3 GM).

98 AUSSME, N.7468, Controffensiva austriaca nei giorni 4 e 5 settembre, 5 September 1917. E4 b.2A (3 GM).

99 AUSSME, Riunione tenuta il giorno 11 settembre 1917 alle ore 10 nell'ufficio di S.E. il Capo di S.M. dell'Esercito. E2 b.29.

100 AUSSME, Qualora la Russia dovesse concludere una pace separate cogl'Imperi Centrali (il che costringerebbe naturalmente alla pace anche la Romania) di quali nuovi elementi di forza potrebbero disporre gli Imperi Centrali da impegnare contro l'Intesa sulle fronti occidentali e quali forze potrebbero loro essere controproposto?, 26 September 1917. E2 b.129.

101 AUSSME, N.4479, Cadorna to War Ministry, 18 September 1917. E4 b.1(1) (13 GM). Alberto Monticone, *La battaglia di Caporetto* (Rome: Studium, 1955), p. 61.

102 AUSSME, N.4523, Cadorna to Sonnino, 28 September 1917. H5 c.9.

103 Gallinari, 'Alfredo Dallolio', 135.

104 AUSSME, Sistemazione artiglierie, 30 September 1917. E4 b.4/5 (17 GM).

105 AUSSME, N.4686, Cadorna to 2ª and 3ª Armies, 3 October 1917; N.4698, Cadorna to Porro, 3 October 1917. E4 b.1/1 (13 GM).

106 AUSSME, N.4484, Cadorna to Capello, 19 September 1917. E4 b.4/5 (17 GM).

107 AUSSME, Nota: Segretaria del capo di stato maggiore, 13 September 1917. E4 b.3A/4 (16 GM).

108 AUSSME, N.505, Capello to Comando Supremo, 21 September 1917. E4 b.4/5 (17 GM).

109 Monticone, *La battaglia di Caporetto*, p. 47.

110 Monticone contends that Cadorna's directives concerned the Bainsizza, that once the defences there were secured a counter-attack was well within Capello's powers, that Cadorna had not openly disapproved his plans, and that therefore Capello was not guilty of any insubordination: Monticone, *La battaglia di Caporetto*, pp. 64–6.

111 AUSSME, N.5757, Capello to Army Corps Commanders, 8 October 1917, p.4. E4 b.1/1 (13 GM).

112 AUSSME, N.5796, Riassunto della conferenza tenuta da S.E. il commandante della 2ª Armata, 9 October 1917, pp. 2, 4. E4 b.1/1 (13 GM). Conferenza tenuta da S.E. il Comandante del IV Corpo d'Armata il 14 ottobre 1917 in Creda. E2 b.131.

113 AUSSME, N.4741, Cadorna to Capello, 10 October 1917. E2 b.131.
114 AUSSME, N.4857, Porro to Cadorna, 16 October 1917; Fo.4835, Cadorna to Capello, 17 October 1917. E4 b.1/1 (13 GM).
115 Monticone, *La battaglia di Caporetto*, p. 68.
116 AUSSME, T.6034, Montuori to Comando Supremo, 18 October 1917. E4 b.1/1 (13 GM).
117 Alberto Cavaciocchi, *Un anno al commando del IV Corpo d'Armata: Il memoriale dell'unico generale che pagò per Caporetto* (Udine: Gaspari, 2006), p. 9.
118 AUSSME, N.6055, Sunto delle parole da S.E. il generale Capello i giorni 17 e 18 ottobre ai Comandi dei Corpi d'Armata II, VII, XXVII, IV, VII, XXIV, 18 October 1917. E4 b.1/1 (13 GM).
119 Roberto Bencivenga, *La sorpresa strategica di Caporetto* (Udine: Gaspari, 1997), pp. 51–2.
120 AUSSME, T.164, Sonnino to Cadorna, 12 September 1917; T.188, Sonnino to Giardino, 18 September 1917. H3 b.14/c.4, 3.
121 AUSSME, N.21229, Offensiva austro-germanica, 6 October 1917. E2 b.129. The head of Italian military intelligence in France, Colonel Nicola Brancaccio, subsequently claimed that the movement of German troops to the Italian front was signalled by the Deuxième Bureau 'from the start' but that nothing was said to him: Nicola Brancaccio, *In Francia durante la guerra* (Milan: Mondadori, 1926), p. 161.
122 AUSSME, Presenza di truppe germaniche e probabile controffensiva nemica sul medio Isonzo, 9 October 1917, p. 2. E2 b.129.
123 AUSSME, N21676, Probabili ragioni dell'attività nemica alla nostra fronte, 12 October 1917. E2 b.129.
124 AUSSME, N.21745, Offensiva austro-germanica, 13 October 1917. E2 b.129.
125 Monticone held that none of the intelligence Cadorna received amounted to alarm signals of a serious threat: Monticone, *La battaglia di Caporetto*, pp. 48–56.
126 AUSSME, N.21973, Offensiva austro-germanica alla nostra fronte, 16 October 1917. E2 b.129.
127 AUSSME, Boll. 2417, 2417 bis, 21 October 1917. E4 b.1/1 (13 GM).
128 Cappellano, *L'Imperial regio Esercito*, pp. 168–70.
129 AUSSME, N.4929, Imminente offensive austro-germanica sulla nostra fronte, 23 October 1917. E4 b.1 (1–1 GM).
130 In one of its many curious findings, the Caporetto Inquiry subsequently concluded that the design for the counter-offensive was good and if well carried out could have broken the enemy's manoeuvre had one of Bongiovanni's divisions (3rd) been properly positioned and another (62nd) sent forward: *Inchiesta*, vol. II, p. 71.
131 AUSSME, N.4907, Cadorna to Capello, 21 October 1917. E4 b.1/1 (13 GM).
132 AUSSME, N.198, Capello to Minister of War [8 December 1917]. E2 b.131.
133 Faldella, *La grande guerra*, vol. II, p. 99; Bencivenga, *La sorpresa strategica di Caporetto*, pp. 68–71, 73; Monticone, *La battaglia di Caporetto*, p. 71.

134 Among the many accusations afterwards levelled at Badoglio one of the most damning was that he had reserved to himself the power to order the start of the Italian bombardment, intending to use telephone lines which were immediately destroyed – as he should have foreseen. According to his own account, his artillery preparations seem to have been exactly in line with both doctrine and orders. AUSSME, Relazione Badoglio, pp. 5, 92–3. H5 b.13/c.1.

135 AUSSME, Nota alla memoria del Tenente Colonello BALDASSARE sull'azione svolta dall'artiglieria del IV e del XXVII C. d'A. il 24 ottobre 1917 [Ricci], 16 June 1920. H5 b.13/c.12.

136 Quo. Andrea Ungari, 'Le inchieste su Caporetto: uno scandalo italiano', *Nuova Storia Contemporanea* vol. 3 no. 2, March–April 1999, 48 fn. 3.

137 *Inchiesta*, vol. II, pp. 207, 209.

138 AUSSME, Relazione dell'azione dell'artiglieria del IV e XXVII C. d'A. negli ulitimi giorni dell'Ottobre 1917, 21 June 1920. H5 b.13/c.12. A complicated system for coordinating infantry with artillery involved waving coloured flags with different numbers, sometimes folded and sometimes open: Ardengo Soffici, *I Diari della Grande guerra: "Kobilek" e "La Ritirata del Friuli" con i taccuini inediti* (Florence: Valecchi, 1986), pp. 120–1 (18 August 1917).

139 Enrico Caviglia, *La dodicesima battaglia [Caporetto]* (Milan: Mondadori, 1935), pp. 87–99. For contrasting views on this issue, see Pieri, *La prima guerra mondiale*, pp. 144–5, and Faldella, *La grande guerra*, vol. II, pp. 76–7, 82–3.

140 Cavaciocchi, *Un anno al commando del IV Corpo d'Armata*, pp. 146, 150–1, 215. The Caporetto Inquiry did not accept criticism of Cavaciocchi for his (mis-)use of reserves, believing that it would have needed 'a prophetic vision of the future' to do otherwise: *Inchiesta*, vol. II, pp. 118–19.

141 Melograni, *Storia politica della Grande Guerra*, vol. II, p. 398.

142 ASV, 'Sulla sistemazione difensiva del settore pel caso di attaco nemico': diary entry 10 October 1917. Archivio del generale Alberto Pariani b.1.

143 *Inchesta*, vol. II, pp. 122–3, 130–1, 133.

144 ASV, Diary entry, 10 October 1917. Archivio del generale Alberto Pariani b.1.

145 Faldella, *La grande guerra*, vol. II, p. 175; Melograni, *Storia politica della Grande Guerra*, vol. II, p. 420..

146 Adriano Alberti, *L'importanza dell'azione militare italiana: Le cause militari di Caporetto* (Rome: Ufficio Storico dello Stato Maggiore dell'Esercito, 2004), pp. 310–11.

147 Alberti holds that M. Plezia and Foni did not fall until the morning of 25 October: *ibid.*, pp. 315, 319–20.

148 Faldella, *La grande guerra*, vol. II, p. 139. See also *Inchiesta*, vol. II, pp. 110–11; Monticone, *La battaglia di Caporetto*, p. 103 fn.19, believed the order to defend Kamno was perfectly clear but impossible to carry out as the enemy had already progressed too far and Farisoglio could not get orders to his troops.

149 Bencivenga, *La sorpresa strategica di Caporetto*, p. 82.

150 AUSSME, Promemoria circa il memoriale presentato dal generale Bongiovanni [by Adriano Alberti], 10 November 1919. H5 b.13/c.2.

151 *Inchiesta*, vol. II, p. 138.
152 Cadorna to Carla [Cadorna], 24 October 1917: Cadorna, *Lettere famigliari*, p. 227.
153 AUSSME, N.4940, Cadorna to Dallolio, 24 October 1917. E2 b.85.
154 AUSSME, F.4933, Cadorna to Capello, 24 October 1917. H4 b.14/c.1.
155 Soffici, *I Diari*, p. 219 (16 October 1917).
156 For Capello's reasoning, see Novello Papafava, *Da Caporetto a Vittorio Veneto* (Rome: Edizoni di Storia e Letteratura, 2012), pp. 124–32.
157 AUSSME, undated note by Porro [?April/May 1935]. H5 b.14/c.12.
158 Cadorna, , *La guerra alla fronte italiana*, p. 496.
159 AUSSME, N.5906, Cadorna to Capello, 28 October 1917. E4 b.2/2 (14 GM).
160 AUSSME, 1921: Note sulle giornate 24–28 Ottobre 1917 [Cavallero], pp. 2–4; Come fu regolato il ripiegamento delle armate 2ª e 3ª dell'ottobre 1917 [Cavallero], 6 March 1935. H5 b.14/c.12.
161 AUSSME, N.4988, Cadorna to Commanders 2nd and 3rd Army, 26 October 1917. E4 b.2/2 (14 GM).
162 AUSSME, N.4999, Cadorna to Commanders 2nd and 3rd Army, 26 October 1917. E4 b.2/2 (14 GM).
163 AUSSME, N. 58856 GM, Zaccone [Army Intendant-General] to Intendenze 2ª and 3ª Armies, 26 October 1917. E4 b.3A/4 (16 GM).
164 Paolo Gaspari, *La battaglia del Tagliamento* (Udine: Gaspari, 1998), pp. 23–7.
165 AUSSME, N.9976, Aosta to Corps Commanders, 26 October 1917; N.9978, Aosta to Corps Commanders, 26 October 1917. E4 b.2/2 (14 GM).
166 AUSSME, N.30R, Aosta to Cadorna, 29 October 1917: E4 b.3A/4 (16 GM); [n.13], Aosta to Corps Commanders, 29 October 1917: E4 b.2/2 (14 GM).
167 Gasparotto, *Diario di un fante*, vol. I, pp. 177, 182 (7 November 1917).
168 Dominioni, *1915–1919*, pp. 235–6 (28 October 1917).
169 Malaparte, *Viva Caporetto!*, p. 121. It was certainly the case that after Caporetto 'clandestine' prostitutes accompanied 3rd Army to the Piave: Sema, *Soldati e prostitute*, pp. 49–50. For a picture of the retreat by troops not animated by the spirit of revolt, see Melograni, *Storia politica della Grande Guerra*, vol. II, pp. 424–33.
170 AUSSME, Viganò to Caneva, 21 September 1918. H4 b.C.
171 AUSSME, Caviglia to Pintor, 26 March 1931. H5 b.10/f.13.
172 Soffici, *I Diari*, pp. 318–19 (31 October 1917).
173 *Ibid.*, pp. 46–7.
174 AUSSME, T.5040, Cadorna to Intendenza Generale, 29 October 1917, E4 b.2/2 (14 GM); T.5194, Cadorna to War Minister, 31 October 1917, H6 b.F.
175 Gaspari, *La battaglia del Tagliamento*, pp. 146–8.
176 On the lengthy and politically complex post-war debates over whether what happened was a betrayal, a strike, a revolution in the making, or a purely military defeat, see Isnenghi, *I vinti di Caporetto*, esp. pp. 9–25, 40–3, 51–8, 77, 84–5, 94–5; Melograni. *Storia politica della Grande Guerra*, vol. II, pp. 435–41.

177 AUSSME, N.5277, Cadorna to Orlando, 3 November 1917. H5 b.14/c.5.
     See Rocca, *Cadorna*, pp. 292–3, 300–1.
178 AUSSME, N.71691, Della Noce to Army Commanders, 6 November 1917.
     E2 b.132.

NOTES TO CHAPTER 6

1 Vittorio Orlando, *Memorie 1915–19* (Milan: Rizzoli, 1960), pp. 504–5; Bertoldi,
   Badoglio, pp. 74–5; Melograni, *Storia politica della Grande Guerra*, vol. II,
   pp. 538–9.
2 AUSSME, T.4559, Diaz to Alfieri, 9 November 1917; T.122867, Alfieri to
   Diaz, 10 November 1917. H5 b.14/c.5.
3 Luigi Grattan, *Armando Diaz Duca della Vittoria. Da Caporetto a Vittorio
   Veneto* (Foggia: Bastogi, 2001), p. 52.
4 Foscari to Colosimo, 8 November 1917: Raffaele Colapietra. 'Documenti
   dell'archivio Colosimo in Catanzaro', *Storia e Politica* vol. 20 no. 3, 1981, 588.
5 Consiglio dei ministri, 9 November 1917: *ibid.*, 590–1.
6 Pietro Pastorelli, 'Le carte Colosimo', *Storia e Politica* vol. 15 no. 2, 1976,
   369–70.
7 AUSSME, Holograph note in French, signed by Foch and Robertson,
   31 October 1917. H5 b.10f.4.
8 Anonymous, 'La fin d'une légende: la mission du Maréchal Foch en Italie (29
   ottobre–24 novembre 1917)', *Révue des Deux Mondes* 20 August 1920, 285–6.
9 Mariano Gabriele, *Gli alleati in Italia durante la prima guerra mondiale
   (1917–1918)* (Rome: Ufficio Storico dello Stato Maggiore dell'Esercito,
   2008), pp. 30–2, 41–4; Gionfrida, *L'Italia e il coordinamento militare "interalleato"*, p. 89.
10 AUSSME, 'Propaganda', 15 December 1917. E2 b.129.
11 Patrick Facon, 'I soldati francesi in Italia, 1917–1918', in Giampietro Berti
    and Piero Del Negro, eds., *Al di qua e al di là del Piave: L'ultimo anno della
    Grande Guerra* (Milan: Franco Angeli, 2001), pp. 52–4.
12 Diary 17 April 1918 (and a similar incident 14 April 1918): Townsend
    Ludington, ed., *The Fourteenth Chronicle: Letters and Diaries of John Dos Passos*
    (London: André Deutsch, 1974), pp. 183, 184. In all, 552 officers were
    charged with abusing their authority and 340 were cashiered; see Bruna Bian-
    chi, 'Le ragioni della diserzione: Soldati e ufficiali di fronte a giudici e psichiatri
    (1915–1918)', *Storia e problemi contemporanei* vol. 5 no. 10, 1992, 21–2.
13 Melograni, *Storia politica della Grande Guerra*, vol. II, p.531
14 Alberto Baldini, *Diaz Duca della Vittoria* (London: Humphrey Toulmin,
    1935), p. 47.
15 Grattan, *Diaz*, pp. 112–21.
16 Spagnol, *Memoriette marziali e veneree*, p. 41.
17 Grattan, *Diaz*, p. 123.
18 AUSSME, Perdite e ricuperi dell'esercito mobilitato dal 20 Ottobre al
    24 Novembre 1917, n.d.; Notizie statistiche sulle forze e sulle perdute,
    20 January 1918. E2 b.131.
19 AUSSME, Morrone to Caneva, 27 December 1918, p. 10. L13 b.145/f.13.

20 AUSSME, Pintor to Calcagna, 11 December 1917; [memorandum by Calcagna], 15 December 1917, pp. 3, 4, 5. E2 b.131.

21 AUSSME, Spirito delle truppe, 20 January 1918. H3 b.14/c.4.

22 Melograni, *Storia politica della Grande Guerra*, vol. II, pp. 471–2.

23 Piero Melograni, 'Documenti sul "morale delle truppe" dopo Caporetto e considerazioni sulla propaganda socialista', *Rivista Storica del Socialismo* vol. 10 no. 32, 1967, 217–18, 220–1, 226–63.

24 Nicola Della Volpe, 'Lo spirito delle truppe in guerra nelle relazioni dei comandi e della censura epistolare', in Piero Del Negro, ed., *Lo spirito militare degli italiani* (Padua: University of Padua, 2002), pp. 79–80.

25 IWM, Delmé-Radcliffe to Wilson, 7 January 1918. Wilson MSS 73/1/11 (22).

26 Report, 20 January 1918: Brig. Gen. Sir James Edmonds and Maj. Gen. H.R. Davies, *Military Operations Italy 1915–1919* (London: HMSO, 1949), p. 136.

27 AUSSME, Relazione sull'esercito italiano compilato dal Gen Fayolle [21 December 1917], p. 13. E2 b.130.

28 AUSSME, T.31245, Orlando to Diaz, 23 November 1917; T.5910, Diaz to Orlando, 24 November 1917. E2 b.130/f.A.

29 AUSSME, N.6149, Diaz to War Ministry, 2 December 1912. E.2 b.130/f.A.

30 AUSSME, T.33629, Orlando to Diaz, 10 December 1917; Promemoria [Badoglio], 11 December 1917; N.6564, Diaz to Orlando, 13 December 1917. E2 b.130/f.A.

31 AUSSME, C.675, Spirito delle truppe e delle predisposizioni nella zona d'operazione, 24 December 1917. E2 b.130/f.A.

32 Mark Cornwall, *The Undermining of Austria–Hungary: The Battle for Hearts and Minds* (London: Macmillan, 2000), pp. 79–94.

33 Alessi, *Dall'Isonzo al Piave*, pp. 211–12.

34 AUSSME, N.7539, Alfieri to Diaz, 15 January 1918. E2 b.132.

35 AUSSME, N.1117, Propaganda pattriotica, 1 February 1917. F3 b.277/f.8.

36 Delmé-Radcliffe to Wilson, 11 April 1918: Cornwall, *The Undermining of Austria–Hungary*, p. 103.

37 Circular 1 February 1918: Angelo Gatti, 'Il servizio P nell'esercito italiano 1918–1919', in Giampetro Berti and Piero Del Negro, eds., *Al di qua e al di là del Piave: L'ultimo anno della Grande Guerra* (Milan: Franco Angeli, 2001), pp. 377–9.

38 Melograni, *Storia politica della Grande Guerra*, vol. II, pp. 512–73.

39 Isnenghi, *Giornali di trincea*, p. 165.

40 *Ibid.*, p. 67.

41 *Ibid.*, pp. 67–8, 74–5, 79–80, 93, 127–9, 137–9, 158, 165, 204, 215.

42 Melograni, *Storia politica della Grande Guerra*, vol. II, pp. 516–17.

43 AUSSME, N.720, Irregolarità nell'andamento dei servizi e deficienze nell'azione dei comandanti, 13 January 1918. F3 b.277/f.3.

44 Circular 4 January 1917: Procacci, *Soldati e prigionieri italiani*, p. 136.

45 AUSSME, N.8050, Azione morale degli ufficiali sulle truppe, 18 February 1918. E2 b.132.

46 AUSSME, N.1670, Diaz to Comandini and Orlando, 23 February 1918; N.1861, Diaz to Alfieri, 7 March 1918. E2 b.130.

47 Forcella and Monticone, *Plotone d'esecuzione*, pp. 386–7, 384.

48 AUSSME, N.2430, Morale delle truppe alla fronte, 5 April 1918. E2 b.130.
49 AUSSME, N.7350, Discorsi di militari in licenza, 9 January 1918. E2 b.132.
50 Malagodi, *Conversazioni della guerra*, vol. II, p. 294 (18 March 1918).
51 Melograni, 'Documenti sul "morale delle truppe" dopo Caporetto', p.218.
52 Melograni, *Storia politica della Grande Guerra*, vol. II, pp. 501–3.
53 Forcella and Monticone, *Plotone d'esecuzione*, pp. 508–12. Diaz also altered
    the procedure of military courts on 25 May, introducing a preliminary stage
    in which the evidence was more carefully tested, but due to its relatively late
    application it apparently had little effect on the overall number of penal cases:
    Magli, *Fucilazioni di guerra*, p. 167.
54 See Appendix B.
55 Faldella *La Grande Guerra*, vol. II, pp. 284–5, 287–8; Angelo Mangone, *Diaz:
    Da Caporetto al Piave a Vittorio Veneto* (Milan: Frassinelli, 1987) pp. 70–8,
    86–8; Grattan, *Diaz*, p. 76 (quo.).
56 Lucio Ceva, 'Notizie sulla battaglia dei Tre Monti', in Giampetro Berti and
    Piero Del Negro, eds., *Al di qua e al di là del Piave: L'ultimo anno della Grande
    Guerra* (Milan: Franco Angeli, 2001), pp. 309–28; Antonino Zarcone, 'L'au-
    tunno 1917 dall'archivio storico dello Stato Maggiore dell'Esercito' in
    Alberto Monticone and Paolo Scandaletti, eds., *Esercito e popolazioni nella
    Grande Guerra: Autunno 1917* (Udine: Gaspari, 2008), pp. 46–7.
57 Gatti, *Un italiano a Versailles*, pp. 147–150 (23 December 1917); Brancaccio, *In
    Francia durante la guerra*, pp. 90–1, 162–4 (22 April 1917; 7 November 1917).
58 AUSSME, N.7660, Diaz to Orlando, 19 January 1918. E2 b.132.
59 Gionfrida, *L'Italia e il coordinamento militare "interalleato"*, pp. 101–8.
60 IWM, Notes on a conversation with General Badoglio at 3 p.m. 21 February
    1918. Delmé-Radcliffe MSS 06/1/1–4 (31).
61 AUSSME, N.14447, Riorganizzazione dell'artiglieria d'assedio, 23 January
    1918. F3 b.277/f.5. N.8094, Schieramento d'artiglieria per la difesa ad
    oltranza, 1 February 1918. E2 b.132.
62 AUSSME, N.306, Direttive per l'impiego dei Corpi d'Armata in difensiva
    (2ª Army), 20 January 1918. E2 b.132.
63 Filippo Cappellano and Basilio Di Martino, *Un esercito forgiato nelle trincee:
    L'evoluzione tattica dell'Esercito italiano nella Grande Guerra* (Udine: Gaspari,
    2008), pp. 154–68.
64 Mangone, *Diaz*, pp. 67, 79–80.
65 AUSSME, N.6977, 'Deployment of forces in depth', 26 December 1917.
    E2 b.132.
66 Melograni, *Storia politica della Grande Guerra*, vol. II, p. 333.
67 Andrea Curami, 'L'industria bellica italiana dopo Caporetto', in Giampetro
    Berti and Piero Del Negro, eds., *Al di qua e al di là del Piave: L'ultimo anno
    della Grande Guerra* (Milan: Franco Angeli, 2001), pp. 549–62; Tremelloni,
    'Aspetti economici della guerra', pp. 275–6, 278–80. Figures for the losses at
    Caporetto vary: Mazzetti gives a total of 3,152 guns, leaving 3,986 still
    available, and quotes another authority stating that the losses had been made
    up by April 1918: Mazzetti, *L'industria italiana nella Grande Guerra*, p. 43.
68 Report, 20 January 1918: Edmonds and Davies, *Military Operations Italy
    1915–1919*, pp. 135–6.

69 AUSSME, Relazione sull'esercito italiano compilato dal Gen. Fayolle, 1 May 1918 [originally dated 26 December 1917], pp. 10–12, 13, 17–18, 19. E2 b.130.
70 AUSSME, T. Orlando to Diaz, 10 January 1918; T.7389, Diaz to Orlando, 10 January 1918; T. Orlando to Diaz, 18 January 1918; T.7778, Orlando to Diaz, 18 January 1918 (with annotation by Diaz). E2 b.130.
71 AUSSME, Diaz to Orlando, 23 January 1918. E2 b.130.
72 Pasqualini, *Carte segrete dell'Intelligence Italiana 1861–1918*, pp. 334–7.
73 Cappellano, *L'imperial regio Esercito*, pp. 130–1, 223–4.
74 AUSSME, N.62865, Ammaestramenti ricavati dalle operazioni in Fiandra e a Lens, 24 January 1918 [British translation of a document by Ludendorff]. E2 b.130.
75 AUSSME, N.12, Modalità d'attacco studiate dai tedeschi, 23 March 1918. F3 b.277/f.3.
76 Cappellano, *L'imperial regio Esercito*, pp. 143–56.
77 AUSSME, N.2990, Progetti nemici alla nostra fronte, 1 February 1918; N.2994, Confronto tra le forze belligeranti, 1 February 1918. E2 b.129.
78 AUSSME, N.6828, Promemoria per S.E. il Capo di S.M.E., 13 March 1918; Attività del nemico, 13 March 1918; N.7161, Attività del nemico, 17 March 1918 [quo.]. E2 b.129.
79 AUSSME, N.8803, Direttive per le operazioni del 1918, 3 March 1918. E2 b.132.
80 Gionfrida, *L'Italia e il coordinamento militare "interalleato"*, pp. 189–90.
81 Diaz to Orlando, 1 April 1918: Grattan, *Diaz*, pp. 128–9.
82 Gionfrida, *L'Italia e il coordinamento militare "interalleato"*, pp. 192–3.
83 Nitti to Diaz, 18 May 1918: Alberto Monticone, *Nitti e la grande guerra (1914–1918)* (Milan: Giuffrè, 1961), p. 277.
84 Nitto to Diaz, 20 May 1918: *ibid.*, p. 278.
85 Nitto to Diaz, 2 June 1918: *ibid.*, p. 280.
86 Porro to Boselli, 23 August 1916: Procacci, *Soldati e prigionieri italiani*, pp. 196–7.
87 *Ibid.*, pp. 172, 198.
88 Morrone to Sonnino, 28 March 1917: *ibid.*, pp. 203–5 (original emphasis).
89 *Ibid.*, pp. 212–16.
90 AUSSME, T., Interior Ministry to War Ministry, 16 September 1918. H4 b.A.
91 Alfieri to Orlando, 3 October 1918: Procacci, *Soldati e prigionieri italiani*, p. 232.
92 Alessandro Tortato, *La prigionia di guerra in Italia 1915–1919* (Milan: Mursia, 2004), pp. 63–72.
93 Procacci, *Soldati e prigionieri italiani*, pp. 221–4 fn.107.
94 Alessandro De Bosdari, *Delle guerre balcaniche: Della Grande Guerra e di alcuni fatti precedenti ad esse* (Milan: Mondadori, 1928), p. 220.
95 Tortato, *La prigionia di guerra in Italia*, pp. 53–5, 98–9, 179–81.
96 Norms for the employment of prisoners in industry and agriculture, 25 May 1916: *ibid.*, pp. 182–3.
97 *Ibid.*, p. 104. Regulations introduced after war was declared on Germany in August 1916 permitted prisoners of war to work for up to ten hours a day for a total payment of 0.5 lire a day.

98 Cornwall, *The Undermining of Austria–Hungary*, pp. 340–1.
99 AUSSME, N.7, Diaz to Foch, 14 May 1918; N. 11030, Diaz to Foch, 28 May 1918. H5 b.10/f.6.
100 AUSSME, Organizzazione del servizio informazioni sul nemico nelle regioni invase, 18 July 1918. H5 b.12/f.4/2.
101 Cappellano, *L'imperial regio Esercito*, p. 174; Tairolli, *Spionaggio e propaganda*, pp. 198–9.
102 Franco Fucci, *Emilio De Bono: Il maresciallo fucilato* (Milan: Mursia, 1989), pp. 46–9.
103 Pethö, *I servizi segreti dell'Austria–Ungheria*, pp. 189–94.
104 Massimo Multari, 'L'esercito italiano alla vigilia della battaglia di Vittorio Veneto', in Lorenzo Cadeddu and Paolo Pozzato, eds., *La battaglia di Vittorio Veneto: Gli aspetti militari* (Udine: Gaspari, 2005), pp. 22–8.
105 Cappellano, *L'imperial regio Esercito*, pp. 143, 182–3.
106 Isnenghi and Rochat, *La Grande Guerra*, pp. 455–8; Fortunato Minniti, *Il Piave* (Bologna: Il Mulino, 2000), pp. 55–65; Faldella, *La Grande Guerra*, vol.II, pp. 352–7; Mario Montanari, 'Caratteristiche e significato della battaglia del Solstizio', in Giampetro Berti and Piero Del Negro, eds., *Al di qua e al di là del Piave: L'ultimo anno della Grande Guerra* (Milan: Franco Angeli, 2001), pp. 329–39.
107 Irene Guerrini and Marco Pluviano, *Francesco Baracca: Una vita al volo* (Udine: Gaspari, 2000), pp. 142–56.
108 Diaz to his wife, 26 June 1918: Grattan, *Diaz*, p. 144.
109 Diaz to Foch, 21 June 1918: Grattan, *Diaz*, p. 160; Foch to Diaz, 24 June 1918: Faldella, *La Grande Guerra*, vol. II, p. 368; Foch to Diaz, 27 June 1918: Grattan, *Diaz*, pp. 160–1.
110 AUSSME, Orlando to Diaz, 1 July 1918. E2 b.132.
111 AUSSME, N.2050, Foch to Diaz, 13 July 1918. H10 b.5/f.6.
112 AUSSME, N.31RP, Diaz to Foch, 29 July 1918. H10 b.5/f.6.
113 AUSSME, N.2692, Foch to Diaz, 6 August 1918 with pencil comments by Diaz. H10 b.5/f.6.
114 AUSSME, T. Foch to Diaz, 12 August 1918; N.12739 G.M., Diaz to Foch, 13 August 1918 (original emphasis). H10 b.5/f.6.
115 Nitti to Diaz, 23 June 1918; Diaz to Nitti, 29 June 1918: Monticone, *Nitti*, pp. 282–3.
116 Alessi, *Dall'Isonzo al Piave*, pp. 241–3, 252–4 (15 and 18 May 1918).
117 Pino, 'La regolamentazione tattica', p. 304.
118 AUSSME, T.234, Diaz to army commanders, 17 June 1918. E2 b.132.
119 Pino, 'La regolamentazione tattica', pp. 295–8, 300.
120 ASV, Badoglio to commanders of 3rd and 8th armies, 26 August 1918. Archivio del generale Alberto Pariani b.14.
121 Bertoldi, *Badoglio*, pp. 87–8.
122 AUSSME, T.41P, Diaz to Orlando, 14 September 1918; T.2392, Orlando to Diaz, 15 September 1918. H5 b.10/f.5.
123 Diaz to Orlando, 17 September 1918: Grattan, *Diaz*, p. 216.
124 Studio di un'operazione offensive attraverso il Piave, 25 September 1918: Mangone, *Diaz*, pp. 191–5 [quo. p.192].

125 Mangone, *Diaz*, p.131.
126 Nitti to Orlando, 20 October 1918: Monticone, *Nitti*, p. 293.
127 Aldovrandi Marescotti, *Guerra diplomatica*, pp. 188–9 (28 October 1918).
128 AUSSME, La battaglia di Vittorio Veneto 24 Ottobre–4 Novembre [n.d.], p. 11. L3 b.70/7.
129 ASV, Diary entry, 11 October 1918. Archivio del generale Alberto Pariani b.1.
130 N.14096, Direttive per l'azione, 12 October 1918: Mangone, *Diaz*, pp. 196–8.
131 Orlando to Diaz, 14 October 1918; Diaz to Orlando, 14 October 1918: Grattan, *Diaz*, p. 218.
132 Grattan, *Diaz*, pp. 185–6, 219.
133 N.14348, Direttive per l'azione, 21 October 1918: Mangone, *Diaz*, pp. 199–202.
134 Cappellano, *L'imperial regio Esercito*, pp. 222–3.
135 *Ibid.*, p. 175.
136 Cornwall, *The Undermining of Austria–Hungary*, pp. 346–50 [quo. p. 349], 362–5. Despite Italians' virtuosity in this field, Cornwall concludes that in the process of undermining Austria–Hungary 'front propaganda had only a small role to play': *ibid.*, p. 444.
137 *Ibid.*, p. 421.
138 Petho, *I servizi segreti dell'Austria–Ungheria*, p. 194.
139 Alessandro Massignani, 'Il servizio informazioni italiano alla vigilia della battaglia di Vittorio Veneto', in Lorenzo Caddedu and Paolo Pozzato, eds., *La battaglia di Vittorio Veneto: Gli aspetti militari*, (Udine: Gaspari, 2005) pp. 156–61.
140 Ferruccio Botti, *La logistica dell'esercito italiano (1831–1981)*, vol. II, *I servizi dalla nascita dell'esercito italiano alla prima guerra mondiale (1861–1918)* (Rome: Ufficio Storico dello Stato Maggiore dell'Esercito, 1991), pp. 746–7, 752–4.
141 Ferrucio Botti, 'La battaglia di Vittorio Veneto dal punto di vista logistico', in Lorenzo Cadeddu and Paolo Pozzato, eds., *La battaglia di Vittorio Veneto: Gli aspetti militari* (Udine: Gaspari, 2005) pp. 132–4, 140–2.
142 Ilari, *Storia del servizio militare in Italia*, vol. II, *La "Nazione Armata"*, pp. 432–5.
143 Di Martino and Cappellano, *I Reparti d'Assalto Italiani*, p. 187.
144 George H. Cassar, *The Forgotten Front: The British Campaign in Italy 1917–1918* (London: Hambledon Press, 1998), pp. 183–98; Gabriele, *Gli alleati in Italia*, pp. 327–44.
145 AUSSME, N.20827/1596, Intercept ore 9.2, 28 October 1918. H5 b.10/f.5.
146 AUSSME, T. Orlando to Diaz, 29 October 1918; T.51, Diaz to Orlando, 29 October 1918; T.52, Diaz to Orlando, 30 October 1918. H5 b.10/f.5.
147 De Martino and Cappellano, *I Reparti d'Assalto Italiani*, pp. 126–33, 190, 193, 196–200; Rochat, *Gli Arditi della Grande Guerra*, pp. 103–5, 108–9.
148 Diaz to his wife, 30 October 1918: Giuliano Lenci, *Le giornate di Villa Giusti: Storia di un armistizio* (Padua: Il Poligrafo, 1998), p. 83.
149 Cassar, *The Forgotten Front*, p. 215.
150 Gabriele, *Gli alleati in Italia*, pp. 377–80; Massignani, 'La guerra aerea sul fronte italiano', p. 44.

151 Melograni, *Storia politica della Grande Guerra*, vol. II, pp. 552–3; Pieri, *La prima guerra mondiale*, pp. 325–6 comes to a more upbeat conclusion.
152 ASV, Diary entry, 27 October 1918. Archivio del generale Alberto Pariani b.1.
153 Aldovrandi Marescotti, *Guerra diplomatica*, p. 194 (30 October 1918).
154 Lenci, *Le giornate di Villa Giusti*, p. 85.
155 Diaz to his wife, 31 October 1918: *ibid.*, p. 88.
156 Francesco Fatutta, 'La ventilata operazione contro la Baviera del dicembre 1918', *Rivista Italiana Difesa* vol. 22 no. 3, 2002, 92–7.
157 ASV, Diary entry, 1 November 1918. Archivio del generale Alberto Pariani b.1.
158 Lenci, *Le giornate di Villa Giusti*, p. 100. According to Hanks, the twenty-four-hour protocol was introduced by Badoglio when the two sides met to sign the armistice at 1500 on 3 November: Ronald W. Hanks, '*Vae Victis*! The Austro-Hungarian Armeeoberkomando and the armistice of Villa Giusti', *Austrian History Yearbook*, vol. XIV (Minneapolis: University of Minnesota Press, 1978), pp. 108–9.
159 Hanks, '*Vae Victis*', p. 114 (using an Austrian source). However, figures are as always uncertain: Cassar points out that according to the Austrian official history there were no more than 260,000 combatants on the Italian front: Cassar, *The Forgotten Front*, p. 215.

NOTES TO CHAPTER 7

1 *Dall'Isonzo al Piave 24 ottobre–9 novembre 1917: Relazione della Commissione d'Inchiesta* (Rome: Stabilimento poligrafico per l'amministrazione della guerra, 1919), vol. II, pp. 551–8.
2 *Ibid.*, vol. II, pp. 263–70, 312–21, 324–45, 358, 397, 520.
3 AUSSME, *Bozze* (proofs): Ambiente funzionamento dei grandi comandi, pp. 4–5. H4 vol. III/f.16.
4 *Relazione della Commissione d'Inchiesta*, vol. II, pp. 555–7.
5 The draft section of the report dealing with Badoglio, which gives brief indications of the sources for its findings, shows that on the crucial issues such as his losing contact with his troops the commission tended to take his word for things and not probe any further: *Bozze* (proofs), AUSSME, H4 b.A.
6 Ungari, 'Le inchieste su Caporetto', 52–4.
7 Ferruccio Parri, 'Badoglio a Caporetto', *L'Astrolabio*, 25 December 1964, 29.
8 Giorgio Rochat, *L'esercito italiano da Vittorio Veneto a Mussolini* (Bari: Laterza, 1967), pp. 72–3, 77, 86, 96–7.
9 Ungari, 'Le inchieste su Caporetto', 59.
10 Sonnino, *Diario 1916–1922*, p. 305 (3 October 1918).
11 Bonin Longare to Sonnino, 15 October 1918: Rodolfo Mosca, 'Autunno 1918: Sonnino, la Francia e la vittoria da spartire', *Storia e Politica* vol. 15 no. 1, 1976, 51.
12 Memoria della delegazione alla conferenza della pace sulle aspirazioni italiane nel riassetto coloniale africano, 1 February 1919: *DDI* 6th ser. vol. II no. 197, p. 138; Sonnino, *Diario 1916–1922*, p. 319 (16 December 1918).
13 Appunti: la vera ... questione: adriatica, 22 February 1919: *DDI* 6th ser. vol. II no. 456, p. 307.

14 See John Gooch, 'Italy before 1915: the quandary of the vulnerable', in Ernest R. May, ed., *Knowing One's Enemies: Intelligence Assessment before the Two World Wars* (Princeton NJ: Princeton University Press, 1984), pp. 205–33.

15 Mosca, 'Autunno 1918', 64; see Sonnino, *Diario 1916–1922*, p. 314 (15 November 1918).

16 Sonnino to Balfour, 2 December 1918: *DDI* 6th ser. vol. I no. 436, pp. 233–6.

17 Giovanni Buccianti, *L'egemonia sull'Etiopia (1918–1923): Lo scontro diplomatico tra Italia, Francia e Inghilterra* (Milan: Giuffrè, 1977), p. 26.

18 Colosimo to Sonnino, 6 December 1918; Promemoria ... relative alle aspirazioni italiane nel riassetto coloniale africano, 24 January 1919: *DDI* 6th ser. vol. I no. 475, pp. 256–7; vol. II nos. 97, 483, pp. 55–63, 329–30.

19 Sonnino, *Diario 1916–1922*, p. 305 (10 October 1918) records a discussion of 'sustainable and desirable' frontier lines with representatives of the army and navy.

20 Diaz to Orlando, 22 January 1919: *DDI* 6th ser. vol. II no. 63, p. 33.

21 Badoglio to Orlando, Sonnino, Colosimo, 28 November 1918: *DDI* 6th ser. vol. I no. 393, p. 198.

22 John Gooch, *Mussolini and his Generals: The Armed Forces and Fascist Foreign Policy, 1922–1940* (Cambridge: Cambridge University Press, 2007), pp. 8–9, 12, 64–5.

23 Consiglio di Stato, 16 December 1918: Colapietra, 'Documenti dell'archivio Colosimo', 616.

24 Rochat, *L'esercito italiano da Vittorio Veneto a Mussolini*, p. 33 fn.33.

25 Badoglio to Orlando, Sonnino, Barzilai, 28 January 1919, all: Promemoria (23 January 1919): *DDI* 6th ser. vol. II no. 141, p. 94.

26 H. James Burgwyn, *The Legend of Mutilated Victory: Italy, the Great War, and the Paris Peace Conference, 1915–1919* (Westport CT: Greenwood Press, 1993), pp. 232–3, 254.

27 *Ibid.*, p. 278.

28 Vittorio Emanuele III to Orlando, 23 January 1919, 27 January 1919, 1 February 1919 [quo.], 4 February 1919: *DDI* 6th ser. vol. II nos. 66, 123, 191, 223, pp. 35, 79, 131, 154.

29 Montanari, *Le truppe italiane in Albania*, pp. 202–16, 222–3, 229.

30 Burgwyn, *The Legend of Mutilated Victory*, p. 302.

31 *Ibid.*, p. 301.

32 Ilari, *Storia del servizio militare in Italia*, vol. II, *La "Nazione Armata"*, p. 497.

33 Vincenzo Gallinari, *L'esercito italiano nel primo dopoguerra 1918–1920* (Rome: Ufficio Storico dello Stato Maggiore dell'Esercito, 1980), pp. 43–50; Anonymous, *L'esercito italiano tra la 1a e la 2a guerra mondiale novembre 1918–giugno 1940* (Rome: Ufficio Storico dello Stato Maggiore dell'Esercito, 1954), p. 7; Ilari, *Storia del servizio militare*, vol. II, *La "Nazione Armata"*, p. 498. Figures vary, sometimes tallying closely and sometimes not: Gallinari cites a third figure for numbers released – 8,622 officers and 865,000 men.

34 Zupelli to Diaz, 12 January 1919: Gallinari, *L'esercito italiano nel primo dopoguerra*, p. 51.

35 Rochat, *L'esercito italiano da Vittorio Veneto a Mussolini*, p. 33.

36 Ilari, *Storia del servizio militare*, vol. II, *La "Nazione Armata"*, p. 499. Rochat suggested that the cause was Zupelli's demonstrable incapacity to organise a programme of assistance for the demobilised soldiery: Rochat, *L'esercito italiano da Vittorio Veneto a Mussolini*, p. 29.

37 *Ibid.*, p. 49.

38 Tittoni to Parliament, 27 September 1919: Gallinari, *L'esercito italiano nel primo dopoguerra*, p. 129

39 Nitti to Tittoni, 28 July 1919: Rochat, *L'esercito italiano da Vittorio Veneto a Mussolini*, p. 58.

40 Ilari, *Storia del servizio militare*, vol. II, *La "Nazione Armata"*, pp. 502–3. Rochat estimates the number at 600,000: *L'esercito italiano da Vittorio Veneto a Mussolini*, p. 59.

41 Giovanna Procacci, 'Italy: From interventionism to Fascism, 1917–1919', *Journal of Contemporary History* vol. 3 no. 4, October 1968, 166.

42 Rochat, *Gli Arditi della Grande Guerra*, p. 125.

43 *Ibid.*, pp. 137–41.

44 Pieri and Rochat, *Badoglio*, pp. 473–4.

45 Nicola Tranfaglia, *La prima guerra mondiale e il fascismo* (Turin: UTET, 1995), p. 164.

46 *Ibid.*, pp. 476–9.

47 Gallinari, *L'esercito italiano nel primo dopoguerra*, pp. 138–51.

48 Tranfaglia, *La prima guerra mondiale e il fascismo*, p. 193.

Appendix A Chiefs of the Italian general staff and war ministers

CHIEFS OF THE ITALIAN GENERAL STAFF

Lt.-Gen. Alberto Pollio	14 June 1908 – 1 July 1914
Lt.-Gen. Luigi Cadorna	27 July 1914 – 8 November 1917
Lt.-Gen. Armando Diaz	8 November 1917 – 21 November 1919
Lt.-Gen. Pietro Badoglio	24 November 1919 – 3 February 1921
Lt.-Gen. Giuseppe Vaccari	3 February 1921 – 11 April 1923

WAR MINISTERS

Lt.-Gen. Paolo Spingardi	4 April 1909 – 19 March 1914
Lt.-Gen. Domenico Grandi	24 March 1914 – 11 October 1914
Maj.-Gen. Vittorio Zupelli	12 October 1914 – 4 April 1916
Lt.-Gen. Paolo Morrone	4 April 1916 – 15 June 1917
Lt.-Gen. Gaetano Giardino	16 June 1917 – 29 October 1917
Lt.-Gen. Vittorio Alfieri	30 October 1917 – 20 March 1918
Lt.-Gen. Vittorio Zupelli	21 March 1918 – 17 January 1919
Lt.-Gen. Enrico Caviglia	18 January 1919 – 23 June 1919
Lt.-Gen. Alberico Alberici	24 June 1919 – 13 March 1920
Prof. Ivanoe Bonomi	14 March 1920 – 21 May 1920
Avv. Giulio Rodinò	22 May 1920 – 15 June 1920
Prof. Ivanoe Bonomi	16 June 1920 – 2 April 1921
Avv. Giulio Rodinò	2 April 1921 – 4 July 1921
Avv. Luigi Gasparotto	4 July 1921 – 26 February 1922

Appendix B   Executions 1915–1918

Sentences handed down by officially constituted war tribunals. Figures in parentheses indicate the number of death sentences commuted.

	1915	1916	1917	1918
January		(3)	4 (8)	13 (4)
February		(1)	13 (6)	12 (4)
March		13 (6)	16 (8)	18 (3)
April		19 (12)	10 (5)	29 (10)
May	(1)	5 (6)	68 (3)	12 (6)
June	4 (5)	30 (6)	44 (9)	30 (8)
July	14 (46)	16 (3)	25 (6)	10 (3)
August	11 (11)	26 (8)	36 (21)	7
September	5 (3)	17 (8)	26 (1)	5
October	6 (4)	13 (8)	17 (7)	1 (1)
November	17 (8)	14 (5)	55 (5)	
December	9 (1)	14 (8)	45 (6)	
Sub-totals	66 (79)	167 (74)	359 (85)	137 (39)
Total	Carried out: 729 Commuted: 277			

Source: *Caporetto Enquiry*, Vol. II, Table 33.

Bibliography

ARCHIVES

Archivio Centrale di Stato
Carte Brusati

Archivio di Stato di Venezia (ASV)
Archivio del Generale Alberto Pariani

Archivio dell'Ufficio Storico dello Stato Maggiore dell'Esercito
E2 Comando Corpo di Stato Maggiore – Carteggio G.M.
E4 Carteggio G.M. del Comando Supremo – 1a G.M.
F1 Comando Supremo – Vari Uffici
F3 Carteggio Sussidario 1a G.M.
F17 S.M.R.E. – Ufficio "R" ed Ufficio "I"
G9 M.G. – Divisione S.M. – Capo di S.M.R.E.
G28 Corpo di S.M. – Campi e Manovre
G29 Addetti Militari
H3 S.I.M.
H4 Commissione d'Inchiesta – Caporetto
H5 S.M.R.E. – Classificato "RR"
L3 Studi Particolari
L7 Eritrea: Ministeriale, comandi, relazioni, memorie storiche
L8 Libia: Diari, Memorie, Sussidario (Guerra Italo-Turca)
L13 Documentazione acquista dal 1968 – "Fondi"

Imperial War Museum (IWM)
Papers of Brigadier-General Sir Charles Delmé-Radcliffe
Papers of General Price-Davies V.C.
Papers of Field Marshal Sir Henry Wilson

Royal Archives Windsor
RA PS/GV – 0.910
RA PS/GV – Q.688

The National Archives
F.O. 45
F.O. 371

SECONDARY SOURCES

AA.VV., *1915–1918: L'Italia nella Grande Guerra* (Rome: Istituto Poligrafico dello Stato, 1970).

Il pensiero di studiosi di cose militari meridionali: Atti del congresso (Caserta: Società Storia Patria di Terra di Lavoro, 1978).

Adamson, Walter L., 'The impact of World War I on Italian political culture', in Aviel Roshwald and Richard Stites, eds., *European Culture in the Great War: The Arts, Entertainment and Propaganda, 1914–1918* (Cambridge: Cambridge University Press, 1999), pp. 89–126.

Afflerbach, Holger, 'Da alleato a nemico: Cause e conseguenze dell'entrata in guerra dell'Italia nel maggio 1915', in Johannes Hürter and Gian Enrico Rusconi, eds., *L'entrata in guerra dell'Italia nel 1915* (Bologna: Il Mulino, 2010), pp. 75–101.

'"Vani e terribili olocausti di vite umane": I moniti di Luigi Bongiovanni prima dell'entrata dell'Italia', in Johannes Hürter and Gian Enrico Rusconi, eds., *L'entrata in guerra dell'Italia nel 1915* (Bologna: Il Mulino, 2010), pp. 125–46.

Alberti, Adriano, *Il generale Falkenhayn: Le relazioni tra i capi di S.M. della Triplice* (Rome: Libreria dello Stato, 1934).

L'importanza dell'azione militare italiana: Le cause militari di Caporetto (Rome: Ufficio Storico dello Stato Maggiore dell'Esercito, 2004).

Albrecht-Carrié, René, 'Italian colonial policy, 1914–1918', *Journal of Modern History* vol. 18 no. 2, June 1946, 123–47.

Aldovrando Marescotti, Luigi, *Guerra diplomatica: Ricordi e frammenti di diario (1914–1919)* (Milan: Mondadori, 1936).

Alessi, Rino, *Dall'Isonzo al Piave: Lettere clandestine di un corrispondente di Guerra.* (Milan: Mondadori, 1966).

Anonymous, *L'emigrazione italiana dal 1910 al 1923* (Rome: Edizioni del Commissariato Generale dell'Emigrazione, 1926).

L'esercito Italiano tra la 1a e la 2a guerra mondiale novembre 1918–giugno 1940 (Rome: Ufficio Storico dello Stato Maggiore dell'Esercito, 1954).

Ascolano, Dario, *Luigi Capello: Biografia militare e politica* (Ravenna: Longo, 1999).

Askew, William C., *Europe and Italy's Acquisition of Libya 1911–1912* (Durham NC: Duke University Press, 1942).

Augias, Corrado, *Giornali e spie: Faccendieri internazionali giornalisti corrotti e società segrete nell'Italia della Grande Guerra* (Milan: Rizzoli, 1994).

Avarna Di Gualtieri, Carlo, 'Il carteggio Avarna-Bollati luglio 1914–maggio 1915', *Rivista storica italiana* vol. 61, 1949, 218–74; vol. 62, 1950, 67–87, 375–94.

Avogadro, Francesco degli Azzoni, *L'amico del re: Il diario di guerra inedito dell'aiutante di campo di Vittorio Emanuele III* (Udine: Gaspari, 2009).

Badoglio, Gian Luca, *Il Memoriale di Pietro Badoglio su Caporetto* (Udine: Gaspari, 2000).

Baldini, Alberto, *Diaz Duca della Vittoria* (London: Humphrey Toulmin, 1935).

Baratieri, Oreste, *Memorie d'Africa (1892–1896)* (Turin: Bocca, 1898).

Baroni, Piero, 'Profilo biografico del generale Vittorio Luigi Alfieri', *Memorie Storiche Militari* 1982, 231–69.

Beach, Jim, 'Issued by the General Staff: Doctrine writing at British GHQ', *War in History* vol. 19 no. 4, November 2010, 464–91.

Bencivenga, Roberto, *La sorpresa strategica di Caporetto: Saggio critico sulla nostra guerra* (Udine: Gaspari, 1997).

Bernardi, Mario, *Di qua e di là dal Piave: Da Caporetto a Vittorio Veneto* (Milan: Mursia, 1989).

Berti, Giampietro and Piero Del Negro (eds.), *Al di qua e al di là del Piave: L'ultimo anno della Grande Guerra* (Milan: Franco Angeli, 2001).

Bertoldi, Silvio, *Badoglio: Il generale che prese il posto di Mussolini* (Milan: Rizzoli, 1993).

Bertolini, Piero, 'Diario (agosto 1914–maggio 1915)', *Nuova Antologia* vol. 222 no. 1221, February 1923, 214–24.

Bianchi, Bruna, 'Le ragioni della diserzione: Soldati e ufficiali di fronte a giudici e psichiatri (1915–1918)', *Storia e problemi contemporanei* vol. 5 no. 10, October 1992, 7–31.

Bissolati, Leonida, *Diario di Guerra* (Turin: Einaudi, 1935).

Boff, Jonathan, 'Combined arms during the Hundred Days campaign, August–November 1918', *War in History* vol. 19 no. 4, November 2012, 464–91.

Bolchini, Piero, 'Milano 1915: Il socialismo e la guerra', *Movimento operaia e socialista* vol. 16, 1970, 261–91.

Bono, Salvatore, 'Lettere dal fronte libico', *Nuova Antologia* no. 2052, 1971, 528–40.

Bosworth, Richard, *Italy, the Least of the Great Powers: Italian Foreign Policy before the First World War* (Cambridge: Cambridge University Press, 1979).

Italy and the Approach of the First World War (London: Macmillan, 1983).

Botti, Ferruccio, *La logistica dell'esercito italiano*, vol. II, *Dalla nascita dell'esercito italiano alla prima guerra mondiale (1861–1918)* (Rome: Ufficio Storico dello Stato Maggiore dell'Esercito, 1991).

Botti, Ferrucio, 'La battaglia di Vittorio Veneto dal punto di vista logistico', in Lorenzo Cadeddu and Paolo Pozzato, eds., *La battaglia di Vittorio Veneto: Gli aspetti militari* (Udine: Gaspari, 2005), pp. 121–48.

Bracco, Barbara, *Memoria e identità dell'Italia della Grande Guerra: L'Ufficio storiografico della mobilitazione (1916–1926)* (Milan: Unicopli, 2002).

Brancaccio, Nicola, *In Francia durante la guerra* (Milan: Mondadori, 1926).

Buccianti, Giovanni, *L'egemonia sull'Etiopia (1918–1923): Lo scontro diplomatico tra Italia, Francia e Inghilterra* (Milan: Giuffrè, 1977).

Burgwyn, H. James, *The Legend of Mutilated Victory: Italy, the Great War, and the Paris Peace Conference, 1915–1919* (Westport CT: Greenwood Press, 1993).

Cabiati, Aldo and Ettore Grasselli, *Le guerre coloniali dell'Italia* (Milan: Corbaccio, 1935).

Caciulli, Vincenzo, 'Gli ufficiali italiani e i trasferimenti di guarnigione: Nota per una ricerca', in *Esercito e città dall'unità agli anni trenta: Convegno nazionale di studio* (Perugia: Deputazione di Storia Patria per l'Umbria, 1989), pp. 169–83.

'La paga di Marte: Assegni, spese, e genere di vita degli ufficiali italiani prima della grande guerra', *Rivista di storia contemporanea* vol. 22, 1993, 569–95.

Cadeddu, Lorenzo and Paolo Pozzato, *La battaglia di Vittorio Veneto: Gli aspetti militari* (Udine: Gaspari, 2005).

Cadorna, Luigi, *La guerra alla fronte italiana* (Milan: Treves, 1934).

Altre pagine sulla grande guerra (Milan: Mondadori, 1926).

Lettere famigliari, ed. Raffaele Cadorna (Milan: Mondadori, 1967).

Candeloro, Giorgio, *Storia dell'Italia moderna*, vol. VI, *Lo sviluppo del capitalismo e del movimento operaio* (Milan: Feltrinelli, 1970).

Storia dell'Italia moderna, vol. VII, *La crisi di fine secolo e l'età giolittiana* (Milan: Feltrinelli, 1974)

Storia dell'Italia moderna, vol. VIII, *La prima guerra mondiale, il dopoguerra, l'avvento del fascismo* (Milan: Feltrinelli, 1978).

Canevari, Emilio and Giorgio Commisso, *Il generale Tommaso Salsa e le sue campagne coloniali* (Milan: Mondadori, 1935).

Capello, Luigi, *Caporetto, perchè? La 2a armata e gli avvenimenti dell'ottobre 1917* (Turin: Einaudi, 1967).

Cappellano, Filippo, *L'Imperial regio Esercito austro-ungarico sul fronte italiano 1915–1918* (Rovereto: Museo Storico Italiano della Guerra, 2002).

Cappellano, Filippo and Flavio Carbone, 'I carabinieri reali al fronte nella Grande guerra', in Nicola Labanca and Giorgio Rochat, eds., *Il soldato, la guerra e il rischio di morire* (Milan: Unicopli, 2006), pp. 167–214.

Cappellano, Filippo and Basilio Di Martino, *Un esercito forgiato nelle trincee: L'evoluzione tattica dell'Esercito italiano nella Grande Guerra* (Udine: Gaspari, 2008).

Caracciolo [di Feroleto], Mario, 'Cadorna, Joffre e i "siluramenti"', *Nuova Antologia* no. 1460, 1933, 189–98.

Caracciolo di Feroleto, Mario, *Memorie di un Generale d'Armata: Mezzo secolo nel Regio Esercito* (Padua: Nova Charta, 2006).

Cardoza, Anthony L., *Agrarian Elites and Italian Fascism: The Province of Bologna 1901–1926* (Princeton NJ: Princeton University Press, 1982).

Cassar, George H., *The Forgotten Front: The British Campaign in Italy 1917–1918* (London: Hambledon Press, 1998).

Castronovo, Valerio, *Giovanni Agnelli: Il fondatore* (Turin: UTET, 2003).

Cavaciocchi, Alberto, *Un anno al commando del IV Corpo d'Armata: Il memoriale dell'unico generale che pagò per Caporetto* (Udine: Gaspari, 2006).

Caviglia, Enrico, *La dodicesima battaglia [Caporetto]* (Milan: Mondadori, 1935).

Ceva, Lucio, *Le forze armate* (Turin: UTET, 1981).

'Veneto e Italia di fronte alla grande guerra: Memorialisti e letteratura di guerra', in *Storia della cultura veneta dell'età napoleonica alla prima guerra mondiale* (Vicenza: Nero Pozzi, 1986).

'Capo di stato maggiore e politica estera al principio del secolo', *Il Politico* vol. 52 no. 1, 1987, 123–35.

'La Grande Guerra nel Veneto: Scrittori e memorialisti', *La Cultura* vol. 26 no. 1, 1988, 82–141.

'La fine della grande guerra ad occidente (Villa Giusti e Compiègne) 3–11 November 1918', *Nuova Antologia* no. 2208, October–December 1998, 119–42.

'Notizie sulla battaglia dei Tre Monti', in Giampietro Berti and Piero Del Negro, eds., *Al di qua e al di là del Piave: L'ultimo anno della Grande Guerra* (Milan: Franco Angeli, 2001), pp. 308–28.

'Comando Militare e Monarchia Costituzionale italiana (1848–1918)', in Lucio Ceva, *Teatri di guerra: Comandi, soldati e scrittori nei conflitti euopei* (Milan: Franco Angeli, 2005), pp. 41–64.

Chickering, Roger, and Forster, Stig (eds.), *Great War, Total War: Combat and Mobilization on the Western Front 1914–1918* (Cambridge: Cambridge University Press, 2000).

Childs, Timothy W., *Italo-Turkish Diplomacy and the War over Libya 1911–1912* (Leiden: Brill, 1990).

Churchill, Winston S., *The World Crisis 1911–1918* (London: New English Library, 1968).

Cilibrizzi, Saverio, *Storia parlamentare politica e diplomatica d'Italia: Da Novara a Vittorio Veneto*, vol. VI, *1916–1917* (Naples: Tosi, 1950).

Colapietra, Raffaele, 'Documenti dell'archivio Colosimo in Catanzaro', *Storia e politica* vol. 20 no. 3, 1982, 584–627.

Conte, Arthur, *Joffre* (Paris: Editions Olivier Orban, 1991).

Corner, Paul and Giovanna Procacci, 'The Italian experience of "total" mobilization, 1915–1920', in John Horne, ed., *State, Society and Mobilization in Europe during the First World War* (Cambridge: Cambridge University Press, 1997), pp. 229–34.

Cornwall, Mark, *The Undermining of Austria–Hungary: The Battle for Hearts and Minds* (London: Macmillan, 2000).

Cortesi, Luigi, 'Il PSI dalla "settimana rossa" al Congresso nazionale del 1918', *Rivista Storica del Socialismo* vol. 10 no. 32, 1967, 1–44.

Cova, Alberto, 'Problemi dell'agricultura cremonese negli anni della Prima guerra mondiale (1914–1920)', in Peter Hurtner and Giorgio Mori, eds., *La transizione dall'economia di guerra all'economia di pace in Italia e in Germania dopo la Prima guerra mondiale* (Bologna: Il Mulino, 1983), pp.153–78.

Cruttwell, C. R. M. F., *A History of the Great War 1914–1918* (Oxford: Clarendon Press, 1964).

Curami, Andrea, 'L'industria bellica italiana dopo Caporetto', in Giampietro Berti and Piero Del Negro, eds., *Al di qua e al di là del Piave: L'ultimo anno della Grande Guerra* (Milan: Franco Angeli, 2001), pp. 549–62.

Dell'Isonzo al Piave 24 ottobre–9 novembre 1917: Relazione della Commissione d'inchiesta (Rome: Stabilimento Poligrafico per l'Amministrazione della Guerra, 1919).

De Biase, Carlo, *Aquila d'Oro: Storia dello Stato Maggiore Italiano (1861–1945)* (Milan: Edizioni del Borghese, 1969).

De Bono, Emilio, *Nell'esercito nostro prima della guerra* (Milan: Mondadori, 1931).

De Bosdari, Alessandro, *Delle guerre balcaniche: Della Grande Guerra e di alcuni fatti precedenti ad esse* (Milan: Mondadori, 1928).

De Caprariis, Vittorio, 'Partiti politici ed opinione pubblica durante la grande guerra', *Atti del XLI Congresso di Storia del Risorgimento Italiano (Trento 9–13 ottobre 1963)* (Rome: Istituto per la Storia del Risorgimento Italiano, 1965), pp. 73–158.

De Chaurand de Ste Eustache, F., *Come l'esercito italiano entrò in guerra* (Milan: Mondadori, 1929).

De Felice, Renzo, 'Ordine pubblico e orientamento delle masse italiani popolare nella prima metà del 1917', *Rivista Storica del Socialismo* vol. 6 no. 20, September–October 1963, 467–504.

De Grand, Alexander J., 'The Italian Nationalist Association in the period of Italian neutrality, August 1914–May 1915', *Journal of Modern History* vol. 43 no. 3, September 1971, 394–412.

De Rossi, Eugenio, *La vita di un ufficiale italiano sino alla guerra* (Milan: Mondadori, 1927).

De Stefano, Natalia, 'Moti popolari in Emilia-Romagna e Toscana (1915–1917)', *Rivista Storica del Socialismo* vol. 10 no. 32, 1967, 191–216.

Del Boca, Angelo, *Gli italiani in Africa orientale dall'unità alla marcia su Roma* (Bari: Laterza, 1976).

Gli italiani in Libia: Tripoli, bel suol d'amore 1860–1922 (Bari: Laterza, 1986).

Del Boca, Lorenzo, *Grande guerra, piccoli generali: Una cronaca feroce della Prima Guerra mondiale* (Turin: UTET, 2007).

Del Negro, Piero, *Esercito, stato, società* (Bologna: Capelli, 1979).

'Ufficiali di carriere e ufficiali di complemento nell'esercito italiano della grande guerra: La provenienza regionale' in M. Canini, ed., *Les fronts invisibles* (Nancy: Presses Universitaires de Nancy, 1985), pp. 263–86.

Della Volpe, Nicola, 'Lo spirito delle truppe in guerra nelle relazioni dei comandi e della censura epistolare' in Piero Del Negro, ed., *Lo spirito militare degli italiani* (Padua: University of Padua, 2002), pp. 71–88.

Di Scala, Spencer M., *Vittorio Orlando* (London: Haus, 2010).

Di Martino, Basilio and Filippo Capellani, *I Reparti d'Assalto Italiani nella Grande Guerra (1915–1918)* (Rome: Ufficio Storico dello Stato Maggiore dell'Esercito, 2007).

Dominioni, Paolo Caccia, *1915–1919 diario di guerra* (Milan: Mursia, 1993).

Dos Passos, John, *One Man's Initiation: 1917* (Ithaca NY: Cornell University Press, 1969).

Doughty, Robert, A., *Pyrrhic Victory: French Strategy and Operations in the Great War* (Cambridge MA: Harvard University Press, 2005).

Duca, Francesco, 'Badoglio e gli inediti su Caporetto', *Storia del XX secolo*, September 1977, 33–44.

Dupint, Amelio, *La battaglia del Piave* (Rome: Libreria del Littorio, 1929).

Edmonds, Brig. Gen. Sir James and Maj. Gen. H.R. Davies, *Military Operations Italy 1915–1919* (London: HMSO, 1949).

Fabi, Lucio, *Gente di trincea: La grande guerra sul Carso e sull'Isonzo* (Milan: Mursia, 1994).

'"Se domani si va all'assalto/soldatino non farti ammazzar...": Appunti e riflessioni sulla vita e la morte del soldato in trincea', in Nicola Labanca and Giorgio Rochat, eds., *Il soldato, la guerra e il rischio di morire* (Milan: Unicopli, 2006), pp. 153–66.

Facon, Patrick, 'I soldati francesi in Italia, 1917–1918', in Giampiero Berti and Piero Del Negro, eds., *Al di qua e al di là del Piave: L'ultimo anno della Grande Guerra* (Milan: Franco Angeli, 2001), pp. 51–7.

Faldella, Emilio, *La grande guerra*, vol. I. *Le battaglie dell'Isonzo (1915–1917); La grande guerra*, vol. II, *Da Caporetto al Piave (1917–1918)* (Milan: Longanesi, 1978).

Falls, Cyril, *The Battle of Caporetto* (Philadelphia PA: J. P. Lippincott, 1965).

Farina, Salvatore, *Le truppe d'assalto italiane* (Milan: La Libreria Militare, 2005).

Farini, Domenico, *Diario di fine secolo* (Rome: Bardi, 1962).

Farolfi, Bernardino, 'Dall'antropometria militare alla storia del corpo', *Quaderni Storici* vol. 42, 1979, 31–58.

Fatutta, Francesco, 'La ventilate operazione contro la Baviera del dicembre 1918', *Rivista Italiana Difesa* vol. 22 no. 3, March 2002, 92–7.

Faucci, Riccardo, 'Elementi di imperialismo nell'Italia prefascista', in Massimo Pacetti, ed., *L'imperialismo italiano e la Jugoslavia* (Urbino: Argalia, 1977), pp. 15–82.

Fava, Andrea, 'Assistenza e propaganda nel regime di guerra (1915–1918)', in Mario Isnenghi, ed., *Operai e contadini nella Grande Guerra* (Bologna: Capelli, 1982), pp. 174–212.

Fay, Sidney B., *The Origins of the World War* (New York: Free Press, 1966).

Ferrari, Paolo and Alessandro Massignani, *Dietro le Quinte: Economia e intelligence nelle guerre del Novecento* (Milan: CEDAM, 2011).

Fiorento, Fiorenza, *Ordine pubblico nell'Italia giolittiana* (Rome: Carecas, 1978).

Forcella, Enzo and Alberto Monticone, *Plotone di esecuzione: I processi della 1a guerra mondiale* (Bari: Laterza, 1968).

Forsyth, D. J., *The Crisis of Liberal Italy* (Cambridge: Cambridge University Press, 1993).

Franzina, Emilio, 'Lettere contadini e diari di parroci di fronte alla prima Guerra mondiale', in Mario Isnenghi, ed., *Operai e contadini nella Grande guerra* (Bologna: Capelli, 1982), pp. 104–54.

Casini di guerra: Il tempo libero dalla trincea e i postriboli militari nel primo conflitto mondiale (Udine: Gaspari, 1999).

French, David, *The Strategy of the Lloyd George Coalition 1916–1918* (Oxford: Clarendon Press, 1995).

Fucci, Franco, *Emilio De Bono: Il maresciallo fucilato* (Milan: Mursia, 1989).

Gabriele, Mariano, *Gli alleati in Italia durante la prima guerra mondiale (1917–1918)* (Rome: Ufficio Storico dello Stato Maggiore dell'Esercito, 2008).

Gadda, Carlo Emilio, *Tacuini di Caporetto: Diario di guerra e di prigionia (ottobre 1917–aprile 1918)* (Milan: Garzanti, 1991).

Galassi, Francesco L., *Hanging off the Windowsill: Italy at War 1915–1918*, ms. n.d.

Gallarati Scotti, Tommaso, 'Idee e orientamenti politici e religiosi al Comando supremo: appunti e ricordi', in Giuseppe Rossini, ed., *Benedetto XV, I cattolici e la prima guerra mondiale* (Rome: Edizioni 5 lune, 1963), pp. 509–15.

Gallinari, Vincenzo, 'Il generale Alfredo Dallolio nella prima guerra mondiale', *Memorie Storiche Militari* 1977, 109–42.

L'esercito italiano nel primo dopoguerra 1918–1920 (Rome: Uffico Storico dello Stato Maggiore dell'Esercito, 1980).

Garrone, Virginia and Alessandro Galante, *lettere e diari di guerra 1914–1918 di Giuseppe ed Eugenio Garrone* (Milan: Garzanti, 1974).

Gaspari, Paolo, *La battaglia del Tagliamento* (Udine: Gaspari, 1998).

Gasparotto, Luigi, *Diario di un fante* (Milan: Treves, 1919).

Gatti, Angelo, *Uomini e folle di guerra* (Milan: Treves, 1921).

Un italiano a Versailles (Dicembre 1917–Febbraio 1918) (Milan: Ceschina, 1958).

Caporetto: Dal diario di guerra inedito (Maggio–Dicembre 1917) (Bologna: Il Mulino, 1964).

Gatti, Gian Luigi, 'Il servizio P nell'esercito italiano 1918–1919', in Giampiero Berti and Piero Del Negro, eds., *Al di qua e al di là del Piave: L'ultimo anno della Grande Guerra* (Milan: Franco Angeli, 2001), pp. 369–401.

Gentile, Emilio, 'Un'apocalisse nella modernità: La Grande Guerra e il Mito della Rigenerazione della politica', *Storia contemporanea* vol. 26 no. 5, October 1995, 733–87.

Gentsch, James F., *Italy, Geography, and the First World War*, PhD thesis, University of London, 1999.

Gibelli, Antonio, *L'officina della guerra: La Grande Guerra e le trasformazioni del mondo mentale* (Turin: Bollati Boringhieri, 1991).

Gibelli, Antonio and Carlo Stiaccini, 'Il miracolo della guerra: Appunti su religione e superstizione nei soldati della Grande guerra', in Nicola Labanca and Giorgio Rochat, eds., *Il soldato, la guerra e il rischio di morire* (Milan: Unicopli, 2006), pp. 125–36.

Gionfrida, Alessandro, *L'Italia e il coordinamento militare "interalleato" nella prima guerra mondiale* (Rome: Ufficio Storico dello Stato Maggiore dell'Esercito, 2008).

Gooch, John, 'Italy before 1915: The quandary of the vulnerable', in Ernest R. May, ed., *Knowing One's Enemies: Intelligence Assessment before the Two World Wars* (Princeton NJ: Princeton University Press, 1984), pp. 205–33.

'Italy during the First World War', in Allan R. Millett and Williamson Murray, eds., *Military Effectiveness*, Vol. I, *The First World War* (London: Allen & Unwin, 1988), pp. 157–89.

Army, State and Society in Italy, 1870–1915 (London: Macmillan, 1989).

'Morale and discipline in the Italian army, 1915–1918', in Hugh Cecil and Peter Liddle, eds., *Facing Armageddon: The First World War Experienced* (Barnsley: Pen and Sword, 1996), pp. 434–47.

Mussolini and his Generals: The Armed Forces and Fascist Foreign Policy, 1922–1940 (Cambridge: Cambridge University Press, 2007).

'Italy', in Richard F. Hamilton and Holger H. Herwig, eds., *War Planning 1914* (Cambridge: Cambridge University Press, 2010), pp. 198–225.

'"The moment to act has arrived": Italy's Libyan war 1911–1912', in Peter Dennis and Jeffrey Grey, eds., *1911 Preliminary Moves* (Canberra ACT: Army History Unit, 2011), pp. 184–209.

Grattan, Luigi, *Armando Diaz Duca della Vittoria: Da Caporetto a Vittorio Veneto* (Foggia: Bastogi, 2001).

Griffith, Paddy, *Battle Tactics of the Western Front: The British Army's Art of Attack, 1916–18* (New Haven CT: Yale University Press, 1994).

Guardione, Francesco, *Il generale Enrico Cosenz* (Palermo: Alberto Reber, 1900).

Guerrieri, Filippo, *Lettere dalla trincea: Libia–Carso–Trentino–Macedonia* (Valagarina: Manfrini, 1969).

Guerrini, Irene and Marco Pluviano, *Francesco Baracca: Una vita al volo* (Udine: Gaspari, 2000).

Hadley, Tim, 'Military diplomacy in the Dual Alliance: German military attaché reporting from Vienna, 1906–1914', *War in History* vol. 17 no. 3, July 2010, 294–312.

Halpern, Paul, *The Mediterranean Naval Situation 1912–1914* (Cambridge MA: Harvard University Press, 1971).

Hanks, Ronald W., '*Vae victis!* The Austro-Hungarian Armeeoberkomando and the armistice of Villa Giusti', *Austrian History Yearbook*, vol. XIV (Minneapolis: University of Minnesota Press, 1978), pp. 94–114.

Hardach, Gerd, *The First World War 1914–1918* (London: Allen Lane, 1977).

Hastings, Selina, *The Secret Lives of Somerset Maugham* (London: John Murray, 2009).

Herrmann, David G., 'The paralysis of Italian strategy in the Italian–Turkish war, 1911–1912', *English Historical Review* vol. 104 no. 411, 1989, 332–56.

Hess, Robert L., 'Italy and Africa: Colonial ambitions in the First World War', *Journal of African History* vol. 4 no. 1, 1963, 105–26.

Heywood, Geoffrey A., *Failure of a Dream: Sidney Sonnino and the Rise and Fall of Liberal Italy 1847–1922* (Florence: Fondazione Luigi Einaudi/Leo S. Olschki, 1999).

Holtferich, Carl-Ludwig, 'Moneta e credito in Italia e Germania dal 1914 al 1924', in Peter Hurtner and Giorgio Mori, eds., *La transizione dall'economia di guerra all'economia di pace in Italia e in Germania dopo la Prima guerra mondiale* (Bologna: Il Mulino, 1983), pp. 665–89.

Hull, Isabel V., *Absolute Destruction: Military Culture and the Practices of War in Imperial Germany* (Ithaca NY: Cornell University Press, 2005).

Ilari, Virgilio, *Storia del servizio militare in Italia*, vol. II, *La "Nazione Armata" 1871–1918* (Rome: Rivista Militare, 1990).

Isnenghi, Mario, *I vinti di Caporetto nella letteratura di guerra* (Vicenza: Marsilio, 1967).

   Giornali di trincea (1915–1918) (Turin: Einaudi, 1977).

   (ed.), *Operai e contadini nella Grande Guerra* (Bologna: Capelli, 1982).

   Il mito della grande guerra (Bologna: Il Mulino, 1989).

Isnenghi, Mario and Giorgio Rochat, *La Grande Guerra 1914–1918* (Milan: La Nuova Italia, 2000).

Joll, James, *The Origins of the First World War* (Harlow: Longman, 1984).

Jonas, Raymond, *The Battle of Adwa: African Victory in the Age of Empire* (Cambridge MA: Harvard University Press, 2011).

Kelikian, Alice A., 'From liberalism to corporatism: The province of Brescia during the First World War', in John A. Davis, ed., *Gramsci and Italy's Passive Revolution* (New York: Barnes & Noble, 1979), pp. 213–38.

King, Jere Clemens, *Generals and Politicians: Conflict between France's High Command, Parliament and Government, 1914–1918* (Westport CT: Greenwood Press, 1971).

Knox, MacGregor, *To the Threshold of Power, 1922–33: Origins and Dynamics of the Fascist and National Socialist Dictatorships*, vol. I (Cambridge: Cambridge University Press, 2007).

Labanca, Nicola, 'I programmi dell'educazione morale del soldato: Per uno studio sulla pedagogia militare nell'Italia liberale', *Esercito e città dall'unità agli anni trenta: Congresso nazionale di studio* (Perugia: Deputazione di Storia Patria per l'Umbria, 1989), pp. 521–36.

  Caporetto: Storia di una disfatta (Florence: Giunti, 1997).

Labanca, Nicola and Giorgio Rochat, *Il soldato, la guerra e il rischio di morire* (Milan: Unicopli, 2006).

Lenci, Giuliano, *Le giornate di Villa Giusti: Storia di un armistizio* (Padua: Il Poligrafo, 1998).

Levra, Umberto, *Il colpo di Stato della borghesia: La crisi del fine secolo in Italia 1898/1900* (Milan: Feltrinelli, 1975).

Lowe, C. J. and F. Marzari, *Italian Foreign Policy 1870–1940* (London: Routledge & Kegan Paul, 1975).

Ludington, Townsend (ed.), *The Fourteenth Chronicle: Letters and Diaries of John Dos Passos* (London: André Deutsch, 1974).

Lussu, Emilio, *Un anno sull'Altopiano* (Turin: Einaudi, 1998).

Mack Smith, Denis, *Italy and its Monarchy* (New Haven CT: Yale University Press, 1989).

Magli, Massimiliano, *Fucilazioni di guerra: Testimoniaze ed episodi di giustizia militare dal fronte italo-austriaco 1915–1918* (Chiari: Nordpress, 2007).

Malagodi, Olindo, *Conversazioni della guerra* (Milan: Ricciardi, 1960).

Malaparte, Curzio, *Viva Caporetto! La rivolta dei santi maledetti* (Milan: Mondadori, 1981).

Malgeri, Francesco, *La guerra libica (1911–1912)* (Rome: Edizioni di Storia e Letteratura, 1970).

Malpensa, Marcello, 'I vescovi davanti alla guerra', in Daniele Menozzi, Giovanna Procacci and Simonetta Soldani, eds., *Un paese in guerra: La mobilitazione civile in Italia (1914–1918)* (Milan: Unicopli, 2010), pp. 295–315.

Mangone, Angelo, *Diaz: Da Caporetto al Piave a Vittorio Veneto* (Milan: Frassinelli, 1987).

Mantoan, Nevio, *La guerra dei gas 1914–1918* (Udine: Gaspari, 2004).

Maravigna, Pietro, *Le undice offensive sull'Isonzo* (Rome: Libreria del Littorio, 1929).

Marchesini, Daniele, 'Città e campagna nel specchio dell'alfabetismo (1921–1951)', in Simonetta Soldani and Gabriele Turi, eds., *Fare gli Italiani: Scuola e cultura nell'Italia contemporanea*, vol. II, *Una società di massa* (Bologna: Il Mulino, 1993), pp. 9–10.

Marcus, Harold G., *The Life and Times of Menelik II: Ethiopia 1844–1913* (Oxford: Oxford University Press, 1975).

Marselli, Nicola, *Gli avvenimenti del 1870–71* (Turin: 1873).

Martini, Ferdinando, *Diario 1914–1918*, ed. Gabriele De Rosa (Milan: Mondadori, 1966).

Marwil, Jonathan, *Visiting Modern War in Risorgimento Italy* (New York: Palgrave Macmillan, 2010).

Mascolini, L., 'Il ministero per le armi e munizioni (1915–1918)', *Storia contemporanea* vol. 91 no. 6, 1980, 933–65.

374   Bibliography

Massignani, Alessandro, 'La guerra aerea sul fronte italiano', in Paolo Ferrari, ed., *La Grande Guerra aerea 1915–1918: Battaglia–industrie–bombardamenti–assi–aeroporti* (Valdagno: Gino Rossato Editore, 1994), pp. 17–55.

'La grande guerra sul fronte italiano: Le truppe d'assalto austro-ungariche', *Italia contemporanea* no. 198, March 1995, 37–62.

Le truppe d'assalto austro-ungariche nella Grande Guerra (Novale: Gino Rossato Editore, 1999).

'The *Regi Carabinieri*: Counterintelligence in the Great War', *Journal of Intelligence History* vol. 1 no. 1, Winter 2001, 130–44.

'Il servizio informazioni italiano alla vigilia della battaglia di Vittorio Veneto', in Lorenzo Cadeddu and Paolo Pozzato, eds., *La battaglia di Vittorio Veneto: Gli aspetti militari* (Udine: Gaspari, 2005), pp. 149–63.

Mazzetti, Massimo, *L'esercito italiano nella Triplice Alleanza: Aspetti della politica estera 1870–1914* (Naples: Edizioni Scientifiche Italiane, 1974).

L'industria italiana nella Grande Guerra (Rome: Ufficio Storico dello Stato Maggiore dell'Esercito, 1979).

'Note all'interpretazione interventista della grande guerra', *Memorie Storiche Militari*, 1979, 95–125.

Melograni, Piero, 'Documenti sul "morale delle truppe" dopo Caporetto e considerazioni sulla propaganda socialista', *Rivista Storica del Socialismo* vol. 10 no. 32, 1967, 217–63.

Storia politica della Grande Guerra 1915/18 (Bari: Laterza, 1977).

Menozzi, Daniele, 'Chiesa e città', in Daniele Menozza, Giovanna Procacci and Simonetta Soldani, eds., *Un paese in guerra: La mobilitazione civile in Italia (1914–1918)* (Milan: Unicopli, 2010), pp. 269–74.

Menozzi, Daniele, Giovanna Procacci and Simonetta Soldani, *Un paese in guerra: La mobilitazione civile in Italia (1914–1918)* (Milan: Unicopli, 2010).

Ministero della Guerra, *Campagna di Libia* (Rome: Comando del Corpo di Stato Maggiore Ufficio Storico, 1922/38).

Storia militare della Colonia Eritrea (Rome: Comando del Corpo di Stato Maggiore Ufficio Storico, 1935–6).

L'esercito italiano nella Grande Guerra, 1915–1918 (Rome: Ufficio Storico dello Stato Maggiore dell'Esercito, 1927–).

Minniti, Fortunato, *Esercito e politica da Porta Pia alla Triplice alleanza* (Rome: Bonacci, 1984).

Il Piave (Bologna: il Mulino, 2000).

Molinelli, Raffaele, 'I nazionalisti italiani e il primo governo di guerra (maggio 1915–giugno 1916)', *Rassegna storica del Risorgimento* vol. 4, 1977, 449–69.

[Montanari, Mario], *Le truppe italiane in Albania (Anni 1914–20 e 1939)* (Rome: Ufficio Storico dello Stato Maggiore dell'Esercito, 1978).

Montanari, Mario, 'Italiani e Serbi in Balcania durante la prima guerra mondiale', *Memorie Storiche Militari* 1982, 207–28.

Politica e strategia in cento anni di guerre italiane, vol. II Part I, *Le guerre d'Africa* (Rome: Ufficio Storico dello Stato Maggiore dell'Esercito, 1999).

'Caratteristiche e significato della battaglia del Solstizio', in Giampietro Berti and Piero Del Negro, eds., *Al di qua e al di là del Piave: L'ultimo anno della Grande Guerra* (Milan: Franco Angeli, 2001), pp. 329–39.

Monticone, Alberto, *La battaglia di Caporetto* (Rome: Studium, 1955).

Nitti e la grande guerra (1914–1918) (Milan: Giuffrè, 1961).

Gli italiani in uniforme 1915/1918: Intellettuali, borghesi e disertori (Bari: Laterza, 1972).

'Sonnino e Salandra verso la decisione dell'intervento', in Alberto Monticone, *Gli italiani in uniforme 1915/1918: Intellettuali, borghesi e disertori* (Bari: Laterza, 1972), pp. 57–87.

'Il socialismo torinese ed I fatti dell'agosto 1917', in Alberto Monticone, *Gli italiani in uniforme 1915/1918: Intellettuali, borghesi e disertori* (Bari: Laterza, 1972), pp. 89–144.

'Problemi e prospettive di una storia della cultura popolare dell'Italia nell prima Guerra mondiale', in Mario Isnenghi, ed., *Operai e contadini nella Grande Guerra* (Bologna: Capelli, 1982), pp. 33–9.

Monticone, Alberto and Paolo Scandaletti (eds.), *Esercito e popolazione nella grande guerra autunno 1917* (Udine: Gaspari, 2008).

Morozzo della Rocca, Roberto, 'I capellani militari cattolici nel 1915–1918', in Giorgio Rochat, ed., *La spada e la croce: I capellani italiani nelle due guerre mondiali* (Bolletino della Società di Studi Valdesi no. 176, 1995), pp. 61–71.

Mortara, Giorgio, *La salute pubblica in Italia durante e dopo la guerra* (Bari: Laterza, 1925).

Mosca, Rodolfo, 'Autunno 1918: Sonnino, la Francia e la vittoria da spartire', *Storia e Politica* vol. 15 no. 1, 1976, 49–69.

Multari, Massimo, 'L'esercito italiano alla vigilia della battaglia di Vittorio Veneto', in Lorenzo Cadeddu and Paolo Pozzato, eds., *La battaglia di Vittorio Veneto: Gli aspetti militari* (Udine: Gaspari, 2005), pp. 18–28.

Mulligan, William, *The Origins of the First World War* (Cambridge: Cambridge University Press, 2010).

Omodeo, Adolfo, *Momenti della vita di guerra: Dai diari e dalle lettere dei caduti 1915–1918* (Turin: Einaudi, 1968).

Orlando, Vittorio Emanuele, *Memorie (1915–1919)* (Milan: Rizzoli, 1960).

Page, Thomas Nelson, *Italy and the First World War* (New York: Scribners, 1920).

Palumbo, Michael, 'German–Italian military relations on the eve of World War I', *Central European History* vol. 12 no. 4, December 1979, 343–71.

Papa, Antonio, 'Guerra e terra 1915–1918', *Studi Storici* vol. 10 no. 1, 1969, 3–45.

Papafava, Novello, *Appunti militari 1919–1921* (Ferrara: STET/Tadei, 1921).

Da Caporetto a Vittorio Veneto (Rome: Edizioni di Storia e Letteratura, 2012).

Parri, Ferruccio, 'Badoglio a Caporetto', *L'Astrolabio* 25 December 1964, 29–35.

Pasqualini, Maria Gabriella, *Carte segrete dell'Intelligence Italiana 1861–1918* (Rome: Ministry of Defence – Edizione fuori commercio, 2006).

Pastorelli, Pietro, 'Le carte Colosimo', *Storia e Politica* vol. 15 no. 2, 1976, 363–78.

Patriarca, Silvana, *Italian Vices: Nation and Character from the Risorgimento to the Republic* (Cambridge: Cambridge University Press, 2010).

Pavone, Claudio (ed.), *Dalle carte di Giovanni Giolitti: Quarant'anni di politica italiana*, vol. III (Milan: Feltrinelli, 1962).

Pedone, Antonio, 'Il bilancio dello stato', in Giorgio Fuà, ed. *Lo sviluppo economico in Italia: Storia dell'Economia Italiana negli ultimi cento anni* (Milan: Franco Angeli, 1974), pp. 203–40.

Pedroncini, Guy, 'Trois maréchaux, trois strategies?', *Guerres mondiales et conflits contemporains* vol. 37 no. 145, January 1987, 45–62.

Pelo, Doriano, 'La "grande Guerra" nelle memorie autobiografiche di Adriano Colocci, marchese, colonello e "disfattista" ', *Storia e problemi contemporanei* no. 9, April 1992, 39–64.

Pethö, Albert, *I servizi segreti dell'Austria–Ungheria* (Gorizia: Editrice Goriziana, 2001).

Petricioli, Marta, *L'Italia in Asia Minore: Equilibrio mediterraneao e ambizioni imperialiste alla vigilia della prima guerra mondiale* (Florence: Sansoni, 1983).

Philpott, William, 'France's forgotten victory', *Journal of Strategic Studies* vol 34 no. 6, December 2011, 901–8.

Pieri, Piero, *Guerra e politica negli scrittori italiani* (Milan: Ricciardi, 1955).

  La prima guerra mondiale (Udine: Gaspari, 1988).

Pieri, Piero and Giorgio Rochat, *Badoglio* (Turin: UTET, 1974).

Pino, Enrico, 'La regolamentazione tattica del Regio Esercito Italiano e la sua evoluzione nell'ultimo anno del conflitto', in Giampietro Berti and Piero Del Negro, eds., *Al di qua e al di là del Piave: L'ultimo anno della Grande Guerra* (Milan: Franco Angeli, 2001), pp. 275–308.

Pinzani, Carlo, 'I socialisti italiani e francesi nel periodo della neutralità italiana (1914–1915)', *Studi Storici* vol. 15 no. 2, 1974, 364–99.

Pisa, Beatrice, 'Una azienda di Stato a domicilio: La confezione di indumenti militari durante la grande guerra', *Storia contemporanea* vol. 20 no. 6, December 1989, 953–1006.

Pluviano, Marco and Irene Guerrini, *Le fucilazioni sommarie nella prima guerra mondiale* (Udine: Gaspari, 2004).

Prato, Giuseppe, *Il Piemonte e gli effetti della guerra sulla sua vita economica e sociale* (Bari: Laterza, 1925).

Procacci, Giovanna, 'Italy: From interventionism to Fascism, 1917–1919', *Journal of Contemporary History* vol. 3 no. 4, October 1968, 153–76.

  'Popular protest and labour conflict in Italy, 1915–1918', *Social History* vol. 14 no. 1, January 1989, 31–58.

  Soldati e prigionieri italiani nella Grande guerra (Turin: Bollati Boringhieri, 2000).

Puccini, Mario, *Caporetto: Note sulla ritirata di un fante della III Armata* (Gorizia: Editrice Goriziana, 1987).

Rastelli, Achille, 'I bombardamenti sulle città', in Paolo Ferrari, ed., *La Grande Guerra aerea 1915–1918: Battaglie–industrie–bombardamenti–assi–aeroporti* (Valdagno: Gino Rossato Editore, 1994), pp. 183–250.

Relazione della Commissione d'Inchiesta, *Dall'Isonzo al Piave 24 Ottobre–9 Novembre 1917* (Rome: Stabilimento poligrafico per l'amministrazione della guerra, 1919).

Renzi, William A., 'Italy's neutrality and entrance into the Great War: A re-examination', *American Historical Review* vol. 73 no. 5, June 1968, 1414–32.

  In the Shadow of the Sword: Italy's Neutrality and Entrance into the Great War, 1914–1915 (New York: Peter Lang, 1987).

Répaci, Antonino, *Da Sarajevo al "maggio radioso": L'Italia verso la prima guerra mondiale* (Milan: Mursia, 1985).

Répaci, Francesco A., *Scritti di economia e finanza*, vol. IV, *La finanza dello stato: Scritti vari* (Milan: Giuffrè, 1974).

Restifo, Giuseppe, 'L'esercito italiano alla vigilia della grande guerra', *Studi Storici* vol. 11, no. 4 1970, 783–93.

Rocca, Gianni, *Cadorna* (Milan: Mondadori, 2004).

Rochat, Giorgio, 'La preparazione dell'esercito italiano nell'inverno 1914–15 in relazione alle informazioni disponibili sulla guerra di posizione', *Risorgimento* vol. 13, 1961, 10–32.

'L'esercito italiano nell'estate 1914', *Nuova Rivista Storica* vol. 45 no. 9, 1961, 295–348.

L'esercito italiano da Vittorio Veneto a Mussolini (Bari: Laterza, 1967/2006).

L'Italia nella prima guerra mondiale: Problemi di interpretazione e prospettiva di ricerca (Milan: Feltrinelli, 1976).

Gli Arditi della Grande Guerra: Origini, battaglie, miti (Milan: Feltrinelli, 1981).

Ufficiali e soldati: L'esercito italiano dalla prima alla seconda guerra mondiale (Udine: Gaspari, 2000).

'L'efficienza dell'esercito italiano nella Grande Guerra' in Giorgio Rochat, ed., *Ufficiali e soldati: L'esercito italiano dalla prima alla seconda guerra mondiale* (Udine: Gaspari, 2009), pp. 27–54.

Rochat, Giorgio and Giulio Massobrio, *Breve storia dell'esercito italiano dal 1861 al 1943* (Turin: Einaudi, 1978).

Rodd, James Rennell, *Social and Diplomatic Memories 1902–1919* (London: Edward Arnold, 1925).

Romano, Sergio, *La quarta sponda: La guerra di Libia 1911/1912* (Milan: Bompiani, 1977).

Romeo, Rosario, *Dal Piemonte sabaudo all'Italia liberale* (Bari: Laterza, 1974).

Rubenson, Sven, *The Survival of Ethiopian Independence* (London: Heinemann, 1976).

Ruffo, Maurizio, *L'Italia nella Triplice Alleanza: I piani operative dello Stato Maggiore verso l'Austria–Ungheria dal 1885 al 1915* (Rome: Ufficio Storico dello Stato Maggiore dell'Esercito, 1998).

Rusconi, Gian Enrico, 'L'azzardo del 1915: Come l'Italia decide l'intervento nella Grande Guerra', in Johannes Hürter and Gian Enrico Rusconi, eds., *L'entrata in guerra dell'Italia nel 1915* (Bologna: Il Mulino, 2010), pp. 15–74.

Russo, Luigi, *Vita e disciplina militare* (Milan: Mondadori, 1992).

Salandra, Antonio, *La neutralità italiana [1914]: Ricordi e pensieri* (Milan: Mondadori, 1928).

Memorie politiche 1916–1925 (Reggio Calabria: Edizioni Parallelo, 1975).

Schiarini, Pompilio, *L'offensiva austriaca nel Trentino* (Rome: Libreria del Littorio, 1929).

Sechi, Salvatore, 'Il morale delle truppe durante la prima guerra mondiale', *Studi Storici* vol. 11 no. 4, 1970, 794–818.

Segreto, Luciano, 'Statalismo e antistatalismo nell'economia bellica: Gli industriali e la Mobilitazione Industriale (1915–1918)', in Peter Hurtner and Giorgio Mori, eds., *La transizione dall'economia di guerra all'economia di pace in Italia e in Germania dopo la prima guerra mondiale* (Bologna: Il Mulino, 1983, pp. 301–34.

Sema, Antonio, *Soldati e prostitute: Il caso della terza armata* (Valdagno: Gino Rossato, 1999).

Serpieri, Arrigo, *La guerra e le classe rurali italiani* (Bari: Laterza, 1930).

Serra, Enrico, 'Caporetto perché', *Nuova Rivista Storica* vol. 84 no. 1, March 1972, 178–85.

Sheffield, Gary and John Bourne (eds.), *Douglas Haig: War Diaries and Letters 1914–1918* (London: Weidenfeld & Nicolson, 2005).

SIFAR, *Il servizio informazioni militare italiano dalla sua costituzione alla fine della seconda guerra mondiale* (Rome: Stato Maggiore della Difesa, 1957) [declassified 1977].

Smith, Leonard V., *Between Mutiny and Obedience: The Case of the French Fifth Infantry Division during World War I* (Princeton NJ: Princeton University Press, 1995).

Soffici, Ardengo, *I Diari della Grande guerra: "Kobilek" e "La Ritirata del Friuli" con i taccuini inediti* (Florence: Valecchi, 1986).

Soldani, Simonetta, 'La Grande guerra lontana dal fronte', in G. Mori, ed., *Storia d'Italia: Le Regioni dall'Unità a oggi – La Toscana* (Turin: Einaudi, 1986), pp. 343–452.

Somgyi, Stefano, 'Cento anni di bilanci familiari in Italia (1857–1956) Part 1', *Annali dell'Istituto G. G. Feltrinelli* vol. 2, 1959, 121–74.

Sonnino, Sidney, *Diario 1914–1916*, ed. Pietro Pastorelli (Bari: Laterza, 1972). *Carteggio 1914–1916*, ed. Pietro Pastorelli (Bari: Laterza, 1974).

Stevenson, David, *Armaments and the Coming of War: Europe 1904–1914* (Oxford: Oxford University Press, 1996).

Spagnol, Tito A., *Memoriette marziali e veneree* (Vicenza: Mario Spagnol Editore, 1970).

Stefani, Filippo, *La storia della dottrina e degli ordinamenti dell'esercito italiano*, vol. I, *Dall'esercito piemontese all'esercito di Vittorio Veneto* (Rome: Ufficio Storico dello Stato Maggiore dell'Esercito, 1984).

Stuparich, Giani, *Guerra del '15* (Turin: Einaudi, 1978).

Tarolli, Vittorino, *Spionaggio e Propaganda: Il ruolo del servizio informazioni dell'esercito nella guerra 1915/1918* (Chiari: Nordpress, 2001).

[Testasecca, Lucangelo],*Lucangelo Bracci Testasecca nel ricordo degli amici e nel suo diario di guerra* (Rome: Edizione Colombo, 1957).

Thompson, Mark, *The White War: Life and Death on the Italian Front 1915–1919* (New York: Basic Books, 2009).

Tomassini, Luigi, 'Industrial mobilization and the labour market in Italy during the First World War', *Social History* vol. 60 no. 1, January 1991, 59–87.

'The home front in Italy', in Hugh Cecil and Peter H. Liddle, eds., *Facing Armageddon: The First World War Experienced* (Barnsley: Pen & Sword, 1996), pp. 577–95.

'Gli effetti sociali della mobilitazione industriale' in Daniele Menozza, Giovanna Procacci and Simonetta Soldani, eds., *Un paese in guerra: La mobilitazione civile in Italia (1914–1919)* (Milan: Unicopli, 2010), pp. 25–57.

Tortato, Alessandro, *Ortigara: La verità negata* (Novale: Gino Rossato Editore, 1999). *La prigionia di guerra in Italia 1915–1919* (Milan: Mursia, 2004).

Toscano, Mario, 'Il problema del confine occidentale durante la prima guerra mondiale', *Rassegna italiana politica, letteraria e artistica* vol. 58 no. 301, June 1943, 243–51.

Tosti, Amedeo, *Storia dell'esercito italiano (1861–1936)* (Milan: Istituto per gli studi di politica internazionale, 1942).

Tranfaglia, Nicola, 'Dalla neutralità italiana alle origini del Fascismo', *Studi Storici* vol. 10 no. 2, 1969, 335–86.

La prima guerra mondiale e il fascismo (Turin: UTET, 1995).

Tremilloni, Roberto, 'Aspetti economici della guerra' in AA. VV., *1915–1918: L'Italia nella grande guerra* (Rome: Presidenza del Consiglio dei Ministri, 1976), pp. 265–98.

Trevelyan, G. M., *Scenes from Italy's War* (London: T. C. & E. C. Jack, 1919).

Ungaretti, Giuseppe, *Lettere dal fronte a Gherardo Marone (1916–1918)* (Milan: Mondadori, 1978).

Ungari, Andrea, 'Le inchieste su Caporetto: uno scandalo italiano', *Nuova Storia Contemporanea* vol. 3 no. 2, March–April 1999, 37–80.

'The Italian Air Force from the eve of the Libyan conflict to the First World War', *War in History* vol. 17 no. 4, November 2010, 403–34.

Valiani, Leo, 'Nuovi documenti sui tentativi di pace nel 1917', *Rivista storica italiana* vol. 75 no. 3, September 1963, 559–87.

'Le origini della guerra del 1914 e dell'intervento italiano nelle ricerche e nelle pubblicazioni dell'ultimo ventennio', *Nuova Rivista Storica* vol. 78 no. 3, September 1966, 593–613.

Valori, Aldo, *La condotta politica della guerra* (Milan: Corbaccio, 1934).

Vandervort, Bruce, *To the Fourth Shore: Italy's War for Libya (1911–1912)/Verso la quarta sponda: La guerra italiana per la Libia (1911–1912)* (Rome: Ufficio Storico dello Stato Maggiore dell'Esercito, 2012).

Vanzetto, Livio, 'Contadini e grande guerra in aree campione del Veneto (1910–1922)', in Mario Isnenghi, ed., *Operai e contadini nella Grande guerra* (Bologna: Capelli, 1982), pp. 72–103.

Veneruso, Danilo, *La grande guerra e l'unità nazionale: Il ministero Boselli* (Turin: SEI, 1996).

Vento, Andrea, *In silenzio gioite e soffrite: Storia dei servizi segreti italiani dal Risorgimento alla Guerra Fredda* (Milan: Il Saggiatore, 2010).

Ventrone, Angelo, *Piccolo storia della Grande guerra* (Rome: Donzelli, 2005).

Vigezzi, Brunello, 'Le "Radiose giornate" del maggio 1915 nei rapport dei Prefetti (Parte Ia)', *Nuova Rivista Storica* vol. 43 no. 3, September–December 1959, 313–43.

'Le "Radiose giornate" del maggio 1915 nei rapport dei Prefetti (Parte IIa)', *Nuova Rivista Storica* vol. 44 no. 1, January 1960, 54–111.

'I problemi della neutralità e della guerra nel carteggio Salandra–Sonnino (1914–1917)', *Nuova Rivista Storica* vol. 45 no. 3, September–December 1961, 397–466.

Da Giolitti a Salandra (Florence: Vallecchi, 1969).

'Politica estera e opinione pubblica in Italia dal 1870 al 1945', *Nuova Rivista Storica* vol. 62 no. 5–6, 1979, 548–69.

'Rosario Romeo, Giolitti, la crisi dello Stato liberale e la prima guerra mondiale', *Storia contemporanea* vol. 25 no. 1, February 1994, 5–36.

Violante, Luciano, 'La repressione del dissenso politico nell'Italia liberale: Stati d'assedio e giustizia militare', *Rivista di storia contemporanea* vol. 5 no. 4, 1976, 481–524.

Visentin, Angelo, 'Esercito e società nella pubblistica militare dell'ultimo secolo', *Rivista di storia contemporanea* vol. 16 no. 1, 1987, 31–58.

Vitale, Ornello, *La popolazione attiva in agricoltura attraverso i censimenti italiani (1881–1961)* (Rome: Instituto di Demografia Università di Roma, n.d.).

Wall, Richard, and Winter, Jay (eds.) *The Upheaval of War: Family, Work and Welfare in Europe 1914–1918* (Cambridge: Cambridge University Press, 1988).

Webster, Richard A., 'From insurrection to intervention: the Italian crisis of 1914', *Italian Quarterly* vol. 5/6 no. 21, Winter–Spring 1961–2, 27–50.

'Autarky, expansion, and the underlying continuity of the Italian state', *Italian Quarterly* vol. 8 no. 32, Winter 1964, 3–188.

Whittam, John, *The Politics of the Italian Army* (London: Croom Helm, 1977).

'War aims and strategy: The Italian government and High Command 1914–1919', in Barry Hunt and Adrian Preston, eds., *War Aims and Strategic Policy in the Great War 1914–1918* (London: Croom Helm, 1977), pp. 85–104.

Winter, Jay, and Robert, Jean-Louis, *Capital Cities at War: Paris, London, Berlin 1914–1919* (Cambridge: Cambridge University Press, 1997).

Woodward, David R., *Lloyd George and the Generals* (London: Associated University Presses, 1983).

Zarcone, Antonino, 'L'autunno 1917 dall'archivio storico dello Stato Maggiore dell'Esercito', in Alberto Monticone and Paolo Scandaletti, eds., *Esercito e popolazioni nella Grande Guerra: Autunno 1917* (Udine: Gaspari, 2008), pp. 39–50.

Zuber, Terence, '"There never was a Schlieffen Plan": A reply to Gerhard Gross', *War in History* vol. 17, no. 4, 2010, 512–25.

Index

Adigrat, 22–6
  battle of (1893) 26
Adua, 18–19, 21–3, 25, 29, 196, 306
  battle of (1896) 27–8
  and Italy's military reputation 28
Ain Zara, battle of (1911) 45
aircraft production 126, 143
air power, *and* military operations 110–11,
  116, 297
air warfare 116–17
Albania, in Italian policy 70; in Italian
  strategy 118–21
Albertone, Major-General Matteo 26–8
Albricci, Lieutenant-Colonel Alberico 58,
  62, 67, 69
Aldovrandi Marescotti, L. 70
Alexiev, General Mikhail 155, 159, 173–4,
  179
Alfieri, Lieutenant-General Vittorio
  248–50, 255, 263, 275, 277
Allenby, General Sir Edmund 288
Alpini 120, 136–7, 140, 222–3, 241, 253,
  262, 279
Alula of Tigray *see* Ras Allula
Amba Alagi, battle of (1895) 25
Andrássy, Count Julius 296
Ansaldo 127–8, 213, 265, 277
anti-militarism 12
Aosta, Emanuele Filiberto duke of 105,
  109, 146, 180, 182–4, 211, 224, 242,
  248, 271, 287, 297, 315–16
Arditi 200–3, 226, 242, 262, 268, 286,
  293–6, 316
Arimondi, Major-General Giuseppe 22–8
Army, Italian
  chiefs of the general staff (functions in
    peacetime) 28–30
  demobilisation of 310–14
  medical service 141
  military budgets: (pre-1914) 11–12,
    24–5; (Abyssinia) 22, 48; (1914–15) 79
  military traditions and 7

mobilisation of 63–6, 88–9
  officer corps, pre-war 13–15, 65; war-
    time 141, 189
  organisation of, pre-war 8–11, 50, 57–8;
    on mobilisation 78–9
  peacetime functions of 7, 12–13
  tactical doctrine, in Abyssinia 24; in
    Libya 47; pre-war 51–2; war-time 116
  war aims 75, 306–8
  war planning, pre-1914 31–8; *and* the
    Libyan war 40–3; *and* the world war
    62–3, 82
Arrighi, Major-General Giovanni 235, 239
artillery, pre-war armament of 50–1,
  79–80
  doctrine of 24, 199, 211, 234, 285
Arz von Straussenberg, General Artur 278,
  300
ascari 23, 25, 28
Asquith, H. H. 179
Assab 17–18
Avarna Di Gualtieri, Ambassador Giuseppe
  67, 69, 75, 78, 96

Badoglio, Lieutenant-General Pietro 182,
  185, 210, 225, 229–30, 234, 236, 238,
  240, 248, 252, 255, 264, 279, 285–6,
  291, 300, 304–5, 307–9, 311–12, 314,
  316
Balbo, Italo 282
Baldissera, Lieutenant-General Antonio
  20–2, 31
Bandini, Major-General Oreste 178
Baracca, Major Francesco 282
Baratieri, Lieutenant-General Oreste 20,
  22–8
  and the battle of Adua 26–7, 28
Barrère, Camille 271, 284
Barzilai, Salavatore 158
Bassi, Major Giuseppe 201
'Battle of the Bridges', *see* Solstice, battle of
Bencivenga, Colonel Roberto 149

Benedict XV, Pope 197
Berchtold, Count Leopold 75
Bersaglieri 168, 171, 201, 242, 244, 253,
    262, 286, 297
Bertolé-Viale, Lieutenant-General Ettore
    19–21, 32
Bertotti, Lieutenant-General Emilio 120–1
Bevione, Giuseppe 39
Bianchi, Riccardo 128, 266
Bir Tobras, battle of (1911) 45–6
Bissolati, Leonida 156, 180, 185–8, 208,
    248–9, 272
Blanc, Alberto 23
Bollati, Count Riccardo 73, 77
Bongiovanni, Lieutenant-General Luigi 83,
    85–7, 224, 229, 233, 239, 304
Bonomi, Ivanoe 309
Boroević, General Svetozar 114, 131, 153,
    211–12, 225, 280, 296
Boselli, Paolo 160, 171, 178–80, 186–7,
    196–7, 203, 244, 246, 273
Bratianu, Ion 72, 176
Breganze, Lieutenant-Colonel Giovanni
    84–5
Briand, Aristide 176, 179, 195
Briccola, Major-General Ottavio 48
Brotti, Colonel Achille 130
Brusati, Lieutenant-General Roberto 103,
    131, 148–50, 152–6, 161, 199
Brusati, Lieutenant-General Ugo 66, 145
Brussilov, General Alexei 159, 200
Bülow, Prince von 75–6, 82
Burian, Istvan 75, 78

Caccia Dominioni, Paolo 166, 193, 243
Cadorna, General Count Raffaele 54
Cadorna, Lieutenant-General Luigi 28, 37,
    49, 52–7, 59–69, 75–6, 78–92, 94–7,
    102–22, 124, 130, 134–7, 139–40,
    142, 144–50, 152–61, 164, 166–80,
    182–8, 190–1, 193, 199, 203–12,
    223–34, 239–44, 246, 248, 250–2,
    259–64, 270, 274, 303–5, 307
    and air power 113
    and alliance strategy 106, 111–13, 147,
        153, 155, 159, 173–5, 190
    and army discipline 13, 80–1, 91–2,
        102–3, 167, 170–1
    and tactical doctrine and method 55–7,
        146, 183
    and war plans 62–3, 82–3, 89–90, 95
Calcagno, Colonel Ricardo 231
Calderari, Colonel Luigi 59
Caneva, General Carlo 43–9, 303–4
Cannoniere, Colonel Alfredo 234

Capello, Lieutenant-General Luigi 47, 118,
    182–5, 200–1, 203, 209–11, 223–6,
    228–30, 233–4, 239–40, 248, 254,
    256, 267, 271, 304
Caporetto, 89, 127, 140, 247–8, 250, 253,
    256, 260, 262, 265–6, 274–5
    battle of (1917) 69, 233–41
    Inquiry 235, 238–9, 253–4, 303–5
Carabinieri 132–4, 137–8, 162–3, 170, 202,
    236, 253, 255, 259, 274, 313
Carcano, Paolo 68, 179
Carlotti, Ambassador Andrea 74, 117,
    173, 205
Casavola, Giannino 122
case di tolleranza, see prostitution
Cavaciocchi, Lieutenant-General Alberto
    230, 233–6, 239–40, 304
Cavallero, Colonel Ugo, 161, 166, 229,
    241, 269, 287–8
Cavan, Lieutenant-General Lord 295–7
Caviglia, Lieutenant-General Enrico 225,
    235, 243, 249, 287, 289–90, 293,
    295–6, 312–15
Chantilly conference (July 1915) 111;
    (March 1916) 155, 159, 173, 175;
    (November 1916) 179–80, 203
Chapperon, Lieutenant-General Alessio
    162
Clemenceau, Georges 270, 299, 308, 310
Coatit, battle of (1895) 23–4
Colosimo, Gaspare 195, 249, 306
Commandini, Ubaldo 254
Como Dagna, Major-General Sabina
    222–3
Conrad von Hoetzendorff, General Count
    35–7, 58, 62, 87, 96, 103, 155, 157–60,
    208, 261–2, 280
Corsi, Rear-Admiral Camillo 40
Cosenz, Lieutenant-General Enrico 17–18,
    21, 28–9, 32
    and war planning 32–3
Crispi, Francesco 19–26, 28, 31
cryptography 71, 130–1
Custoza
    1st battle of (1849) 15
    2nd battle of (1866) 15–17, 28–30, 82

Dabormida, Major-General Vittorio 26–8
D'Alessandro, Lieutenant-General Felice
    212
Dallolio, Lieutenant-General Alfredo 80,
    84, 107, 122–4, 128, 204–5, 220–1,
    228, 235, 249, 265–6, 316
D'Annunzio, Gabriele 55, 196, 274, 310,
    316–17

De Bono, Lieutenant-General Emilio 14, 280
De Bosdari, Ambassador Alessandro 74
De Chaurand de Ste Eustache, Lieutenant-General Felice 156, 169
De Cristoferis, Lieutenant-Colonel Tommaso 19
De Marchi, Major-General Ernesto 294
De Martini, Giacomo 74
De Medici, Colonel Giulio 236
Della Noce, Lieutenant-General Giuseppe 135–6
Delmé-Radcliffe, Brigadier-General Charles 179, 254, 257, 264
Depretis, Agostino 19
dervishes 20, 22, 23, 43
Diaz, Lieutenant-General Armando 84–6, 130, 248–9
    as chief of general staff (1917-18) 247–52, 254–7, 259–61, 263–8, 270–2, 274, 278–9, 282–93, 295–300, 304–5, 307, 312, 314, 317
Di Giorgio, Lieutenant-General Antonino 133, 191, 222, 241, 244
Di Robilant, Lieutenant-General Carlo Felice 19, 144, 316
Di Rudinì, Antonio 22
Di San Giuliano, Antonio 61
    and Albania 118–19
    and the Libyan war 39–40, 43, 47
    and the outbreak of the world war 61–2, 64–5
Di San Marzano, Lieutenant-General Alessandro 20
Djemal Pasha 59
Dobro Pole, battle of (September 1918) 287
Dogali, battle of (1887) 19, 21
Dos Passos, John 251
Douhet, Colonel Giulio 187–8

Edmonds, Brigadier-General Sir James 100
Egidi, Colonel Silvio 234
Einaudi, Luigi 123
Elia, Lieutenant-General Vittorio 189
Ellena, Major-General Giuseppe 27
Enver Bey 60
Eritrea, colony of 14, 19, 21–4

Falkenhayn, General Erich von 58, 83–4, 87, 155, 189
Fara, Colonel Gustavo 45–6
Faravelli, Admiral Luigi 44
Farisoglio, Major-General Angelo 239
Fayolle, General Émile 254, 266–7
Ferrari, Cardinal 196

Ferrero, Gulgielmo 6
FIAT 124, 212
Finzi, Lieutenant-Colonel Cesare 279
Fiume, seizure of 314, 316
Foch, General Ferdinand 84, 207, 248, 250, 270–1, 278, 283–4, 286–8, 296, 299, 312–13
Franchet d'Espérey, Marshal Louis 287–8
Franchetti, Leopoldo 195
Franz Ferdinand, Crown Prince 37, 58–9
Franz Josef, Emperor 58, 81, 87
Freemasons, 46, 54, 75, 81, 92, 180, 248, 304
French, General Sir John 90
Frugoni, Lieutenant-General Pietro 104, 109–10, 115, 147–8, 157, 170, 189

Gabba, Colonel Melchiore 244
Galliano, Major Giuseppe 26, 28
Gandolfi, Major-General Antonio 22
Garibaldi, Giuseppe 7, 23, 29
Garibaldi, Peppino 92
Garioni, Lieutenant-General Vincenzo 343
Garrone, Eugenio 140
Garrone, Giuseppe 140
Garruccio, Colonel Giovanni 161
Gasparotto, Luigi 98–9, 101–2, 242
Gazzera, Colonel Pietro 300
Genè, Major-General Carlo 19
Germany, Italian declaration of war on 146, 177–8
Giardino, Lieutenant-General Gaetano 201, 248, 250, 252, 256, 268, 270–1, 284, 290, 293, 315
Giolitti, Giovanni 12, 14, 22, 40, 43, 45–7, 49, 54, 92–4, 136
Gladstone, W. H. 18
Govone, Colonel Ugo 15
Grandi, Lieutenant-General Dino 61, 64–9, 79–80
Graziani, Lieutenant-General Andrea 245
Graziani, General Jean-César 290, 295–6
Grazioli, Lieutenant-General Francesco Saverio 201, 293, 315
Greece
    in Italian policy 70–2
    in Italian strategy 119–20
Grey, Sir Edward 76
Guardia di Finanza 133

Hankey, Lieutenant-Colonel Maurice 248
Hervé, Gustave 197
Hindenburg, Field Marshal Paul von 85, 189, 204, 278, 282, 299
House, Colonel Edward 306

ILVA 127, 213
Imperiali, Ambassador Marquis Guglielmo 76, 78
Isonzo
1st battle of (June 1915) 109
2nd battle of (July 1915) 112
3rd battle of (October 1915) 115–16
4th battle of (November 1915) 117–18
5th battle of (March 1916) 147–8
6th battle of (August 1916) 176, 180–5, 188
7th battle of (September 1916) 185
8th battle of (October 1916) 185–6
9th battle of (November 1916) 186
10th battle of (May 1917) 208–11
11th battle of (August 1917) 202–3, 224–5
Isvolsky, Count Alexander 179

Jagow, Gottlieb von 73, 77
Janushkevich, General N. N. 90
Joffre, General Joseph 90–1, 111, 116, 120, 153, 173–80, 182, 203
Johannis, Emperor 20–2

Karl I, Emperor 204, 278, 280, 299
Kassala 18, 22–4
Khartoum 17–18
Kitchener, Field Marshal Lord 173

Labriola, Arturo 219
Lansing, Robert 296
Lausanne, treaty of (1912) 48–9
Lequio, Lieutenant-General Clemente 104, 157, 168–9
Levi, Primo 71
Litta Modigliani, Major-General Vittorio 244
Lloyd George, David 203, 206, 248, 299, 310
Ludendorff, General Erich 204
Lussu, Emilio 171
Luzzi, Lieutenant-General Guido 157

Macallé, 25
siege of (1896) 26
Magenta, battle of (1859) 15, 208
Malagodi, Olindo 82, 198
Malaparte, Curzio 102, 243
Mambretti, Lieutenant-General Ettore 169, 222–3
Mancini, Pasquale S. 17, 40
Maravigna, Lieutenant-General Pietro 133
Marchetti, Colonel Odoardo 155, 231, 260

Marchetti, Colonel Tullio 130–1, 152–3, 161, 279, 291–2
Marieni, Lieutenant-General Giovanni Battista 285
Marinetti, Filippo Tommaso 39
Marro, Colonel Prospero 173
Marselli, Nicola 8
Martini, Domenico 158
Martini, Ferdinando 63, 195
Massaua 17–20, 23–6
masturbation 166
Maugham, W. Somerset 92
Mazzella, Archbishop Orazio 164
Mazzini, Giuseppe 7
Megiddo, battle of (September 1918) 288
Melograni, Piero 164
Menelik of Showa 20–4, 26–7
Menotti Serrati, Giacinto 197, 220
Messe, Major Giovanni 280
Metemma, battle of (1889) 20
military brothels, see prostitution
military intelligence, Austrian 95–6, 131–2
military intelligence, Italian
  and army morale 254, 291
  estimates of enemy forces and intentions 90, 112, 114, 117, 150–3, 204–5, 208, 224, 227, 230–1, 269, 279, 284, 291–2
  and lesson learning 269, 282, 284–5
  structure and organisation of 129–30, 161–2, 267–8
  and the Libyan war 42
Millerand, Alexandre 90
Minozzi, Don Giovanni 164
Mocenni, Major-General Stanislao 23–5
Moltke, General Helmuth von (the elder) 29
Moltke, General Helmuth von (the younger) 35–7, 58, 61, 62
Mombelli, Lieutenant-General Ernesto 173
Montuori, Lieutenant-General Luca 182, 222–3, 230, 232, 234, 236, 241, 277, 280, 304
Moris, Colonel Maurizio 113
Morrone, Lieutenant-General Paolo 138, 156, 158, 160, 167, 187, 191, 253, 274, 276
Mussolini, Benito 92, 99, 196, 305, 315, 317

Nava, Lieutenant-General Luigi 104, 144
Nicholas II, Tsar 159, 173
Nicholas, Grand Duke 89, 111
Nigra, Count Costantino 18
Nitti, Francesco 127, 260, 271–2, 284, 288, 305, 310, 313–17
Nivelle, General Henri 204, 207–8, 224

Ojetti, Ugo 145
Omodeo, Adolfo 102
Orero, Major-General Baldassare 21
Orlando, Vittorio 128, 157, 197, 244,
   248–50, 253–5, 257–8, 260, 263, 267,
   270–2, 275, 277, 282–3, 298–9, 303,
   305–8, 310, 313, 315
Ortigara, battle of (June 1917) 222–3
Osio, Lieutenant-General count Egidio 32
Ouchy, secret treaty of (1912) 48

Painlevé, Paul 207
Palatsin, General F. F. 179–80
Paratore, Senator 305
Pariani, Colonel Alberto 40, 289, 298, 300
Peace Note, German (December 1916) 219
Peace Note, Papal (August 1917) 221, 255
peace settlement 308–9
Pecori-Giraldi, Lieutenant-General
   Guglielmo 45–6, 149, 156, 315
Pelizzo, Bishop Luigi 166
Pellegrini, Lieutenant-Colonel Giulio 236
Pelloux, Lieutenant-General Luigi 29
Pershing, General John J. 286
Pétain, General Philippe 263
Petrograd conference (February 1917) 205
Pettiti di Roreto, Major-General Carlo 156
Piacentini, Lieutenant-General Settimo
   173, 185, 309
Pieri, Piero 161
Pirozzi, Major-General Nicola 105
Piscecelli, Lieutenant-Colonel Maurizio
   236
Plumer, General Sir Herbert 254, 266
Poincaré, President Raymond 195
Pollio, Lieutenant-General Alberto 14, 17,
   35, 53–4, 57–8, 62, 104, 110, 248
   and tactical and strategic doctrine 51–2
   and the Libyan war 45–7, 50
   and war planning 35–8
Porro, Lieutenant-General Carlo 156–7,
   161, 177, 179–80, 201, 203, 229, 240,
   252, 304
Porta, Major-General Felice 169
Primerano, Lieutenant-General Domenico
   23, 25, 29
prisoners of war
   Austro-Hungarian 275–7
   Italian 272–5
propaganda, Austrian 256
propaganda, Italian 256–9, 291
prostitution 166–7

Ragni, Major-General Ottavio 48
Raimondo, Orazio 305

Rapallo conference (November 1917) 248
Rapallo, treaty of (1922) 316
Ras Alula of Tigray 19, 21
Ras Maconnen of Harrar 23
Ras Mengesha of Tigray 22–3
religion, role of 163–4
Ricci, Lieutenant-General Giuliano 234,
   288
Ricotti-Magnani, Lieutenant-General
   Cesare 18–19
Risorgimento, wars of 6
Robertson, General Sir William 174,
   205–7, 250
Rocca, Major-General Francesco 241
Rochat, Giorgio 163
Rodd, James Rennell 73, 76
Romania
   in Italian policy 71–2
   in Italian strategy 173, 176–7
Rome, capture of (1870) 15
Rome conference (January 1917) 204
Romei Longhena, Major-General Count
   Giovanni 159, 205
Rommel, Erwin 238, 240
Ropolo, Lieutenant-Colonel Edoardo 59,
   91
Rostagno, Major-General Gustavo 169
Ruelle, Lieutenant-General Carlo 134
Russia
   military convention with (1915) 88
   military conversations with 90–1
Russian Revolution
   February 1917 205–6, 219
   October 1917 257

Saati 18–20
Sadowa, battle of (1866) 15
Said Ahmed el-Sherif 46
Salandra, Antonio 49, 58, 61, 64–8, 72–3,
   75–7, 79, 81, 88, 91–4, 105–7, 111,
   115–18, 120–1, 136, 144, 146,
   155–60, 173, 196, 276
Saletta, Lieutenant-General Tancredi
   as 3rd chief of the general staff 29–30
   in Ethiopia 18–20
   and war planning 33–5
Salonika 119–20, 147, 159, 174–6, 180
   and Italian strategy 172, 174, 176, 178,
   190
Salsa, Major Tommaso 24
San Martino, battle of (1859) 15
Sarrail, General Maurice 177–8
Sazanov, Count Sergei 173
Schlieffen, General Alfred von 32, 35
Sciara Sciat, battle of (1911) 44, 48

Senafé, battle of (1895) 23–4
Senussi 44, 46, 60, 72
Servizio P, see propaganda, Italian
sex, casual 166
  see also prostitution
SIM *see* military intelligence
Smaniotto, Colonel Ercole 279
Soffici, Arnaldo 243
Solferino, battle of (1859) 15, 208
Solstice, battle of the (1918) 279–82,
  285–91, 296
Sonnino, Sidney 64, 67–8, 71–3, 75–8,
  81–2, 88, 93, 107, 111, 118–21, 144,
  155–8, 160, 172–4, 176, 178, 195–6,
  204, 206, 249, 263, 273–5, 277, 284,
  298, 306–8, 310
Spingardi, Lieutenant-General Paolo
  13–15, 35, 43, 47, 49, 66, 110, 277
St. Jeanne de Maurienne, treaty of (1917)
  307
Strafexpedition 155–61, 168, 170–1, 174,
  176–8, 180, 188, 191, 201, 223
Stuparich, Giani 97, 101
Supreme War Council 248, 262–3, 271,
  286, 312
Switzerland, in Italian strategy 175–6, 179
syphilis 99

Talaat Bey 60
Tassoni, Lieutenant-General Giulio 244
Tedesco, Francesco 120
teleferiche 182
Tettoni, Lieutenant-General Adolfo 67–9,
  216
Thaon di Revel, admiral Paolo 64, 71–2,
  77, 250, 307–8, 310
Tittoni, Ambassador Tommaso 74, 155
Toselli, Major Pietro 25
Tranfaglia, Nicola 316
Tre Monti, battle of (1918) 262
Treaty of Berlin (1878) 39
Treaty of London (1915) 78, 92, 299
  negotiations leading to 76–8
trench newspapers 258
Treves, Claudio 197
Triple Alliance 58, 61–2, 69–70, 74–5, 85
Triple Entente 62, 70, 73
Triplice see Triple Alliance
Turati, Filippo 197
'Turin Days' (August 1917) 220–1

Turkey
  and the Libyan war 39, 40, 42–3, 44,
  46, 47–9
  threat to Italy at the outbreak of the
  world war 59–60, 72–3

Uccialli, treaty of *see* Wichale
Umberto I, King 22, 30
Ungaretti, Giuseppe 99

Vaccari, Colonel Giuseppe 242
Valenzano, Colonel Gioacchino 27
Vanzo, Lieutenant-General Augusto
  225
venereal disease 141, 163, 166–7
Venizelos, Eleftherios 71
Versailles conference, *see* peace settlement
Vickers-Terni 126
Villa Giusti, armistice of 299–300
Villani, Major-General Giovanni 236, 238
Vittorio Emanuele II, King 7, 15
Vittorio Emanuele III, King 30, 35, 60,
  145, 173, 204, 248, 308
Vittorio Veneto, battle of (1918) 16, 247,
  286, 288–9, 293, 298, 305
  air power and 297
  course of 293–8
  logistics of 292–3
  plans and operational directives for
  286–90

Waldersee, General Alfred von 58
Wangenheim, Ambassador Baron von 60
war aims, Italian 194–8, 305–8
Weber, General Viktor 298, 300
Weygand, Colonel Maxime 206
Wichale, treaty of (1889) 23
Wilson, President Woodrow 196–7, 288–9,
  298, 306, 308
wine, importance of 164–6

Zimmerman, Arthur 73
Zoppi, Lieutenant-General Ottavio 148–50,
  154, 169, 200, 293–5, 316
Zuccari, Lieutenant-General Luigi 37,
  104–5
Zupelli, Lieutenant-General Vittorio 36,
  68, 76, 79–81, 83–5, 94–5, 108, 110,
  113, 120–2, 128, 139, 144–5, 258,
  298, 311–12